HUC UNDIQUE GAZA CONGERITUR

Volume II
(February 3, 1785 to January 26, 1786)

Wesley E. Pippenger
and
James D. Munson, Ph.D.

HERITAGE BOOKS
2018

HERITAGE BOOKS
AN IMPRINT OF HERITAGE BOOKS, INC.

Books, CDs, and more—Worldwide

For our listing of thousands of titles see our website
at
www.HeritageBooks.com

Published 2018 by
HERITAGE BOOKS, INC.
Publishing Division
5810 Ruatan Street
Berwyn Heights, Md. 20740

International Standard Book Number
Paperbound: 978-1-888265-91-0

INTRODUCTION

The Virginia Journal and Alexandria Advertiser continued on into Volume II, without a break. In the volume's first issue we find:

> *The* Virginia Journal and Alexandria Advertiser*, has now completed its first volume, the Editor therefore takes this opportunity of returning his sincere and grateful thanks to his friends and customers, for the patronage and encouragement they have given to his design.*
>
> *It is with the highest pleasure, he reflects on the many instances of their kindness, and indulgence, in the conducting of his paper; but as he has also experienced their great politeness to him, as a citizen, he thinks himself bound by every tie to make the utmost exertions in his power, for the future emolument and instruction of his subscribers.*
>
> *He is now determined to preserve in the publication of his paper, agreeable to the plan and sentiments he has already laid before the public — happy to merit their approbation, and to be thought worthy of their attention. The constant and great expence attending the printing business lays the Editor under necessity of informing his friends and customers, that he shall be much obliged to them for the punctual payment of what may be due on the subscription for his paper last year; and also that they would pay one half of the subscription for the ensuing year, as it will comfortably enable the Editor to proceed in his work, to their great advantage and emolument.*
>
> *GEORGE RICHARDS*
> *Alexandria, January 27, 1785.*

ALEXANDRIA AND THE YEAR 1785

The states in America were united in name, but not yet in thought. They dealt separately with matters of currency, duties on imports, and such as the pirates of Algiers. The Algerines not only stopped and boarded ships, but took them into port, sold the vessels and the cargo, and put the crew and passengers into slavery.

Even more pressing for Alexandrians were other nations' changing trade and navigation regulation — especially those of Great Britain and France. When still British subjects, American producers, merchants, and shippers had built successful commercial ties in the Caribbean, the British Isles, and Europe. Now, Americans were being hampered, if not harassed, both in maintaining their old business, and building new relations.

Overarching this abroad were the tensions between disputatious Austria, Prussia, France, England, the Republic of Holland, Turkey, and Russia. Overarching this at home, problems between the Indians and whites affected frontier settlement. Also, Great Britain refused to hand over the frontier posts of the North West, saying it would not do so until Americans satisfied their pre-war indebtedness to British business houses.

As did other Americans, Alexandrians wondered if the states, newly united, could act in concert but remain separate. Alexandria was founded, shaped, and lived or died based on trade and transportation. It could not survive in the 1785 world — let alone prosper — by itself.

NOTICE

Our Notice to the Reader, which follows, gives insight into our working methods, conventions used, and the purpose of our typography and layout. Even a quick reading of this will markedly increase the reader's ease, speed and accuracy in finding information.

Wesley E. Pippenger
Arlington, Virginia

James D. Munson
Arlington, Virginia
April 1999

NOTICE TO THE READER

We serve researchers and general readers alike. We occasionally condense, but usually transcribe verbatim. Advertisements, in particular, we do verbatim. Our indexing tries to anticipate the widest range of interests, and reports down to the smallest detail.

INDEX GUIDELINES

- The entire text of an advertisement is given when it first appears. When repeated in later issues, we refer back to that first appearance.
- Each item is indexed as a main entry. Linens, rum, hats, scissors, salt—each an index entry of its own.
- Sailing vessels whose type is not specified are listed by name under "Ships." Where the vessel type *is* stated in the newspaper, each vessel is listed by name under its type: Brigs, Snows, Sloops, Schooners, Frigates, etc. Vessel names are in *italics.*
- Ship captains are indexed by surname, as are other named individuals; there is no separate "captain" listing. The subheading will show given names, plus Captain, Capt., or [Capt.].
- Other ship personnel: lieutenant, mate, cook, seaman, etc., are listed under "ship."
- The heading "ship" (not "Ship**s**") contains incidents affecting a specific vessel: sunk, aground, dismasted, and the like. Here we also record instances of the remarkable ship-to-ship communication, called "speaking." For example, Capt. Smith reports that, at a given location, he "spoke the ship *Verity*, Capt. Thomas, all aboard well."
- Waterways are listed by type (rivers, bays, capes etc.) and are cross indexed by name: Delaware Bay, Potomack River.
- People in the 18th century were more fearful of forces of nature than we of the 20th century—they being less equipped to deal with resulting damage and destruction. Therefore, we have separately indexed natural wonders, weather, astronomy, earthquakes, and the like.
- All African Americans are under "Negroes," the term then in use. If identified as a slave, the individual is under "slaves." Those mentioned only by given name only are listed at the end of the index and without a surname, for instance "[ ], Jack."
- Runaways are indexed only by page number; the abstract gives the race, gender, nationality, master, free, servant, slave, and so on.
- Because of the cultural significance of the color black in clothing and accessories, all instances of black textiles, findings, or notions are so indexed: black crepe, black gloves, black ribbons, black bombazine, etc.

Layout and Typography

Finding an item in a page of dense text can be exhausting. We have tried to make it easy for readers by breaking the text mass into smaller units.

- The end of a newspaper issue and beginning of another is indicated by a line if three black bars: 
- **Bold type** highlights news sources and dates, i.e. **Paris, April 20**.
- The symbol "■" marks divisions of major news sources. Where one news source gives a number of paragraphs on different subjects, we have used " ... " as in: Madame Pompadour has been absent now from Paris for two weeks ... Floods in Lorraine have carried away several bridges ... At Avignon a balloon ascension, etc.
- In the index, only proper nouns or occupations are capitalized.

1785/02/03, Vol. I No. 53

Page 1. HOOE AND HARRISON, Have for Sale at their Store, Osnaburgs, Ravens duck, brown rolls, Russia duck, Holland's ditto, white-lead, Red ditto, Spanish brown, red ochre, yellow ditto, white vitriol, verdigrease, brimstone, sand-glasses, spy-glasses, sheet-lead, sheet copper, German steel, loglines, deepsea ditto, houseline, marline, hamberline, sail twine, seine ditto, sheet-tin in boxes, steel wire, tar, turpentine, English and Dutch cordage, anchors of different sizes, mould candles, hyson, bohea and souchong tea, black pepper, single refined sugar, candied ditto, gin in cases, muskets, butter pots, water pitchers, queen's china, glass ware, delf bowls, long and short pipes, violins, looking-glasses, hatchets, carpenters' and joiners' tools, scythes, bolting-cloths, blankets, flannels, hats, cotton stockings, yarn and worsted ditto, diaper napkins, cambricks, lawns, check shirts, gauze handkerchiefs, old hock in bottles, &c. ALX, Jan. 26, 1785 [see like ad Vol. I No. 52] ■ DANIEL and ISAAC M'PHERSON, Have for Sale, WEST-INDIA and New-England rum, molasses, brown sugar, salt, sail-duck, cordage, brown rolls, dowlas, fine and coarse mens' and womens' shoes by the box or dozen, glass ware by the box, paints, gunpowder, spades, shovels, coarse and fine hats, black pepper, soap and candles by the box, with many other articles of dry-goods and hard-ware, all of which they will sell on reasonable terms for Cash or Country Produce. ALX, Jan. 25, 1785 [see like ad Vol. I No. 52] ■ ALL PERSONS INDEBTED TO THE Copartnership of HARPER and FENNER, which dissolved the 22d of November last, are once more requested to make immediate Payment.--Constant Attendance is given at the Store by EDWARD HARPER. ALX, Jan. 26, 1785. N.B. Those Gentlemen who are indebted for Cash lent, are most particularly requested to call and discharge the same. E.H. [see like ad Vol. I No. 52] ■ A PERSON OF A LIBERAL PRO-fession is desirous of trying a benevolent Experiment, by instructing an honest NEGRO LAD in a Business that will give him, if ingenious and docile, an accurate Knowledge of the English Language, and besides rendering him really a rational Creature, will enable him, in due Time, to earn handsome Wages.--Inquire at the Printing-Office [see like ad Vol. I No. 52]. ■ TO BE SOLD, A Stout strong hearty young NEGRO MAN, who is well acquainted with all kinds of country business, is a good pit sawyer, has worked in a smith's shop, and has some knowledge of that business; he is, perhaps, one of the best cutters and grubbers in the State, and can hew well with the broad-ax; to any person moving to a new settlement this fellow would be extremely valuable.--Inquire of EDWARD HARPER. N.B. His wife is also for sale, who is a healthy strong willing Wench, well acquainted with plantation or house work.--Inquire as above [see like ad Vol. I No. 52]. ■ TO BE SOLD, On board the Sloop *Polly*, Capt. Mark Clark, at Col. Lyle's Wharf, Rhode-Island cheese, cranberries, chairs, potatoes, butter, cyder, oil, hops, spruce, and mackerel. ALX, Jan. 25, 1785 [see like ad Vol. I No. 52] ■ PUBLIC VENDUE OF LANDS. On Tuesday the 22d of February next, will be Sold to the highest Bidder, at the Vendue-Store in ALX, the three following Tracts of valuable Land, situated in Fairfax Co., viz. ONE Tract, lying within four miles and an half of ALX, on Holme's-Run, containing agreeable to survey, 252 acres, 150 of which are woodland and well timbered; the cleared land is under good fence, 25 acres whereof are good meadow and now laid down with Timothy, and as much more may be made at a small expence; this tract is well watered, there being a number of fine springs on it, and there are on the premises a tolerable dwelling-house with a good brick chimney and two rooms on the lower floor, and a small apple orchard.--Another Tract, containing 300 acres, lying on the south-side of the middle Branch of Great-Hunting Creek, and is likewise about four miles and an half from ALX; this tract has about 200 acres of woodland, the remainder being cleared is under tolerable fence; there are on the premises a good mill-seat, where formerly was a mill, 50 or 60 acres of meadow land, and an overseer's house, two barns and an apple and peach orchard.--The other Tract joins the last, and contains 75 acres of well timbered woodland.--The terms are, one third in ready money at the time of signing the deeds, one third in nine months, and for the remaining third a credit of eighteen months will be given, on bond with good security.--The plots are now lodged in the hands of the Vendue-Master, and may be seen at any time before the sale on application to him, and the land will be shewn by applying to the Subscriber, who lives near ALX. BALDWIN DADE, January 24, 1785 [see like ad Vol. I No. 52] ■ FOR SALE, A Valuable TRACT of LAND, lying in Prince William County, Va., about two miles from Dumfries, eight from Colchester, and twenty-four from ALX, containing 2150 acres; this land is well adapted to farming and planting, is very well timbered, and has the advantage of a large never failing stream running through it, upon which may be got one or more good mill seats. Also, another valuable Tract of Land, containing upwards of 800 acres, lying in Washington County, Md., about one mile from the river Potomack, eight from Hagar's-Town, and twenty-six from Frederick-Town: This tract is altogether of the rich limestone lands in Connicocheague valley, and is generally acknowledged to be equal in soil and produces as highly as any land in the county [further purchase details]... For terms of the Virginia tract, apply to Col. BAILEY WASHINGTON, of Stafford Co., and of the other to Col. RICHARD DAVIS, who lives near the premises, or to the Subscriber, who owns the lands. PEREGRINE FITZHUGH. Jan. 3, 1785 [see like ad Vol. I No. 49] ■ The Subscriber has on Hand a Quantity of Medicines, among which are Glauber's and Epsom's Salts, Peruvian Bark, Jalap, Rhubarb, Emetic Tartar, Magnesia, &c. which he will sell on reasonable Terms. CHARLES WORTHINGTON. George-Town, Jan. 15, 1785 [see like ad Vol. I No. 51] ■ FOR SALE, FOR CASH OR COUNTRY PRODUCE, A Few Pipes of choice Madera Wine, Jamaica Rum fit for present Use, of high Proof and excellent Flavour. Claret in small Boxes of 2½ and 3 Dozen each. A few Kegs of Scotch-Barley and Herrings. WILLIAM HUNTER, jun., ALX, Jan. 18, 1785 [see like ad Vol. I No. 52] ■ To be Sold at Public Vendue on the Premises, on Tuesday the 3d Day of April next, A Valuable PLANTATION, lying within six miles of ALX, containing 200 acres, whereon is a good dwelling-house, with two rooms on a floor, and a good brick chimney; a good kitchen, meat-house, corn-house with a room below, stable, and other out-houses, a spring of good water within 100 yards of the door, a good apple and peach orchard, and a young orchard; about 8 acres of meadow cleared and well laid down in Timothy, and a quantity more may be made.--The land produces good Indian-corn, tobacco, and small grain, and all under very good fence; there are 35 bushels of wheat sown on the land in one body, and looks as well as any in the county.--One-third of the purchase-money to be paid down, one-third in twelve months after, and the other third at the expiration of twelve months more, on giving bond with approved security for the two payments, and may be entered upon immediately after the day of sale.--On the same day will also be sold for ready-money, horses, cows, hogs, corn, fodder, hay, farming utensils, and household and kitchen furniture. On Thursday the 6th of April next, will be sold in ALX, a Lot of Ground on Queen-street, containing 61 feet front and 122 feet back, whereon is a good two-story brick-house, with four fireplaces on a floor and two in the cellar, a good store-room, and rents at 100l. per year; there is an addition to it of two rooms above and a cellar below, that rents at 30l. per year, and a good spring of water on the Lot.--Also, a Lot on the same street, 30 feet front and 122 feet back, whereon is a good house not finished, with a good cellar below, with a fireplace.--Also, another Lot on the same street, being a corner Lot, containing 30 feet front and running 122 feet on Pitt-street, whereon is a log-house with a brick chimney.--Also, a Lot on Pitt-street, 61 feet front and 123 feet back, whereon is a good tan-yard and mill-house.--The terms of sale for the Lots will be the same as for the above Plantation.--Good deeds will be made for the Plantation and Lots by SAMUEL M'LEAN. Jan. 26, 1785 [see like ad Vol. I No. 52] ■ NOTICE is hereby given, that a petition will be presented to the next General Assembly, relative to draining the marsh adjoining this town, and to condemn certain lands, the property of Charles Alexander, Esq., for the use of public buildings and other purposes. ALX, January 25, 1785. ■ FOUND, By Cab, a Slave belonging to Mr. Richard Arell, A BOLT of OSNABURGS, marked 147,222 thus 222.--The Owner may have it again by applying to SAMUEL ARELL. Dec. 3, 1784 [see like ad Vol. I No. 45] ■ TO BE SOLD at the PRINTING-OFFICE, A Variety of Writing-Paper, Dutch Quills, Paper Hangings, Blank Books, gilt and common Letter Paper, Sealing-Wax, Wafers, Inkpowder, Pounce, Ink-stands, Black Lead Pencils, Common Prayer Books, from Two to Ten Shillings; Boston's Fourfold State, Russel's Sermons, Psalters, &c.&c.&c.

Page 2. *By the Brig May, Capt. Haskell, which arrived here last Friday from London, we have the following Advices, viz.* ■ **HAGUE, October 24.** His Excellency, M. De Reischach, Envoy Extraordinary from his Imperial Majesty, has not conferred with government members here since the Scheldt River ship affair; he will not demand anything before the courier returns from the Emperor. Meanwhile, there are State troop movements. The Bois de Luc garrison is on the march, and two cavalry companies from Hoorne and two from Enkhuysen are now at Breda. The Rotterdam garrison is en route there; the Baden-Dourlach regiment, garrisoned at Arnheim, will be relieved as soon as the Arnheim Burgesses request their departure ... Last Wednesday the States of Holland conferred on the disagreement between the and the Amsterdam Magistracy, resolution of which is expected by Wednesday next ... At the request of their High Mightinesses, the Prince of Orange ordered Vice-Admiral Reynst to dispatch war ships to convoy merchant vessels during the winter from the Baltic and Archangel. A frigate and cutter are ordered out ... The Prince Stadtholder departs immediately for Breda and other frontier cities to inspect the State's defense preparations. Major General Dumoulin, most excellently skilled in tactics and engineering, departed the 16th for Ecluse, in Flanders. ■ **LONDON, October 30.** According to yesterday's mails, there is reason to believe that the French will not assist the Dutch against the Emperor. The following, from the Hague, refers. The dispatches to their High Mightinesses which the courier brought from Paris, the 19th, we hear were urgent enough to occasion an immediate answer, via the same courier. We understand that the French Minister disapproves of matters having been carried to such extremity as make negotiation difficult, while the Emperor considered himself the injured party; the 1756 treaty, promising assistance by 25,000 men to an attacked Austria, places France in an embarrassing situation. Another account is similar but in stronger terms ... *Extract of a genuine letter from* **Brussels, October 21**. It is currently reported here, that his Prussian Majesty has refused the Imperial troops the liberty of marching through any part of his dominions in their route to the Low Countries. If true, bloody Continental war will result, for the Emperor declares he will not relinquish his demands; opening the Scheldt and possession of Maestricht being only a part of them. Should he have naval assistance, the Republic of Holland has everything to dread. I hear the agent from Zealand, long resident here to effect mediation, is on the eve of his departure ... *Extract of a genuine letter from* **Antwerp, October 20.** During the past 5-6 days we expected to see the Scheldt opened, but such seems no longer imminent. Last Saturday, the Prince de Ligne (a General in the Imperial service) arrived here and was given the keys to the town by the Burgo-master. We are now entirely under military government by 6000 troops stationed within the city, and two regiments of dragoons are quartered in an adjacent hamlet to observe movements by a large Dutch army at Bergen-op-Zoom, about four hours march from here. The pavement on the Key, or Quay, is entirely taken up, and the engineers work day and night in raising batteries, now nearly completed. Forges are erected near the platforms, on which 48-pounder guns are planted, to fire red hot balls into Dutch men of war, should they venture up the Scheldt to attack the city. The Dutch have offered to return the ship they took at the Scheldt's mouth, the Captain having been liberated after 24 hour imprisonment. This is refused, and we hear the Emperor has greatly increased his demands, as the vessel's capture visited indignity of the Imperial flag. Expresses between Brussels and the Hague pass here all hours of the day and night, the gate leading to the former being left open for that purpose under a Captain's guard. Nonetheless, those who pretend to be in the secret believe the Scheldt will be opened after a little blustering, and Antwerp declared a free port. For, unless the King of Prussia joins the Dutch, the threats of their High Mightinesses must end *in fume.* [As smoke, or vapor--Eds.] ... *Extract of a letter from* **Kilkenny, October 20.** Last Monday a party of the 20th foot, quartered at Cashel, were called on to assist in reclaiming some lands near the city which had been forcibly with-held from the lawful owner. On their arrival, they found well armed defenders fortified and dug in. Five soldiers were killed, eleven wounded, and withdrew without accomplishing their mission. The defenders' casualties are not known. ■ **November 1.** By advices from **Flanders**, all appears hostile. The Emperor appears resolved to vindicate the honor of his insulted flag, more particularly rouzed from the indignity suffered to the latter ship, in which Mr. Le Roi, an eminent engineer, was deputed by the spirited Joseph, merely to receive the insult. In consequence, his Imperial Majesty has reinforced the Antwerp garrison, and erected batteries to guard the Scheldt. His Highness Prince Charles of Ligne arrived the 18th with his regiment, bringing troop total to upwards of 6000--in addition to the 5000 employed to watch the Dutch at Maestricht. All the frontier towns are filling with soldiers who declare *We are going to fight the Dutch.* On the other side, the Stadtholder has toured Holland's frontiers and directed all of the Republic's troops to take up defense of places most vulnerable to the Emperor's forces ... *A puff Ministerial.* ["puff" is an exaggerated statement. --Eds.] A communique says the additional ships the East India Company is sending to China will employ 2000 additional seamen. A commentator points out that an Indiaman's crew is less that 100, and the Company will send no more than three extra ships--but something must be said as a palliative for imposing the commutation tax. Further, as a reward for the India Company's kindly treatment while he was out of office, he now gives them the tea bill. Although the public pays for this, the various and singular advantages flowing from his administration should occasion no murmur even should every article be doubly taxed ... The Minister will have to ask Parliament for a million more for tax deficiencies, two millions for debt due the Bank, and to impose fresh taxes to raise nine millions for unfunded debt ... In case of war we will repent the last change in Administration: the Dutch certainly will be able to bring thirty sail of the line to sea, and if they look once more into the Medway, with what force can we oppose them? ... From the Dutch newspapers in Friday's mail, France is not disposed to champion the Dutch against the Emperor. If France withholds aid, the Hollanders will be in difficulty, unless the King of Prussia aids his relation, the Prince of Orange. By treaty, if the Austrian Emperor is attacked, France is to supply him with 25,000 men. As the Dutch were the first aggressors, France can not side with the Republic without an absolute and direct breach of treaty ... Letters from **Baltimore, Maryland** dated **September 16** report many North Carolinians have sent spirited remonstrances to Congress over the recent imposts. Also, Marylanders are greatly discontent with the new government; a general meeting of principal planters has been advertised, to seek means of redressing their grievances ... A gentleman who left **Calais** last Tuesday says just as they sailed a Philadelphia ship with tobacco was lost on the French coast ... Letters from the continent received Saturday mention the Dutch fleet fitting out at the Texel: the *Orange* of 50 guns; *Zaal Bloom*, 44; *Jason*, 36; *Hoorne*, 24; and *Phoenix* cutter. Commodore Jan Brace, commanding, makes haste lest the winter block up the ports and prevent his getting out ... From Elbinge, they write that Dutch captains of ships there have lately taken out burgessoise (a sort of certificate) which entitles them to use and sail under the Prussian flag. Becoming general, this is the surest indication of war ... Dutch trade may be greatly interrupted by the more than forty privateers now lying ready in Ostend's harbour ... Since last Tuesday 44 ships from the West Indies, Virginia, Philadelphia, Hudson's Bay, and the Baltic have arrived in the river [London.] **November 4.** About one o'clock this morning an express arrived at the Marquis of Carmarthen office, with dispatches from Lord Viscount Torrington, his Majesty's Minister Plenipotentiary at the Court of Brussels, saying letters of recall had been sent to the Imperial Minister at the Hague. All the troops in Austrian Flanders were in motion; and every warlike preparation was making with the utmost expedition. ■ **HARTFORD, January 11.** Last November 26 the Governor of the Bahamas islands ruled that Indian corn may be imported in American vessels. The supply of local corn there is insufficient to provide subsistence to the great number of Negroes and the poor. The shortfall is due to the continued drought ... They write from Quebec of a most severe north-easter on November 26. The storm surge destroyed many wharves and the stores built thereon. Several craft were ruined, and great damage done to the larger shipping. ■ **NEW YORK, January 17.** *Extract of a letter from* **Boston,** *dated* **January 2, 1785**, *to a gentleman in this city*: The writer forwards an earnest and polished narrative for "those who delight in actions of generosity and humanity": how the French vessel, *Postilion*, struck upon reefs near the Bahamas, and was fortuitously sighted by the small sloop *Active*, Capt. Burkett, of Messrs. Clark & Nightingale, Providence, Rhode Island; despite high winds and seas, the *Active* hove to until all hands were transferred from the wreck; Captain Burkett, unasked, gave up his cabin to the *Postilion's* distinguished passengers--Comte and Comtesse de Broglio--for the remainder of the 25 day trip to Providence; how the courtesies and kindnesses extended to all the rescued by those of the *Active* were matched by the people of Providence, and then of Boston (to which the titled couple were forwarded); how the Captain and his employers refused compensation for any ship's stores expended (including six crates of oranges from the cargo);

Page 3. [The Postilion Story (*continued*)] How even the Boston broker, Mr. Hayes, refused the customary commission for transferring the Comte's funds from Providence to Boston; and for all of which the French Captain, the Comte and Comtesse expressed their gratitude to Messrs. Clark & Nightingale. The writer quotes C & N's modest response that Captain Burkett's conduct was only "consistent with the dictates of humanity, and perfectly agreeable to the desire we have of rendering every service in our power to any of your polite and hospitable nation," &c. &c. &c. ■ **January 19.** At a January 14 meeting of the Merchants of this city, at the city tavern, the following gentlemen were chosen a standing commercial committee for the ensuing year: John Nesbit, Charles Petit, Thomas Fitzsimons, Samuel Howell, John Nixon, Isaac Hazelhurst, John Ross, Modecai Lewis, Clement Biddle, George Clymer, John Wilcox, Tench Coxe, Richard Wells ... Private letters by the British Packet arrived at **New York** say the Emperor's troops have taken Fort Lillo, a Dutch fort on the Flanders side of the Scheldt--and that the republic's forces had taken one of the Emperor's forts; that the Empress of Russia has entered an alliance with the Emperor; that France and Prussia were to join the United Netherlands; and that by the disposition of the several belligerent powers, the war was likely to prove very serious ... His Most Christian Majesty's packet *la Courier de l'Amerique*, Chevalier Aboville, arrived at Sandy Hook in 49 days from Port l'Orient ... We hope in a day or two to be able to give more particular accounts of the affairs now taking place in Europe. **January 22.** Extract of a letter from **Altena (Germany)** dated **November 5, 1784:** Last Sunday a courier from Vienna brought news that war is declared by the Emperor against Holland ... Extract of a letter from **Bristol, October 20:** A society of gentlemen in and about **London** and **Westminster** are considering erecting a college in Bermuda. Both Oxford and Cambridge are become such sinks of vice and profligacy that a lad risks ruin in return for a smattering of what custom stiles a liberal education. The islands are in every way favourable to education, manners and morality. In point of health and temperature of air they are exceeded by no spot on the globe. Three, four or five years in this plan would see the boys return very different characters from what our universities now annually present us with ... Extract of a letter from **New York,** dated **January** 18: The U.S. Congress met as scheduled here on the 11th, in City Hall. Six States are already here, the rest expected daily; when all are assembled, they will proceed to business. ... Letters from New Hampshire say a very large coal mine has been discovered at the extremity of Gaspee Bay, in north eastern Nova Scotia. Timber for fencing, building, &c., is so scarce in many parts of these States that we wish for coal imports to our capital towns. We could thus save our forests for more valuable uses than mere firing, and employ thousands in a brisk trade, in no way prejudicial to our political interests. ■ **ALX, February 3**. Copy of a Letter from a Gentleman in Spain to his Friend in this Town, dated October 28, 1784.

SIR,

My last to you was dated the 1st Instant, by Captain -----, who was detained by contrary Winds, and did not get to Sea until the 10th--I am sorry to inform you he was the following Day captured by the Moors and carried into Tangiers. I have a Letter from him of the 19th, wherein he seems to think there is some Prospect of the Vessel's being released; but that nothing could be determined until Orders arrived from the Emperor, which would require some time. For my own Part, I have my Apprehensions, and think that the small Value of the Prize is the only Circumstance in Favor of her being restored. However, I have recommended Capt. ----- to a Friend at Tangiers; and I have in a particular Manner requested our Minister at Madrid, to exert his Influence in his Behalf; and I shall do every thing in my Power to save the poor People at least from Slavery. After the pacific Declarations of this perfidious African, I confess that this unfortunate Event was as unexpected as chagrining; and, till some Arrangement, too long neglected, takes Place with him on Behalf of Congress, it is needless to warn you against sending any Vessels into these Seas under American Colours. I now hear he has five large Cruisers out and getting more ready. Although the Vessel was luckily covered, it will be impossible to effect any further Insurance on your Flag, except at high Premiums. You must in Future make Use of Vessels with Passes for any of the Southern Parts of Europe.

A late London Paper says, "That Mr. Orde's Opinion of the perilous Situation of Ireland, through the Medium of Mr. Dundas, has occasioned Perplexities, that have induced this *Political Phaeton* to call up the brightest of his advising Friends for Assistance." ■ The Brig *Fitzhugh*, Capt. — , from London, is arrived in this River, after a long Passage. The *Peggy*, Capt. Nixon, from this Port, is arrived at Dover. The *Tyger*, Capt. Harrison, also from this Port, is arrived at London. ■ DIED.] Capt. JAMES PARSONS, much esteemed and deservedly lamented. ■ NAVAL-OFFICE, ALX. *Inward Entries*. Sloop *Betsy*, J. Ingraham, and Brig *Zephyr*, B. Lee, from Boston; Brig *May*, W. Haskell, London. *Cleared Outwards*. Brig *Commerce*, J. Hill, for Lisbon.

The VIRGINIA JOURNAL and ALEXANDRIA ADVERTISER, has now completed its First Volume, the Editor therefore takes this Opportunity of returning his sincere and grateful Thanks to his Friends and Customers, for the Patronage and Encouragement they have given to his Design.

It is with the highest Pleasure, he reflects on the many Instances of their Kindness, and indulgence, in the conducting of his Paper; but as he has also experienced their great Politeness to him, as a Citizen, he thinks himself bound by every Tie to make the utmost Exertions in his Power, for the future Emolument and Instruction of his Subscribers.

He is now determined to persevere in the Publication of his Paper, agreeable to the Plan and Sentiments he has already laid before the Public--happy to merit their Approbation, and to be thought worthy of their Attention.

The constant and great Expence attending the Printing Business lays the Editor under Necessity of informing his Friends and Customers, that he shall be much obliged to them for the punctual Payment of what may be due on the Subscription for his Paper last Year; and also that they would pay one Half of the Subscription for the ensuing Year, as it will comfortably enable the Editor to proceed in his Work, to their great Advantage and Emolument.

GEORGE RICHARDS.

ALX, January 27, 1785 [see like ad Vol. I No. 52].

ANECDOTE

Alcibiades being blamed by all his friends for cutting the tail of his dog that was remarked by every one for his beauty, told them he did it that the Athenians might amuse themselves by blaming him for that, and so he might escape a worse censure; which was no bad policy, as when people envy or find fault with small matters, they often pass over greater.

PRICES CURRENT, ALX. / Tobacco, 28s. per Ct. / Fine Flour, 30s. per Barrel. / Wheat, 6s. per Bushel. / Jamaica Spirits, 4/6 per Gallon. / Windward Rum, 3s. per Ditto. / Continental Rum, 2/2, to 2/4 per Ditto. / Molasses, 1/6 per Ditto. / Muscovado Sugar, 38s. to 47s. per Ct. / Salt, 6s. per Bushel, by Retail. Exchange, 36.

To be Sold at the Vendue-Store, on Saturday next the 5th Instant, the following Goods, viz.

Broadcloths, coarse ditto, kerseys, baizes, corduroys, fustians, dowlas, Irish linens, gauzes, muslins, printed linens, calicoes, silk and linen handkerchiefs, osnaburgs, shoes, hats, stockings, glass, Liverpool china, soap and pipes in boxes, ladys' and gentlemens' gloves, loaf sugar, rum, Liverpool bottled beer in hogsheads, and many other articles. ☞ At private sale, a valuable healthy Young Negro Fellow. C. COPPER, Vendue-Master, ALX, Feb. 2, 1785.

FRANCIS FABRIT, Lately from France, Proposes opening a DANCING-SCHOOL at Mr. Reeder's Tavern, where regular attendance will be given every Friday and Saturday, and where the English and French modes of Dancing will be taught. Private tuition will be given to any Gentlemen and Ladies desiring the same, on any other day but that of public teaching.--The terms may be known by applying to the Subscriber at Mr. Reeder's. ☞ He proposes beginning his School on Friday at 9 o'clock, A.M. ALX, Feb. 1, 1785 ■ THE BRIG *MAY*, CAPTAIN HASKELL, from LONDON, which arrived here on Friday last, has a Number of Goods on board for different Gentlemen on this River.--The Captain requests they may be immediately sent for as his Stay here will be but short. ALX, Feb. 2, 1785 ■ TWENTY DOLLARS REWARD. STRAYED or stolen from the Subscribers some time in May last, a bay MARE, about fourteen hands and an half high, six years old, marked GR, though not easily discerned, has a number of grey hairs round the root of her tail, and is a natural trotter.--A bay horse COLT, one year old, was lost at the same time, and is supposed to have been taken off with her.--Whoever delivers the said Mare and Colt to the Subscribers, shall receive the above reward, or Ten Dollars for Either. RICHARD ARELL, GEORGE MASON, ALX, Jan. 28, 1785 ■ WHEREAS THE COPARTNER-ship of CALLENDER, LEWIS and COMPANY, is dissolved, it is requested that all Persons who are indebted to the Rope-Walk, or have any Demands against it, will bring in their Accounts for Settlement. ☞ The Subscriber begs Leave to inform his Friends and Customers, that he intends carrying on the Ropemaking Business in all its Branches.--Any Orders for Cordage or white Rope will be particularly attended to.--As he superintends this Business himself, he makes no Doubt of giving Satisfaction to those who will favor him with their Custom. ELEAZER CALLENDER, Fredericksburg, Jan. 26, 1785 ■ WILLIAMS, CARY, And COMPANY, Have the Pleasure to inform their Friends and the Public in General, that they have just received by the *May*, Capt. Haskell from London, a neat, general and elegant Assortment of all Kinds of European and East-India GOODS, amongst which are, LADYS' bell hoops, pads, fancy coloured ostrich feathers, barometers, microscopes, perspective glasses, printed linens, calicoes, cambricks, lawns, muslins, ladys' Morocco, stuff and leather shoes, mens' shoes, mustard in bottles, hair powder, starch and blue, threads, tapes, pins, needles, all kinds of Hardware, among which are the newest fashioned plated buckles, castings, nets, twine, ladys' and gentlemens' gloves, a variety of fans, ladys' work baskets, stuff and silk petticoats, copper tea-kettles, iron pots, all kinds of worsted and yarn hose, tablecloths, napkins, smoothing-irons, copper scales and weights, and a variety of other articles too tedious to mention, which they intend to dispose of on the most reasonable terms, by wholesale only. ALX, Feb. 1, 1785 ■ STRAYED or stolen from Mr. Michael Gretter's door, on Thursday the 27th ult. a black MARE, about fourteen hands high (with a saddle and bridle) marked by a pack-saddle along the back with white spots, suckled a foal, and shod all round.--Whoever will secure said Mare, if found within ten miles of this town, shall receive Four Dollars Reward, from Mrs. GRETTER, and if stolen, Six Dollars for her and the thief, paid by the Subscriber, living in Fairfax County, within three miles of the old Court-House. WILLIAM SWINK, Feb.

3, 1785 ■ Just received, and to be Sold on the most reasonable Terms, at the Printing-Office, A GREAT VARIETY OF ELEGANT PAPER-HANGINGS, Feb. 3, 1785.

Page 4. Poetry. "On Bribery." ■ Brenton, Va., Prince William Co., Jan. 8, 1785. On Monday the 4th of April next, if fair, if not the next fair Day, will be offered for Sale, at Mr. William M'Daniel's Tavern, in the Town of Dumfries, ABOUT 4000 acres of LAND, being part of that noted tract of land, called and well known by the name of the Brenton-Tract; it lies about 17 miles from Dumfries, 30 or 35 miles from ALX, and 28 from Fredericksburg.--At Dumfries the nighest navigation, there is always a good and ready market for every kind of country produce, and the two last mentioned towns are the most considerable on the two rivers of Potomack and Rappahannock.--This land produces very good tobacco, wheat, corn, &c. is particularly well adapted to farming, being very level, can always be improved with little expence, and is remarked for its superior excellence in producing wheat; there is on it some land which may be converted into good meadow land, and 12 or 14 good merchant mills within 30 miles, three of them as nigh as 8 miles.--The tobacco made on the land is esteemed among the best carried to Dumfries, the best inspection on Potomack.--The land will be laid off in lots of 1, 2 or 300 acres.--Three years credit will be given, provided the interest is regularly and punctually paid.--Bond carrying interest from the day of sale, with approved and sufficient security, will be required.--The land will be shewn by the subscriber living on the premises.--Several blooded Nags will be sold at the same time. DANIEL CARROLL BRENT [see like ad Vol. I No. 51] ■ JONATHAN SWIFT and CO. Have for Sale, at their Store on Capt. Harper's Wharf, a general Assortment of European Goods, suitable to the Season, which they will sell by the Package or Piece at a very moderate Advance, viz. Broadcloths of all colours and prices, corduroys, royal ribs, velvets, velverets, sarrandines, crapes, camblets, cambleteens, linens, dowlas, osnaburgs, carpetings, gauzes, millenary, ladies' calamanco and lasting shoes, misses Morocco ditto of different colours, gentlemens' shoes and boots, beaver, castor and felt hats, canvas, cordage, porter in hampers, an assortment of hardware, fowling-pieces, 10d. and 20d. nails, elegant looking-glasses, cut glass, and a few crates of queen's ware for sterling cost and charges. ☞ Their terms are for ready-money, for which they allow two and an half per cent.--They will give the market price, in cash or goods, for good Tobacco. ALX, Jan. 10, 1785 [see like ad Vol. I No. 50] ■ ELIZABETH HANNAH, INFORMS the Public, that she has lately removed to a large commodious house of Mr. Andrew Wales's, on the bank-head, being a pleasant [healthy] situation, where she proposes continuing her school, and will take, if timely applied to, ten young ladies as boarders.--Her terms for boarding and tuition are Thirty Pounds per annum. ALX, Jan. 17, 1785 [see like ad Vol. I No. 52] ■ ☞ Choice LAMPBLACK to be Sold at the Printing-Office ■ M'CREA and MEASE, Have just arrived an Assortment of GOODS, which they propose selling on the most reasonable Terms; amongst them are Cloths, shalloons, calamancoes, durants, camblets, denims, checks, striped hollands, bedbunts, messinets, silverets, taffetas, nonsopretties, tapes, glassware, window glass, clear and spotted lawns, striped and figured ditto, ditto handkerchiefs, fine souflee and needle-work'd aprons, threads, Dutch lace and edging, silk ferrets, Barcelona handkerchiefs, black and white lace, blond ditto, ladies' fashionable trimmed cloaks, hats and bonnets, Cyprus and other gauzes, knee and other garters, mens' and womens' gloves, silk [mitts], ribbons, counterpanes, Irish linens, osnaburgs, quality bindings, ladies' stays, writing-paper, inkpowder, pins, needles, milled and common flannels, mens', womens' and boys' thread, cotton and silk hose, spelling-books, pocket-books, hair broom-heads, brushes, sieves, table knives and forks, clasp and pen knives, rasors, shaping and other scissors, bar-lead, shot, coffee-mills, sleeve-buttons, plated spurs and buckles, spectacles, blank account books, quills, bridles, curry-combs, horsewhips, money-scale with weights, twist, sewing silk, shirt-buttons, cottons, calicoes, coatings, &c.&c. It is useless to say any thing respecting the terms on which these goods will be sold--Whoever applies at the Post-Office, will find them agreeable. ALX, Jan. 4, 1785 [see like ad Vol. I No. 49] ■ TO BE SOLD, A VERY valuable TRACT of LAND, lying on Aquia-Run, in Stafford Co., Va., not more than one mile from Aquia Warehouse, about six miles from Dumfries, and twelve miles from Fredericksburg, containing Six Thousand Acres; it is well watered, abounding with timber, and is calculated for planting or farming.--On this land are several valuable mill-seats... For further particulars inquire of the Subscriber opposite to Lower-Marlborough, in Md., or to Colonel BAILEY WASHINGTON, near to and adjoining the premises, who will shew the land. WILLIAM FITZHUGH, October 13, 1784 [see like ad Vol. I No. 37] ■ FOR SALE, A Valuable TRACT of LAND, lying in Frederick Co., Va., containing 1100 acres, within eight miles of Winchester, on the main road from thence to Philadelphia, and within two miles of three merchant mills [further and payment description]...

The price may be known by applying to Mr. Charles M'Donald on the premises, or to Mr. Nathaniel Burwell of Carter's Grove, on James-River, or to the Subscriber in York County, near Williamsburg. NATHANIEL BURWELL, jun. Nov. 19, 1784 [see like ad Vol. I No. 43] ■ FOR SALE, A PLANTATION, within 8 miles of Winchester, containing 400 acres--the lands are rich, level, and but very little broken with limestone, about 60 acres of which are cleared, and under good fences, has a large new barn, and a pretty good overseer's house.--Also 300 acres of unimproved Land, lying about 2 miles from the above place.--Likewise three very well improved Lots in the borough of Winchester, in a very advantageous part of the town for any kind of business.--Cash, Tobacco, or Military Certificates will be received in payment, and the terms made known by applying to the Subscriber. JOSEPH HOLMES. Winchester, Nov. 25, 1784. ☞ Also for sale, a large and neat Assortment of MERCHANDIZE, which he will sell for very little more than first cost, for Cash or Tobacco. J.H. [see like ad Vol. I No. 34] ■ WANTED, As an Apprentice to a genteel Business, A Smart active Lad, who can be well recommended.--Inquire at the Printing-Office. ALX, Jan. 23, 1785 ■ JOHN MURRAY And COMPANY, Have for Sale on the best Terms for Cash or Produce of any Kind, NEW Beef in Barrels, Molasses, Green Tea, Tallow Candles in Boxes, Coffee, Sugars, New-England Rum in Hogsheads, Tierces and Barrels.--Also a General Assortment of European and India GOODS, by Wholesale or Retail. ☞ They will purchase Tobacco, Hemp or Flour, at such a Price and give such Pay as cannot fail to satisfy the Seller, at their Store in Fairfax-Street, opposite the Court-House. ALX, Jan. 19, 1785 [see like ad Vol. I No. 51] ■ The Subscriber has on Hand, and is selling on low Terms, by the large or small Quantity, A VERY LARGE AND GENERAL ASSORTMENT OF MEDICINES, And sundry other Articles necessary for Practitioners of Physic and Surgery. ☞ His Medicinal Shop is now moved to the extreme Part of Cameron-street, leading from the Court-House directly towards the Church, where Orders from Gentlemen of the Profession and others will be speedily and punctually complied with. WILLIAM BROWN, ALX, Jan. 18, 1785 [see like ad Vol. I No. 51].

THE SHIP *HAZARD*, Capt. NEW, now lying at ALX, will take in Tobacco consigned to FORREST and STODDERT, London, at Seven Pounds, Sterling, per Ton.--She will sail early in February.--The Tobacco will be insured to receive Ten Guineas per Hogshead in case of Loss.

BENJAMIN STODDERT.

George-Town, Jan. 15, 1785.

ALL PERSONS HAVING CLAIMS against the estate of Mr. JOHN THORNTON, deceased, late of Loudon Co., are desired to make them known, that provision may be made for the payment thereof; and all those indebted to said estate, are requested to make payment to SAMUEL LOVE, jun. Executor. Loudon Co., January 15, 1785 [see like ad Vol. I No. 51] ■ FORTY DOLLARS REWARD. RAN away from the Subscriber the 24th of August last, a remarkable black strong-made Negro Man, named PETER, late the property of Mr. Benjamin Foreman, about 5 feet 9 inches high, about 22 years of age, but appears older [additional details]. MICHAEL M'KEWAN. [torn] Martinsburg, Berkeley Co., Dec. 27, 1784. N.B. Said Negro was raised with Mr. John Werington, and formerly belonged to Mr. Alexander Catlet near Seneca in Maryland [see like ad Vol. I No. 51] ■ ROBERT LYLE, WILL Rent the house and Store he now lives in, and Part of a House and Store opposite the Printing-Office that is not quite finis[hed], for one or more Years.--He has for Sale, a few Pipes and Hogsheads of Coniac and Spanish Brandy, a few Chests of Bohea, Green and Souchong Teas, Loaf Sugar by the Hogshead, Nails by the Cask, and an Assortment of Dry-Goods too tedious to mention. ALX, Jan. 19, 1785 [see like ad Vol. I No. 51] ■ THE SUBSCRIBER WILL LEASE out a Lot of Ground, 28 feet front on Royal-Street, adjoining the north end of Mr. Richard Arell's brick house, and extending back easterly 123 feet 5 inches, being part of the late Mr. Piper's lot, rent free, on condition the lessee erect such buildings as the parties can agree on.--Those who take it soon may have the lot for seven years and nine months. WILLIAM RAMSAY, ALX, Jan. 3, 1785 [see like ad Vol. I No. 49] ■ ALX: Printed by GEORGE RICHARDS, and COMPANY, at the Corner of Fairfax and Princess Street--by whom Advertisements, &c. are thankfully received for this Paper,--and where Printing is performed with Care and Expedition.

1785/02/10, Vol. II No. 54

Page 1. WILLIAMS, CARY, And COMPANY, have goods for sale, just arrived by the *May*, Capt. Haskell [see like ad Vol. II No. 53] ■ HOOE AND HARRISON, Have for Sale at their Store, Osnaburgs, etc, [see like ad Vol. II No. 53] ■ DANIEL and ISAAC M'PHERSON, Have for Sale, WEST-INDIA and New-England rum, etc. [see like ad Vol. II No. 53] ■ EDWARD HARPER offers for sale stout strong hearty young Negro man [see like ad Vol. II No. 53] ■ WILLIAM HUNTER, jun. offers for sale a few pipes of choice Madera Wine [see like ad Vol. II No. 53] ■ PEREGRINE FITZHUGH offers land for sale in Prince William County [see like ads Vol. I No. 49 and Vol. II No. 53] ■ WILLIAM SWINK offers reward for strayed or stolen mare from Michael Gretter's door [see like ad Vol. II No. 53] ■ CALLENDER, LEWIS and COMPANY is dissolved; ELEAZER CALLENDER will continue ropemaking business [see like ad Vol. II No. 53] ■ Choice LAMPBLACK to be Sold at the Printing-Office ■ **VENICE, September 22.** Chevalier Emo reports that on September 6 he was with his squadron on the Barbary coast. The Bey of Tunis forwarded proposals to him via the Venetian Consul, to which Emo replied he could undertake no negotiations until the Tunisians had made indemnification for insulting the Republic's flag. The Regency assures it will grant such, and we may hope our differences will be satisfactorily resolved. ■ **LONDON, October 29.** Letters dated the 18th from Dutch Flanders report Austrian troop movements towards Antwerp, possibly to total 10,000 men there in 24 hours. Austrian villages near Lillo are barricaded by wagons, trees, &c. ... Extract of a letter from **Strasburg, October 16**: The writer, with the banker Mr. Zolicoffer, witness the diving descent of Mr. Henri de Clermont--a young Swiss balloonist. [The ebullient and detailed account of his "unrivaled performance", together with particulars of his balloons' construction and operation, the amazing ascension, provisions carried, journey aloft, and his miraculous survival run almost two columns: the longest and most colorful report of this 18th century fascination.--Eds.]

Page 2. [The Great Balloon Adventure (*continued*)] ... Extract of a letter from **Rotterdam, October 16**: on the 1st or 3rd of this month a triple alliance in support of the Barrier treaty was concluded at Paris between these states and the Courts of Berlin and Versailles. England will be forced into the war; the Emperor has called upon his Britannic Majesty (in his capacity of Elector) to join the Westphalian circle to compose the army which is to assemble at Brabant next March ... Extract of a letter from **Stockholm, October 8:** Northern powers, especially the Empress of Russia seem uneasy by our Court's putting our frontier in a state of defense, and augmenting our troops. To address the concerns relayed by the Court of St. Petersburgh's Ambassador, and as the matter has been improperly reported in the newspapers, the Minister of State (Baron de Creutz) issued for publication a verbatim transcript--translated from the German--of the Swedish clarification. Contrary to rumor, Sweden is not preparing for war; no troops assembled, and the magazines at Carlscrone only those authorized by new regulation for the sea service. To preserve his military and defensive system, he orders training maneuvers. His deteriorating fleet is undergoing routine repairs. His artillery, useless in the capital (in view of his conviction of the Empress' friendship) has of course been redeployed to the frontiers where it belongs. The reported 20,000 men mustered in Scandinavia are working on the Christianstadt and Landscron fortifications. Far from having the least hostile design, these actions are pacific measures, tending to the preservation of that repose by which the King is become dear to his people. ■ **Nov. 3.** Extract of a letter from **Dublin, October 26:** Yesterday delegates from counties, cities and towns met for seven hours at the William Street exhibition room . Mr. D'Arcy put the case for extreme secrecy in the face of corrupt men, corrupt times, and iniquity unparalleled even by Nero's. Accordingly he requested the galleries be cleared, and all non-delegates to withdraw; his motion was agreed to without a division. On the motion of Sir Edward Newenham, Colonel William Shawman was unanimously elected president, and John Talbot Ashenhurst, Esq. Unanimously chosen secretary, to the congress. ■ **Nov. 11**. From a respectable correspondent: on Saturday the 30th, the Emperor of Germany at Brussels declared war against the States General. ■ **Nov. 12.** From Flushing, on the 3rd, they write that Dutch Admiral Reynst has dispatched two vessels of 16 guns up the Scheldt, to reinforce the *Dauphin* cutter, to be stationed between fort Cruithanz and Stoitagre. As the Emperor has ships of force in that area, the States may wish to cover troops crossing the river. ■ **Nov. 13.** An authoritative source cites word reaching Brussels of a skirmish in the fort Lillo area between Imperial troops and the Dutch--to the disadvantage of the latter ... The whole of the Germanic body are in ferment over the Emperor's affairs with the Dutch. Protestant Electors side with him, but some ecclesiastics of the contrary persuasion side with (and are in the pay of) France. If the French abide by their treaty with Holland, the contest will be obstinate; if the Courts of Versailles and Vienna are in accord, the Hollanders' situation will be desperate, and they must give up their claims ... Extract of a letter from **Blois, France, October 31:** All France believes English-French peace will not last long, with war almost certainly to break out first in the East Indies. The cabinet is unanimous concerning Ireland, wishing equitable concession and exact equality ... Extract of a letter from **Brussels, November 8:** Last night the Dutch broke a dike near Lillo, drowning several persons. Their attempt on a second was prevented by Imperial troops. Ostend is alarmed, and makes an extraordinary effort to complete the ramparts there. ■ **Nov. 14.** A Dunkirk letter received yesterday reports word received there reports a clash between Imperial and Dutch forces. The Dutch were attempting some new works at fort Lillo; The Emperor's troops attacked, but were repulsed with 7 killed, 15 wounded ... Reliable letters from **Portendie, Sept. 5**, on the Guinea coast, indicate that disputes between the French at Goree and the Moorish King, Alley Courie, remain unsettled. The latter captured the Governor's large snow bound to Europe with a valuable cargo, and seizing and carrying up to the country the entire crew and a lady of distinction ... Yesterday Lord George Gordon attended the Dutch Ambassador to St. James's, dressed in a great coat, with a large belt slung over his shoulder, and in that a broad sword, and a Dutch cockade in his hat; upon coming to the bottom of the stairs, he there halted until the Ambassador returned, when he drew his sword and saluted the Ambassador, declaring at the same time, that he would protect to the utmost of his power, the Dutch Protestants and their interests. ■ **NEW YORK, January 19.** There now being in town sufficient (9) representatives in Congress, they sit daily in their city hall rooms, on the dispatch of national business. ■ **PHILADELPHIA, January 28.** *Extract of a letter from a gentleman at* ***Amsterdam*** *to his friend in New York, dated the* ***25th of November, 1784****:* The Ambassador at the Court of Vienna being recalled, and his departure from Gravenhague having effectually taken place the first instant, without taking leave, and our minister at Vienna, having been instructed to do the same, we are now at open war with the Emperor. Twenty thousand Croats march toward our frontiers. The insurance upon Dutch vessels from America to Holland is twenty per cent ... Private letters from Amsterdam say war has actually broken out between the Emperor and the Republic; the Emperor has ordered 80,000 troops to march toward the Low Countries. In consequence, 40,000 Prussians and 40,000 French auxiliaries are moving to join the United Provinces' forces.

Page 3. **BALTIMORE, February 1.** The ship *Aldborough*, Capt. Moatt, arrived here from Cadiz on the 1st; spoke the *Galliot* -----, commanded by William Richey, from London for Virginia. She had lost her bowsprit and some sails, and was then bearing away for Bermuda. ■ **ALX, February 10**. Some very useful Discoveries have been made at Milan by the Chevalier de Marco Barbaro, Chamberlain to the Court of Bavaria, on fermented Grain, employed in sowing. Each Grain has produced above 15 Ears. Upwards of 600 Farmers, whom he has supplied with Grain thus prepared, to sow their Lands, are lavish in their Praises of it. The Chevalier de Marco has repeated his Experiments on different Kinds of Grain, and particularly on Rice, which he has sown on dry Land, where it thrives, after this Preparation, as if it was in Water. This last Discovery, in particular, will become of great Benefit to the World, as it is well known that the Stagnation of the Waters, necessary to the Cultivation of Rice, are hurtful to the Salubrity of the Air, and caused it to be excluded from many Countries. ■ Arrivals at Baltimore. Ship *Aldborough*, J. Moatt, from Cadiz; Sloop *Dolphin*, W. Willis, Hispaniola; Schooner *Ellicott*, A. Parrott, Boston. ■ NAVAL-OFFICE, ALX. *Inward Entries*. None. *Cleared Outwards*. Sloop *Polly*, D. Peoples, for Philadelphia; Schooner *Industry*, J. Foster, Beverley; Sloop *Lark*, S. Brown, Boston; Brig *Greenwich*, C. Collins, Lisbon.

GEORGE RICHARDS announces completion of the paper's first volume [see like ad Vol. II No. 53]

Messieurs Richards and Company,

WE wish to inform the public through the channel of your paper, that laws, on similar principles, have passed the Assemblies of Virginia and Maryland, for establishing a Company to open and extend the navigation of the River Potomack, by which the said Company are allowed to raise by Subscription a capital stock of Fifty Thousand Pounds, sterling, for completing the said work, in shares not less than One Hundred Pounds, sterling, each. It is stipulated that the work shall begin in one year after the Company is formed, and the River made navigable from the highest part of the North-Branch, that has water sufficient, to the Great Falls in three years, and be completed from thence to tide-water in ten years after the said Company is formed; and for the encouragement the Company are vested in perpetuity with tolls, agreeably to the Act [a few copies of which may be had at the Printing-Office].

The Collectors are vested with power sufficient to enforce the payment of the tolls. The property invested in this fund is declared to be real estate, and the same is to be forever free from payment of any tax, imposition or assessment whatsoever. The probability of success in this business has been so well ascertained to the different Assemblies, that they have each ordered their Treasurer to subscribe for the State Five Thousand Pounds, sterling, so that one fifth of the capital is already secured. The two States have also given directions to have a wide road cut from the head of the navigation on the North-Branch to the most convenient head waters of the Ohio, by which such an easy, extensive and inland intercourse will be opened as has not yet been discovered; and what is farther encouraging it opens a communication with a country that is said to be the most healthy, commodious and fertile of any in America. Hence the great advantages that must inevitably flow to our country, from the success of this scheme, joined to the private emoluments that are like to accrue to the adventurers, afford such great encouragement, that we doubt not the remaining subscriptions will soon be filled up. Books are now opened for this purpose at the city of Richmond by Jaquelin Ambler and John Berkley, Esquires, Joseph Holmes and Edward Smith, Esquires, at Winchester, and by the Subscribers at ALX. The books will be continued open till the 10th of May next, and a general meeting of the subscribers called on the 17th of said month, to choose a President and Directors for carrying on the work.

JOHN FITZGERALD,
WILLIAM HARTSHORNE,
ALX, Feb. 9, 1785

PRICES CURRENT, ALX. / Tobacco, 29s. per Ct. / Fine Flour, 30s. per Barrel. / Wheat, 6s. per Bushel. / Jamaica Spirits, 4/6 per Gallon. / Windward Rum, 3s. per Ditto. / Continental Rum, 2/2, to 2/4 per Ditto. / Molasses, 1/6 per Ditto. / Muscovado Sugar, 38s. to 47s. per Ct. / Salt, 6s. per Bushel, by Retail. Exchange, 36.

To be Sold at the Vendue-Store, on Saturday next the 12th Instant, Saturday the 19th, and Monday the 21st, a Variety of valuable Merchandise, among which are the following Articles, viz.

A Quantity of good sound Dutch blankets, sold for the benefit of the insurers; a parcel of the best London superfine broadcloths in half pieces of the following colours, white, green, olive, grey, London brown, mixt, prune, garnet, drab, &c. coarse and narrow ditto, corduroys, linseys, flannels, swanskins, a parcel of yard-wide Irish linens lately imported, Russia sheeting, dowlas, diaper, osnaburgs, canvas, printed linens, calicoes, ribbons, osnaburg thread, pins, garterings, plated buckles, plated table and tea spoons, large elegant looking-glasses, mens' and womens' shoes, hats, saddles, suits of mens' ready made clothes and shirts, queen's and glass ware in crates and hogsheads, a general assortment of the best finished joiners' and carpenters', coopers' and smiths' tools in small parcels, among them are a variety of planes of most kinds complete, such as smoothing, single and round, double-ironed, jack, fore, raising, hollows and rounds, bead, sash, fillister, O's, OG's, screw, rabbit, table, grooving, &c. adzes, hammers, drawing-knives, axes, frows, augers, chisels, brass, iron-rimed and wood stock locks of the best kinds, stirrups, candlesticks, steel coffee mills, curry combs, vices, reap-hooks, &c. Also loaf sugar, muscovado ditto in tierces and barrels, soap and pipes in boxes, Port wine in half pipes and quarter casks, Liverpool bottled ale in hogsheads, tanners' oil, mackerel, spades, shovels, cutting knives, crosscut and hand saws, plain silver watches, womens' set shoe buckles, mens' knee ditto, gold set broaches, &c. ☞ On Tuesday the 22d, will be sold, the three Tracts of Land lying near town, as advertised in this paper by Mr. Dade. C. COPPER, Vendue-Master, ALX, Feb. 10, 1785.

THE Vestries of the different parishes throughout the State, being by an act passed the last session to be dissolved on Easter day next, and the Vestries being by the same act empowered to levy all arrearages and legal demands against the parishes, notice is hereby given to all persons having claims against the Vestry of Fairfax Parish, that the Vestry will meet at the vestry-house, near the Falls church, on Wednesday the 16th day of March next, for the purpose of settling all claims and levying all arrearages; and all persons having demands against that parish, or who have undertaken the care of the parish poor, are desired to attend: And the members of the Protestant Episcopal Church are hereby informed that an election of vestrymen will be held at the vestry-house, on the Monday in next Easter week, agreeably to the directions of the beforementioned act. DAVID GRIFFITH, Minister, R.T. HOOE, W. PAYNE, Church Wardens, Feb. 10, 1785.

THE BRIG *MAY*, Captain HASKELL, from LONDON, which arrived here on Friday last, has a Number of Goods on board for different Gentlemen on this River.--The Captain requests they may be immediately sent for, as his Stay here will be but short. ALX, Feb. 2, 1785 ■ THE Subscriber has on hand about Eleven Hundred Pounds, sterling, worth of MEDICINES, SHOP-FURNITURE and SURGEON'S INSTRUMENTS, a large proportion thereof not yet opened, and all imported from Europe within eight months past; which quantity being found much too large for the common demand of this place, he will divide the whole with any gentleman in want of such a supply, and sell one half at first cost by the invoice:--Any person inclining to purchase will find the Medicines well assorted, and laid in on as advantageous terms as any that have been imported since the peace; and they may be divided for the most part without breaking packages.--The other half he will retail by the pound, for ready money or short credit, at an advance of 25 per cent. on the original cost, which is considerably lower than they are sold by retail any where on the continent. W. BROWN, ALX, Feb. 8, 1785. ■ RICHARD ARELL and GEORGE MASON offer twenty dollars reward for strayed or stolen MARE [see like ad Vol. II No. 53] ■ WHEREAS some evil minded Person or Persons have maliciously reported that I have given up my House, and quit entertaining Gentlemen--I therefore think it my Duty to inform the Public in general, and my former Customers in particular, that I still keep my House for the Accommodation of Gentlemen as usual. JOHN LOMAX, ALX, Feb. 9, 1785. ■ WILLIAM LOWRY, And COMPANY, Have for Sale the following European GOODS, for Cash, Tobacco, Gensang, Snakeroot, Sarsaparilla, Skins, or short Credit, viz. Superfine and refine cloths, cassimers, tablecloths, ratteens, coatings, Salisbury cloths, a variety of Irish linens, calicoes, calamancoes, russels, tammies, durants, moreens, satinets, lastings, corduroys, fustians, jeans, cotton and linen checks, souflee, striped, spotted and plain gauzes, handkerchiefs, ribbons, modes, satins, Marseilles quilting, muslin stripes, German cords, demities, nankeens of the best quality, cotton, thread and worsted hose, writing-paper, wafers, pens, quills, blank books, counting-house ditto, sealing-wax, threads, pins, laces, bag buttons, twist, bindings, hardware, ironmongery, nails, &c. ☞ As W. Lowry proposes shortly to return to England, it is earnestly requested that all those indebted to the house would make speedy payment.--They will give Cash for good Tobacco. ALX, Feb. 8, 1785. ■ ALL PERSONS HAVING ANY Demands against the Subscriber are requested to bring them in that they may be settled; and those whose accounts have been long standing, would much oblige him by settling them immediately, and thereby prevent trouble and expence. JOHN LOMAX, ALX, Feb. 10, 1785 ■ FRANCIS FABRIT proposes opening a dancing-school [see like ad Vol. II No. 53] ■ TO BE SOLD, THREE valuable Negro MEN, well acquainted with Ropemaking Business.--Inquire of CHARLES STEWART at Annapolis, Feb. 9, 1785 ■ THE DRAWING OF THE GEORGE-TOWN ACADEMY LOTTERY is unavoidably put off till the Third Monday in May next. George-Town, Feb. 2, 1785 ■ Just received, and to be Sold on the most reasonable Terms, at the Printing-Office, A Variety of elegant PAPER-HANGINGS.

Page 4. Poetry. "On Truth." ■ M'CREA and MEASE, Have just arrived an Assortment of GOODS [see like ad Vol. II No. 53] ■ WILLIAM FITZHUGH offers for sale land on Aquia-Run in Stafford County [see like ads Vol. 1 No. 37 and Vol. II No. 53] ■ MICHAEL M'KEWAN offers fourty dollars reward for runaway Negro man named Peter [see like ad Vol. II No. 53] ■ DANIEL CARROLL BRENT offers about 4,000 acres for sale called the Brenton Tract [see like ad Vol. II No. 53] ■ NATHANIEL BURWELL, jun. offers for sale 1,100 acres of land in Frederick County [see like ads Vol. I No. 43 and Vol. II No. 53] ■ JOSEPH HOLMES offers for sale a 400-acre plantation near Winchester [see like ads Vol. I No. 34 and Vol. II No. 53]. ■ EDWARD HARPER seeks persons indebted to copartnership of Harper and Fenner [see like ad Vol. II No. 53] ■ A PERSON OF A LIBERAL PRO-fession is desirous of trying a benevolent Experiment, by instructing an honest NEGRO LAD in a Business that will give him, if ingenious and docile, an accurate Knowledge of the English Language, and besides rendering him really a rational Creature, will enable him, in due Time, to earn handsome wages.--Inquire at the Printing-Office ■ TO BE SOLD at the PRINTING-OFFICE, A Variety of Writing-Paper, Dutch Quills, Paper Hangings, Blank Books, gilt and common Letter Paper, Sealing-Wax, Wafers,

Inkpowder, Pounce, Ink-stands, Black Lead Pencils, Common Prayer Books, from Two to Ten Shillings; Boston's Fourfold State, Russel's Sermons, Psalters, &c.&c.&c. ■ BALDWIN DADE offers for sale at public vendue three tracts of land situated in Fairfax County [see like ad Vol. II No. 53] ■ SAMUEL M'LEAN offers for sale a 200-acre plantation within a few miles of ALX [see like ad Vol. II No. 53] ■ NOTICE is hereby given, that a petition will be presented to the next General Assembly, relative to draining the marsh adjoining this town, and to condemn certain lands, the property of Charles Alexander, Esq., for the use of public buildings and other purposes. ALX, January 25, 1785 ■ TO BE SOLD, On board the Sloop *Polly*, Capt. Mark Clark, at Col. Lyle's Wharf, Rhode-Island cheese, cranberries, chairs, potatoes, butter, cyder, oil, hops, spruce, and mackerel. ALX, Jan. 23, 1785 ■ ALX: Printed by GEORGE RICHARDS, and COMPANY, at their Printing-Office on Fairfax--by whom Advertisements, &c. are thankfully received for this Paper,--and where Printing is performed with Care and Expedition.

1785/02/17, Vol. II No. 55

Page 1. DANIEL and ISAAC M'PHERSON, Have for Sale, WEST-INDIA and New-England rum, etc. [see like ad Vol. II No. 53] ■ WILLIAMS, CARY, And COMPANY, have goods for sale, just arrived by the *May*, Capt. Haskell [see like ad Vol. II No. 53] ■ WILLIAM FITZHUGH offers for sale land on Aquia-Run in Stafford County [see like ad Vol. II No. 53] ■ JOHN LOMAX seeks to settle accounts of long standing [see like ad Vol. II No. 54] ■ TO BE SOLD, THREE valuable Negro MEN, well acquainted with the Ropemaking Business.--Inquire of CHARLES STEWART at Annapolis, Feb. 9, 1785 ■ W. BROWN has for sale medicines, shop-furniture and surgeons instruments [see like ad Vol. II No. 54] ■ WILLIAM LOWRY, And COMPANY, Have for Sale European Goods [see like ad Vol. II No. 54] ■ FRANCIS FABRIT proposes opening a dancing-school [see like ad Vol. II No. 53] ■ RICHARD ARELL and GEORGE MASON offer twenty dollars reward for strayed or stolen MARE [see like ad Vol. II No. 53] ■ THE DRAWING OF THE GEORGE-Town ACADEMY LOTTERY is unavoidably put off till the Third Monday in May next. George-Town, Feb. 2, 1785. ■ **PARIS, October 9.** The Count d'Oels (Prince Henry of Prussia) seems to have recovered from his recent slight indisposition, but remains confined to his apartments by important private affairs. A treaty of confederacy has been completed between Prussia, France, Holland and the Grand Seigneur which will effect whatever they please when they have revenged themselves on Austria and Russia. ■ **HAGUE, November 19.** The substance of a circular letter of October 23, 1784, sent to all the Ministers of the Emperor of Germany at the foreign Courts, and considered in Europe a DECLARATION of war: You know the claims of his Imperial Majesty against the States General, his offer of amicable settlement and the Brussels conferences to that end. The Dutch non-performance, the closing of the Scheldt, the change in Europe from that which prevailed at the conclusion of the Munster Treaty means the Scheldt is not the real object. Although the Emperor sought amicable accommodation with the Republic, they have blocked negotiations and held to a claim not only illegitimate but contravening a number of treaties. To validate his rights, his Imperial Majesty dispatched a ship from Antwerp, with ample warning of possible violent responses should his ship be denied free passage. The subsequent action, which insulted our flag, has been publicly reported in some detail. His Imperial Majesty can only regard that as an effective declaration of war by the Republic. Consequently, he ordered the recall of the Baron de Reischach, his minister at the Hague, to quit Holland without taking leave of the States General, and to assemble in the Low Countries an army of 80,000 Imperial troops--to be augmented as circumstances may require. Objective observers will agree that these are the natural consequences of an hostility so manifest, and a fact by which his Imperial Majesty's dignity has been so grievously wounded. Please explain these matters, in person.

Page 2. [The German-Dutch matter (*continued*)] Per contra, the paper delivered by the Dutch Ministers at Brussels to Comte Belgiojoso: In response to his Imperial Majesty's orders as received from his Excellency Comte Belgiojoso, that the Republic's conduct is responsible for an insult to his flag, and the Baron Reischach recalled, the Ministers Plenipotentiary of the Republic of the United Provinces protest any hostile aggression, and maintain they were but supporting their incontrovertible right. The Republic persists in their peaceable dispositions but--if his Imperial Majesty is not swayed--the republic will do whatever is necessary, however disagreeable, as the right of nature and nations entitles it to. [signed] at Brussels, October 30, 1784: BARON HOP, W. A. LESTEVENON, P. VAN LEYDE, P.E. VAN de PERRE ■ **LONDON, November 4.** M. L'Abbe de Crillon received from Madrid the 8th of last month a print of an amphibious animal found in the mountains of Chile. It is a carnivore, 11 feet long, scales, beared chin, broad forehead with ox-like horns, an ass's ears, breast and facial features with some resemblance to a man; its enormous jaws are set with six inch teeth; one of its two tails seizes its prey, the other used for defense; its bellow horrible, its effluvia very offensive like that Virgil ascribed to the harpy Cylaeno. This one is a male; the captured female escaped and terrorizes Chili's inhabitants, requiring a whole sheep per day. Brought to Madrid September 25, he will be conveyed to Paris the end of winter ... Lunardi has challenged Blanchard to a 3-heat balloon race: with, across, and against the wind. Bets placed in the St. James neighborhood exceed £50,000. ■ **Nov. 16.** The high population of the United Provinces may be attributed to their great trade, and many manufactories and fisheries. Some reckon the population at two and a third million, while Susmilch and other political arithmeticians say two and a half millions--a million in the province of Holland, alone. Most of the first class, the old nobility, are now extinct, and the vacancies not filled up, as the States General confer neither rank nor nobility. Some Counts or Barons, so made by the late Emperor, bear the titles but are not permitted the ancient nobility's privileges ... Yesterday, news from Brussels reported M. De Reischach, his Imperial Majesty's late envoy to the Hague and immediately met with the Governor. It appears the Dutch, via the Grand Pensioner, declared to the Envoy that the States General in concert with the other Seven United Provinces will insist on the sovereignty of the river Scheldt. Such is in accord with both the 1648 Munster treaty and that of Aix la Chapelle in 1731, agreed to by his Imperial Majesty's predecessor--as Duke of Brabant and Austria, and Count of Flanders, further guaranteed by several powerful courts. The States were further concerned by the unexpected departure of the much esteemed Envoy. They hope his Imperial Majesty will not plunge into war with a people who have high regard for his justice and his person--a neighbour with whom they wish to live on terms of mutual convenience and respect. ■ **Nov. 18.** The French Monarch recently published a plan by which Captains of inactive naval ships may receive two-thirds pay, but may not leave the kingdom without permission. Absentees forfeit their pay. The hope is to prevent them from engaging in foreign service, and have experienced officers on hand for the navy when required. This country should do the same ... On the 6th of this month, at Achencrue, Scotland, died Richard Oswald, Esq., lately a Commissioner from England to Versailles for negotiating the peace ... Extract of a letter from **Oran, October 26**: On Sunday the 26th, Don Pedro Guelphi, commanding officer here, learned that Moors had appeared in our garden ground about nine o'clock. Our drums beating to arms caused the enemy to retreat precipitously, carrying away things pilfered from the inhabitants, and cutting down the fruit trees. We estimated them to be a full 8000. We pursued, and they dug in along the hollow roads. Don Andrea de Dasas repulsed those of the enemy who had fallen upon his troops. The enemy gave way, carrying off a great number of their dead; our loss was trifling. The enemy--the entire Turkish force under the Bey--joined him with five pair of colours on the heights, from which he witnessed the affair from six in the morning till one in the afternoon. ■ **PHILADELPHIA, Feb. 1.** By an authentic letter from **Dublin**, by the last packet, via New York, we learn of a credit revolution The national bank has reduced the paper speculation whose excess enables adventurers with little or no property to make a great figure and sport away upon other men's substance. Business people are retrenching and being more frugal. None but persons of real property will survive this ordeal ... In this mercantile world, public spirit and private corruption pass at par in Ireland. The good and the wise seem to lose out to corruption and power. Rutland is plastered with panegyrical addresses by the minions of the court and their dependents. Charlemont also, who tends to destroy that harmony on which the hopes of Ireland were founded, is addressed 'on his manly and constitutional answer,' in spite of the sons of liberty opposition. May the flame which animated Americans kindle in the bosom of the Irish, and lead them to an effectual opposition of the oppressions of their tyrants, and a determination to be really free! ■ **BALTIMORE, February 8.** A late Irish newspaper mentions the Irish Parliament meets the 2nd, and the English Parliament the 21st of January, to afford the former to draw up some trade matters before the repeal in England of the navigation act, as far as it relates to Ireland. ■ **ALX, February 17.** On Tuesday, the 8th Instant, being the Election of the Mayor, Aldermen and Common-Council, of this Town, the following Gentlemen were chosen: JAMES KIRK, Esq., Mayor; JAMES KEITH, Esq., Recorder; DAVID ARELL, JOHN FITZGERALD, RICHARD CONWAY, and WILLIAM HERBERT, Esquires, Aldermen; Messieurs WILLIAM HARTSHORNE, SAMUEL ARELL, WILLIAM HUNTER, jun., BENJAMIN SHREVE, PETER WISE, and WILLIAM LYLES, Common-Councilmen. ■ A Letter from Philadelphia mentions, that the December *Packet* was arrived at New-York; but the Letters brought by her had not come to Hand.--That it was reported the Quarrel between the Emperor and the Dutch was compromised.--And that two American Vessels had been taken by the Algerines.

On the 10th Instant departed this Life, in the 69th Year of his Age, WILLIAM RAMSAY, Esq., a Gentleman generally esteemed for the humane and generous Sentiments of his Heart, as well as for his Uprightness and Integrity, throughout a long and active Life:--This Gentleman first proposed and promoted the Establishment of the Town of Alexandria, and was its first Inhabitant.--He was consoled on the Verge of Life, with the Reflection of having acted his Part well, and of having reared, and leaving to represent him, a numerous and amiable Family, in Possession of as much Happiness as generally falls to the Lot of Humanity.--Thus he met the lingering but certain Approach of Death with a Composure and Resignation of Mind very remarkable and truly exemplary.--His Remains were interred on the 12th in the Episcopal Church-Yard, and attended by very numerous and respectable Company, preceded by the Brotherhood of Free-Masons in Procession, with the Solemnities usual of such Occasions.

NAVAL-OFFICE, ALX. *Inward Entries*. Brig *Industry*, C.C. Russel, from Boston; Schooner *Virginia*, S. Davis, Hispaniola. *Cleared Outwards*. Schooner *Harrington*, H. Williams, for New-York or Philadelphia. ■ Messieurs PRINTERS, Please to inform Mr. Patton, through your Paper, that it would become the Character of a Gentleman to insert Truth in Public Prints, if he means to take spiteful Liberties against another.--Had Mr. Patton waited till next Day, which was the proper Stage-Day, he would not have been disappointed of accompanying Col. Jameson to ALX. NATHANIEL TWINING.

PRICES CURRENT, ALX. / Tobacco, 29s. per Ct. / Fine Flour, 30s. per Barrel. / Wheat, 6s. per Bushel. / Jamaica Spirits, 4/6 per Gallon. / Windward Rum, 3s. to 3/3 per Ditto. / Continental Rum, 2s. to 2/2 per Ditto. / Molasses, 1/6 per Ditto. / Muscovado Sugar, 38s. to 45s. per Ct. / Salt, 6s. per Bushel, by Retail. / Corn, 3s per Bushel / Exchange, 40.

WILLIAM HARTSHORNE And COMPANY, Have for sale at their Store in ALX, A Quantity of molasses, coffee and muscovado sugar, just arrived in the Schooner *Virginia*, Capt. Davis, from the West-Indies.--They have also for sale, by large or small quantities, alum salt, continental rum, bar-iron, steel, train oil, mackerel, soap and candles by the box, with a variety of dry-goods as usual. ☞ They give Ready-Money and a good price for Wheat and Indian-Corn. February 14, 1785 ■ Fairfax County, Feb. 16, 1785. ON MONDAY NEXT, BEING Court-Day for this County, will be let at the Court-House, to the Persons who will perform the Services for the least Money, the Repairs to be made on the Court-House and Gaol of this County.

Page 3. Just Imported from London, in the Brigantine *Fitzhugh*, now opening for Sale by ROBERT ALLISON, A Large and general Assortment of DRY-GOODS, suitable for the present and approaching Season, which will be Sold on the lowest Terms for Cash, Tobacco, Flour and Wheat. ALX, Feb. 15, 1785 ■ LEERTOUWER, HUYMAN, And HUIBERTS, Have imported in the last Vessels from Holland, Superfine, middling and coarse broadcloths, German osnaburgs, Ravens duck, Russia sheeting, ditto drilling, fine and coarse Dutch linens, calicoes, chintzes, coarse hats, diapers, checks, silk handkerchiefs, gauzes, a variety of ribbons, laces, half-bleached sewing thread from No. 16 to 50, nonsopretties, tapes, ready-made shirts, worsted stockings, 8 by 10 window-glass, nails of all sizes, padlocks, coffee-mills, candlesticks with handles, lamps with ditto, shovels, hatchets, frying-pans, chafing-dishes, trevits, gridirons, smoothing-irons, table knives and forks, chopping-knives, powder, shot, all kinds of paints, glass and queen's ware, blue and white coffee-cups, Dutch gin in cases and jugs, French cordials in large and small boxes, Frontigniac wine in cases of 12 bottles.--They have also for sale continental rum in hogsheads, tierces and barrels, and a variety of other articles, which they intend to dispose of on the most reasonable terms, by wholesale only. ALX, Feb. 15, 1785 ■ Just imported from London, and to be Sold by Wholesale, by WILLIAM DEAKINS, jun., At his Store in George-Town, the following Articles, viz. Superfine, fine and coarse broadcloths, duffils, Bath coatings, fearnoughts, powder, shot, bar-lead, candles, soap, camblets, corduroys, black alamodes, silk and linen handkerchiefs, cloth cardinals, Irish sheetings, dowlas, Irish linens, pewter basons, dishes and plates, tin and glass ware of all kinds, bed tickings, German osnaburgs, brown rolls, thread and silk stockings, gauzes, cambricks, diaper tablecloths, working canvas, black silk florentines, rich brocaded lustrings, fashionable bonnets, ditto silk cardinals and shades, worked muslin aprons, saddler's ware and tools, lump sugar, double and single refined ditto, all kinds of teas, ginger, sulphur, nails of all sorts, guns, andirons with brass heads, locks, hinges, desk furniture, brass chafingdishes, candlesticks, spades, pickaxes, several pair of fashionable pint silver cans, fashionable set knee-buckles, gold sleeve-buttons, mens' and womens' gloves, blond and thread lace, a great variety of ostrich feathers, seine twine, saltpetre, &c.&c. February 14, 1785 ■ TO BE SOLD, On Monday the 7th of March next, before Mr. WILLIAM M'DANIEL's Door, in the Town of Dumfries, TWELVE SLAVES, belonging to the personal estate of the Rev. Mr. JAMES SCOTT, deceased, consisting of Men, Women and Children; and on Friday in the same week, at Westwood, in Prince-William County, the remainder of the Household Furniture, belonging to the said estate, consisting of tables, chairs, bedsteads, one bed and furniture, a neat pier glass, and other articles too tedious to enumerate.--Credit will be allowed for all sums exceeding Forty Shillings for twelve months, the purchasers giving bond and approved security, to bear interest from the date, if not punctually paid. T. BLACKBURN, Administrator. ☞ Those who have claims against the said estate are desired to bring them in, that provision may be made for payment; and those indebted to it, either by bond or open account, are requested to discharge the same as speedily as possible. Rippon-Lodge, Feb. 8, 1785 ■ TEN GUINEAS REWARD. RAN away on the 21st of January last two English servants, viz. WILLIAM CASEY, about five feet seven or eight inches high, twenty-eight years of age, by trade a bricklayer; his head is rather large, has brown straight hair, and a scar on the left side of his chin.--WILLIAM HUBBLE, about five feet six inches high, twenty-six years of age, by trade a bricklayer, and has dark brown hair sometimes tied.--They have been at ALX and sold some of their clothes and tools.--Whoever apprehends the said Men, and gives notice to EDWARD VIELLER, at Annapolis in Maryland, shall receive the above reward, or FIVE GUINEAS for either of them, and all reasonable charges. Feb. 3, 1785 ■ ALMANACKS, For the Year of our Lord One Thousand Seven Hundred and Eighty-Five, may be had at the Printing-Office, ALX, Wholesale and Retail.

[Top right column two and three ripped away from microfilm copy.]

TO THE PUBLIC. PROPOSALS for printing by subscription [ ] complete translation of the Odes, Epodes [ ] Secular Poems of Horace, in English verse; which [ ] it is the first work of that nature ever attempted [in] America, it is hoped, will meet with every encour[age]ment from the candid and judicious citizens of [the] States. The five books, together with every [ ]ticular Ode and Epode, are addressed to [ ] distinguished civil and military characters amo[ ]. Besides the literal translations from the original, [ ] are a number of Imitations and Paraphrases, e[ ] adapted to the meridian of this country, a[ ] genius of its inhabitants. It is likewise propo[sed] to publish a few poetical translations from Virgil [ ] Tibullus, Anacreon, and our own Beveridg[ ] two or three modern Latin Odes.--Also a [ ] of Original Poems, consisting of Pastorals, E[nglish] Satires, Letters, Songs; Masonic, New-Year's, Bir[th]-Day and other Odes; Fables, Epigrams, Epitaphs, Rebuses; Distichal Panegyrics, on Ladies of Distinction, and other Poetical Miscellanies.--To which will be added a Pastoral Drama, on the Birth-Day of our late Commander in Chief, and the Return of Peace; inscribed to the Governor of Pennsylvania, with a Prologue written by a Lady, a Critical Preface addressed to the Subscribers, and an Epistle Dedicatory of the whole, to his Excellency General Washington. The above work is the production of a young gentleman, late an officer of rank in the American army. It is therefore to be expected that every gentleman civil and military, in the United States, who wish to encourage the arts and sciences [in this] rising Empire, will patronize a work, which [we] presume, cannot fail to merit their approbation, more particularly as it is a Cyon of American growth, and as such is entitled to the countenance and protection of the sons and daughters of freedom in this western hemisphere. Such ladies and gentlemen who are pleased to honor this work with their subscriptions, will have their places of abode, names, rank and titles, whether literary, civil or military, inserted in the book, as laudable encouragers of arts and genius,

CONDITIONS,

This work is intended to be printed in a large handsome octavo volume, on a good paper with a neat type, and to contain between three and four hundred pages.--It will be sent to press as soon as five hundred subscribers have signed their names. The price to each subscriber will be Three Dollars, a sum hardly adequate to so arduous an undertaking; the half of which is to be paid at the time of subscribing, to enable the printer to expedite the work, and the residue at the delivery of the book. It is to be observed that no more volumes will be printed than the exact number subscribed for; and they who enter their names for more than a dozen books, will have the usual discount allowed them. Subscriptions will be received by Col. Thomas Chase, at Boston; Col. Samuel Wyllis, in Hartford,

Connecticut; Dr. Charles M'Knight, New-York; Mr. Isaac Collins, Printer in Trenton, New-Jersey; Col. Thomas Proctor, High Sheriff of Philadelphia; Col. Eleazer Oswald, at the Coffee-House, Messrs. Dunlap and Claypoole, Printers, and Major Samuel Nicholas, at the Conestogoe-Waggon in Philadelphia; Mr. John Barnaby, Merchant, Head of Elk, Cecil-County; Mr. John Carnan, near the Head of Bohemia; the Rev. Dr. Smith, Provost of the College at Chester-Town; Mr. James Ryan, Merchant, Mr. William Murphy, Bookseller, Messrs. Goddard and Langworthy, and Mr. Hayes, Printers, and at Major William Brown's, and Mr. T. DeWitt's Coffee-Houses in Baltimore-Town; Messrs. F. and S. Green, Printers in Annapolis; Mr. Charles Allen, Merchant in Cambridge, E.S. of Maryland; Col. Fitzgerald, and the Printers in ALX; Mr. William Carr and Mr. Richard Graham, Merchants, Dumfries; John Lewis, Esquire, and Col. William M'Williams, Fredericksburg; Mr. John Stockdell, Merchant, and Mr. James Hayes, Printer in Richmond; Mr. William Knox, Merchant in Petersburgh, Virginia; and by Dr. Ramsey, Major Weede, and Dr. Fallen, in Charleston, South Carolina. ■ FIVE POUNDS REWARD. ON the 22d of last month was stolen out of my stable, a bay HORSE, with black mane and tail, black legs, has several saddle-spots, is crest fallen and branded upon the near buttock B, about 15 hands high, 12 years old, trots and gallops easy, but cuts his ancles a little with his hind shoes; he was Major George Washington's saddle-horse during the invasion in 1781, and mine for several years before and since.--It is supposed he is stole by a Frenchman that calls himself PEILLON, who is of a middle size, dark complexion, about 30 years old, is well dressed, and wore here a blue coat with a red waistcoat with three rows of buttons.--Whoever brings the said horse to me shall have the above reward, and double on conviction of the thief. JOHN BROWNLOW. Fredericksburg, Feb. 8, 1785.

[Portion of top right column ripped away from the microfilm copy; text taken from like ad run the following day.]

ONE HUNDRED DOLLARS REWARD. RAN away from the subscriber on the night of the 12th instant, a likely black raw-boned country-born Fellow, named WILL, who is very artful and roguish, and is supposed to have been guilty of felony which is the supposed cause of his elopement; he is about forty years of age of the middle size, stands wide between the knees, and when standing stoops in his knees, has long slim feet, large ancles, long heels, and has a hump on his breast; he is a very hardy fellow in plantation business, drives carriages well, a good ploughman, can stock ploughs, understands stacking] and mowing, and can do the common carpenter jobs necessary on a plantation; having a variety of clothes his dress cannot be described.--Eight Dollars will be given if taken up twenty-five miles from home or under, and reasonable travelling charges paid if brought home, and so in proportion to the amount of the above reward.--Said Negro is supposed to be in company with white men on their way to the southern States. LEWIS ELLZEY, Feb. 14, 1785. ■ NOTICE is hereby given to whom it may concern, that I intend to apply to the next General Assembly of the Commonwealth of Virginia, to have a deed recorded that I got from JOHN MOXLEY, of Loudon County, for a tract of land in Hampshire County, on Patterson's Creek, for which I have paid the whole consideration, and missed having it recorded through my ignorance of the laws of the said Commonwealth.--The said John Moxley was to have made me a deed, but was prevented by death. CONRAD MYRE, February 10, 1785 ■ Just received, and to be Sold on the most reasonable Terms, at the Printing-Office, A Variety of elegant PAPER-HANGINGS ■ MICHAEL M'KEWAN offers fourty dollars reward for runway Negro man named Peter [see like ad Vol. II No. 53] ■ A petition is to be presented relative to draining the marsh adjoining ALX [see like ad Vol. II No. 54] ■ TO BE SOLD at the PRINTING-OFFICE, A Variety of Writing-Paper, Dutch Quills, Paper Hangings, Blank Books, gilt and common Letter Paper, Sealing-Wax, Wafers, Inkpowder, Pounce, Ink-stands, Black Lead Pencils, Common Prayer Books, from Two to Ten Shillings; Boston's Fourfold State, Russel's Sermons, Psalters, &c.&c.&c.

Page 4. [Top of left column ripped away from microfilm copy] ■ DAVID GRIFFITH, R.T. HOOE and W. PAYNE give notice regarding the abolishment of vestries [see like ad Vol. II No. 54] ■ DANIEL CARROLL BRENT offers about 4,000 acres for sale called the Brenton Tract [see like ad Vol. II No. 53] ■ WILLIAM HUNTER, jun. offers for sale Madera Wine, Jamaica Rum, etc. [see like ad Vol. II No. 53] ■ Goods for sale from the Brig *May*. Captain Haskell, from London [see like ad Vol. II No. 54] ■ NATHANIEL BURWELL, jun. offers for sale 1,100 acres of land in Frederick County [see like ads Vol. I No. 43 and Vol. II No. 53] ■ BALDWIN DADE offers for sale at public vendue three tracts of land situated in Fairfax County [see like ad Vol. II No. 53] ■ JOSEPH HOLMES offers for sale a 400-acre plantation near Winchester [see like ads Vol. I No. 34 and Vol. II No. 53] ■ CALLENDER, LEWIS and

COMPANY is dissolved; ELEAZER CALLENDER will continue ropemaking business [see like ad Vol. II No. 53] ■ SAMUEL M'LEAN offers for sale a 200-acre plantation within a few miles of ALX [see like ad Vol. II No. 53] ■ PEREGRINE FITZHUGH offers land for sale in Prince William County [see like ad Vol. II No. 53]. ■ WILLIAM SWINK offers reward for strayed or stolen mare from Michael Gretter's door [see like ad Vol. II No. 53] ■ ☞ Choice LAMPBLACK to be Sold at the Printing-Office ■ ALX: Printed by GEORGE RICHARDS, and COMPANY, at their Printing-Office on Fairfax--by whom Advertisements, &c. are thankfully received for this Paper,--and where Printing is performed with Care and Expedition.

1785/02/24, Vol. II No. 56

Page 1. LEERTOUWER, HUYMAN, And HUIBERTS, Have imported in the last Vessels from Holland a selection of goods [see like ad Vol. II No. 55] ■ WILLIAM DEAKINS, jun. has for sale an assortment of goods just imported from London [see like ad Vol. II No. 54] ■ W. BROWN has for sale medicines, shop-furniture and surgeons instruments [see like ad Vol. II No. 54] ■ CHARLES STEWART at Annapolis has three valuable Negro men for sale [see like ad Vol. II No. 54] ■ ROBERT ALLISON has for sale a large assortment of goods just imported from London [see like ad Vol. II No. 55] ■ WILLIAM LOWRY, And COMPANY, Have for Sale European Goods [see like ad Vol. II No. 54] ■ T. BLACKBURN has for sale 12 slaves belonging to the personal estate of the late Rev. Mr. JAMES SCOTT [see like ad Vol. II No. 55] ■ WHEREAS sundry persons from ALX have made a practice of going on my land and cutting wood, and have also been dealing with my Negroes, I do hereby give this public notice, that I have employed a man to guard my property, and that any person found trespassing, or dealing with my Negroes in any manner whatever, shall be prosecuted with the utmost vigor. THOMAS H. HANSON, Feb. 14, 1785 ■ WILLIAM HUNTER, jun. offers for sale Madera Wine, Jamaica Rum, etc. [see like ad Vol. II No. 53] ■ WILLIAM HARTSHORNE And COMPANY, Have for sale items just arrived in the Schooner *Virginia* [see like ad Vol. II No. 55] ■ JOHN LOMAX denies malicious reports that he has given up his house [see like ad Vol. II No. 54] ■ LEWIS ELLZEY offers one hundred dollars reward for runaway fellow named Will [see like ad Vol. II No. 55] ■ EDWARD VIELLER, at Annapolis, offers ten guineas reward for two runaway English servants [see like ad Vol. II No. 55] ■ CONRAD MYRE notifies public he intends to record deed from John Moxley, of Loudon County [see like ad Vol. II No. 55].

Page 2. **LEGHORN, October 29.** Bombardment by the Venetian squadron, Chevalier Emo commanding, destroyed two thirds of Susa, in the Tunisian territories. **Paris, Nov. 13:** Orders have been expedited for victualing troops destined for Flanders. Tomorrow the Dutch Ambassadors will receive their answer from the Count de Vergennes; that from Vienna cannot be looked for before the 28th. The King's interference with the Emperor has been of the most pressing nature, though in terms of friendship and alliance. ■ **LONDON, Nov. 27.** *Extract of a letter from* ***Amsterdam, Nov. 25:*** News from Utrecht says the Colleges of State of that province will arm all inhabitants, country and town, aged 18-60 ... Thirty-two British officers are said to have been murdered by Tippo Saib, after the surrender of Badinore: two per day, in order of seniority, by scalding oil upon their heads--this to force confessions of the garrison treasure's supposed hiding place! In consequence of Tippo Saib's cruelty to General Matthews and his officers, officers in the Company's service vow that in future they will neither give nor take quarter. ■ **December 1.** Extract of a letter from **Florence, Oct. 20:** The Duchess of Albany arrived here the 7th at the house of the Pretender, her father; he had not seen her since she was six. The Grand Duke immediately sent one of his gentlemen to compliment her. The Pretender, having wished the theatre box given her might be distinguished from the common ones, the Grand Duke ordered it ornamented as for the Grand Duchess: with tapestry fringed with gold. When the Duchess of Albany went to the opera, the court and the city honored her passage; as she is both young and beautiful, being dressed in the Parisian taste, and ornamented with her father's jewels, she cut a splendid figure. Her father was enchanted, and it is hoped she will make him happy in his old age ... A letter from Lisbon says two American ships loaded with wheat and flour would not off-load until their commanders were assured both that they would be paid in cash and not afterwards stopped for having so much Portugal money aboard. They were put on guard by--just as they arrived in the harbour--an English vessel being stopped on that account, and released only at the intercession of the English Consul. ■ **DUBLIN, November 15.** Last Saturday, in his Majesty's Court of King's Bench, Counsel was heard in behalf of Stevens Reily, Esq; on a rule to shew cause why an attachment should not issue against him, for having, as High Sheriff of the county of Dublin, convened and presided at meetings of his bailiwick on last July 31 and August 9, for illegal purposes. Counsel for the Crown: the Right Hon. The Attorney General, the Solicitor General, Prime Serjeant, and -----. Counsel for the defendant: Counselors Caldbeck, Sheridan, Hussey (the Recorder), and Smith. Opening statements being incomplete at a late hour, the Court adjourned until tomorrow ... The Castle Hacks say the long-wished for protecting duties will eventually be granted. Two persons are named as plenipotentiaries from our Parliament, to meet with the English Ministry as to mode and quantum of sums, articles on which they are to be imposed, and similar regulations. ■ **CHARLESTON, December 28.** Yesterday put in here in distress, the brig *Friendship*, Captain Murray, from Halifax, bound to Virginia ... Piracy under American Colours: The schooner *Free-Mason*, formerly the *Nancy*, the property of the subscriber, was piratically taken away from him by the Captain and his crew, having just gone ashore for information previous to entry, on the 3rd instant, within sight of Cape Francois, in the island of Hispaniola. A reward of one hundred Spanish milled dollars for information leading to the recovery of vessel and cargo. The schooner is remarkably long; Philadelphia built, 25 tons burthen, 55 feet keel, and from 13 to 14 feet bean; painted on her sides white, yellow, red and green, and on her stern are emblems of Masonry on the deck is fixed a large false cable [sic; probably *cabin*; see following text - Ed.], at the end of which is the binnacle, and an iron stove for baking; the entrance to the cabin is by two steps, and through a double door painted green, the inside is papered, white and yellow; a small distance from the steps is a contrivance for depositing provisions, &c. that locks with a French padlock; in the cabin are four keeping places, two of which serve as presses, and contain sundry merchandises, silks, Flanders linen and lace, and paper hangings. **Description of the Crew**: *Francis Hughes*, the Captain, a native of Port Louis, in Brittany; about 25 years old, 5 feet 4 inches high, yellow complexion, with black hair and eye brows. *Theobald Bush*, an Irishman, about 30 years old, 5 feet 2 inches high, chestnut coloured hair and eye brows, and very much marked with the small pox. *John Pilot*, a native of the environs of Bourdeaux; about 28 years old, 5 feet 3 inches high, very meagre, black hair and eye brows, and remarkable small eyes. *Marson Besie*, a native of Brittany, about 28 years old, 5 feet 1 inch high, full faced, and very large eyes. *Peter Pauget*, a native of Berne, about 35 years old, 5 feet 1 inch high, very lean, and black complexion. *Thomas Carwin*, a native of Pumage, in Normandy, cabin boy, a likely youth, about 15 years old, and 5 feet high. **CHARLES TRAVERS**, Kingston, Jamaica, Nov. 19, 1784. As the subscriber returns to Hispaniola, he requests of any who can give information of the above atrocious act of piracy, to declare the same to Mr. A. Lido, merchant of this town. ■ **NEW YORK, Feb. 8.** We feel extreme concern in announcing the death of Major Robert Malaysian, formerly a merchant in Maryland; a bilious disorder has deprived the world of a most amiable ornament of society, the loss of which is sincerely regretted by a very extensive acquaintance in Europe and America. He died in Philadelphia. ■ **PHILADELPHIA, Feb. 12.** We hear from New York that a few days ago Congress appointed Mr. Gervais of South Carolina, Mr. Osgoode of Massachusetts Bay, and Mr. Walter Livingston of New York, Commissioners to the Board of Treasury ... Several gentlemen arriving here from New York say that the December British packet reached there last Saturday with the news that the Emperor of Germany has given up his claim for opening the Scheldt, as he found that other European powers--so far from countenancing him--had declared in favour of Holland. This is confirmed in letters by the packet brought, whose Captain also mentioned it to our correspondent ... Last Monday arrived here Colonel Francis Johnson, one of the Commissioners for holding a treaty with the Indians, who says the treaty satisfactory to both parties was concluded about twelve days ago at Fort M'Intosh. At this treaty the State purchased of the Indians all the land within this State's original grant. They fixed the bounds of the Indian territories with this State, which neither party are to transgress, and any crime committed will be punished by the suffering party agreeable to the laws of their country. They have also opened the trade into the Indian country ... Last Friday, the 21st, at a meeting in Philadelphia of the Philosophical Society, for promoting useful knowledge, the following gentlemen were elected members, viz.: Frederick Eugene Francis, Baron de Beelen Bertholff, Imperial Counsellor of Commerce to the United States, Brussels. Samuel Gustavus, Baron Hermelin, of Stockholm; Sweden. William Bradford, Esquire, Attorney General of Pennsylvania. Edward Burd, Esquire, Prothonotary of the Supreme Courts of Pennsylvania. Dr. Adair Crawford, Physician of St. Thomas's Hospital; London. Doctor John Carson of Philadelphia. The Reverend Manasseh Cutler of Ipswich, Massachusetts. The Count de Guichen, Lieutenant General in the French Naval Armies; France. Andrew Ellicot, Esquire, Maryland. Doctor William Griffiths of Philadelphia. Doctor Hugh James of Montenegro Bay, Jamaica. Mr. Joseph Mandrillon, Merchant of Amsterdam. Brigadier General Thaddeus; Kozenzook. Mr. Henry Herchell of Bath, England. Doctor James McHenry of Baltimore, Maryland. James Madison, Esquire, of Virginia. The Reverend Henry Muhlenberg of Lancaster, Pennsylvania. Christ. Fred. Michaelis, M.D. of Gottenburg[h]. The Honorable Mann Page, Esquire, of [Fredericksburg], Virginia. Thomas Payne, Esquire, Author of Common Sense. Charles Petit, Esquire, of Philadelphia. Dr. Robert Percival, Professor of Chymistry, Trinity College, Dublin. The Reverend Doctor Richard Price, F.R.S. London. The Reverend Joseph Priestly, L.L.D.F.R.S. Birmingham. The Reverend Doctor Samuel S. Smith, Vice President of the College of Nassau Hall, Princeton, New Jersey. Monsieur Jean Baptist Siie, junior, Surgeon and Professor of Anatomy; Paris. Colonel George Wall, of the Supreme Executive Council of Pennsylvania. Mr. Benjamin Workman, Teacher of Mathematics in the University of Pennsylvania. Extract from the minutes, SAMUEL MAGAW, one of the Secretaries. ■ **Feb. 14.** The affairs of Europe seem pregnant with consequences alarming to humanity. Though remote from that theatre, we lament the turbulence of those spirits, that for mere punctilios of court etiquette can involve whole kingdoms in the horrors of war, and want only to massacre thousands of their inhabitants. ■ **Feb. 15.** The sloop *Susannah*, Capt. William Earle, jun. of Providence, arrived at Charleston, South Carolina from the Mississippi River, where the Spaniards would allow him neither to trade nor proceed up to New Orleans. Soldiers boarded him, and dispatched a boat to New Orleans. Eight days later it returned with orders for him to put to sea immediately. Prior to this, several other American and British vessels had also been compelled to quit the river. ■ **February 16.** Extract of a letter from **London**, dated **Nov. 30:** A revolution in the French Ministry has been threatened; as the Queen disapproves of France's arms turned against her Imperial brother, whilst Vergennes urges a due observance of national faith, pledged to Holland ... Imperial troops destined for the Low Countries: **Infantry.** The regiments of Ligne, Kaunitz, Clairfayt, Vierset, Murry, Bonder, Preyst, Latterman, Dentmeister, Migazzi and Tillier. Two battalions of Croats, with 280 Chasseurs, 132 artillerists, four battalions of militia levied on the frontiers, 300 Chasseurs of Tyrol, a body of 500 hussars, and another 600 Boulons. **Cavalry and Dragoons.** The regiments of Cobourg, Tuscany and Arberg, with four divisions, and their squadrons of reserve; the regiments of Warmser, with five divisions. The **artillery** is very large, and the Generals of this numerous army are Messrs. Alton and Slade for the infantry, and Harrach and Lelier for the Cavalry. ■ **Feb. 17.** Last Thursday arrived here Arthur Lee, Esq., one of the Honorable Commissioners of the United States for Indian Affairs, en route New York to report to Congress their proceedings with the northern and western Indians. ■ **ALX, February 24.** On Thursday, the Third Instant, was married at Annapolis, the Honorable JOHN F. MERCER, Esq., one of the Delegates representing this Commonwealth in the Congress of the United States, to Miss [Sophia] SPRIGGS, eldest Daughter of Richard SPRIGGS, Esq., of that City. ■ His Britannic Majesty's Packet *Speedy*, Captain D'Auvergne, will sail from New-York, with the Mail for Falmouth, on the 4th of next Month. The Mail will be closed the preceding Day. ■ NAVAL-OFFICE, ALX. *Inward Entries.* Brig *William and Henry*, T. Simmons, from Salem; Schooner *Adams*, A. Row, Gloucester; Ship *Leda*, S. Dunn, Hispaniola. *Cleared Outwards.* Schooner *Success*, S. Parker, for Nova-Scotia; Brig *Ann*, G. Fanshaw, Liverpool; Brig *May*, W. Haskell, Patuxent.

Page 3. [S]TATE of the PUBLIC TAXES to be collected in the year 1785, due under the Revenue Law for 1784. On land.--30s. in the 100l. or 1½ per cent. *ad valorem*, to be collected in manner following: 20s. in the 100l. or 1 per cent. ad valorem, distrainable for the 10th of October last, and payable into the Treasury the 10th of November last; and the remainder or 10s. in the 100l. being half per cent. *ad valorem*, distrainable for the 31st of January, 1785, and payable into the Treasury the 25th of March, 1785.

On all slaves of both sexes and of all ages, 10s. each.

On every free male above the age of 21 years, 10s.

On every horse, mare, colt and mule, except covering horses, 2s.

On every covering horse, the sum such horse covers one mare at the season.

On cattle of all ages, for each 3d.

On all riding carriages 6s. per wheel.

On every billiard-table, 15l.

On every ordinary license, 5l.

The above taxes for the year 1784, on free males and property, as also the tax on slaves are distrainable for the 31st of January, 1785, and payable into the Treasury on or before the 25th day of March, 1785.

By an act of the last session of Assembly one half of the above taxes due under the revenue law for the year 1784, on land, slaves, free males and property, are remitted, and the other half are distrainable for the 1st day of September next, and payable into the Treasury the 1st of November following.

J. AMBLER, Treasury-Office, Jan. 31, 1785.

Note. — Specie, Auditor's warrants for interest on military certificates; and civil list warrants may be paid to the sheriffs or other collectors in discharge of any of the public taxes whatsoever, due for the year 1784; but the taxes on land and slaves must be paid at the Treasury either in specie, warrants for interest on military certificates, or civil list warrants, except one-tenth or two shillings in the pound of the land tax which may be paid in bills of credit, [r]emitted agreeable to the resolutions of Congress of the 18th of March, 1780.

Note also. — That's Auditor's warrants or the undermentioned funds will be received at the Treasury in discharge of all other taxes due under the revenue law for the year 1784, except the taxes on land and slaves, viz.:

Warrants on the contingent and military funds.

Warrants for pensions and present relief to disabled officers and soldiers.

Warrants for payment of money lent the public on requisition of the General Assembly in May, 1780, or Governor Jefferson.

Warrants for interest on Loan-Office debts registered, or which shall be registered before the 1st day of May next.

Warrants for interest at the rate of five per cent. per annum, due for slaves executed; warrants for which interest shall issue on the 1st day of January annually.

Warrants on the unappropriated 2-10ths of the taxes of 1783.

Warrants to venire-men and witnesses attending criminal prosecutions where the attendance has been since the October General Court in the year 1783.

Warrants to apprehenders of horse stealers.

There are likewise to be under the Certificate Law the following taxes, viz.

On land, 20s. for every 100l. or one per cent. ad valorem.

On every free male above the age of 21 years, 10s.

On all slaves above the age of 16 years, 10s.

On every horse, mare, colt and mule, each 2s.

On cattle of all ages, each 3d.

On all riding carriages, 5s. per wheel.

On every billiard-table, 15l.

On every ordinary license, 4l.

These taxes are distrainable for the 31st of January, 1785, and payable into the Treasury at the same time with the taxes under the revenue law.

All sheriffs, collectors of taxes and inspectors, are hereby required to be punctual in making their collections and paying the same into the Treasury agreeable to the several periods directed by law, as nothing will induce a delay in me from proceeding to move for judgment against them on failure. They are likewise further required to take notice that all applications for suspensions of executions must hereafter be made to his Excellency the Governor, who, with advice of Council, has power to remit the interest and damages on judgments where it may appear reasonable so to do.

The certificate tax may be discharged wither in specie, military or militia audited certificates, Treasury tobacco notes which are payable to inlisted soldiers at the rate of 20s. per hundred, or any specie warrant whatsoever. L. WOOD, jun., Solicitor, Solicitor's-Office, Jan. 31, 1785.

☞ Choice LAMPBLACK to be Sold at the Printing-Office. ■ Messieurs Richards and Company, I Had no Intention of troubling you farther, with Stage Matters, till I saw a Piece in your last Paper signed NATHANIEL TWINING, saying, "It would become the Character of a Gentleman, to insert Truth in Public Prints, if he means to take spiteful Liberties against another,"--Now I think it a Duty to inform the Public, that it was the said Twining, who told me the Stage would set off on Saturday, and at the Time appointed found three of the Horses ready harnessed, and the people at the Office uneasy at his having rode off the other.--Let them then judge what Credit is due to his Assertions for the future. JAMES PATTON, ALX, Feb. 23, 1785. ■ ANECDOTE of the KING of PRUSSIA [text not given here].

PRICES CURRENT, ALX. / Tobacco, 30s. per Ct. / Fine Flour, 30s. per Barrel. / Wheat, 6s. per Bushel. / Jamaica Spirits, 4/6 per Gallon. / Windward Rum, 3s. to 3/3 per Ditto. / Continental Rum, 2s. to 2/2 per Ditto. / Molasses, 1/6 per Ditto. / Muscovado Sugar, 38s. to 45s. per Ct. / Salt, 6s. per Bushel, by Retail. / Corn, 3s per Bushel / Exchange, 40.

TO BE LET, ON GROUND-RENT FOR EVER, SUNDRY Lots of Ground adjoining this Town. The Ground will be shewn, and the Terms made known by Mr. OLIVER PRICE in ALX, or the Subscriber. DAVID GRIFFITH, ALX, Feb. 24, 1785. ■ TEN DOLLARS REWARD. WAS taken away from the Subscriber's Plantation, on Shenandoah, Berkely County, near the Blomary, a likely young Virginia-born NEGRO WENCH, about 17 years of age, full-breasted, remarkably black, round-faced, and upwards of 5 feet high: She took with her a coarse white [linsey] jacket, a striped [linsey] petticoat, a white linen coat and apron, a white handkerchief, straw hat, very ordinary shoes and stockings, and was brought up to plantation work.--She was taken off by GEORGE LEWIS, a Dutchman, who speaks broken English, and formerly lived at ALX, but of late was a waggoner to Capt. Brady: He is a short thick fellow, of a pale complexion, and has light brown hair; had on when he went away a pea jacket lined with white flannel, a pair of breeches of the same colour, and a felt hat half worn.--Whoever apprehends the said Fellow and Wench, and secures them so that I get them again, shall receive the above reward, and reasonable charges paid if brought home. BENJAMIN RANKINS, Feb. 13, 1785. ■ Just received, and to be Sold on the most reasonable Terms, at the Printing-Office, A Variety of elegant PAPER-HANGINGS. ■ THE Subscriber having purchased a farm in the upper part of Fairfax County, means to decline the practice of physic in ALX; he will therefore consider himself much favored if all those who are indebted to him will prepare for an immediate settlement:--He will hold himself in readiness to discharge any accounts that are against him, presented any time after the 20th day of next month, relying much upon the punctuality of such as stand in arrears for his professional services; and he is sorry to add, that his late engagements will shortly oblige him to enforce a settlement with such as have a considerable time shewn too great an unwillingness thereto.☞ He will sell on very low terms for cash, wheat or tobacco, his Shop with the greatest part of his Medicines and Shop-Furniture. ELISHA C. DICK, ALX, Feb. 23, 1785 ■ For Sale on the Premises, under the Will of the late Rev. JOHN SCOTT, upon Thursday the 14th Day of next April, TWO TRACTS of LAND, lying on Town-Run and Elk-Run in the lower end of Fauquier County, and joining on Brenton; the one containing 832 acres, the other 678; considerable more than one half of these Tracts of Land is still in woods, there being on the first but one plantation, on the other two, one of which is small; they lie level, and the soil is good, and well adapted to the culture of tobacco, Indian-corn, and wheat; there is a meadow on each tract, and more may be made, there being a considerable quantity of low ground fit for that purpose; the situation is about 25 miles from Fredericksburg, 18 from Dumfries, and 30 from ALX; possession will be given to the purchaser of the larger tract immediately, and of the other at the end of the year, with 4000 lb. of crop tobacco, for which it is rented for the present year only.--One fourth of the purchase-money to be paid when possession is given, the remainder in four annual payments, the purchaser giving bond with approved security, bearing interest from the date.--Any person inclinable to purchase may see the lands before the sale by applying to Mr. HENRY D. HOOE, who lives in the neighbourhood.

Also for sale upon the premises, on Thursday the 21st of April next, 1200 acres of LAND on Wolf-Run in Fairfax County, about 16 miles from ALX, and 15 from Colchester; two-thirds of this land is in woods, the soil fertile, and exceedingly well watered; there are several orchards and other small improvements on it, and the whole is at present rented for 4500 pounds of crop tobacco.--The terms the same as the foregoing, and the lands will be shewn by Mr. Edwards in the neighbourhood.--Any person inclinable to treat privately for either of the above tracts of land before the day of sale will please to apply to the Subscriber. ELIZA SCOTT, Executrix, Prince-William County, Feb. 14, 1785. ☞ For Sale at Fauquier Court-House, on Monday the 20th of March next, several high bred Fillies of the Arabian, *Fearnought* and Liberty breed, a young Bay Horse suitable for a carriage or the saddle, and several blooded Colts.--Six months credit will be given, the purchasers giving bond with approved security, bearing interest from the date if not punctually paid. E. SCOTT. ■ RICHARD ARELL and GEORGE MASON offer twenty dollars reward for strayed or stolen MARE [see like ad Vol. II No. 53] ■ JOHN LOMAX seeks to settle accounts of long standing [see like ad Vol. II No. 54] ■ SAMUEL H. M'PHERSON, At Messieurs Hooe and Harrison's Store, No. 7, Has for sale, Port wine, porter, cheese, ticks of feathers, and a pretty general assortment of European GOODS, cheap for cash, country produce, officers, soldiers, and any kind of liquidated certificates. ALX, Feb. 23, 1785.

Page 4. Poetry. "Life." ■ SAMUEL M'LEAN offers for sale a 200-acre plantation within a few miles of ALX [see like ad Vol. II No. 53] ■ NATHANIEL BURWELL, jun. offers for sale 1,100 acres of land in Frederick County [see like ad Vol. II No. 53] ■ ALMANACKS, For the Year of our Lord One Thousand Seven Hundred and Eighty-Five, may be had at the Printing-Office, ALX, Wholesale and Retail ■ Offer to the Public to print by subscription a complete translation of the Odes, Epodes and Secular Poems of Horace, etc. [see like ad Vol. II No. 56] ■ JOHN BROWNLOW, Fredericksburg, offers reward for stolen horse [see like ad Vol. II No. 55] ■ DAVID GRIFFITH, R.T. HOOE and W. PAYNE give notice regarding the abolishment of vestries [see like ad Vol. II No. 54] ■ DANIEL CARROLL BRENT offers about 4,000 acres for sale called the Brenton Tract [see like ad Vol. II No. 53] ■ MICHAEL M'KEWAN offers forty dollars reward for runaway Negro man named Peter [see like ad Vol. II No. 53] ■ CALLENDER, LEWIS and COMPANY is dissolved; ELEAZER CALLENDER will continue ropemaking business [see like ad Vol. II No. 53] ■ THE DRAWING OF THE GEORGE-Town ACADEMY LOTTERY is unavoidably put off till the Third Monday in May next. George-Town, Feb. 2, 1785 ■ ALX: Printed by GEORGE RICHARDS, and COMPANY, at their Printing-Office on Fairfax--by whom Advertisements, &c. are thankfully received for this Paper,--and where Printing is performed with Care and Expedition.

1785/03/03, Vol. II No. 57

Page 1. DAVID GRIFFITH has for lease sundry lots adjoining ALX [see like ad Vol. II No. 56] ■ LEERTOUWER, HUYMAN, And HUIBERTS, Have imported in the last Vessels from Holland a selection of goods [see like ad Vol. II No. 55] ■ WILLIAM DEAKINS, jun. has for sale an assortment of goods just imported from London [see like ad Vol. II No. 54] ■ W. BROWN has for sale medicines, shop-furniture and surgeons instruments [see like ad Vol. II No. 54] ■ CONRAD MYRE notifies public he intends to record deed from John Moxley, of Loudon County [see like ad Vol. II No. 55] ■ Just received, and to be Sold on the most reasonable Terms, at the Printing-Office, A Variety of elegant PAPER-HANGINGS. ■ SAMUEL H. M'PHERSON has for sale at Hooe and Harrison's Store, Port wine, etc. [see like ad Vol. II No. 56] ■ RICHARD ARELL and GEORGE MASON offer twenty dollars reward for strayed or stolen MARE [see like ad Vol. II No. 53] ■ JOHN LOMAX seeks to settle accounts of long standing [see like ad Vol. II No. 54] ■ BENJAMIN RANKINS offers ten dollars reward for Negro Wench taken away from plantation on Shenandoah [see like ad Vol. II No. 56] ■ EDWARD VIELLER, at Annapolis, offers ten guineas reward for two runaway English servants [see like ad Vol. II No. 55] ■ THOMAS H. HANSON warns again persons tresspassing or dealing with his Negroes [see like ad. Vol. II No. 56] ■ ALMANACKS, For the Year of our Lord One Thousand Seven Hundred and Eighty-Five, may be had at the Printing-Office, ALX, Wholesale and Retail ■ ROBERT ALLISON has for sale a large assortment of dry goods just imported from London [see like ad Vol. II No. 55] ■ W. BROWN has for sale medicines, shop-furniture and surgeons instruments [see like ad Vol. II No. 54] ■ ELIZA SCOTT, executrix of Rev. Mr. John Scott, dec., offers for sale two tracts of land on Town-Run and Elk-Run in Fauquier County [see like ad Vol. II No. 56].

Page 2. **RICHMOND, January 4.** *In the House of Delegates, Wednesday, the 17th of November, 1784.* RESOLVED, that it is the opinion of this Committee, that acts ought to pass for the incorporation of all societies of the Christian Religion, which may apply for same. The resolution... was agreed to by the House, Ayes 62, Noes 23. [There follows the text of *An Act for incorporating the* **PROTESTANT EPISCOPAL CHURCH**, with provisions for it to enjoy ownership of property, structures, books, plate and ornaments the property of the late established church before January 1, 1777, its corporate legal responsibilities, acquisition of additional property, selection of clergymen and church officers, composition and election of vestries, financial accounting, and payment of debts in arrears since 1777.] To begin to put in effect the new provisions, a convention will be held in Richmond next May 18. [signed] MILES SELDEN, BENJAMIN BLAGROVE, DAVID GRIFFITH. ■ **LONDON, December 4.** Copy of a letter from the Right Honorable Lord George Gordon, President of the Protestant Association, to the Right Honorable Mr. Pitt, First Lord of the Treasury: Several hundred seamen, many lately from India, and among them Acting Lieutenants, Mates and Midshipmen of the Royal Navy have petitioned that they are willing, ready and able to serve the United Protestant States of Holland against the King of the Romans, and all their Popish enemies--signed by Edward Robinson, and 34 other seamen, at the Kettle Drum, Radcliff Highway, November 17, 1784. Several officers of distinction in the land service, a field officer of the Connecticut line in the province of Massachusetts, an Irish brigade officer in France, and some Athole Highlanders--among others--are of like disposition. I acquaint you, as Prime Minister, of this that you may convince Baron Van Lynden of the general good disposition of the people of these kingdoms to comply with his Excellency's request, and to renew again their old friendship with Holland upon the righteous and solid foundation of the protestant interest. [signed] I am &c, G. GORDON, Welbeck Street, Nov. 17, 1784.

Page 3. Copy of a letter from...Mr. Pitt...to G.G. from Downing Street, Nov. 19, 1784: My Lord, I have hitherto returned no answer...because I did not think it my duty to enter into a correspondence...the subject. But having been informed that many seamen have been induced to quit their occupation in expectation of being employed to serve against the Emperor, I think it proper to remind you that whatever steps you have taken, have been without the smallest degree of authority or countenance from his Majesty's ministers, and that it is for your Lordship to consider what consequences may be expected from them. [signed] I am &c., W. PITT ... Letter from G.G. to Mr. Pitt: It was very rude of you not to answer my two letters sooner.... The seamen's hearts are warm towards the States of Holland.... As soon as you, and the rest of his Majesty's ministers, are pleased to authorize and countenance these honest endeavours of the seamen to support those protestant states, I will make proposals to the Dutch Ambassador and to the States of Holland, to take them into immediate pay. The consequences may fall upon the heads of the King's servants if they advise their Sovereign tp take part against the Protestant interest. [signed] I am &c, G.G., Welbeck Street, Nov. 19, 1784. ■ **NEW YORK, February 17.** There are a number of counterfeit French guineas in circulation, but badly executed and easily detectable by their lightness ... The English newspapers have long misidentified the commander of the British forces in India. They name, in error, Lieutenant General Mathew. The commander is, rather, Major General Meadows--the same who served under Generals Howe and Clinton in this country, highly respected by all the military, British and American, during several years of the late contest. ■ **PHILADELPHIA, February 14.** Frances Hughes, mariner, was yesterday committed to gaol by his Honor the Judge of the Admiralty, being charged with piracy in running away with the schooner *Free Mason*, the property of Mr. Charles Travers, on her late voyage from Philadelphia to Hispaniola. ■ **ALX, March 3**. The Ship *Helena*, Capt. Crawford, from Glasgow, via Teneriffe, is arrived in James River. On the 14th of January he spoke with the Brig *Sea-Horse*, Capt. Simon Davis, from Boston, bound to Barbadoes; on the 19th, spoke with the *Three Friends*, Capt. Gram[e], from St. Croix to Georgia, in Distress, whom he supplied with Provision and Water; and on the 26th, spoke with the Brig *Patton*, Captain William Waters, from New-London for Hispaniola. ■ By an Act of the last Session of Assembly one Half of the Taxes of 1785, due under the Revenue Law, are remitted, and not the Taxes of 1784, as mentioned in our last. ■ NAVAL-OFFICE, ALX. *Inward Entries*. None. *Cleared Outwards*. Brig *Richmond*, J. Green, for Rhode-Island; Schooner *Adams*, A. Row, Cape-Ann; Schooner *Hope*, J. Butler, Boston; Sloop *Anchorsmith*, G. Dunham, Philadelphia; Ship *Iris*, T. Cole, Lisbon; Schooner *Polly*, J. Humphries, Baltimore. ■ On Saturday next, the 5th Inst., will be Sold at the Vendue-Office, opposite the Court-House, A VARIETY OF WET AND DRY GOODS, AS USUAL. C. COPPER, Vendue-Master, ALX, March 2, 1785. ■ WEST-INDIA GOODS, Of every Kind, to be Sold on very low Terms, for Cash, Tobacco, Hemp or Flour, by JOHN MURRAY AND CO. Also, a few Cags of fine old Coniac Brandy, and Frontigniac Wine in small Cases. ☞ They will exchange a small Quantity of Salt to receive Fish in Payment early in the Season. ALX, March 1, 1785. N.B. A general Assortment of European GOODS as usual. ■ ROBERT ADAM, Has for sale, old Jamaica spirits, West-India rum, coffee, sugar and cocoa.-- Also, a general Assortment of DRY-GOODS, and QUEEN'S-WARE, which he will sell on very reasonable terms, for cash or country produce.--He has to let, on Ground-Rent for ever, Twenty-Nine LOTS under the bank, all made ground, between Water and Union streets, and also on the east side of Union-street, and thence running along Princess-street, all of which are very well calculated for trade, and the accommodation of tradesmen, and very convenient to deep water, where vessels of any burthen may load and unload.--The terms may be known by applying to said Adam, Mr. John Lomax, or Mr. William Ward, where a plan of said Lots may be seen. March 1, 1785. ■ ALL persons that are indebted to the estate of Doctor WILLIAM RUMNEY, deceased, are once more desired to come and pay off their balances, so that the subscriber may be enabled to pay off the debts due from that estate, those who do not comply with this request, in three months from this date, may expect that suits will be immediately commenced against them. ROBERT ADAM, Executor, March 1, 1785 ■ ALL persons indebted to the estate of Mr. THOMAS KIRKPATRICK, deceased, are requested to make immediate payment, or their accounts and bonds will be put into the hands of an attorney; and all those who have claims against the estate are desired to bring them in, that they may be adjusted and paid. ROBERT ADAM, ROBERT M'CREA, JOHN GIBSON, WILLIAM HUNTER, jun., Executors, ALX, March 2, 1785 ■ To be Sold on Thursday the 7th Day of April next, agreeable to the last Will and Testament of William Douglass, Esq., deceased, at his late Dwelling-House, for Ready-Money, A TRACT of LAND in the Parish of Shelburne, in Loudon County, Virginia, containing 150 acres, near said dwelling-house, formerly purchased of Edward Dulin, whose heir will join in the conveyance, on the purchasers paying to him the first purchase-money, which is infinitely short of the value of the land; at the same time will also be sold for ready-money, 30 acres of LAND called the Smith's-Shop-Field, contiguous to said dwelling-house, purchased of Thomas Awbrey; also 70 acres of LAND adjoining the Smith-Shop-Field, likewise purchased of Thomas Awbrey; and also all the right and title of 535 acres of LAND, purchased of John Sinclair, known by the name of Hawling's Bottom, on Potomack River, of which the said William Douglass died in possession of only 365 acres; likewise a vacancy of 8 acres adjoining said Hawling's land, for which there is a deed, and 12 acres of LAND more adjoining said 8 acres, lying on the river, purchased of Thomas Awbrey.--The reason that the dwelling-house and other improvements of the said William Douglass, together with 900 acres of land to which they belong, are not now advertised, is that they are included in two mortgages with which the subscriber does not choose to intermeddle until the equity of redemption is foreclosed, as he thinks them encumbered beyond what they will sell for.--The plots will be shewn and explained on the day of sale to such persons as may be disposed to purchase; and as the day of sale has been put off two different times, owing to the badness of the weather, if the above day should be foul, the premisses advertised will be sold the next fair day. HUGH DOUGLASS, Executor, Feb. 14, 1785 ■ ☞ FOR the Accommodation of travelling Gentlemen and others, the Subscriber will let Boys and Horses.--The Boys can be well recommended, and are acquainted with most of the Public Roads and Towns in Virginia.--Inquire at Messrs. Lomax, Ward, or Wise's Taverns. ROGER CHEW, ALX, March 1, 1785 ■ FOR SALE, A Few Gross of empty Bottles.--Inquire of Capt. ROBERTSON on board the *Lilly*, or DANIEL and ISAAC M'PHERSON. ☞ A Person well recommended to act as Second Mate of a Ship, will meet with encouragement by applying as above. ALX, March 1, 1785 ■ WRIGHT and LONG, Taylors and Ladies Habit-Makers, from Philadelphia, TAKE this method of informing their friends and the public in general, that they have commenced business at the corner of King and Royal streets, next door to Mr. M'Knight's.--Such gentlemen as please to favor them with their custom may rely on being served with the greatest elegance and despatch.--Said WRIGHT and LONG take the liberty of returning their sincerest thanks to those who have already been pleased to favor them with their commands, and hope, by their skill and attention to business, to merit a continuance of their favors. ALX, Feb. 22, 1785 ■ To be Sold at Public Vendue, on Saturday the 12th Instant, A LOT of GROUND in this town, adjoining the lots of Robert Adam, Esq., fronting on Queen-street 20 feet, and extending back 88 feet 3 inches.--The terms will be one half the money in hand and the balance in 6 weeks from the day of sale, and a good and sufficient title will be made by the subscriber.--At the same time will be rented my HOUSE on Princess-street, in the situation it now stands, to the person who will finish it for the shortest Time. ISABELLA ELTON. ALX, March 1, 1785 ■ The sale of the LANDS I advertised a few weeks ago, is postponed from unavoidable causes, the Maryland Tract to the 20th of March, and the Virginia Tract to the 2d day of April.--They will then be sold upon the terms communicated in the postscript of the advertisement above alluded to. PEREGRINE FITZHUGH, Feb. 27, 1785 ■ TO BE SOLD, A Warrant for Four Thousand acres of LAND, on the Western Waters of this State, the property of a late Continental Officer.--For Terms inquire of the Printers. ■ Left on the Counter of Messieurs Shreve and Lawrason's Store. AN Auditor's Interest Certificate.--The owners may have it again by applying at said store, and paying the charge of this advertisement. ALX, March 1, 1785 ■ RAN away from the subscriber a likely young Negro Fellow, named JACOB, about 21 years of age, a brownish complexion, a steadfast look when talked with, big lips, a long high nose, with a scar on the top rather between his eye-brows, from a slight kick of a horse; he walks with his legs close and turns his toes in; is about 5 feet 5 or 6 inches high, is a very sensible artful fellow, and may probably make his way across Potomack or towards Baltimore, as he has travelled considerable distance back and endeavoured to get free:--He had on when he went away a coarse brown cloth coat with buttons of the same, with a red plush cape to it, an osnaburg shirt, and old green jacket, and new white country cloth breeches.--Whoever takes up said Negro and secures him so that I may get him again, shall have Twenty Shillings more than the law allows, paid by SAMUEL MITCHELL, Charles County, Feb. 23, 1785 ■ To be Rented for the ensuing Season, THE Fisheries at Belvoir, one of which is allowed to be one of the best Herring Fisheries on Potomack River,--The other Shores are not much inferior.--For Terms apply to BATTAILE MUSE ■ Berkely County, Feb. 11, 1785. BY a power of attorney to me directed from Nathaniel Lyttleton Savage, Esq., I am authorised to sell on the 29th of March next, the PLANTATION whereon Mr. Rich. Willis lately moved from, lying in the aforesaid County, near Keys's Ferry; it contains Four Hundred acres, has a neat well finished dwelling-house on it, some out-houses, a good spring, a large stream running through it, and about 8 or 10 acres of valuable meadow-ground; the land is good in quality, level and in a neighbourhood of genteel families. The purchaser upon paying half the cash down, and giving bond with approved security for the balance to be paid in six months, will have possession given on the first of January next, and an undoubted title, by GILES COOK, jun.

Page 4. Poetry. "Verses written extempore in praise of a GOOSEQUILL." ■ WILLIAM HARTSHORNE

And COMPANY, Have for sale items just arrived in the Schooner *Virginia* [see like ad Vol. II No. 55] ■ ELISHA C. DICK closes his practice of physic in ALX; sells his shop with medicines and shop-furniture [see like ad Vol. II No. 56] ■ DAVID GRIFFITH, R.T. HOOE and W. PAYNE give notice regarding the abolishment of vestries [see like ad Vol. II No. 54] ■ JOHN LOMAX seeks to settle accounts of long standing [see like ad Vol. II No. 54] ■ DANIEL CARROLL BRENT offers about 4,000 acres for sale called the Brenton Tract [see like ad Vol. II No. 53] ■ LEWIS ELLZEY offers one hundred dollars reward for runaway fellow named Will [see like ad Vol. II No. 55] ■ T. BLACKBURN has for sale 12 slaves belonging to the personal estate of the late Rev. Mr. JAMES SCOTT [see like ad Vol. II No. 55] ■ WILLIAM FITZHUGH offers for sale land on Aquia-Run in Stafford County [see like ad Vol. II No. 53] ■ JOHN LOMAX seeks to settle accounts of long standing [see like ad Vol. II No. 54] ■ THE DRAWING OF THE GEORGE-Town ACADEMY LOTTERY is unavoidably put off till the Third Monday in May next. George-Town, Feb. 2, 1785 ■ Offer to the Public to print by subscription a complete translation of the Odes, Epodes and Secular Poems of Horace, etc. [see like ad Vol. II No. 56] ■ CHARLES STEWART at Annapolis has three valuable Negro men for sale [see like ad Vol. II No. 54] ■ JOHN LOMAX denies malicious reports that he has given up his house [see like ad Vol. II No. 54] ■ ALX: Printed by GEORGE RICHARDS, and COMPANY, at their Printing-Office on Fairfax--by whom Advertisements, &c. are thankfully received for this Paper,--and where Printing is performed with Care and Expedition.

1785/03/10, Vol. II No. 58

Page 1. JOHN MURRAY and CO. offers for sale West-India Goods [see like ad Vol. II No. 57] ■ ROBERT ADAM has for sale old Jamaica spirits, West-India rum, etc. [see like ad Vol. II No. 57] ■ ROBERT ADAM, executor of Dr. William Rumney seeks settlement of accounts [see like ad Vol. II No. 57] ■ DANIEL and ISAAC M'PHERSON have for sale a few gross empty bottles [see like ad Vol. II No. 57] ■ DAVID GRIFFITH, R.T. HOOE and W. PAYNE give notice regarding the abolishment of vestries [see like ad Vol. II No. 54] ■ An Auditor's Interest Certificate found at Shreve and Lawrason's Store [see like ad Vol. II No. 57] ■ TO BE SOLD, A Warrant for Four Thousand acres of LAND, on the Western Waters of this State, the property of a late Continental Officer.--For Terms inquire of the Printers ■ DAVID GRIFFITH offers on ground rent sundry lots adjoining ALX [see like ad Vol. II No. 56] ■ WRIGHT and LONG, Taylors and Ladies Habit-Makers announce opening of business [see like ad Vol. II No. 57] ■ ISABELLA ELTON to sell a lot fronting on Queen-street [see like ad Vol. II No. 57] ■ PEREGRINE FITZHUGH delays sale of lands previously advertised [see like ad Vol. II No. 57] ■ SAMUEL MITCHELL, Charles County, offers reward for return of runaway Negro fellow named JACOB [see like ad Vol. II No. 57] ■ BATTAILE MUSE offers for rent the fisheries at Belvoir [see like ad Vol. II No. 57] ■ The Executors of the estate of THOMAS KIRKPATRICK seek settlement of accounts [see like ad Vol. II No. 57] ■ HUGH DOUGLASS, Executor of the last Will and Testament of William Douglass, deceased, offers for sale land in Shelburne Parish, Loudon County [see like ad Vol. II No. 57] ■ GILES COOK, jun., Berkely County, wishes to sell plantation whereon Mr. Rich. Willis lately removed from [see like ad Vol. II No. 57] ■ ROGER CHEW offers for lease Boys and Horses [see like ad Vol. II No. 57].

Page 2. **LONDON, December 1.** The vigor of Old Frederick's mind is daily giving way to the obligations of mortality. He is aware that his Prussian Majesty will take the field in favor of the Dutch, but does not consider it as important as England's politicians do. He is determined to risk the issue of a campaign, and to support his own dignity, which must be sullied, if his opposition to the Dutch is abandoned ... Betts are laid that a certain *crack-brained popular* gentleman *(Lord George Gordon)* will be in the Tower in less than three months; and indeed his present conduct favors very much offence to the constitution of the country, and the dictates of common sense ... *Copy of a letter from the Right Honorable* Count O'Rourke, *to the Right Honorable* Lord George Gordon. *Cary street, opposite Lincoln's Inn, Nov.* 24, 1784. My Lord George, I SHALL be glad to know what motive or what interest you can have in being so vehement against the ancient Catholic religion? [The writer continues with an ornate scolding: that the Gordon family was Catholic down to and including Lord George's grandfather; that the O'Rourke family has lineage more ancient, and is not for religious persecution; toleration has diffused through the world, and men accept that no particular mode of worship will open the road to heaven; did not your Lordship partake of that blessing; Catholics are considered good subjects of our King; forget the odious word Papist; that O'Rourke was in a Scotch regiment (Lord Lewis Drummond, commanding) in the French service, wherein men of different religions lived like friends; anent the regiment, O'Rourke concludes: it would have been fortunate for you had you passed a few years in it; it might have given you a more liberal way of thinking, and kept you out of a vast deal of trouble; it is not too late to mend; and when your lordship pleases to call on me, I shall be happy to enlarge on the subject with you, and perhaps, if you are not predetermined, I may be able to convince you that you are wrong. I have the honor &c, O'ROURKE. P.S. I should be glad to know who is this officer in the Irish Brigade you so pompously mention...I am sure you can have no influence over him...to join in your present schemes. I must also remark, that when you speak of the Emperor, you should observe the respect due to so great a public, and so illustrious a private character. ... Lord GEORGE GORDON's Answer states he is answerable to his constituents, and accountable to government and the magistrates; if he has broken any laws he is not responsible for his public conduct to O'Rourke or any other private individual. G.G. therefore declines the offer to call upon him to enlarge upon the subject. Signed at Welbeck street, Nov. 29, 1784. ■ **TENERIFFE, December 18.** A bark arriving here the 14th from the island of Hierro brings a tale of a most melancholy event there on the 7th. On the 6th a vessel flying white colours put ashore 37 people, among them 5-7 women, some with babies. They came ashore on a S.W. beach whose only exit inland was a narrow defile through otherwise inaccessible rocks. Nearby islanders secured the opening, and some went to the principal town to the Governor, Don Juan Briz Calderon. Briz convened a Cavildo (council). Because of the plague in Europe, an order prohibited vessels being admitted until no danger of infection could be determined. However, against strenuous objections by some Cavildo members, Briz ordered that the people on the beach be killed. Refusing the plea that the islands' Governor General be informed, and his ruling sought, Briz took a party of militia to the spot. Firing the first fatal shot himself, he threatened the reluctant militiamen with instant death if they did not continue the massacre. None of the people offered resistance, nor could they escape--their ship having sailed off after landing them. All were slaughtered. The Governor General, at first unbelieving, was convinced by letters from Briz, himself. He has commenced action by which those responsible will meet with condign punishment. The victims' nationality is not known, but is generally supposed to be from Ireland or Scotland, going to America. ■ From the *Bahama Gazette*. **NASSAU, January 8.** We hear that a 1000 troop reinforcement has been sent from the Havana to New Orleans. The vast numbers of Americans settling on the Louisiana frontiers, and their uneasiness at being kept from the free navigation of the Mississippi, gives the Spanish government good grounds of jealousy and distrust ... The detachments to Florida, Louisiana and South America have so much reduced Cuba's military that a considerable part of the Havana's garrison duty is done by the militia ... Don Antonio Claracony Sanz, the islands' governor under Spanish dominion, is confined in the Moro castle. Whether he will be court martialed or sent home to Spain is not known ... Don Galvez, lately appointed to the government of Cuba, &c. &c. Was daily expected at the Havana when the sloop of war *Porcupine* left there ... It will not now be denied that the very few articles we want from the American States, may be brought from thence in our own vessels. To allow foreigners a participation in any branch of commerce, to which we are fully adequate ourselves, might be deemed a species of political suicide. **January 15.** *Extract of a letter from St. Augustine, December 5, 1784:* Governor Tonyn's preference in this country chagrins the Spaniards, but is a favourable circumstance for the British inhabitants. His conduct as a faithful servant of the crown, and a steady friend to the unfortunate loyalists, was never more conspicuous than at the present crisis. Regardless of hints and open statements to lessen his consequence with them, he steadily perseveres in advancing their interests, and alleviating their distress .,.. When the *Tartar* left London, it was reported the government contemplated establishing a free port in these islands. ■ **CHARLESTON,** (*South Carolina*) Feb. 3. *Extract of a letter from a gentleman in London, to his friend in this city:* The writer warns that American credit was never so low as at present; several American business houses have stopped for want of remittances from America. America has made no provision for payments on either interest of principal of Continental or State debt. The assembly's prohibiting debt recovery is thought highly unjust. Discard all private animosities. Be just. Be magnanimous in peace as you have been brave and honorable in war. ■ **ALX, March 10.** Last Friday evening, being very Dark, a Sailor belonging to a Ship in this Port, in attempting to come ashore on a Plank, fell in and was drowned. And on Sunday Afternoon, a Lad, belonging to a Brig from Whitehaven, fell out of a Boat, and [*Continued on Page 3*].

Page 3. [Lad (*continued*)] was also drowned, notwithstanding Attempts were made to save him. ■ NAVAL-OFFICE, ALX. *Inward Entries*. Schooner *Nelly*, J. King, from Maryland; Ship *Astrea*, N. West,

St. Eustatia; Ship *Triton*, T. Lewis, Boston; Brig *Liberty*, J. Nixon, New-York; Schooner *Peggy*, R. Quirk, Leogan. *Cleared Outwards*. Ship *Liberty*, J. Read, for Falmouth, Brig *Hope*, T. Cragg, Whitehaven.

PRICES CURRENT, ALX. / Tobacco, 30s. per Ct. / Fine Flour, 30s. per Barrel. / Wheat, 6s. per Bushel. / Jamaica Spirits, 4/6 per Gallon. / Windward Rum, 3s. to 3/3 per Ditto. / Continental Rum, 2s. to 2/2 per Ditto. / Molasses, 1/6 per Ditto. / Muscovado Sugar, 38s. to 45s. per Ct. / Salt, 6s. per Bushel, by Retail. / Corn, 3s per Bushel / Exchange, 40.

JONATHAN SWIFT and CO. TAKE the earliest opportunity in town and country, that they have received, per the ship *Ceres*, Captain St. Barb, from London (via Boston) an additional assortment of European GOODS, which they will dispose of at a moderate advance for cash, bills of exchange or tobacco.--They have received, per the ship *Triton* from Boston, West-India and New-England rum, molasses, Port wine, tea, coffee, chocolate, allspice, cheese, butter, soap, candles, beef, mackerel, mens' and womens' leather shoes, womens' coarse calamanco and lasting shoes; a few tons of iron hollow ware, and many other articles.--They discount 2½ per cent. for ready-money, and give the market price as usual, in cash or goods, for good tobacco. ALX, March 5, 1785 ■ M'CREA and MEASE, Have for Sale on the most reasonable Terms, A Quantity of Dry LISBON SALT, and an Assortment of DRY-GOODS.--Also, several small LOTS, on the most principal Streets in this Town. ALX, March 8, 1785.

On Saturday next, the 12th Inst. will be Sold at the Vendue-Office, opposite the Court-House,

IRISH linens, canvas, osnaburgs, calicoes, fine dimity, diaper tablecloths, black bonnet and sewing silk, Persian, plain, spotted and striped gauze, plain figured and gauze ribbons, wash-leather gloves, tapes, osnaburg thread, womens' and girls' stays, plated buckles and spoons, and a considerable parcel of well assorted queen's ware.--Also a large quantity of excellent cheese and butter, candles, soap, chocolate, coffee, allspice, Port wine, &c.&c.&c. ☞ Cash will be advanced to transient persons who may be in immediate want, and have goods for public sale (on depositing them in the hands of the Vendue-Master) in order to give proper time for public advertising. C. COPPER, Vendue-Master, ALX, March 9, 1785.

FOR SALE, A LOT of GROUND, valuable situated on the east side of Royal-street, between King and Prince streets, containing 22 feet in front and running back 70 feet, subject to a small ground-rent.—A purchaser of the Lot may have with it at cost, about 4000 feet of scantling, properly sized for a two story brick house and kitchen, a hundred tons of good building stone, the most part drawn to the Lot, and near a thousand bushels of shells for lime.

Likewise an unimproved well situated LOT of GROUND, having west front of 25 feet on St. Asaph's-street, and running back 95 feet 5 inches between Wolf and Wilkes's streets, clear of ground-rent.—A special warrant will be given the purchaser. —The terms are ready cash, for which it may be had very cheap.

Also, a valuable LOT of GROUND in the town of Norfolk, containing 90 feet by 113 in Glasgow-Square, well situated for any kind of public business. —Terms, a credit for half the purchase-money, or saleable merchandise for the whole, will be received in payment, and a good title made thereto.—Inquire of C. COPPER. ☞ For want of employ.—A Virginia born Negro BOY about 15 years of age; he is an active lively lad, a complete waiter and understands taking care of horses. ALX, March 8, 1785 ■ TO BE SOLD, BY PORTER AND INGRAHAM, MOLASSES per hogshead, New-England rum and sugar per hogshead or barrel.—They have remaining on hand a neat and general assortment of European GOODS, which they will sell by whole-sale or retail, at a very moderate advance, for cash or produce. ALX, March 7, 1785.

FOR LIVERPOOL,

THE Ship *RAPPAHANNOCK*, MARK TOWELL, Master. She is a fine new ship, between 3 and 400 hogsheads of tobacco burthen, is now ready to begin to load at Fredericksburg, will take in 150 hogsheads on freight, with liberty of consignment, at £.7. sterling, per ton, delivered along-side; the remaining part of her cargo being engaged it is expected she will sail in all March or very early in April.--She has excellent accommodations for passengers.

I intend to Liverpool in this ship, and to return in her so as to be here early in September with a fall cargo, shall be happy to execute any commands my friends and acquaintance choose to favor me with, in which shall endeavour to give them satisfaction.--For freight or passage apply to the subscriber.

I earnestly request all those indebted to me by bond or open account to make immediate payment, or at least a settlement before the first of April, those who do not may expect them put into the hands of an attorney.

JOHN BROWNLOW.

Fredericksburg, March 2, 1785.

N.B. I have for sale about £.2000 sterling cost of European Goods, and a considerable quantity of West-India Goods, upon the lowest terms, as I mean to break up my store, and a SLOOP about 70 hogsheads burthen, 8 years old and well found; also, an excellent PHAETON and pair of HORSES. J. BROWNLOW.

FOR SALE, A LOT of GROUND in ALX, situated on Fairfax-street, about 39 feet in front by 123 feet in depth, with the conveniency of a 10 feet alley.--On the Lot is a STORE with a counting room, a back shed, a good cellar, and also a stable. The whole at present occupied by Messrs. Hunter, Allison and Company. Also a LOT of GROUND in Dumfries, near the landing, containing 122 feet in front by 108 feet in depth, on which is a brick house 54 feet by 28 feet, a granary and bale-house each 30 by 18 (which may at a small expence be converted into stores) and a good stable. — The whole will be sold together or separate as purchasers may incline. And to be Let on Ground-Rent for ever, a LOT in ALX, containing 44 feet on Fairfax-street, and 123 feet on Gibbon-Street. — For terms apply to WILLIAM WILSON, ALX, March 8, 1785 ■ CRAIK AND COMPANY, At their Store near the Corner of Fairfax and King Streets, have just opened and ready for sale a large and general Assortment of MEDICINES, consisting of PERUVIAN Bark, Red Bark, Jalap, Rhubarb, Ipecacuanha, Gentian, Orange Peel, Zedoary, Valerian, Liquorice, Senna, Glauber Salts, Epsom Ditto, Nitre, Salt of Wormwood, Ditto of Steel, Ditto of Tartar, Ditto of Hartshorn, &c. Flower of Sulphur, Sulphur of Antimony, Crude Antimony, Tartar Emetic, Cream of Tartar, Calomel, Aloes, Manna, Magnesia, Alum, Cantharides, Sago, Gum Camphor, -- Opium, -- Assafoetida, -- Guaci, -- Arabic, -- Ammoniac, &c. PATENT MEDICINES, TURLINGTON's Balsam, Hooper's Pills, Lockyer's Ditto, Anderson's Ditto, Bateman's Drops, Jesuit's ditto, Haerlem Oil, Greenough's Tincture, Hill's Balsam, James's Powders, Squire's Elixir, Godfrey's Cordial, Stoughton's Bitters, &c. The above are a fresh Importation of the first Quality, and will be Sold in large or small Quantities, upon as good Terms as they can be purchased any where upon the Continent. — Orders from Gentlemen or [Practitioners] in any Part of the Country, will be carefully executed upon the shortest Notice. ALX, March 9, 1785 ■ Messieurs RICHARDS and COMPANY, WE wish to inform the public that a Company has been formed to raise funds to make the Potomack River navigable [see like ad Vol. II No. 54].

FOR LONDON,

THE Ship *ASTREA*, a fine fast sailing ship with good accommodations for passengers. — She is expected to sail by the middle of April, and will take 200 hogsheads on freight at £.7 sterling, per ton, with liberty of consignment. — For freight or passage apply to Capt. NATHANIEL WEST, on board, at Conway's wharf, or to WILLIAM HARTSHORNE and COMPANY.

ALX, March 3, 1785.

N.B. Captain West has a few hogsheads of good English sugar and coffee for sale on board said ship.

JOHN HUFF, Post-Rider from Winchester to ALX, RETURNS his thanks to the gentlemen who have encouraged him in his undertaking, and hopes his conduct and punctuality have been such as merit future encouragement. — He makes no doubt they are sensible of the mutual advantages, which both towns, as well as the intervening places, have received, by a regular conveyance, and wishes to inform them that he purposes, with their patronage, to engage for another year. — Subscriptions are taken in at Mr. M'Guire's tavern, Winchester; at Mr. Roper's tavern, Leesburg; and at the Printing-Office, ALX. ■ WANTED, A Person to take charge of a Mill, Bake-House and interest adjoining, consisting of valuable meadows and some upland, distant about 20 miles from ALX; a single man well recommended, will only answer. — The above interest will be let, with or without the stock on it, if an agreeable offer is made in a few weeks. — Apply to Colonel FITZGERALD. ALX, March 8, 1785 ■ PATRICK GOOLDING, returns his sincere and grateful thanks to the ladies and gentlemen of this town, and the public in general, for the kind encouragement he has hitherto met with since his arrival here. He respectfully informs them that he keeps his SCHOOL in the room that Mr. M'Iver kept his in, where he faithfully promises to pay the strictest attention to the education and improvement of the children committed to his care. He would willingly instruct a few young ladies and gentlemen, at their houses in the evenings. ALX, March 8, 1785.

Page 4. Poetry. "Universal Discontent." ■ ELISHA C. DICK closes his practice of physic in ALX; sells his shop with medicines and shop-furniture [see like ad Vol. II No. 56] ■ DANIEL CARROLL BRENT offers about 4,000 acres for sale called the Brenton Tract [see like ad Vol. II No. 53] ■ THE DRAWING OF THE GEORGE-Town ACADEMY LOTTERY is unavoidably put off till the Third Monday in May next. George-Town, Feb. 2, 1785 ■ W. BROWN has for sale medicines, shop-furniture and surgeons instruments [see like ad Vol. II No. 54] ■ ELIZA SCOTT, executrix of Rev. Mr. John Scott, dec., offers for sale two tracts of land on Town-Run and Elk-Run in Fauquier County [see like ad Vol. II No. 56] ■ LEWIS ELLZEY offers one hundred dollars reward for runaway fellow named Will [see like ad Vol. II No. 55] ■ SAMUEL H. M'PHERSON has for sale at Hooe and Harrison's Store, Port wine, etc. [see like ad Vol. II No. 56] ■ Just received, and to be Sold on the most reasonable Terms, at the Printing-Office, A Variety of elegant PAPER-HANGINGS ■ RICHARD ARELL and GEORGE MASON offer twenty dollars reward for strayed or stolen MARE [see like ad Vol. II No. 53] ■ BENJAMIN RANKINS offers ten dollars reward for Negro Wench taken away from plantation on Shenandoah [see like ad Vol. II No. 56] ■ WILLIAM FITZHUGH offers for sale land on Aquia-Run in Stafford County [see like ad Vol. II No. 53] ■ JOHN BROWNLOW, Fredericksburg, offers reward for stolen horse [see like ad Vol. II No. 55] ■ CONRAD MYRE notifies public he intends to record deed from John Moxley, of Loudon County [see like ad Vol. II No. 55] ■ CHARLES STEWART at Annapolis has three valuable Negro men for sale [see like ad Vol. II No. 54] ■ ALX: Printed by GEORGE RICHARDS, and COMPANY, at their Printing-Office on Fairfax—by whom Advertisements, &c. are thankfully received for this Paper,—and where Printing is performed with Care and Expedition.

1785/03/17, Vol. II No. 59

Page 1. Messieurs RICHARDS and COMPANY, wish to inform the public that a Company has been formed to raise funds to make the Potomack River navigable [see like ad Vol. II No. 54] ■ The Ship *Astrea* is to soon sail for London [see like ad Vol. II No. 58] ■ Colonel FITZGERALD seeks a person to take charge of a mill, bake-house and interest adjoining [see like ad Vol. II No. 58] ■ JONATHAN SWIFT and CO. have for sale goods just received on the Ship *Ceres*, Captain St. Barb, from London (via Boston) [see like ad Vol. II No. 58] ■ JOHN BROWNLOW gives notice of his new Ship *Rappahannock*, and seeks to sell goods and close his store [see like ad Vol. II No. 58] ■ The Executors of the estate of THOMAS KIRKPATRICK seek settlement of accounts [see like ad Vol. II No. 57] ■ JOHN HUFF, Post-Rider from Winchester to ALX, thanks customers and seeks additional subscriptions [see like ad Vol. II No. 58] ■ M'CREA and MEASE, have for sale dry Lisbon salt, etc. [see like ad Vol. II No. 58] ■ PORTER and INGRAHAM have for sale molasses per hogshead, etc. [see like ad Vol. II No. 58] ■ WILLIAM WILSON has for sale a lot of ground on Fairfax-street, and a lot of ground in Dumfries [see like ad Vol. II No. 58] ■ C. COPPER, vendue-master, has for sale a lot of ground on Royal-street, a lot of ground on St. Asaph's street, and a lot of ground in the town of Norfolk; offers employment of Negro Boy [see like ad Vol. II No. 58] ■ An Auditor's Interest Certificate found at Shreve and Lawrason's Store [see like ad Vol. II No. 57] ■ Just received, and to be Sold on the most reasonable Terms, at the Printing-Office, A Variety of elegant PAPER-HANGINGS.

Page 2. **RICHMOND.** In the **HOUSE** of **DELEGATES**, Friday the 24th of December, 1784: **A MOTION** was made, and the question put that the third reading of the engrossed Bill establishing a provision for teachers of the Christian religion, be postponed until the fourth Thursday in November next. It was resolved in the affirmative. Ayes 45. Noes 38. On a motion by Mr. Brackenridge, seconded by Mr. Zane, ordered that the voter names be inserted in the record. **Affirmative**: Wilson Cary Nicholas, Edward Carter, Samuel Sherwin, Nicholas Cabell, Michael Bowyer, Zachariah Johnston, John Trigg, Moses Hunter, Archibald Stuart, John Nicholas, Samuel Hawes, Jacob Morton, French Strother, Spencer Roane, William Gatewood, William Pickett, George Clendinnen, Ralph Humphries, Isaac Vanmiter, Turner Southall, Nathaniel Wilkinson,

Benjamin Pope, Francis Peyton, John Glenn, Robert Sayers, John Brackenridge, John Kearnes, James Maddison, Charles Porter, Benjamin Lankford, William Mayo, William Ronald, John Bowyer, John Hays, Gawin Hamilton, John Hopkins, Isaac Zane, John Taylor (of Southampton), Thomas Towles, Mann Page, William Brent, Thomas Edmonds (of Sussex), John Howell Briggs, James Montgomery and Thomas Matthews. **Negative:** John Cropper, Thomas Parramore, Benjamin Harrison, Bernard Markham, Carter Henry Harrison, James Pendleton, William Watkins, Joseph Jones (of Dinwiddie), Miles King, George Wray, Alexander Henderson, John Marshall, Thomas Smith, James Hubbard, Garland Anderson, Bartlett Anderson, John Scasbrook Wills, Philip Barbour, Joseph Jones (of King George), William Thornton, James Ball, Richard Bland Lee, William Anderson, Francis Corbin, William Curtis, Willis Riddick, Kinchen Godwin, Daniel Sandford, Lyttleton Eyre, John Thornton, Richard Bibb, Edmund Ruffin, Thomas Walke, Carter Bassett Harrison, John Allen, Richard Lee, Nathaniel Nelson, and Henry Tazewell ... Following the above, the House moved to publish the Bill, the motion to postpone, and the above voter list, in handbills (12 copies of each to each General Assembly member) to be distributed in their counties, the people thereof to signify their opinion of such a Bill to the next Assembly Session ... A BILL *Establishing a* PROVISION *for* TEACHERS *of the* CHRISTIAN RELIGION: WHEREAS the general diffusion of Christian knowledge hath a natural tendency to correct the morals of men, restrain their vices, and preserve the peace of society, which cannot be effected without competent provision for learned teachers, who may be thereby enabled...to instruct such citizens, as from their circumstances and want of education, cannot otherwise attain such knowledge; it is judged that such provision may be made by the Legislature, without counteracting the liberal principle heretofore adopted and intended to be preserve by abolishing all distinctions of pre-eminence amongst the different societies or communities of Christians: [verbatim text of the Bill is here summarized - Eds.] a percent or amount [left blank] of land taxes shall be collected by County Sheriffs, directions for a public accounting specified; after deducting a five per cent fee, the sheriffs to turn the remainder over to the Vestry, Elders or Directors of each society; safeguards for the funds; funds to be solely for provision of Ministers or Teachers of each society's gospel, except that Quakers and Menonists may use funds as they think best calculated to promote their particular mode of worship; sums not appropriated to uses as specified above shall be accounted for and placed into the Public treasury, disposed of by the General Assembly for encouragement of seminaries only in the counties in which the particular sums were raised. *A Copy of the Engrossed Bill* [signed] JOHN BECKLEY, C.H.D. ■ **PARIS, December 2.** By courier arrived at the Count de Merci's we learned the Emperor persists in his intentions. Although his Imperial Majesty has not yet spoken, his answer probably will conform with the word brought by the courier. In consequence, two armies are being assembled; the Prince of Conde has solicited command of the second, its van guard to be commanded by M. De Boiullie. Marischal de Broglio will be general of the first, its van guard commanded by M. De Rochambeau. The States General, it is said, will request M. De Maillebois to command their forces; it is thought the King will grant him permission. ■ **LONDON, November 25.** A number of our navy Lieutenants requested the Admiralty for leave to engage in the Emperor's service, but received a peremptory refusal ... Authentic Intelligence, from a gentleman just arrived from the Continent: Mons. De Vergennes's politics prevail, and France means to take a part with the Dutch ... The Queen is highly incensed--her letters to Vienna are less than they have even been ... Three encampments of France's forces, each of 20,000 men, will take place in the Low Countries. **Dec. 18.** The Prince Stadtholder has appointed Prince Frederick of Hesse Cassel, Lieutenant General in the service of the Republic, to be Governor of Maestricht, in lieu of the Prince of Nassau Weilbourg. **Dec. 20.** The foreign prints speak with the same uncertainty of the present contest between the Dutch and the Emperor. There is nothing decisive in either side's proceedings. **Dec. 21.** The Emperor has prepared for this for four years, and his trips to France and Russia were made from a political point of view. No doubt he has reached understanding with both courts, and anticipates their support ... Our Government has contracted for large quantities of grain, saying the supply must be as great as during the most violent rage of the late war. No reason was given. If we are not to be personally involved with the war on the continent, we are at least to enter into the interest of one of the powers, and furnish them with supplies. We leave the comment to our readers. ■ **CHARLESTON** *(South Carolina) Feb.* 8.The following is a real extract from a letter of the celebrated Dr. Franklin, to a friend in London, as the sagacity of remarks which it discovers, will easily evince. "The political world, within the last half century, has assumed a variety of aspects, and from present appearances, it is still as unsettled as ever. The States of Europe are ripe for slavery, and their respective governments are ready and prone to take every advantage of the people. It is not easy to decypher the various problematical governments of the several powers on the continent; but there is none of them which does not seem very interested in the politics of England. Your patriots have certainly served your country. The reform which they broached is the only expedient the poor peasantry of England have yet in reserve to protect themselves from plunder and despotism. The Irish may probably make a bad cause of a very good one. The flame in that country seems too rapid and fierce to be lasting; those of property expect nothing but ruin from the idleness and dissipation of their dependents; and in this situation it requires more public spirit than they have yet discovered to refuse a bribe. The Scotch are a selfish, but cool, intrepid and ingenious people. They will carry their object, because they adopt no measures which are not rational, and plausible! How truly respectable and great does the French King appear, in the midst of there political intrigues and impending revolutions. His memory will go down to posterity, loaded with glory; it will be said of him, that he protected the States General from the savage grasp of imperial tyranny. It is not impossible but it may also be said of him, that both Ireland and Scotland were emancipated by his means from their present miserable subjection to their haughty English task masters." ■ **NEW YORK, February 23.** Married last October 26, at Pool, England: Dr. Sylvester Gardiner, formerly of Boston, aged 80, to Miss Catherine Goldthwait, of 28 [sic], daughter of Thomas Goldthwait, Esq., late of Penobscot, in New England. Mr. Goldthwait had a son of 24, not long since married to the widow Primate, of Walthamstowe, aged 70, so that the father can say what few people can boast of--that he has a son-in-law and a daughter-in-law, both of whom are several years older than himself, he being only 66 ... The following Address of the Artificers, Tradesmen and Mechanics of this city, to the Continental Congress, was made a few days ago: From our superior sufferings in the late glorious struggle for freedom, we cannot be insensible of the great change produced in the blessings of peace, and or ungrateful to your August body. We are indebted to your wisdom, fortitude and resolution in directing us to victory, and thus for our domestic happiness. We therefore most cordially welcome your arrival in this city. We sincerely hope our representatives will coincide with the other States in augmenting your power to every exigency of the Union. We trust soon to see the completion of the great temple which has been reared to liberty, and that the names of its architects will be handed to remotest posterity with never fading laurels. Signed by order: Robert Boyd, jun, Daniel Niven, Henry Bicker, John Stagg, John Burger, Edward Meeks, Jeremiah Wool. To which the Secretary of the Congress replied: The Congress is grateful for your cordial welcome and expressions of support; and that, while acknowledging the goodness of Divine Providence in concluding the American revolution, they experience additional gratitude in contemplating the happiness of those who have suffered so severely by the calamities of war. CHARLES THOMSON, Secretary.

Page 3. **March 1.** By the snow *Sophia Magdalena*, Capt. Loftenburgh, arrived last Friday from Lisbon, we have positive assurances that the Emperor of Germany had declared war against the United States of Holland. ■ **PHILADELPHIA, March 4.** An extract of a letter from **London, Nov, 26**, describes in detail the five month political maneuvering of Pitt's party against the Bedford's. Mr. Pitt has won, Lord Camden has been seated, Mr. Nepean (one of the commissioners) bringing the privy seal to the cabinet and placing it in custody of the noble Earl. Key figures: Earl Gower, Lord Shelburne, the Duke of Grafton, and Mr. Prat as emissary and negotiator in Ireland. The Earl of Shelburne and the Earl Temple with be made Marquises. Mr. Pitt triumphs by keeping the Earl of Shelburne out, without throwing him into the opposite scale ... Some gentlemen, regarding the great importance of agriculture, met here last Tuesday and formed a society to promote improvements within the States--similar to what have advanced the husbandry in Europe such as to raise our apprehensions. Americans should be inspired with active endeavours to keep pace, if not equal Europeans, in this ... It appears by the foreign papers that the Austrians and Dutch are unwilling to go to extremes without doing everything in their power to avoid them. The Emperor's answer will determine the whole, and is anxiously awaited by the Dutch. It is remarkable that the States General have no allies, unless it be true France has promised assistance; it is equally remarkable that the other powers do not seem to interpose as mediators. **March 7.** Extract of a letter from **Caen, Normandy**, dated **Dec. 10** to a gentleman in New York: "There is a new circumstance which bids fair to embarrass trade. War is certainly declared by the Emperor against the Hollanders.--Hostilities commenced the 6th instant. The Imperial forces attacked several Dutch forts, which induced them to open their sluices, and cause a most direful inundation, which has drowned a great part of the Imperial Low Countries.-- The mediation of France has been rejected by the Emperor, and there is great reason to fear that this unlucky quarrel will set all Europe in flames." ■ **ALX, March 17**. "A Gentleman reading in the Annual Register for 1781, ingenious 'Thoughts on the Rot in Sheep, by Benjamin Price,' and therein meeting with the following Assertions, viz. 'Salt is pernicious to most Insects; they never infest Gardens where Sea-Weed is laid:' It immediately occurred to him, that, if so, the loss of various excellent young Plants, destroyed by Insects in the Beginning of Spring might be prevented, by laying fresh Sea-Weed near the Plants, or, when Distance hinders the obtaining of Sea-Weed, Hay well steeped in a strong Brine. It is supposed, that the salted Hay, if not fouled with Dirt, will afterward be an acceptable Food to Cattle." ■ Extract of a Letter from a Gentleman in Lisbon to his Correspondent in this Town, dated December 1, 1784. "The War, of late declared between the Emperor and States of Holland, is supposed will have some Influence on our East-India Goods, which have hitherto sold to such an enormous Loss for the Proprietors.--In the North great Speculations have already taken Place--Nobody chooses to sell at the old Prices here.--We wish and hope it will be the same Case with you, that our Teas may come to a good Market." ■ The *Chance*, Captain Stafford, from London, is arrived in James-River. ■ NAVAL-OFFICE, ALX. *Inward Entries*. Brig *Dolphin*, S. Babson, from Martinico; Schooner *Lottery*, T. Mann, Baltimore; Brig *Marquis de la Fayette*, B. Bradhurst, Aux Cayes. *Cleared Outwards*. Ship *Heer Adams*, M. Collins, and Ship *Lyon*, J. Chase, for l'Orient; Ship *Hazard*, T. New, London; Sloop *Dolphin*, B. Rice, Philadelphia; Ship *Stanley*, J. Woods, Liverpool.

On Monday next the 21st Instant, being Fairfax Court-Day, will be Sold at the Public Vendue-Store, opposite the Court-House,

TWO valuable Virginia-born SLAVES, one a Man about 33 years of age, a complete sawyer; the other a Lad about 19 years old who has been some time at the carpenters' business.--Rum in hogsheads, coffee in bags and barrels, allspice in bags, a quantity of Rhode-Island cheese and butter, candles, soap, chocolate, sailcloth, white and brown Irish linens, calicoes and printed linens, womens' stays, shirts, shoes, osnaburg thread, sewing silk, ribbons, tapes, garterings, gauzes, modes, diapers, pins, Morocco-leather pocket-books with silver clasps, silver watches, plated buckles, carpenters' axes, nails, &c.&c.&c. CYRUS COPPER, Vendue-Master, ALX, March 14, 1785.

AT PRIVATE SALE. ☞ Hadley's quadrants, scales, dividers, spy-glasses of the best kind, Moore's navigation, seamans' assistants, mariners compasses, blank journals, German and common steel, pit and crosscut saws, BOHEA and GREEN TEA in quarter chests, all of which will be sold very reasonable for ready cash. C. COPPER.

OBSCURITY,

Imported from England last Fall, by Messieurs Benjamin and John Crocket,

STands this season at Harmony-Hall, about 12 miles from Baltimore-Town, and three miles from Dr. Lyon's and Samuel Owing's Mills, and will begin to cover on the 25th of March next, at Six Guineas a Mare, and One Dollar to the Groom. He is a dark chestnut, 16 hands three inches high, well proportioned, and equal in figure to any horse on the continent, was bred by Lord Milford, got by Col. O'Kelly's *Eclipse*, his dam (which is own sister to Croney) by *Careless*, his grandam by *Cullen Arabian*, his great grandam by *North-Country Diamond*, great great grandam by a son of Sir John Harper's Barb, and out of the *Old Child Mare*, who was the dam of Lord Tracy's *Whimsey*, and great great grandam of Careless. This horse was six years old last grass; at four years old he won a match of 200 Guineas, and a £.50 plate. *Eclipse*, his sire, was never beat, and is now the first stallion in England; Careless the sire of his dam, won nine King's plates, and was never beat.

Pasturage will be provided for Mares, at Three Shillings per week, and good care taken of them, but will not be answerable for escapes, or other accidents.--To prevent trouble, it is requested the Money may be sent with the Mares.

Feb. 24, 1785. JOHN FORMAN.

RAN away from the Subscriber living in Augusta County, on the 18th of January last, an Irish Servant Man, named JEREMIAH FLANNERY, of a fair complexion, speaks much on the brogue, about 22 years of age, about 5 feet 7 or 8 inches high, a little knock-kneed, stoops a little when he walks, slender made, has short brown hair that just ties behind, and is a breeches-maker by trade: He had on and took with him a sky-blue cloth coat, with long skirts and lappelled at the breast, a new felt hat, check shirt with some white patches on it, one white ditto, a pair of old buckskin breeches, two pair of stockings, half-worn shoes, and a blackish hunting-shirt.--I expect he will change his name and clothes.--Whoever takes up said Servant and delivers him to me, shall have THREE POUNDS Reward, and reasonable charges, if taken in this State, and if out of the State, TWENTY DOLLARS Reward, paid by WILLIAM ANDERSON, Feb. 7, 1785. ■ To be SOLD Cheap for Cash or Flour, on Board the Brig *Dolphin*, lying at Captain Conway's Wharf, ABOUT FORTY CASKS OF GOOD MOLASSES, ALX, March 16, 1785.

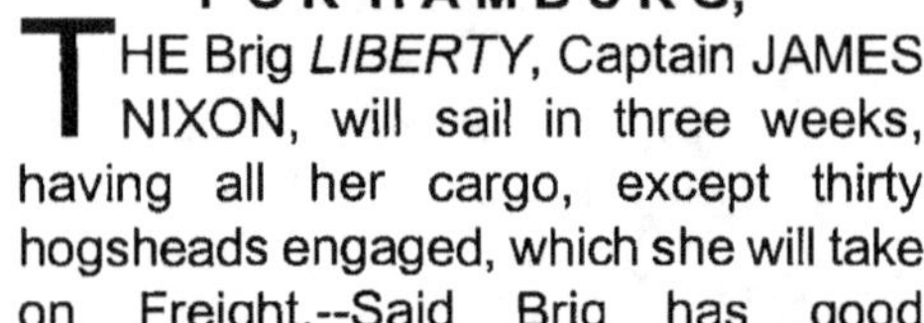

FOR HAMBURG,

THE Brig *LIBERTY*, Captain JAMES NIXON, will sail in three weeks, having all her cargo, except thirty hogsheads engaged, which she will take on Freight.--Said Brig has good accommodations for Passengers, and will take three or four.--For terms apply to the Captain on board, at Captain Conway's wharf, or to JOHN MURRAY and CO. at their store in Fairfax-street, where may be had very cheap, pickled codfish in barrels, Jamaica and West-India rum, liver oil, chalk, an assortment of iron castings, spermaceti candles, a few thousand feet of well seasoned Albany boards clear of knots for inside work. ALX, March 15, 1785.

THE Subscriber begs leave to acquaint his friends and the public in general, that after many years private and public practice in the hospitals in Europe and America, he has settled at Mr. John Short's, where he designs following his profession.--Any family honoring him with their business, may depend on every attention being paid them, by their most obedient and most humble servant, J. APEDAILE. ALX, March 12, 1785 ■ TO BE SOLD in Berkeley County, TWO Thousand Five Hundred acres of LAND, adjoining to the land I have given to my son, Mr. James Wormeley.--The goodness and fertility of this land are so well known, that any particular description of its soil is unnecessary.--It is convenient to merchant-mills, saw-mills, the market-town of Winchester, to churches, and meeting-houses.--I shall be in Berkeley in May or the beginning of June.--In my absence either my son, Mr. James Wormeley, may be applied to, or Mr. Nicholas Roper who lives near the land, will shew it, and receive proposals from those who wish to become purchasers.--It may be laid off in lots of two or three hundred acres, or more or less in quantity, or sold in one body to suit the purchasers.--Six months credit will be given for half the sums, and twelve for the other half.--Interest from signing the bonds will be required in failure of payment at the time they shall become due. RALPH WORMELEY, Rosegill, March 3, 1785 ■ FOUND, By Laz, a Slave belonging to M'Crea and Mease, A Box, containing a Parcel of Leather INK-HOLDERS.--The Owner may have it again by applying at the Post-Office, proving Property, and paying the Charge of this Advertisement. ALX, March 15, 1785 ■ BATTAILE MUSE offers for rent the fisheries at Belvoir [see like ad Vol. II No. 57] ■ LEWIS ELLZEY offers one hundred dollars reward for runaway fellow named Will [see like ad Vol. II No. 55] ■ CHARLES STEWART at Annapolis has three valuable Negro men for sale [see like ad Vol. II No. 54] ■ DYER, Hair Cutter and Dresser from London, DRESSES ladies' and gentlemens' hair in the most elegant and approved manner.--He may be found at his lodgings at Mr. Storm's facing Mr. Biterman's, brewer, in Queen-street. ☞ He makes ladies' curls, dressing, plain and elastic cushions, and all kinds of false hair, in such a manner as not to be easily discovered. ALX, March 15, 1785.

Page 4. Poetry.

EPIGRAMS

DICK, after drunk, when crop-sick, gravely swore
That whilst he breath'd, he never wou'd drink more;
Dick daily tipsy grows, nor perjur'd thinks
Himself, but swears he breaths not whilst he drinks.

❀ ❀ ❀

I heard last week, friend Edward, thou wast dead;
--I'm very glad to hear it too, cries Ned.

CRAIK and COMPANY have for sale at their store on the corner of Fairfax and King streets, an assortment of medicines [see like ad Vol. II No. 58] ■ PATRICK GOOLDING thanks his customers and wishes to continue his school in the room that Mr. M'Iver kept his in [see like ad Vol. II No. 58] ■ GILES COOK, jun., Berkely County, wishes to sell plantation whereon Mr. Rich. Willis lately removed from [see like ad Vol. II No. 57] ■ RICHARD ARELL and GEORGE MASON offer twenty dollars reward for strayed or stolen MARE [see like ad Vol. II No. 53] ■ DANIEL and ISAAC M'PHERSON have for sale a few gross empty bottles [see like ad Vol. II No. 57] ■ HUGH DOUGLASS, Executor of the last Will and Testament of William Douglass, deceased, offers for sale land in Shelburne Parish, Loudon County [see like ad Vol. II No. 57] ■ BENJAMIN RANKINS offers ten dollars reward for Negro Wench taken away from plantation on Shenandoah [see like ad Vol. II No. 56] ■ DANIEL CARROLL BRENT offers about 4,000 acres for sale called the Brenton Tract [see like ad Vol. II No. 53] ■ ROBERT ADAM has for sale old Jamaica spirits, West-India rum, etc. [see like ad Vol. II No. 57] ■ ROBERT ADAM, executor of Dr. William Rumney seeks settlement of accounts [see like ad Vol. II No. 57] ■ JOHN MURRAY and CO. offers for sale West-India Goods [see like ad Vol. II No. 57] ■ W. BROWN has for sale medicines, shop-furniture and surgeons instruments [see like ad Vol. II No. 54] ■ ROGER CHEW offers for lease Boys and Horses [see like ad Vol. II No. 57] ■ WRIGHT and LONG, Taylors and Ladies Habit-Makers announce opening of business [see like ad Vol. II No. 57] ■ PEREGRINE FITZHUGH delays sale of lands previously advertised [see like ad Vol. II No. 57] ■ ALX: Printed by GEORGE RICHARDS, and COMPANY, at their Printing-Office on Fairfax--by whom Advertisements, &c. are thankfully received for this Paper,--and where Printing is performed with Care and Expedition.

1785/03/24, Vol. II No. 60

Page 1. CRAIK and COMPANY have for sale at their store on the corner of Fairfax and King streets, an assortment of medicines [see like ad Vol. II No. 58] ■ RALPH WORMELEY offers for sale 2,500 acres of LAND in Berkeley County [see like ad Vol. II No. 59] ■ JOHN HUFF, Post-Rider from Winchester to ALX, thanks customers and seeks additional subscriptions [see like ad Vol. II No. 58] ■ Just received, and to be Sold on the most reasonable Terms, at the Printing-Office, A Variety of elegant PAPER-HANGINGS ■ M'CREA and MEASE, have for sale dry Lisbon salt, etc. [see like ad Vol. II No. 58] ■ JONATHAN SWIFT and CO. have for sale goods just received on the Ship *Ceres*, Captain St. Barb, from London (via Boston) [see like ad Vol. II No. 58] ■ WILLIAM WILSON has for sale a lot of ground on Fairfax-street, and a lot of ground in Dumfries [see like ad Vol. II No. 58] ■ C. COPPER, vendue-master, has for sale a lot of ground on Royal-street, a lot of ground on St. Asaph's street, and a lot of ground in the town of Norfolk; offers employment of Negro Boy [see like ad Vol. II No. 58] ■ PORTER and INGRAHAM have for sale molasses per hogshead, etc. [see like ad Vol. II No. 58] ■ J. APEDAILE who practiced in hospitals in Europe and America has settled at Mr. John Short's [see like ad Vol. II No. 59] ■ About 40 casks of good molasses for sale from on board the Brig *Dolphin* [see like ad Vol. II No. 59] ■ LEWIS ELLZEY offers one hundred dollars reward for runaway fellow named Will [see like ad Vol. II No. 55] ■ WILLIAM ANDERSON offers reward for runaway Irish servant named Jeremiah Flannery [see like ad Vol. II No. 59] ■ BATTAILE MUSE offers for rent the fisheries at Belvoir [see like ad Vol. II No. 57].

Page 2. Moore-Hill, March 14, 1785.
To the FREEHOLDERS of FAIRFAX COUNTY.
GENTLEMEN,

AMONG other reports injurious to me and altogether unfounded, one, I am told, prevails, that my situation, as a debtor, has been the cause of my voting in Assembly against opening the courts of justice, to the immediate recovery of British claims, thereby, for the sake of my own private benefit, suffering a violation of the treaty of peace.

I consider this the most malignant calumny that could have been invented against me, either as your representative, or as a trading man.--As to the first, that motives of private Interest could prevail against your good and that of the community; and as to the last, because it might, if possible, draw into doubt my credit as a merchant; with regard to this I can assure you, gentlemen, that I have the most honorable, and the most ample testimony of the purity and propriety of my conduct, from those with whom I was formerly most happily connected, and from whom I am now obliged to draw money which is due to me, because the debtors to British merchants are not, I presume, yet able to discharge their debts, inasmuch as very little has been paid to me, although the circumstances of those indebted to the concern of which I have been a member, promise payments as speedily as any, I believe, in the State.

But, gentlemen, what most concerns you in this business is, that your representative, for the sake of his private interest, should have voted for a measure opposed to the national honor and the public [wealth]. You have seen lately an estimate of our national debt which must be secured, and in time paid.--You know that large importations of goods must be made, and that these must be regularly paid for.--When you consider therefore these things, you will be pleased to compare the balance of your trade with the amount of the debts of your citizens, and say, or let any one of you say, whether the laws ought to permit the unrestrained demands of creditors, or whether it be prudent or just that the tranquility of the State should be hazarded by the experiment. I hesitate not to say, that it is not prudent, and that it is not just, and that the creditors of the citizens, cannot, or do they think so, nor do they expect payments in any other mode, than agreeable to the resolution of the Assembly in May last, in the forwarding of which I took an active part.

Gentlemen, I have particular interest in the speedy recovery of British debts, having been a partner formerly with British merchants.--I owe not one shilling to any British subject, unless it be for transactions begun in the year 1784; on the contrary, very considerable sums are due to me for former transactions. But, gentlemen, it has ever been a rule with me since I have been your representative, in all questions where my private interest *did* come into competition with the public good, to regard only the latter; and it is to be lamented, that there does exist a mind so sordid as to be influenced by contrary motives, or to harbour such conjectures as to the minds of others.--I can, through the whole of my representation, justify my conduct to every rational unbiassed man, nor can it be said, that I have attended to my private security and right as a citizen, other than by supporting the following clause in the bill respecting British debts, which did not pass.

Provided that no citizen of this Commonwealth, of approved fidelity and attachment thereto, and who has been resident therein since the 19th day of April, 1775, and may have been in partnership with British merchants prior to that date, shall in any manner be affected by this act, but after establishing in the High Court of Chancery his share of any copartnership with any such British merchant or merchants, shall be entitled to receive a like share of each debt in the same manner as other good citizens are.

It has been alledged that the county is at this time under a bad representation.--So far as the allegation concerns me, *I do deny it*, and defy any person to satisfy you thereof by fair and open measures.

ALX, March 22.

I, last evening, was informed that report has raised two other motives in me for giving my voice as above stated; the one, that I meant to depreciate the British claims in order to become a purchaser of them; the other, most atrocious indeed! that by preventing the fulfilment of the treaty of peace I meant to bring on another war.--As to the first of these let any man take this paper in his hand and present or transmit it to those with whom I have had correspondence, and let them say whether I have ever in the most distant manner hinted such a design.--I assure you, gentlemen, that although I have the best opinion of Virginia rights, yet I desire nothing more, in the debts of her citizens, than what is now justly due to me.--As to the last, what reasonable man can believe I should have inclination for or an interest in a renewal of the calamities of war? The thing is absurd as it is false: It is the old leaven of malice and wickedness, and not the unleavened bread of sincerity and truth. All other calumnies are refutable immediately; these, incredible as they must appear to every dispassionate man, can be fully refuted only by time, in the interval of which it is not my desire to be in the public walks.--I came thither at the desire of a majority of you, and while I have been there I have uniformly consulted the public good, in preference to any private interest whatever, and with truth I assure you, that the best of my skill and abilities, I have ever been your faithful representative.

ALEXANDER HENDERSON.

■ **MADRID, December 3.** The King rewarded the principal officers in the late expedition against Algiers. Lieutenant General Don Barcelo is appointed commander in chief of the naval armament destined to cruise off the islands of Baleiro and the Barbary coast. Admiral Don Francisco de Cisneros, second in command, has been invested with the cross of the order of Charles III with a pension. His Majesty has also promoted many of the brigadiers, Captains of the line of battle ships, frigates, and other inferior officers. ■ **LONDON, December 14.** Report in a letter from **Newcastle, Dec.11**: Sunday morning a fleet of some 150 vessels sailed from Yarmouth roads. About 4:00 p.m., between Cromer and the floating light, a violent storm of heavy rain and S.S.E. winds separated the fleet; the increasing gale split all the sails into shivers, so that it was impossible to work the ships, and many were drove ashore. Some foundered at sea with loss of all hands. From **Sunderland** we learn that Monday about 30 keels were found sunk in the river, mostly laden with coals. Several ships broke from their moorings, but with little damage. That day a sloop from Leith, laden with barley, drove between the giers [sic]; the Master and Mate drowned, but two men, ship and cargo saved. On Tuesday morning the coast wore an awful appearance, covered with wrecks and bodies; upwards of 50 sail on shore between there and Hartlepool, and about 60 between it and Shields. We hear from **Seaton**, near Hartlepool, that the coast there presents a most melancholy and distressing scene of ships, some upon the rocks, others upon the sands, others at anchor some distance from shore, which appear in the utmost danger, and the sea running so high, that it is impossible to give them any assistance from shore. There are about 16 on shore near Hartlepool, one of which has no living creature on board, and appears to be a light collier. There has been a great fall of snow in Cleveland, particularly on the mountains near Kirkleatham, Gainsborough, and Stolkesly. ■ **CHARLESTON, February 14.** The Honourable William Moultrie, Esq.

Is elected Governor and the honorable Charles Drayton, Esq. the Lieutenant Governor of this State. The honorable John Ewing Calhoun, Thomas Sumpter, George Haig and Daniel Huger, Esqs. are elected members of the Privy Council. Honorable Charles Pinckney, Jacob Read, John Bull, David Ramsey, and John Kean, Esqs. are elected Delegates to the Congress of the U.S. **Feb. 17.** A gentleman from the western part of North Carolina says a body of Spaniards have taken post at Muscle Shoals, and are building a fort. The Chicamawga tribe have abandoned and burnt their towns, and moved off to some distant part, greatly disgusted with the attempts of individuals to get their country without a purchase. ■ **BOSTON, February 21.** Last January 20 was born to Mr. Amariah Chase of Sutton, a son of the fifth generation from Mr. Isaac Chase, of that town, now 97 years of age.--There is something very peculiar respecting this child, as he has now living 6 grandfathers and 7 grandmothers, 57 uncles and 63 aunts. ■ **NEW YORK, March 7**. This State's Legislature has ordered the quota of troops required by Congress to garrison frontier posts to be immediately raised; barracks are repairing for their reception. ■ **PHILADELPHIA, March 7.** Extract of a letter from **l'ORIENT, Dec. 20, 1784**, to a gentleman in New York: The packet boat, *Courier de New York*, was stopped as she was going out of port, by order of the Court, by an officer who came express from Paris; I assure you it was to send to India the news of a war which appears inevitable. The English have declared openly to the Emperor that he may depend on their assistance, and they are arming their fleet with the greatest activity ... Last Friday morning, Messrs. Hallam and Allen paid one hundred pounds to this city's overseers of the poor--the production of the labours of those two gentlemen at the theatre Tuesday the 1st; a very crouded audience were greatly entertained and amused by lectures, pantomime, &c., their satisfaction heightened by their contributing to the relief of the poor. **March 12.** The Captains of his Britannic Majesty's Packets have instructions to take aboard at Falmouth any indigent U.S. citizen who applies, and land them in New York, free of charge. They are to do the same for British citizens in New York, to Falmouth ... The Emperor of Germany has commissioned two gentlemen now at Charleston to collect specimens of flora and fauna. They have already been very successful, and the cabinet in Vienna will receive no inconsiderable addition from South Carolina's unbounded natural variety ... Authentic advices by the last French packet say his Most Christian Majesty, ever disposed to render these United States every advantage in his power, has established free ports in the French West Indies for American traders. Which of the islands is yet to be announced ... A letter from **Amsterdam, October 11:** When an Imperial brig from Antwerp made an attempt to pass the Dutch commander on the Scheldt, he fired on her and drove her back. Politicians hereabouts see this as a declaration of war, and from preparations throughout Europe, we believe it will be general. These States have purchased two cutters, one for £3000, the other £2800 sterling. "In all these revolutions, America will apparently be neutral, and have an opportunity to rise superior to the losses occasioned by the war. The commercial part of her subjects may certainly derive great advantages by shipping, being employed as carriers for the contending parties, exclusive of their having an opportunity to put off their products to greater advantage than heretofore." ■ **BALTIMORE, March 15.** Captain Robert Ewart, in the Ship *Washington*, arrived here since our last, from Jamaica and Port au Prince, the latter of which he left three weeks ago. He says that Don Galvez, Governor of Havana, sailed with 7 sail of the line, and 10,000 land forces, against the Musquito Shore--to take possession of it in right of His Most Catholic Majesty; that the Spanish army landed and summoned the British forts to surrender; that Don Galvez permitted a vessel to go with dispatches to the Governor of Jamaica, in consequence of which a British ship of the line with several frigates, 1800 land forces, 10,000 stand of arms--supposed to be for the use of the natives in the British interest-- were dispatched to support and defend the invaded country. This affair occasioned great alarm in Jamaica, where the militia were called up, as on the eve of war ... From Kingston, Jamaica, comes word that the pirate and murderer Maurice Keaton was executed at Cuckold's point on December 27, near Port Royal. His body was then suspended in chains to a lofty gibbet. He met his fate with resignation, penitence, and fortitude; he told the crowd he welcomed death as a relief from his sorrows. He then forbade the executioner to take away the ladder, saying he would jump off himself when he was ready, which he accordingly did in about two minutes. Thomas Twentyman, one of his accomplices, died in the gaol of Kingston.

Page 3. **ALX, March 24**. Last Thursday Evening the Sons of St. Patrick gave an elegant Ball at Mr. Lomax's. ■ The *Triton*, Capt. Young, from this Port for Liverpool, arrived at the Cove of Cork on the 26th of November. ■ *Abstract from the Act to amend the Act, entitled "An Act to amend and reduce the several Acts of Assembly for the Inspection of Tobacco, into one Act." Be it enacted by the General*

Assembly, That the Inspectors at several warehouses within this Commonwealth, shall, on or before the first day of April next, give bond with sufficient security in the Court of the County where such warehouses may be, in the sum of two thousand pounds, payable to the Governor and his successors, with condition for the due accounting for and paying the tax or duty on tobacco, and they shall be allowed two and a half per centum for collecting and paying the said tax into the Treasury. Every inspector hereafter appointed, shall, before he enters upon his office, give the like bond and security; copies of which bonds shall be by the Clerk of the Court transmitted to the Solicitor within 2 months, under penalty of 200 pounds in case of failure. If the Inspectors at any warehouse shall neglect or fail to account for and pay the tax or duty on tobacco at the times required by law, for every such neglect or failure they shall forfeit and pay the sum of 500 pounds, to be recovered on motion by the Solicitor, in the General Court, on giving the parties ten days previous notice in writing of such motion.

AND WHEREAS frauds have been committed by persons receiving duplicate notes for tobacco, alledging the original to have been lost or mislaid: For prevention whereof in future, *Be it enacted*, That no person shall be entitled to receive such duplicate note from the Inspectors, until he shall first have advertised the loss of the original, at the Court--house of the County in which such inspection may be, on the Court day, and at the Inspection where the said duplicate note shall be granted, and shall moreover give bond with sufficient security, to the Inspectors, in double the amount of the tobacco so claimed, to indemnify the person who may thereafter produce the original note, the value by him paid for the same. ■ NAVAL-OFFICE, ALX. *Inward Entries.* Schooner *Polly*, J. Humphries, and Sloop *Nancy*, J. Garlick, from Baltimore; Sloop *Commerce*, S. Packard, Providence; Ship *Hope*, T. Barnard, New-York. *Cleared Outwards.* Sloop *Lottery*, T. Mann, for Baltimore; Schooner *Virginia*, S. Davis, Surinam; Sloop *Commerce*, S. Packard, New-York.

By the UNITED STATES, in CONGRESS Assembled, February 23, 1785. *Resolved,*

THAT the quarter-master general, commissary of purchases, commissary of issues, commissary of forage, and all the late heads of departments, or their successors or agents, be required, without delay, to forward to the board of treasury or to the comptroller, a list of their respective deputies who have been duly authorized to issue certificates. That the heads of departments aforesaid, and each of their deputies who have not settled their accounts, and all other persons who have issued certificates of debts due by the United-States, loan-office certificates, and certificates of final settlement excepted, be required forthwith to deliver to the board of treasury, or to some commissioner of accounts in the State where such persons reside, a fair abstract of all the certificates which they have issues, and they shall specify those certificates for which they have taken receipts as for cash paid, and a copy of those abstracts shall be transmitted by the board of treasury to the several commissioners of accounts, to whom they may be of use in detecting frauds.

That a copy of these resolutions be published in the Gazettes or public Newspapers of the several States, and that if any person or persons so required as aforesaid, shall refuse or neglect for the space of two months, from such publication, to deliver a full and just account of the certificates he or they have issued, the board of treasury, or in case it is not at the time organized, the comptroller shall take proper steps for causing him or them to be prosecuted according to law.

Resolved, That the commissioners of accounts be instructed, to be careful how they admit charges against the United States, on certificates which are not duly supported by the authority of Congress, and the accounts of the officers who have issued them.

CHARLES THOMSON, Secretary.

PRICES CURRENT, ALX. / Tobacco, 30s. per Ct. / Fine Flour, 30s. per Barrel. / Wheat, 6s. per Bushel. / Jamaica Spirits, 4/6 per Gallon. / Windward Rum, 3s. to 3/3 per Ditto. / Continental Rum, 2s. to 2/2 per Ditto. / Molasses, 1/6 per Ditto. / Muscovado Sugar, 38s. to 45s. per Ct. / Salt, 5s. per Bushel, by Retail. / Corn, 3s per Bushel / Exchange, 40.

FOR LONDON,

THE BRIG *FITZHUGH*, Captain JENKINS, lying at Boyd's-Hole, takes in Tobacco consigned to Forrest and Stoddert, London, at Seven Pounds, sterling, per ton.--It is expected she will be loaded by the last of March. BENJAMIN STODDERT.

George-Town, March 8, 1785.

FOR LONDON,

THE Brig *MARQUIS DE LA FAYETTE*, a new strong built vessel, has good accommodations for a few passengers, and will most assuredly sail by the 15th of next month, as one half of her cargo is now along-side.--A few tons of Tobacco will be taken on freight at Thirty-Five Shillings, sterling, per hogshead, with liberty of consignment.--For further particulars apply to Captain Benjamin Bradhurst, on board said Brig, or to WILLIAM LYLES and CO.
ALX, March 22, 1785.

ALL persons having claims against me on my own account, are desired to bring them in and receive payment.--I will attend at ALX at the Courts in April and May next to pay off such claims; and at Dumfries, at the Courts to be held in the month of May. ☞ The creditors of GLASSFORD and HENDERSON will oblige me much by prosecuting their claims in the Court of Chancery agreeable to law, where every facility will be given by me for the most speedy recoveries; and for that purpose such creditors who live in the Counties of Loudon and Fairfax, will, I hope, meet me at ALX on the third Tuesday in April; and those who live elsewhere on the first Tuesday in May next. This trouble would not be proposed could a sum sufficient for the discharge of the debts of that concern (which are inconsiderable) be collected by ALEXANDER HENDERSON, Moore-Hill, March 14, 1785.

MAGNOLIO,

STANDS at Mount Vernon, and covers mares for Five Pounds the season.--Good pasturage may be had for mares at Three Shillings per week, and all possible care taken of them, but will not be answerable for escapes or other accidents that may happen to them. *Magnolio* if five years old the first day of June next, a chestnut colour, near sixteen hands high, finely formed, and thought by all who have seen him to be perfect.--He was got by the *Ranger Arabian*, his dam by *Othello* son of *Crab*, her dam by *Morton's Traveller*, and her dam was *Selima* by the Godolphin Arabian. LUND WASHINGTON, March 21, 1785.

January 28, 1785.

ECLIPSE,

Imported last Summer,

STANDS this season at Collington Meadows, in Prince-George's County, Maryland, and will begin to cover on the 20th day of March next, at Six Guineas a mare, and One Dollar to the groom; his colour is a fine chestnut with a small blaze, and one white hind foot, full fifteen hands and a half high, great bone, and very handsome. Good pasturage for mares at 2/6 per week, but will not be answerable for escapes or other accidents. The money to be sent with the mares.

RICHARD B. HALL.

London, February 26, 1784.

Esteemed friend, WE have procured you a horse of the first running blood, as you desired, and got by the celebrated *Eclipse*. Enclosed is his pedigree, attested by Mr. Tattersall, whose veracity may be depended on, and who is allowed to have the most extensive knowledge of the turn of any man in this country.

OXLEY and HANCOCK.

Richard B. Hall,

THIS is to certify, that the chestnut [sic] horse I sold Mr. Oxley was bred by the late Sir John Shelley, Bart., and was got by *Eclipse*, out of *Phoebe*, full sister to *Apollo*. Phoebe was got by *Regulus*, her dam by *Cottingham*, grand-dam by Snake, great grand-dam by the *Bald Galloway*, great great grand-dam by Lord Carlisle's *Turk*. *Cottingham* was got by Mr. Hartley's blind horse. This horse was five years old last grass. Witness by hand this 16th of February 1784.

RICHARD TATTERSALL.

N.B. The horse won several plates and matches, &c.&c. R.T.

THE Subscriber has for Sale a Young Negro WOMAN, about fifteen years of age who was raised in his house.--She is active, healthy, likely, and remarkably sensible, uncommon pains have been taken to instruct her, and indeed few can excel her when she pleases; but the perverseness of her temper and the connections she has formed, induce him to part with her.--Credit will be given if required. He takes this opportunity to request all those who have open accounts with him, for dealings at his store before the war, to come and pay them, and those that are unprepared to comply with this request, upon closing their accounts by bond, with security if required, shall have a further indulgence. He wants an Assistant of ability, integrity, sobriety and assiduity. ☞ For a good price in ready-money he will sell a LOT or two in town. JOHN MUIR, ALX, March 24, 1785 ■ George-Town, March 18, 1785. Will be SOLD to the highest Bidder on the 20th Day of April next, if fair, if not the next fair Day, SEVERAL valuable LOTS in this Town, on one of which is a convenient House, calculated for a Store and the reception of a small family.--The terms of sale will be known on the day of sale. BERNARD O'NEILL, WILLIAM DEAKINS, jun. ■ THE Subscriber meaning to Practice the Law in the Superior Courts of this Commonwealth, will attend at Richmond during the ensuing General Court, and in the intervals of the Courts will receive and transact business at the Town of Fredericksburg. JOHN F. MERCER, Fredericksburg, March 15, 1785 ■ George-Town, March 18, 1785. Will be SOLD to the highest Bidder on the 20th Day of April next, if fair, if not the next fair Day, A NUMBER of valuable LOTS in the Addition to this Town, agreeable situated, convenient to the river, and well worth the attention of new adventurers.--The terms of sale will be made known on the day of sale. WILLIAM DEAKINS, jun. ■ Dumfries, March 10, 1785. ON Thursday the 7th Day of April next, being Prince William Court Week, will be Let at the Court-House Door, at 4 o'Clock in the Afternoon, the Building of a large Two Story Brick Prison, when the Plan, Dimensions and Times of Payment will be made known to the Bidders. HENRY LEE, RICHARD GRAHAM, ALEXANDER LITHGOW, Commissioners. ■ JOHN MASON AND COMPANY, WITH the greatest respect beg leave to inform the ladies and gentlemen of ALX, and the public in general, that they intend carrying on the Goldsmith, Jewelry, Watch and Clock Making businesses in all their different branches, at their shop in Royal-street, near Doctor Dick's, where all orders from any part of the country will be obeyed with the greatest care and expedition. They also flatter themselves that the early experience they have received in some of the most elegant manufactories in Europe, together with their particular attention to please, will enable them to give general satisfaction to all those who favor them with their commands, which will be executed in the neatest manner, on reasonable terms.--They will give the utmost value for old gold, silver, lace, and watches, in exchange. ☞ All kinds of Engraving done on the shortest notice. ALX, March 20, 1785 ■ THE Subscribers will, on notice, execute deeds to such persons as are entitled to CARROLLSBURGH LOTS, where deeds have not been already executed and recorded.--If any of the Lots are for sale, an answer will be given on the terms being made known to H. ROZER, D. CARROLL, N. YOUNG, March 4, 1785 ■ TO BE LET, ON GROUND-RENT FOR EVER, TWO LOTS, situated on Water-street, 25 feet in front by 123 feet 5 inches in depth.--The terms will be made known by applying to the Subscriber. JAMES ADAM, ALX, March 20, 1785 ■ To be Rented, until the 20th Day of March, 1786, THE STOREHOUSE and other Improvements at the Falls of Potomack, in Virginia, belonging to RICHARD THOMPSON and THOMAS MAGRUDER.--For Terms apply to either of them at the House of the Subscriber in George-Town, Maryland. RICHARD THOMPSON, March 23, 1785.

Page 4. Poetry. "From the Hibernian Magazine; The Extent of Life's Variety." ■ Messieurs RICHARDS and COMPANY, wish to inform the public that a Company has been formed to raise funds to make the Potomack River navigable [see like ad Vol. II No. 54] ■ RICHARD ARELL and GEORGE MASON offer twenty dollars reward for strayed or stolen MARE [see like ad Vol. II No. 53] ■ CHARLES STEWART at Annapolis has three valuable Negro men for sale [see like ad Vol. II No. 54] ■ W. BROWN has for sale medicines, shop-furniture and surgeons instruments [see like ad Vol. II No. 54] ■ ROGER CHEW offers for lease Boys and Horses [see like ad Vol. II No. 57] ■ DANIEL CARROLL BRENT offers about 4,000 acres for sale called the Brenton Tract [see like ad Vol. II No. 53] ■ JOHN FORMAN offers for sale horse *OBSCURITY* [see like ad Vol. II No. 59] ■ DYER, Hair Cutter and Dresser from London announces opening of business [see like ad Vol. II No. 59] ■ The Brig *Liberty*, Captain James Nixon, to sail for Hamburg [see like ad Vol. I No. 59] ■ The Ship *Astrea*, Captain Nathaniel West, to sail for London [see like ad Vol. II No. 58] ■ John Brownlow announces the Ship *Rappahannock*, Mark Towell, master, to sail for Liverpool [see like ad Vol. II No. 58] ■ TO BE SOLD, A Warrant for Four Thousand acres of LAND, on the Western Waters of this State, the property of a late Continental Officer.--For Terms inquire of the Printers. ■ PATRICK GOOLDING thanks his customers and wishes to continue his school in the room that Mr. M'Iver kept his in [see like ad Vol. II No. 58] ■ Colonel FITZGERALD seeks a person to take charge of a mill, bake-house and interest adjoining [see like ad Vol. II No. 58] ■ Parcel of Leather INK-HOLDERS found by Laz, a slave belonging to M'Crea and Mease [see like ad Vol. II No. 59] ■ ALX: Printed by GEORGE RICHARDS, and COMPANY, at their Printing-Office on Fairfax--by whom Advertisements, &c. are thankfully received for this Paper,--and where Printing is performed with Care and Expedition.

1785/03/31, Vol. II No. 61

Page 1. TO BE SOLD, A Warrant for Four Thousand acres of LAND, on the Western Waters of this State, the property of a late Continental Officer.--For Terms inquire of the printers ■ ALEXANDER HENDERSON, Moore-Hill, seeks to settle outstanding accounts and those of Glassford and Henderson [see like ad Vol. II No. 60] ■ JOHN MUIR offers a young Negro woman for sale [see like ad Vol. II No. 60] ■ BERNARD O'NEILL and WILLIAM DEAKINS, jun. offer for sale several lots in George-Town [see like ad Vol. II No. 60] ■ JOHN MASON AND COMPANY announce opening of their business of Goldsmith, Jewelry, Watch and Clock Making [see like ad Vol. II No. 60] ■ Commissioners in Dumfries solicit bids to build prison [see like ad Vol. II No. 60] ■ H. ROZER, D. CARROLL and N. YOUNG will execute deeds to persons entitled to lots in Carrollsburgh [see like ad Vol. II No. 60] ■ JAMES ADAM offers for ground-rent for ever two lots on Water-street [see like ad Vol. II No. 60] ■ RICHARD THOMPSON has for rent a storehouse at the Falls of Potomack [see like ad Vol. II No. 60] ■ About 40 casks of good molasses for sale from on board the Brig *Dolphin* [see like ad Vol. II No. 59] ■ WILLIAM DEAKINS, George-Town, offers for sale a number of lots in the Addition to Georgetown [see like ad Vol. II No. 60] ■ LEWIS ELLZEY offers one hundred dollars reward for runaway fellow named Will [see like ad Vol. II No. 55] ■ Messieurs RICHARDS and COMPANY, THE House of Delegates of this State having ordered the bill, establishing a provision for the Teachers of the Christian Religion, to be published, accompanied with a request that the people may signify to the next session of Assembly their opinion respecting the adoption of such a bill; and a copy thereof having appeared in your Journal, I beg leave, through the same channel of communication, to submit to my fellow-citizens a few thoughts, which have occurred to me on this interesting subject.

As an advocate for the essential rights and interests of Christianity; as an enemy to every measure that may serve to disturb that general harmony in the community, which is the only source of public happiness; and as a sincere friend to the Clergy themselves, I do not hesitate to declare my opinion, that no such bill, as that now under consideration, ought ever to be passed into law. For taking into view the aspect which it has upon these several important objects, to me it appears liable to objections far more powerful than any arguments which can be offered in its defence.

The *principle* on which it is founded is totally *inadmissible--That legislative aid is necessary to the support of the Christian Religion, or of its authorized Teachers or Ministers*. "The diffusion of Christian knowledge hath indeed," as the framers of the bill have justly remarked, "a natural tendency to correct the morals of men, to restrain their vices, and to preserve the peace of society." "For whatsoever things are true, honest, just, pure, lovely, and of good report, or in any respect virtuous and praiseworthy," contributing to the improvement of human nature, to sweeten the intercourse of mankind in every relation of life, and to strengthen those obligations which bind them together in any religious, or civil association;--all these things are uniformly inculcated, under the sanction of the highest authority, and of the most persuasive motives, in every part of this excellent system. But the Divine Author of it has no where informed us, that the persons whom he calls to be Teachers of his doctrines and laws, are thereby constituted officers of civil government, or that it is the business of the Legislature to provide by law for their support. When he commissioned the Apostles, the first Ministers of his Church, to go and teach all nations the knowledge of his religion, he made no mention of any provision to be made for them, by the legislatures of the several countries where they should preach the gospel; but left them to depend for this, under his providential care, upon the voluntary contributions of the people, by whom they should be received, and to whom they should impart their instructions and ministrations. On the same footing, I conceive, it was intended, that the Ministers of the Gospel should stand in every age. All the security and encouragement which he saw fit to give in this case was, "that he would be with them," and all their regular and faithful successors, by his spirit and providence, "at all times, even unto the end of the world." And the Teacher, or Minister, who cannot freely consent to take upon him the pastoral charge of a people, trusting to the author of this promise, not only to bestow all needful spiritual aid for the exercise of his ministry, but also to add all such things as may be necessary to his temporal subsistence in some other way, more desirable, than that of his forcing it from the flock committed to his care, by the operation of the pains and penalties of law, has ground to suspect that his views are not quite so pure and disinterested as they ought to be, and that his labours in such circumstances are not likely to be either acceptable or useful.

The tendency of these observations is not, I persuade myself, to weaken the obligations of Christians to afford an adequate support to their approved Teachers or Ministers. This is acknowledged to be their duty, established by an authority much higher [*Continued on Page 2*].

Page 2. (*continued*) than that of any Legislature on earth: For "the Lord himself hath ordained, that they who preach the gospel, should live by the gospel." And it doubtless becomes the people, as cheerfully to impart to such a suitable supply of temporal things, as it becomes these, "to be instant in season, and out of season," in all zealous desires and endeavours, to promote their eternal interest...

That the Church of Christ stands not at least in any need of such interposition of government, is abundantly evident, not only from the consideration that Christ's kingdom is not of this world, and accordingly not indebted to the protection or favor of the rulers of the world, for its stability or prosperity; but by undeniable facts, more powerful than any reasoning, from them, that could be used on the subject...

As this bill is thus founded on a principle, which appears to be dishonorable and injurious to Christianity, *so in its operation, if passed into a law, it may naturally be expected to destroy much of that good understanding and affection, which ought ever to subsist between the different members of the same civil community.* If the people conceive, that Christianity and its Teachers stand in no need of the aid of law for their support; that the Assembly, being delegated for the sole purpose of conducting the affairs of civil government, have no right to interfere in the peculiar concerns of religion; and that the interposition of their authority, in matters so foreign from the business of their appointment, is usually no less prejudicial to the true interests of the Church of Christ, than it is in itself unwarrantable (and such I am persuaded are the prevailing sentiments of the citizens of this State;) the tax, which such a law would impose, will never be collected, but by measures very undesirable, and perhaps, in may instances, not without force and violence... [To be concluded in our next.] ■ **LONDON, December 14.** The Emperor's Envoy waited on his Prussian Majesty to advise that his Imperial Sovereign, displeased with Dutch conduct, was about to send 80,000 men against them. The King of Prussia replied that the Prussian Ambassador at Vienna would be informing the Emperor that Prussian troops also were on the move. The King did not grant the Envoy a particular audience, but received him while pointing out to six of his Generals some geographical dispositions, on the map ... From Vienna we learn that the Peace or War question will soon be determined; from the works at the arsenal and the appointments of a commission of war, the latter seems inevitable. France has good reason for not taking part; Prussia is afraid of France, and it is believed the Mareschal de Lascy has p[text missing] as the Emperor has ordered prepared his campaign equipage. His Majesty leaves Vienna [word missing] in 10 or 12 days. But the Prince of Kaunitz has persuaded the Emperor to delay until receiving responses from the Courts of Russia, France and Prussia to his intimation he plans to send an army into the Netherlands. **December 21.** The militia is to be formed for one month next spring ... As of last October 31st, the total of the ordinary of the British navy: 111 ships of the line, 14 of 50 guns, 84 frigates, 43 sloops--in all, 252 ships ... Extract of a letter from **Newcastle, December 8:** "Every hour brings us fresh accounts of wrecks and losses, above 100 vessels are totally lost and ashore, upon this coast; few of them will be got off. Never was such a stroke to this port before." ... Extract of a private letter from **Paris, December 12:** A stranger arrived at the Hotel of the Comte de Mercy here, Friday evening. However incredible it may at first appear, I hear it may be the Emperor, incognito, to confer in person with the French Cabinet. The Comte, who is the Imperial Ambassador here, and the above incognito, have been twice at Court ... Same letter, **December 13**, Two in the Morning: the stranger is the Imperial Joseph. The Dutch Envoy has sent this information to the Hague, but our messenger will reach London first--unless the bad weather should again stop the Packets at Calais. The Emperor's coming here is mysterious, and bodes no good for the Dutch ... A majority of the German Electors are decidedly with the Emperor; indeed, opening the Scheldt would be universally beneficial to the Empire, introducing trade and more money ... Every mail from Ireland this past fortnight brings favorable news. The rage of party begins to subside in all parts of the country; the people understand that Mr. Pitt is preparing some commercial regulations which will place the two kingdoms' trade on a more equal footing. ■ **CHARLESTON, February 28.** Mr. Fusdan, lately from England, has erected at Winnsborough in this State, a horse powered saw mill, sawing 800-1000 feet of plank per day. ■ **HARTFORD, March 7.** Last Monday the Governor and State Council met here at the State house. They decided the General Assembly should not be called, considering some late dispatches from Congress respecting the interest of the Dutch loan. After appointing a fast, and issuing a proclamation to prevent the spread of small pox in

Litchfield county, they adjourned. ■ **NEW YORK, March 10.** The Hon. Henry Knox, Esq., late a Major General in the army of the United States, has by Congress been appointed Minister of War, for the direction of all our military affairs ... A correspondent says the Emperor of Morocco, who ordered several American vessels seized, used the pretext that we did not honor him with a reply to his overtures for friendly connexions. We are certain reasons for silence will be entirely satisfactory. In the near future the Flag of liberty, in every quarter of the globe, will be as free from Barbarian insults as the nation to which the flag belongs, by its virtues giving dignity to its supporters, and incessantly increasing its lustre ... Col. William Palfrey, an American gentleman, who left here for France in 1781 to be our Consul there, and who was supposed to have been lost at sea, was captured by an Algerine Corsair, and is now a slave at the oar. [*New Haven Gaz.*] ... **Extract of a letter from Cork, Oct. 27.** The *Ocean*, Capt. Moore, (belonging to Glasgow) is arrived here from Jamaica. Captain Moore fell in with a vessel off Newfoundland, from this kingdom to America, with emigrants, in so great distress, that had he not providentially come across them, the whole must have perished. His humanity led him to take the people on board, and has brought them in here. The vessel almost immediately went down after the people were taken out.

Page 3. **PHILADELPHIA, March 25.** Extract of a letter from **St. Eustatia, January 30, 1785:** "A vessel arrived here from St. Kitt's commanded by an Irishman, who had brought out near 100 convicts, destined for Nova Scotia, whose passages were all paid by the King of Great Britain, at the rate of £5 sterling, per head... But instead of bringing them to the port intended, he landed them on one of the Cape de Verd islands, where they were indiscriminately murdered by the natives, on a supposition they were infected with the plague. The inhuman Captain proceeded to the West Indies, and was selling the ship's provisions at St. Kitt's, when a letter was received by the Governor of that island, from the Governor of Teneriffe, containing an explicit account of this villainous transaction. The Captain being informed of this, slipt his cable and ran into St. Eustatia, where he expected to be safe. But the Governor of St. Kitt's immediately sent a sloop after him with a letter to the Governor of St. Eustatia, requesting him not to afford protection to such a villain; in consequence of which he was arrested and confined in the fort." ■ **RICHMOND, March 26.** If true that the Spaniards are building a fort in the western part of North Carolina, with intent to molest or cut off settlers in the new States, we should be roused to immediate opposition against them; we should invite the natives of Spanish colonies in America to throw off these tyrants, under the promise of considering them as united in the same league as ourselves. ■ **BALTIMORE, March 26.** On Wednesday afternoon departed this life, at his house in Market street, Doctor JOHN STEVENSON, aged 67, native of Londonderry, Ireland, and of a very respectable family. A Baltimore resident almost 40 years, he was one of its most eminent merchants; he was the first exporter of wheat and flour from this port, and consequently laid the foundation of its present commercial consequence. It was his heart's delight to promote and see the increase and prosperity of this town in particular, and the State in general. He was distinguished for a nervous and manly understanding, sprightly wit, steady friendship, a high sense of integrity and honor, and an unbounded hospitality. ■ **ALX, March 31**. The Honorable John Haring, John Lawrence, and Melancton Smith, Esquires, are elected Delegates to represent the State of New-York in Congress. ■ By the *Pearce*, Capt. -----, which arrived in Patuxent River a few Days since, we have received London Papers as late as the 14th of January, which mention, That M. Maillebois sets out for Holland in a few Days, and that several general Officers will accompany him as Volunteers. The States of Holland give this General an Appointment of 100,000 Crowns a Year, and allow him a similar Sum for his Equipages before he takes the Field. To this they add an Annuity of 100,000 Livres, whether there be Peace or War.--That the King of Prussia has ordered a large Body of Forces to hold themselves in readiness to march the Movement the Imperial Troops are in Motion, that they may oppose their marching through any Part of the Prussian Territories.--That the Prussian Ambassador, at Vienna, has Orders to leave that City, and return Home as soon as the Imperial Troops begin to move towards the Dutch Provinces.--And that several Officers in the Service of the Dutch have arrived at Berlin, for the Purpose of purchasing Arms and Clothes for the Use of the light Troops raising in the Dutch Provinces. ■ The *Union*, Capt. Holliday, from Virginia, is arrived at Clyde. The *Friendship*, Capt. Caldwell, from Virginia for London, with Tobacco, arrived at Spithead on the 12th of January. The *Mary-Ann*, Capt. Priestman, from Maryland is arrived at Falmouth. ■ On Thursday the 16th of December died at Glasgow, in the 64 Year of his Age, Mr. DANIEL BAXTER, Bookseller. ■ NAVAL-OFFICE, ALX. *Inward Entries.* Sloop *Bathsheba*, J. Ingraham, from Newport; Brig *King Taminy*, O. Goodwin, Martinico; Brig *Betsy*,

T. Perkins, Maryland; Brig *Ann-Maria*, J. Robertson, Barbadoes; Sloop *Experience*, J.W. Miller, Cadiz. *Cleared Outwards*. Sloop *Hetty and Matilda*, H. Arys, for Charleston; Ship *Watson*, W. Hayden, Amsterdam; Brig *William and Henry*, T. Simmons, Rappahannock. ■ ☞ Constant Employment and the highest Wages, will be given to reputable JOURNEYMEN PRINTERS, on Application to the Printers hereof, or to Messrs. GODDARD and LANGWORTHY, Printers in Baltimore.

Virginia, to wit:
In the NAME of the COMMONWEALTH,
To All whom it May Concern.
CHARLES HELLSTEDT, having been recognized by the United States in Congress assembled, as Consul in the United States of America, from his Majesty the King of Sweden, to reside at Philadelphia; it is hereby declared, that the privileges, pre-eminence, and authority belonging to such character and quality, are due to him. In testimony whereof, PATRICK HENRY, Esquire, our Governor, hath hereunto set his hand, and caused the seal of the Commonwealth to be affixed, at Richmond, this 12th day of March, 1785, and ninth of the Commonwealth. P. HENRY. Attest, A. BLAIR, C.C.

PRICES CURRENT, ALX. / Tobacco, 30s. per Ct. / Fine Flour, 30s. per Barrel. / Wheat, 6s. per Bushel. / Jamaica Spirits, 4/6 per Gallon. / Windward Rum, 3s. to 3/3 per Ditto. / Continental Rum, 2s. to 2/2 per Ditto. / Molasses, 1/6 per Ditto. / Muscovado Sugar, 38s. to 45s. per Ct. / Salt, 4s. per Bushel, by Retail. / Corn, 3s per Bushel / Exchange, 40.

FOR AMSTERDAM, To sail positively by the 1st of May, having Four-Fifths of her Cargo engaged, THE Ship *HOPE*, T. BARNARD, Master, being American property and one of the first ships out of the continent for safety and sailing.--For freight or passage apply to
JOSIAH WATSON.
ALX, March 29, 1785.

WILLIAM LYLES and CO. announce sail of the Brig *Marquis de la Fayette* [see like ad Vol. II No. 60] ■ ROBERT ADAM has for sale old Jamaica spirits, West-India rum, etc. [see like ad Vol. II No. 57] ■ FOR SALE, The following TRACTS of LAND lying in Washington County, and on Potomack River, viz. THE Resurvey on Sugar-Bottom, containing 360½ acres; the Resurvey on Dogwood-Plains, 263½ acres; the Resurvey on Walnut-Level, 255 acres; and the Resurvey on Horse-Lick, 302-1/4. These Lands lay on the main road from Frederick-Town to Fort-Cumberland, about 70 miles from the former, and 14 miles only from Bath.--They are of the first quality, and will be sold uncommonly cheap for ready-money. The price may be known by application to Doctor THOMAS of Frederick-Town, Mr. WILLIAM BAILEY of George-Town, or the Subscriber. THOMAS H. HANSON, ALX, March 28, 1785 ■ ☞ THE Stages will begin to run as usual on the fourth day of April next, viz. From Philadelphia to Baltimore in two days, from Baltimore to ALX in one day, from ALX to Fredericksburg in one day, and from Fredericksburg to Richmond in one day; from Richmond to the Southward they will run as usual.--The Stages will start from each post precisely at four o'clock in the morning.--The starting days from ALX will be Tuesdays, Thursdays and Saturdays, and will arrive at Baltimore and Fredericksburg the same evenings. March 30, 1785 ■ Just arrived in the Brig *Ann-Maria*, and to be Sold on reasonable Terms for Cash, Flour, Wheat, or Indian-Corn, by RICHARD CONWAY, A Parcel of good BARBADOES RUM.--He has also for Sale, a few Pieces of Superfine Broadcloth, and good Sugar in Barrels. ALX, March 30, 1785 ■ WHEREAS it hath been industriously propagated that I have quit keeping a public house, I beg leave to inform the public, that I have no such intention, but on the contrary have lately furnished my house with the best liquors, &c. for the accommodation of gentlemen, and will kindly thank any who may please to favor me with their custom. THOMAS ROPER, Leesburg, March 26, 1785 ■ TO BE RENTED, And immediately possession given, THE House and Store adjoining the gaol, where the Subscriber now lives.--For the conveniency of a young man, the Store, Counting-room and Cellar will be rented separately.--Apply to ROBERT BRYCE. ALX, March 31, 1785 ■ AN elegant CHARIOT with Harness, and a Pair of firm well-broke bay HORSES of full Size, to be Sold, either together or separate, as may best accommodate the Purchaser.--Tobacco or cash will be taken in Payment. JOSIAH WATSON, ALX, March 28, 1785 ■ TWENTY DOLLARS REWARD. RAN away from the Subscriber, and has been ever since March, 1781, a Negro Man, named JACOB, about four or five and twenty years of age, about 5 feet 10 inches high, very strait and well made, somewhat of an Indian colour, round-faced, with fine even white teeth; he is very chatty, affects to talk politely, and seems very ready, obliging and complaisant.--Shortly after he went away he enlisted with Capt. Bradford, in Col. Voce's regiment of the Pennsylvania line, while laying at the Head of Elk, on their way to Virginia, and when in Virginia he played some prank for which he was confined, and afterwards made his escape.--He is a strong active fellow, very expert at mowing, cradling, reaping, and all plantation business.--Whoever secures said fellow so that the Subscriber may get him again, shall be entitled to the above reward, and all charges paid, MARY DULANY, Annapolis, Maryland, March 24, 1785 ■ THE Subscriber, in expectation of a meeting of the Town Council, deferred certain proposals to the citizens so long as to leave no room for their publication in this Week's Journal. They will be published soon, if necessary. In the mean time they may be seen at the Printing-Office, or in the hands of the public's most humble Servant, CHARLES M'IVER, ALX, March 31, 1785 ■ ALL persons indebted to the estate of Benjamin Ogle, Esq., of Berkely County, deceased, are once more desired to come and pay off the balances, that the subscriber may be enabled to pay the debts due from that estate. Those who do not comply with this request in one month from this date, may expect that suits will be immediately commenced against them, by WILLIAM HARDAGE, Executor. Shenandoah, March 24, 1785 ■ ALL that stand in arrears with the Subscriber [is] desired to settle the same in one month [from] this date; and all that have any claims ag[ainst Ben]jamin Ogle, Esq., or the Subscriber, are [requested to] bring them in, that they may be adjusted [torn away]. WILLIAM HAR[DAGE], March 31, 1785 ■ LUND WASHINGTON offers for sale horse *MAGNOLIO* [see like ad Vol. II No. 60] ■ ☞ If Mr. NATHANIEL GREENE, late of Rhode-Island, will apply to Messrs. GODDARD and LANGWORTHY, Printers in Baltimore, either in Person or by Letter, he may hear of something greatly to his Advantage.

Page 4. Poetry. "Friendship: An Ode." ■ The Brig *Liberty*, Captain James Nixon, is shortly to sail for Hamburg [see like ad Vol. II No. 59] ■ Benjamin Stoddert announces sailing for London the Brig *Fitzhugh* [see like ad Vol. II No. 60] ■ John F. Mercer, Fredericksburg, announces his practice of law in that town [see like ad Vol. II No. 60] ■ DANIEL CARROLL BRENT offers about 4,000 acres for sale called the Brenton Tract [see like ad Vol. II No. 53] ■ JOHN FORMAN offers for sale horse *OBSCURITY* [see like ad Vol. II No. 60] ■ RICHARD B. HALL offers for sale horse *ECLIPSE* [see like ad Vol. II No. 60] ■ RICHARD ARELL and GEORGE MASON offer twenty dollars reward for strayed or stolen MARE [see like ad Vol. II No. 53] ■ DYER, Hair Cutter and Dresser from London announces opening of business [see like ad Vol. II No. 59] ■ Just received, and to be Sold on the most reasonable Terms, at the Printing-Office, A Variety of elegant PAPER-HANGINGS ■ RALPH WORMELEY offers for sale 2,500 acres of LAND in Berkeley County [see like ad Vol. II No. 59] ■ Parcel of Leather INK-HOLDERS found by Laz, a slave belonging to M'Crea and Mease [see like ad Vol. II No. 59] ■ JOHN HUFF, Post-Rider from Winchester to ALX, thanks customers and seeks additional subscriptions [see like ad Vol. II No. 58] ■ WILLIAM WILSON has for sale a lot of ground on Fairfax-street, and a lot of ground in Dumfries [see like ad Vol. II No. 58] ■ WILLIAM ANDERSON offers reward for runaway Irish servant named Jeremiah Flannery [see like ad Vol. II No. 59] ■ J. APEDAILE who practiced in hospitals in Europe and America has settled at Mr. John Short's [see like ad Vol. II No. 59] ■ ALX: Printed by GEORGE RICHARDS, and COMPANY, at their Printing-Office on Fairfax--by whom Advertisements, &c. are thankfully received for this Paper,--and where Printing is performed with Care and Expedition.

1785/04/07, Vol. II No. 62

Page 1. WILLIAM WILSON has for sale a lot of ground on Fairfax-street, and a lot of ground in Dumfries [see like ad Vol. II No. 58] ■ ROBERT ADAM has for sale old Jamaica spirits, West-India rum, etc. [see like ad Vol. II No. 57] ■ JOHN MUIR offers a young Negro woman for sale [see like ad Vol. II No. 60] ■ JOSIAH WATSON offers for sale an elegant chariot, etc. [see like ad Vol. II No. 61] ■ WILLIAM LYLES and CO. announce sail of the Brig *Marquis de la Fayette* [see like ad Vol. II No. 60] ■ Conclusion of the Piece begun in our last. CAN any satisfactory reason be assigned, why Episcopalians, Baptists, Methodists, Presbyterians, and all other Christian communities, by whatever name distinguished, should not be permitted, equally with the people called Quakers, and the Menonists, to place the money raised from their members in their respective general funds, to be employed for the advancement of the interests of the religion, on as extended a scale as they may think proper to adopt? Would there be any danger, or impropriety, in conceding this privilege to all societies without distinction, especially when it may happen that they do not want the supplies which the proposed law might give them, for the particular purposes therein specified? By administering to the necessities of their indigent and helpless members, by establishing schools for the instruction of their children, on plans most conformable to their own sentiments of a Christian education, and by various other measures, they might perhaps be able to serve the cause of Christianity, with full as much credit and advantage, as by bestowing superfluous revenues upon the clergy, or adding useless appendages to churches... [Continued on Page 2].

Page 2. (*continued*) ... I have now finished my remarks on this obnoxious bill; and the importance of the subject shall be my only apology, for having so long repassed on the time and patience of those who may think proper to favor them with a perusal. If my sentiments happen to coincide with those of any respectable number of my fellow-citizens, I persuade myself they will also think with me, that measures should be early concerted, to prevent such a bill from obtaining the sanction of a law... VIGILARIUS.

VENICE, Nov. 22. Chevalier Emo's bombardment of Susa, Africa, was successful, reducing it to ruins without a man lost. Five were wounded, among them Sieur Moro, second in command, whose toes were crushed. Of the squadron's 260 bombs discharged, 200 took effect. **Vienna, Dec. 11.** From Lintz we hear that the regiments of Tillier, Preiss, and Deutschmeister, arrived there on the 4th in good condition. After receiving cannon and ammunition appointed for them, they continued towards the Netherlands via Nuremburg. **Frankfurt, Dec. 27.** The Emperor's equipage under Captain Truber de Steinfeld, arrived here day before yesterday from Hanau, escorted by four horse Chasseurs, and after some repose continued toward Brussels ... A letter from **Paris dated the 26th, at night**, says 50 infantry regiments, 15 of cavalry, 5 of Hussars, 21 of dragoons, one of Chasseurs, four and a half of artillery--in all, 96 and a half regiments, are appointed to take the field ... **Petersburgh, Dec. 8.** Since Georgia has been under the protection of our Sovereign, a small body of troops have been stationed there, who have had several skirmishes with the inhabitants of the neighboring districts, one of the last of which was attended with much bloodshed ... **Hague, Jan. 2.** The States of Holland and West Friesland will assemble next Wednesday. The 26th of last month The Prince Stadtholder, in quality of Captain general, dispatched orders for the augmentation of troops of the Republic, conformably to the resolutions of the States General of the 15th of the same month. **Jan. 7.** M. De Wassenaar de Staremberg, Ambassador Extraordinary from the States General to the court of St. Petersburgh, is recalled ... We hear from Franckfort that the Imperial troops suffer prodigiously from the inclemency of the season, and that the desertion on their march increases daily ... It is confidently reported here, since yesterday, that several Austrian regiments have received orders to turn back ... Another report says some Swiss officers in the service of the Republic, and some recruits, have been made prisoners of war by the Emperor's troops. **Constantinople, Dec. 1.** The Sublime Porte will send a Minister of the second rank to Madrid, to compliment his Catholic Majesty in the name of the Grand Seignior ...The Spanish Minister confers with the Divan on the differences between his king and the Regency of Algiers. Acaugi Bachi is dispatched to Algiers with proposals on the disagreements between Spain and that Regency ... Captain Pacha's fleet has returned to port, but some of the crews have the plague; that terrible disorder has not yet subsided ... The dispute between the Emperor and the Dutch has raised insurance rates 8 and 10 per cent in the ports of the Levant. **Leyden, Jan. 2.** They write from the Hague that the States General have already replied to the Memorial presented them last month on the 24th by M. De Kalatchow, Envoy Extraordinary from the Empress of Russia. **Cologne, Dec. 31.** Letters from Venice mention the Republic is putting all her ships of war into commission, and making great exertions to increase her maritime strength. This is said to be in consequence of the rejection of the propositions made by the States General relative to the affair of the merchants Chomel and Jordan. ■ **LONDON, January 6.** The business of the ensuing Parliament, say the Quidnuncs of the day, is to consist merely in repealing old laws, and altering some late ones, so that the next sessions will be only a *new edition* of the former, with alterations and amendments, *cum notis variorum ... A translation of a letter said to have been written by the Empress of all the Russia to his Prussian Majesty:* [The Empress' salutary opening reaffirms the total friendship and accord she believes exist between Russia and Prussia. She holds the Emperor's claims to be just and moderate.] Nature has granted the use and advantage of the river to the Low Countries; Austria alone, by virtue of the law of nature and the nations is entitled to its exclusive use. The equity and disinterestedness of Joseph II can only impart this right to other people, it belonging exclusively to his States. Austrian sentiments merit esteem and attention, but Dutch avidity and judgement assumed on the basis of the Treaty of Muncaster are notorious and blamable in every respect. Holland merits no assistance of any foreign power. The consequences they draw on themselves must be submitted to the moderation of the Emperor alone. I am firmly resolved to assist him with all my land and sea forces, as if the welfare of my own Empire was in agitation. I hope my sentiments will meet with the success which our reciprocal friendship deserves, and which has never been interrupted. [signed] CATHERINE. **Jan. 14.** We understand a tax on coals is again in agitation, and likely to be part of Mr. Pitt's budget. He has ever proved himself a friend to the poor, and therefore it is no wonder he takes such pains totally to rescue them from expensive articles--having succeeded with **light**, he now means to deprive them of *fire!* A correspondent says our good young minister proceeds from virtuous principle--that the cold will drive the poor to bed very early in the evening, and compel them to be industrious during the day to keep warm. Some people would suppose we could enjoy the produce of our country more cheaply at home than abroad, but the contrary is the fact, coals being sold at Holland five and twenty per cent cheaper than in the metropolis ... A letter from **Venice, dated December 17:** The differences between us and Holland cannot be amicably resolved. Our Senate has voted to make war on the United Provinces rather than pay the 600,000 florins demanded by the States General. Our arsenal workers labor day and night, and we intend to repel force with force. Our squadron, Chevalier Emo commanding, put into Trapani about a week ago. The *Bravoura*, of 80 tons, thought lost, has been saved ... The answer to the demand why France is fitting so many men of war at Brest (four sail extraordinary of the line, and four frigates, fitting out) is they are to relieve some ships on foreign stations which must come home for repair. So unsatisfactory to the British is this answer that they have ordered two sloops of war off that port, to observe; and, should they sail together, to follow them to their destination. The Dutch fleet equipped at the Texel is under the same suspicion, and a cutter is stationed to give notice of their sailing. Extract of a letter from **Constantinople, Nov. 8.** Extraordinary news is circulating here that the Spanish Minister at the Porte has requested it to bring about peace between his Catholic Majesty and the Algerines, to which the Ottoman Minister has agreed. The Spanish initiative, should it be true, would appear to be the result of a system prevailing at the Court since the retreat of his Catholic Majesty, a system of which the treaty with the Regency of Tripoli has been one effect. It would not be astonishing if the Spanish Government were tired with expenses, in a great measure unfruitful, to subjugate the Barbarians, whose excursions extremely incommode the mercantile navigation and commerce of the kingdom.

Page 3. **PHILADELPHIA, March 25.** A letter from Cape Gratios a Dios, January 25, 1785, says the natives declare they would rather die than come under the Spanish government ... A letter dated **Black River, Musquito Shore, Feb. 19** says Great Britain seems inclined to protect the Musquito Shore, so American vessels will find it dangerous to come this way. At this moment the cannon from the ships off the bar announce the arrival of two men of war, and a large transport ship with 400 soldiers, and a suitable train of artillery, from Jamaica, for the defence of this settlement ... A letter from **Newport, Rhode Island, March 8** reports our General Assembly passed the five per cent act, they to appoint the collection officers, the money to be paid into the general treasury ... A gentleman from **New York, March 17**, writes I believe the Colonel Palfrey capture and enslavement story to be false. A gentleman --a very great friend of the United States-- in the Emperor of Morocco's dominions, writes regularly here. A letter from him gives the correct account of recent captures by the Barbarians mentions not a word about the *Shillelah*, in which the unfortunate Palfrey sailed. I conclude that he is not in slavery, but died--as we all must--and rests now in a watery grave. **April 1:** Extract of a letter from **Plank Bridge, North Carolina, Jan. 2:** I condole with you on the loss of our friend T. Sawyer. On December 25, in lat. 36, 50, and long. 70 there started a butt [the end of a hull plank came loose - Eds.] about ten o'clock in the morning, and by one she had sunk to the surface of the water. The *Irish Volunteer*, Capt. Ferguson, from Portsmouth, Virginia bound to Ireland hove to and offered relief. When the wreck struck the ship rather hard, the offended Captain stamped and swore, ordered them to fill away the topsails, and let them all go to hell together, and bore away and left them. The seas broke over them so rapidly that they dropped off one by one until all perished, except Malachi Norris. He was taken off by a schooner bound for Norfolk, Virginia; he says our friend was the last to drop off, and could he have survived fifteen more minutes, he would have been saved as well ... A correspondent says the Muscle Shoals are in the Western part of the South, and not-as reported--in the western part of North Carolina. They are on the Cherokee River, which flows through the Ohio to the Mississippi. The Cherokee is said to be navigable to its forks, on the Western part of North Carolina. It is navigable by vessels of greater size to the Muscle Shoals. [See M'Murray's new Map of the United States.] ■ **RICHMOND, April 2.** On Thursday died, at the Glebe near this city, the Rev. Miles Selden, incumbent of Henrico Parish. ■ **ALX, April 7**. The Honorable Thomas Jefferson, Esq., of this State, is said to have been appointed by Congress, Minister to the Court of France, in the Room of Dr. Franklin, who, on Account of his advanced Age, has Leave to return to America. ■ The *Amelia*, Captain John Throckmorton, from this Port, is arrived at London. ■ MARRIED.] Mr. JOHN DUNDAS, Merchant, to Miss NANCY HEPBURN. -- Capt. JOHN ROBERTSON, to Miss BETSY MOXLEY.

On Saturday last departed this Life, Mrs. ANN RAMSAY, Relict of late WILLIAM RAMSAY, Esq., in the 55th Year of her Age.—The amiable Character of this Lady, exemplified in her Conduct as a Wife, a Mother and a Neighbour, as it procured her through Life the general Esteem and Affection of all who knew her, will render her Loss long regretted, not only by her nearer Relations, but by the Inhabitants of this Town and Neighbourhood of every Rank and Description, to whom her Benevolence and Humanity, displayed in numberless good Offices, and her agreeable Deportment have heretofore been a social Blessing and Comfort.--On Monday her Remains were interred with every Mark of Respect, contiguous to the Grave of her late deceased Husband.

NAVAL-OFFICE, ALX. *Inward Entries.* Snow *Resolution*, J. Gyllenspetz, from Lisbon; Sloop *Susanna*, C. Young, Providence; Schooner *Lottery*, T. Mann, Baltimore. *Cleared Outwards*, Ship *Paragon*, H. Hughes, for Madera; Brig *Union*, S. Gardner, Lisbon.

On Monday next the 18th Inst. will be Sold at the Vendue-Office, opposite the Court-House, A VARIETY OF WET AND DRY GOODS, Among which are Three large and elegant LOOKING-GLASSES.

C. COPPER, Vendue-Master.

ALX, April 6, 1785.

On Tuesday the 26th Inst. will be Sold at Public Vendue, for the Benefit of the INSURERS, THE Brigantine *INDUSTRY*, with all her MATERIALS, as she now lies at Capt. HARPER's Wharf.--An Inventory of Materials may be seen by applying to Captain CHARLES RUSSELL, on board said Brigantine, or at my office.

C. COPPER, Vendue-Master.

ALX, April 5, 1785.

To be Sold at Public Vendue, on Tuesday next the 12th Instant, A LOT of GROUND, situated on the South side of King-street, between Royal and Pit [sic] streets, opposite Mrs. ELIZABETH GRETTER's, 30 feet front and running back 72 feet.--The situation of this Lot is truly valuable being central in the town, and on the principal street leading from the Back Country.--The terms of payment are, one third in hand, one third in three months, and the remaining third in six months after the day of sale, on bond with security.--A general warranty will be made the purchaser. CYRUS COPPER, Vendue-Master, ALX, April 5, 1785. ■ Bladensburg, April 2, 1785. ALL persons indebted to the estate of CHRISTOPHER LOWNDES, deceased, either by bond, note or open account, are desired to make payment. It is expected that those who cannot conveniently discharge their balances, will settle their accounts and renew their obligations. Persons having claims against the estate, are desired to present them legally attested, to BENJAMIN LOWNDES, FRANCIS LOWNDES, Administrators. ■ RICHARD CONWAY has for sale a parcel of good Barbadoes Rum [see like ad Vol. II No. 61].

THE BEAUTIFUL ARABIAN, Will cover mares until the 1st of August at Strawberry-Hill, three miles from ALX, at Four Guineas each, or Two Guineas the single leap.--Good pasturage at Three Shillings per week, but I will not be answerable for escapes or accidents.

GEORGE GILPIN.

April 5, 1785.

WILLIAM HUNTER, jun. Has for Sale, by the Piece or Package, for Cash, Country Produce, or good Bills of Exchange. PLAIN, striped, corded, figured and spotted lawns, white crapes, demi muslins, lastings, calamancoes and tammies, copperplate furniture, shags, satin florentines, printed handkerchiefs, chintz shawls, silk gauzes, thread ditto, ribbons, printed velverets, nuns' thread, English coloured ditto, carpets, a few crates of earthern [sic] and glass ware. Also, Madera wine in pipes, claret in boxes, and a few puncheons of old Jamaica spirits. ALX, April 7, 1785. ■ Just arrived in the Snow *Resolution*, Capt. Gyllenspetz, from Lisbon, and to be Sold on reasonable Terms, by WILLIAM WILSON, The following Articles, viz. SALT, Lisbon wine in quarter casks, Lemons in boxes, Oranges in ditto, Figs in frails, Bohea tea in chests, China bowls in sets of 3 or 5 each, India chintzes, Superfine plain muslins, Striped muslins, Striped and check'd ditto, Corded ditto, Silks, Bandana handkerchiefs, Superfine India cotton clothes excellent for summer wear. ☞ He wants to purchase wheat and Indian-corn. ALX, April 4, 1785. ■ JONATHAN SWIFT and CO. Have for Sale, at their Store on Captain Harper's Wharf, a general Assortment of European Goods, which they will dispose of by the Package or Piece, Cheap for Cash, Bills of Exchange, Flour, Wheat or Tobacco, viz. BROADCLOTHS of all colours and prices, hunters, plains, cassimers, denims, shags, stockinets, queen's cord, honey-combs, corduroys, cordelures, royal ribs, velvets, velverets, jeans, jeanets, fustians, calicoes, chintzes, linens, dowlas, osnaburgs, metal and death-head buttons, sewing silk, twist, tapes, garterings, bindings, carpetings, patent beaver, castor and felt hats, ladies' riding hats, gilt and plain looking-glasses, gold, silver, tortoishell and pinchbeck watches, ladies' calamanco and lasting shoes, misses' Morocco ditto, mens' and womens' leather ditto, queen's-ware, cut glass, fowling-pieces, hardware, grindstones, nails, duck, cordage, &c.&c. They have lately received, per Ship *Triton*, from Boston, New-England rum, molasses, port wine, hyson and souchong tea, coffee, chocolate, allspice, soap, candles, butter, cheese, beef, mackerel, iron castings, &c.--They discount 2½ per cent. for ready-money, and give the market price as usual, in cash or goods, for good tobacco. ALX, April 5, 1785 ■ The Ship *Hope*, T. Barnard, master, to sail for Amsterdam [see like ad Vol. II No. 61] ■ THE Subscriber will Rent the House and Store he now lives in, for one year or term of years, also a large Store fit for wholesale store, opposite the Printing-Office, and two or three Rooms of a house adjoining the same, if wanted. Possession will be given by the 20th instant. He will sell THREE LOTS, in fee-simple.--If they are not sold by the 1st of May next, he will Let them on Ground-Rent.--For terms apply to ROBERT LYLE, April 4, 1785 ■ The Subscriber begs leave to inform the public, that he has opened a Tavern, in the house lately occupied by Miss Susanna[h] Franklin, in the town of Dumfries, where he is accommodated with every thing requisite for the regularly keeping a genteel house. Those gentlemen who will please to favor him with their custom may be assured that every exertion in his power shall be used, in order to render them the most agreeable satisfaction, and such favors he gratefully acknowledged, by their most humble servant, WILLIAM TEBBS, April 2, 1785 ■ THE Subscriber has for sale, clear of Ground-Rent, several LOTS of GROUND, situated on Wilkes and St. Asaph's Streets;--also about 100,000 Bricks, very convenient for building on one or two of said Lots.--He will let, for one or more Years, a commodious well-fitted Store, with a good Cellar under it.--He wishes to inform his former Customers and Masters of Vessels, that he has lately built a BAKE-HOUSE near his Dwelling-House, on King-Street, the second Door from Capt. Jesse Taylor's, where he again carries on the Biscuit-Baking Business, and has now some good Bread on Hand. ADAM LYNN, April 4, 1785.

Page 4. Poetry. "An Epitaph on a COUNTRY COBBLER" [Dick Hall]. ■ John F. Mercer, Fredericksburg, announces his practice of law in that town [see like ad Vol. II No. 60] ■ Benjamin Stoddert announces sailing for London the Brig *Fitzhugh* [see like ad Vol. II No. 60] ■ RICHARD B. HALL offers for sale horse *ECLIPSE* [see like ad Vol. II No. 60] ■ JOHN MASON AND COMPANY announce opening of their business of Goldsmith, Jewelry, Watch and Clock Making [see like ad Vol. II No. 60] ■ JAMES ADAM offers for ground-rent for ever two lots on Water-street [see like ad Vol. II No. 60] ■ H. ROZER, D. CARROLL and N. YOUNG will execute deeds to persons entitled to lots in Carrollsburgh [see like ad Vol. II No. 60] ■ RICHARD THOMPSON has for rent a storehouse at the Falls of Potomack, [see like ad Vol. II No. 60] ■ ALEXANDER HENDERSON, Moore-Hill, seeks to settle outstanding accounts and those of Glassford and Henderson [see like ad Vol. II No. 60] ■ LEWIS ELLZEY offers one hundred dollars reward for runaway fellow named Will [see like ad Vol. II No. 55] ■ JOHN HUFF, Post-Rider from Winchester to ALX, thanks customers and seeks additional subscriptions [see like ad Vol. II No. 58] ■ LUND WASHINGTON offers for sale horse *MAGNOLIO* [see like ad Vol. II No. 60] ■ Just received, and to be Sold on the most reasonable Terms, at the Printing-Office, A Variety of elegant PAPER-HANGINGS ■ WILLIAM DEAKINS, George-Town, offers for sale a number of lots in the Addition to Georgetown [see like ad Vol. II No. 60] ■ WILLIAM

HARDAGE, Shenandoah, seeks to settle accounts of Benjamin Ogle, Esq., of Berkely County, deceased [see like ad Vol. II No. 61] ■ BERNARD O'NEILL and WILLIAM DEAKINS, jun. offer for sale several lots in George-Town [see like ad Vol. II No. 60] ■ MARY DULANY offers reward for return of runaway Negro man named JACOB [see like ad Vol. II No. 61] ■ THOMAS H. HANSON offers for sale land in Washington County on Potomack River [see like ad Vol. II No. 61] ■ THOMAS ROPER, Leesburg, informs public of recent furnishings for accommodating gentlemen [see like ad Vol. II No. 61] ■ ROBERT BRYCE offers for rent house adjoining the gaol [see like ad Vol. II No. 61] ■ TO BE SOLD, A Warrant for Four Thousand acres of LAND, on the Western Waters of this State, the property of a late Continental Officer.--For Terms inquire of the printers ■ ALX: Printed by GEORGE RICHARDS, and COMPANY, at their Printing-Office on Fairfax--by whom Advertisements, &c. are thankfully received for this Paper,--and where Printing is performed with Care and Expedition.

1785/04/14, Vol. II No. 63

Page 1. TO BE SOLD, A Warrant for Four Thousand acres of LAND, on the Western Waters of this State, the property of a late Continental Officer.--For Terms inquire of the printers ■ WILLIAM WILSON offers for sale goods recently arrived in the Snow *Resolution* [see like ad Vol. II No. 62] ■ JONATHAN SWIFT and CO. offer for sale at their store on Captain Harper's Wharf, a general Assortment of European Goods [see like ad Vol. II No. 62] ■ The Ship *Hope*, T. Barnard, master, to sail for Amsterdam [see like ad Vol. II No. 61] ■ ROBERT LYLE offers to rent house and store he now lives in [see like ad Vol. II No. 62] ■ Mr. NATHANIEL GREENE to apply to Printers in Baltimore [see like ad Vol. II No. 62] ■ WILLIAM HUNTER, jun. offers for sale goods [see like ad Vol. II No. 62] ■ Winchester, April 2, 1785. ON Tuesday the 3d day of May next, being the 1st day of Frederick Court, will be let at the Court-House door, at 4 o'clock in the afternoon, the building of a two-story Court-House, fifty feet long and forty wide; the first story to be 14 feet high, and the second 10, and to be finished in a complete manner; a plan of which, and time of payment will be made known that day to the bidders, who are to take notice, that bond with sufficient security for the punctual performance will then be required. To be sold at the same time and place to the highest bidder, the present Court-House, conditioned to be removed off the lot where it now stands within 30 days after the day of sale. EDWARD M'GUIRE, PHILIP BUSH, JOSEPH HOLMES, Commissioners. ■ WILLIAM TEBBS informs the public that he has opened a Tavern in the house lately occupied by Miss Susannah Franklin, in Dumfries [see like ad Vol. II No. 62] ■ JOHN HUFF, Post-Rider from Winchester to ALX, thanks customers and seeks additional subscriptions [see like ad Vol. II No. 58] ■ JAMES ADAM offers for ground-rent for ever two lots on Water-street [see like ad Vol. II No. 60] ■ John F. Mercer, Fredericksburg, announces his practice of law in that town [see like ad Vol. II No. 60].

For the VIRGINIA JOURNAL, &c. Messieurs PRINTERS, WHATEVER melancholy it may excite, it will, I believe, be readily allowed; that the history of mankind, is replete with absurdities and contradictions. There are but few events, on which, we can either dwell with pleasure; or bestow unmingled applause. The most illustrious, almost constantly afford an opportunity, for indulging sentiments of the most opposite cast.--In short, it would appear to be a settled law of our natures, that admiration and abhorrence reign by turns.

Perhaps, the American revolution, if not without example, is at least one of those singular ones, where the mind filled with wonder alone, is held in no doubtful balance.--Reason, whose progress even among those, who are styled the learned, is extremely slow; and who, it may be truly said, seldom reaches the great mass of mankind; has here, at length, obtained a complete triumph, over the long night of superstition, and bigotry... [*Continued* on Page 2].

Page 2. (*continued*) ...The bill of rights, was not the work of an Assembly, but of a Convention: And in my apprehension, if they mean any thing, it is, that all Assemblies should consider it, as a rule of conduct given them by the people.--And here, it may be justly observed, that the natural rights of man, are never likely to be so well defined, and attended to; as when, from causes of great and general danger, the selfish and ambitious aims of individuals, are lost in the single, but power consideration of mutual safety... I must bet their attention to the bill establishing religious freedom, drawn up by a Committee appointed by the House in 1776, to revise, and digest the laws; consisting of Thomas Jefferson, George Wythe, Edmund Pendleton.--Names, that will long, long indeed, be dear to this State... To conclude; in my opinion, the best instructions which can be given to our representatives on this occasion, will be, to enjoin them to support with all their might this excellent bill, and in all their acts, to remember the bill of rights. A FRIEND TO THE BILL OF RIGHTS. ■ [Entire text given for "A Bill for establishing religious Freedom."] ■ **VIENNA, Dec. 18.** Our troops' march will be only 40 days, instead of 56. France's proposals are unacceptable to our Court, and France in the end says it cannot desert the Dutch. Our Sovereign still insists: open the Scheldt or war. **Hague, Jan. 5.** News from Germany is not favorable to the Republic. Success of the Court of France's conciliation efforts seems unlikely, and the Emperor rigidly perseveres in his Scheldt claims. Russia's real intent is not clear, but probably will espouse the Emperor's cause. This should induce the European powers to prepare opposing so formidable a confederacy. The Court of Versailles's precautionary armament readiness would seem to validate this. Every day the celerity of the Austrian armies' movements increases; it is certain, however, the Emperor cannot attempt anything considerable without doubling the forces now intended for the Netherlands. Letters from Guelderland report the greatest defence activity there, fearing it to be one of the first objectives of the Emperor. ■ **LONDON, January 6. Extract of a letter from Paris, Dec. 31:** Count de Mercy and M. De Brantsen confer daily with the other commissioners whose Courts are concerned in the negotiations ongoing here. We fear success is not promising, as the King busies himself several hours daily in his cabinet with Old De Vergennes, and the Marquis de Segur is planning and preparing for the worst. **Jan. 14.** There are agents now in **London** purchasing horses for the Imperial army's artillery. This is cheaper than sending for them to Hungary, the distance being immense. Several have already been embarked at Dover and landed at Ostend. Each horse is computed to cost the Emperor above £50 before he arrives at his destination. However, this is a trifle to what every horse landed in America last war cost us: not less than £200, considering the number that died on the passage ... A gentleman just arrived from **Paris** says the rage for ballooning is such there that several showmen have what they call balloon stands round the Boulevards. For a livre or two any body who chooses is let up to a certain height, and pulled down by a string attached for that purpose. A recent accident, however, makes people a little more cautious. The string gave way, and the balloon took its flight half over Paris before descending. The person was a young man about nineteen. He came down in a nobleman's courtyard and, as the servants saw his descent, they got together a parcel of beds, straw, &c. By which he escaped unhurt, although almost frightened to death ... A letter from **Leghorn** reports: Two Dutch vessels (names unknown) were taken December 2nd within two leagues of this port by the Algerines, and we suppose were carried into Algiers. Trade is much hindered here, for the Barbary corsairs are masters of the Mediterranean, and unless European powers unite to drive them into their ports--for there is no hope of taking them--there will be no trading to any part of the Levant, excepting by the British who pass unmolested. ■ **PHILADELPHIA, April 2.** The Committee of Assembly, to whom the petitions against the bank were referred, have reported a resolution, That a bill be brought in to repeal the act for incorporating said bank. This report was agreed to by the House ... Extract of a letter from **Whitehaven, England, Dec. 7.** "Friday last was opened at Lonningfoot, in the parish of Lamplugh, a new iron forge, constructed for making plate work and edge tools. There were present upwards of a hundred people, on the occasion, when a spade was begun and completed in a few minutes. The machinery, which is carried by water, is allowed to be exceedingly well executed. The works are the property of Mr. Atkinson, of Bank End, and were constructed by Mr. George Ford, of Egremont, very much to his credit as an artist. An entertainment was given at Bank End by the proprietor, to a great number of tradesmen from this town, Egremont, and the neighbourhood, who afterwards adjourned to the works, which were opened in the manner above mentioned." **April 4.** Extract of a letter from **New York, March 23.** "I am sorry to acquaint you that the bill for granting the 5 per cent to Congress was thrown out by our legislature, so that no fund can now be established for the payment of either principal or interest of the continental debts; by this means, many of the most meritorious of our citizens who trusted their all on the faith of the promises, are now cut off from every hope of relief at present." ... The snow *Sophia Magdalena*, Peter Lofwenburg, master, [possibly Loswenburg - Eds.] which arrived New York February 24 from Lisbon fell in, off the island of Madeira, with three Algerine corsairs. Notwithstanding Captain Lofwenburg had a Mediterranean pass, yet he crouded all his sails, and night coming on, escaped being detained and plundered by those piratical infidels ... By the Shelburne papers it appears the loyalists are in great distress for provision; without speedy relief, some violent commotion must ensue. **April 8.** Extract of a letter from **Hamburg, Dec. 20:** A political writer calculates the number of German troops, hired by the English, who perished in the American war to be

11,853: 3,015 Brunswickers, 6,500 Hessians, 981 of the principality of Hanau, 461 Anspachers, 722 Waldeckers, and 126 of Anhalt Zerbst ... Extract of a letter from **Kingston** (Jamaica), **March 5:** By the schooner *Ruth*, Capt. Bonnyman from Black River, we are informed the *Belisarius* which lately sailed from here with troops destined for the Bay, had arrived there several days before he sailed. The report of the arrival of Don Galvez, with ten sail of the line and 7000 troops--which certain politicians considered indicative of a speedy rupture with Spain, appears to be rather exaggerated; we learn from more reliable sources of the Spanish Admiral's arrival at Laguira, with only two ships and a small number of troops. He was hourly expected at the Havana. ■ **BALTIMORE, April 8.** A London newspaper states that last January 1st the prices of gold and silver there were: gold in coin and bars--£3.17.10 ½ per ounce; pieces of eight (pillar large and small, and Mexican large, and new)--5s.1d. per ounce; silver in bars--5s. 2 1/4 per ounce ...

Page 3. Lloyd's list, printed in London Jan. 4, 1785 advises that the *Plymouth*, Capt. Foster, from Virginia, was arrived at Falmouth--and that an American brig was lost within 4 or 5 miles of Wicklow. ■ ALX, April 14. The General Assembly of South-Carolina have lately passed an Act for raising a Tax on all Shipping, for defraying the Expence of laying out Buoys, and erecting a Light-House and Beacons, as leading Marks in the Harbour of Charleston; and also for erecting Beacons for George-Town and Beaufort. ■ At the present Sessions of the General Court, now sitting at Richmond, the following Criminals were capitally convicted: Thomas Martin from this County; William Delafield, from Mecklenburg; and John Lane, from Culpepper [sic]; for Horse-stealing. John Fowler, from Albemarle, was also capitally convicted, for breaking open a Store. ■ A late Jamaica Paper says, "The Representation to the King from the Loyalists settled on the Bahama-Islands, presents the most faithful Picture of the Situation of those unfortunate Men." ■ Last Week as a Negro Man was digging under the Bank, unfortunately a large Mass of Earth fell upon him and fractured his Thigh. ■ The Ship *Grace*, from New-York, is arrived at Charleston. ■ MARRIED.] Mr. RICHARD WEIGHTMAN to Miss BETSY CHEW. ■ NAVAL-OFFICE, ALX. *Inward Entries.* Ship *Paragon*, J. Knight, from Boston. *Cleared Outwards.* Schooner *Lottery*, T. Mann, for Baltimore; Sloop *Susanna*, C. Young, Rhode-Island.

PRICES CURRENT, ALX. / Tobacco, 30s. per Ct. / Fine Flour, 30s. per Barrel. / Wheat, 6s. per Bushel. / Jamaica Spirits, 4/6 per Gallon. / Windward Rum, 3s. to 3/3 per Ditto. / Continental Rum, 2s. to 2/2 per Ditto. / Molasses, 1/6 per Ditto. / Muscovado Sugar, 38s. to 45s. per Ct. / Salt, 4s. per Bushel, by Retail. / Corn, 3s per Bushel / Exchange, 40.

JOHN MURRAY and COMPANY, Have for Sale, at their Store on Fairfax-Street, very cheap for Cash, Tobacco, Flour or Gensang, Muscovado Sugars, Loaf Ditto, Coffee and Chocolate, Spermaceti Candles, Tallow Ditto, Molasses, Frontigniac Wine, Swedish 12d. Nails, at 7d. per Pound by the Cask, Best Connecticut Beef and Pork, Train Oil, Chalk, Alum Salt, Iron Dogs, Tea-Kettles and Pots, Dutch Ovens, Bar Lead, &c. Also, a general assortment of EUROPEAN GOODS suitable for the Season; a genteel Parcel of striped, figured and plain Muslins and Lustrings; a Quantity of Cotton Cards, at Twenty-Two Shillings per Dozen. ☞ About Twenty Hogsheads of Tobacco is wanted on Freight for the Brig *Liberty*, Captain Nixon, who will sail for Hamburg in a few Days. ALX, April 12, 1785.

FOR LIVERPOOL,

To sail positively by the 20th Instant, as she has all her Cargo engaged, THE FAST SAILING BRIG *BETSY*; she has good accommodations for a few passengers.--For further particulars apply to Captain THOMAS PERKINS on board the said Brig.
ALX, April 12, 1785.

To be Let on Ground-Rent for ever, to the highest Bidder, on Tuesday the 21st Day of June next, on the Premises, ABOUT 200 LOTS of GROUND, adjoining the Town of ALX, pleasantly situated and convenient to the best water in that town. The Lots have, in general 20 feet front, and some of them 43 feet 5 inches; and in depth they are, some 75 feet, some 83 feet, some 96 feet, and many of them 123 feet 5 inches.--They will be let free from rent for one year from the day of sale. DAVID GRIFFITH, April 14, 1785 ■ Winchester, March 30, 1785. THE Parish of Frederick, in the County of Frederick, being at present without a Minister of the Protestant Episcopal Church, legally inducted the Vestry of the said Parish have therefore determined to proceed to the appointment of one, at the Church in Winchester, on the First Thursday in May next, pursuant to an act of the last session of the General Assembly. Published by order of the Vestry, J. PEYTON, Clerk. ■ THE Subscribers to the scheme for opening and extending the navigation of Potomack River, are desired to take notice, that a meeting of the Subscribers will be held on the 17th of next month, at the house of Mr. John Lomax, in the town of ALX, to elect Directors, &c. for carrying on the work, agreeable to laws passed in the States of Virginia and Maryland. WILLIAM DEAKINS, jun., BENJAMIN STODDERT, JOHN FITZGERALD, WILLIAM HARTSHORNE, Managers, ALX, April 9, 1785 ■ WILLIAM HEPBURN, Has for Sale, by Wholesale and Retail, A Fine Assortment of IRISH LINENS, and other GOODS, suitable to the Season. ☞ He has also for Sale, a few Hogsheads of excellent SPIRITS.

☞ LANDS AND NEGROES FOR PUBLIC SALE. To be Sold by Public Vendue at the Baltimore Furnace, about two Miles from Baltimore Town, on the 9th Day of May next, at 10 o'Clock in the Forenoon,

BETWEEN forty and fifty Slaves, consisting of Women, Girls and Boys, a considerable number of which are very likely. The terms of sale for them are, three years credit, on the purchasers giving bond with approved security, on interest, to be paid annually.

Also on the 16th day of May next, at 10 o'clock in the forenoon, at Major Brown's Coffee-House, in Baltimore-Town, will commence the sale of that famous TRACT of LAND called PHILIPSBURGH, containing about 900 acres, lying very near said Town, which was advertised by us on the 13th of September last for Sale, therefore shall now only add, that most of it is good farming Land, exceedingly well wooded, with a considerable quantity of ship and other timber.--It will be laid off in lots of various sizes according to their situations, as part of it lies on Patapsco-River and Harris's-Creek, we apprehend there may be several good and convenient ship-yards, while those lots at a greater distance from navigation, will be commodious for gentlemens' country-seats, small farms, gardens, pastures, &c.&c. The terms of sale of this Land are, one shilling in the pound of the purchase money to be paid down in cash the next day after the sale, and three years credit to be given on the residue, on giving bond with two or more approved securities, with legal interest, to be paid annually. Any person desirous to view the premises before the day of sale, are requested to apply to Mr. Miles Love, at Gorsuch's-Point, near said town.

Also, to be sold, at the time and place last abovementioned, about 150 acres of LAND, lying about one and a half miles from Baltimore-Town, on which stands the Mount-Royal Forge, with other very considerable improvements.--This Land will be laid out in several lots as it may be thought will best suit the purchasers. It has been suggested to us, that there are several valuable mill-seats on this land, exclusive of the one where the forge now stands, we therefore recommend it to those gentlemen inclinable to speculate, to view the premises, which will be shewn by Mr. Zachariah M'Cubbin, Surveyor in said Town, who will also shew the plats of the whole of the above Lands. The terms of sale of this last mentioned Land are the same as those of Philipsburgh, except that the one-fifth of the purchase-money of this is to be paid down in cash the next day after the sale, instead of one shilling in the pound.--Attendance will be given at the different times and places of sale, by

CLEMENT BROOKE,
JOHN MERRYMAN.

Baltimore, March 30, 1785.

To be Sold at Public Vendue, on Wednesday the 4th of May next, at the Round-House, at the Little-Falls, for Ready-Money, FOUR NEGROES, some household Furniture, and a serviceable Mare, belonging to the Estate of Thomas Stubblefield, deceased. JOANNA STUBBLEFIELD, Administratrix. Fairfax County, April 13, 1785.

--Open his Mouth and look in.--

RAN away from the Subscriber, living at Hooe's-Ferry, on the 25th of March last, DAVY, a small black Negro man slave, very thin, visage, most of his teeth decayed by the venereal disorder, with an entire loss of the palate of his mouth, which occasions him to snuffle so exceedingly that it is difficult to understand him. Whoever apprehends the said slave and brings him to me, or secures him in any gaol so that I get him again, shall receive a reward of FIVE GUINEAS, provided he is taken 20 miles from home, if less than 20 miles, ONE GUINEA. GERARD HOOE.

Hooe's-Ferry, April 1, 1784.

AS my intended change of residence, makes it necessary that I should bring my affairs in this Town to a pretty speedy settlement, I have to request in solicitous terms, that all those who stand in arrears for my late professional services, will be so obliging as to call at my house immediately, either to make payment or give their notes for the sums that may be respectively due from them.--I am particularly desirous to have this business accomplished in *this* month, having concerns to the northward that will demand my attention the ensuing one. ELISHA C. DICK, ALX, April 8, 1785 ■ To be Rented for One Year from the First of May next, THE HOUSE and GARDEN, now occupied by Mr. Patrick Murray, and situated on the Corner of King and Pitt Streets.--Also, to be rented for a Term of Years, a new Two-Story HOUSE on the Wharf, near the Ferry-Landing; it is 30 by 24 Feet, and may be easily finished for a Dwelling-House or Store.--Also, to be Rented on Ground-Rent for ever, several LOTS of GROUND on the Wharf, on Princess and Union Streets, one of which is a Corner-Lot, with a South and East Front, containing 70 by 50 Feet, and would do well for a Tavern, being near the Ferry-Landing.--Also, to be Rented or Sold, the Whole or Part of a LOT, on Princess and St. Asaph's Streets, with a South and East Front, containing 176½ Feet Front, and 63 in Depth; it lies high up, and pleasantly situated on the South-East Corner of the Square where Mr. Charles Lee lives.--Likewise, to be Let on Ground-Rent for ever, a LOT of GROUND, situated between Queen and Princess Streets, on Pitt-street, containing 86 Feet by 123½.--Also, 2000 acres of patent Land, in the County of Monongalia, about 5 Miles from Morgan's-Town, and 3 from the River Monongalia, which will be Sold low for Cash or Soldier's Certificates, or exchanged for Land in this County.--The Terms may be known by applying to WILLIAM HEPBURN. ALX, April 13, 1785 ■ To be Sold at Public Vendue, on Monday the 16th of May next, if not sold before at private Sale, A Valuable LOT of GROUND in fee simple, situated on Fairfax-street, containing between 28 and 29 feet front, and 98 feet back.--The terms of sale will be made known on the day of sale, or at any time before on applying to C. COPPER, Vendue-Master, ALX, April 14, 1785 ■ STOLEN, supposed to have been conveyed away last court-day, a wide-mouthed SILVER CAN, which holds rather more than a pint, the crest on one side a greyhound's head, with a ducal coronet round the neck, in a wreath of flowers, and the mark of the goldsmith's company at the bottom. Whoever brings the said Can to Mr. Norton's, shall receive a very genteel reward, adequate to its value, and no questions asked about it. All goldsmiths and others are desired to stop it and the person who brings it, if offered for sale. Winchester, April 8, 1785 ■ March 30, 1785. Fairfax County, to wit: WHEREAS Michael Gretter, of the said County and Gaoler thereof, came before me David Arell, one of the Justices of the Commonwealth of Virginia, in the County aforesaid, and made oath on the Holy Evangelists of Almighty God, that JOHN TOMKINS, confined at the suit of John Douglas; JACOB HELMES, bound over to the grand jury on suspicion of stealing a watch; JOHN WEBB, bound over to the grand jury for receiving of stolen corn from a Negro; FRANCIS JOHNSON, on suspicion of stealing; THOMAS CLARKSON, for want of security for his good behaviour; and Negro TOM, a runaway from Loudon gaol; broke out of gaol in the night between the 29th and 30th instant, and are now going at large.--These are therefore, in the name of the Commonwealth aforesaid, to require all Sheriffs, Mayors, Bailiffs, Constables and Headboroughs within this Commonwealth, and every of them in their respective counties, cities, towns and precincts, to seize and retake the said prisoners, so escaped and going at large as aforesaid, and being so retaken, forthwith to convey and commit to the prison where such prisoners are usually kept, within the county where they or any of them shall be, there to be safely kept until discharged by due course of law. Given under my hand and seal the day and year first above mentioned, DAVID ARELL (L.S.) ■ WANTED, As an Apprentice to a genteel Business, A Smart active Lad, who can be well recommended.—Inquire at the Printing-Office, ALX, Jan. 13, 1785.

Page 4. Poetry. "I Will Be Happy." ■ WILLIAM WILSON has for sale a lot of ground on Fairfax-street, and a lot of ground in Dumfries [see like ad Vol. II No. 58] ■ THOMAS H. HANSON offers for sale land in Washington County on Potomack River [see like ad Vol. II No. 61] ■ MARY DULANY offers reward for return of runaway Negro man named JACOB [see like ad Vol. II No. 61] ■ Just received, and to be Sold on the most reasonable Terms, at the Printing-Office, A Variety of elegant PAPER-HANGINGS ■ ROBERT ADAM has for sale old Jamaica spirits, West-India rum, etc. [see like ad Vol. II No. 57] ■ JOSIAH WATSON offers for sale an elegant chariot, etc. [see like ad Vol. II No. 61] ■ THOMAS ROPER, Leesburg, informs public of recent furnishings for accommodating gentlemen [see like ad Vol. II No. 61] ■ ROBERT BRYCE offers for rent house adjoining the gaol [see like ad Vol. II No. 61] ■ WILLIAM HARDAGE, Shenandoah, seeks to settle accounts of Benjamin Ogle, Esq., of Berkely County, deceased [see like ad Vol. II No. 61] ■ LEWIS ELLZEY offers one hundred dollars reward for runaway fellow named Will [see like ad Vol. II No. 55] ■ LUND WASHINGTON offers for sale horse *MAGNOLIO* [see like ad Vol. II No. 60].

On Monday next the 18th Inst. will be Sold at the Vendue-Office, opposite the Court-House, A VARIETY OF WET AND DRY GOODS, Among which are Three large and elegant LOOKING-GLASSES.

C. COPPER, Vendue-Master

ALX, April 6, 1785.

C. COPPER offers for sale Brigantine *Industry* and all her materials [see like ad Vol. II No. 62] ■ CYRUS COPPER, offers for sale at public vendue a lot of ground opposite Mrs. Elizabeth Gretter's [see like ad Vol. II No. 62] ■ BENJAMIN and FRANCIS LOWNDES, Bladensburg, administrators of Christopher Lowndes, deceased, seek to settle accounts [see like ad Vol. II No. 62] ■ RICHARD CONWAY has for sale a parcel of good Barbadoes Rum [see like ad Vol. II No. 61] ■ ADAM LYNN has for sale several lots of ground on Wilkes and St. Asaph's streets, and he has lately built a bake-house near his dwelling-house on King Street [see like ad Vol. II No. 62] ■ ☞ Constant Employment, and the highest Wages, will be given to reputable JOURNEYMEN PRINTERS, on Application to the Printers hereof, or to Messrs. GODDARD and LANGWORTHY, Printers, Baltimore. ■ ALX: Printed by GEORGE RICHARDS, and COMPANY, at their Printing-Office on Fairfax--by whom Advertisements, &c. are thankfully received for this Paper,--and where Printing is performed with Care and Expedition.

1785/04/21, Vol. II No. 64

Page 1. Subscribers to the scheme for opening and extending navigation of Potomack River are notified of an upcoming meeting [see like ad Vol. II No. 63] ■ JOHN MURRAY and COMPANY, Have items for Sale at their Store on Fairfax-Street [see like ad Vol. II No. 63] ■ DAVID GRIFFITH offers for sale about 200 lots of ground adjoining ALX [see like ad Vol. II No. 63] ■ Capt. Thomas Perkins announces departure of the fast sailing Brig *Betsy* [see like ad Vol. II No. 63] ■ Elisha C. Dick seeks to settle outstanding accounts [see like ad Vol. II No. 63] ■ Printing-Office seeks smart active lad as apprentice [see like ad Vol. II No. 53] ■ WILLIAM HEPBURN has for sale a fine assortment of Irish linens, etc. [see like ad Vol. II No. 63] ■ Clement Brooke and John Merryman, Baltimore, offer for sale lands and Negroes for public sale [see like ad Vol. II No. 63] ■ Reward offered for return of stolen silver can to Mr. Norton, Winchester [see like ad Vol. II No. 63] ■ WILLIAM HEPBURN offers for rent the house and garden now occupied by Mr. Patrick Murray; several lots on the Wharf on Princess Street, others [see like ad Vol. II No. 63] ■ C. COPPER offers for sale a lot on Fairfax-street [see like ad Vol. II No. 63] ■ DAVID ARELL gives notice that six persons escaped from the Fairfax County gaol [see like ad Vol. II No. 63] ■ Joanna Stubblefield to offer for sale four Negroes, household furniture, etc. [see like ad Vol. II No. 63].

Page 2.

LONDON, Jan. 14. All the French newspapers say they are equipping at Brest four ships of the line and four frigates; the British Ambassador has demanded to know the squadron's destination ... A letter from the **Hague, Jan.7** reports a body of Swiss recruits coming to assist the States General were taken prisoner, together with their commanding officer, by the Emperor's troops. Another group of 250 from the Rhinegrave of Salm, designed for the same service, have also been interrupted. These will cause much disturbance, as they confirm the Emperor will leave no stone unturned to revenge the injury received from the United Provinces. We also hear the Prince of Orange will make a vigorous attack on the Low Countries unless he perceives the Emperor will soon come to some accommodation. **Jan. 29.** Dispatches received Saturday from Paris state the dispute was settled between the Emperor and the Dutch: for the Emperor giving up his pretensions to the Scheldt, the Dutch will give him Maestricht, together with three bailiwicks on the Mease, and a sum of money to reimburse his expenses ... By yesterday's mail, the Dublin papers say the Attorney General declares the congress an illegal assembly, and vows to prove it. Mr. Flood declares he will meet him on that question. It is of the utmost moment, and involves points which every subject should understand ... The narrow and illiberal system which governed the British cabinet heretofore with respect to Irish intercourse is now dropped, and the measures to be adopted have the warmest approbation of the friends of both kingdoms ... A **Gibraltar, Dec. 26th** letter says the Turks are fitting out several stout armed vessels at Algiers, &c., from 12-26 guns each, to be manned by renegadoes of all nations--in order to cruise the Western Ocean for the American vessels sailing from Europe. This unexpected stroke will hurt American shipping. Many American vessels have been waiting five or six months in Mediterranean ports, fearful of being taken; the Turks strictly examine every vessel, and make immediate prizes of those without passes ... By the miserable conduct of our affairs during the late war, the consequence of this country is so much sunk in the eyes of other powers of Europe, that no reference is made to us, on the present dispute between the Emperor and the Dutch: While France is actually the arbitress of Europe. **Feb. 9.** Our Minister at Paris, the Duke of Dorset, reports seven French ships of the line, with 1500 troops aboard, have just sailed from Brest for the Mauritius and Isle of Bourbon in the East Indies. **Feb. 11.** In the House of Commons of Ireland on Friday the 4th, the Right Honorable Thomas Orde delivered a message from his Majesty, which concluded: His Majesty has observed with great concern the recent popular disturbances, and is highly satisfied with the constant and strenuous endeavours of his faithful Commons in Ireland to reject every effort to dictate to the legislature. He is persuaded that proper attention will be given such internal regulations as necessary to secure his Irish subjects' peace and security, as well as the commercial objects between his kingdoms, upon equitable and lasting principles. And they may depend on his ready concurrence in measures for closer ties between the two countries. ■ **CHARLESTON, March 31**. The American Company opened their theatre Monday evening with a tragedy called the Roman Father. The spectators were agreeably surprized to find the large room over the Exchange metamorphosed into an elegant little theatre, fitted up with great taste and spirit. With regard to the merits of the performers, it is but justice to say that they have been received by crouded audiences with loud and reiterated marks of approbation. ■ **HARTFORD, March 28.** Congress have transmitted to the Court of Spain a very spirited remonstrance respecting the navigation of the Mississippi: Shewing that all the right in that territory formerly belonging to Great Britain was confirmed to the United States by the treaty of peace, and that if they refuse to do us justice in that particular, it was in our power to do ourselves justice. ■ **NEW HAVEN, March 31.** We hear Congress has granted a sum of money to be disposed of in subsidies to the piratical States of Barbary--a method the European States are obliged to use to conciliate the favor of descendants of him whose hand was against every man. ■ **NEW YORK, April 2.** A letter from St. Martin's, dated the 14th ult. Says, "I hear that fourteen sail of vessels are arrived at different islands, dismasted." ... **April 4.** We hear the Hon. John Lewis Gervais, Esq., has declined acceptance of appointment as a Commissioner of the Board of Treasury. We also hear the Hon. William Patterson, Esq., of New Jersey has accepted appointment as a Judge of the Federal Court lately instituted to determine the controversy between this State and Massachusetts ... Last Thursday arrived his most Christian Majesty's packet, *Le Courier de New York*, Mons. Deveau commanding, in 62 days from l'Orient. In her came passenger M. De Chateaufort, Esq., Consul of France for the Carolinas. **April 5**. James Gardoqui, Esq., Spanish Minister to the United States, is arrived at the Havana whence he is soon to sail for Philadelphia. **April 6.** Extract of a letter from a gentleman in **Charleston, South Carolina**, to his friend in this city: I am pleased Congress is seated in New York, where I think it probable they will remain until a war or domestic convulsion obliges them to quit it; as to a federal town I am persuaded it will not, nor cannot be built for many years to come; the United States will not contribute for that purpose, till the debt of the late revolution is paid to themselves and their foreign creditors, this State has already come to that determination, and it is reasonable to suppose that the rest will follow the example. ■ **PHILADELPHIA, April 11.** A February 8th letter from London reports the failure of the imperial East India Company established at Ostend in 1781 or 1782--which will be attended with very alarming and serious consequences to the merchants of London ... Extract of a letter from **London, Feb. 4:** On account of the Barbary corsairs, there is no insurance yet fixed on American bottoms. Those on English bottoms, from London to Boston, are five guineas per cent, and to New York, two guineas and a half; to Philadelphia, Charleston, and Annapolis, ditto; From Liverpool, Bristol and Glasgow to New York, the insurance is fixed at the same price ... Extract of a letter to a friend in this city from a gentleman in **Amsterdam, Oct. 6, 1784**: Two American ships, Messrs. Green, and Bell commanding, bound to the East Indies, have both been at Cape of Good Hope, and will probably get their business done at China. They may be expected back about March next. ■ **BALTIMORE, April 15.** A paragraph from his Britannic Majesty's speech to his Parliament last January 25, stresses attention be paid to completing commercial arrangements between Great Britain and Ireland. A system of reciprocal advantage best ensures the prosperity of all the dominions ... Extract of a letter from **Cadiz, January 6**: A very formidable armament is preparing here against the spring to attack Algiers; they are to be joined by the Portuguese and Venetians, also the combined forces of some other nations which, when together, will form one of the most powerful fleets that ever went against that regency. A number of officers of high rank from the different nations will embark on this expedition, amongst whom French and Spanish officers; yet many of the most considerate politicians think it will only be putting the Spanish kingdom to a vast expence, without being able to do any material injury to the Algerines, whose daring insolence of late has become very alarming. ■ **ALX, April 21**. His Excellency Patrick Henry, Esq., Governor of this Commonwealth, has issued a Proclamation, suspending for a Time the Operation of an Act of Assembly, passed at the last Session, entitled, "An Act for amending the several Laws, for regulating and disciplining the Militia, and guarding against Invasions and Insurrections," in the Counties on the Western Waters, until the first Day of January next. Charles Simms and David Stewart, Esquires, are elected Delegates to represent this County in the General Assembly for the Ensuing Year.

Extract of a Letter from a Gentleman in Philadelphia to another in this Town, dated March 8, 1785.

I am exceedingly pleased with the Accounts you give me of the Improvements proposed to be made in the interior Navigation of Virginia, and think it an Object well worth of Attention of your Legislature.--However, your Wishes and the Inducement of my Friends Society, might operate on my Inclination to become an Alexandrian, and a Resident in "the favored State of the Thirteen," still I cannot yet clearly see my Interest in the Change, speaking as a commercial Man, or admit the Opinion you would seem to inculcate of the decline of this City, which you adopt from the Idea that the Imports exceed our Exports in Value, seven to one.--Admitting this Assertion for a Moment, I cannot possibly give into your Conclusion.--Trade, like every Thing else, has its Ebbs and its Floods, and is continually fluctuating.--The present Overstock of Importation, proceeding principally from the erroneous Ideas of the Europeans on the Profits of the American Trade, is merely a temporary Evil, and will remedy itself by its own Operation.--I might go further and prove that this Circumstance, apparently injurious, is in fact in favor of the State, and advantageous to the Bulk of the Community, prejudicial only to the mercantile People.--For the want of quick Returns to Men of slender Capitals, must in may Instances, as we have already seen, produce Failures, by which Events the unpaid Amount of their European Debts will be so much saved to the Public, or in other Words, a certain Value in Property introduced into the Country, for which no equivalent is returned: But a Benefit founded on private Injustice or private Misfortune, never Wish to uphold.--Suffice it then to observe, that these Bankruptcies will discharge the superfluous Individuals engaged in Commerce, and oblige them to turn their Attention to those Manufactures, that the present population of this Country will support, or to the Cultivation of our Land, where they will find an extensive and unbounded Field for the Exertion of their Usefulness.--Trade being thus regulated, like a prudent Family, will receive no more than it pays for,--and this it will be enabled to do with more facility, as the Farmers of Pennsylvania, recovering now, as they have not yet done, from the Impoverishment of War.--And notwithstanding the prohibitory Acts of the European Powers, they cannot be equal to the entire Prevention of our West-India Trade, where under some Cover or other we shall always find a Market for our Produce, when the Price is not so immoderately advanced as it is now, by the partial and temporary Causes I have beforementioned, exclusive of the Sales, we may find from Time to Time, among the different European Nations, according to their Necessities, often arising from the failure of their Crops.--Independent of these Advantages and the great Fertility and high Cultivation of the Soil of this State, which supply our City, situated as it is in the Centre of a rich Country, and at the Head of a fine Navigation.--Philadelphia has also other Conveniencies, in the Superiority of Capital, its Precedence, and Establishment, which bear down many smaller Obstacles, and add surprising Facilities to its Commerce, without taking into Consideration the indefatigable Industry of its Citizens.--Advantages which in a very great Degree have made it the Emporium of Commerce for a great Part of the American Coast, as is proven by the Documents extracted from our Custom-House, where within the last Twelvemonth, an astonishing Proportion of Coasting Vessels have been cleared, and by this Means rendered it the Theatre of Interchange to a vast Amount.

Feeling, as I do, a sympathetic Joy in the flourishing Condition of its Sister Towns, as a Philadelphian, I cannot yield the Advantages of our City to those of any other place, especially when I myself am an Eye-Witness of its thriving Situation, and see in the short Space of a single Summer Six Hundred new Brick Houses rise to augment its Opulence and its Grandeur.

Page 3. By a Gentleman of Credit from Shenandoah County, we have the following Intelligence of an uncommon Accident, which lately happened there: A Negro Man, going to Visit his Wife, was, it is supposed, attacked by a Gang of Wolves, as his Body has been found, with his Knife, and two Wolves dead by him. ■ DIED.] On board the Ship *Stanley*, now in this Port, from Liverpool, Captain JOHN WOODS. ■ NAVAL-OFFICE ALX. *Inward Entries.* Sloop *Dolphin*, O. Stewart, from Philadelphia; Brig *Triton*, G. Young, Liverpool. *Cleared Outwards.* Ship *Lily*, W. Robertson, for London; Brig *Ann-Maria*, J. Robertson, Barbadoes.

PRICES CURRENT, ALX. / Tobacco, 30s. per Ct. / Fine Flour, 30s. per Barrel. / Wheat, 6s. per Bushel. / Jamaica Spirits, 4/6 per Gallon. / Windward Rum, 3s. to 3/3 per Ditto. / Continental Rum, 2s. to 2/2 per Ditto. / Molasses, 1/6 per Ditto. / Muscovado Sugar, 38s. to 45s. per Ct. / Salt, 4s. per Bushel, by Retail. / Corn, 3s. per Bushel / Exchange, 40.

To be Sold at the Vendue-Store, on Saturday the 30th Instant, the following Goods, viz.

RUM and molasses in hogsheads, muscovado sugar in barrels, coffee in casks and bags, green tea, a choice assortment of Irish linens, sagathies, a variety of black, souflee, spotted and striped gauzes, gauze aprons and handkerchiefs, ribbons, garterings, Scotch threads, printed linens and calicoes, check shirts, ladies' stuff shoes, cutlery, hardware, chests of carpenters' tools complete, Peruvian bark, patent medicines, 4½ and 5 inch cables, fine brass wire metal sieves, with a variety of other articles.

C. COPPER, Vendue-Master.

☞ Ready cash, as usual, advanced to those who want, and have goods for public sale.

ALX, April 20, 1785.

JOSEPH MARIE PERRIN, Hath lately removed from the Corner of Fairfax and Queen Streets to his own House on Royal-Street, opposite to the Court-House, where he will sell by Wholesale or Retail, BLACK modes, lustrings, florentines, satin of divers colours, black brunellas, a large assortment of ribbons, ladies' kidskin gloves, calicoes, chintzes, hairpowder, ladies' fans, hats, silk stockings, and a variety of other articles. ALX, April 21, 1785 ■ ☞ *SPRING GOODS.* JONATHAN SWIFT and CO., Have for Sale, at their Store on Captain Harper's Wharf, A General Assortment of SPRING GOODS, which they will dispose of on the most moderate Terms, for Cash, Bills of Exchange. Furs, Wheat, Flour or Tobacco.--Excellent London Porter in Hampers, a few Barrels of Mess Beef and Pork, and West-India Goods of all Kinds. ALX, April 19, 1785 ■ Dumfries, April 18, 1785. **DAVID FORBES**, HAS for sale at this place, a general assortment of MEDICINES, amounting to £.2000 sterling cost, which he will sell as low as any on the continent; they are lately imported and, I think, good. Also, four sets of instruments complete, and six sets of pocket instruments. ■ ALL Persons indebted to the Estate of FRANCIS DADE, Esq., Attorney at Law, are requested to make immediate Payment of their Accounts to WILLIAM HUNTER, jun., of this Place, who is properly authorized to receive the same, and grant Discharges.--Those failing may expect Suits will be commenced against them. TOWNSHEND DADE, Administrator, ALX, April 20, 1785 ■ TO BE LET, ON GROUND-RENT FOR EVER, SUNDRY LOTS of GROUND, situated on Fairfax, Prince and Royal Streets.--The Terms may be known by applying to the Subscriber, who will attend at Mr. Wise's Tavern for that Purpose on the Third Monday in the next Month, being Court-Day. NATHANIEL C. HUNTER, April 20, 1785 ■ JESSE TAYLOR, Has just imported in the Brig *Triton*, Capt. Young, from Liverpool, the following Goods, viz. Flowered and striped muslins, Printed, flowered, and bordered Marseilles quilting, and jeanets, Princes, Prussian and Dutch cords, Silk, lorrets and velvet cords, Snowdenets and queen's ditto, Plain and corded demities, Counterpanes, Paolian rib and rib delures, Satinets and beavers, Dyed jeans and jeanets, Honeycombed, and figured velverets, Flowered and spotted ditto, Corduroys and cordurets, Black, blue and red velvets, Pillow, and pocket fustians, Furniture and apron check, Cotton and linen ditto, Check and silk handkerchiefs, Striped Hollands, Printed linens, and cottons. The foregoing, with a great variety of other Goods now on hand suitable for the season, he will sell by wholesale or retail, cheap for cash or country produce. ALX, April 18, 1785. ■ **WILLIAM LOWRY and CO.** Have the pleasure to inform their Friends and the Country Traders, that they have just received their Spring Assortment, which will be sold on reasonable Terms, by Wholesale only, for Cash, Produce, or short Credit; they consist of the following Articles, viz. A General assortment of superfine, refine, and 7/8 cloths, cassimers, cassinets and other fashionable articles for summer wear, a variety of printed cottons, calicoes and linens, printed, silk, bandano, romal and lawn handkerchiefs, cambricks, a general assortment of souflee, striped, plain and spotted gauzes, ribbons, modes, sarsenets, thread edgings, silk mitts, pelongs, &c. jeans, fustians, Washington cords, Elliot's stripes, cordureens, cotton satinets, king's cords, demities, German cords, muslin stripes, and a variety of other Manchester goods; mens', womens', and youths' cotton and thread hose, womens' shoes, calamancoes, russels, durants, camlets, wildbores, tammies, cotton and linen checks, 4-4 and 7/8 Irish linens, 9-8 wide Irish sheetings, a few osnaburgs, a neat assortment of hardware in which is a variety of metal buttons, plated and brass buckles, spurs, pewter spoons, knives, &c. an assortment of foolscap [type of paper]. post and other writing paper, blank books, quills, pens, inkpowder, wafers, &c. An elegant FORTE PIANO for sale, price 16 guineas.--Also, a neat Finger ORGAN, with diapason only, price 30 guineas. All those and many other articles are received in addition to their former assortment. ALX, April 19, 1785 ■ THE Copartnership between WRIGHT and LONG being mutually dissolved, they request those indebted to them would please to make immediate payment; and all those to whom they are indebted are requested to bring in their accounts, and they shall be paid.--Attendance for the above-mentioned purposes is regularly given by Edward Long, who carries on the Taylor's Business in all its branches. ☞ Said WRIGHT also carries on his Business in the house of Mr. John Saunders. ALX, April 19, 1785.

Loudon County, April 16, 1785. RAN away from the Subscriber on the 22d of March, a Mulatto Man, named HARRY, but calls himself HARRY JACKSON; he is about 5 feet 9 or 10 inches high, well made and very active, has a scar on his forehead, is fond of liquor, and can work at the shoemaking business: He took with him his common working cloaths, which were cotton, but it is probable he may have got others.--I have reason to apprehend that he is lurking about the lower end of Fairfax County as he has many relations there.--Whoever delivers the said Fellow to Col. DENNIS RAMSAY in ALX, or to the Subscriber, shall receive EIGHT DOLLARS reward. THADDEUS M'CARTY.

Fredericksburg, April 11, 1785. RAN away from the Subscriber this morning, a French servant man, named CHARLES DEGEAU, about 5 feet 7 or 8 inches high, 24 or 25 years of age; he has black curled hair, of a dark complexion, and tolerable good features.--He took with him when he went away a fustian jacket and breeches and grey surtout coat; but as he had a variety of cloathing, it is uncertain what he may wear. He speaks the French and German languages, but English imperfectly.--Whoever apprehends said servant, or secures him in any goal on the continent shall have TEN DOLLARS re[ward, by]. GA[RLAND THOMPSON]. ■ To be Sold, or exchanged for Land in Loudon, Fairfax, Prince-William, Fauquier, Frederick, or Berkely Counties, the following Tracts or Parcels of Land on the Western Waters, viz. ONE TRACT of 1191 acres, in Monongalia County, situated on Papaw-Creek, a branch of Monongalia River, about 6 miles from said river, which is navigable a considerable distance above the said creek; this Land is well stocked with sugar-tree, poplar, white and black oak timber; and as there is a convenience for building mills on it, a saw-mill will be very advantageous, there being a great demand for plank for the purpose of boat-building, to transport emigrants to the lower parts of that country. One other TRACT in the same County, containing 1000 acres, lying on the waters of Morgan's-Run, about 3 miles from a good landing on Cheat-River, where the boat-building business is carried on; and would also be an excellent place for a saw-mill, there being a great quantity of good timber on the tract. On this Land, I am credibly informed, there is a large body of iron ore, and sufficient streams of water to erect any kind of Iron-Works on, and timber to support them. Also, several TRACTS of LAND in Jefferson County, containing 2925 acres; as this Land was located at an early period, I expect it is of an excellent quality. Likewise, an undivided moiety (or half) of 28256½ acres of located LAND, in a good part of the country as the Locator informed me. I have also in the town of Leesburg, THREE unimproved LOTS to sell, well situated, containing in front 47 feet each; and extending back 102 feet, with the priviledge of a 10 feet alley to each Lot. For terms apply to the Subscriber in said town. SAMUEL CANBY, Leesburg, April 11, 1785.

REPUBLICAN,

Bred by the late Mr. William Brent of Stafford County, stands at my stable in Brent-Town, Prince-William County, five years old, about 15½ hands high, and will cover mares this season till the first day of August next ensuing, at THREE POUNDS.--Those who will be pleased to favor me with their custom, are desired to send the cash or their notes of hand with their mares, payable by the first of August next.--Good pasturage, gratis, for all mares that come a distance, and the greatest care shall be taken of them, but I will not be liable for escapes or other accidents.

Republican was got by True-Whig out of *Young Selima*, sister to the noted *Chatham*; Selima was got by Col. Baylor's imported *Fearnought*, out of Mr. William Brent's *Ebony*; she was out of Col. Tasker's *Selima*, by *Othello*, both imported by him; *True-Whig* was got by *Regulus*, out of the noted swift and high bred horse *Apollo's Dam*; *Regulus* was bred by Col. Baylor, and got by his horse *Fearnought* out of *Jenny Dismal*, who was got by *Old Dismal*; he won one thousand guineas sweepstakes, and five King's plates without ever being once beaten; his sire the *Godolphin Arabian*; *Jenny Dismal*'s dam was got by Lord Godolphin's *Whitefoot*; *Regulus*, while the property of Mr. Fitzhugh, won at Aquia, £.50, at Port-Royal, £.50, at Annapolis two of £.50 each; at Upper Marlborough, £.50, at Leed's-Town, £.60, and at Fredericksburg the jockey-club purse of 100 guineas, where he carried ten stone.

JOHN T. FITZHUGH.

April 1, 1784.

ALX and NORFOLK PACKET. THE Schooner *ROVING NANCY* will sail as a Packet from ALX to Norfolk, being well calculated for freight or passage, and will sail on the 1st and 20th of each month.--She is now laying at the County Wharf. EZEKIEL HUDNALL, Master. ALX, April 18, 1785 ■ GERARD HOOE offers reward for return of runaway black Negro man named DAVY [see like ad Vol. II No. 63] ■ **M'MURRAY'S MAPS OF THE** UNITED STATES are received at the Printing-Office, and ready to be delivered to the Subscribers. ALX, April 21, 1785.

Page 4. Poetry. "The Bee, Written by Mr. Nicholls." ■ TO BE SOLD, A Warrant for Four Thousand Acres of LAND, on the Western Waters of this State, the property of a late Continental Officer.--For Terms inquire of the Printers. ■ WILLIAM WILSON offers for sale goods recently arrived in the Snow *Resolution* [see like ad Vol. II No. 62] ■ JONATHAN SWIFT and CO. offer for sale at their store on Captain Harper's Wharf, a general Assortment of European Goods [see like ad Vol. II No. 62] ■ ROBERT LYLE offers to rent house and store he now lives in [see like ad Vol. II No. 62] ■ Mr. NATHANIEL GREENE to apply to Printers in Baltimore [see like ad Vol. II No. 62] ■ WILLIAM HUNTER, jun., offers for sale goods [see like ad Vol. II No. 62] ■ Commissioners, Winchester, open bids for building a new court-house [see like ad Vol. II No. 63] ■ WILLIAM TEBBS informs the public that he has opened a Tavern in the house lately occupied by Miss Susannah Franklin, in Dumfries [see like ad Vol. II No. 62] ■ WILLIAM WILSON has for sale a lot of ground on Fairfax-street, and a lot of ground in Dumfries [see like ad Vol. II No. 58] ■ THOMAS H. HANSON offers for sale land in Washington County on Potomack River [see like ad Vol. II No. 61] ■ BENJAMIN and FRANCIS LOWNDES, Bladensburg, administrators of Christopher Lowndes, deceased seek to settle accounts [see like ad Vol. II No. 62] ■ ☞ Constant Employment and the highest Wages, will be given to reputable JOURNEYMEN PRINTERS, on Application to the Printers hereof, or to Messrs. GODDARD and LANGWORTHY, Printers in Baltimore. ■ ROBERT ADAM has for sale old Jamaica spirits, West-India rum, etc. [see like ad Vol. II No. 57] ■ THOMAS ROPER, Leesburg, informs public of recent furnishings for accommodating gentlemen [see like ad Vol. II No. 61] ■ MARY DULANY offers reward for return of runaway Negro man named JACOB [see like ad Vol. II No. 61] ■ ADAM LYNN has for sale several lots of ground on Wilkes and St. Asaph's streets, and he has lately built a bake-house near his dwelling-house on King Street [see like ad Vol. II No. 62] ■ WILLIAM HARDAGE, Shenandoah, seeks to settle accounts of Benjamin Ogle, Esq., of Berkely County, deceased [see like ad Vol. II No. 61] ■ C. COPPER offers for sale Brigantine *Industry* and all her materials [see like ad Vol. II No. 62] ■ J. PEYTON, Winchester, seeks minister for the Protestant Episcopal Church [see like ad Vol. II No. 63] ■ ALX: Printed by GEORGE RICHARDS, and COMPANY, at their Printing-Office on Fairfax--by whom Advertisements, &c. are thankfully received for this Paper,--and where Printing is performed with Care and Expedition.

1785/04/28, Vol. II No. 65

Page 1. C. COPPER has items for sale at Vendue-Store [see like ad Vol. II No. 64] ■ Subscribers to the scheme for opening and extending navigation of Potomack River are notified of an upcoming meeting [see like ad Vol. II No. 63] ■ Commissioners, Winchester, open bids for building a new court-house [see like ad Vol. II No. 63] ■ Elisha C. Dick seeks to settle outstanding accounts [see like ad Vol. II No. 63] ■ Reward offered for return of stolen silver can to Mr. Norton, Winchester [see like ad Vol. II No. 63] ■ JESSE TAYLOR offers for sale goods just imported in the Brig *Triton* [see like ad Vol. II No. 64] ■ JONATHAN SWIFT and CO. Have for Sale a general assortment of SPRING GOODS [see like ad Vol. II No. 64] ■ WILLIAM HEPBURN has for sale a fine assortment of Irish linens, etc. [see like ad Vol. II No. 63] ■ JOSEPH MARIE PERRIN has opened his own house on Royal-Street [see like ad Vol. II No. 64] ■ DAVID FORBES, Dumfries, has for sale a general assortment of MEDICINES [see like ad Vol. II No. 64] ■ TOWNSHEND DADE seeks to settle accounts for estate of Francis Dade, Attorney at Law [see like ad Vol. II No 64.] ■ NATHANIEL C. HUNTER has for rent sundry lots on Fairfax, Prince and Royal Streets [see like ad Vol. II No. 64] ■ SAMUEL CANBY, Leesburg, offers for sale or exchange tracts in Monongalia and Jefferson counties [see like ad Vol. II No. 64] ■ GARLAND THOMPSON, Fredericksburg, offers reward for runaway French servant man named Charles Degeau [see like ad Vol. II No. 64] ■ Joanna Stubblefield to offer for sale four Negroes, household furniture, etc. [see like ad Vol. II No. 63] ■ M'Murray's Maps of the U.S. are ready for delivery to subscribers [see like ad Vol. II No. 64].

Page 2.

BERLIN, January 5. The political journal of last month lists the land forces of Europe in time of peace: Austria, 290,000; Russia, 470,000; Prussia 224,434; France, 192,000; the United Low Countries, 37,000; Great Britain and Ireland, 58,000; Sweden, 49,000; Denmark, 67,000; Poland, 15,000; Turkey, 210,000; Venice, 8000; Naples & Sicily, 30,000; the See of Rome, 5000; Tuscany, 3000; Sardinia, 40,000; Spain, 98,000; Portugal, 20,000; Saxony, 26,000; Brunswick, 16,000; Bavaria, 24,000; Wurtemburg, 6000; Hesse Cassel, 2000. ■ **UTRECHT, March 3.** Letters from the Hague dated the 2nd differ from those last received. A courier arrived at Vienna brings word the Emperor refuses to resume negotiations. It is probable his demand is very great, and the States will never accede to it. Thus, we still say Dutch and German soldiers will be the only competent judges of the dispute. ■ **PARIS, February 3.** There remains little doubt of the dispute between the Emperor and Holland being brought to an amicable conclusion; the Emperor seems more disposed than before to comply with the Republic's moderate proposition. It appears the Emperor was so moved by the last dispatches from Petersburg. The Compte de Maillebois' departure is again postponed. ■ LONDON, March 10. One of the King's messengers who is arrived with dispatches from the Earl of Torrington at Brussels brings word that it is universally believed there that the Emperor and the Dutch are far from an accommodation. The Prince of Ligne, commander in chief of Austrian forces in the Low Countries, continues tirelessly augmenting garrisons in all the towns; he puts even the frontier villages in the same state of defense by planting such epaulment round them, and breaking up the roads, as would prevent any sudden incursions. The Dutch continue putting their military on a most respectable footing, but it was expected they would have to ask the Court of Versailles for leave to march troops through France. Otherwise it would be almost impossible for the auxiliaries, particularly those from the Swiss cantons, to enter Holland in safety. Even in that case, they must be carried from French ports by sea to the Maese [sic] ... Government have resolved to increase the military establishment in Canada to six regiments, supplied with rations like those in our garrisons ... RETURN for WESTMINSTER: The house admitted the deputy clerk of the crown, who presented to the Speaker the precept given him that day from Thomas Corbet, Esq., High Bailiff of Westminster, setting forth that pursuant to an order of the house, he had scrutinized the legality of votes polled in the late election, and that upon casting up the books, after deducting the unqualified votes, there appeared for Lord Hood 6588, Hon. C.J. Fox 6126, Sir Cecil Wray 5895. And that Lord Hood and Mr. Fox having a majority of votes, he returned them to represent the city of Westminster in Parliament ... **MANCHESTER, March 1, 1785:** Resolved unanimously, that too liberal concessions are held out to Ireland by abridging those of this kingdom, if duties and bounties on English and Irish manufactures are equal, our higher labour costs and inland duties will give Ireland such an advantage as to make it the emporium of the fustian trade. ■ **KINGSTON,** (Jamaica) **March 12.** His Honor the Lieutenant Governor has received orders from England by the last packet to fill up this island's regiments with the full peace establishment of 500 men each. Recruiting parties to accomplish this are actually beating up for volunteers in Canada and Nova Scotia, and will shortly do so here. **March 16.** A gentleman arrived from the Spanish Main reports a considerable force of Spaniards has attacked the Samblas Indians, but were repulsed with three of their best officers and a great number of men lost. Immediately after the action, the Dons intrenched themselves upon the sea beach, under cover of their shipping. When these advices came away, they daily expected 2000 reinforcements from Carthagena with which they mean to proceed to leeward to receive the *submission* of the Musquito Indians. With singular satisfaction we observe the firm, consistent, wary conduct of this government, and determined resolution to protect and encourage at all hazards our infant settlements on the Musquito shore. They are hourly becoming of dearer consequence to the mother country, and may yet be a thorn festering in the side of Spain, which no art will be able to cure or extract. **March 19.** The arms of Spain were never more poorly regarded than now. Take the defeat of the Armada in good Queen Bessy's days, Rodney's defeat of Langara, Elliott's destruction of their floating batteries; their triple defeats by the Infidels before Algiers. The most recent stain on these proud and solemn Quixotes by a handful of untutored savages--the Samblas Indians--makes them a laughingstock anywhere on earth public transactions are faithfully recorded. The extensive territory annexed to the Musquito shore is of the last importance to Great Britain, both as a country producing many valuable commodities, and as a port opening an inroad to the richest Provinces of Spain--the foundation of their wealth and power. For in case of a war or revolt among their American subjects, a handful of British veterans stationed in that country might so divide the Dons' strength as to render them like wrens against the talons of eagles. ■ **CARTHAGENA, October 4.** Joachin Navarro, wife of Francis Huertas, in the St. Anthony quarter here, between the 7th and 8th of last month, gave birth to a monstrous child. It was baptized, named Jean Raimond, and lived only three days. An autopsy was performed by Don Gaspez de Villaquesa, assistant to the Surgeon Major of the fleet, and Don Vincent Ocagna, Surgeon in Ordinary, the report of which and the body being sent to the Society of Natural History at Madrid. The infant's exterior and most of its members were well formed, but it had three legs, a double os pubis, three groins each with an orifice; in the stomach cavity were two lungs attached to a single trachian artery; the great lobes being separated by the mediastinum; in size the heart was equal to two, distinguished by the auriols; in the epigastic region in the cavity of the belly, there was no stomach, and the inferior part of the oesophagus exceeded the usual size; the colon had neither the common exterior nor direction, but formed a stomach, from the lower part of which descended a membrane for performing the office of the rectum, being terminated by the anus; this kind of stomach was filled with excrement; and the two reins [kidneys--Eds.], which had the natural position, were of extraordinary size. ■ **CHARLESTON,** (South Carolina) **April 6.** Everyone who views our revolution as affording "an asylum to the distress and persecuted of all nations" must feel a pang from the progress European luxury has made here, bidding fair to annihilate the beneficent consequences of our emancipation, and enervating the new world inhabitants equally with those of the old. To such it must give the highest satisfaction that the different States are turning their attention to checking the process of importation, the great fund and source of dissipation and luxury. ■ **HARTFORD, April 5.** A correspondent observes that no laws can be better calculated to confirm knaves in the practice of villainy than those of Connecticut. A vile fellow is convicted of stealing or forgery--he is sentenced to be whipped, to sit on a wooden horse for an hour or two, and to a month's imprisonment; which is just enough to rivet his vicious principles, to harden him, and then he is let loose seeking revenge. A deliberate villain was never reclaimed by such momentary sufferings. If death is too severe, and Newgate will not confine him, give him the dungeons in chains for life. Better for the State to support them in prison for a single offence, than that of repeated convictions. ■ **NEW YORK, April 12.** A gentleman reports the English fortifying it and training militia in expectation of a French war. However, the English actions in the West suggest they will oppose United States claims to the western posts and Indian trade ... Henry Hamilton, Esq., Lieutenant Governor of Quebec, issued a proclamation on the 9th about reports of illicit trade between people of the neighbouring American States and inhabitants of Quebec Province. All such illicit trade is strictly prohibited, with several acts of Parliament regulating and restraining the plantation trade. **April 13.** Last evening arrived the ship *Mercury*, Captain Bateman, in 28 days from London ... The latest European prints leave us uncertain about a continental war. One account tells us that their disputes are coming to a jarring head; another holds that pacification is imminent, via negotiations of mediating powers. April 20. **PHILADELPHIA, April 14.** Congress have directed the commissioners for holding treaty talks with the southern Indians to meet at Charleston, South Carolina on May 16, that they notify the Indians of time and place, and prepare to carry out the further duties of the commission with all possible and convenient dispatch ... The first week in February there were imported into London from the United States, 5064 pounds of Ginseng: from Philadelphia 300; New York 350; Baltimore 2000; Maryland 650; Potomack 1764. During the same space, 724,596 pounds of Tobacco: from Philadelphia 4204; Virginia 674,089; Maryland 43,000; New York 2,418; Georgia 885. ■ **BALTIMORE, April 22.** Extract of a letter from **Nassau, New Providence, March 25**: Great discontents in the Bahama Islands in consequence of Governor Maxwell's behavior towards the American loyalists; the Governor to prevent ill effects of their clamours, with great art and privacy procured an address to be presented him by some of his dependents, expressing their approbation of his conduct as governor. This being diametrically opposite to the real sentiments of the loyalists and other inhabitants, they circulated a paper, signed by 126 respectable gentlemen in and near this town, in which they not only disapprove of the address' fulsome language, but utterly renounce its sentiments; declaring they had every cause to depre[illegible]ate Mr. Maxwell's return to that country, as the greatest evil which could possibly befall the Bahama Islands...

Page 3. Price of tobacco per pound in London, March 4: Maryland yellow [torn]. Middle brown 1/8. Long leaf 1/8 ½. Virginia, York River 1/9. James River 1/9. Str[torn] 1/8. Carolina 1/8 ... Insurance [rates; page too torn, and fragments too offset to decipher.-- Eds.] ■ **ALX, April 28.** [illegible] with Pleasure we inform the Public, that the [subsc]riptions opened in this Town, for opening the Navigation of Potomack River, are selling so fast, that in all Probability that gre[at] and important Work will be immediately carried into Execution. ■ A Letter from Barbadoes, dated January 29, to a Gentleman in New-York, says "The Secretary of State (at the British Court) having recommended to our Governor to take the Sentiments of the People at large in this Island, relative to the Propriety of making Barbadoes a Free-Port, we had several Meetings on that Subject, and the 9th of February is fixed for the meeting of the Merchants, Planters, &c. to argue this grant Point." ■ Last Tuesday Morning as a Drayman was receiving Goods from the Loft of a Store in this Town, unfortunately a Hamper of Porter flipped out of the Slings, which fell on him, fractured his Leg, and otherwise bruised him to such a Degree, that his Life is despaired of. ■ Last week a Child was found drowned in the Well of a Cellar in this Town.--It is supposed it fell in while at Play. ■ The General Assembly of Pennsylvania have made Choice of Charles Pettit and James Wilson, Esquires to represent that State in Congress, in the Room of Joseph Reed, Esq., deceased, and Matthew Clarkson, Esq., resigned. ■ John Peyton and Richard B. Lee, Esquires, are chosen Delegates to represent the County of Loudon in the General Assembly, for the ensuing Year. ■ A few Days since the Ship *Potomack*, Captain Bradstreet, from London, passed by this Port for George-Town. ■ The *Abby*, Childs, from Virginia, for Liverpool, after losing both her Masts and Bowsprit, in going into Dublin Harbour, struck on the Bar and bilged. ■ The *Virginia Hero*, Nicholson, for Virginia, sailed from Gravesend the Beginning of March. ■ NAVAL-OFFICE, ALX. *Inward Entries*. Sloop *Phoebe*, J. Cartwright, from Surinam; Sloop *Polly*, J. Humphries, and Schooner *Lottery*, Z. Mann, Baltimore; Schooner *Mary*, T. M'Clain, and Sloop *Charmin[g] Polly*, J. Ellwood, Philadelphia; Schooner *Mary*, [D.] Johnston, Jamaica; Sloop *St. George*, W. Denny, Grenada; Sloop *Edward*, E. Hammond, New-York. *Cleared Outwards*. Brig *Dolphin*, S. Babson, for Gloucester; Sloop *Betsy*, J. Ingraham, Boston; Brig *Marquis de la Fayette*, G. Dunham, London; Brig *Betsy*, T. Perkins, Liverpool; Schooner *Lottery*, Z. Mann, Baltimore. ■ By the UNITED STATES in CONGRESS assembled, March 17, 1785. WHEREAS it must conduce to the Preservation of Public Credit, and the equal Distribution of Justice that the Amount of the National Debt be ascertained with the utmost Expedition; and as Delay in the Settlement of Accounts tends to render them obscure, and to encourage Frauds by preventing the Means of detecting them; *Resolved,* That all Persons having unliquidated Claims against the United States be, and they are hereby required within Twelve Months from the Date hereof, to deliver a particular Abstract of such Claims to some Commissioner in the State in which they respectively reside, who is authorized to settle Accounts against the United States; and any Person or Persons neglecting to deliver their Claims as aforesaid, except at the Board of Treasury; provided that in those States where there is no Commissioner of Accounts, the Citizens of such State or States shall be allowed one Year for delivering their Claims from the Time when a Commissioner shall have been appointed and enter on the Duties of his Office. That all Persons who shall neglect to deliver in a particular Abstract of their Claims aforesaid, shall be excluded from the Benefit of Settlement or Allowance. CHARLES THOMSON, Secretary.

PRICES CURRENT, ALX. / Tobacco, 30s. per Ct. / Fine Flour, 28s. per Barrel. / Wheat, 6s. per Bushel. / Jamaica Spirits, 4/6 per Gallon. / Windward Rum, 3s. to 3/3 per Ditto. / Continental Rum, 2s. to 2/2 per Ditto. / Molasses, 1/6 per Ditto. / Muscovado Sugar, 38s. to 43s. per Ct. / Salt, 4s. per Bushel, by Retail. / Corn, 3s. per Bushel / Exchange, 40.

Just imported in the Schooner *St. George*, Captain Denny, from Grenada, and to be Sold by WILLIAM WILSON, RUM in puncheons and barrels, of high proof and well flavoured, Muscovado sugar in barrels, A few pipes of old Madera wine, London particular quality, And a few boxes of mould candles. ALX, April 26, 1785 ■ **FOR SALE,** THE SCHOONER *ST. GEORGE* how lying in this harbour, a British vessel of about 40 tons burthen, and a good sailer.--An inventory of which will be shewn by the subscriber.--For terms apply to WILLIAM WILSON. ALX, April 26, 1785 ■ JOHN MURRAY and COMPANY, Have items for Sale at their Store on Fairfax-Street [see like ad Vol. II No. 63] ■ WILLIAM LOWRY and CO. Have for sale a Spring Assortment, an elegant Forte Piano, Finger Organ [see like ad Vol. II No. 64]. ☞ They have removed to the store where Mr. Henry Lyles lately kept his store, on Fairfax-Street, near King-street, ALX, April 19, 1785 ■ To be Sold at Public Auction, on Friday the 20th of May next, if not sold before at private Sale, THE STOREHOUSE and other Improvements at the Falls of Potomack, in Virginia, belonging to RICHARD THOMPSON and the late THOMAS MAGRUDER.--For Terms apply to the Subscriber in George-Town, Maryland. RICHARD THOMPSON. ☞ On Saturday next he will sell at Public Auction, for Ready-Money only, several LOTS of GROUND, in Fee-Simple, well situated, either with or without Improvements. George-Town, April 26, 1785 ■ A PERSON, who is well acquainted with business aid trade in general, having been brought up in that line from his youth, and can satisfy any person of his abilities and character, offers his service to any gentleman, as an assistant in a wholesale or retail store. As he is well acquainted with bookkeeping and other accounts, he flatters himself he will give satisfaction to any merchant who may please to employ him. He is engaged to the latter end of this month with merchants at Elk-Ridge landing, at the expiration of which time he proposes to be in this town. A line directed to A.B. and left with the Printers will be duly attended to. ALX, April 5, 1785. ■ DAVID GRIFFITH offers for sale about 200 lots of ground adjoining ALX [see like ad Vol. II No. 63] ■ Just imported by the Subscriber, in the Brig *Triton*, George Young, Master, from Liverpool, and to be Sold cheap for Ready-Cash, at the Vendue-Store, opposite the Court-House, SINGLE and double refined loaf sugar, Liverpool ale of the best quality in bottles, and Cheshire cheese in hampers, Also for sale, bohea, common, green, and hyson tea, muscovado sugar in barrels, molasses, coffee, chocolate, West-India and Continental rum, with a variety of DRY-GOODS. CYRUS COPPER, ALX, April 26, 1785.

TO BE SOLD OR FREIGHTED, **THE Brig *TRITON***. She is strong fast sailing vessel, built since the war, is well sound, and will carry about 800 barrels. Inquire of
CYRUS COPPER.
ALX, April 26, 1785.

ALX and BALTIMORE PACKET. THE Schooner *LOTTERY*, ZACHARIAH MANN, Master, will ply constantly as a Packet from ALX to Baltimore twice a Month, and touch at Annapolis, or at any Place on the River Potomack, where Freight may offer.--Goods, on Freight from this to Baltimore (in the Absence of the Master) will be received by Messrs. Williams, Cary and Company, Merchants in ALX.--Care will be taken of Goods, &c. committed to his Charge, and the Favors of the Public gratefully acknowledged. April 25, 1785 ■ WE the Subscribers, being informed that Major Samuel Cox is again offering the mill and lands adjacent for sale, that he is at present possessed of on Goose-Creek, Loudon County; [in consequence whereof, we think proper to inform the] public, that we, in January 1779, made a fair purchase of said mill and lands, which will appear from an instrument of writing entered into with said Cox on the date aforesaid.--Said Cox refusing to make us deeds for the same agreeable thereto, we in the aforesaid year brought suit to compel him, which is yet undetermined. ROBERT WRIGHT, JOSEPH BRADEN, JAMES CROOKS. Loudon County, April 22, 1785 ■ WILLIAM HARDAGE, Shenandoah, seeks to settle accounts of Benjamin Ogle, Esq., of Berkely County, deceased [see like ad Vol. II No. 61] ■ THADDEUS M'CARTY, Loudon County, offers reward for runaway Mulatto man who calls himself HARRY JACKSON [see like ad Vol. II No. 64].

Page 4. Poetry. "The ANT and the CATERPILLAR. A FABLE." ■ WILLIAM HEPBURN offers for rent the house and garden now occupied by Mr. Patrick Murray; several lots on the Wharf on Princess Street, others [see like ad Vol. II No. 63] ■ THOMAS H. HANSON offers for sale land in Washington County on Potomack River [see like ad Vol. II No. 61] ■ C. COPPER offers for sale a lot on Fairfax-street [see like ad Vol. II No. 63] ■ WILLIAM WILSON has for sale a lot of ground on Fairfax-street, and a lot of ground in Dumfries [see like ad Vol. II No. 58] ■ Clement Brooke and John Merryman, Baltimore, offer for sale lands and Negroes for public sale [see like ad Vol. II No. 63] ■ GERARD HOOE offers reward for return of runaway black Negro man named DAVY [see like ad Vol. II No. 63] ■ EZEKIEL HUDNALL, master, announces that the Schooner *Roving Nancy* will sail as a Packet from ALX to Norfolk [see like ad Vol. II No. 65] ■ DAVID ARELL gives notice that six persons escaped from the Fairfax County gaol [see like ad Vol. II No. 63] ■ Copartnership of WRIGHT and LONG is dissolved, they seek to settle accounts; Wright carries his business in the house of John

Saunders [see like ad Vol. II No. 65] ■ JOHN T. FITZHUGH offers breeding with horse *REPUBLICAN* [see like ad Vol. II No. 65] ■ ☞ Constant Employment and the highest Wages, will be given to reputable JOURNEYMEN PRINTERS, on Application to the Printers hereof, or to Messrs. GODDARD and LANGWORTHY, Printers in Baltimore ■ J. PEYTON, Winchester, seeks minister for the Protestant Episcopal Church [see like ad Vol. II No. 63] ■ ALX: Printed by GEORGE RICHARDS, and COMPANY, at their Printing-Office on Fairfax--by whom Advertisements, &c. are thankfully received for this Paper,--and where Printing is performed with Care and Expedition.

1785/05/05, Vol. II No. 66

Page 1. DAVID GRIFFITH offers for sale about 200 lots of ground adjoining ALX [see like ad Vol. II No. 63]. ■ JESSE TAYLOR offers for sale goods just imported in the Brig *Triton* [see like ad Vol. II No. 64] ■ JONATHAN SWIFT and CO. Have for Sale a general assortment of SPRING GOODS [see like ad Vol. II No. 64] ■ DAVID FORBES, Dumfries, has for sale a general assortment of MEDICINES [see like ad Vol. II No. 64] ■ ROBERT WRIGHT, JOSEPH BRADEN and JAMES CROOKS, Loudon County, notify public of Samuel Cox's inappropriate attempt to sell the mill on Goose-Creek [see like ad Vol. II No. 65] ■ JOSEPH MARIE PERRIN has opened his own house on Royal-Street [see like ad Vol. II No. 64] ■ CYRUS COPPER has for sale items just imported in the Brig *Triton*; the Brig *Triton* is for sale [see like ad Vol. II No. 65] ■ The Schooner *Lottery*, Zachariah Mann, Master, will ply constantly as a Packet from ALX to Baltimore twice monthly [see like ad Vol. II No. 65] ■ THADDEUS M'CARTY, Loudon County, offers reward for runaway Mulatto man who calls himself HARRY JACKSON [see like ad Vol. II No. 64] ■ THOMAS ROPER, Leesburg, informs public of recent furnishings for accommodating gentlemen [see like ad Vol. II No. 61] ■ WILLIAM WILSON has for sale items just imported in the Schooner *St. George*; the Schooner *St. George* is for sale [see like ad Vol. II No. 65] ■ WILLIAM LOWRY and CO. Have for sale a Spring Assortment, an elegant Forte Piano, Finger Organ [see like ad Vol. II No. 64] ☞ They have removed to the store where Mr. Henry Lyles lately kept his store, on Fairfax-Street, near King-street, ALX, April 19, 1785 ■ GERARD HOOE offers reward for return of runaway black Negro man named DAVY [see like ad Vol. II No. 63] ■ M'Murray's Maps of the U.S. are ready for delivery to subscribers [see like ad Vol. II No. 64].

Page 2.

STRASBURG, Feb. 25. Serious preparations for war are making here. The King's Commissary, the Jew Cerf Berlin, has collected provisions and forage for a two hundred thousand man army. The same activity is exerted in all other frontier towns, where a great number of convents are converted into stores and magazines. ■ **BRUSSELS, December 10.** Present important affairs of state do not prevent his Imperial Majesty's finding the leisure to attend to his favorite object-- the reform of religious houses. He sent the following to the superiors of the Mendicant Friars in the Austrian Netherlands: We intend a reform amongst the Mendicant Orders beneficial to religion and the welfare of the state, by employing each individual of those said orders in the cure of souls, the instruction of youth, &c. We write this with the advice of the most serene Governors of the Netherlands, directing you to lay within the space of one month, before our privy council: 1st. The number and situation of the convents; 2dly the name, age and time of profession of every individual of every convent; 3rdly the time, age, and year of entering of postulants and novices; 4thly, the function of each individual both within and out of the monasteries. To the above you will add an exact and correct list of the various objects, and of the produce arising from alms bestowed on each convent in particular. And whereas the number of mendicants is by far too numerous in town and country, you shall deliver your opinion on the most proper means of effecting a re-union of some of the said convents, together with the parishes in which the friars might be employed, and in what manner. Finally, we strictly enjoin, till our pleasure is further known, that no novice be in future admitted to your order, without the express consent of our Governor General, to whom you may apply whenever you think it indispensable to admit novices in any monastery. Being, &c. (Signed) JOSEPH. Kuls, Vt. Tm. De Ksul. ■ **AIX LA CHAPPELLE, March 3.** The plan of the approaching campaign is arranged. The difficulties advanced by the Porte regarding the limits induced the Court of Versailles to establish on her frontiers towards Turkey a camp of 30,000 men for holding in check the numerous garrison of Belgrade and environs; also, 30,000 men in Moravia, and 70,000 under Field Marshall Loudohn at Colin, to prevent Prussian troops from traversing the mountains. ■ **LONDON, March 3.** Extract of a letter from the English Consul at **Algiers, Feb. 11:** People here are preparing for the proposed Spanish visit next spring. I believe even a force three times that of the immortal Elliot at Gibralter would not last a week, or even an hour, before this city. Before reaching here, the Spaniards must silence not only the castle's formidable artillery, but that of the 500 toises long mole--plus the fire of the newly raised battery called the Devil's battery (in honor of that name at Gibralter.) If that is surmounted, they will stand against a most numerous and warlike army; well disciplined and of a formidable appearance. The Spaniards will repent their obstinate rashness. More successful would be reducing those pirates with gold; that seducing metal would operate with much greater force on the minds of an avaricious but brave people than all the attempts against a place so well fortified. **March 4.** We hear that the day of the cabinet meeting to determine what part the Court of France would take in the dispute between the Emperor and the Dutch, the Queen intercepted the Prime Minister, Count Vergennes, and accosted him: "Sir, I hope you will not forget today that the Emperor of Germany is my brother." To which the Count replied, "No, Madam, I certainly shall not; neither will I forget that the Dauphin is your son." ... Extract of a letter from Madras, Sept. 15, 1784: The great Nizam, and likewise the Mahratas, are jealous of Tippoo, who has struck rupees on his own name, an honor never usurped by any Prince of Indostan before. He calls himself Tippoo Sultan Babadar, and everything that is great. Tippoo has disciplined his infantry in the same manner as we do, and in English. No troops but ours can oppose him. Had the war lasted until now, he might well have driven us into the sea. It is probable we shall soon have a war. We must, however, be paid from somewhere else than our treasury, which is drained to a piece ... **St. James's, March 4**. Yesterday at levee at St. James, Mr. John Temple kissed the King's hand on being appointed consul from Great Britain to America. ■ **DUBLIN, Feb. 26.** Last Saturday a poor Summerhill man with two sacks of potatoes on a horse, in Darby Square, fell through the pavement into a 40 foot deep cavern, at whose bottom were many coffins, bones, &c. The oldest inhabitants knew nothing of any vaults or caverns there. It is supposed it is a Danish burying place. **March 15.** A gentleman from London reports an Indiaman lately arrived there brought a most extraordinarily sized ostrich, in perfect health despite a tedious, seven month passage. Male, it is from the Suez desert between Egypt and Arabia, nearly 14 hands high. **March 16.** A number of counterfeit dollars are in circulation, so well executed their baseness is discovered only by cutting, or the most strict examination. Unexampled sheriffs' activity has located a cache of them, as well as counterfeit half guineas, which they seized after a strict search. **March 17.** A tax upon emigrants would oblige numbers to stay at home, to be starved. This would produce spectacles to gratify the hatred and malignancy of tax framers, who are resolved to try what consequences may result from insult, despair, and distress. Broken spirit and tame submission are what they flatter themselves with; but wrongs infinitely less than those we suffer often rouze the spirit of vengeance. The castle hacks talk of dismembering the empire; but they care not a rush for the universal discontents that oppressive taxes, now to be raised, have caused. No, no,--they seem to forget that a trifling STAMP ACT lost America FOR EVER to England--that this single measure, founded in tyranny and folly has, from the zenith and pride of power, reduced her to such a situation, that she is scoffed at and despised by surrounding nations; and yet, with their experience the *boy minister*, apeing the conduct of Lord *Buffoon,* is carrying the same measure here with tenfold severity. ■ **KINGSTON,** (*Jamaica*) **March 9.** The present sugar cane crop promises to be rich and abundant ... A gentleman just arrived from Hispaniola reports the port of Cape Nicola Mole is shut against all American vessels, by command of his Most Christian Majesty, and is hereafter to be considered only as the King's port. ■ **BOSTON, April 6.** By Captain Elwell, bound from Virginia to Lisbon, who arrived here yesterday, we learn that near the Newfoundland banks he spoke with a vessel bound to Philadelphia, the master of which declared he fell in with a Liverpool ship, from which he learned of a Moorish cruiser having captured six American vessels, and had the Masters of them on board. In consequence of which Captain Elwell thought it best to tack about and proceed for this port. ■ **NEW LONDON, April 15.** We have advice by Captain Joseph Phillips, who arrived here last week (passenger) from St. Martin's, that the island of St. Bartholomew, ceded to Sweden by the King of France, was taken possession of about the first of last month, by the subjects of the former, who had allotted out the lands for the purpose of erecting buildings; that it was made a free port for all nations, and probably would soon become a place of considerable consequence for commerce. ■ **PHILADELPHIA, April 25.** Extract of a letter from **Cadiz, February 14:** Don Barcelo gives up the command of the squadron destined against Algiers; the command goes to Don Antonio D'Acre. The fleet takes a large quantity of artillery, which are now fitting out in this arsenal ... A letter from **Lisbon:** the

Queen has decreed no American ship to pay any duty in any of her ports provided they carry their own country's products, only; also, no American ships to be searched by any of her officers when they are ready to get under sail--a privilege no other nation's ships have ... Extract of a letter from **Cape Francois, March 3**: A recent edict published here prohibits spermaceti candles and flour, on pain of confiscation of both vessel and cargo. Please publish immediately. This severe edict will remain in force for some time. Sugar and coffee are also prohibited on the same penalty ... **April 27.** A gentleman arriving on the *Harmony*, from London, was told the day he sailed that a house in London had received a **Gibralter letter of February 14**, to the following purpose: 'Our letters from Barbary mention, that the American vessel lately taken, together with all her crew, are ordered to be released, and that the Dey had issued strict orders, forbidding his cruisers to capture or molest and **VESSELS** belonging to the **UNITED STATES** of **AMERICA**. **April 29.** Extract of a letter from **Fort M'Intosh, April 12:** Only two of our prisoners are yet brought in by the Indians, the remainder expectedly shortly. These two are fine little boys, can speak no English, know not their parents or names, or from whence they were taken; one of them made an effort to leave us, and resume barbarism. This country may in time be a rich and populous settlement. Well watered, the land seems good, but frequent conflagrations have destroyed much of the timber in some parts. I toured about 30 miles up Beaver Creek to a beautiful old Indian town called Kuskuscoes, where there were once about 100 houses. There are frequent migrations to Kentucky by this river, yet it seems probable some may stop here, once this country is ready for inhabiting. This garrison is healthy ... A most intelligent gentleman writes from **Dublin, March 5:** Politics rival all ancient and modern precedents in infamy, corruption, tyranny and depravity. Our nation is like a mushroom: one day growing, the next in dissolution. Foremost in the ranks of tyranny is the Attorney General, prosecuting everyone concerned in convening the counties &c. To choose Delegates to Congress--and every printer who has published their resolutions. Mr. Magee [proprietor of the Dublin Evening Post] was today liberated from Newgate, after a long confinement for contempt of Court: But he has yet to be tried for several fabricated offences, which will throw him on a special jury, who will find him guilty right or wrong. Mr. Rorke of Bridge street, is to be confined for six months, besides paying a large pecuniary mulct. Poor Kidd [one of the proprietors of the Dublin Morning Post] lies there now, and is to be tried for new offences. Amidst all these persecutions, the work of infamy rolls on in Parliament with uncommon celerity. No reform--no protecting duties--no beneficial act: and, wonderful to tell, a resolution of both houses "that the revenues shall be made equal to the expenditures." The new taxes astonish and alarm every man: an additional half penny on newspapers, and a shilling on every ten lines of advertisements, besides a shilling for each advertisement, as such; and so in proportion to the number of columns in each paper. These taxes are with the double view of preventing the sale of papers, and the publication of volunteer and county resolutions, which you know are generally long. The other taxes are equally mischievous and oppressive, and their [sic] is no opposing them.

Page 3. **BALTIMORE, April 29.** A Somerset County gentleman informs us that Mr. James Diamond, of the same county, has invented an instrument calculated to determine the right line, distance, bearing, and magnitude of any object by sight only, whether accessible or inaccessible, without change of place or station, by an entirely new method. Such an instrument must be highly acceptable to those in gunnery, navigation, surveying, &c. There is not even the slightest hint of its principles in Euclid, or any other ancient or modern author--which is no small honor to the inventor, and to this country in general. ■ **ALX, May 5**. Extract of a Letter from a Gentleman in Boston to his Friend in this Town, dated April 14, 1785. "Yesterday arrived here the *Cincinnatus*, Capt. --- Farris, in 20 Days from London, with not more than Half a Cargo on Board, owing to the British being unwilling to freight in American Bottoms.--They have laid an additional Tax of 1d. per lb. on Tobacco; 7s. per Cent. on Rice; on Whale and other Oil, 20s. per Ton; and an enormous Tax on all American Produce.--The People here are highly exasperated against the English, and it is doubtful whether they will suffer a further Importation of British Goods.--A Merchant from Halifax, who brought with him here a large Quantity of British Goods, amongst which were a Parcel of ready-made Clothes, all which he advertised would be sold lower than any were ever before sold here.--The Merchants and Tradesmen took the Alarm and wrote violently and spiritedly against such a Step, consequently the Sale of the ready-made Clothes is put off.--A Town Meeting will be called Tomorrow, to take into Consideration these important Matters, and what will be their Issue God only knows." ■ On Monday Evening last, being the Anniversary of King Tamminy, an elegant Ball was given at Mr. Lomax's Tavern. ■ NAVAL-OFFICE, ALX. *Inward Entries*. Schooner *Barbadoes*, J. Seymore, from Barbadoes; Ship *Young Daniel*,

S. Wybrants, Lisbon; Schooner *General Jones*, E. Veale, North-Carolina. *Cleared Outwards*. Sloop *Polly*, M. Clark, for Boston; Sloop *Molly Beverly*, J. Christie, Charleston; Sloop *Dolphin*, A. Stewart, Philadelphia; Schooner *Mary*, T. M'Clain, Washington; Ship *Jenny*, D. Deshon, Amsterdam.

From the PENNSYLVANIA PACKET *and* DAILY ADVERTISER,

To the PRINTERS, IT is very extraordinary, that in this country of liberty, our fine ladies and fine gentlemen should be the slaves of the most despotic, most cruel, most relentless tyrant in the world. With what face can they boast that they are the sons and daughters of freedom, when it is notorious that, in the most important article of their lives, they bow their necks to the arbitrary mandates of a monarch, who tortures and renders them ridiculous, for his amusement. Fashion is the tyrant I mean; and certainly a more lawless, fantastical tyrant never existed. He pays no regard to the remonstrances of sense and reason, than an archbishop to a country curate, or a prime minister to a private gentleman. The first intention in cloathing our bodies, is, to keep them warm; and reason tells us, that every article of dress which is neither convenient nor ornamental, is absurd; but fashion tells us, that our shoes must terminate in a point as sharp as that of a bodkin, and, in obedience to her commands, we immediately cramp our toes, and hobble along the streets like fine ladies in China. Reason and experience inform us that there can be no beauty without proportion; but fashion assures us that a short waist is the ton, and all our females instantly resemble the monstrous figures in the Dutch pictures of the last century, or rather Dutch skippers, with a dozen pair of breeches. Nature and common sense would tell us, that in the head-dress of a woman, nothing is so graceful and so becoming as their own shining locks, in flowing ringlets on their necks; but fashion, in broken English assures their ladyships, that nothing is so much the ton, as to be unnatural; that every hair on the lady's head must be pasted and distorted in a diametrical opposition to its natural position; that a certain number of curls are to stick out behind, at five inches distant from the head, and as perfectly stiff as if they were made of wood and stone; that an immense horse tail must be fixed to their heads, so large, that it cannot be mistaken for their own hair, and so plastered as to resemble no hair at all. But what provokes me most is, that our fools of fashion are held in perpetual derision by the creatures they employ; by milliners and hairdressers, who disguise them for their amusement. If I were a prime minister, I would transfer the burthen of taxation from the rational, the industrious part of the community, to these useless instruments of fashion, and their silly employers, and thus render them, in some measure, useful to society. Your's, &c.

SOCIUS.

FOR SALE, On very reasonable Terms, **A quantity of Lisbon Salt**, on board the *Young Daniel*, Captain Wybrants, now lying at the County Wharf.--Apply to WILLIAM WILSON. ALX, May 2, 1785.

To be CHARTERED to any PORT in EUROPE

The Dutch Ship *YOUNG DANIEL*, Captain WYBRANTS, with a Mediterranean pass; she is an exceeding strong, good vessel, of about 500 hogsheads of tobacco burthen.--For terms apply to

WILLIAM WILSON.

☞ He has for sale, a quantity of CORDAGE and CANVAS.

ALX, May 2, 1785.

☞ NEW TEAS. **Jesse Taylor**, Has just imported, in the Ship *Young Daniel*, Capt. Wybrants, A Quantity of TEAS, which he will sell by the Quarter Chest, on reasonable Terms for Cash, Country Produce, or a short Credit. ALX, May 3, 1785 ■ **Robert Lyle**, INFORMS his friends and customers in general, that he has removed his store higher up Fairfax-street, opposite the Printing-Office. He thanks the public in general for their former custom, and would be glad of a continuation of their favours. Said Lyle has DRY and WET GOODS for sale as usual. He will sell THREE LOTS of GROUND, in fee-simple, or will ground-rent them for ever. N.B. He has a few chests of GREEN and BOHEA TEA for sale. ALX, May 5, 1785 ■ WINCHESTER RACES. ON Wednesday the 25th of May next, will be run for over the course near this Town, a purse of THIRTY POUNDS, free for any horse, mare or gelding. Aged horses carrying ten stone, six years old nine stone seven pounds, five years old eight stone and ten pounds, four years old seven stone and ten pounds, and three years old a feather.--On Thursday the 26th, will be run for over the same ground, a purse of TWENTY POUNDS, free for any horse, mare or gelding (the winning horse the preceding day excepted) carrying the same weights, and the best two in three two mile heats for each purse. The horses to be entered with Mr. EDWARD M'GUIRE the day preceding the race.

Subscribers paying entrance twenty shillings, and non-subscribers thirty for the first purse, or double at the post; and for the second, a subscriber fifteen shillings, and a nonsubscriber twenty, or double at the post. And on Friday the 28th, will be run for, the entrance-money of both days, or sweepstakes, free for any horse, mare or gelding (except those of the two preceding days) carrying the same weights, and also the best two in three two mile heats. All disputes to be settled by the managers. Winchester, April 26, 1785 ■ TO BE LET, On reasonable Terms, A Good STOREHOUSE for wet and dry goods, on Clements-Bay, in St. Mary's-County, about five or six miles from Llewellin's Warehouse; the tide flows within two or three yards of the doors of said store, and vessels of considerable burthen may lay within twenty yards of the shore in a fine pleasant harbour. The above house has a cellar below, a store, a counting room and granary, and is well situated for custom.--Any person inclinable to rent the same, may have it for one, two, three or more years, by applying to the Subscriber on the premises. JAMES HEARD, April 23, 1785 ■ Just arrived in the Schooner *Barbadoes*, Captain Seymour, from Barbadoes, and to [be] sold by **Richard Conway**, A Quantity of good RUM, on reasonable Terms, for Cash, Flour or Indian-Corn. He has on Hand very good SUGAR in Barrels, to sell as above. ALX, May 5, 1785.

On Thursday the 12th Instant, will be Sold at Public-Vendue, THE SCHOONER *St. GEORGE*, with all her tackle and apparel as she came from sea, now lying off Harper and Watson's wharf, she is a fast sailing vessel, has good accommodations, will carry about five hundred barrels, is well found, her rigging and sails nearly new, and has a British register.--The terms are one half ready cash, for the other half a credit of six weeks will be allowed, on bond with security if required.--Inventory of her materials may be seen at the Vendue-Store.

On the same day, weather permitting, will positively be sold for ready cash, Dr. DICK's Shop, together with a lease of near five years to come of the Lot on which it stands, subject to a ground-rent of Seven Pounds Ten Shillings per annum.--It is an excellent stand for a retail store, being situated on the west side of Royal-street near the corner of King-street.--The purchaser will have the privilege to remove the house off the lot at any time before or at the expiration of the lease, and be put in possession clear of back-rent to the time of sale.

C. COPPER, V. Master.

☞ On Saturday next, will be sold at the Vendue-store, as usual, a variety of wet and dry GOODS. ALX, May 4, 1785.

DROPPED from my servant's horse, at the Bridge near the Church, about eight o'clock last evening, a pair of black SADDLE-BAGS with an iron lock, which contained a number of bonds, receipts, and other papers in a red pocket-book, some Continental State money, a State land warrant for about 15 or 1600 acres of land in my own name, two certificates in the name of Francis Willis, jun. of Berkeley County, one for £.20 the other for 20 odd pounds, both dated 1783; two tobacco notes, one in the name of Thomas Allison, the other in the name of Daniel Stone, marked and numbered ALX Warehouse, D.S. No. 798, 1127, 111, 1016; T.A. No. 807, 1121, 116, 1005; also, a large sum of gold.--Whoever has found the bags, and will deliver them with the papers to Mr. COPPER, Vendue-Master, may keep the gold and no questions will be asked. All persons will please to take notice not to take up any bonds due me without my assignment, nor to purchase the above tobacco notes.--Among the number of bonds there are two replevy bonds, given by Mr. Henry Whiting to His Excellency George Washington, one for £.159,8s. the other for £.50; one bond given by Col. Anthony Thornton for £.100 payable the first day of June next; one bond given by Robert B. Carter for 6000 lb. of crop tobacco; one bond given by Cuthbert Harrison, Esq., for 1100 lb. of tobacco; one bond given by William Heale, Esq., for 1150 lb. of tobacco, with other bonds and accounts which I do not remember. BATTAILE MUSE, ALX, May 3, 1785.

Frederick County, Virginia, April 26, 1785.

RAN away from the Subscriber on the 17th instant, an Irish servant lad, named JOHN COURTNEY; he is about 16 or 17 years of age, of a fair fresh complexion, dark hair of a moderate length, a sly reserved countenance, speaks slow and much on the Irish accent. His clothes, unless changed, are a drab coloured coarse cloth lappelled waistcoat, made without skirts and lined with linen, and one half of the sleeves is of a lighter colour than the rest, a red striped flannel jump under it, a pair of old blue plush breeches, and has either a pair of old black worsted or coarse white yarn stockings on; he took

two pair of old shoes with him, one of which has small nails in the edges of the soles and heels.--He can write and possibly may forge himself a pass.--I will give THREE POUNDS for apprehending and securing him in any gaol, so that I may hear of him, or if brought to me will give one shilling per mile going and returning besides other reasonable charges.
JOHN CORDELL.

NOTICE is hereby given to all persons who have any just demands against me, to bring in their accounts that they may be settled and payed; and all persons who are indebted to me are likewise requested to make immediate payment, as I am very desirous of having all my accounts closed. JOHN OSBURNE, Loudon County, April 26, 1785.

Page 4. Poetry. "A Rural Ode." ■ WILLIAM WILSON has for sale a lot of ground on Fairfax-street, and a lot of ground in Dumfries [see like ad Vol. II No. 58] ■ Employment sought by person now engaged with merchants at Elk-Ridge landing [see like ad Vol. II No. 65] ■ THOMAS H. HANSON offers for sale land in Washington County on Potomack River [see like ad Vol. II No. 61] ■ Copartnership of WRIGHT and LONG is dissolved, they seek to settle accounts; Wright carries his business in the house of John Saunders [see like ad Vol. II No. 65] ■ Clement Brooke and John Merryman, Baltimore, offer for sale lands and Negroes for public sale [see like ad Vol. II No. 63] ■ JOHN T. FITZHUGH offers breeding with horse *REPUBLICAN* [see like ad Vol. II No. 65] ■ EZEKIEL HUDNALL, master, announces that the Schooner *Roving Nancy* will sail as a Packet from ALX to Norfolk [see like ad Vol. II No. 65] ■ Subscribers to the scheme for opening and extending navigation of Potomack River are notified of an upcoming meeting [see like ad Vol. II No. 63] ■ NATHANIEL C. HUNTER has for rent sundry lots on Fairfax, Prince and Royal Streets [see like ad Vol. II No. 64] ■ SAMUEL CANBY, Leesburg, offers for sale or exchange tracts in Monongalia and Jefferson counties [see like ad Vol. II No. 64] ■ RICHARD THOMPSON offers to sell the storehouse, etc. of Richard Thompson and the late Thomas Magruder [see like ad Vol. II No. 65] ■ TOWNSHEND DADE seeks to settle accounts for estate of Francis Dade, Attorney at Law [see like ad Vol. II No 64.] ■ GARLAND THOMPSON, Fredericksburg, offers reward for runaway French servant man named Charles Degeau [see like ad Vol. II No. 64] ■ ALX: Printed by GEORGE RICHARDS, and COMPANY, at their Printing-Office on Fairfax--by whom Advertisements, &c. are thankfully received for this Paper,--and where Printing is performed with Care and Expedition.

1785/05/12, Vol. II No. 67

Page 1. WILLIAM WILSON has a quantity of Lisbon Salt for sale; Ship *Young Daniel*, Captain Wybrants to be charted to any port in Europe [see like ads Vol. II No. 66] ■ ROBERT LYLE has removed his store higher up Fairfax-street where he has wet and dry goods for sale [see like ad Vol. II No. 66] ■ JAMES HEARD has for sale a good storehouse and goods on Clement's-Bay, St. Mary's County [see like ad Vol. II No. 66] ■ JOHN OSBURNE, Loudon County, seeks to settle accounts [see like ad Vol. II No. 66] ■ RICHARD CONWAY has items for sale just arrived in the Schooner *Barbadoes* [see like ad Vol. II No. 66] ■ C. COPPER, Vendue-Master to sell the Schooner *St. George* [see like ad Vol. II No. 66] ■ BATTAILE MUSE seeks to find lost pair of black saddle-bags, containing many papers and money [see like ad Vol. II No. 66] ■ THOMAS ROPER, Leesburg, informs public of recent furnishings for accommodating gentlemen [see like ad Vol. II No. 61] ■ George-Town, May 7, 1785. On Wednesday the 15th of June next, will be sold in this Town to the highest Bidder, SUNDRY NEGROES, both male and female, amongst whom are several likely boys and girls, from ten to fifteen or sixteen years of age; also, horses, cattle, plantation utensils, household furniture and sundry other articles too tedious to particularize, the property of the late Mr. THOMAS MAGRUDER, deceased. The terms of sale for the Negroes will be one third ready-money or tobacco, one third more by the first of October next, and the remaining one third by the first of February, 1786. Tobacco, wheat or other produce, will be received at market-price, in discharge of the two last mentioned payments.--For the stock &c. one half ready-money, and the remainder by the first of October next.--The purchasers of any article to give bond with approved security, to bear interest from the date, if not paid by the time or times abovementioned. At the same time will be offered for sale, a TRACT of very valuable LAND, adjoining to Mrs. Mary Berry, about 4 miles from Upper-Marlborough, in Prince-George's County, called Magruder's Vale, and containing 159 acres. Also, on Wednesday the 27th day of July next, will be sold one third part of a LOT of GROUND, in the town of Upper-Marlborough. Time will be given for part of the money, if required, and deeds given immediately on securing payment to BASIL MAGRUDER, WILLIAM B. MAGRUDER, RICHARD THOMPSON.

☞ All persons having demands against the estate of the late Mr. THOMAS MAGRUDER, are desired to bring in their accounts, properly proved, to WILLIAM B. MAGRUDER at George-Town, who is empowered to receive and settle them; and in order to hasten the payment, the Subscribers earnestly solicit all those indebted to the said estate, either by bond or open account, to make immediate payment, as no indulgence can be given. BASIL MAGRUDER, WILLIAM B. MAGRUDER, RICHARD THOMPSON, Executors. ■ JOHN CORDELL offers reward for return of runaway Irish servant lad named JOHN COURTNEY [see like ad Vol. II No. 66] ■ TOWNSHEND DADE seeks to settle accounts for estate of Francis Dade, Attorney at Law [see like ad Vol. II No 64.].

Page 2.

LONDON, Feb. 28. An indignant correspondent who saw Lord North honored with a blue ribbon for the loss of thirteen colonies imagines he will yet see Mr. Pitt blue ribboned for the loss of commerce and manufactures of Great Britain by extravagant grants to Ireland, rising in her demands. Perhaps the two ribboned patriots will hereafter cut their jokes in coalition in parliament, upon all sober, serious friends to their country ... *Bon Mot*: On the first night representation of School for Scandal, Mr. Cumberland said he could find nothing in it to make him *laugh*. Mr. Sheridan on hearing this said "What an ungrateful man, not to laugh at my *comedy*, when I laughed at his *tragedy* from the first to the last scene!" **March 4.** The nabob of Arcot, a well meaning gentleman, hearing the lady of an English nabob wished to take from India a diamond of peculiar lustre, sent a small bag of his choicest, with his compliments, requesting the lady to choose any one of them; but the English nabob, fancying all of them, returned nothing but his compliments to the unsuspecting Indian! **March 5.** North America was severed from us either by Lord North's measures, or the persevering opposition given them by Mr. Fox. Now, they act uniformly together to further dismember the Empire. Impunity hath made them bold! ... *A lesson for Duelists* relates how two friends had a falling out, and one challenged the other to a duel. By agreement, the challenger came to breakfast at the other's house, before going to the dueling ground. There they breakfasted with the friend's wife and children. After the meal, the host remarked that the wife and children who had just left the room depended solely on him for their subsistence. "Unless you can stake something equal, in my estimation, to the welfare of seven persons...I cannot think we are evenly matched." "We are not, indeed!" replied the other, giving him his hand, and they became firmer friends than ever. ■ **BOSTON, April 13.** To the Freemen of this Commonwealth, particularly the ancient supporters of the Public Good, the Tradesmen of Boston. [There follows a passionate review of the impending ruin of the State's trade and navigation, the elements of which follow. - Eds.] Almost all our money has gone to England for the last three years' imports, leaving little or none to live on, pay taxes, support State and federal government, tending to ruin of our commerce and fishery, and the breaking of our national faith ... The Whale fishery, once support of thousands, yielding England $800,00 per annum , is stymied by a duty of £18 per ton on oil; we are thereby deprived of 50% of the natural and commercial means of remittance ...British regulation deprives us of the carrying trade to Great Britain, Nova Scotia, Newfoundland, Quebec, or the English West Indies; thereby as much of our Rum, Lumber, Fish and Flour as formerly shipped to those places is left on hand, our navigation discouraged and much of it neglected ... Any American built ship is prohibited in British trade, thus cutting off our ship building, and thus a great means of remittance ... A 7/ sterling duty on rice of Americans or carried in American bottoms cuts off that formerly considerable remittance ... An extra duty of 1d sterling, per pound, of American tobacco, or carried in American bottoms stops that source of remittance, or results in a loss of it ... Our vessels are sent back from British ports without being permitted to off-load their freight--which ought to teach us to send theirs back, likewise ... As a natural consequence credit of Americans in England is gone, and a swarm of British Agents, British Factors, and British Merchants, are sent among us, and are daily increasing: a set of men unprincipled in their attachment to America, natural enemies to her prosperity, alienated from her by the political separation which was the happy effect of the late glorious revolution; they intend to drain us to the last penny, rejoice over our ruin, and reduce us to poverty ... Rouse, rouse then my countrymen! Warn them to leave by a certain day with their property and effects, or have them seized. More Refugees, Agents and Factors and shiploads of their goods are expected hourly. Refuse them landing, and send them back.! Assure them the spirit of 1775 lives, and repeated injuries will raise in us, as well as in our old friends the Chuckataw Indians, to a flame!. Let them go back quietly, giving them sufficient provision at reasonable prices for their return passage, but let them have no more! ... Be not afraid! Let us form a body as ready and firm as in former times, when the interest of the community was not more in danger than now! Let us honor ourselves, and we cannot fail of honoring our country. [signed] **JOYCE**, jun. ... Bostonians! A meeting is to be held on Friday next--though timid Whigs and Cringing Panders may cry no Mobs and Riots. Patriots....! Be assured that the voice of the people is the voice of God. [signed] **LIBERTY**. **April 18.** At a large and respectable Meeting of the Merchants, Traders, and others, convened at Faneuil hall, on the 16th instant, to consider the alarming state of our Trade and Navigation, the following Votes were unanimously agreed to. WHEREAS there is no U.S.-Great Britain commercial treaty; and certain British Merchants, Factors and Agents residing here expect further supplies imported in British bottoms, greatly to the hindrance of freight in all American vessels; and as many more such persons are daily expected to arrive, thus threatening an entire monopoly of British importations in such merchants' hands--greatly to the prejudice of this country: ... Therefore, to prevent their remaining (unless approved of by the selectmen) and to discourage sale of their merchandise--We the Merchants, Traders and others of the town of Boston, DO AGREE: First, that a Committee draft a petition to Congress on this matter, and that it be empowered to write the State's several seaports requesting them to join us in a similar application to Congress immediately to regulate the trade of the United States; further, that representatives to Congress be instructed to draft regulations to put our commerce on equal footing. VOTED: That the Committee write merchants in the several seaports of the other United states, recommending that their representatives apply to their legislatures to vest such power (if not already done) in Congress to achieve the desired ends, Congress making regulations to do so. VOTED: We pledge that neither we nor our subordinates will directly or indirectly purchase and goods of, nor have any commercial regulations with the British now here or to arrive (excepting persons approved as aforesaid). VOTED: we will not lease or sell any warehouse, shop, house or any other place for the sale of such goods, now will we employ persons who will assist said merchants, Factors, or Agents in their business--for we feel all such British importations are calculated to drain us of currency and impoverish this country. VOTED: that a Committee be appointed to wait on such as already have leased such places for the disposal of such merchandise, and inform them of this meeting's resolve. VOTED: That we encourage the manufactures and produce of this country [illegible] to promote them. VOTED: That a Committee be appointed to make immediate application to the Governor and Council of this Commonwealth, requesting the Naval Officers of this State to deny landing of goods from Great Britain's dominions consigned to or the property of the aforesaid persons, until the legislature meets. VOTED: That copies of these resolutions be printed and dispersed among the inhabitants, that they may be adopted and carried into execution, with that temper which is consistent with the character of good citizens. ■ **PHILADELPHIA, May 3.** It is confidently asserted that the Court of London has positively determined not to give up the posts on our frontiers, alleging that the United States have not complied with the terms of the treaty.

ALX, May 12. Last Monday a Man was found dead in a Brick-Yard, near this Town. As he was much intoxicated the preceding Night, it is thought his Death was occasioned by an immoderate Use of strong Drink. ■ On Saturday last a public Examination of the ALX Latin School was held in the Court-House in this Town. At Ten o'Clock the Examination began, at which a Number of learned Gentlemen and others were present, when after a minute and particular Examination of the first Class, the Judges declared themselves incapable of determining whether Master M'CREA, Master TAYLOR, or Master WILSON, was best entitled to the Prize for that Class, and left the Determination thereof to Fortune, which decided it in Favor of Master TAYLOR. The Prize of the second Class was adjudged to Master HARTSHORNE. At Three o'Clock in the Afternoon the Youths delivered their Orations which they had previously prepared, from a Stage erected in the Court-House for that Purpose, in the Presence of a crowded and respectable Audience, from whom they received great and general Applause. The Prizes allotted to the best Speakers were adjudged to Master WILSON and Master M'CREA.

Page 3. The *Virginia*, Capt. Scott, is arrived in Rappahannock, from London. ■ MARRIED.] DAVID ARELL, Esq. to Miss PHOEBE CAVERLY. ■ DIED.] Mr. JOHN ELLIS, Merchant. -- Mr. HUGH GIBNEY, Bricklayer. ■ NAVAL-OFFICE, ALX. *Inward Entries*. Sloop *Polly*, L. Hill, from North-Carolina; Brig *Martha*, G. Slacom, Lisbon; Brig *Cesar*, J. Atkinson, Whitehaven; Ship *Mary*, J. Andrews, London; Schooner *Lottery*, Z. Mann, Baltimore. *Cleared Outwards*. Ship *Triton*, T. Lewis, for l'Orient; Ship *Ranger*, J. Knight, London; Ship *Eagle*, A. Hallott,

Lisbon; Sloop *Bathsheba*, J. Ingraham, and Sloop *Judith*, S. Martin, New-England; Schooner *Peggy*, R. Quirk, Barbadoes; Sloop *Diligence*, W. Miller, Bermuda; Sloop *Edward*, E. Hammond, New-York. ■ ☞ A Meeting of the INHABITANTS of ALX is requested, at the Court-House, on Saturday the 14th Instant, to take into consideration a Letter and Memorial, from the Chamber of Commerce of New-York. By orders of the Commercial Committee, WILLIAM HUNTER, jun., May 7, 1785 ■ **James Hendricks and Co.**, Will have open and ready for Sale in a few Days, A Handsome assortment of DRY-GOODS, received by the last vessels from Europe, which with what they had on hand makes their assortment very general for the season, all which they will sell at a low advance for cash, good bills on Europe, or country produce. ALX, May 11, 1785 ■ To be Sold at the Vendue-Store, on Monday next, being Court-Day, EXCELLENT Sugar in Barrels, and a great Variety of GOODS, as usual. C. COPPER, Vendue-Master, ALX, May 10, 1785 ■ To be Sold at Public Vendue, on Monday the 16th Instant, TWO LOTS of GROUND situated between Wilkes and Gibbon streets; one 24 feet in front, and the other 23 feet 3½ inches, by 75 feet deep.--The terms are one half cash and the other half in six months.--Good titles will be made. C. COPPER, Vendue-Master, ALX, May 9, 1785 ■ **Philip Dalby**, Is now opening for sale at his Store on the Corner of Royal and Cameron Streets, and near the Market-House, a large Assortment of Goods, consisting of HOSIERY, cutlery, ironmongery, stationary, hats, persians, modes, ribbons, gloves, handkerchiefs of various kinds, linen and cotton checks and stripes, furniture ditto, muslins, muslin cords, jeans, jeanets, denims, satinets, demities, white nankeens, with many other articles suitable to the present season, which he will dispose of by wholesale only, for cash, produce, or short credit. ALX, May 7, 1785. ■ ☞ SPRING GOODS. **Robinson, Sanderson and Rumney**, Have the Pleasure to inform their Friends and the Public, that they are now landing from on Board the *Cesar*, Capt. Atkinson, from Whitehaven, A Large and general assortment of EUROPEAN GOODS, suitable to the season, which will be disposed of by wholesale only, at their store on Fairfax-street, on the very lowest terms. ALX, May 11, 1785.

EIGHT DOLLARS REWARD.

RAN away from the Subscriber on the 2d instant, living within 7 miles of Mr. Keys's ferry, and within 12 of Harper's ferry, an Irish servant lad, named PHILIP LOUGHEREY; he is about 5 feet 7 or 8 inches high, about 18 years of age, has dark brown hair, and very fresh in the face: He is very impertinent, and very much given to swearing and strong liquor: He had on when he went away, a short brown coating coat, lined with brown shalloon half-worn, white broadcloth jacket with blue backs to it, two pair of old breeches, one of jean, the other of spotted swanskin, mended on the knee with worsted plush, an old felt hat broke in the crown, a pair of light blue stockings, and a pair of shoes half-worn with large square brass-buckles in them. Whoever will apprehend said servant, and secure him so that his Master may get him again, shall receive the above reward, [plus] reasonable charges paid if brought home.

DAVID KENNEDY.

Berkeley County, May 3, 1785.

William Hartshorne And Company, HAVE just imported in the *Mary*, Captain Andrews, from London, an assortment of Spring GOODS, which they will sell on reasonable terms for cash, or country produce, by wholesale and retail.--Those whose accounts are more than three months standing, will particularly oblige us by paying their balances, as we are informed by our friends in England, that no such credits can be had there as formerly.--Those who cannot pay immediately, will please to settle their accounts and give their bonds for the balance.--We hope the law limiting credits to six months, will be our excuse for this request, especially when it is considered, that those who sell goods, are the only people affected by it, as appears by some late determinations in our General Court.--Several valuable LOTS, well situated in Alexandria, may be had on Ground-Rent.--Inquire of WILLIAM HARTSHORNE. ALX, May 9, 1785 ■ **Jesse Taylor**, has just imported in the *Martha*, Captain Slacom, from Lisbon, LISBON wine, red and white port, best and second hyson, sequin, singlo, green and bohea teas, which he will sell on reasonable terms for cash or country produce. ALX, May 10, 1785 ■ **Richard Conway**, Has imported from Lisbon, in the Brig *Martha*, Gabriel Slacom, Master, which he will sell on reasonable Terms, for Cash or Country Produce, **Salt, Lisbon and Oporto Wines**. ALX, May 10, 1785. ■ Agreeable to the last Will and Testament of FOUSHEE TEBBS, Gentleman, deceased, will be Sold at his late Mansion-House, and Twelve-months Credit given, on Thursday the 16th Day of June next, SEVERAL likely SLAVES, the stock of horses, cattle, sheep, hogs, household and kitchen furniture; also a TRACT of LAND, beautifully situated on Quantico-Creek, between Potomack River (of which it has a full view) and Dumfries, within one mile and an half of the latter, and well watered and timbered, containing upwards of 300 acres; also, one other TRACT, lying on Potomack River and Powell's-Creek, including the fishery called Curry's-Bay, containing about 30 acres, one other TRACT of LAND lying within 4½ miles of Dumfries, and on the main road leading to the same, containing 200 acres; and on Friday the 17th of June next will be sold in Dumfries, the HOUSES and LOTS in said town, the property of the said FOUSHEE TEBBS; also, on Tuesday the 2d day of August next, will be sold on the said terms at Winchester, one TRACT of LAND, within 7 miles of said town, containing about 550 acres: and at the same time and place will be sold two other TRACTS of LAND, lying in Hampshire and adjoining the manor lands in the said County, containing about 560 acres. A further description of the said Lands and Lots will be unnecessary, as those who wish to become purchasers I suppose will first view the premises. An undoubted title and immediate possession will be given, reserving the priviledge of the tenants continuing on the said Lands till the expiration of the year, but the rents to be forfeited to the purchasers. I shall attend at the said several places for the above purposes. Bond with approved security will be required. As I am desirous of settling the accounts of the estate as soon as possible, all persons that are indebted to or have any demands against it, are desired to settle their respective balances, as the situation of the affairs of the estate will not admit of a long indulgence, and I am anxious to discharge the debts due from the estate to its creditors. WILLOUGHBY TEBBS, Executor. April 27, 1785.

C U B,

FORMERLY the property of Colonel Francis Thornton, is in high perfection at the Subscriber's, and will cover mares the ensuing season at Sixteen Dollars.

Cub is from the first stock in England and Arabia, as appears from his pedigree, which is so well known, to insert it now will be useless.

The uncommon strength, activity, and great performance of Cub's colts on the turf, renders him in estimation equal to any horse on the continent.

I have exceeding good pasturage at 2/6 per week, but will not be answerable for escapes or other accidents. WILLIAM COURTS.
March 13, 1785.

Henry Lyles, Has for sale at his Store on Fairfax-Street, the fourth Door from King-Street, the following Articles, which he will retail on low Terms, for Cash only, SUPERFINE broadcloths and cassimers, a large assortment of buttons and other trimmings, osnaburgs, brown Holland and Irish linens, superfine Marseilles and mock quiltings, superfine and fine white and coloured jeanets, corded demities, velvets, corduroys and king's cords, chintzes and calicoes, brocades, lustrings, tiffanies, English persians and black modes, a beautiful assortment of ribbons, black and white souflee gauzes, souflee, lawn, cambrick and common linen handkerchiefs, cambricks, fine and coarse lawn, worked muslim and lawn aprons, tamboured, flowered and book muslins, tablecloths, womens' stays, mens' and womens' silk, cotton and thread stockings, knit and silk shag waistcoat patterns, womens' calamanco and mens' leather shoes, mens' Woodstock, beaver and dogskin gloves, womens' best French red, white and coloured ditto, skeleton and straight wires, garters, silk purses, quality and shoe bindings, nonsopretties and tapes, nuns, osnaburgs, white, brown and coloured threads, furniture 3-4 and 5-4 checks, large and small looking-glasses, wool cards, hair sieves, bottle corks, copper and iron tea-kettles, japanned tea-trays, salvers and candle-boxes, tin, queen's and glass ware, castors, toys, fig-blue, loaf sugar, brass mariners' compasses, quarter hour glasses, stone jugs from 1 to 3 gallons, brushes of different kinds, gunpowder and shot, best scented hair-powder, pomatum and blackball, inkpowder, inkstands, writing paper, red and black sealing-wax, wafers, slates and pencils, best temple and common spectacles, snuff-boxes, tortoishell, horn and ivory combs, gun locks, table, clasp and pen knives, rasors, scissors, corkscrews, taperbits, fish-hooks, chain spurs, thimbles, curtain-rings, hat-hooks, knitting pins, japanned hair, gilt and pound pins, tea-spoons, ear-rings, d[arn?]ing and sewing needles, stock, closet, trunk, cupboard and pad locks, hinges, sheep-shears, thumb latches, hammers, gimblets, augers, tapborers, chisels, gouges, rules, plain-irons, steel spring rat-traps, broad and narrow hoes, ship-carpenters' axes and adzes, hand and crosscut saws, 24d. 20d. 10d. 8d. 6d. and 4d. nails, saddles, bridles, girths, cruppers, surcingles, stirrup-leathers, straps, saddle-cloths, portmanteaus and leather bags, red and yellow ochre, bohea and hyson tea; also, about two thousand weight of choice bacon. ALX, May 9, 1785

■ WHEREAS some malicious persons have circulated a report that I intend to quit keeping public house, I therefore give this notice to inform my friends and the public in general, that I have no such intention, but on the contrary have supplied myself with a stock of liquors, and am in every other respect able to entertain such as may please to favor me with their custom.--The Subscriber has also two good saddle-horses which he will hire to any gentlemen on reasonable terms. ROBERT SIM. Hawkins's Ferry, opposite to ALX, May 11, 1785. ■ To be Sold cheap, and the Payments made easy, AN exceeding valuable and well improved FARM, containing 355 acres, situated about 4 miles from Winchester, in the County of Frederick, adjacent to the road leading from thence to Staunton, convenient to several merchant mills, and to places of worship of various denominations. It is remarkably well timbered and watered, and has a good proportion of meadow made and to be made.--There are on the premises about 90 acres of Land clear, a good dwelling-house, kitchen, barn, and other necessary buildings; a more particular description may be unnecessary, but the Subscriber takes the liberty of assuring the public, that in his opinion it is the most valuable Farm (of its extent) in that part of the country of which there is any prospect of the sale.--For terms apply to SAMUEL PLEASANTS, Merchant in Philadelphia, or to the Subscriber near Winchester, ALEXANDER WHITE. Woodville, April 29, 1785 ■ FOR SALE, FOUR Hundred acres of LAND, in the County of Loudon, on the main road from Winchester to ALX, 12 miles above Newgate, and 14 below Leesburg; on this Land is a plantation with about 70 acres cleared, in proper order for farming or cropping, for which the Land is well adapted, a good barn, out-houses, and a tolerable dwelling-house, with a variety of fruit trees, several parcels of meadow made, and others which may be reclaimed; grain may be sowed on the place this fall, and possession delivered on the 1st of January next. Cash, tobacco, merchants notes payable in six months, or Negroes from 15 to 30 years of age, will be received for one half the purchase, and four years credit will be given for the remainder, on giving bond with approved security, to bear interest from the date if not punctually paid.--The price will be made known by applying to RICHARD GRAHAM, Esq., in Dumfries, or to the Subscriber near the premises. GEORGE RALLS, May 3, 1785.

Page 4. Poetry. "The Stage of LIFE." ■ JONATHAN SWIFT and CO. Have for Sale a general assortment of SPRING GOODS [see like ad Vol. II No. 64] ■ JOSEPH MARIE PERRIN has opened his own house on Royal-Street [see like ad Vol. II No. 64] ■ Clement Brooke and John Merryman, Baltimore, offer for sale lands and Negroes for public sale [see like ad Vol. II No. 63] ■ ☞ A few Barrels of choice LAMPBLACK may be had at the Printing-Office. ■ WILLIAM WILSON has for sale a lot of ground on Fairfax-street, and a lot of ground in Dumfries [see like ad Vol. II No. 58] ■ Employment sought by person now engaged with merchants at Elk-Ridge landing [see like ad Vol. II No. 65] ■ Subscribers to the scheme for opening and extending navigation of Potomack River are notified of an upcoming meeting [see like ad Vol. II No. 63] ■ CYRUS COPPER has for sale goods imported in the Brig *Triton*; the Brig *Triton* to be sold or freighted [see like ad Vol. II No. 65] ■ The Schooner *Lottery*, Zachariah Mann, Master, will ply constantly as a Packet from ALX to Baltimore twice monthly [see like ad Vol. II No. 65] ■ ROBERT WRIGHT, JOSEPH BRADEN and JAMES CROOKS, Loudon County, notify public of Samuel Cox's inappropriate attempt to sell the mill on Goose-Creek [see like ad Vol. II No. 65] ■ M'Murray's Maps of the U.S. are ready for delivery to subscribers [see like ad Vol. II No. 64] ■ WILLIAM WILSON has for sale items just imported in the Schooner *St. George*; the Schooner *St. George* is for sale [see like ad Vol. II No. 65] ■ WILLIAM LOWRY and CO. Have for sale a Spring Assortment, an elegant Forte Piano, Finger Organ [see like ad Vol. II No. 64] ☞ They have removed to the store where Mr. Henry Lyles lately kept his store, on Fairfax-Street, near King-street, ALX, April 19, 1785 ■ Winchester Races to be held starting Wednesday the 25th of May next [see like ad Vol. II No. 66] ■ GERARD HOOE offers reward for return of runaway black Negro man named DAVY [see like ad Vol. II No. 63] ■ ALX: Printed by GEORGE RICHARDS, and COMPANY, at their Printing-Office on Fairfax-street--by whom Advertisements, &c. are thankfully received for this Paper,--and where Printing is performed with Care and Expedition.

1785/05/19, Vol. II No. 68

Page 1.

CONSTANTINOPLE, January 9. By a ship arrived here from Alexandria with the tribute Egypt pays the Grand Seignior, we learn the kingdom is in a most melancholy situations. Murad Bey reigns as a cruel and sanguinary tyrant, oppressing trade, ruining the inhabitants, and disturbing the Franks--a striking example of the misfortunes despotism causes. **Jan. 26.** In the last fortnight several have died of the plague in Galata and Pera, so that several of the usual assemblies have been discontinued. The

Spanish, Swedish and Prussian hotels were shut on their respective sovereigns' birthdays ... The Grand Seignior has deposed Selim Effendi the Chiaux Bachi, whose annual revenues were 30,000 piastres ... The Dutch man of war lately arrived at Smyrna caused uneasiness to the Imperial Minister, who petitioned the Porte that the government intervene to prevent Dutch hostilities here; the Captain Pacha received orders to hinder any such Dutch proceedings. ■ **PETERSBURGH, January 21.** Letters from Kiachta and Irkutsh, in Siberia, say the Chinese have cut off all commerce with Russia, reducing Imperial revenue by 100,000 roubles. The Chinese motive is unknown, but accommodation of the difference is hoped for. ■ **PARIS, March 4.** We fear war inevitable, although we hardly think the Emperor will engage for so small an object, at such a distance, with a power with easy natural defences, and who may rely on France's protection. ■ **HAGUE, March 10.** It seems the Empress of Russia has replied to the King of Prussia's letter regarding the exchange of territory at issue between the Emperor and the Elector of Bavaria; the Emperor has said it will be to no one's disadvantage, not contrary to the Treaty of Teschen, and even to the advantage to the Duke of Deux Ponts (presumptive heir to the Elector of Bavaria.) The King of Prussia has replied, but the manner not publicly known ... Several public prints have mentioned suspicions of treason against the city of Maestricht, saying it was discovered through the channel of a great Potentate. We are assured this was by the Rhine-Graaf of Salm, who avers he had them from the King of Prussia whilst he was in Berlin. Their High Mightinesses required that Nobleman to appear before their Secret committee last Saturday; on Monday a serious conference was held, whose results are not yet public. **LONDON, February 23.** The key elements of the official paper sent by his Most Christian Majesty to the Emperor: Having no ulterior motive, and with the Emperor's welfare his only concern, the King feels the Dutch only supported a right (not opening the Scheldt) secured them by treaty--a treaty which they see as a basis for their prosperity, and even existence. The States General and the Emperor should resume the negotiations begun in Brussels, thus preventing hostilities and perhaps leading to equitable arrangements. Any opposite conduct by the Emperor might cause such general uneasiness as to make most of the powers think themselves obliged to take certain precautions and measures. Indeed, the king must assemble troops on his own frontiers. Besides, the king cannot be indifferent to the fate of the United Provinces, nor see them attacked, as he is about to conclude an alliance with them. The King renews his offer of mediation, confirms his personal sentiments with regard to the Emperor, and hopes to see extinguished the first seeds of a war whose consequences cannot be calculated. **March 9.** Letters from Lisbon by yesterday's mail confirm a marriage next May between the Royal families of Portugal and Spain. This junction between the infant Don Louis of Portugal (youngest son of Queen Isabella) and the infanta Charlotta Louisa of Spain, is to prevent the extinction of the Braganza family, neither the Prince of Beira, nor Don Pedro Xavier, the Queen's other son, having any issue by their aunts, to whom they are married. Papal dispensation is not required; the parties are not of such near kin. However, by this alliance Portugal will be more closely linked to the house of Bourbon, from which it has been the constant policy of this country to keep them as much as possible separate. **March 13.** A Paris letter says the French Minister at Berlin has written Mons. Vergennes that the King of Prussia's Minister at Vienna declares the Emperor determined to annex Bavaria. This caused the King of Prussia immediately to order forage and provisions for two armies, one 180,000 and the other 80,000; he is resolved to take the field as soon as the frost will permit his troops to march ... Despatches received late Monday night from the Duke of Dorset in Paris are said to report that matters between the Emperor and the Dutch are unlikely to be brought to an accommodation; war between them is looked on as inevitable ... The French Court has ordered Count Dillon to prepare a 20,000 man encampment in Flanders, near the Mountaise, the beginning of May--as some interesting events may be expected by that time ... By a **March 1 letter from Berlin** we learn that Austrian troop movements begin making the Court uneasy. The Emperor's three proposed spring encampments seem more offensive than defensive in nature. The opening of the Scheldt is not the Emperor's only object, in consequence of which he has ordered purchase of 10,000 horses; several contractors have offered to furnish every requisite for transporting the artillery and equipages. The Emperor will supply the officers' horses at his expense. The Elector of Saxony has been solicited to furnish 12,000 of his troops to join with 30,000 Prussians in establishing a camp at Koenigstein; a Prussian army of 80,000 is to be assembled in the environs of Schweidnitz, to penetrate into Bohemia and Moravia, if required. **March 21.** The conduct of administration respecting the new system for Ireland, is so far entitled to general praise, as it has been done wisely--the time, in which candor and caution have been so well shewed off, has been occupied most warily in disseminating all over the kingdom, the best fabricated explanations ... A stop is put to the negotiation for restoring the town of Negapatnam, with its dependencies in the East Indies, to the Dutch, it having been discovered that a bargain was going on between the States and the French for that purpose. ■ **CHARLESTON** (*South Carolina*), **April 18.** Extract of a letter from a **Delegate in Congress** to a gentleman here, dated **March 28**: "The interruption lately given by the Barbary corsairs to our trade is so serious a consideration, that Congress are taking such steps, as I hope will in future effectually secure our commerce from their depredations." ... Yesterday forenoon a young gentleman, lately from Europe, went into his lodging's necessary and cut his throat; he had lost so much blood before he was found that all medical assistance was in vain, and he expired this morning. The supposed cause: the loss of a cargo of goods had reduced him to poverty and despair ... A sloop from Hispaniola with sugar, molasses, coffee &c. was lost last Friday night on our bar, and only three men saved ... We hear the Brig *Vry van Dwinglandy*, Captain Schram, en route this port from Amsterdam, is entirely lost, and every person on board perished. **April 25.** From Savannah we hear that on the 10th General Greene and Colonel Hawkins to take a view of the islands and [Continued on Page 2].

Page 2. [Gen. Greene's Tour (*continued*)] inland navigation of that state, and to visit his Excellency Don Vincent Emanuel De Zespedes, Governor of East Florida, and returned the Sunday following. They were received at St. Augustine with courtesies, and military honors for the General. A Captain and 50-man guard for his quarters were modestly refused by the general as being no longer in a military character. Centinels were placed at his quarters, and the different guards of the garrison paid him Lieutenant General's honors. They were entertained by the Governor in a most splendid and elegant manner. The Commandant, the Treasurer, the Secretary and every other officer of his Catholic Majesty in East Florida seemed to vie with each other in those traditional Spanish marks of unaffected friendship. The General was escorted to St. John's by the Colonel Commandant of horse and a party of dragoons; he was received by the officer commanding at that post, and from thence attended by the Colonel Commandant through inland navigation to the river St. Mary's, where the Commodore commanding his Catholic Majesties ships received him with the Spanish flag displayed at his foretop, and a 13 gun salute. After an elegant entertainment by the Commodore, he was attended by the Commodore in his barge (with another 13 cannon salute) to Cumberland Island, Georgia, where the Spanish took leave of our general and the colonel. Such attention as paid by the officials of East Florida to a great and beloved General must see United States citizens return the same to every officer of his Catholic Majesty who may come among them... A few days ago the Honorable Major General Greene returned here from Savannah. ■ **PROVIDENCE, April 22.** Friday last arrived in the river the ship *Hope*, Capt. Swain, of this port, 24 days from Land's End of England, laden with salt. As the Captain could not procure on freight, he therefore purchased a load of salt at Lymington. Several American vessels came out with Capt. Swain in ballast.■ **NEW YORK, May 2.** Mr. Loudon: Please to insert the undermentioned notification in your paper, as some designing person took the opportunity yesterday afternoon, of taking a paper from the Coffee House, giving the same information. [signed] A Customer. "One of the ships from England, and not permitted to land her goods at **BOSTON**, was on Sunday at the Narrows." ... On Friday last arrived his most Christian Majesty's packet *Le Courier d'Europe*, Capt. Cornick, in 37 days from l'Orient. **May 7.** Yesterday arrived the ship *Duke of Buccleugh*, Capt. Richie, in 38 days from London, by whom we learn the English Ministry on March 23 received advice by express from Paris: the Emperor's troops have begun their march against the Dutch territories. It is supposed Maestricht and the adjacent counties will be the first scenes of hostilities. War seems to be commenced, without a doubt. ■ **PHILADELPHIA, May 7. STAMP ACT!** The Commonwealth of Massachusetts have passed an act, imposing duties on licensed vellum, parchment, and paper. By this *patriotic measure* the following articles are subject to the [summarized] **IMPOSITIONS** annexed:

Real estate deed--1/
Bond, other than to Judge of Probate--1/
Charter Party--1/
Promissory Notes of Hand, 6£ or greater--3d
Original Writ, Clerk of Common Pleas-6d
Original Writ, Justice of the Peace--3d
Writ of Execution, Clerk of Supreme Judicial Court--9d
Writ of Execution, Justice of the Peace--4d
Policy of Insurance--1/
Newspaper--2/3d
Almanack--1d
Register of Vessels--1/
Foreign Clearance--9d
Clearance, Vessel not wholly owned by citizen of this or any other of the U.S.--12/
Certificate to practice as Attorney, Court of Common Pleas--6£
Ditto, Supreme Judicial Court--9£
(Persons not already admitted to practice in either above court must obtain a

certificate, and paid the duty.)
Certificate to degree: Barrister at Law--12£
(Persons not already with Barrister at Law
degree must obtain same, and
Paid the duty.)

It is a little extraordinary, says a correspondent, that the people of Boston, hitherto foremost in the cause of justice and liberty, should be the first to adopt the measures of oppression. Even in England, where a blind submission is generally paid their tax masters, the STAMPS and EXCISE were always considered and generally complained of as grievous and oppressive. Indeed, the very words must sound harsh and disagreeable in the ears of freemen, whatever their political situation and circumstance. **May 18.** Extract of a letter from **New York, May 11:** The ship *Empress of China*, Capt. Green, is arrived here in 4 months 19 days from Canton. It is said she has brought back all the money that was sent in her; her cargo having purchased more than would load her twice. ■ **ALX, May 19**. Last Tuesday, being the Day appointed by the States of Virginia and Maryland, relative to opening the inland Navigation of the River Potomack, a Meeting was held at Mr. Lomax's Tavern, consisting of a very numerous Assembly of the first People in the respective States.--DANIEL CARROLL, Esq.; President of the Assembly of Maryland, being appointed to the Chair, the Subscription Books were read as the Acts direct, when it appeared that Forty Thousand Three Hundred Pounds was subscribed, a Sum far beyond what was requisite to incorporate the Company.--The Company was of Course established, and proceeded to the Election of a President and Directors, when the following Gentlemen were appointed: His Excellency GEORGE WASHINGTON, President; GEORGE GILPIN, JOHN FITZGERALD, THOMAS JOHNSON, and THOMAS S. LEE, Esquires, Directors. This great and important Work is to be immediately begun.--The vast Consequence that must derive to the Middle States when completed, cannot be elucidated but by Time, the Discoverer of all great Events. The next Great Meeting is appointed to be held at George-Town on the First of August next. ■ We hear from the Southward of a very destructive Insect having got among the new Wheat, in the Neighborhood of Richmond, by which many Crops have received great Damage.--These Insects have been, from Time to Time, observed further Southward. ■ The *Lion*, Capt. Campbell, is arrived in this River from Glasgow, under Jury-Masts, after a Passage of 9 Weeks. She lost her Masts in a Gale of Wind after being 15 Days at Sea. ■ NAVAL-OFFICE, ALX. *Inward Entries*. Brig *Glory*, G. Richmond, and Ship *Fortune*, T. Halder, from London; Sloop *Dove*, S. Packard, New-York; Schooner *Polly*, T. West, Baltimore. *Cleared Outwards*. Ship *Astrea*, N. West, for Halifax and London; Schooner *Lottery*, Z. Mann, and Sloop *Hero*, J. Humphries, Baltimore; Snow *Resolution*, J. Gyllenspetz, Lisbon; Ship *Leda*, S. Dunn, Europe; Sloop *Sally*, P. Godfrey, Bermuda. ■ Letter to the Honorable the Representatives of the People of the State of New-York, re: a slow or absent restoration of trade since peace and independence... The decay of those manufactures which formerly made a part of our exports, together with the check agriculture has received from the advanced price of labour and the devastations of war, have been high prejudicial to the commerce of the State... No power is invested in the Representative Sovereignty of America to regulate trade, but that right is reserved to the respective states who cannot possibly use if for common benefit: 1). Because not being enabled to form treaties, trade cannot in their hands be made the basis of commercial impacts. 2). Because no regular system can be adopted by thirteen different Legislatures, pursuing different objects, and seeing the same object in different lights, and 3). Because if it were even to be presumed, that they would at all times and in every circumstance, sacrifice partial interests to the general god, yet the want of harmony in their measures, and a common force would for ever defeat their best intentions. Memorialists observe it will be necessary either that trade of the States continues to labour under all these inconveniences which arise from want of commercial treaties, or that the power of regulating trade be transferred to that Honorable Body... that these reflections are confirmed by daily experience, and that though they are well informed, no endeavours have been wanting on the part of the U.S. Congress, to procure such treaties... Memorialists pray the U.S. Congress be granted power to regulate trade... *By order of the Chamber*, JOHN ALSOP, President.

PRICES CURRENT, ALX. / Tobacco, 28s. per Ct. / Fine Flour, 28s. per Barrel. / Wheat, 6s. per Bushel. / Jamaica Spirits, 4/6 per Gallon. / Windward Rum, 3s. to 3/3 per Ditto. / Continental Rum, 2s. to 2/2 per Ditto. / Molasses, 1/6 per Ditto. / Muscovado Sugar, 38s. to 42s. per Ct. / Salt, 3s. per Bushel, by Retail. / Corn, 3s. per Bushel / Exchange, 40.

George-Town, May 19, 1785.
THE Ship *POTOMACK PLANTER*, Capt. RICHARD JOHNS, lying at George-Town, takes Tobacco consigned to Forrest and Stoddert, London, at Seven Pounds, sterling, per ton. She will sail early in June.
BENJAMIN STODDERT.

TO BE SOLD, IN FEE-SIMPLE, FOUR LOTS of GROUND on Princess-street, between Fairfax and Water streets, containing 24 feet front each, and 100 feet in depth, with the privilege of a 9 feet alley; also, 3 LOTS on Fairfax-street, between Princess and Oronoko streets, 22½ feet front each and 114 feet 5 inches in depth, with the privilege of the same alley.--One third of the purchase-money to be paid in three months, one third in six months, and the remainder the first of April 1786.--Bond with approved security will be required.--As to the situation of the Lots I shall only observe, the first four stand on the street leading to the public ferry and public warehouses. WILLIAM HUNTER, jun. ☞ If not sold before, they will be put up at Public Vendue on Saturday the 18th of June next, on the same terms. ALX, May 19, 1785 ■ On Saturday next, will be sold at the Vendue-Store, A Quantity of Irish linens, osnaburgs, paper-hangings, handkerchiefs, fustians, rum, muscovado sugar, with a variety of other articles. C. COPPER, Vendue-Master. ALX, May 19, 1785.

On Monday the 23d instant, will be sold at Public Vendue,

THE SCHOONER *MOLLY*, with all her tackle and apparel as she now lies at Conway's Wharf. She will carry about 400 barrels, is not more than 4 months old, remarkably strong built, and completely fitted for sea.--The terms of sale are one half cash, the remainder in two months, for which bond and security will be required. The inventory may be seen at the Vendue-Store.

C. COPPER, Vendue-Master.
ALX, May 19, 1785.

On Thursday the 26th instant, will be sold at Public Vendue,

THE Brigantine *TRITON* with all her tackle and apparel.--She is a strong well built vessel, burthen about 800 barrels, well fitted, a good sailer, and not more than 18 months old.--An inventory of her materials, &c. may be seen at the Vendue-Store.

C. COPPER, Vendue-Master.
ALX, May 18, 1785.

LOST in December last, an AUDITOR's CERTIFICATE, granted to the Subscriber for militia service as Lieutenant in Capt. Robert Sandford's company of Fairfax militia, amounting to Twenty-Two Pounds Eight Shillings, dated November 21, 1783, and signed by H. Randolph and J. Pendleton, jun.--All persons are forewarned from receiving the above described Certificate, as an affidavit to the loss of it has been made and lodged in the Auditor's-Office at Richmond, in order to obtain a new Certificate and stop the old one if ever it makes its appearance in that office, and to enable me to discover, by tracing it, the person who has found and secreted it. THOMSON MASON, Fairfax County, May 16, 1785 ■ TO BE LET, A PART of a HOUSE, situated on King-street, and second door from the corner of Royal-street, suitable for either a wholesale or retail store, with a counting-room and cellar. Any person inclining to hire, may have it fitted agreeable to his liking, and have possession about the first of June next.--It is a good stand for business.--For terms apply to WILLIAM M'KNIGHT, ALX, May 17, 1785 ■ **RUM**, Of an excellent Quality, made and sold by the Hogshead or larger Quantity, cheap for Cash or Country Produce, by WILLIAM LYLES and COMPANY, ALX, May 17, 1785 ■ Just arrived, and to be sold by **Herbert and Potts**, At their store on the corner of Fairfax and Queen streets, a general assortment of MERCHANDISE, consisting of the following articles, viz. Superfine, second and coarse broadcloths of a variety of colours, calamancoes, tammies, shalloons, duroys, yard-wide and 7/8 Irish linens of all prices, calicoes, chintzes, black and white satins, lustrings, modes, persians, sarsenets, black, white and coloured Barcelona handkerchiefs, velverets, corduroys, drawboys, white cotton, linen and worsted furniture checks, cotton and silk gown patterns, cotton stripes, striped Hollands, pillow fustians and jeans, buckram, twist, Marseilles quilting, plain, corded and figured demities, garterings, Manchester tapes, striped ditto, silk, cotton and thread stockings, gauzes, cambricks, lawns, plain, striped and tamboured muslins, white cotton counterpanes, black silk, breeches patterns, ribbons, sheetings, osnaburgs, German linen, bed ticks and bunts, checks, drillings, men and womens' white and coloured gloves and mitts, a large assortment of buttons, buckles, spurs, sleeve-buttons, stock and pad locks, knob, cupboard, book-case, desk, drawer, chest, portmanteau and saddle-bag ditto, desk-furniture, polished and japanned snuffers, tobacco and snuff boxes, spectacles with steel and paper cases, chests with carpenters' tools complete, knives and forks, files of every kind, pins, Whitechapel and common needles, darning needles, leather, paper and brass inkpots, brass and iron candlesticks, tea-kettles, coffee-pots, chafing-dishes, curry-combs and brushes, sweeping, dusting, paint, clothes, hearth, shoe and carriage brushes, horsewhips, men and boys' fine and coarse hats, iron and brass wire sieves, hair sifters, thimbles, shaving-boxes, ivory and horn combs, comb-brushes, shoemakers and carpenters' hammers, lathing hammers, steel and iron plate handsaws, jack, smoothing and moulding planes, coopers' adzes, dowelling mills and bits, drawing-knives, tap and bung borers, spike and small gimlets, inch and half, inch, 5/8 and ½ inch augers, chisels and gouges assorted, plane-irons, steelyards, crates with earthen and stone ware, brass skillets, castings, brass cocks, pepper, coffee and corn mills, sickles and scythes, spades and shovels, 20d. 12d. 10d. 8d. 4d. and 3d. nails, writing and letter paper, quills, powder and shot, saddles and bridles, girths, surcingles, stirrup leathers and saddlestraps, saddlecloths, china in sets, white, brown and coloured threads, pocket-books, cinnamon, mace, cloves and nutmegs, pepper, ginger, watch strings, chains, keys and seals, breast pins, linen handkerchiefs, assorted boxes of cutlery, &c. men and womens' leather shoes, marble chimney pieces and side-board slabs, a pair of very elegant pier looking-glasses, hair pins and gimped fringe.--Also a number of other articles. ALX, May 18, 1785.

Westmoreland, May 1, 1785.
FOR LONDON,
To sail early in June,

THE copper bottom Ship *STANLEY*, British built, with a Mediterranean pass to the newest cut, will be ready in a few days to take on board Tobacco in Yeocomoco, on consignment to,
T. BLANE.

ALX, May 19, 1785.
SUCH as may incline to ship Tobacco to the address of Mr. BLANE, will please to forward their orders to their obedient servant,
WILLIAM HUNTER, jun.

ALX, May 17, 1785. As the ALX LATIN SCHOOL has been understood by some to be private, and confined to a few families, I take this method of informing the public that any number of scholars will be admitted, and proper care always taken to provide teachers in proportion to the growth of the school. Gentlemen who send their children to this school, may depend that I shall give every assistance in my power to forward them in their education, as I am fully determined to co-operate with those gentlemen, who have evidenced so warm a desire to establish a permanent and respectable school in ALX. The house in which the school is at present taught, is convenient, and in a healthy situation, a little removed from the hurry and bustle of the town. It is expected we shall in a little time be able to give encouragement to teachers in various branches of literature, as a very considerable sum is already subscribed for building a school-house upon a lot of ground generously bestowed to the public for that purpose. The terms of admittance may be known by applying to WILLIAM M'WHIR. ■ Just imported in the last vessels from Europe, and to be sold by **Randle Mitchell and Son**, At their store on the east side of Fairfax-street, near Mr. William Herbert's dwelling-house; the following general assortment of GOODS and MERCHANDISE, which they will sell on the very lowest terms for cash or country produce, viz. IRISH sheeting linens, 7/8 and yard-wide ditto, osnaburgs and ticklenburgs, Russia sheetings and drillings, brown and white dowlas, 6-4 and 7-4 bed bunts and ticks, best patterns of chintzes and calicoes, a great variety of printed cottons, printed linens, diapers, cambricks and lawns, 5-4, 6-4, and yard-wide muslins, book muslins, diaper tablecloths, men, women, and boys' thread and cotton stockings, flowered and plain gauzes and gauze handkerchiefs, India, bandano and silk ditto, romal and check linen ditto, spotted and bordered linen ditto, plain and bordered kenting ditto, black taffetas and persians, blue, green and striped ell-wide and narrow persians, modes, black and coloured pelongs and satins, blue, green and cloth-coloured fine cassimer cloths, India nankeens, plain and striped mantua silks, 6-4 and 7-4 fine and superfine broadcloths, pillow fustians and jeans of all colours, jeanets, corduroys, velvets, velverets, sagathees, dorseys, moreens for womens' petticoats, white cotton Marseilles for ditto, white jeans, demities, shalloons, rattinets, durants, tammies, calamancoes, camblets, men and womens' worsted stockings, threads, bobbins and tapes of all kinds, silk and cotton laces and ferrets, a great assortment of broad and narrow ribbons, fine wilton cloths, black and coloured Barcelona silk handkerchiefs, cravats, sewing silks of all colours, broad and narrow worsted bindings, coat and breast wrought, plain, metal and plated buttons, coat, breast, silk and hair ditto, womens' fine and coarse Leghorn hats, womens' worsted shoes, writing-paper, ink-powder, playing-cards, wafers, wrapping-paper, pasteboard, whalebone, wool and cotton cards, men and boys' castor hats, men and boys' felt ditto, table knives and forks, penknives of all sorts, pocket and cuteau knives, rasors, womens' scissors, sleeve-buttons plain and stone set, best English and German steel, men and womens' saddles, iron pots, plated, plain and wrought men and womens' buckles, pins and needles, assorted, spectacles, coffee-mills, copper coffee-pots and sauce-pans, shoe-tacks and awl-blades, an assortment of queen's ware, cups, saucers, plates, dishes, bowls, &c. an assortment of glass-ware tumblers, decanters, glasses, &c. 7 by 6, 7 by 9, and 8 by 10 window-glass, an assortment of brushes, plough-lines, traces, halters, leather collars, bedcords, madder, redwood, allum and copperas, glue, hair-sieves, an assortment of ironmongery, best indigo, allspice, pepper, cinnamon, mace, nutmegs, cloves, mustard, soap, candles, muscovado and loaf sugars, brandy, Jamaica spirits, common rum, Teneriffe and port wines, claret in bottles, bohea and green teas, 8d. 10d. 12d. and 20d. nails, frying-pans, handsaws, hammers, chisels, &c. an assortment of saddlery of most kinds, gunpowder and shot, &c.&c. ☞ The low terms they intend to do business on, puts it out of their power to credit; but they hope those who purchase from them, will find it their interest to pay cash. They have their goods on such terms as to be able to supply any country store in the wholesale way greatly to their advantage. ■ THIRTY DOLLARS REWARD. ON the evening of the 9th inst. was taken up at the Stage-Office, a LETTER directed to the Subscribers. Whoever discovers the person or persons, so that they be brought to justice, shall receive the above reward. JOHN DUNDAS and CO., ALX, May 17, 1785 ■ To be sold or rented for a term of years, A HORSE SNUFF-MILL, in excellent order, and built on the most approved plan; also, a complete set of implements for carrying on the tobacco manufacturing business. Any person inclined to purchase or rent, may depend on a great share of custom, as the Subscriber intends leaving off the business, and there is at present no person who carries it on in this place; also, a TWO-STORY BRICK HOUSE, contiguous to the Mill, with two good rooms on a floor, and very agreeably situated.--He will also sell, or rent on ground-rent for ever, several LOTS of GROUND, well situated, and in that part of the town which has the appearance of a more rapid improvement than any other.--The terms will be made easy to the purchasers, and if rented the price will be moderate. JACOB COX, ALX, May 18, 1785 ■ ☞ A great Variety of BLANKS, printed on good Paper, may be had at the Printing-Office.

Page 4. Poetry. "An Evening SOLILOQUY." ■ WILLIAM HARTSHORNE and COMPANY offer for sale goods just imported in the Ship *Mary*, and several Lots well situated in ALX may be had on ground-rent [see like ad Vol. II No. 67] ■ ROBERT SIM gives notice that he is not quitting his public house and has recently supplied it [see like ad Vol. II No. 67] ■ **James Hendricks and Co.** will have ready for sale in a few days an assortment of dry goods [see like ad Vol. II No. 67] ■ **Richard Conway**, has for sale salt, Lisbon and Oporto wines [see like ad Vol. II No. 67] ■ WILLOUGHBY TEBBS, Executor of the Last Will and Testament of Foushee Tebbs, has for sale slaves and several tracts of land [see like ad Vol. II No. 67] ■ ALEXANDER WHITE, Woodville, has for sale a 355-acre farm in Frederick County [see like ad Vol. II No. 67] ■ WILLIAM COURTS offers horse CUB for breeding [see like ad Vol. II No. 67] ■ **Robinson, Sanderson and Rumney**, have for sale European Goods [see like ad Vol. II No. 67] ■ **Philip Dalby**, has goods for sale at his store on the corner of Royal and Cameron streets [see like ad Vol. II No. 67] ■ **Daniel and Isaac M'Pherson**, Have just imported in the *Cesar*, Capt. Atkinson, from Whitehaven, an assortment of GOODS, among which are the following articles, viz. WHITE and coloured jeans and jeanets, linens, checks, check handkerchiefs, bed-ticks, durants, duroys, calamancoes, osnaburgs, cottons and calicoes of different kinds, bindings and ferrets of different kinds, striped hollands, black modes, fans, mens' and womens' gloves, sewing silk, Irish linens, sheetings, a variety of hardware, scythes, sickles, nails, spades, shovels, iron pots and ovens, loaf sugar, &c.&c. all which they will sell on reasonable terms for cash or country produce. ALX, May 12, 1785 ■ **Jesse Taylor**, has just imported in the Ship *Martha*, Lisbon wine, etc. [see like ad Vol. II No. 67] ■ DAVID GRIFFITH offers for sale about 200 lots of ground adjoining ALX [see like ad Vol. II No. 63] ■ DAVID KENNEDY, Berkeley County, offers reward for return of runaway Irish servant lad named Philip Lougherey [see like ad Vol. II No. 67] ■ M'Murray's Maps of the U.S. are ready for delivery to subscribers [see like ad Vol. II No. 64] ■ ALX: Printed by GEORGE RICHARDS, and COMPANY, at their Printing-Office on Fairfax-street--by whom Advertisements, &c. are thankfully received for this Paper,--and where Printing is performed with Care and Expedition.

1785/05/26, Vol. II No. 69

Page 1. WILLIAM LYLES and COMPANY has rum for sale [see like ad Vol. II No. 68] ■ **T. BLANE**, Westmoreland, has for sale the copper-bottom Ship *Stanley* [see like ad Vol. II No. 68] ■ Property of the late Mr. THOMAS MAGRUDER, deceased, for sale in George-Town [see like ad Vol. II No. 67] ■ ROBERT SIM gives notice that he is not quitting his public house and has recently supplied it [see like ad Vol. II No. 67] ■ WILLIAM HARTSHORNE and COMPANY offer for sale goods just imported in the Ship *Mary*, and several Lots well situated in ALX may be had on ground-rent [see like ad Vol. II No. 67] ■ WILLIAM M'KNIGHT has for rent part of a house on King-street [see like ad Vol. II No. 68] ■ **James Hendricks and Co.** will have ready for sale in a few days an assortment of dry goods [see like ad Vol. II No. 67] ■ **Richard Conway**, has for sale salt, Lisbon and Oporto wines [see like ad Vol. II No. 67] ■ **Robinson, Sanderson and Rumney**, have for sale European Goods [see like ad Vol. II No. 67] ■ **Jesse Taylor**, has just imported in the Ship *Martha*, Lisbon wine, etc. [see like ad Vol. II No. 67] ■ ☞ A great Variety of BLANKS, printed on good Paper, may be had at the Printing-Office. ■ **Philip Dalby**, has goods for sale at his store on the corner of Royal and Cameron streets [see like ad Vol. II No. 67] ■ **Daniel and Isaac M'Pherson**, Have just imported in the *Cesar*, Capt. Atkinson, from Whitehaven, an assortment of goods [see like ad Vol. II No. 68] ■ BENJAMIN STODDERT will take on tobacco for Ship *[Potomack] Planter*, to sail early in June [see like ad Vol. II No. 68] ■ WILLIAM HUNTER, jun. has for sale in fee-simple four lots on Princess-street [see like ad Vol. II No. 68] ■ ALEXANDER WHITE, Woodville, has for sale a 355-acre farm in Frederick County [see like ad Vol. II No. 67].

Page 2.

LONDON, March 15. They write from the Hague that the States General Assembly, having collected the votes of the Seven provinces relative to the Emperor's demands, have given their ultimate answer: No, declaring they cannot comply with such hard conditions. Copies were given all foreign ambassadors at the Hague, and also to Paris and the several Courts with whom the Dutch are allied, so that affairs are now hastily coming to a crisis. **March 19.** As Mr. England is about to take Mr. Ireland into partnership, *share and share alike*, it is but fair Ireland assist in paying some *small* debts of honor of Mr. England's--a few trifles not amounting to more than 150 millions! **March 25.** The French Court has ordered preparation of an encampment for a considerable body of troops in French Flanders. The King of Prussia has begun encampments. The Empress of Russia's intentions are not known, but no doubt will follow the example of her neighbours; even the Turks begin to march troops towards the Bender. From all this, there is reason to expect a general war in a few months. ■ **CHARLESTON** (South Carolina) **April 24.** From a **Philadelphia** gentleman to his friend in this city: [Elements of a rapturous appreciation of one Dr. Moyes, lecturing to numerous ladies and gentlemen in the College Hall, and on other occasions. - Eds.] To a lament that we know so little of the evolution of our ideas in infancy, or the first act of reasoning, the doctor felt we begin to think earlier than expected, and lose our early ideas by after impressions. Blind since 18 months old, he remembers having a plaid gown, and seeing a boy driving his herd to pasture; perhaps he can remember that because he has seen nothing since to obliterate those ideas. Speaking of Dr. Priestly's doctrine of the soul sleeping after death until the resurrection, commented he "startled from this opinion as if it involved something like annihilation," for he enjoyed so much pleasure in thinking he could not bear the thought of suspending it for 1000-10,000 years. He speculated on future pleasures of the soul: we live before birth only with the one sense of feeling, and thereafter with five senses. Who knows how many more may be added after death? A single sense more may enable us to comprehend spirit as easily as we now comprehend light and sound! After this he dwelt on the wonderful powers and faculties of the mind, particularly memory. It brings us nearer our duty than any other. The faculty of recalling the past is only exceeded by that of the Deity--which enables foreseeing the future. ■ **SALEM, May 3.** The Constitution declares that "the Liberty of the Press is essential to the Security of freedom in a State." But if a legislature lays such taxes on the Press, that amounts to a prohibition of *Reading* by one person, they can impose taxes which withhold it from *10,000* or more. Thus the lately passed *Stamp Act* will prevent some citizens from being informed, thus tending to destroy Freedom, and thereby a flagrant violation of the natural and constitutional rights of the people. Since our last, several good customers have signified their intention of discontinuing taking this paper on commencement of the *Stamp Act*; one declared he would rather pay double stamp duty to *increase* newspaper circulation, than submit to an act which will inevitably tend to their *suppression*. Mr. Gill, late Publisher of the Continental Journal in Boston, notified his customers in last Thursday's papers: "The subscriber (not being fond of *Stamp Acts*, having experienced the ill effects of two heretofore) informs his late customers, that he has discontinued the Continental Journal, &c. JOHN GILL." ■ **BOSTON, April 18.** The General Court in their last session was pleased to pass a Stamp Act, a name heretofore held in an opprobrious light, and highly disgustful to us. The two-thirds of a penny stamp on newspapers will see the Poor deprived of the entertainment and political knowledge therein, and tend towards a majority of inhabitants of the States being politically ignorant. It is hoped the Honorable Members of the General Court will reconsider the clause, repeal same, and free the public from that bar to political wisdom. A correspondent observes that an additional duty on tea--6d on common, 1/ on the best kinds--together with an additional shilling per gallon of rum would afford government a much larger revenue than can possibly be raised by the stamp act. The act is thought by many will be attended with more cost and trouble, than it will yield profit. ■ **ALX, May 26.** Last Saturday the *Henry*, Capt. Dennison, arrived here from Cadiz.--He informs, that the British Consul there had received Letters from Tangiers, mentioning that the Vessel bound to this Port from Cadiz, and taken and carried in there, had been ordered by the Emperor of Morocco to be delivered up, and the People set at Liberty; and that no more American Vessels were to be molested by his Subjects, until it was known whether the United States were disposed to be *friendly* or not. ■ Last Friday Francis Johnson and John Montgomery were convicted of Petty Larceny, and ordered to receive Thirty Lashes at the Public Whipping-Post. On the Afternoon of the same Day a Cart with Dry Goods, was robbed on the Road to Colchester of a Trunk.--Johnson and Montgomery are both taken up and committed to the Gaol here as Perpetrators of the Robbery.--A great Part of the Goods were found on Montgomery. ■ NAVAL-OFFICE, ALX. *Inward Entries.* Brig *Glasgow*, J. Patrick, from St. Ubes; Brig *Eglington*, P. Woodrow, Liverpool; Ship *Henry*, J. Dennison, Cadiz. *Cleared Outwards.* Brig *Zephyr*, B. Lee, for l'Orient; Brig *King [Taminy]*, O. Goodwin, Gottenburg; Ship *Hope*, T. Barnard, Amsterdam; Sloop *Phoebe*, J. Cartwright, Barbadoes; Sloop *Charming Polly*, J. Elwood, Philadelphia.

ALX, May 17, 1785.

THIS Day, and at this Town, pursuant to the Act of the General Assembly of the Commonwealth of Virginia for opening and extending the Navigation of Potomack River, and pursuant to the Act of the General Assembly of the State of Maryland for the same Purpose, there was a general Meeting of the Subscribers to the Undertaking, who proceeded to the Choice of a Chairman, and elected Daniel Carroll, Esq., to that Office, and appointed Charles Lee, Esq., Clerk of the Meeting. The Books that had been opened for receiving Subscriptions at the City of Richmond, at the Towns of ALX and Winchester, in Virginia; and at the City of Annapolis, at George-Town, and Frederick-Town, in the State of Maryland, being produced and examined, and Subscriptions therein appeared to be as follow, viz.

In the Richmond Book, One Hundred Shares;
In the ALX Books, One Hundred Thirty-Five Shares;
In the Winchester Books, Thirty-One Shares;
In the Annapolis Books, Seventy-Three Shares;
In the George-Town Books, Forty-Two Shares;
In the Frederick-Town Books, Twenty-Two Shares;

Amounting in all to Four Hundred and Three Shares, which mad a Capital of Forty Thousand and Three Hundred Pounds, Sterling Money.

On a Motion made and seconded, *Resolved*, That the Subscribers now present in Person, together with those represented by Proxy, proceed to the Choice of a President and Directors of the Potomack Company, and that the President and Directors now to be chosen, shall continue in Office until the First Monday in the Month of August, which shall be in the Year One Thousand Seven Hundred and Eighty Six.

Resolved, That at every General Meeting, in taking the Votes of the Proprietors, each Proprietor shall give in his Vote or Votes at the Clerk's Table in Writing, and where the Vote or Votes shall be given by Proxy, that the Name of each Constituent be also inserted.

Ordered, That Charles Simms and James Keith be a Committee, to examine the Deputations to act and vote as Proxy, and to make Report thereof to this Meeting; who have made Report accordingly,

Resolved, That the Deputations from Thomas Blackburn to William Brown, from Thomas Johnston to Abraham Faw, and from John Lynn to Abraham Faw, to act and vote for them respectively, appearing to have been executed before one Witness only, are illegal and insufficient, and that the said Thomas Blackburn, Thomas Johnston, and John Lynn, be not admitted to vote by their respective Proxies aforesaid.

The Proprietors present in Person, as well as the absent Proprietors by their respective Proxies, having given in their Votes in the Manner beforementioned for the Choice of a President and Four Directors of the Potomack Company, and the said Votes being duly examined and accounted, a Majority of Votes was in Favor of his Excellency George Washington to be President, and in Favor of Thomas Johnston, Thomas Sim Lee, John Fitzgerald, and George Gilpin, Esquires, to be Directors; and thereupon his Excellency George Washington was declared by the Chairman to be elected President, and the said Thomas Johnston, Thomas Sim Lee, John Fitzgerald and George Gilpin, Directors of the Potomack Company.

Ordered, That the names of the Proprietors who were present in proper Person, and also of those who voted and acted by Proxy at this Meeting, with the Names of such Proxies respectively, be inserted on the Minutes.

Present in proper Person. His Excellency George Washington, Daniel Carroll, Robert Peter, Samuel Davidson, William Deakins, jun., Charles Worthington, Thomas Beall of George, Henry Townsend, James M. Lingan, Benjamin Stoddert, John Boucher, Bernard O'Neill, Lyonel Bradstreet, Thomas Cramphin, George Digges, James Johnston, Abraham Faw, Horatio Gates, Peter B. Bruin, Edward Beeson, Edward Smith, Joseph Holmes, John Gunnell, Charles Little, Roger West, Lund Washington, William Hepburn, Henry Lyles, William Lowry, Benjamin Shreve, John Harper, William Scott, Daniel M'Pherson, William Brown, William Hartshorne, George Gilpin, Leven Powell, Charles Simms, Robert T. Hooe, William Ellzey, Samuel M. Brown, Joseph Janney, Daniel Roberdeau, John Allison, Baldwin Dade, Benjamin Dulany, James Lawrason, James Keith, Alexander Henderson, David Stewart, William Lyles, John Potts, jun., William Herbert, Dennis Ramsay, Richard Conway, John Fitzgerald and Charles Lee.

Present by Proxy.--Jaquelin Ambler, Agent for the Commonwealth of Virginia, by his Excellency George Washington, Joseph W. Harrison by Dennis Ramsay, Richard Harrison by Robert T. Hooe, Thomas Lewis by Charles Simms, Robert Macky by Edward Smith, Henry Ridgely, jun., by William Deakins, jun., William Baley by William Deakins, jun., George Scott by Robert Peter, and James Rumsey by Peter B. Bruin.--Also, Baker Johnston, George Schnitzell, Thomas S. Lee, Joseph Chapline, Philip Thomas, Thomas Beaty, Joseph Sim, John F. Ameling, Thomas Gauntt, Thomas Hawkins and Patrick S. Smith, severally and respectively by Abraham Faw; also, Alexander White, Philip Pendleton, William Drew, Moses Hunter, William Bready, William M'Kewan, James Campbell, Henry Bedinger, George Scott, George Hite, Walter Baker, Abraham Shepherd, Benjamin Beiler, and Cornelius Wynkoop, severally and respectively by Horatio Gates.

Resolved, That the Writings concerning the Deputations to act and vote as Proxy, be delivered, together with the Subscription Books and the Minutes of this Meeting, to the President and Directors; and that a general Meeting of the Potomack Company be held at George-Town, in the State of Maryland, on the First Monday in August next.

CHARLES LEE, Clerk of the Meeting.

Page 3.

PRICES CURRENT, ALX. / Tobacco, 28s. to 29s. per Ct. / Fine Flour, 28s. per Barrel. / Wheat, 6s. per Bushel. / Jamaica Spirits, 4/6 per Gallon. / Windward Rum, 3s. per Ditto. / Continental Rum, 2s. to 2/2 per Ditto. / Molasses, 1/6 per Ditto. / Muscovado Sugar, 35s. to 38s. per Ct. / Salt, 3s. per Bushel, by Retail. / Corn, 3s. per Bushel / Exchange, 40.

☞ JUST RECEIVED, and to be SOLD by the Printers hereof, "A REPLY to the Address to the Roman Catholics of the United States of America--By the Author of a Letter to the Roman Catholics of the City of Worcester."--Also, The Discovery, Settlement and present State of KENTUCKEY, containing an Essay towards the Topography and Natural History of that Country, to which is prefixed a new and correct Map of that Country, drawn from accurate Surveys.--By JOHN FILSON. ■ TO BE SOLD, At the Printing-Office, A Variety of Blank Books, consisting of Ledgers, Journals, Cash-Books, Letter-Books, &c.&c. Also, Stoughton's Bitters, Anderson's Pills, Daffy's

Elixir, Balsam of Honey, Squire's Elixir, Bateman's Drops, Godfrey's Cordial, &c.&c.&c. ■ **Robert Broket**, From Ireland, BEGS leave to offer his services to the public, as STONECUTTER and BRICKLAYER.--He can cut, engrave and polish marble for chimney pieces, &c.--Plans and drawings may also be done by him, agreeable to the taste of any who may please to employ him. Any commands shall be strictly attended to, and executed with despatch and care; and he flatters himself, will be done in such a manner as to merit future encouragement.--Inquire at Mr. M'Gachen's. ALX, May 24, 1785. ■ ALL persons indebted to the estate of Mr. THOMAS KIRKPATRICK, deceased, are requested to make immediate payment, or their accounts and bonds will be put into the hands of an attorney; and all those who have claims against the estate are desired to bring them in, that they may be adjusted and paid. ROBERT ADAM, ROBERT M'CREA, JOHN GIBSON, WILLIAM HUNTER, jun., Executors, ALX, May 12, 1785 ■ WILLIAM COURTS offers horse CUB for breeding [see like ad Vol. II No. 67].

THIRTY DOLLARS REWARD.

RAN away from Cuthbert Harrison, about the 20th of April last, a NEGRO FELLOW about 21 years of age, named DICK, remarkably stout, tall and well made, of a very black complexion; he has been much used by horses and is a good waggoner, but fond of spiritous liquor, and when he drinks a little too much appears stupid, drowsy and very much inclined to sleep; it is supposed he is making for Pennsylvania, as he was heard to say that the Negroes in that State had been set free; he was cloathed in the usual manner, and believe he wears a yarn or worsted cap. Whoever takes up said Slave and secures him in any gaol, and gives notice to the Subscribers, so that he is recovered again, shall receive TEN DOLLARS, if in the neighbourhood or 10 miles from home, TWENTY DOLLARS if 20 miles from home, and if 30 miles or out of this State, the above reward, and all reasonable expences paid if delivered to the Subscribers living on Goose-Creek, on the road leading from ALX to Snicker's-Gap.

LEVEN POWELL,
SIMON TRIPLETT.

Loudon County, May 20, 1785.

THE Trustees of the George-Town Academy, have come to the absolute determination, to commence the DRAWING of the LOTTERY on Thursday the 9th day of June next, and what tickets may then be on hand will be taken by the Trustees on account of the school.--All those who have any of the tickets unsold, are desired to return them to the Managers, at least five days before the drawing. ☞ On the same day will be sold at Public Vendue, a large TWO-STORY STONE HOUSE, with the Lot on which it stands, convenient situated on the main street near the centre of George-Town. ROBERT PETER, BENJAMIN STODDERT, WILLIAM DEAKINS, jun., Managers, George-Town, May 20, 1785. ■ **Leertouwer, Huyman, and Huiberts**, Have left in the care of Messieurs HOOE and HARRISON, for sale, the following GOODS, viz. WINDOW-GLASS 8 by 10, wood-axes, shovels and tongs, cutting-knives, scythes, frying-pans, chafing dishes, bird shot, gin in cases, French cordials, &c.&c. ALX, May 20, 1785. ■ SAMUEL CANBY, Leesburg, offers for sale or exchange tracts in Monongalia and Jefferson counties [see like ad Vol. II No. 64] ■ THE Parish of Norborne in the County of Berkeley, being at present without a Minister of the Protestant Episcopal Church, legally inducted, the vestry of the said Parish have therefore determined to proceed to the appointment of one, at the Church in the Parish aforesaid, on or before the first day of October next, pursuant to an act of the last session of the General Assembly. Published by order of the Vestry, THOMAS RUTHERFORD, MORGAN MORGAN, Church-wardens, Berkeley County, May 16, 1785 ■ George-Town, May 20, 1785, WHEREAS my Wife MARGARET MAGUIRE has absented herself from my bed and board, I do hereby forewarn all persons from dealing with her on my account as I will not pay any debts of her contracting. PATRICK MAGUIRE. ☞ I will sell, on Thursday the 9th day of June next, to the highest bidder, THREE valuable LOTS in this Town, well situated for business, one of which is well improved.

A CHARTER WANTED,

For the *EGLINGTON*,

A Fine new British built Brigantine, of 360 hogsheads of tobacco burthen, with a Mediterranean pass.--If a Charter should not offer soon, she will sail in about two months for Liverpool, and will take 150 hogsheads on freight, at Seven Pounds, sterling, per ton, with liberty of consignment.--She is a strong, tight, good vessel, and will be ready to receive tobacco in 8 or 10 days.--For terms apply to Mr. JAMES MUSCHETT, Merchant in Dumfries, or the Subscriber.

H. STEUART.

Loudon County, May 23, 1785.

DAVID GRIFFITH offers for sale about 200 lots of ground adjoining ALX [see like ad Vol. II No. 63] ■ JOHN FORMAN offers for breeding horsè *OBSCURITY* [see like ad Vol. II No. 60] ■ WILLOUGHBY TEBBS, Executor of the Last Will and Testament of Foushee Tebbs, has for sale slaves and several tracts of land [see like ad Vol. II No. 67] ■ RAN away from the Subscriber on the 15th instant a tawny NEGRO WOMAN, named ANN, about 19 years of age, and of a middle size.--Also, ran away on the 18th instant, another wench, called BET, about 32 years of age, of nearly the same complexion.--They took with them, a variety of cloathing, among which were the following, viz. One Indian Persian gown, two calico ditto, and one striped cotton and silk ditto, &c. Whoever takes up said slaves, and brings them to the subscriber, shall have a satisfactory reward, besides what the law allows. RAPHAEL BOORMAN, Cornwallis's Neck, Maryland, May 19, 1785.

Page 4. Poetry. "SOLILOQUY on a Spring Morning." ■ **Herbert and Potts**, at their store on the corner of Fairfax and Queen streets, have for sale a general assortment of MERCHANDISE [see like ad Vol. II No. 68] ■ THOMSON MASON seeks lost auditor's certificate [see like ad Vol. II No. 68] ■ ☞ A few Barrels of choice LAMPBLACK may be had at the Printing-Office. ■ **Randle Mitchell and Son**, have goods for sale just imported in the last vessels from Europe [see like ad Vol. II No. 68] ■ JOHN DUNDAS and CO. offer reward for return of a letter directed to the subscribers [see like ad Vol. II No. 68] ■ GEORGE RALLS offers for sale 400 acres of land in Loudon County [see like ad Vol. II No. 67] ■ **Henry Lyles**, has for sale at his store on Fairfax-street, goods listed [see like ad Vol. II No. 67] ■ JACOB COX offers for sale or rent a horse snuff-mill and a two-story brick house contiguous to the mill [see like ad Vol. II No. 68] ■ WILLIAM M'WHIR solicits additional students of the ALX Latin School [see like ad Vol. II No. 68] ■ ALX: Printed by GEORGE RICHARDS, and COMPANY, at their Printing-Office on Fairfax-street--by whom Advertisements, &c. are thankfully received for this Paper,--and where Printing is performed with Care and Expedition.

1785/06/02, Vol. II No. 70

Page 1. **Herbert and Potts**, at their store on the corner of Fairfax and Queen streets, have for sale a general assortment of MERCHANDISE [see like ad Vol. II No. 68] ■ JOHN FILSON is selling new books on Roman Catholics [see like ad Vol. II No. 69] ■ The Printing-Office is selling blank books, ledgers, journals, etc. [see like ad Vol. II No. 69] ■ WILLIAM LYLES and CO., is selling rum [see like ad Vol. II No. 68] ■ WILLIAM HARTSHORNE and COMPANY offer for sale goods just imported in the Ship *Mary*, and several Lots well situated in ALX may be had on ground-rent [see like ad Vol. II No. 67] ■ JACOB COX offers for sale or rent a horse snuff-mill and a two-story brick house contiguous to the mill [see like ad Vol. II No. 68] ■ THOMSON MASON seeks lost auditor's certificate [see like ad Vol. II No. 68] ■ WILLIAM M'KNIGHT has for rent part of a house on King-street [see like ad Vol. II No. 68] ■ ☞ A few Barrels of choice LAMPBLACK may be had at the Printing-Office. ■ T. BLANE, Westmoreland, has for sale the copper-bottom Ship *Stanley* [see like ad Vol. II No. 68] ■ **Daniel and Isaac M'Pherson**, Have just imported in the *Cesar*, Capt. Atkinson, from Whitehaven, an assortment of goods [see like ad Vol. II No. 68] ■ The George-Town LOTTERY will commence drawing on Thursday the 9th day of June next [see like ad Vol. II No. 69] ■ H. STEUART and JAMES MUSCHETT seek charter for new Brigantine *Eglington* [see like ad Vol. II No. 69] ■ ☞ A great Variety of BLANKS, printed on good Paper, may be had at the Printing-Office.

Page 2.

LONDON, March 21. The Irish Parliament, in consequence of Mr. Orde's propositions, have imposed new taxes amounting to 56,000£ per year. This was carried by surprise in the moment of good humour, and a formidable opposition will form in Ireland to any material alteration. The Duke of Rutland has wrote to the minister asking to be recalled in the event of proposition alterations, or not being finally adjusted this session. We cannot control the Irish Parliament, nor dictate on what materials they shall lay duties; are not our iron and steel in danger--if the Irish import duty free from Russia or Sweden--whilst we, foolishly enough since American ingratitude is confirmed, continue to load them with ponderous duties ... Kirwall and other northern villages will petition against the Irish trade bill. This petition may be termed an *aurora borealis*, expected to *illustrate* the business. ■ **KINGSTON,** (*Jamaica*) **March 26.** *From the Bahama Gazette of February 12, 1875.* Best informed opinion is that Parliament will not allow the Americans the least intercourse with our West India islands, other than in British bottoms; that trade between Great Britain and the United States will be equally free to both; that all trade between them and our continental colonies will be entirely prohibited--in other words, that the present regulations prescribed by the King in Council, will be adopted by the legislature. There is no doubt British shipping and resources are fully sufficient for the regular supply of our colonies. Regard for the national welfare dictates pursuing every measure that can afford employment to our own seamen. ■ **HALIFAX** (*Nova Scotia*) **April 26.** By his Excellency JOHN PARR, Captain General and Commander in Chief, in and over his Majesty's Province of Nova Scotia, the islands of St. John and Cape Breton, and their dependencies, Vice Admiral of the same. **A PROCLAMATION.** WHEREAS it has been represented to me that many frauds and impositions have been committed and a clandestine trade carried out by United States vessels, under pretence of importing provisions into this province: I do therefore, with consent and advice of his Majesty's Council, forbid importing all kinds of provisions beginning 30 days from now, except in vessels of his Majesty's subjects, and navigated according to law. Collectors of his Majesty's Customs, Revenue Officers, and others whom it may concern, are to take notice and govern themselves accordingly. Given, etc., at Halifax, April 25, the 25th year of his Majesty's reign. **J. PARR** By his Excellency's command, Rich. Bulkley. GOD SAVE THE KING. ■ **WORCESTER, May 12.** Regarding driving British factors from this Commonwealth: let them be served as Britain serves us--every British factor settling here paying a 10-15% duty on all his imported goods. Better than disturbing the public tranquility, we have a legal right to do this, and will be considered just. ■ **NEW YORK, May 16.** A gentleman on board the *Empress of China* has furnished us with an account of their reception in China, as taken from his journal. Last July 17 we made the island of Java, anchoring in the Straits of Sunda the following evening. We were happy to find there two ships of our good allies, the French. The Commodore, Mons. D'Ordelin and his officers welcomed us in a most affectionate manner. As his own ship was immediately bound for Canton, he invited us to go in company. We cheerfully accepted, and he gave us his night and day signals, and instructions for navigating the China seas should we become separated. Arriving at Macao August 23, the French Consul for China and others of his nation came aboard to congratulate and welcome us to that part of the world, and introducing the Americans to the Portuguese Governor there. The little time we were there was entirely taken up by the good offices of the Consul, the gentlemen of his nation, and those of the Swedes and Imperialists--other Europeans having repaired for Canton. We finished our outbound voyage three days later. Before anchoring, we saluted the shipping in the river with 13 guns, answered by the Commodores of the European nations, each of whom, sent an officer to compliment us on our arrival. These visits were returned by the Captain and Supercargoes in the afternoon, who were again saluted by the ships as they finished their visit. The French assisted us in coming to safe and convenient moorings, furnished us part of their bankfall, and insisted we share their Canton quarters until we were settled. Arriving at Canton August 30, and the following two days, we were visited by Chinese merchants and chiefs of the several European establishments--treated by them in all respects as a free and independent nation. The Chinese were very indulgent to us and happy in the contemplation of a new people, opening to them a fresh source of commerce to their extensive Empire. After four months there, experiencing from all hands every possible attention, we set sail for America December 28, and happily arrived here on the 11th instant. ■ **PHILADELPHIA, May 21.** His Excellency William Greene, Esq., is elected Governor and the Honorable Jabez Bowen, Esq., Lieutenant Governor of Rhode Island ... On the 13th of last month Congress made the following resolution: Any State which settled with and paid officers and privates of their late lines in the army of the United States, in accordance with the resolution of July 1, 1784 relative to proofs of claims, may charge such payments to the United States (if not already settled for by the Paymaster General. ... Last April 19, the delegates of Massachusetts, pursuant to an act of their Legislature, made a deed of Cession of their western territory to the United States in Congress assembled ... The poor Loyalists and refugees in the Province of East Florida, totally abandoned by their late most gracious Sovereign, George III of Britain, have petitioned in a very humble manner, Charles III of Spain, for a small tract of his country. They ask to be granted "in fee simple the jurisdiction and sole direction of the internal government of that country, from which your Majesty's troops are now withdrawn, lying between St. John's and St. Mary's river, in this province, including the islands on the sea shore, situate between those rivers," for which we will gladly pay tribute and acknowledge you Lord of the soil. "We will defend the frontier and stand in defence of the Province against every power but that of our mother country." We have not heard if any answer has been given this request. ■ **ALX, June 2**. His Excellency Patrick Henry, Esq., Governor of this Commonwealth, has issued a Proclamation, offering a Reward of Fifty Pounds for apprehending and securing William Baker, of Hampshire County, supposed to be an Accessary to the Murder of a certain Monsieur le Brun. ■ The Legislature of Rhode-Island have lately passed an Act for laying an Impost of Seven and a Half per Cent. on all British Goods imported into that State, in British Vessels, in addition to the Impost of Two and a Half per Cent. on imported Goods. ■ The *Ann*, Captain Marvin, from London, is arrived in the River, and hourly expected here. ■ DIED.] Mr. CYRUS COPPER, Vendue-Master. ■ NAVAL-OFFICE, ALX. *Inward Entries.* Sloop *Betsy*, B. Stonehouse, from Boston; Sloop *Hero*, J. Humphries, Sloop *Pimento*, J. Hutchins, and Schooner *Lottery*, Z. Mann, Baltimore; Brig *Patient Mary*, W. Sliegh, New-York. *Cleared Outwards.* Schooner *Barbadoes*, J. Seymour, for Barbadoes; Sloop *Hero*, J. Humphries, and Schooner *Lottery*, Z. Mann, Baltimore. ■ The Address of the Convention to the Members of the Protestant Episcopal Church in Virginia. [full text given]. For more than Eight Years our Church hath languished under Neglect. We will not however believe that her Friends have revolted, and therefore trust that a knowledge of her present Condition will rekindle their former Affections... Of what is the Church now possessed? Nothing but the Glebes and your Affections. Since the Year 1776, she hath been even without regular Government, and her Ministers have received but little Compensation for their Services. Their Numbers are diminished by Death and other Causes, and we have as yet no Resource within ourselves for a Succession of Ministers. Many Churches stand in need of Repair, and there is no Fund equal to the smallest Want. By the favor of Providence indeed the Protestant Episcopal Church is incorporated by Law, and under this Sanction are we now assembled. We have accepted the Invitation of a Convention, lately holden at New-York, to send Deputies to another to be holden at Philadelphia in the fall. We shall not enter into a Revision of Doctrine and Worship, until their Return and Report of the Sentiments of those of our Communion, with whom they may be associated. We have however organized the Government of the Church... Signed by Order of the Convention, JAMES MADISON, President. Attest ROBERT ANDREWS, Secretary. Richmond, May 25, 1785.

Page 3. ANECDOTE. A PROFESSED and boasting votary of infidelity and universal scepticism, taking occasion, in company, to discharge the whole artillery of his wit and ridicule, against the commonly received notions of a God, and a future state of retribution, particularly the *vulgar chimera* of an everlasting Hell for impenitent sinners of the human race...

PRICES CURRENT, ALX. / Tobacco, 26s. to 28s. per Ct. / Fine Flour, 28s. per Barrel. / Wheat, 6s. per Bushel. / Jamaica Spirits, 4/6 per Gallon. / Windward Rum, 3s. per Ditto. / Continental Rum, 2s. per Ditto. / Molasses, 1/6 per Ditto. / Muscovado Sugar, 35s. to 38s. per Ct. / Salt, 3s. per Bushel, by Retail. / Corn, 3s. per Bushel / Exchange, 40.

Colin MacIver and Co., Have just imported in the Brig *Eglington* from Liverpool, the following Goods, viz. AN excellent and complete assortment of ladies', mens' and youths' drab and black hats, 3/4 and 7/8 linen checks, 7/8, yard, and one yard and 3/8 common ditto, Wigan and furniture ditto, striped Hollands, striped cottons light and dark grounds, cotton and linen handkerchiefs, white linen and sheetings, 3/4, 7/8 and yard-wide bedtickings, 6-4, 1/2, 7/4 and 8/4 bedbunts and Holland tapes, which, with a variety of other goods not on hand, they will sell on the lowest terms for cash or country produce. ALX, June 1, 1785. ■ ALL those indebted to the late Partnership of DOW, MAC IVER and CO. by bond, note or book account, are earnestly requested to make immediate payment to the Subscriber, in whose hands the books and papers of the said Company are left.--There being a necessity for a settlement of the affairs of the said Company, no further indulgence can be given.--Those who neglect to comply with this notice within six weeks from this date, may expect to be dealt with as the law directs, without any respect to persons. COLIN MAC IVER, ALX, June 1, 1785. ☞ I have for sale a likely young NEGRO FELLOW, who can be recommended for honesty and industry. C.M. ■ Just IMPORTED, and to be SOLD by **Jordan and Poyer**, At Mr. Wales's Store, near Capt. Harper's Wharf, BARBADOES RUM in Hogsheads and Barrels, and best Muscovado SUGAR in Ditto. ☞ They want to purchase a Quantity of Flour, and a few Pounds of Snakeroot. ALX, June 1, 1785.

TEN DOLLARS REWARD.

RAN away from the Subscriber, on the night of the 24th instant, an Irish servant man, named JOHN BUCKLY, a hatter by trade, 29 or 30 years of age, about 5 feet 5 or 6 inches high, a thick clumsy made fellow, of a sandy complexion, large beard, short thick sandy hair inclining to curl, has a sober deceitful countenance, and is capable of the greatest ingratitude; he can write a tolerable hand, will probably forge a pass and travel as a journeyman hatter looking for work;--He had on and took with him a light coloured cloth coat, a dark brown short ditto, with jacket and breeches nearly of the same colour, a pair of black stuff breeches, and a light coloured coating surtout with a velvet collar, all of them the worse for wear; two check and one white shirts, one pair of osnaburg trousers, one pair of black stockings not fellows, and a good pair of shoes with yellow buckles.--I have reason to believe he is enticed away by the villainy of a certain HENRY HOWARD, also by trade a hatter, a short well set man, dressed in a short blue coat, brown corduroy jacket and overalls of the same, has worked journey-work in many different parts of Virginia, and went off at the same time, supposed in company.--Whoever apprehends and secures said servant man in any gaol, so that I may hear of him and get him again, shall be intitled to the above reward, and if brought home all reasonable charges shall be paid by HENRY BUDD, ALX, May 28, 1785.

Hooe and Harrison, Have for Sale, at their Store in ALX, LEMONS, Jar Raisins, Jesuits' Bark, Cork Wood, Cadiz Salt, and a Variety of other GOODS too tedious to mention. ALX, June 1, 1785 ■ **Daniel and Isaac M'Pherson**, Have for Sale, MADERA wine by the pipe, hogshead and quarter-cask, citron by the box, West-India rum by the hogshead and barrel, brown sugar, salt, train oil, and a few gross of bottles. ALX, June 1, 1785. ■ STOLEN from the Brig *Industry* on the night of the 26th instant, a YAWL; she rowed with four oars, was payed with turpentine, some of the bottom plank worm-eaten and very leaky.--ONE GUINEA will be given for the recovery of the Boat, and on conviction of the thief TWO GUINEAS. D. and I. M'PHERSON. ALX, May 30, 1785.

For Sale, by the Subscriber,

A Small FARM, containing 154 acres, lying in the County of Spotsylvania, within 7 miles of Fredericksburg; there is on it a dwelling-house with two rooms below and two above stairs, with every other convenient out-house, and a large barn; it is about one half cleared and is in good order for cropping, having several different enclosures under good fences, among which there are some pretty good meadow ground, and a tolerable orchard of different kinds of fruit.--This place would suit either a farmer or tradesman, particularly a tanner, there being on it an excellent situation for a tanyard, having a never failing spring so situated as to be made to convey the water into the vats without the assistance of a pump.--Hides might easily be procured from the butchers in town, and there is a plenty of bark near the place.--Likewise, another TRACT of LAND, containing 510 acres, lying in the same County, about 20 miles from town; there are on it a small dwelling-house and a pretty good orchard.--This place is remarkable for its fine range for all kinds of stock, which may be raised in any quantity at very little expence of feeding, is well watered, and situated in a most healthy part of the country.--For terms apply to DAVID GALLOWAY, jun., Fredericksburg, May 24, 1785.

STRAYED away from ALX on Saturday the 21st of May, a sorrel MARE, seven years old, full blooded, fourteen hands and an half high, has a cut upon her neck under the mane about three inches long, and it is supposed she is gone towards Mr. Israel Lacey's in Loudon, as she came from thence.--Whoever finds her shall receive SIX DOLLARS reward and all reasonable charges paid, by applying to Mr. Israel Lacey in Loudon, or Williams, Cary and Company, ALX.
ALX, June 1, 1785.

Will be sold to the highest bidder at Leesburg, on the Second Monday in July next, A Valuable PLANTATION, containing 1225 acres, situated within 25 miles of Dumfries, Colchester or ALX, and on the road leading from either place to Leesburg.--A great part of this plantation is fine tobacco land, and there is one but what is very good for farming, and well timbered. The payments will be made easy to the purchaser.--The above land will be sold either in lots or otherwise, and may be had at private sale. WILLIAM MONROE, May 15, 1785 ■ A SCHOOL will be opened by the Subscriber in a few days, next door to Robert M'Crea, Esquire's, where he will teach reading, writing, vulgar and decimal arithmetic.--As he can be well recommended, both for his learning and morals, by some of the first characters in Philadelphia, and will make it his constant endeavours to deserve, so he hopes to meet with the encouragement of a generous public.--Any who may please to favor him with their commands will find him at Mr. M'Knight's, or he will wait on them at their dwellings. EDMUND EDMONDS, ALX, June 1, 1785 ■ The Churchwardens of Norborne Parish, Berkeley County, seek a minister [see like ad Vol. II No. 69] ■ **Jonathan Swift and Co.**, Have for Sale, at their Store on Captain Harper's Wharf, A General Assortment of European and West-India GOODS, which they will dispose of on the most moderate terms, for Cash, Bills of Exchange, Produce, or short Credit, with security.--They have excellent Hyson, Souchong and Bohea Tea in chests and half chests, London Porter in small hampers and a few barrels of Mess Beef and Pork. ALX, June 1, 1785 ■ THE Subscribers have just received Nine Packages of Merchandise, marked AB in a diamond, from No. 1 to 9, which were imported in the Ship *Amelia*, John F. Throckmorton, from London.--The owner may receive them by applying to JONATHAN SWIFT and CO., ALX, June 1, 1785.

On the 20th day of September next if fair, if not the next fair day, will be SOLD on the Premises,

A Valuable TRACT of LAND, lying in Stafford County, Virginia, well watered and abounding with good timber. The south bounds of the Land are within 12 miles of Fredericksburg, and the north bounds about 5 miles from Dumfries, both considerable and growing towns. The east bounds are about one mile from Aquia Warehouse, and crosses Aquia-Run at the fork, where the north and south branches divide, each extending westward through the whole Land, and will furnish several valuable mill seats. At the fork of the two branches on the eastern bounds, and where both may be included there is a remarkable convenient seat with abundance of water for a large merchant mill and saw-mill, with plenty of stone for building, and heights to erect mills of any construction. Adjoining to this seat are upwards of 1000 acres of uncleared Land, abounding with timber proper for a saw-mill, such as large white oak and pine, of the latter many large enough for ships lower masts. The annual rents now on the Lands are upwards of 22,000 pounds of tobacco, and there are upwards of 4000 acres still unsettled. It is a remarkable healthy place, and from its number of branches and small natural meadows, affords good grazing for stock. The whole is laid off in 32 Lots, from 150 to 350 acres, for the conveniency of purchasers. A draught may be seen, and the Land shewn, by an application to Col. BAILEY WASHINGTON, whose residence is adjoining.--The conditions and terms of sale are as follow: The Lots to be sold respectively at Public sale to the highest bidder, in sterling money, or good London bills of exchange. Gold and silver will be taken at its value, and crop tobacco of 1000 pounds net, inspected within the year, will be received in discount at such price as may be agreed on. Deeds to be given with a general warranty. One third of the purchase-money to be paid down, one third in two years, and the other third in three years from the day of sale, with legal interest to be paid annually. Bonds to be given with approved security, and if the annual interest, being demanded, is not paid within three months after it becomes due, the indulgence of credit shall be forfeited, and a suit may be commenced to recover both principal and interest. Any purchaser making the second and third payments, or any part of either on the day of sale, will be allowed a discount of 10 per cent. on such sum. Any person or persons inclinable to purchase the whole before the day of sale, shall have it at a moderate price on paying down one half the purchase-money, and giving bond on interest with approved security, conditioned as above, for payment of the other half within five years from the time of sale.

WILLIAM FITZHUGH, May 30, 1785.

Mount-Airy, May 27, 1785.

RAN away from the Subscriber's plantation near the Woodyard in Prince-George's County, State of Maryland, a Mulatto man, named NICK, a carpenter by trade, 35 years of age, about 5 feet 9 or 10 inches high, is round shouldered and stoops as he walks. Whoever takes up the said Slave and brings him to the Subscriber, shall have EIGHT DOLLARS reward and reasonable charges, paid by

BENEDICT CALVERT.

Patrick Maguire warns public of his absent wife and that he will not honor any debts she contracts; has for sale three valuable lots [see like ad Vol. II No. 69].

Page 4. Poetry. "To STELLA: On her giving the Author a Gold and Silk Net Purse of her own weaving. By the late Dr. Johnson." ■ **Leertouwer, Huyman, and Huiberts**, have glass and other items for sale [see like ad Vol. II No. 69] ■ WILLIAM HUNTER, jun. has for sale in fee-simple four lots on Princess-street [see like ad Vol. II No. 68] ■ Executors of the estate of THOMAS KIRKPATRICK, deceased, seek settlement of accounts [see like ad Vol. II No. 69] ■ JOHN DUNDAS and CO. offer reward for return of a letter directed to the subscribers [see like ad Vol. II No. 68] ■ LEVEN POWELL and SIMON TRIPLETT, Loudon County, seek runaway Negro fellow named DICK [see like ad Vol. II No. 69] ■ SAMUEL CANBY, Leesburg, offers for sale or exchange tracts in Monongalia and Jefferson counties [see like ad Vol. II No. 64] ■ JOHN FORMAN offers for breeding horse *OBSCURITY* [see like ad Vol. II No. 60] ■ **Robert Broket**, seeks employment as a stonecutter and bricklayer [see like ad Vol. II No. 69] ■ RAPHAEL BOORMAN, Cornwallis's Neck, Maryland, seeks runaways Ann and Bet [see like ad Vol. II No. 69] ■ M'Murray's Maps of the U.S. are ready for delivery to subscribers [see like ad Vol. II No. 64] ■ **Randle Mitchell and Son**, have goods for sale just imported in the last vessels from Europe [see like ad Vol. II No. 68] ■ WILLIAM M'WHIR solicits additional students of the ALX Latin School [see like ad Vol. II No. 68] ■ ALX: Printed by GEORGE RICHARDS, and COMPANY, at their Printing-Office on Fairfax-street--by whom Advertisements, &c. are thankfully received for this Paper,--and where Printing is performed with Care and Expedition.

1785/06/09, Vol. II No. 71

Page 1. DAVID GRIFFITH offers for sale about 200 lots of ground adjoining ALX [see like ad Vol. II No. 63] ■ **Jonathan Swift and Co.**, Have for Sale, at their Store on Captain Harper's Wharf, A General Assortment of European and West-India GOODS; Nine packages marked A.B. are found, owner sought [see like ads Vol. II No. 70] ■ DANIEL and ISAAC M'PHERSON have for sale Madera wine; offer reward for return of yawl stolen from the Brig *Industry* [see like ads Vol. I No. 70] ■ Israel Lacey seeks return of mare strayed from ALX [see like ad Vol. II No. 70] ■ WILLIAM MONROE offers for sale at Leesburg a valuable 1225-acre plantation [see like ad Vol. II No. 70] ■ COLIN MAC IVER and CO. have for sale goods just imported in the Brig *Eglington* from Liverpool; Colin Mac Iver seeks to settle accounts from the late partnership of Dow, Mac Iver and Co. [see like ads Vol. II No. 70] ■ DAVID GALLOWAY, Fredericksburg, offers for sale a small 154-acre farm, and a 510-acre tract of land, both in Spotsylvania County [see like ad Vol. II No. 70] ■ RAPHAEL BOORMAN, Cornwallis's Neck, Maryland, seeks runaways Ann and Bet [see like ad Vol. II No. 69] ■ ☞ A few Barrels of choice LAMPBLACK may be had at the Printing-Office. ■ **Hooe and Harrison**, Have for Sale, at their Store, Lemons, etc. [see like ad Vol. II No. 70] ■ **Jordan and Poyer**, have just imported and to be sold at Mr. Wales's Store, Barbadoes Rum, etc. [see like ad Vol. II No. 70] ■ **Robert Broket**, seeks employment as a stonecutter and bricklayer [see like ad Vol. II No. 69] ■ HENRY BUDD offers ten dollars reward for return of runaway Irish servant man named JOHN BUCKLY [see like ad Vol. II No. 70] ■ EDMUND EDMONDS announces his opening of a school in ALX [see like ad Vol. II No. 70].

Page 2.

LONDON, April 4. Leghorn letter says a Venetian vessel, called a polacre, was taken off there by the Moors, and carried into Algiers. The Barbarians are so intolerably insolent, that they stop ships of all nations, even the English, unless they have passes; so that presently they are masters of the Mediterranean sea, and have stopped almost all trade to every port that lies near the same ... Accounts from the continent in the last mail state the King of Prussia lies so dangerously ill as to afford little hope of his recovery. He is about 73, born in 1712 ... there is difficulty between our civil Governors in America and the Congress over the evacuation of Niagara, Detroit and other posts on the upper lakes. General Haldiman refused to give them up, though they come within the American boundary line, and his conduct has been in some measure approved by Ministers; so that the 29th and 31st regiments are ordered immediately to relieve the 8th regiment, now in possession of those forts. **April 8.** The continent is certainly in a state of political fermentation. The Dutch and the Emperor are ready to engage immediately, if a peace cannot be concluded upon. The French prepare to assist the Dutch, but wish not to offend the Emperor. Old Frederick marches and countermarches his troops. An intestine infection saps the vitals of the Republic of Holland; and the Stadtholder perhaps owes his quiet tenure of his seat to the necessity for a show of unanimity. The Spaniards, Portuguese, Venetians and Maltese, are preparing for the annual drubbing which they go to receive before Algiers. Add to this, that the Empress has every reason to suspect designs of the most hostile nature against her favorite Crimea, and from a quarter not the most agreeable. Transylvania is still in a state of inactive confusion, since the rebellion. And Old England, neighbour-like, has her trials and troubles. *Give us peace in our time, O Lord!* ... HOUSE of COMMONS, *Monday, April 4.* TRADE with AMERICA. [The verbatim transcript of proceedings, but here condensed. - Eds.] *The Chancellor of the Exchequer* brought up a bill to extend last year's act which dispenses with certain instruments by U.S. vessels entering ports of Great Britain. *Mr. Fox* wished not to obstruct, but facilitate the bill's passage. Nonetheless, U.S.-Great Britain permanent commercial arrangements had not yet been made, as expected. He proposed continuing parliamentary discussion of such, but changing the expiry of the present act from April 1785 back to September 1785. *The Chancellor of the Exchequer* felt it impracticable to establish in the present session such a permanent system. Mr. Pitt successfully moved a second reading as well as the house going into a committee on the said bill. *Mr. Fox*, in committee, reiterated his view and moved the bill's end-date be September 1, 1785. *Mr. Jenkins* disapproved, asserting insufficient time for such an important commercial treaty. *Mr. Eden* held that ill consequences were neither known nor apprehended for want of the treaty, and he gave the bill his hearty support. The committee then passed the original form of the bill, Mr. Fox's amendment consequently lost. The house resumed, Mr. Gilbert made a report of the bill, and it was ordered engrossed ... Petition from the captors of Penobscot, for head money, asking the reward of the head money granted but not yet received. *The Chancellor of the Exchequer* was averse, fearing it would set a precedent, and moved a three month postponement. *Sir George Collier* objected to hesitating about a matter of such obvious justice and urgent necessity on a claim so thoroughly validated. He then narrated [in great detail] the Penobscot action, of which he was the commander. He added that he could not sit still, or to abandon the brave companions of his victory. *Mr. Eden* having stated the necessity of inquiry, and expatiated on the merits of those who had conquered, the motion was put and carried. **April 11.** Notwithstanding the States of Holland behaved in a manner derogatory to every principle of gratitude and justice towards this country during the late war, there are strong political reasons for our preventing the Dutch from being crushed. If the Dutch provinces are divided, it is our insular situation only will protect this kingdom. ■ **ST. GEORGE'S** (*Grenada*) **May 14.** Letters from the neighbouring French islands say the late Arrêt, for regulating their trade with foreigners, is carried out with the utmost rigor. Several English vessels whose Masters had through ignorance neglected to conform as prescribed by the Arrêt, have been seized--among them the schooner *Fan-Fan*, from this port, in ballast, which had only touched at St. Lucia to land a passenger. ■ **CHARLESTON, May 18.** The organizing of a militia being an object of great moment, especially in the interior of this State, his Excellency the Governor set out for Camden a few days ago to effect this. **May 19.** A letter from a passenger aboard the ship *Fanny*, Capt. Overton, tells of the ship's loss. She sailed from this port last February, for Liverpool, and on March 1 was overset in a gale of wind. They had to cut away her masts, by which means she righted, but they were in that deplorable condition until April 1, when they were taken off by a vessel and carried into Newbury Port. ■ **NEW YORK, May 19.** The Minister of War directs the uniform for frontier service troops to be *blue*, faced with *red* and lined with *white* for the infantry; *blue* faced and lined with *red* for the artillery; the cockades to be *black*. Discarding the union cockade does not seem to be met with general approbation. It is therefore to be lamented, that any regulation should take place that will excite jealousy or create uneasiness in the minds of our allies, who afforded us succour in the moment of distress and difficulty. **May 21.** We learn that when the ship *Empress of China* received a salute at Canton from one of the harbour ships, the charge in one of the saluting guns had not been drawn, which killed two Chinese on the spot. This brought on the resentment of 30,000 natives, who secured the English ship's gunner. The commanders and ships companies of all the British, french, American, Danish, Swedish, Dutch &c. vessels combined to recover him. Business was suspended for a week, and after an equitable trial the man was acquitted and enlarged. The Chinese ancient good humor returned, for their investigation found no premeditation and concluded it mere Chance Medley. China is governed by excellent laws, rigidly enforced, otherwise what could be done by so many myriads of inhabitants as compose the immense Empire of China? **May 23.** By a ship arrived at Portsmouth, in 40 days from Brest, the Consul of France in Boston received the pleasing intelligence of the happy delivery of her Majesty of France, of a Prince; on whom has been conferred the title of Duke of Normandy. ■ **PHILADELPHIA, May 30.** A New York paper of Friday last says, "The port of Havana is again opened for the reception of American produce, and the admission of all American vessels.

This event will give new life to our trade, which for some time past has been in a very languid state." **June 3.** On April 23 Congress published an ordinance about the disposal of the western territory. The land is to be surveyed, laid out in six mile square townships, and the board of treasury to sell it by public vendue, at not less than one dollar per acre, in specie or certificates, in addition to the survey expence (rated at $36 the township.) ... From the ***New York Gazette,* May 31**. Recent letters via South Carolina report from Dominica the pleasing prospect of a valuable commerce between this country and Spanish dominions on the Main. Last December the Spanish Superintendent and Consul appointed John Skey Eustace (native of this State, late a federal army colonel, and practitioner of law in Georgia) to be Inspector general of their trade with America. He has sailed from Dominica for Alveres, on the Spanish main, where much of their treasure from Mexico to Peru is lodged until shipment to Old Spain. This appointment is deemed most honorable and lucrative, supposed worth £10,000 sterling per annum. Colonel Eustace's distinguished abilities and lively genius had rendered him a favorite with that polished Courtier and Statesman ... The brig *Apollo*, Tyrie, from the Bay of Honduras to London, was totally lost February 21 on Glover's Reef ... A gentleman arrived from Dublin says that by April 20 every vessel expected from America with flaxseed was arrived, and that the *Friendship*, from New York, had lost her bowsprit; and that Captain Bell died the day of his arrival ... The present difficulties in our commerce, will, it is to be hoped, produce what every wise man wishes, viz. An enlargement of the power of that Honorable Body which alone can protect the United States from the insults and abuses of the Barbarians, whether civilized or uncivilized. While their tendency is to this valuable object, the friends of this country behold them with satisfaction... Yesterday arrived his Most Christian Majesty's Packet *Le Courier de la Martinique*, in 27 days from l'Orient; and the brig *Peggy*, Captain Dekay, from Bristol in 49 days ... Extract of a letter from **London, April 9:** Our letters from the Continent give a clearer picture than the newspapers, so we enclose translations for your use: **Vienna, March 19**. From Constantinople we hear constantly that the Turks are making extraordinary preparations for war, by sea and land; a corps of 6000 Janissaries has been out in quarters on cantonment in the environs of Belgrade ... The Venetians continue to arm against the States of Holland. The Prussian Ambassador's memorial delivered to the Venetian Minister here made very little impression. Most likely the Dutch and Venetians will be the first to commence hostilities this season. It is said the Empress of Russia has already settled with her powerful allies the means to ascertain the crown of Poland (when vacant) to one of the Great Duke's children; and that, for this reason, France has done all in her power to raise the Turks out of their usual inactivity. In case of war, Russia is likely to assist Austria against the Turks, and very likely a Russian army will appear on the Turkish frontiers, even before the negociation or the war with Holland begins.

Page 3. **ALX, June 9**. Last Saturday arrived in this Town the justly celebrated Mrs. CATHERINE MACAULAY GRAHAM, on her Way to Mount-Vernon, the Seat of His Excellency General WASHINGTON. ■ Extract of a Letter from Captain James Ervine, now a Prisoner at Mogador, South Barbary, to a Gentlemen in this Town, dated April 1, 1785. "Soon after our Arrival at Tangiers we were ordered to Morocco and carried before the Emperor, who informed us he was at Peace with our Nation; but soon after ordered us to this Place, where we are to remain Prisoners, till Congress may think proper to send an Ambassador to our Relief. This is the ultimate Determination of the Emperor. We hope, which is all the Comfort we have under our dreadful Situations, they will be speedy and favorable to our Wishes, and restore us again to our Families and Friends." ■ A few Days ago the Sloop *Molly Beverly*, Capt. Christie, arrived here from Charleston. In Lat. 36, 28, N. Long. 74, 40, W. he spoke the Brig *Active*, Captain Jenny, from Baltimore, bound to Antigua, out 3 Days, all well. ■ The [*Janet*], Captain Chisholm, from Glasgow, is arrived at Norfolk. ■ MARRIED.] At Richmond, Colonel MICHAEL RYAN, to Miss FRANCES DUDLEY. DIED.] Major WINDSOR BROWN. ■ NAVAL-OFFICE, ALX. *Inward Entries*. Sloop *Dolphin*, A. Stewart, and Sloop *Speedwell*, W. Scott, from Philadelphia; Brig *Jenny*, M. Griffing, Barbadoes; Sloop *Molly Beverly*, J. Christie, Charleston; Schooner *Jesse*, S. Davis, Grenada; Brig *Jane and Elizabeth*, J. Frazer, George-Town. *Cleared Outwards*. Ship *Henry*, J. Dennison, for Baltimore; Sloop *Dolphin*, A. Stewart, Philadelphia; Brig *Liberty*, J. Nixon, Hamburg; Brig *Martha*, G. Slacom, St. Eustatia. ■ M. CAPUS, from Barbadoes, proposes teaching in this Town Dancing, and Vocal and Instrumental Music.--He may be spoke with at Mr. SHORT's. ■ ☞ It is requested that the Subscribers to the Scheme for erecting a House for a Grammar School in ALX, and those who wish to interest themselves therein, will meet at the Court-House on Saturday next, at 10 o'Clock, A.M. for the Purpose of arranging and carrying into Effect the Design of said Subscription. ALX, June 7, 1785. ■

Just imported, and to be sold by **William Hartshorne And Company**, BARBADOES and Grenada RUM, Muscovado SUGAR, COFFEE, Smiths' Anvils and Vices, Soap and Candles by the Box, and a Variety of DRY-GOODS as usual. ALX, June 9, 1785 ■ By the PRESIDENT and DIRECTORS of the POTOMACK COMPANY, May 31, 1785. ORDERED, That the Proprietors of the said Company pay into the hands of WILLIAM HARTSHORNE, Treasurer of the said Company, on each share Five Pounds, sterling, on or before the fifteenth day of July next, and also the further sum of Two Pounds Ten Shillings, sterling, on or before the first day of October next. GEORGE WASHINGTON, THOMAS JOHNSTON, THOMAS S. LEE, GEORGE GILPIN, JOHN FITZGERALD. Four hundred and three of the give hundred shares in the Potomack Company having been subscribed, books are now opened at Mr. William Hartshorne's, Treasurer, in ALX, to receive the first subscriptions that may be offered to make up the ninety-seven remaining shares. ■ ADVERTISEMENT. THE President and Directors of the Potomack Company, will meet at ALX on Friday the first day of July next, to agree with a skillful person to conduct the opening and improving the navigation of Potomack River, from the Great Falls to Payne's, and from the upper part of the Shenandoah to the highest place practicable on the North Branch, and also to agree with two Assistants and Overseers; also, that liberal wages will be given to any number not exceeding one hundred good hands, with provisions and a reasonable quantity of spirits; that a further encouragement will be given to such as are dexterous in boring and blowing rocks, in which service a proportion of the men will be employed; and that the conductor of the work, or some other person authorized, will attend at Seneca on the third day of July next, and at Shenandoah on the sixth day of July next, to contract with the men who may offer for this service. By order of the Board, JOHN POTTS, jun., Secretary. ■ **Richard Conway**, has for sale salt, Lisbon and Oporto wines [see like ad Vol. II No. 67] ■ **W. Mounsher and Co.**, Have for Sale, TWO very handsome single riding CHAISES and a very elegant SULKY, entirely new.--They may be seen at Mr. WARD's Tavern. ALX, June 7, 1785. ■ Just imported, and to be sold by **James Ramsay**, At Mr. Watson's store on the Wharf, A SMALL Quantity of choice Muscovado SUGAR and RUM in hogsheads and barrels. ALX, June 7, 1785. ■ BATTAILE MUSE seeks to find lost pair of black saddle-bags, containing many papers and money [see like ad Vol. II No. 66] ■ LEFT in the Subscriber's stable, by a stranger, name unknown, on the 13th of May last, a dark bay HORSE, saddle and bridle, supposed to be 11 or 12 years old, with a hanging mane and switch tail both black, two fore feet white, 13 hands and upwards high, branded on the near buttock NR, and has a small slit on each ear.--The owner is desired to come, prove property, pay charges and take him away, otherwise he will be sold in fourteen [days] from this date. THOMAS REEDER, ALX, June 6, 1785. ■ FOR SALE, FOURTEEN LOTS of GROUND, in the town of Leesburg, the smallest of which has 40 feet in front and 85 feet in depth; the others are of different sizes.--Also for sale, an elegant Teem of Horses with a stout Waggon, a handsome riding Horse and a young Mare.--Likewise, an active Negro Boy and Girl, both young.--The terms of sale are, Ready-Money or Produce for the Negroes and Horses; but credit will be given for part of the purchase of the Lots. PATRICK CAVAN, Leesburg, June 7, 1785. ☞ Said Cavan has TWO HOUSES, situated on the Main-street, which he wishes to Rent, and possession will be given immediately.--Also, another HOUSE, of which possession will be given in a few months. ■ FOR SALE, A SAW-MILL (generally known by the name of Bruce's) together with about 1250 acres of LAND in the County of Orange, a great proportion of which is in good timber.--There is on this tract an exceeding pretty Farm, extending about a mile on the River Rappadan, sufficient to work four or five hands to great advantage.--The mill is now at work, and saws near 100,000 feet of plank annually, which is generally carried to Fredericksburg by an exceeding good road, the distance being only about 26 miles.--My price is £.1500 military certificates issued by this State, or, I will barter for merchandise, Negroes, horses, or any kind of country produce.--I will also sell my Military LAND WARRANTS, containing 7777 acres and two-thirds, the greater part of which are already located on Gasper's River, by the best judges in the Western Country.--For these I will take one dollar per acre, in certificates as aforesaid, or barter in like manner. BURGES BALL, Culpepper, May 27, 1785. ■ AS JOHN DUNDAS and COMPANY intend to move their Store on the 11th of next month to the late dwelling-house of Mr. William Hepburn, the Store, with a neat well finished counting room and bed room (which may answer for a small family) a good loft and a cellar under the whole, which they now occupy, and has lately been completely repaired, will be to rent at that time.--Also, the DWELLING-HOUSE and Garden thereunto adjoining, now in the tenure of Mr. Patrick Murray; possession of which will be given on the 1st of November. JOHN DUNDAS, ALX, June 7, 1785. ☞ The said John Dundas and Co. have for sale at their Store, a neat assortment of MERCHANDISE, suitable to the present season, which they will sell for cash, country produce, or on short credit. ■ The Churchwardens of Norborne Parish, Berkeley County, seek a minister [see like ad Vol. II No. 69] ■ BENEDICT CALVERT, Mount-Airy, seeks return of runaway Mulatto man named NICK [see like ad Vol. II No. 70].

TEN DOLLARS REWARD

RAN away from the Subscriber on the 9th of April last, a yellow strong NEGRO WENCH, named KATE: She had on and took away with her, three linsey petticoats, and one striped linsey jacket.--Any person who will take up said Wench, and return her to the Subscriber, living on Shenandoah near the Bloomery, shall receive the above reward and have all reasonable charges paid.

BENJAMIN RANKINS.

June 4, 1785.

Newport, Charles-County, June 1, 1785. RAN away from the Subscriber on the 8th day of December last, a Mulatto Man SLAVE, who calls himself STEPHEN BUTLER; he is a lusty Fellow, about 6 feet 2 inches high, thick visaged, has a small scar on his right cheek bone and a large one on his side, occasioned by the cut of a knife in a fray.--His clothes I cannot describe, as it is probable he has changed them.--He plays on the violin, and can work a little at coopering, sawing and wheel work, but is a tolerable good house-carpenter.--He is very well known as a runaway for 30 years past, and is about 50 years of age.--He has been frequently concealed by white people, having ran away upwards of one hundred times, some of whom I could now mention, but for the present small content myself by forbidding, at their peril, any person whatever from harbouring or concealing him.--He is an artful insinuating fellow, a great liar, and a coward; but if taken into custody will endeavour to make his escape.--Whoever will bring the said Slave to his Master, shall receive, if taken in the County, TEN DOLLARS reward, and if out of the County, TWELVE DOLLARS, and if 50 miles from home, or out of the State, TEN POUNDS and all reasonable charges, paid by LEONARD BOARMAN. ■ RAN away from the Subscriber, a Negro Man, called EMANUEL, about 30 years of age, 5 feet 5 or 6 inches high, very square made and of a dark brown complexion, with remarkable large eyes.--I remember no particular marks or scars, except his being some years ago burnt in the hand, the traces of which may perhaps yet remain.--He is very sensible and has a number of friends and associates among the lower class of whites.--I make no doubt he has procured a pass.--He was taken off in a vessel, and I understand passes for a freeman by the name of JAMES.--Whoever secures the said Negro in any gaol whatever, shall receive a reward of SIX POUNDS. SPENCER BALL, Northumberland County, June 3, 1785. ■ ☞ A great Variety of BLANKS, printed on good Paper, may be had at the Printing-Office.

Page 4. Poetry. "The SETTING SUN." ■ WILLIAM LYLES and CO., is selling rum [see like ad Vol. II No. 68] ■ **Leertouwer, Huyman, and Huiberts**, have glass and other items for sale [see like ad Vol. II No. 69] ■ WILLIAM HUNTER, jun., has for sale in fee-simple four lots on Princess-street [see like ad Vol. II No. 68] ■ SAMUEL CANBY, Leesburg, offers for sale or exchange tracts in Monongalia and Jefferson counties [see like ad Vol. II No. 64] ■ WILLIAM HARTSHORNE and COMPANY offer for sale goods just imported in the Ship *Mary*, and several Lots well situated in ALX may be had on ground-rent [see like ad Vol. II No. 67] ■ Executors of the estate of THOMAS KIRKPATRICK, deceased, seek settlement of accounts [see like ad Vol. II No. 69] ■ JOHN FORMAN offers for breeding horse *OBSCURITY* [see like ad Vol. II No. 60] ■ BENJAMIN STODDERT announces the Ship *Potomack [Planter]* will consign for tobacco and sail in early June [see like ad Vol. II No. 68] ■ H. STEUART and JAMES MUSCHETT seek charter for new Brigantine *Eglington* [see like ad Vol. II No. 69] ■ JOHN FILSON is selling new books on Roman Catholics [see like ad Vol. II No. 69] ■ WILLIAM FITZHUGH offers for sale a valuable tract of land in Stafford County [see like ad Vol. II No. 70] ■ LEVEN POWELL and SIMON TRIPLETT, Loudon County, seek runaway Negro fellow named DICK [see like ad Vol. II No. 69] ■ The Printing-Office is selling blank books, ledgers, journals, etc. [see like ad Vol. II No. 69] ■ ALX: Printed by GEORGE RICHARDS, and COMPANY, at their Printing-Office on Fairfax-street--by whom Advertisements, &c. are thankfully received for this Paper,--and where Printing is performed with Care and Expedition.

1785/06/16, Vol. II No. 72

Page 1. DAVID GRIFFITH offers for sale about 200 lots of ground adjoining ALX [see like ad Vol. II No. 63] ■ WILLIAM LYLES and CO., is selling rum [see like ad Vol. II No. 68] ■ **William Hartshorne And Company**, have for sale Barbadoes and Grenada

Rum, etc. [see like ad Vol. II No. 71] ■ WILLIAM HUNTER, jun., has for sale in fee-simple four lots on Princess-street [see like ad Vol. II No. 68] ■ BURGES BALL, Culpepper, has for sale a saw-mill and 1250 acres of Land in Orange County [see like ad Vol. II No. 71] ■ **Hooe and Harrison**, Have for Sale, at their Store, Lemons, etc. [see like ad Vol. II No. 70] ■ The President and Directors of the Potomack Company authorize payment of dividends, etc.; John Potts, jun., Secretary of the Company announce upcoming meeting [see like ad Vol. II No. 71] ■ THOMAS REEDER seeks owner of horse left by a stranger in his stable [see like ad Vol. II No. 71] ■ PATRICK CAVAN, Leesburg, offers for sale 14 lots of ground and other property in the town of Leesburg [see like ad Vol. II No. 71] ■ DANIEL and ISAAC M'PHERSON have for sale Madera wine; offer reward for return of yawl stolen from the Brig *Industry* [see like ads Vol. I No. 70] ■ WILLIAM FITZHUGH offers for sale a valuable tract of land in Stafford County [see like ad Vol. II No. 70].

Page 2.

HAGUE, March 25. The States of Holland have assembled two days sooner than intended on account of the last declaration of the Emperor. The following are a fuller account than previous published. His Imperial Majesty demands: I. Deputies sent by the States of Holland to Vienna, to make excuses; II. Absolute sovereignty of the Scheldt, Antwerp to Stastinger, free trade and navigation the entire length, toll and duty free; III. Sixteen millions of Dutch florins as compensation for the city of Maestricht for the Emperor to completely quit his claim; IV. Cession of the counties of Vrendoven, and Outer Maese; V. The forts of Kruischans and Frederick Henry to be demolished; VI. Cession and resignation of the forts of Lillo and of Liefkenshoek to his Imperial Majesty; VII. Sluices in Flanders and on the Maese be restored to the Emperor, that we may no longer be able to overflow his territory; VIII. Indemnification of the damages which his subjects have sustained by the inundations. ■ **LONDON, April 1.** Yesterday died in Cary street, Lincoln's Inn, Count O'Rourke, descended from the Sovereigns of his county, now Leitrim, in Ireland. Oliver Cromwell stripped his family of an estate worth £70,000 annually. The Count had been in the Imperial and French service, and had the order of St. Louis conferred on him by the French King for his bravery. He had presented a memorial to the King in consideration of his family being stripped of such an immense fortune (which is in part enjoyed by the Crown) to allow him a pension. **April 14.** An order has been sent Ireland for two more regiments to prepare to embark for foreign service; the number going abroad from there now totals 4800, of which 3000 go to the Leeward Islands, where, on the exchange of garrisons, there is to be an augmentation of 300 in the island of Antigua, 250 at St. Kitt's, 200 at Barbadoes, 150 at St. Vincent's, and proportionately in the other, smaller islands. The reason: the French have not reduced their soldiers in Martinique, and in St. Lucia are collecting a garrison near equal to that at the outbreak of the late war. Jamaica is to be augmented with a whole regiment and artillery company, according the plan of the administration and the Governor, Lord Dunmore. The soldiers are, however, to be employed as labourers on the new fortifications, to be commenced as soon as possible after the new Governor arrives ... We have just heard, from good authority, that peace is concluded between the Emperor and the Dutch. ■ **DUBLIN, April 8.** The additional taxes, the minister reckons, will be £140,000 per annum but--as the Financier's business is to be rather too low in his computation--we may expect them to be £190,000. Fixed; irrecoverable. For what? A return for propositions which may never pass--in hopes of blessings we many never enjoy--the price is stipulated--the price is paid--and we are left to chance to seek the value. Well may we be called a blundering nations ... A caution to seamen: Captain Gillis, of the *Three Brothers*, belonging to Belfast, on his last voyage home from America discovered an island or large rock in lat. 57:25, off the island of Torry, N.E. coast of Ireland, 65 leagues--not described in any of our charts. It seems of considerable dimensions, and at a distance wears a conical appearance. A range of sunken rocks branches to the eastward of the above island for 3 or 4 miles, highly dangerous for vessels to approach. ■ **PHILADELPHIA, May 13.** An extract from a letter of a young student of the university of Copenhagen, to his friend in America, is inserted not only because it breathes the finest sentiments of liberty and feeling of humanity, but that it also exhibits a striking picture of the miseries attendant on absolute government [The full column text is intricate, flowery, and undoubtedly the result of several drafts. We summarize here - Eds.] "I am still desolate from our parting, and question my reason for being, and even my being a student here. When I inform my parents, the are happy enough not to comprehend my meaning.... Remember the farm we so admired, where we so often walked with the gentle M-----? Her father has been ordered off it; his Lord, struck with its beauties, wants to add it to his own domain. The old man is detailed to the most desolate and barren part of the estate. Have you a more deplorable instance among your poor Negroes? And this amidst a people who boast of the mildness and equity of their laws. The rich will not be independent, and the poor cannot. And yet we are continually trying to promote national industry. Who would guess we have eight quarto volumes about domestic husbandry and scarcely eight acres together? A stranger the other day was asked if he had seen the Flora Danica, and how he liked it? He replied he was sorry to find so many plans he did not know, and so few he did. *Monsieur n'est pas bontanique aparement*, was all that was said, to so sensible, so cutting a reproof. Would I were no more! Would I could rescue this land from its evils; how gladly, like Decius [also, possibly Declus--Eds.] would I plunge into the gulph of death. Sometimes I could drown my horrid thoughts in blood! If vassalage and taxes deprive a man of his child, his cattle and his corn, he will either abandon his home land or summon up a resolution more formidable--having nothing to lose but his life, with which he would readily part. Oh Penn! Oh Berstoff! Names dear to humanity; with what reverence do I pronounce them! And whilst chisel and pencil are used to transmit warriors and heroes to posterity, a silent tear of rapture shall oft record your worth, and every feeling heart be your temple of adoration. Adieu my dear friend, it grows late.... **June 3.** The committee of merchants and traders of Philadelphia request the different printers to publish, in their respective papers, the following [summarized -- Eds.] memorial and the resolutions of the Assembly taken thereon: It has been considered and lamented that a full and direct power over U.S. commerce has not been given Congress. Hence the intercourses of the States are liable to be perplexed and injured by various and discordant regulations; we are thus on unequal footing with other nations who may treat each of the States knowing their power remains severally among them. However tenacious some of our States have been, soon the general welfare will suffer. We hope a recommendation from Congress to the States for vesting it with the powers over U.S. commerce would be well received. We pray you to try to procure such a recommendation from Congress. [signed Thomas Fitzsimons, Charles Petit, John Ross, Isaac Hazelhurst, Mordecai Lewis, Tench Coxe, John M. Nesbitt, John Nixon, John Wilcocks, Samuel Howell, George Clymer, Clement Biddle, Richard Wells ... STATE of PENNSYLVANIA In General Assembly, Friday, April 8, 1785. A.M. The memorial was read the second time, whereupon, Resolved that it is the opinion of this house that the privilege of the States individually to control and regulate their own trade is no longer compatible with the general interest and welfare of the U.S., productive of mutual inconveniences and injustices among ourselves, and that the systems of nations can exclude us and not be consistently or effectually counteracted but by a unity of councils in the great representative body of the United States. Resolved therefore, that Congress be requested to devise such a system of commercial powers as they ought necessarily to be vested with, to be recommended to the States, and that Congress be assured of finding the most suitable disposition on the part of Pennsylvania to comply therewith. Extract from the Minutes, SAMUEL BRYAN, Clerk Gen. Assem. ■ **ALX, June 16.** It is said that the Citizens of Philadelphia have experienced every Conveniency from the Emission of Paper Money, it being in equal Credit with Gold and Silver. ■ The *Nancy*, Captain Kelso, is arrived in James River, from Glasgow. ■ The *Blandford*, Capt. Troop, *Lydia*, Capt. Watson, and *Neptune*, Capt. Bell, are arrived at Glasgow from James River. ■ Extract from Lloyd's Marine List of April 1, 1785. "The *Cato*, Tucker, from the West-Indies to Virginia, foundered at sea." ■ NAVAL-OFFICE, ALX. *Inward Entries*. Sloop *Bathsheba*, J. Ingraham, from Rhode-Island; Sloop *General Washington*, T.J. Lake, Philadelphia; Schooner *Surprize*, L. Laiezou, Baltimore. *Cleared Outwards*. Sloop *Dove*, S. Packard, for Rhode-Island.

FOR LONDON,

THE Brig *JANE and ELIZABETH*, JOHN FRAZER, Master, now lying at ALX, and will positively sail by the first of July.--Any person wanting a passage, may apply to Messieurs WILLIAMS, CARY and COMPANY, or to the Master on board.

June 16, 1785.

Page 3.

On Saturday the 18th instant, and on Monday the 20th instant, will be sold,

A GENERAL assortment of WET and DRY GOODS, consisting of rum, sugar, coffee, hyson tea in quarter chests, soap, claret in bottles, &c. coarse and fine cloths, printed linens, calicoes, gauzes, muslins, silks, coarse and fine Irish linens, handkerchiefs, thread, thread and cotton stockings, boots and boot legs, &c.&c.

SAMUEL ARELL, Vendue-Master.

ALX, June 16, 1785.

FOR GLASGOW,

THE Brigantine *JANET*, Captain CHISHOLM, will be at ALX in a few days, where, and at Quantico, she is to load with tobacco for Glasgow. She will take 100 hogsheads on freight with liberty of consignment, and will positively sail by the 25th of July.--For terms apply to Mr. ALEXANDER CAMPBELL in Dumfries, or the Subscriber.

WILLIAM WILSON.

ALX, June 14, 1785.

To be Sold on the 2d of July next, to the highest bidder, at the Vendue-Store in ALX, FOUR LOTS of GROUND with a south front on Prince-street of 20 feet each, and running back 100 feet to a 10 feet alley, and are marked on the plan No. 3, 4, 5 and 6; three other LOTS on the same square 22 feet front to the west on Washington-street, and in depth 100 feet, No. 7, 8 and 9.--Number 6 is the corner of Prince-street (which is 66 feet wide and of Washington-street which is 100 feet wide) distant from the bank of the river about 500 yards.--The situation of these Lots are equal to most of the unimproved parts of this town, the ground being high and the lower end of Prince-street better improved with wharves and stores than any other.--They will absolutely be sold for what they will fetch, subject to an annual ground-rent of 10s. currency, per foot, not to commence till the -- day of November next; each of these Lots must be improved in the course of next summer, or security given for the punctual payment of the rent.--A plan may be seen at the Printing-Office. ALX, June 16, 1785. ■ THE Subscriber takes this method of informing the public, that he intends opening a SCHOOL in Martinsburg, for the instruction of youth in the Latin and Greek languages, English grammar and mathematics, where those who are desirous of having their youth instructed in any or all those branches of literature, may depend that the greatest attention shall be paid to their improvement and morals, by their humble servant. JOHN CLARK. ☞ The School will be opened the first of June. Martinsburg, May 23, 1785. ■ **Richard Weightman**, Taylor and Habit-Maker, BEGS leave to acquaint his friends and the public, that he has removed from Mrs. Gretter's on King-street, to a convenient house on Fairfax-street, near the Printing-Office, where all favors will be gratefully received and executed as usual. ☞ An APPRENTICE is wanted to the above business. ALX, June 15, 1785. ■ EDMUND EDMONDS announces his opening of a school in ALX [see like ad Vol. II No. 70] ■ Israel Lacey seeks return of mare strayed from ALX [see like ad Vol. II No. 70] ■ ☞ The BRETHREN of LODGE NO. 39, are earnestly requested to meet at the Lodge Room at 10 o'Clock A.M. on Friday the 24th Instant. By Order of the Master, SAMUEL ARELL, Secretary, Thursday June 16, 1785. ■ **Hooe and Harrison**, HAVE to let upon Ground-Rent, several LOTS of LAND in this town, and some upon their Wharf.--Also to let by the year, the HOUSE in which Mr. Joseph Caverly lately dwelt; a new STORE and DWELLING-HOUSE under one roof, on their Wharf; and two STORES with cellars adjoining their dwelling-house. ALX, June 15, 1785. ■ **Williams, Cary and Co.**, Have just received per the *Britannia*, Captain Lambert, a general assortment of European and East-India GOODS, which they propose selling on the most reasonable terms by wholesale, consisting of Superfine cloths, cassimers, 7/8 Irish linens from 15d. to 2/2. 9-8 sheetings, dowlas, checks, muslins, lawns, cambricks, gauzes, a variety of ribbons, ½ ell and 3/4 modes from 2s. upwards, durants, scarlet cloaks, silk petticoats, striped ticks, bedbunts, dyed pillow jeans and jeanets, corduroys, cotton counterpanes, mens' and womens' cotton and thread hose, a variety of hardware, roasting jacks, an assortment of nails, fishing seines, butt soles, mens' coarse and fine shoes, a few elegant sofas, a few hogsheads of choice Grenada rum, a few tubs of German steel and some indigo, with many other articles too tedious to mention. ALX, June 15, 1785. ■ **Elias Noah**, Merchant, Is just arrived at the house of Mr. John Wise, at the Fountain Tavern, where he is now opening a general assortment of SPRING GOODS, suitable for the season, which he will dispose of on the most reasonable terms for cash or country produce.--His stay in this place will be eight or ten days.--He wishes to freight a vessel for Philadelphia, of about 40 hogsheads burthen. ALX, June 15, 1785. ■ ☞ *WANTED IMMEDIATELY, A WET NURSE with a good Breast of fresh Milk, who can be well recommended.--Inquire at the Printing-Office, June 16, 1785.* ■ WHEREAS the Common Council did on the 9th of this present month unanimously determine, that a Market-House 73 feet in length and 24 feet in width and a story above the same, should be immediately built; and whereas the said Council have appointed us the Subscribers to prepare a plan for the said house and also for letting the same to the lowest bidder, we do, in compliance with the said order, hereby give this public notice, that the said building will be let to the lowest bidder at three o'clock on Saturday the 18th instant, at the Court-House.--The payments will be made convenient and agreeable to the undertaker or undertakers, and a plan of the building seen by applying to Mr. OLIVER PRICE. RICHARD CONWAY, WILLIAM LYLES, PETER WISE, ALX, June 11, 1785. ■ TO BE LEASED, SUNDRY TENEMENTS in Fairfax County within 5 miles of the Lower Falls of Potomack, 10 of George-Town, and 12 of ALX.--The Land is remarkably fertile, well watered and healthy; it is divided into Lots containing from 150 to 200 acres each, on which are several houses, orchards, &c. a considerable proportion of each Tenement consists of low ground, which may at a small expence be converted into meadow.--The vicinity of these Farms to commercial towns, fisheries, merchant mills, &c. must render them peculiarly convenient to the tenants.--Also, another TRACT in the same County, lying on Wolf-Run, near the confluence of Occoquan and Bull-Run, of which there are three improved Tenements to let, containing 200 acres each; the land is of a good quality, well watered and situated in a healthy country, within 16 miles of Dumfries and Colchester and 25 of ALX.--Also, two TRACTS in Fauquier County, one on Little-River in the upper part of that County, about 40 miles from ALX and 45 from Dumfries and Fredericksburg, of which there remains two or three Tenements to let. The other is situated on Carter's-Run, near the Rappahannock-Mountain, and contains 620 acres on which there is a good dwelling-house with 8 rooms and a cellar complete, all necessary out-houses, garden and orchard; a considerable quantity of improved meadow land is on this tract, and two valuable mill seats; the soil is equal to any in the County of Fauquier and the situation perfectly healthy.--For further information those who are inclined to rent may apply to Mr. GEORGE SMITH, living near the Lower Falls of Potomack, in Fairfax County, who has power to let out the above described Lands on leases for a term of years, or lives. WILLIAM SCOTT, June 8, 1785. ■ **William Wilson**, Has received by the *Janet* from Glasgow, and the last vessels from London and Liverpool, A General assortment of DRY-GOODS, which he will sell by the package or piece on reasonable terms.--He will give short credit, and produce will be received in payment. ALX, June 15, 1785.

FOR LONDON

THE Ship *FORTUNE*, Captain HALDEN, lying at George-Town.--She will take in Tobacco consigned to FORREST and STODDERT, London, at Seven Pounds, sterling, per ton.

BENJAMIN STODDERT.

George-Town, June 10, 1785.

George F. Norton, EMBRACES this opportunity of returning his grateful thanks to his friends in particular, and the public in general, for the encouragement he has met with since his commencement of business, and begs leave to inform them that he has just imported by the *Amelia*, Captain Throckmorton, from London, an elegant and fashionable assortment of European and India MERCHANDISE, consisting of the following articles, viz. Superfine broadcloths blue, brown, drab and a variety of other colours, Cassimers and buckrams, Plain, changeable, brocaded, striped and fancy lustrings of the newest and most fashionable colours in wear, Rich coloured satins, Florentines, Modes of all widths and prices, Persians and sarsenets of all colours, Ladies' silk, satin and stuff shoes, Black and white piquet gauzes, Ribbons of the newest taste, Ladies' stays neatly made, Laces and edgings of all kinds, A choice collection of chintzes and calicoes, A large assortment of silk and satin quilts, A most beautiful assortment of ostrich feathers and Italian flowers, Book, jaconet, sprigged and striped muslins, Cambricks, Clear lawns, Needle worked muslin and lawn aprons and handkerchiefs, A great variety of pocket handkerchiefs, Thread, cotton and silk hose for men, women and children, Mens' and womens' silk gloves and mitts, Silk and satin cloaks, bonnets and chip hats, Mens' best beaver hats, Black, white and underlined with green ditto, Ladies balloon, princess royal and Dunstable ditto, Mens' neatest calfskin and buckskin boots, Mens', womens' and childrens' leather shoes, Ladies' fashionable Italian

Morocco slippers, Sole leather of the first quality, Gloves and mits of various colours, Irish linens of all widths and prices, Irish and Russia sheetings, Best German ticklenburgs, osnaburgs and hempen rolls, Marseilles and mock quilting, Plain and corded dimities, India nankeens, Jeans, jeanets and fustians, Corduroys and cotton stripes, Damask and diaper tablecloths, Russels and calamancoes, Tammies and durants, Shalloons and rattinets, Cutlery well assorted, Cards, Tin and copper ware, Stationary of all sorts, Scythes and sickles, A large assortment of groceries, Medicines assorted, A large quantity of bag, basket, plated and gilt buttons of the first quality and fashion, An extensive collection of ironmongery and hardware, Trimmings of all sorts, Paints assorted, Shot and bar lead, Pewter dishes, basons, porringers, tea and table spoons, Porter in bottles, [Gloucester] and Cheshire Cheese, candles, sweet oil, and Castile soap, Earthen and glass ware, Gunpowder, &c.&c. All of which being laid in on the very best terms, he is enabled and determined to dispose of them on the lowest advance for cash, country produce, military and militia certificates. Winchester, June 13, 1785.

STRAYED from the Commons of ALX about the 24th of last Month, an aged bay HORSE, about 15 hands high, has a black mane and tail, the two fore feet and off hind foot white, a blaze in his face, and a brand mark, supposed ED, on his near hip, which can only be seen at a short distance.--Whoever has taken up the said Horse, and will deliver him to the Subscriber in ALX, shall receive ONE GUINEA reward with all reasonable charges.

PHILIP DALBY.

ALX, June 14, 1785.

☞ Advertisements omitted will be in our next.

Page 4. Poetry. "Simplicity." ■ **Jonathan Swift and Co.**, Have for Sale, at their Store on Captain Harper's Wharf, A General Assortment of European and West-India GOODS; Nine packages marked A.B. are found, owner sought [see like ads Vol. II No. 70] ■ **Jordan and Poyer**, have just imported and to be sold at Mr. Wales's Store, Barbadoes Rum, etc. [see like ad Vol. II No. 70] ■ LEONARD BOARMAN, Newport, Charles-County, offers reward for return of runaway Mulatto man slave called Stephen Butler [see like ad Vol. II No. 71] ■ **Richard Conway**, has for sale salt, Lisbon and Oporto wines [see like ad Vol. II No. 67] ■ COLIN MAC IVER and CO. have for sale goods just imported in the Brig *Eglington* from Liverpool; Colin Mac Iver seeks to settle accounts from the late partnership of Dow, Mac Iver and Co. [see like ads Vol. II No. 70] ■ JOHN DUNDAS and COMPANY intend to move their store on the 11th of next month; have for sale a neat assortment of merchandise [see like ad Vol. II No. 71] ■ **W. Mounsher and Co.**, have for sale two riding chaises, etc. [see like ad Vol. II No. 71] ■ **James Ramsay**, has just imported a small quantity of Muscovado sugar and rum [see like ad Vol. II No. 71] ■ BATTAILE MUSE seeks to find lost pair of black saddle-bags, containing many papers and money [see like ad Vol. II No. 66] ■ Executors of the estate of THOMAS KIRKPATRICK, deceased, seek settlement of accounts [see like ad Vol. II No. 69] ■ JOHN FORMAN offers for breeding horse *OBSCURITY* [see like ad Vol. II No. 60] ■ DAVID GALLOWAY, Fredericksburg, offers for sale a small 154-acre farm, and a 510-acre tract of land, both in Spotsylvania County [see like ad Vol. II No. 70] ■ WILLIAM MONROE offers for sale at Leesburg a valuable 1225-acre plantation [see like ad Vol. II No. 70] ■ The Printing-Office is selling blank books, ledgers, journals, etc. [see like ad Vol. II No. 69] ■ ALX: Printed by GEORGE RICHARDS, and COMPANY, at their Printing-Office on Fairfax-street--by whom Advertisements, &c. are thankfully received for this Paper,--and where Printing is performed with Care and Expedition.

1785/06/23, Vol. II No. 73

Page 1. WILLIAM LYLES and CO., is selling rum [see like ad Vol. II No. 68] ■ **William Hartshorne And Company**, have for sale Barbadoes and Grenada Rum, etc. [see like ad Vol. II No. 71] ■ WILLIAMS, CARY and COMPANY announce sailing of the Brig *Jane and Elizabeth* by the first of July [see like ad Vol. II No. 72] ■ WILLIAM WILSON announces the Brigantine *Janet* will sail by the 25th of July [see like ad Vol. II No. 72] ■ BENJAMIN STODDERT announces the Ship *Fortune* will take in Tobacco consigned to Forrest and Stoddert [see like ad Vol. II No. 72] ■ Four Lots of Ground to be sold at the-Store [see like ad Vol. II No. 72] ■ The Printing-Office is selling blank books, ledgers, journals, etc. [see like ad Vol. II No. 69] ■ **Hooe and Harrison**, have to let upon Ground-Rent, several Lots of Land in this town [see like ad Vol. II No. 72] ■ **William Wilson**, has received by the *Janet* from Glasgow, a general assortment of dry goods [see like ad Vol. II

No. 72] ■ **Williams, Cary and Co.**, Have just received in the *Britannia*, a general assortment of European and East-India Goods [see like ad Vol. II No. 72] ■ **Elias Noah**, Merchant, will sell goods at the house of Mr. John Wise, at the Fountain Tavern [see like ad Vol. II No. 72] ■ **Richard Weightman**, Taylor and Habit-Maker, has removed to a house on Fairfax-street, and seeks an apprentice [see like ad Vol. II No. 72] ■ JOHN CLARK, Martinsburg, intends to open a school there [see like ad Vol. II No. 72] ■ The Brethren Lodge No. 39 is to meet on Friday the 24th instant [see like ad Vol. II No. 72] ■ The President and Directors of the Potomack Company authorize payment of dividends, etc.; John Potts, jun., Secretary of the Company announce upcoming meeting [see like ad Vol. II No. 71] ■ **James Ramsay**, has for sale at Mr. Watson's Store a small quantity of choice Muscovado sugar and rum [see like ad Vol. II No. 72] ■ BENEDICT CALVERT, Mount-Airy, seeks return of runaway Mulatto man named NICK [see like ad Vol. II No. 70] ■ BENJAMIN RANKINS offers reward for return of runaway Negro wench named Kate [see like ad Vol. II No. 71] ■ ☞ A great Variety of BLANKS, printed on good Paper, may be had at the Printing-Office.

Page 2.

PARIS, March 30. The following is the picture drawn in France of Great Britain: the British metropolis has realized Chancellor Bacon's prophecy. She is now mistress of all the treasures of India. Her great credit has raised her to such a degree of power, that she employs for the isles alone more than 500 ships and 10,000 seamen. The commerce between Jamaica and the Spanish provinces likewise employs a great number. The Negro trade produced last year upwards of fifteen millions of livres. Exportation of cane is always considerable; it produces annually more than 2,000,000 sterling. India produces an annual revenue of 200,000,000 of livres (tournois) and the expences of government. England maintains near 50,000 national soldiers, distributed in garrison at Jamaica, the other islands, America, Ireland, Canada, Nova Scotia, and Africa. Their cavalry is not numerous, but it is superior in appointment, in the choice of men and horses, to any other in Europe; but Great Britain principally reckons upon the strength of her navy, which at present consists of 177 ships of the line; 19 guard ships in the several ports, about a dozen on different services in India, America, and the islands; 90 in ordinary, and 44 upon the stocks. The total amounts to 627. ■ **VIENNA, March 19.** The Free Masons, for some time threatened with a dissolution by their enemies, are now in highest of spirits in consequence of the Emperor's ordinance: all public officers in the imperial dominions are commanded to second the Free Masons' endeavours, for promoting the success of their society. Also, the ordinance commands dissolution of those societies bearing the name but unrecognized by the general body of Free Masons. ■ **DUBLIN, April 2.** Yesterday, Mr. Thomas Cary surrendered to Caleb Jenkin, Esq., one of the high sheriffs, to stand trial on a charge of high treason, found against him in November last, on the examination of James Dowling ... A gentleman was lately comparing the pension list of Ireland to Noah's ark. Being asked the reason, he replied that it admitted both clean and unclean beasts; and that it saved from sinking many who would otherwise not be able to keep their heads above water. ■ **St. GEORGE's** (*Grenada*) **April 16.** We are authorized to release the following which both reflects great honor on the French government and may be of service to this colony. His Excellency the General received a letter from M. Le Vicomte de Damas, inclosing two copies of an Arrêt of the Superior Council of Martinique against Millet and others, condemning them to the Gallies for stealing slaves from this island. M. Damas expressed hope that this example of severity, by preventing a repetition of the crime, will put the inhabitants of the islands of this government in a state of ease and security, with respect to the safety of their property. ■ **St. GEORGE's** (*Bermuda*) **April 30.** Within these few days eight whales have been killed close to our shores, viz. Two pair by the boats off the West End, and four brought into harbour by the St. George's boats ... Extract of a letter from **London, Jan. 29.** So lucrative has the iron trade become, in consequence of the late great improvements in smelting furnace construction, that it is expected more metal will be made in the next five years than in the last twenty. Also, the large sums exported for foreign iron from Sweden, America, &c. Will now remain in our own country. **May 7.** By letters from Turk's island we learn that since the last rains they have made large quantities of salt, and continue to be successful. Salt sold at 2s. per bushel, and likely to keep so. ■ **NEW YORK, June 1.** Extract of a letter from **London, April 1:** His Majesty, the King of Great Britain, on March 24 went to the House of Peers and gave royal assent to Mr. Pitt's Newfoundland trade bill, which, in several stages had been opposed by members of the late ministry in both houses ... Accounts from Minorca mention the plague having broke out in Tripoli ... On March 11, the Sieur

Mochain of the Royal Academy of Sciences, at eight in the evening discovered a new comet in the constellation Andromeda, which was not then perceptible to the naked eye. At 8:26 the altitude of this comet was 7 degrees 8 minutes, and its northern declination 26 degrees 35 minutes. **June 9.** Capt. M'Lellan, in a schooner from Eustatia, arrived at Falmouth in New England the latter end of last month. The Captain informs that an American vessel, lately touching at St. Kitt's for water, was forbid anchoring on any pretence whatever; and that at another English island an American vessel was fired on for hoisting her colours ... Capt. Christopher Dyer, in a brigantine from Falmouth, New England, has had his vessel and cargo seized for attempting to sell at an English West India island. **June 10.** A correspondent observes this is the grand era for establishing the most essential concerns to these States--to frustrate the designs of a nation whose power we have shaken off, but who still wishes our ruin. We must begin by casting aside party views and parochialism, uniting to promote the public welfare. Britains trade policy has greatly distressed us, and will continue so until we counteract with a similar system of our own. We have insensibly hurryied into a connexion with her even while she has been prosecuting measures to embarrass us, in the discharge of debts we wantonly contract. We afforded every indulgence to her vessels, and peacefully suffered her merchants to pursue British commerce among us with any restriction, extra duties or hindrance whatever. ■ **PHILADELPHIA, June 8.** Everyone interested in this State's welfare must regret the persons bent on depreciating the new paper money. It is clear that without this sucedaneum, all business will stop for want of a circulating medium. This will involve the fate of everyone, high and low, rich and poor. They must be diabolically possessed who try so hard to compass what will bring calamity on an entire community, without any advantage to themselves; or even if they had, who could set their own paltry interest against the general welfare ... Much has been said on the poverty of the times: many the specious remedies proposed, few touching on the right key. Profusion and luxury, the sure concomitants of wealth, whether real or imaginary (and how imaginary our wealth has been is but too well known) have so far depraved our morals and taste, that very few live within the bounds of their income; and we generally rate the consequence of individuals, not by their virtue, their produce, or their integrity--but by their pomp, parade, and splendid living. This has excited a most destructive spirit of emulation in dress, the influence of which has caused so many to squander away their substance on gewgaws, ornaments, and expensive entertainments. What in all countries has ever been the result of such a procedure, has come to pass here. General bankruptcy, want, ruin and disgrace, threaten to overtake us in our revels, unless a speedy alteration takes place. But *remove the cause, and the effect will cease.* "Let us be frugal, industrious, and temperate, and we shall presently be rich; our mechanics will be employed; we shall be enabled to pay our debts; and hard money will become plenty." **June 13.** On Wednesday the 1st, the following melancholy accident happened at the paper mill of Mr. Simon Steddikorn, near this city: A young man, named Benjamin Andrews, being employed to do some work about the paper press, the ketch unfortunately broke, and the bar struck him in the forehead, with such violence, that it fractured his skull, and he expired in the prime of life, on Monday last. **June 15.** We are informed that Congress, some time since, came to the following resolution respecting the petition of sundry Boston merchants (the purport of which was to pray Congress to apply to the several States to invest it with authority to regulate their foreign trade, so as to avert the union's impending ruin from the hostile systems of trade of European powers) viz. "Ordered, that the petition lie, until Congress shall take into consideration the report of their committee, on an application to the States, to invest Congress with the power of regulating trade, under certain provisoes." ■ **BALTIMORE, June 14.** Since PAPER MONEY has been emitted at Philadelphia, it is said, that the citizens at large have experienced every conveniency from it, and that it passes equal in credit with gold and silver. [The writer approves, and proceeds with three quarters of a column of fine prose in support of each aspect of American resources, needs, and prospects.] Let us instruct our general Assembly representatives *prudently* to emit paper currency; and let our patriotic conduct and exertions afford them every support in this salutary undertaking, which will facilitate our commerce, relieve our poor, and make us feel the blessings of INDEPENDENCE. ■ **ALX, June 23**. A late English Paper mentions, that the principal Manufacturers of Manchester are so much enraged at the daily Oppression of arbitrary Excise Laws, that they have universally put Notices up in their Warehouses, expressive of their Abhorrence of these destructive Laws, and that they will deliver no more Work out after the 2d Day of May, by which Resolutions thousands of industrious Poor will be totally destitute of Bread. ■ DIED.] At his Seat at Richland, Col. WILLIAM BRENT. ■ NAVAL-OFFICE, ALX. *Inward Entries.* Ship *Ann*, A. Huie, from Glasgow;

Schooner *Lottery*, T. Mann, Baltimore; Sloop *Judith*, S. Martin, and Sloop *Friendship*, O. Reed, Rhode-Island; Brig *Glory*, D. Jackson, Whitehaven; Sloop *Polly*, J. Elwood, Philadelphia. *Cleared Outwards*. Ship *Young Daniel*, S. Wybrants, for Lisbon; Brig *Industry*, P. Morie, Madera; Sloop *Surprise*, J.T. [Brooks], Surinam; Schooner *Lottery*, T. Mann, Baltimore, Sloop *Molly Beverly*, W. Wade, Charleston; Schooner *Nancy*, N. Spooner, Barbadoes.

On Saturday the 25th instant, will be sold at the Vendue-Store, A GENERAL assortment of WET and DRY GOODS, consisting of rum, sugar, coffee, hyson tea in quarter chests, soap, claret in bottles, beef and Mackerel in barrels, &c.&c. coarse and fine cloths, printed linens, calicoes, gauzes, muslins, silks, coarse and fine Irish linens, handkerchiefs, threads, thread and cotton stockings, boots and boot legs, &c.&c.

SAMUEL ARELL, Vendue-Master.
ALX, June 23, 1785.

☞ On Saturday next will be let at the Court-House, at three o'clock P.M. to the lowest bidder, the building of a Gallery and Cupula to the Church.--A plan may be seen at Mr. RICHARD ARELL's, ALX, June 23, 1785. ■ THOSE who have BOOKS belonging to the late WILLIAM RAMSAY, Esq., are requested to return them to WILLIAM RAMSAY, ALX, June 20, 1785.

Page 3. **Jesse Taylor**, Has lately imported from different markets, AN assortment of DRY-GOODS suitable for the season; also, best and second hyson, sequin, green and bohea teas, Lisbon and Oporto wines, loaf sugar, &c. which, with a few hogsheads of West-India rum and crates of queen's china, he will sell by wholesale or retail for cash, country produce, or short credit. ALX, June 17, 1785. ☞ Amongst the above goods are a large assortment of saddlery. ■ The Subscriber has for SALE, TWO LOTS OF LAND, in the County of Loudon, containing 150 acres each, situated on the road from Colonel [Leven] Powell's to ALX, 20 miles above Newgate and fifteen from Leesburg, convenient to several mills on Goose-Creek and Little-River; the quality of this land is exceeding fine for corn, wheat or tobacco and under a good fence, and there may be made a small meadow. As both lots join each other, I will either sell them together or separate as may best suit the purchaser. Grain may be sown this fall and possession given the first of February 1786. Any gentleman inclinable to purchase, may see the land and know the terms, by applying to Colonel LEVEN POWELL, living near the premises, or Mr. WILLIAM DUVALL in ALX. Also for sale, another TRACT containing 200 acres, situated 5 miles from ALX on the main road to Colchester, on which there is at least 60 acres of meadow land, the rest high land fit for corn, wheat or tobacco. As to this land it needs no recommendation being allowed by all gentlemen who have seen it, to be equal, if not superior to any land in the State. Any gentleman inclinable to purchase may know the terms by applying to Major WILLIAM JOHNSTON, on the premises, or Mr. WILLIAM DUVALL. DENNIS M. JOHNSTON, ALX, June 20, 1785. ■ PATRICK CAVAN, Leesburg, offers for sale 14 lots of ground and other property in the town of Leesburg [see like ad Vol. II No. 71] ■ WHEREAS a certain JOHN FISHER THROCKMORTON, Master of the Snow *Amelia*, or *Lady Johnston*, now lying at the port of Nangomy, in Potomack, has reported to Colonel Robert T. Hooe, that he the said Throckmorton delivered unto me the Subscriber, in London, several letters for the said Col. Hooe: I hereby deny ever having such letters, and mean to prove by Mr. Jonathan Swift, that his reports are false and malicious; and in consequence of the same, shall commence an action against him for defamation. WILLIAM TAYLOR, June 17, 1785.

TWENTY DOLLARS REWARD.

RAN away this morning from the Subscriber, a very likely Mulatto man, named SANCHO, about 5 feet 4 inches high, about 26 years of age, and his hair straight for his colour: He had on and took with him one dark broadcloth coat with a brown velvet cape and buttons at the sleeves, one short dark country coat, white cloth jacket and breeches, two pair of yarn stockings, one pair of old boots, one pair of old shoes and a new felt hat with red lining. He is very artful and sensible, is a middling good carpenter and can do something at most kinds of work.--It is expected he has a pass and will change his name.--Whoever takes up said fellow and secures him so that his Master may get him again, shall receive TEN DOLLARS if twenty miles from home, and if above that distance the above reward, and reasonable charges paid if brought home. JAMES PERRY.

Montgomery County, Maryland, June 20, 1785.
☞ I expect he will endeavour to get on board some ship or go the back country.

ALL persons indebted to the estate of Mr. ABRAHAM BARNES, deceased, are requested to make immediate payment, or their accounts and bonds will be put into the hands of an Attorney; and all those who have any just claims against the said estate are desired to bring them in properly adjusted, that provision may be made for payment. ROBERT BOGGESS, Executor, June 20, 1785. ■ **Daniel and Isaac M'Pherson**, Have for sale on the most reasonable terms, for cash or country produce, **Tar, pitch, turpentine**, indigo, sail duck and cordage, with a variety of other articles. ALX, June 20, 1785. ■ THE Partnership between LOWRY and M'KENNA being this day dissolved by mutual consent, it is earnestly requested that all those who stand indebted to this house make immediate payment, especially those whose accounts are more than three months on their books. Mr. Lowry proposing shortly to embark for England in order to bring over a spring assortment, offers his services to his friends in the commission line, and hopes his conduct will merit the thanks of those who employ him. ☞ A few cases of *excellent* old port for sale, at the store, next door to Mr. Henry Lyles's, ALX, June 21, 1785. ■ FOR SALE, THE noted TRACT of LAND, called Clarksburgh, in the County of Shenandoah, Virginia, on the main road leading from Winchester to Stantown, where it crosses the North River, containing about 1600 acres, about 400 of which are low grounds, in a bend of the river equal to most lands on the western waters, 200 acres cleared and in good order for cropping, with a dwelling-house 38 by 30 feet, five rooms below stairs, four of them with fire places, a kitchen, store-house, smith's-shop, barns, stables, &c.--Likewise, a neat well contrived distillery.--The lands will be shewn to any person wanting to purchase by Colonel T. Beale or Mr. Reuben Moore, who live near the premises.--Distant payments for one half the purchase-money and a good title made by the Subscriber, living near Dumfries, Virginia. BURR HARRISON, June 20, 1785. ■ ALL persons indebted to the estate of the late JOHN WOOD, Captain of the Ship *Stanley*, are requested to make immediate payment to the Subscriber; and all those who have any demands against said estate are desired to have them immediately proved according to law, and bring them in so that they may be paid.--All such are to take notice that as I intend closing his accounts as soon as possible, I will not pay, or hold myself accountable for any account not furnished me in the course of three months from this date. JESSE TAYLOR, Administrator, ALX, June 17, 1785. ■ THE creditors of HUGH GIBNEY, deceased, are desired to send in their accounts for settlement; and to enable the Subscriber to discharge the same, all those indebted to his estate are earnestly requested to make immediate payment to JOSEPH FULLMER, Administrator, ALX, June 18, 1785. ■ WHEREAS extending the navigation of Potomack, causes may persons to be desirous of possessing property on the river, before any very rapid rise takes place, which must inevitably be the case so soon as some few of the obstructions are removed: I therefore offer to such as are inclined to purchase, 456 acres of LAND, situated at Fort-Cumberland, lying on the river and adjoining to the new town of Washington, which is now rapidly improving, and promises at a future day to be one of the most considerable towns in this State.--Part of this land is reputed equal to any under heaven, and I am well informed of its produce being from forty to sixty bushels of Indian-corn per acre. Valuable as this land is, for cash or tobacco I will sell or give it in exchange for property, in or near to George-Town or ALX. GEORGE FRENCH, George-Town, June 17, 1785. ■ BURGES BALL, Culpepper, has for sale a saw-mill and 1250 acres of Land in Orange County [see like ad Vol. II No. 71] ■ **W. Mounsher and Co.**, have for sale two riding chaises, etc. [see like ad Vol. II No. 71] ■ JOHN DUNDAS and COMPANY intend to move their store on the 11th of next month; have for sale a neat assortment of merchandise [see like ad Vol. II No. 71] ■ WILLIAM SCOTT has for sale sundry tenements in Fairfax County and Fauquier County [see like ad Vol. II No. 72] ■ PHILIP DALBY offers reward for return of stray horse [see like ad Vol. II No. 72] ■ LEONARD BOARMAN, Newport, Charles-County, offers reward for return of runaway Mulatto man slave called Stephen Butler [see like ad Vol. II No. 71].

Page 4. Poetry. From the European Magazine, "The Fair Thief, by the late Earl of Egremont." ■ WILLIAM FITZHUGH offers for sale a valuable tract of land in Stafford County [see like ad Vol. II No. 70] ■ **George F. Norton**, has for sale goods just imported by the *Amelia*, Captain Throckmorton, from London [see like ad Vol. II No. 72] ■ JOHN FORMAN offers for breeding horse *OBSCURITY* [see like ad Vol. II No. 60] ■ **Richard Conway**, has for sale salt, Lisbon and Oporto wines [see like ad Vol. II No. 67] ■ SAMUEL CANBY, Leesburg, offers for sale or exchange tracts in Monongalia and Jefferson counties [see like ad Vol. II No. 64] ■ WILLIAM MONROE offers for sale at Leesburg a valuable 1225-acre plantation [see like ad Vol. II No. 70] ■ HENRY BUDD offers ten dollars reward for return of runaway Irish servant man named JOHN BUCKLY [see like ad Vol. II No. 70] ■ ALX: Printed by GEORGE RICHARDS, and COMPANY, at their Printing-Office on Fairfax-street--by whom Advertisements, &c. are thankfully received for this Paper,--and where Printing is performed with Care and Expedition.

1785/06/30, Vol. II No. 74

Page 1. A list of the Fortunate Numbers in the George-Town Academy Lottery [Note: Chart giving numbers drawn and dollars awarded is reproduced below]. ■ **William Hartshorne And Company**, have for sale Barbadoes and Grenada Rum, etc. [see like ad Vol. II No. 71] ■ **Hooe and Harrison**, have to let upon Ground-Rent, several Lots of Land in this town [see like ad Vol. II No. 72] ■ **William Wilson**, has received by the *Janet* from Glasgow, a general assortment of dry goods [see like ad Vol. II No. 72].

Page 2.

LONDON, April 22. Captain Lyon of the ship *Matty and Betty*, who arrived Liverpool April 21, reports as follows. On the 9th, about 30 leagues west of Cape Clear, he fell in with the ship *George*, Benjamin Curtis, Master, from Virginia bound for Ostend, who on February 13 in lat. 50, long. 9, 40, had the upper works stove in on the starboard side; on the 19th lost their water casks off the deck; the 29th the boatswain fell out of the maintop, and died April 3rd; March 30 the carpenter and another man were washed overboard, which obliged them to scuttle the longboat, the sea making a fair breach over the ship, to throw three hogsheads of tobacco over board to ease the bows. Captain Curtis had but 8 men left, and they were at the pumps every half hour. The same day, Captain Lyon fell in with the brig *Live Oak*, Captain M'Bride, from New Providence for London, out eight weeks and three days. Captain M'Bride, on March 9, spoke with the ship *Commerce*, Captain Robert Mercer, from London for Philadelphia, lat. 46, 47, long. 36, 57, fourteen days from the Downs ... A new coinage of guineas and half guineas to the amount of £30,000 is now going on at the Mint in the Tower, from fresh dies, by order the Lords of the Treasury, and will be issued shortly. **May 6.** A private letter from Amsterdam says advice from Cadiz says the *Vrow Geertruydenberg*, bound to that port, was taken within sight of the harbour by two Barbary corsairs, but a French man of war lying there slipt her cable, went in chase of them, retook the Dutch ship, sunk one of the corsairs, took the other, and brought her with the Dutch ship into Cadiz. **UTRECHT, April 19.** We are much surprised to hear from Graaf that the General Baron Van Monster, the Governor, in order to secure that place from attack, flooded its environs--by which seven villages of the Elector Palatine (who is absolutely neuter in the affair) are under water. Mr. Cornet, Envoy Extraordinary from the Elector, has complained to their High Mightinesses. ■ **KINGSTON, May 14.** The following, we are assured, are extracts from the Prince of Oranges letter to their High Mightinesses the States General, last February, relative to the weak and defenceless state of the Republic: "How often have we foretold the probable consequences of the want of unanimity and mutual good will? And how unfortunately have our predictions been verified, by the event on the appearance of troubles and disputes between two powerful neighbours, France and England? The Republic was in no wise interested in those troubles and disputes, nor ought it to have taken any part in them, except by avoiding the very measures it pursued,--measures which through the weak and defenceless state of the country, produced a war that endangered all our domestic rights and foreign possessions. The dangers of those measures appeared to us so imminent, that we thought it our duty to set it forth in its fullest extent to the inhabitants of these Provinces, in the hope, that they might at least be delayed till the country should be in a better posture of defence. No credit, however, was given to our advice and predictions, that those measures would terminate in a most hazardous war; and yet the event proved them to have been but too well founded. The same circumstances attended the Republic's accession to the Armed Neutrality,--a measure we in truth considered as advantageous to the Republic only on account of its weak and defenceless situation, but what we clearly perceived must give so great umbrage to the power against which it was formed, that it would necessarily be followed by a speedy declaration of war; consequently that treaty of neutrality would, in the end, prove detrimental instead of useful, unless we could obtain some particular dispensations in our favor, and here too our apprehensions were justified by the event. By such means we have lost a dear ally, whose friendship would *now* be of more avail to the States than that of any other power in Europe." **May 18.** The Barbary corsairs, since the repulse of the Spaniards at Algiers are become so exceeding troublesome, that some European powers have had to fit out light frigates to cruise against them. The Spaniards and Portuguese have sent some ships into the Mediterranean to meet with these banditti. A swarm has been seen in the Corsican seas, and the Genoese have dispatched several Xebecs after them. Should they meet, a warm engagement is expected. The pirate squadron's Commodore carries a death's head and battle axe, by way of ensign ... Although earlier accounts could not be entirely depended on, from the Musquito Shore, we can now assert a kind of treaty has been made between the English and Spanish commanding officers, who met in the city of Truxillo for that purpose. It stipulates that English settlers shall remain in quiet and peaceful possession of the country for two years, while both parties will try to accelerate a special treaty between the courts of London and Madrid, respecting all claims of each to the territory there. ■ **PORTSMOUTH, (N.E.) June 3.** Extract of a letter from a gentleman in Cadiz, to his friend in **Kittery, April 12.** Turks have been cruising off this island, taking two American vessels--one of Baltimore, one of Philadelphia--but did not enslave the crews. One

A LIST of the Fortunate NUMBERS in the GEORGE-TOWN ACADEMY LOTTERY.

☞ Those Numbers which have no Figures annexed to them are Prizes of Four Dollars each.

No.	Dol.	No.	Dol.	No.	Dol.	No.	Dol.	No.	Dol.	No.	Dol.	No.	Dol.	No.	Dol.	No.	Dol.	No.	Dol.	No.	Dol.	No.	Dol.
2		254		460	100	730		959		1190		1477	8	1755		1981		2255		2524		2757	
4		64		64		34		62		91		79	10	57		82	8	58		26		60	
6		73		70		37		67		1205		80		58		83	50	60		30		62	
9		79		77	8	42		73		6		81	200	65		87		63		35		79	
20		81		501	25	43		74		8		83		71		93	25	87	10	42		83	
21		84		2		45		84		10		85		75	25	97		91		47		85	
23		87		6		47		87		12		87		76		99		93		50		86	
25		92		11		51		92		14		90		81	10	2000		94		53		90	
27		97	100	12		52		93		23	50	1510		85	8	2		2304		58	8	91	10
29		98		15		54	100	1001		34	10	23		87		3		19		59	10	96	8
32		301	50	18	10	59	500	2		39		26		93	8	7		34		60		2803	
38		2		22		66		3	10	42		29		96	10	11	25	35		61	8	15	200
39	10	6		23		68	100	9		46	10	31		98	50	12		37		65	25	26	25
41		7		24		76		12	8	59		33		1800		14		40		69		27	
42		8		32		77		19		63		36		1		16		48		71		28	
46		10		38		79		24		64		50		2		18		51		73		30	
48		11		42	10	81		25		65		56		7		20	100	56	8	81		33	
61		14	10	45	8	84		26	8	70		61		8		21		57		83		34	
62		17		49		85		37		75	8	63	10	9	8	23		58		87		35	
67		23		53		96		38		85		69		13		30		72		89		37	8
71	8	24		60		98		45		88		71		15		31		73		2606		38	
73		27		63		802		46	8	95	8	79		17		33	8	87		8		43	
80		37		64		3		49	8	1301		82		19	8	48		88		10		49	
81	8	46		70		11		50		2		83	8	23		67		92		12		54	
82		47	200	71		17		52	8	4	8	86		26		77		93		14		64	
88		53		77	25	20		53		8		89	25	27		85	8	99	50	20		72	
96		62		85		22		62		15	8	98		30		90		2400		23		75	
99		64		87		31		64		16		1600	8	34		92		4	8	26		77	
101	50	68	8	89		32		65		23		3		35	10	95		8		29	10	79	
2		70		90		39		67		32		11		36		97		10		30		81	
6		72	50	97		40	10	68		34		14		37		99		11	25	32		86	
11		76		607		42		74		38		16		42		2102		13		34	10	88	
17	25	80		11		45		77		39		17	10	53		9		20		38		92	
20		81	8	18		47		81		47		19		54		13		23		39		94	8
27		87		20		49		94		69		20		57		14		28		40		2906	
33		91		29		50		97	25	77		29		59		19		29		44		8	8
36		95		31		67		99		86		32		60		26		31		48		10	
37		400		32		72		1100		93		37		61		35		38		55		14	
42	50	1		33		79		6		95		40		62	~~50~~	38		43		56	10	21	10
52		4		36		83		8		97		45	8	72	200	42		50		66		37	
58		7	8	37		86		14		98		46		83		43		54		71		38	8
66		9		38		96		20		99		54		90		44		60		73		57	
67		10		43		900	10	22		1400	8	57		95		47	8	62		79	25	62	
68		12		44		1	8	31		3		70		99		51		63		81		66	
70		17		45		5		32		8		72		1900		52		65		86	8	70	1000
71		19		51		7		37		9		74	8	9		60		67		91		72	
77		21		52		12		39		25		78		10	8	72		73		94		75	
80		26		58	8	13		47		30		79		20		77		76		95		78	
90	8	28		59		16		48		35		82		24		80		77		2711		98	
91		34		63		17		49		43	50	1700		31		81		78		17		3000	100
93		37		71		25		51		44		5		35		82		83		19			
95	100	41		76		33		53		48		16		40	10	89		89		24	25		
201	25	43		89		35		55		52		17		42	25	2201		96		25			
10		45		91		36		56		55		33		45		9		99		30			
21		46		93	10	40		58		57		35		52		21		2500		31			
24		47		700		41		65		58		40		58	500	35		1	8	34			
29		49		3		42		67	8	66		42		63		38		12		36			
30		50		4		44		68	8	68		46		65		42		15		38	8		
34		52		12		48		74		70		48		76		46	10	16	10	49	8		
36		53		14		49		82		73		51	10	79	10	53		18	100	51			
38		56		24		58		83		75		52	25	80		54		19	8	53			

of the Captain's letter to Mr. Harrison, a merchant in Cadiz, says if Congress will pay them a certain sum of money every year, and settle a trade with them, our ships may pass; otherwise they will make slaves of all they can take. We also have advice from Algiers that the Algerines are fitting out three sail of privateers to cruise off Cadiz, for American ships. ■ **NEW YORK, June 14.** Sunday arrived here from Shelburne, Nova Scotia, a sloop load of refugees, in violation of a law of this State, which deems it misprision of treason for them to return; despite that, they had rather trust the mercy of the country they have so grossly injured, than remain any longer in that horrid place, where meagre want and oppression stalk unrivaled ... Monday the 9th the schooner *Keats*, Christian Miller, Master, was piratically run away with from Copelano's wharf, in Halifax, by four men: Richard Powell, William Buckley, George Taylor and William Durisian. The master having gone on board about eleven or twelve o'clock at night, and asleep in his cabin, was awakened by uncommon motion of the vessel. On going on deck he was astonished to find himself a sea, and Halifax light bearing west about three leagues. He was made to understand he was a prisoner, and the pirates proceeded westward, landing him on Bald Tusket island. He stayed four days, making a raft tied with cod line given him by the pirates, upon which he fastened himself and committed himself to the sea. The wind setting on shore brought him to land after about 24 hours. After experiencing many hardships, he arrived at Shelburne Sunday the 29th. ■ **PHILADELPHIA, June 16.** By the ship *Alexander* we learn the bankers of Glasgow, owing to the great importation there of dollars, will take them at no more than four shillings, and at 4/2. The former value of a dollar was four shillings, six pence, sterling. **June 18.** A New York paper of last Tuesday reports: From Boston we learn of a report current there of British frigates firing on our fishermen fishing on the Grand Bank of Newfoundland. ■ **ALX, June 30.** Last Friday, being the Anniversary of St. John the Baptist, the Brethren of Lodge No. 39, met at their Lodge-Room, from whence they walked in Procession to the Presbyterian Meeting-House; and after hearing an elegant and well adapted Discourse, suitable to the Occasion, preached by the Rev. Mr. M'Whir, they proceeded in the same Order to Mr. REEDER's Tavern, where they dined, and spent the Afternoon in the greatest Hilarity. ■ The British Packet *Greyhound*, Capt. Dunn, in 6 Weeks from Falmouth, arrived at New-York the 18th Instant. ■ NAVAL-OFFICE, ALX. *Inward Entries.* Sloop *Speedwell*, B. Prince, from St. Croix. *Cleared Outwards.* Brig *Patient Mary*, W. Sleigh, for Cork; Schooner *Virginia*, S. Davis, West-Indies; Sloop *Judith*, S. Martin, Sloop *Friendship*, O. Reed, and Sloop *Bathsheba*, J. Ingraham, Rhode-Island; Sloop *General Washington*, T.J. Lake, Philadelphia; Brig *Cesar*, J. Atkinson, Whitehaven; Schooner *Mary*, D. Johnston, Barbadoes. ■ ANECDOTE of the Author of the BATH GUIDE. SOME years ago as Mr. Ansty was returning home, with some jovial companions, through Bath about three in the morning, they accidentally met with the watch, who was regularly crying the hour.--In the mirth of hearth they were in, this was construed by some of the bucks to be a sort of satire upon them for keeping bad hours. Mr. Ansty therefore insisted that the fellow should cry past eleven o'clock instead of three, on pain of corporal punishment.--After some remonstrance the poor man was obliged to comply--but before he had finished his oration, suddenly recollecting himself, he said shrewdly, I know the *hour* I am to call, but *pray, gentlemen, what sort of weather would you chuse to have? Sunshine*, you scoundrel, to be sure--*Sunshine*--Upon which (notwithstanding its raining at the time violently) the accommodating watchman gravely cries out in the proper key--Past eleven o'clock, and by *particular desire, a sunshining night.*

From the *Gentleman's Magazine*, for November 1782. Description of a Monument erected in Westminster Abby, for Major JOHN ANDRE, designed by ROBERT ADAM, Esq., Architect, and executed in Statuary Marble by Mr. P.M. Van Gelder, Sculptor.

THIS Monument is composed of a Sacrophagus,
elevated on a pedestal, upon the pannel of
which is engraved the following inscription:
Sacred to the Memory
of Major JOHN ANDRE,
Who, raised by his Merit, at an early Period of
his Life, to the Rank of Adjutant-General
of the British Forces in America, and
employed in an important but hazardous Enterprise, fell a Sacrifice to his
Zeal for his King and Country
on the 2d of October, 1780,
aged 29, universally be-
loved and esteemed by
the army in which
he served, and la-
manted even by
his Foes,
His Gracious Sovereign King George III, has
caused this Monument to be erected.

On the front of the Sarcophagus, General Washington is represented in his tent, at the moment when he had received the report of the court-martial held on Major Andre; at the same time a flag of truce arrived from the British army, with a letter for General Washington, to treat for the Major's life. But the fatal sentence being already passed, the flag was sent back without the hoped for clemency in his favor. Major Andre received his condemnation with that fortitude and resolution which had always marked his character, and is represented going, with unshaken spirit, to meet his doom.

On the top of the Sarcophagus, a figure of Britannia, reclined, laments the premature fate of so gallant an officer. The British lion too seems instinctively to mourn his untimely death.

PRICES CURRENT, ALX. / Tobacco, 26s. to 28s. per Ct. / Fine Flour, 28s. per Barrel. / Wheat, 5/6 per Bushel. / Jamaica Spirits, 4/6 per Gallon. / Windward Rum, 3s. per Ditto. / Continental Rum, 2s. per Ditto. / Molasses, 1/8 per Ditto. / Muscovado Sugar, 35s. to 42/6 per Ct. / Salt, 3s. per Bushel, by Retail. / Corn, 3s. per Bushel / Exchange, 40.

☞ BROADCLOTHS. **Jonathan Swift and Co.**, Have for sale at their store on Capt. Harper's wharf, A General assortment of the most fashionable coloured broadcloths both fine and coarse, which they will dispose of for the sterling cost and charges, which were selected from the first manufactories in England, and are as low charged as any ever imported.--Also, a general assortment of DRY GOODS, suitable for the season, which they will dispose of at a very moderate advance for cash, bills, produce, or short credit with security.--They have on hand excellent London porter in small hampers, New-England rum, chocolate, pimento, hyson, souchong and bohea teas in chests and ½ chests. ☞ They discount 2½ per cent. for ready money as usual. ALX, June 30, 1785 ■ TO BE LET, THE Store now occupied by Mr. MARTIN BROWN.--Also, to be let on ground-rent for twelve years, three Lots on King-street, 23 feet front by 76 feet deep, one of which fronts the whole depth of St. Asaph-street.--The tenant may build as he pleases and dispose of his house at the expiration of the term.--For further particulars inquire of ADAM LYNN, ALX, June 28, 1785.

Page 3.

On Saturday the 2d of July, will be sold at the Vendue-Store,

A QUANTITY of WET and DRY GOODS, consisting of West-India and Continental rum in hogsheads and barrels, tea in quarter chests, sugar, chocolate, soap, claret in bottles, broadcloths, linens, calamancoes, calicoes, fustians, corded demities, cambricks, lawns, silk, thread and cotton handkerchiefs, threads, checks, knives and forks, shoes, an elegant assortment of cutlery, a few hogsheads of tobacco, 5 or 6000 feet of inch plank, 8000 18 inch green cypress shingles, and a variety of other articles.

SAMUEL ARELL, Vendue-Master.

ALX, June 30, 1785.

THE Subscriber begs leave to inform the public, that having finished his studies under the celebrated Mr. Peale of Philadelphia, in Portrait Painting, he is now ready to exert himself to the utmost of his abilities in taking LIKENESSES in oil, and flatters himself he shall please those who may employ him.--He may be seen at Mr. Lownes's in Fairfax-street. CHARLES PEALE POLK, ALX, June 28, 1785. ■ TO BE LET, And possession given on the 25th of July. A Convenient DWELLING-HOUSE on Water-street, opposite Hooe and Harrison's stores.--Apply to D. and I. M'PHERSON. ☞ They have for sale, a quantity of West-India rum and muscovado sugar in hogsheads and barrels, and Madera wine by the pipe, hogshead and quarter cask. ALX, June 28, 1785. ■ THE Subscriber takes this method to acquaint the public and his friends in particular, that he intends keeping a BOARDING-HOUSE at Bath this season, at the sign of the White Horse (the old place) where every thing requisite will be furnished for the accommodation of those gentlemen and ladies who may favor him with their company, and they may be assured, that every exertion in his power shall be made, to render the place and time agreeable, and shall be very thankful for all favors conferred on their most obedient humble servant, JOSEPH BUTLER, Berkeley County, June 15, 1785. ■ Just imported in the *Speedwell*, Capt. Prince, from the West-Indies, and to be sold by **Robert Donaldson**, At Mr. WILLIAM HUNTER, junior's store, A FEW puncheons of high proof rum by the hogshead, and a small quantity of muscovado sugar of the first quality by the Barrel.--Also, a few pieces of white and dyed jeans, German cords, denims, muslinets and printed linens, by the piece.--Also, white cotton counterpanes at a very moderate advance. ALX, June 27, 1785. ■ WILLIAM SCOTT has for sale sundry tenements in Fairfax County and Fauquier County [see like ad Vol. II No. 72]. ■ Just imported by the Subscriber, in the *Janet* from Glasgow, and last vessels from London and Liverpool, **A general assortment of** DRY GOODS, which he will sell on reasonable terms by the package or piece. ALEXANDER CAMPBELL, Dumfries, June 25, 1785. ■ ALL persons indebted to the estate of the late Mr. CYRUS COPPER of ALX, deceased, are requested to make immediate payment to the Subscriber; and those who have any demands against the said estate are desired to bring in their claims and receive payment. ELIZABETH COPPER, Administratrix, ALX, June 29, 1785. ■ RAN away from the Subscriber, on Saturday the 11th instant, a Negro woman, named WINNY, about 17 years of age, has been lately corrected for her misbehaving, the marks of which may possibly still appear, has a very stubborn temper and surly countenance.--Whoever apprehends said Negro and brings her home, shall receive 20s. if taken in the County, and if out of the County 40s. and all reasonable charges paid. LAWRENCE HOOFF, ALX, June 27, 1785. ■ WILLIAM FITZHUGH offers for sale a valuable tract of land in Stafford County [see like ad Vol. II No. 70] ■ PHILIP DALBY offers reward for return of stray horse [see like ad Vol. II No. 72] ■ **Robert Lyle**, Has for sale at his store, opposite the Printing-Office, HYSON, green, souchong and bohea teas, French and Spanish brandy, Jamaica spirits and rum, wine, a general assortment of DRY-GOODS suitable for the season, amongst which are mens' hats of all kinds and womens' ditto full trimmed and feathered.--Said Lyle has to rent 2 or 3 rooms of a house.--Possession will be given immediately.--Also, 4 rooms of another house which will be ready in three weeks from this time.--He has also to rent or sell, one LOT of GROUND 25 feet on Fairfax-street, by 75 or 80 in depth.--Also, two LOTS on Royal-street, 27 feet in front each, by 60 deep.--Also to be rented, the STORE opposite the Printing-Office.--For terms apply as above. ALX, June 30, 1785. ■ TO BE LET, For one or more Years, and Possession given the First of August next, THE noted PUBLIC HOUSE so long kept by Mr. JOHN LOMAX.--The Situation, Conveniencies, Out-Houses, &c. are so universally known as to make it needless to particularize them.--For terms apply to JOHN WISE, ALX, June 30, 1785. ■ **George F. Norton**, has for sale goods just imported by the *Amelia*, Captain Throckmorton, from London [see like ad Vol. II No. 72] ■ The Printing-Office is selling blank books, ledgers, journals, etc. [see like ad Vol. II No. 69].

Page 4. Poetry. "Verses Written in a LADY's PRAYER-BOOK." ■ **Jesse Taylor**, Has lately imported from different markets, an assortment of dry goods [see like ad Vol. II No. 73] ■ Four Lots of Ground with a south front on Prince-street will be sold at the Vendue-Store [see like ad Vol. II No. 73] ■ DENNIS M. JOHNSTON has for sale two lots of land in Loudon County [see like ad Vol. II No. 73] ■ BURR HARRISON has for sale a noted tract of land called Clarksburgh, in Shenandoah County [see like ad Vol. II No. 73] ■ **Daniel and Isaac M'Pherson** have for sale tar, pitch, turpentine, etc. [see like ad Vol. II No. 73] ■ The Partnership between Lowry and M'Kenna is dissolved and request that accounts are settled; Lowry to soon leave for England [see like ads Vol. II No. 73] ■ WILLIAM TAYLOR, London, denies having received from John F. Throckmorton letters [see like ad Vol. II No. 73] ■ ROBERT BOGGESS, Executor of Abraham Barnes, deceased, seeks to settle accounts [see like ad Vol. II No. 73] ■ BENJAMIN STODDERT announces the Ship *Fortune* will take in Tobacco consigned to Forrest and Stoddert [see like ad Vol. II No. 72] ■ JAMES PERRY offers reward for return of runaway Mulatto man named SANCHO [see like ad Vol. II No. 73] ■ GEORGE FRENCH offers for sale 456 acres of Land at Fort-Cumberland [see like ad Vol. II No. 73] ■ THOSE who have BOOKS belonging to the late WILLIAM RAMSAY, Esq., are requested to return them to WILLIAM RAMSAY, ALX, June 20, 1785. ■ **Williams, Cary and Co.**, Have just received in the *Britannia*, a general assortment of European and East-India Goods [see like ad Vol. II No. 72] ■ WILLIAM WILSON announces the Brigantine *Janet* will sail by the 25th of July [see like ad Vol. II No. 72] ■ WILLIAMS, CARY and COMPANY announce sailing of the Brig *Jane and Elizabeth* by the first of July [see like ad Vol. II No. 72] ■ WILLIAM LYLES and CO., is selling rum [see like ad Vol. II No. 68] ■ JESSE TAYLOR, Administrator of the estate of the late JOHN WOOD, Captain of the Ship *Stanley*, seeks to settle accounts [see like ad Vol. II No. 73] ■ JOSEPH FULLMER, Administrator of HUGH GIBNEY, deceased, seeks to settle accounts [see like ad Vol. II No. 73] ■ **Richard Weightman**, Taylor and Habit-Maker, has removed to a house on Fairfax-street, and seeks an apprentice [see like ad Vol. II No. 72] ■ JOHN CLARK, Martinsburg, intends to open a school there [see like ad Vol. II No. 72] ■ ☞ A great Variety of BLANKS, printed on good

Paper, may be had at the Printing-Office. ■ ALX: Printed by GEORGE RICHARDS, and COMPANY, at their Printing-Office on Fairfax-street--by whom Advertisements, &c. are thankfully received for this Paper,--and where Printing is performed with Care and Expedition.

1785/07/07, Vol. II No. 75

Page 1. WILLIAM LYLES and CO., is selling rum [see like ad Vol. II No. 68] ■ JESSE TAYLOR, Administrator of the estate of the late JOHN WOOD, Captain of the Ship *Stanley*, seeks to settle accounts [see like ad Vol. II No. 73] ■ WILLIAM WILSON announces the Brigantine *Janet* will sail by the 25th of July [see like ad Vol. II No. 72]. ■ **Robert Donaldson** has for sale goods imported in the *Speedwell*, Capt. Prince, from the West-Indies [see like ad Vol. II No. 74] ■ LAWRENCE HOOFF offers reward for return of runaway Negro woman named WINNY [see like ad Vol. II No. 74] ■ GEORGE FRENCH offers for sale 456 acres of Land at Fort-Cumberland [see like ad Vol. II No. 73] ■ ALEXANDER CAMPBELL, Dumfries, offers for sale goods imported in the Ship *Janet* [see like ad Vol. II No. 74] ■ ELIZABETH COPPER, Administratrix of the estate of the late Mr. CYRUS COPPER, deceased, seeks to settle accounts [see like ad Vol. II No. 74] ■ ROBERT BOGGESS, Executor of Abraham Barnes, deceased, seeks to settle accounts [see like ad Vol. II No. 73] ■ JAMES PERRY offers reward for return of runaway Mulatto man named SANCHO [see like ad Vol. II No. 73] ■ **Richard Weightman**, Taylor and Habit-Maker, has removed to a house on Fairfax-street, and seeks an apprentice [see like ad Vol. II No. 72] ■ JOSEPH FULLMER, Administrator of HUGH GIBNEY, deceased, seeks to settle accounts [see like ad Vol. II No. 73] ■ WILLIAM RAMSAY requests return of books belonging to the late WILLIAM RAMSAY [see like ad Vol. II No. 73] ■ THE Subscribers to M'MURRAY's Maps of the United States of America are requested to call at the Printing-Office for them.

VERSAILLES, April 17. The Sieur Doray, an officer of cavalry, on April 15 presented to the King a clock of his own invention, which was executed by the Sieur Lamy Gonge, of Versailles. The globe inclosing the clock represents a Montgolfier, or balloon, which every Sunday at the last stroke of twelve rises from the marble pedestal, and takes up a gallery in which are seen figures representing two aerial travelers. To the ingenuity of the device, this work adds great skill in the execution. ■ **ELSINEUR, March 19.** Several Copenhagen merchants have stopped payment, and among the rest the agent Wulfert, who has failed for two tons of gold. ■ **LISBON, April 9.** Last Saturday this Court received the news of the celebration of the marriage of the infant Don Juan of Portugal with the infanta of Spain. ■ **VENICE, April 10.** As the differences between us and Holland may very likely end in war, we are with alacrity putting our forces on a respectable footing; besides the fleet under the Chevalier Emo, and that at Corfu, three more sail of the line are ready, and will go out of port in a few days with several smaller warships. There are nearly 30 Sclavonian xebecs, some of 30 and 36 guns, so shortly our sea forces in case of a rupture can annoy the Dutch trade in the Levant very much. ■ **LONDON, May 1.** Saturday evening an express arrived at the Foreign Secretary's St. James office, from the Earl of Chesterfield, his Majesty's Ambassador at Madrid; which, on account of its importance, was immediately carried to the King at Windsor. A memorial from the Court of Madrid, the Catholic King is become the accuser in the affair of the British logwood cutters on the Musquito Shore: that the British were the first aggressors, have gone beyond the stipulated boundaries, ill-treated Spanish subjects, and using the officers of his Catholic Majesty with insult and insolence. This is from the report sent home to Spain by Don Galvez, Governor of the Havana, and will become a British-Spanish bone of contention unless speedily settled. **May 4.** Hindering a Emperor-Dutch peace accord are differences between the United Provinces; some are ready to submit to any condition, others disposed to risk war rather than accede to the demands of Joseph II. Of the latter, the Province of Guelderland is the most obstinate. **May 5.** Admiral Campbell takes leave of the King at St. James tomorrow before going to his command at Newfoundland, of which he is sole Governor. The *Salisbury* man of war of 50 guns awaits him at Spithead, together with the *Hebe* frigate of 36 guns, and *Merlin* of 18 guns, also going to that station. The *Winchelsea* and *San Leocadiz* frigates, part of the same squadron, same as last year, sailed from Spithead last Saturday ... General Haldimand goes out in the *Salisbury* of 50 guns, with whom he is to make a survey of Newfoundland fortifications, and from thence by a frigate to his government at Quebec. **May 3.** Extract of a letter from **Cadiz, April 8.** A few days ago a ship from Bourdeaux was chased into here by an 18 gun Algerine bark. A King's frigate of 32 guns pursued it and gave it a broadside; they returned one, and a most desperate and bloody conflict ensued lasting upwards of four glasses. A sloop of war's incessant and well directed fire carried away the Barbarians' main mast and killed many. The Algerines still would not strike, but tried (in vain) to grapple the sloop. Finally they set fire to the powder and blew themselves up, together with a number of Christian slaves on board, who all perished ... The despatches received Wednesday at the Secretary of State's office, from Sir G.A. Elliott, Governor of Gibraltar, dated as late as the 20th of last month, contain little news. Commodore Sir John Lindsey had not arrived, the appointed time of his cruise not being expired. The *Thetis* frigate had been in 2 or 3 times, the only man of war visiting for nearly two months. The Spaniards are rebuilding part of the town at St. Algesiras, and the posts of St. Roque thrown down during the siege are nearly reinstated; the Spaniards are as busy as the General who repairs the Old Rock's fortifications ... Gibraltar letters, via a ship arrived at Portsmouth in 22 days, say the Algerines have commenced hostilities against the British flag by the capture of two ships which they carried into port. The English Consul at Leghorn notified Commodore Lindsey, who sent a sloop to investigate and demand a restoration. Receiving no answer, a second application was intended ... From Grand Cairo we hear that on the 3rd of last month, when the Beys and other great officers of that city went up to the castle to pay their respects to the Pacha (Governor of Egypt in the name of the Porte), about 60 persons, most of them nobility who had been banished, conspired to make away with many of the Beys. They gained entrance, well armed, in disguise, to the Pacha's preference chamber. Their plot did not entirely succeed. The Emir Hatch (the conductor of the Caravan of Mecca), observing a commotion among the Pacha's people, gave a sign to Hussan Bey. He just at that moment saluting the Pacha, received a considerable wound in his side from a pistol bullet., but was not prevented by this from making a stout resistance. He drew his sabre and, supported by other Beys, repelled the conspirators. One Bey only remained in his place.--The Emir Hatch had his Chiaoux (secretary) killed. The Chiaoux Crayassi was dangerously wounded, as were many principal officers, and several people killed. The government determined to depose the Pacha, and did so the same day; his advisors were banished. The Janissary Aga is making the strictest search for the contrivers of this conspiracy, which was intended to end by setting the city on fire. Punishment has been inflicted on many grandees convicted of involvement in the plot ...Extract of a letter from **Amsterdam, March 30.** From the Dutch Consul at Leghorn the States received word that the Senate of Venice concluded a ten-year treaty of alliance, offensive and defensive, between the two Imperial Courts of Russia and Vienna, during which the republic is to keep up 30 men of war for the service of those powers. The news is not agreeable here, considering the disputes between Holland and Venice ... A letter from **Amsterdam, April 5,** rumours of peace are one day destroyed by those of the next, but we believe peace negotiations are revived with vigor at Paris; we think they will succeed, as the ruling party of this country depends for its power on the preservation of tranquility, and we suppose will sacrifice much to attain it. Peace at any rate suits our circumstances better than war. **May 6.** Extract of a letter from **Berlin, April 8:** Prince Dolgorwsky (the Russian minister) asked our August Sovereign the reason for his troop movements. He replied it seemed strange her Russian Majesty was more attached to the house of Austria's interest, affecting the quiet of Europe, and risking loss of ; that he, as member of the Empire, and guarantee of the interest of all other Sovereigns of the same Empire, and as puissance in particular, would do all in his power, even if alone, to sustain in the rights of Germany, an upright balance in Europe. The Prince answered in accord with his instructions, that his mistress found the Dutch behaviour more strange, and difficult to explain their resistance to the Emperor's just demands--unless encouraged by other powers, his Prussian Majesty in particular. Such an act would surprise Europe, not projects against Germany and the political balance, which, without doubt, had no other foundation than the chimerical fearfulness which his Majesty intended to sow among the other powers; that being assured of the justness of Joseph II's intentions, the Empress found needless all precautions which they might believe to have a right to take, and that all the care they took to detach her from her illustrious ally became absolutely superfluous. ... A letter from **Paris, April 28**, says the latest letters from Petersburgh confirm the Turks' movements have excited uneasiness, and especially the numerous Tartary tribes who may this spring pour down--not upon Crimea--but upon the other provinces belonging to Russia. Government is at great pains to contain any intelligence on this, but the precautions have only increased doubts of the merchants who had speculated on Black Sea trade, and are now against engaging. The Government is obliged to furnish Cherson and other parts of Crimea with provisions ... A letter from **Tangiers, Morocco,** says the Emperor, wishing favorable treatment of the

Dutch, at their Consul's request granted permission to sell the *Citta de Vienna's* cargo (wrecked on that coast) on account of the Dutch merchants. He also ordered the 15 Moors who forced the Captain of the wrecked vessel to land them near Ceuta, to be sent in irons to Morocco. He sent formal complaint to the Emperor of Germany against the Captain of the above vessel, and ordered his garda-costas in future to fire on all vessels, without distinction who attempt on any pretence to land men anywhere other than established ports. This produced a number of memorials from European Consuls requesting exception be made in case of shipwreck ... A current report says the ministry will submit a bill to Parliament, soon after the next recess, to constitute a board of commissioners to study permanent measures which might be taken to regulate commerce between Great Britain and the U.S. ... Extract of a letter from **Paris, April 21:** Some preliminary articles for an accommodation between the Court of Vienna and the Republic of Holland have been signed by the Emperor's Ambassador and those of the U.S. Others pretend nothing has been done, pending completion of diplomatic exchanges. Another courier from Vienna is expected in order to know if the Emperor will desist from some articles the States General cannot admit as foundation of reconciliation. Arrangements require considerable time, owing to the distance between the Courts ... Extract of a letter from **Malaga, April 2:** A 26 gun Algerine rover a few days since had the audacity to chase a sloop from here, under the San Isadore fort, who firing on the renegado, he returned several shot, one of which dismounted an 18 pound cannon from the ramparts and killed 3 men; the pirates metal must from this have been very heavy. The *San Carlos* of fifty, a new ship and the *Agnesia*, of 28 guns, are fitting out now as garda-costas, to prevent these outrages and to protect the coasting trade--nearly stopped from the lawless proceedings of these Barbarian marauders. Those infidels now have 27 sail of vessels at sea from 40 to 16 guns, and are said to be preparing several more. It is something astonishing that the Barbary powers who build none but contemptible gallies should get provided such stout ships. It is more than probable that some of the European states are at bottom of these disorders, fomented to serve purposes not yet revealed. One grand effort will be made this summer to subdue those pirates, who are a terror to all who have a Mediterranean trade, the Dutch and English only excepted. ■ **NASSAU,** (*Bahama*) **May 22.** The brig Hawk, belonging to this port, arrived yesterday from Baltimore with flour, Indian corn, &c. Several other British vessels are expected from the continent. There appears no doubt of our having in future ample supplies of every article wanted from America--by vessels NAVIGATED ACCORDING TO LAW. This is the best antidote to dire warnings by some of the consequences of refusing admittance to American vessels here, and it removes every plea for dispensing with laws observance of which have brought the wealth, prosperity, and naval power of Great Britain. ■ **CHARLESTON, May 19.** Some villains must have spread in the Emperor of Morocco's dominions ideas derogatory to the U.S., otherwise the Moors would not have dared transgress the laws of nations in capturing our vessels. As the black Monarch and the British are friends, perhaps we owe this to the latter. Perhaps the Moors think us too insignificant a people to demand satisfaction for this insult--and it is probable that neglecting this affair would confirm them in this opinion. It is incumbent on Congress to send a deputation to demand an eclaircissement ... Another correspondent says if we let the Moors continue, an American vessel will not be safe in Madeira, much less Malaga, or any French Mediterranean port. Hence, an American vessel cannot get insurance to the Mediterranean without a pass and British colours. **June 8.** Yesterday Mr. Parker, a merchant here, committed suicide with a pistol, despite seeming his usual self the night before, and yesterday morning. When found, his appearance indicated his having struggled in the most poignant sensation during the dissolution of his natural frame. The Coroner's inquest found a verdict of *felo de fe.* ■ **PARR, May 7.** Thursday last arrived the sloop *Three Friends*, Captain Taylor, eight days from Boston, in whom came passengers Captain John Keaquick, and Mr. Robert Younghusband, late Master and Mate of the brig. *Lovely Lass*, of this port, that was cast away last December 20, on the North Edisto, in South Carolina. These gentleman, after saving what they could from the wreck, proceeded to Charleston, and took passage on the ship *Fanny*, for Liverpool. On March 1st she met with a gale in which she overset, and Captain Keaquick with one or two others were washed overboard, but fortunately were got on board again when the ship righted, which she did immediately on the masts being cut away; in this wretched situation they remained for several days, till they were taken off by the brig *Active*, Captain Anthony Ludlum, from London, bound to Boston, where they arrived safe. Captain Keaquick and Mr. Younghusband conceive themselves much indebted to the humanity of Captain Ludlum for the generous treatment they received from him while on board his vessel. ■ **ALBANY, June 16.** Last Sunday arrived in this city his Excellency Governor Clinton, his Secretary, and Colonel Floyd; and set off yesterday accompanied by the Commissioners of Indian affairs, and several gentlemen of this city, to hold a treaty at the German Flatts, with the Oneyday and Tuscarora Indians.

Page 3. **NEW YORK, June 24.** A report prevails that the Havana is opened to the reception of American vessels--*seek and ye shall find--dollars.* ■ **PHILADELPHIA, June 27.** Extract of a letter from **Danville, in Kentucky, May 31:** Our second convention is now sitting, and has resolved to petition the Legislature of Virginia at their next session for an act of separation. An address on the expediency of the measure will also be handed out to the people. Several late acts of the Virginia Assembly, which operate grievously on this district, anticipated the application at an earlier period than was generally thought of; though perhaps it may be better for us in the end. This new State is to be called *"The Commonwealth of Kentucky"* and by computation contains 30,000 souls, which must be vastly increased before a separation can take place. The savages still do mischief, chiefly about the Ohio river, but not of any considerable consequence ... Extract of a letter from Charleston, South Carolina, June 4: The present scarcity of cash has made this place dismal--nothing now talked of but the want of Money. Indeed our old merchants are almost ruined for want of it. No crops last year from our planters, and very little hopes this year; so that God knows what will become of them. British merchants will be, I'm afraid, the ruin of not only this State, but all America; they eagerly catch at every dirty advantage they can take. I wish and hope the people will not remain long dormant; now is the time to rouse and send these ministerial agents and factors from among us ... His Excellency the Governor of Massachusetts has issued a proclamation discountenancing prophanity and irreligion throughout that Commonwealth. **June 28.** Saturday last arrived here the ship *Van Berkel*, Captain Campbell, in six weeks from Amsterdam. Letters of May 10, via this vessel, say that although recruiting and other war preparations are carried on, they were in great hope of successful peace negotiations. We have no particulars ... We hear that last Thursday Congress pursuant to the March 7 resolution proceeded to elect a Minister Plenipotentiary to succeed Mr. J. Adams at the Court of the United Netherlands--and elected William Livingston, Esq. [His Excellency W.L., the present Governor of New Jersey; a gentleman in high esteem for his many patriotic and unwearied exertions.] Congress also elected Mr. Roger Ogden a deputy secretary of Congress ... By the *Bahama Gazette* of the 11th we learn the utmost discontent prevails among the British merchants and loyalists, who oppose the collection of taxes they deem oppressive, and unconstitutionally imposed on them, by an illegal assembly ... In the *St. Christopher's Gazette* of the 11th are advertised the sales of the ship *Polly* otherwise the *Friends*) and the brig *Ruth*, with their cargoes of lumber, condemned in the court of Vice Admiralty of that island, for *breach of the laws of trade* ... The Legislature of New York passed an act granting a bounty on hemp raised with the State, of eight shillings per cwt. As further encouragement for growing hemp and manufacturing cordage and linseed oil, they laid the following duties: on every hundred weight of foreign cordage, four shillings; on every hundred weight of white rope or yarns, four shillings; on every hundred weight of foreign hemp, two shillings; on every gallon of foreign linseed oil, four pence; on every pair of shoes, six pence; on every pair of boots, two shillings; the produce of these duties to be applied to the payment of the above bounties ... The above act has a clause for laying a duty of 1½% on goods imported into the State by a foreigner, and not consigned to a citizen, more than paid by citizens of that State, or of the United States ... And another clause, subjecting to a penalty of one hundred pounds and cost of suit, any person who shall sell as slave any Negro or other person brought into that State after the 1st--every person so sold to be free ... And two clauses on the manumission of slaves: if the slaves be under 50 and able to provide for themselves, the manumittor is not obliged to indemnify the State for any expence it might incur by such manumitted slave ... the last clause of this very salutary act states slaves shall have the privilege of being tried by jury in all capital cases, according to the course of common law ...The Legislature of Delaware has abolished all fairs formerly held there ... Every man, whether from self interest or patriotism, must rejoice that our principal States have at last asked for the only radical cure for our distress: to invest congress with the power to regulate our trade, and thus counteract the illiberal and impolitic systems operating so banefully throughout the States ... Recent letters from Europe report the Pope opened two ports--Civita Vecchia on the Mediterranean, and Ancona on the Adriatic gulph--for admitting American vessels with perfect reciprocity. He has also nominated persons at each to render every service to Americans arriving there, stipulating that subjects of the papacy meet with similar treatment in U.S. ports. We hear that application for this, for the purpose of opening new markets for New England cod fish, was made by the American commissioners in Europe to the Pope's

Nuncio at Paris, who transmitted it to the Pope, by whom he was empowered to conclude the business as above ... Extract of a letter from **Cork, April 1.** Easterly winds are keeping many homeward bound vessels (from America and the West Indies) off this coast, and in great want of the necessaries of life. Merchants of this city have at their own expence despatched a fast sailing cutter to cruise off Cape Clear, laden with bread, water, beef, pork and fresh provisions to bring relief. Management is entrusted to a confidential person, who goes supercargo, and who has orders to relieve whoever is in distress, regardless of country or whither they are bound. He is also ordered to accept even the smallest return for assistance, as the gentlemen promoting this consider themselves amply rewarded by the pleasure of benevolent action. The humane idea was not sooner suggested, than, in order to carry it into immediate effect, liberal subscription was filled up with alacrity. ■ **ALX, June 7**. Yesterday the Brig *Ann-Maria*, Capt. Robertson, arrived here in 24 Days from Barbadoes, at which Place he was seized and detained several Days; but fortunately obtained Permission to sail. ■ Capt. Robertson informs, that the Schooner *Peggy*, Capt. Quirk, from this Port, arrived off Bridge-Town [Barbadoes] about the first of June, at which Place he went on Shore to make Report, where being informed he would positively be seized, returned immediately on Board his Vessel and made Sail.--The Government Brig was despatched after Capt. Quirk in Order to carry him into Barbadoes, but luckily he outsailed her. ■ Last Sunday arrived here the Sloop *Polly*, Capt. Bartlett, from Boston, in which came Passengers the Hon. Major General LINCOLN and Son. ■ Last Thursday one Moore, a Journeyman Taylor, put a Period to his Existence by drowning himself in the Potomack. ■ The *Hope*, Capt. Cragg, from this Port for Whitehaven, is arrived at Cork. ■ NAVAL-OFFICE, ALX. *Inward Entries.* Sloop *Hero*, J. Humphries, and Sloop *Betsy*, P. Duncan, from Baltimore; Sloop *Polly*, W. Bartlett, Boston; Sloop *Sally*, J. Blake, Gloucester. *Cleared Outwards.* Sloop *Charming Polly,* J. Elwood, for Philadelphia; Brig *Jane and Elizabeth*, J. Frazer, London; Sloop *Hero*, J. Humphries, Baltimore; Sloop *Speedwell*, B. Prince, New-York. ■ **I will sell cheap a very** beautiful LOT, with a south Front of 30½ Feet and 123 Feet deep, in a healthy and improved Part of ALX. WILLIAM BAKER, July 4, 1785.

On Tuesday the 19th of July will be sold, EIGHT LOTS, on Columbus and Oronoko streets, 20 and 22 feet in front and from 80 to 123 feet in depth, two of which are subject to a rent of 5s. and the rest 6s. per foot.--The proprietors have an estate in fee in the said Lots and will grant the liberty of purchasing them out in 20 years.--A plan of the Lots, and the terms, may be seen at the Vendue-Store.--At the same time will also be sold, Five LOTS of GROUND on the east side of Fairfax-street to the southward of its intersection with Wilkes-street, containing 20 feet each in front and 80 feet in depth, subject to an annual rent of 12s. per foot.--Plan and terms also may be seen at the Vendue-Store.
☞On Saturday next, as usual, will be sold at the Vendue-Store, a variety of WET and DRY GOODS, among which are a few hogsheads of tobacco and a pipe of excellent claret.--Also a Negro Girl about 13 years of age.

SAMUEL ARELL, Vendue-Master.
ALX, July 7, 1785.

THE Subscriber being regularly bred to the Practice of Physic, in which he has practices successfully for several years, respectfully offers his service in that line to those who may please to honor him with their commands. FOSTER SWIFT. ☞ He may be spoke with at Mr. Short's near Col. Hooe's. ALX, July 5, 1785. ■ TO BE SOLD at Public Vendue, on Tuesday the 19th Instant, **Two Lots of Ground in fee**-simple, situated on Wolf-street, between Water and Fairfax streets, containing 20 feet each in front, and 86 feet 6 inches in depth to a 10 feet alley.--The terms of sale are one-third in hand, one-third in 3 months, and the remainder in 6 months.--Also to let on ground-rent, several Lots on Fairfax-street, containing 20-feet each in front, and 113 feet 5 inches back to a 10 feet alley.--A plan may be seen by applying to DENNIS RAMSAY. ALX, July 7, 1785.

A CHARTER WANTED,

For the ship ANN, ALEXANDER HUIE, Master, of about 360 hogsheads of tobacco burthen.--She has a Mediterranean pass, and now lies at Quantico.--For terms apply to

HUIE, [REID] and CO.

Dumfries, June 29, 1785.

TO BE SOLD, A LOT of GROUND at the corner of Wolf and Washington streets, containing 22 feet front on Washington-street and 73 feet on Wolf-street.--Also, seven other Lots joining the above, with the same front on Washington-street and 73 feet deep, subject to an annual ground-rent of one dollar per foot.--As the purchase-money will be but small, ready pay will be expected, when a deed shall be given the purchaser with a special warranty.--The rent is not to begin till the 26th of October next; each lot to be improved with a dwelling-house in three years, otherwise the rent to be 10s. per foot instead of one dollar.--I have also several lots on Fairfax-street, near the corner of Gibbon-street, which I will rent on moderate terms to such as can improve immediately.--A plan of the lots on Wolf-street may be seen at the Printing-Office. WILLIAM HARTSHORNE. Who has just received, New-England rum, molasses, raisins in jars, and hollow iron ware, which will be sold cheap for Cash. ALX, July 6, 1785. ■ THE Subscribers at the American Flat, in the town of Bath, have procured a number of the best houses, convenient to the springs, for the reception of genteel boarders.--They contain upwards of 40 private rooms, many of them large and convenient. They also propose to establish Stages, to run between Baltimore and Bath the present season.--Previous notice will be given in the *Maryland Journal*, when and where they intend to start. JAMES RUMSEY, NICHOLAS ORRICK, Bath, Berkeley County, June 24, 1785. ■ RAN away from the Subscriber on Saturday the 26th ult. an apprentice Lad, named JOHN GRIMES, about 17 years of age, by trade a sailmaker.--Whoever will return said apprentice to his Master, shall receive a reward of ONE SHILLING currency. JOSEPH ROBERTSON. ALX, July 7, 1785.

Page 4. Poetry. "To Death." ■ **Jonathan Swift and Co.** have for sale at their store on Capt. Harper's wharf, a general assortment of the most fashionable coloured broadcloths, etc. [see like ad Vol. II No. 74] ■ CHARLES PEALE POLK begins to paint portraits [see like ad Vol. II No. 74] ■ D. and I. M'Pherson to rent a convenient dwelling-house on Water-street; have for sale West-India rum and muscovado sugar [see like ad Vol. II No. 74]. ■ **Robert Lyle**, has for sale at his store, opposite the Printing-Office, Hyson, green, souchong and bohea teas, etc. [see like ad Vol. II No. 74] ■ JOSEPH BUTLER, Berkeley County, intends on opening a boarding-house at Bath [see like ad Vol. II No. 74] ■ ADAM LYNN to rent store now occupied by Mr. Martin Brown [see like ad Vol. II No. 74] ■ **William Wilson**, has received by the *Janet* from Glasgow, a general assortment of dry goods [see like ad Vol. II No. 72] ■ WILLIAM FITZHUGH offers for sale a valuable tract of land in Stafford County [see like ad Vol. II No. 70] ■ WILLIAM MONROE offers for sale at Leesburg a valuable 1225-acre plantation [see like ad Vol. II No. 70] ■ BURR HARRISON has for sale a noted tract of land called Clarksburgh, in Shenandoah County [see like ad Vol. II No. 73] ■ ☞ A great Variety of BLANKS, printed on good Paper, may be had at the Printing-Office. ■ **Jesse Taylor**, Has lately imported from different markets, an assortment of dry goods [see like ad Vol. II No. 73] ■ **Daniel and Isaac M'Pherson** have for sale tar, pitch, turpentine, etc. [see like ad Vol. II No. 73] ■ The Partnership between Lowry and M'Kenna is dissolved and request that accounts are settled; Lowry to soon leave for England [see like ads Vol. II No. 73] ■ DENNIS M. JOHNSTON has for sale two lots of land in Loudon County [see like ad Vol. II No. 73] ■ WILLIAM TAYLOR, London, denies having received from John F. Throckmorton letters [see like ad Vol. II No. 73] ■ JOHN WISE has for rent the noted Public House so long kept by Mr. John Lomax [see like ad Vol. II No. 74] ■ The Printing-Office is selling blank books, ledgers, journals, etc. [see like ad Vol. II No. 69] ■ ALX: Printed by GEORGE RICHARDS, and COMPANY, at their Printing-Office on Fairfax-street--by whom Advertisements, &c. are thankfully received for this Paper,--and where Printing is performed with Care and Expedition.

1785/07/14, Vol. II No. 76

Page 1. WILLIAM LYLES and CO., is selling rum [see like ad Vol. II No. 68] ■ SAMUEL ARELL, Vendue-Master has for sale eight lots on Columbus and Oronoko streets, and five lots on the east side of Fairfax-street [see like ad Vol. II No. 75] ■ **William Wilson**, has received by the *Janet* from Glasgow, a general assortment of dry goods [see like ad Vol. II No. 72] ■ ROBERT BOGGESS, Executor of

Abraham Barnes, deceased, seeks to settle accounts [see like ad Vol. II No. 73] ■ JAMES PERRY offers reward for return of runaway Mulatto man named SANCHO [see like ad Vol. II No. 73] ■ **WANTED,** A GOOD MILCH COW.--Inquire at the Printing-Office, July 14, 1785. ■ FOSTER SWIFT announces his practice as Physic [see like ad Vol. II No. 75] ■ DENNIS RAMSAY has for sale two lots on Wolf-Street between Water and Fairfax Streets, etc. [see like ad Vol. II No. 75] ■ HUIE, REID and CO. announce the sailing of the Ship *Ann* [see like ad Vol. II No. 75] ■ WILLIAM HARTSHORNE has for sale a lot at the corner of Wolf and Washington streets, and one on Fairfax-street near the corner of Gibbon-street [see like ad Vol. II No. 75] ■ JAMES RUMSEY and NICHOLAS ORRICK, Bath, Berkeley County, have purchased houses for receiving genteel boarders [see like ad Vol. II No. 75] ■ JOSEPH ROBERTSON offers reward for runaway apprentice lad named JOHN GRIMES [see like ad Vol. II No. 75] ■ Commentary "On Marriage" follows: MEN by marriage become, in every sense, nearer related, or closer connected, with the rest of the species. Our wives are thus rendered as dear to us as ourselves, and the remoter degrees of affinity made proportionable objects of our attention. By marriage we are rendered more beneficient and less selfish, find our hearts and capacities enlarged, our natural affection and compassion, our friendship and benevolence, improved, refined and exalted. Marriage teaches us more sensibly to feel the misfortunes and necessities of others, and acquaints us with the various changes and turns in life, and with whatever belongs to men to know and practice. When single, we only see the world in gross and in general; when married we see it in detail and particular, and view those things singly, and one by one, which we before was in the heap [text continues].

Page 2. **VIENNA, April 16.** Government entertain the most sanguine expectations of tobacco culture in Hungary. So great the foreign market demand, it is considered an important article of commerce. Two Trieste merchants lately bought 12 quintals at Segodin and Groz Niklos at 7 - 8 ½ florins per quintal. ■ **LONDON, May 6.** Extract of a letter from **Portsmouth, April 12:** Yesterday at the quarter sessions here a hatter was fined £140 for fourteen hats sold to one person without proper stamps. The hatter used lesser value stamps than required, cut in two, and so artfully concealed by the hat ticket of the hatter's address partly over them that only one of the trade could have discovered the fraud ... A few days since an attorney at the Temple sent his employer a bill for £122; the client thought this an overcharge, and applied to a person authorized to tax such accounts. The latter made a deduction of £110, leaving only £12 to be paid by the client. As he had advanced £15 to the lawyer he now--instead of having £107 to pay--would have a return, when he can get it ... Extract of a letter from **Petersburgh, March 21:** The Count de Bruce, commander in chief at Moscow, reported [great detail given, here omitted-Eds.] an extraordinary astronomical phenomenon of the sun, double circled with five meteor-like smaller suns, and a bright crescent with horns turned down. It lasted from noon to sunset. General D'Archarow reported the same phenomenon was observed at Ustufchna and at Tocherepow. ■ **KINGSTON, May 21.** Last Monday arrived at Port Royal his Majesty's ship *Swan*, from the Musquito Shore. By her we learn the *Janus*, *Flora* and *Iphegenia* had sailed for Truxillo, and the *Bull Dog* for the Bay of Honduras; that all was quiet at the Shore, but that no peace treaty had been agreed to when she sailed. The troops enjoy better health than expected in so disagreeable a climate. **May 28.** Advices from Hispaniola say that in consequence of repeated orders from Old France, strict and vigorous measures are employed to prevent all intercourse with foreigners, except through the free port recently established, and that only for certain articles. The ports of Cape Francois, Cape Nicola Mole, Port au Prince, and Aux Cayes are shut against all ships but their own, on pain of confiscation of vessel and cargo ... The ship *Diligence*, Captain Haye, arrived last Sunday from Anamaboc with upwards of 400 slaves. She was overtaken on her passage, about two degrees southward of the line, by a dreadful thunder storm, in which a flash of lightning struck the fore-top-gallant-mast which immediately fell to the deck, killing eight slaves outright. Seventeen others were so dreadfully wounded by the mast splinters and the force of the fluid [lightning] they died shortly thereafter. The Captain and crew, although stunned by the shock, were not materially hurt. Such are the effects of lightning--the most extensive, the most rapid and powerful agent in the whole universe! ■ **LITCHFIELD, June 21.** On Saturday the 12th, a grist mill in Livingston's Manor, containing upwards of 1000 bushels of wheat, was set on fire by lightning and, with its contents, entirely consumed. ■ **NEW YORK, July 4.** Last Saturday was the public reception of his Catholic Majesty's Minister; Mr. Jay (Minister of Foreign Affairs) conducted him to the Congress Chamber, where his credentials were in a ceremony presented by the Secretary of the Spanish Legation to the Secretary of Congress. After which, that Hon. Body the members of Congress, the new

Minister, and other gentlemen were entertained with an elegant dinner at the house of his Excellency the President. **July 6.** Last Monday being the anniversary of the complete Independence of the Thirteen United States of North America (which declared on the fourth of July, 1776) the same was ushered in with the firing of cannon, succeeded by the ringing of bells. In the morning and at noon, the French packet, commanded by Captain Tuvache, which has been beautifully decorated, fired a salute, and the day was spent with that conviviality which that subject inspired ... A magnificent dinner was provided by Mr. Bradford, at the Coffee House, at the instance of the Honorable Congress, at which were present John Jay, Esq; the French, Dutch and Spanish Ambassadors, and several other gentlemen.... After dinner the following toasts were drank, each succeeded by a discharge of thirteen cannon:

1. The United States of America.
2. The King of France.
3. The King of Spain.
4. The United Netherlands.
5. The King of Sweden.
6. Concord between nations.
7. Universal empire to law and justice.
8. May the happiness of the people be the sole ambition of the rulers.
9. The fourth of July, 1776.
10. The memory of those who have fallen in defence of their country.
11. The late Commander in Chief, and the officers and soldiers who have hazarded their lives, to defend the rights of their country.
12. May simplicity of manners, industry and frugality, distinguish the character of an American.
13. Liberty, peace and happiness to all mankind.

Their Excellencies the Ambassadors, accompanied by a number of gentlemen, retired about eleven, and his Excellency the President with the rest about one o'clock ... That truly band of brothers, the sociable Society of the Cincinnati, also held their anniversary meeting at Mr. Cape's, where the utmost hilarity prevailed, and after an elegant dinner, the following toasts were drank, under a discharge of cannon:

1. The United States; and may true republican principles govern them.
2. Congress.
3. His Most Christian Majesty.
4. The United Netherlands..
5. His Catholic Majesty.
6. His Excellency General Washington.
7. The friendly powers in Europe.
8. The Governor and State of New York.
9. The memory of our brethren who have gallantly fallen in defence of liberty.
10. May the happiness of America never be interrupted by foreign attacks, or domestic commotions.
11. Our brethren the Cincinnati.
12. The Fair of America, and federal measures.
13. The Day.

At noon the members of the Cincinnati waited on his Worship the Mayor and corporation, at the City Hall, to congratulate them on the day; from thence, preceded by constables, they paid their compliments to his Excellency the President of Congress, and after mutual congratulations, returned to Mr. Cape's for a collation provided by the Corporation, enjoying a degree of pleasure unknown to many pseudo citizens. A correspondent observes of the Society that "nothing could do more honor to human nature, than the brotherly love and unfeigned testimonies of veneration which each member...demonstrated on the celebration of independency on the 4th instant; recollecting with ineffable pleasure, the glorious event brought about by their...exertions; and what distinguishes them still more conspicuously, is, their general, ardent disposition to support pure and uncontaminated the republican principles and federal confederation of their country...." ■ On Monday the 27th ultimate arrived at his house in New London (from England, via Nova Scotia) the Right Reverend Doctor Samuel Seabury, Bishop of the Episcopal Church in Connecticut, to which diocese he was consecrated by three bishops last November 15th, after a most excellent sermon by a Bishop of the Episcopal Church at Aberdeen in Scotland, concerning the pure and apostolical establishment. ■ **PHILADELPHIA, June 29.** The Hon. Rufus King, Nathaniel Gorham, Theodore Sedgwick, Nathan Dane, and John Hancock are chosen to represent Massachusetts in Congress ... **July 7**. The Annual Meeting of the Pennsylvania Society of the Cincinnati, 04 Jul 1785, elected officers for the ensuing year: Arthur St. Clair - President; Thomas M'Kean - Vice President; Francis Johnson - Treasurer; A.G. Claypoole - Ass't Treasurer; William Jackson - Secretary; Richard Fullerton - Ass't Secretary. [Continued on Page 3.]

Page 3. [Society of the Cincinnati (*continued*)] The following, with the officers, were appointed a standing committee for the ensuing year:

John Dickinson	William Macpherson
Samuel Nicholas	Richard Humpton
Rev. Wm. Rogers	T.L. Moore
Matthew M'Connell	

Resolved, That the institution of the Society, with the proceedings hitherto, and of each annual meeting, be printed, and that the standing committee direct the publication. W. JACKSON, Secretary ... Last Monday about 6 o'clock p.m., a little above Frankfort, a young woman was raped; the culprit was apprehended and jailed the same evening. We judge that a crime of so aggravated a dye, and so injurious to society, will most probably soon prove the cause of his exit from this world ... **July 8.** Last Tuesday the Congress appointed the Hon. Judge John Rutledge, Esq., of South Carolina, Ambassador to the United Netherlands vice Governor Livingston who had declined the appointment ... Messrs. John and Robert Baldwin, printers of Cork's *Volunteer Journal*, have had to stop publishing, on account of some late taxes laid upon their business. In their April 25, 1785 notice they thank the public for its support, but--by the government's determination to suppress the kingdom's free papers via the oppressive STAMP ACT--it is not worth their while to go on. ■ **ALX, July 14**. Last Monday Afternoon there were frequent heavy Gusts of Thunder here, accompanied with Hail and much Rain, during which the Lightning struck the Conductor affixed to the House of William Herbert, Esq., which it followed, without any further Damage than breaking some of the Windows, although the Shock was so great as to throw the Conductor down.--The great Quantity of Rain which fell, did considerable Damage to several new Buildings, particularly a new Brick Building which it entirely destroyed. We hear from the Country, that much Damage has been done by the Hail, which was so amazingly large as to cut down Fields of Corn; and we are apprehensive more Damage has been done than we have yet heard of. ■ We hear from Frederick County, that two Boys lately went into the River Shenandoah to bathe and were both unfortunately drowned. ■ Accounts from Boston mention, that the Bridge now building over Charles-River, considering the Magnitude of the Work, goes on rapidly. ■ NAVAL-OFFICE, ALX. *Inward Entries*. Brig *Ann-Maria*, J. Robertson, and Schooner *Adventure*, R. Saunderson, from Barbadoes; Schooner *Venture*, J. Scarborough, and Sloop *Nightingale*, B. Pierce, North-Carolina; Schooner *Lottery*, Z. Mann, Baltimore; Sloop *Dolphin*, A. Steuart, Philadelphia. *Cleared Outwards*. Brig *Jenny*, M. Griffing, for Barbadoes; Sloop *Polly*, J. Blake, Gloucester; Schooner *Lottery*, Z. Mann, Baltimore.

On Monday next, being Court-Day, will be Sold at the Vendue-Store,

A Variety of Wet and Dry Goods, as usual,

Among which are, Claret Wine in Bottles, and a few Hogsheads of Tobacco.

SAMUEL ARELL, Vendue-Master.

ALX, July 14, 1785.

Richard Conway, HAS for Sale, Barbadoes Rum and Spirits by the Hogshead, Muscovado and clayed Sugar in Barrels, and Lisbon Wine in Quarter-Casks. ALX, July 13, 1785. ■ TO BE LET, A Neat and convenient DWELLING-HOUSE, situated on Royal-street, consisting of ten rooms, with good cellars underneath, a kitchen adjoining the house, and every other convenience suitable for a large family; also a large kitchen garden.--There is also a draw-well of excellent water contiguous to the back part of the house, and few houses in ALX can boast of being so well and conveniently supplied with that valuable article.--Any person who may be desirous of renting the above premises, may, by applying to the Subscriber, if terms can be agreed on, have immediate possession of the same, excepting four rooms in the house, which will be reserved by the proprietor three or four months for himself. JOHN SUTTON. ☞ As John Sutton intends going to England this fall, he wishes those who are indebted to him would be kind enough to make payment; and all who have any open accounts against him are desired to bring them in for payment. ALX, July 12, 1785. ■ ALL persons indebted to the estate of JOHN MILLS, Esquire, deceased, or to his Administrators on behalf of his estate, are once more requested to make immediate payment; a reluctance to bringing suits generally, hath induced the Administrators heretofore to give greater indulgence than has been approved by the creditors of the estate. All those concerned will please to take notice, that suits will now be brought indiscriminately for all that remain unpaid, returnable to August Court, the Administrators not deeming themselves justifiable in granting any further time, which they might, perhaps, do in many cases, were they acting for themselves. ROBERT T. HOOE, CHARLES SIMMS, WILLIAM BROWN, Administrators, ALX, July 14, 1785 [see like ad Vol. I No. 46] ■ Town of ALX, July 1, 1785.

NOTICE is hereby given to all persons who may be concerned in the lands which may bind on Washington-street, when extended the width of 100 feet, and in the lands which may bind on Franklin-street, when extended in the manner it was laid off by the executors of John Alexander, that the Common Council have it under consideration to present a plan to the next General Assembly for laying off the lands adjoining the said Town, reaching to the distance of one mile westwardly of the Court-House, parallel with King-street, and to be bound southerly by Hunting-Creek, and northerly by Four-mile-run, so that a perfect uniformity may be preserved with regard to the streets of the said Town; and all persons concerned in the premises are hereby requested to suspend any improvements thereon until the said plan is exhibited to the public, which shall be done on the last Thursday of this Month. By order of Council, OLIVER PRICE, Clerk of Council. ■ To be sold at Public Vendue, on Monday the 22d day of August next, TWO small LOTS of GROUND in fee-simple, each 20 feet front and about 46 feet back, advantageously situated, having a south front on Queen-street, between Fairfax and Royal streets.--Also, a number of small lots on Pitt and Gibbon's streets, about 20 feet front each, subject to a moderate ground-rent, which will be make known at the time of sale.--The Subscriber has also for sale, a lease for three good lives, all existing, of a PLANTATION of LAND in Fairfax County, containing 218 acres, about 18 miles from ALX and about 10 from George-Town; the land is well watered and well timbered, the greatest part clear, has good improvements thereon, excellent in quality for tobacco, corn and wheat, about 40 acres of meadow may be made, and watered by never failing springs. JOHN GRAHAM, ALX, July 14, 1785. ■ For sale at the foot of the Ridge, near Snicker's-Gap, Loudon County, Virginia, A TRACT of LAND, containing about 2500 acres, it is not of the first quality but good farming land; there is on this tract mine tenements, it is well watered, some improved meadow land, and a large quantity of ground capable of being reclaimed and converted into fine timothy meadow.--The terms may be known by applying to me in Westmoreland County, or to Mr. JEREMIAH SANFORD on the premises, who will shew the land. JOHN AUGUSTINE WASHINGTON, July 4, 1785. ■ **LOST**, A LARGE GOLD WATCH with a gold face, maker's name unknown.--Whoever has found it and will return it to the Printing-Office, shall receive a reward of THREE GUINEAS, July 8, 1785. ■ On Tuesday the 19th inst. will be sold at Public Vendue, TEN LOTS, beautifully situated on Washington and Duke streets, No. 1, 2, 3, have each an east front of 21 feet, and No. 4, of 22 feet on Washington-street, and run back 112 feet to 11½ feet alley; the last of these has the additional convenience of an alley of the same width on the whole extent of its south side. No. 5 is a corner lot with a south front of 23½ feet on Duke-street, and extending in depth on Washington-street 80 feet to the alley last mentioned. No. 6, 7, 8, 9, 10, have each a south front also of 20 feet on Duke-street, and an equal depth with No. 5, terminating on the same alley.--These lots possess the advantages of the fronts which are generally preferred; they lie nearly on a level with some of the highest and pleasantest in town, and on two very desirable streets, as Washington-street is 100 feet wide, and Duke-street from the natural progress of improvements down the river, must soon become nearly central in that direction. They will be sold subject to moderate ground-rents, proportioned to their respective situations and advantages. The plan and terms may be seen at the Vendue-Store. SAMUEL ARELL, Vendue-Master, ALX, July 14, 1785. ■ **LENT**, TO some gentlemen whose names are forgotten, a book entitled "Voltaire's Miscellanies," 2 vols. of "Cook's Voyages" and a box of types.--Those gentlemen by returning them would exceedingly oblige, EDWARD HARPER, ALX, July 12, 1785. ■ WHARF BUILDING. **David Shaon**, WHOSE possession it is, being here for the present season, and desirous to be as useful as possible to the inhabitants whilst he stays, invites the earliest application to him at Mr. Roberdeau's wharf, of such who would not be disappointed, when it may not be in his power to serve them, as now he can command any reasonable number of good workmen from Baltimore who await his orders. He professes also the capacity of building a complete pile-driver, one being sufficient for the whole place, and recommends the driving of large piles on the outside walls of every wharf, which is the custom in Baltimore even in the Bason; but is more peculiarly suitable here from the steepness with which the channel of Potomack is formed. Such a machine is too expensive to be born by an individual, therefore if made at more general expence he will give proof of the disinterestedness of his advice. ALX, July 12, 1785. ■ STOLEN or strayed from the Subscriber's plantation in Prince-George's County, Maryland, about two miles and a half from ALX Ferry, on the 16th of last month, two very likely MARES, one between 8 and 9 years old, 15 hands high, short tail, of a bay colour, blind of one eye, and is thought to be with foal; the other 4½ years old, 13 hands high, a dark bay, well-made, has a pretty head, a wild breed and is very lively.--Any person who will take up said mares and send me word, if within 15 miles from me, shall receive ONE

GUINEA reward, and if further TWO GUINEAS, and reasonable charges paid. PETER SAVARY, July 14, 1785.

STOP THE VILLAIN!

ON June the twenty-seventh day,
My Negro fellow ran away,
His name is CALEB, and his age,
Is twenty-six, or near that stage;
A strong built fellow and looks fly,
I think five feet nine inches high;
Although a black, inclin'd to yellow,
He is a cunning artful fellow;
He speaks so soft, with so much art,
As if the tale came from his heart;
When spoken to he'll always smile
With an intention to beguile.
Waistcoat and breeches, if I'm right,
Also his coat and shirt, were white.
He took with him some other clothes,
But what they were they're wise who knows;
The man that finds, and will detect him,
May rest assur'd I'll not neglect him,
But will reward him for his pain,
That is to say if need require,
If not, TWO POUNDS shall be his hire;
In Martinsburg of Berkeley County,
There I'll be found to pay the bounty.
July 1, 1785. JOSEPH MITCHEL.

RAN away from the Subscriber on Sunday the 10th instant, an apprentice Lad, named JAMES LACEY.--Whoever will deliver the said apprentice to his Master, shall receive ONE SHILLING reward. WILLIAM WARDEN, ALX, July 11, 1785.

Page 4. Poetry. From the European Magazine, "EPITAPH On Dr. JOHNSON." ■ WILLIAM BAKER offers lot for sale [see like ad Vol. II No. 75] ■ The Partnership between Lowry and M'Kenna is dissolved and request that accounts are settled; Lowry to soon leave for England [see like ads Vol. II No. 73] ■ D. and I. M'Pherson to rent a convenient dwelling-house on Water-street; have for sale West-India rum and muscovado sugar [see like ad Vol. II No. 74] ■ DENNIS M. JOHNSTON has for sale two lots of land in Loudon County [see like ad Vol. II No. 73] ■ JOSEPH BUTLER, Berkeley County, intends on opening a boarding-house at Bath [see like ad Vol. II No. 74] ■ ☞ A great Variety of BLANKS, printed on good Paper, may be had at the Printing-Office. ■ **Jonathan Swift and Co.** have for sale at their store on Capt. Harper's wharf, a general assortment of the most fashionable coloured broadcloths, etc. [see like ad Vol. II No. 74] ■ CHARLES PEALE POLK begins to paint portraits [see like ad Vol. II No. 74] ■ **Robert Lyle**, has for sale at his store, opposite the Printing-Office, Hyson, green, souchong and bohea teas, etc. [see like ad Vol. II No. 74] ■ ADAM LYNN to rent store now occupied by Mr. Martin Brown [see like ad Vol. II No. 74] ■ ALEXANDER CAMPBELL, Dumfries, offers for sale goods imported in the Ship *Janet* [see like ad Vol. II No. 74] ■ ELIZABETH COPPER, Administratrix of the estate of the late Mr. CYRUS COPPER, deceased, seeks to settle accounts [see like ad Vol. II No. 74] ■ **Robert Donaldson** has for sale goods imported in the *Speedwell*, Capt. Prince, from the West-Indies [see like ad Vol. II No. 74] ■ JOHN WISE has for rent the noted Public House so long kept by Mr. John Lomax [see like ad Vol. II No. 74] ■ The Printing-Office is selling blank books, ledgers, journals, etc. [see like ad Vol. II No. 69] ■ WILLIAM FITZHUGH offers for sale a valuable tract of land in Stafford County [see like ad Vol. II No. 70] ■ LAWRENCE HOOFF offers reward for return of runaway Negro woman named WINNY [see like ad Vol. II No. 74] ■ BURR HARRISON has for sale a noted tract of land called Clarksburgh, in Shenandoah County [see like ad Vol. II No. 73] ■ THE Subscribers to M'MURRAY's Maps of the United States of America are requested to call at the Printing-Office for them. ■ WILLIAM RAMSAY requests return of books belonging to the late WILLIAM RAMSAY [see like ad Vol. II No. 73] ■ ALX: Printed by GEORGE RICHARDS, and COMPANY, at their Printing-Office on Fairfax-street--by whom Advertisements, &c. are thankfully received for this Paper,--and where Printing is performed with Care and Expedition.

1785/07/21, Vol. II No. 77

Page 1. RICHARD CONWAY has for sale Barbadoes rum [see like ad Vol. II No. 76] ■ **Jonathan Swift and Co.** have for sale at their store on Capt. Harper's wharf, a general assortment of the most fashionable coloured broadcloths, etc. [see like ad Vol. II No. 74] ■ CHARLES PEALE POLK begins to paint portraits [see like ad Vol. II No. 74] ■ **Robert Lyle,** has for sale at his store, opposite the Printing-Office, Hyson, green, souchong and bohea teas, etc. [see like ad Vol. II No. 74] ■ JOSEPH MITCHEL offers reward [text in prose] for return of runaway Negro fellow named CALEB [see like ad Vol. II No. 76] ■ JOHN SUTTON has for sale a dwelling-house on Royal-street; intends to go to England this fall and wishes to settle accounts [see like ad Vol. II No. 76] ■ PETER SAVARY offers reward for return of stolen or strayed mares in Prince-George's County, Maryland [see like ad Vol. II No. 76] ■ OLIVER PRICE, Clerk of Council, requests citizens to suspend improvements along Washington and Franklin streets [see like ad Vol. II No. 76] ■ JOHN GRAHAM has for sale two small lots on Queen-street, and a plantation in Fairfax County [see like ad Vol. II No. 76].

From the MARYLAND JOURNAL, &c.

M O N E Y

[The author, who signs himself PHILADELPHUS, leads off with a witty discourse on money, how everyone wishes to have it, and the disagreeableness in the want of it, such as now. Why not, then, do as many suggest and simply print more? [Continued on Page 2].

Page 2. [Money (*continued*)] He demonstrates that such leads to inflation, and inflation to ruinous consequences.--Eds.] ■ **LONDON, March 24.** An Irish gentleman, who danced with great spirit, at Hampstead assembly, noticed a macaroni imitating him in a most extravagant manner. Eventually feeling himself the object of mirth, the Irishman asked the mimic why the mimic-ing. The latter piously claimed that he always danced like that. The Irishman said he would observe the macaroni throughout the evening, and should the macaroni once vary from this style, he would break every bone in the macaroni's body. The poor macaroni was obliged to subscribe to the sentence, to the amusement and satisfaction of all. ■ **CHARLESTON, June 27.** Last Sunday at St. Michael's church, Miss Storer superbly sang three anthems from Handel's Messiah. A genteel collection was made at the church door for a charitable purpose ... Yesterday two gentlemen dueled, one of them--the challenger--receiving a slight hurt on his thumb. The wounded party, (whether from a just consciousness of his being the aggressor, from a sense of his own corpulency, which made the match unequal, from a certain tremor which incommoded him, or from some other cause) fired his pistol in the air--and the affair terminated. **July 01.** French individuals of rank are mocked for their excessive subscription to the "advantages of commerce" ... A melting sermon being preached in a country church, all the congregation fell a weeping, but one man, who being asked why he did not weep with the rest, Oh! Said he, "I belong to another parish." ■ **BOSTON, June 22.** Rumor says this Commonwealth is daily losing property to the royal robbers of Nova Scotia, supposedly already 20 miles within the State line. Act! Even a scowl of resentment would sink them into a state of non-existence ... The curse which once dispersed the Jews though the world seems to have fallen on the Refugees, some of whom sailed a few weeks ago to form a settlement on the Musquito shore ... The conduct of Great Britain, in draining us of our cash, restricting our commerce, aspersing our national character, keeping possession of our frontier garrisons, &c. Certainly look ominous; add to this, that TWO regiments are ordered out of England, to relieve the 8th, one of the regiments that have been stationed in Canada several years ... By the Falmouth papers it appears several people are trying to convince the three eastern counties of this state to break away as a separate state. But as the rage for revolution seems only confined to a few individuals, we are apprehensive no disagreeable consequences will arise therefrom. ■ **NEW YORK, July 7.** The legislature of the State of Vermont dissolved on the 18th ult. They sat only 17 days, and in that short time passed twenty-one acts. ■ **RICHMOND, July 16.** By a gentleman just arrived from the back country, we learn that a Powles valley family was attacked by Indians a fortnight ago, killing two men and four children, and carrying off the children's mother ... Last Monday evening lightning struck a house here, knocking down part of the chimney and tearing off a number of gable-end boards. ■ **ALX, July 21.** By a Gentleman lately from Charleston we learn, that a Number of Vessels were arrived there from Africa with Slaves, and among them were two Ships belonging to the Royal Company of Denmark. ■ We are informed, that much Mischief has lately been done by the Indians to the white Inhabitants settled near Cumberland-River. ■ It is said, that a Halifax Company is to be immediately formed in London, on the same Plan of Monopoly as the East-India Company. ■ Last Tuesday Afternoon as two Carpenters were at Work on a Scaffold near the Top of a House, the Supporters of the Scaffold gave way, when they both fell and were very much hurt. ■ ANECDOTES of GAMING among the ANCIENTS. It is somewhere recorded, that Cobelon the Lacedemonian, being sent to Corinth, with a commission to conclude a treaty of friendship and alliance, when he saw the Captain and Senators of that city playing at dice, returned home without doing any thing, saying, that he would not so much sully the glory of the Spartans, as that it should be said they made a league with gamesters.--Hence it should seem this honest heathen took every man addicted to gaming for a fool or a knave, and therefore resolved to have no dealings with men who could not be depended on. The perniciousness of gaming was so well understood by the grand impostor Mahomet, that he thought it necessary to prohibit it expressly in the Alcoran, not as a thing in itself naturally evil, but only morally so, as it is a leading step to the greatest vices. ■ ANECDOTE of Doctor YOUNG. THE Doctor walking in his garden at Welwyn, in the company with two Ladies (one of whom he afterwards married) the servant came to tell him a Gentleman wished to speak with him. "Tell him, says the Doctor, I am too happily engaged to change my situation." The ladies insisted upon it that he should go, as his visitor was a man of rank, his patron, his friend; and, as persuasion had no effect, one took him by the right arm, the other by the left, and led him to the garden-gate; when finding resistance was vain, he bowed, laid his hand upon his heart, and in that expressive manner for which he was so remarkable, spoke the following lines: "Thus Adam look'd when from the garden driven, And thus disputed orders sent from Heaven; Like him I go, but yet to go am loth; Like him I go, for Angels drove us both. Hard was his fate, but mine still more unkind: His Eve went with him, but mine stays behind." ■ NAVAL-OFFICE, ALX. *Inward Entries*. Brig *Fanny*, W.B. Smith, from Maryland. *Cleared Outwards*. Sloop *Sally*, J. Blake, for Gloucester; Schooner *Lottery*, Z. Mann, [Baltimore]; Brig *Janet*, W. Chisholm, Glasgow.

PRICES CURRENT, ALX. / Tobacco, 26s. per Ct. / Fine Flour, 27s. per Barrel. / Wheat, 5s. per Bushel. / Jamaica Spirits, 4/6 per Gallon. / Windward Rum, 3s. per Ditto. / Continental Rum, 2s. per Ditto. / Molasses, 1/8 per Ditto. / Muscovado Sugar, 35s. to 42/6 per Ct. / Salt, 2/6 per Bushel, by Retail. / Corn, 3s. per Bushel / Exchange, 40.

On Saturday next will be Sold at the Vendue-Store, **A Variety of Wet and Dry Goods, as usual,** Among which are, Claret Wine in Bottles, and a few Hogsheads of Tobacco.

S. ARELL, Vendue-Master.

ALX, July 21, 1785.

Reward for lost gold watch returned to the Printing-Office [see like ad Vol. II No. 76] ■ JOHN WISE has for rent the noted Public House so long kept by Mr. John Lomax [see like ad Vol. II No. 74].

Page 3. To be let on Ground-Rent for ninety-nine years, renewable for ever, on the payment of an alienation, to the highest bidder, on Monday the 8th of August next, if fair, or the next fair day, on the Premises, TWELVE or Fourteen valuable LOTS of GROUND in George-Town, at and near the center of said town, fronting Water and Bridge streets and Fishing-lane; most of the lots have 40 feet front and from 62 to 133 feet deep. Two of them are improved, on one of which is the Store lately occupied by Capt. Thomas Richardson, deceased, and the other improvement may be converted into a store at a small expence. The first year's rent will be expected on the day of sale, and afterwards in half yearly payments, at the expiration of the first 18 months; but if this should not be generally agreed to on the day of sale, the advance part will be given up and rents made payable half yearly.--The plot may be seen in my hands at any time before the day of sale. ROBERT PETER, George-Town, July 8, 1785. ■ FIVE POUNDS REWARD. STRAYED or stolen from the Subscriber last night, a black HORSE, about 15 hands high, two white hind feet, no brand but many saddle spots, not docked, and about 8 years old. He is supposed to be carried off by a certain JOHN MONTGOMERY, alias TOWNSEND, an Irishman, about 5 feet 8 inches high, dark complexion and black hair, who goes about the country as a ditcher or jobber. A Negro LAD, the property of Mrs. Neal, is also missing and supposed to be gone with Montgomery. The Negro is named NED, about 20 years of age, light complexion, large swelled eyes, and appears to half a little. On conviction of the thief the above reward will be paid, or FOUR DOLLARS with reasonable expences, on delivery of the horse to the Subscriber in Port-Tobacco. ROBERT FERGUSSON, Port-Tobacco, July 14, 1785. ■ THIRTY DOLLARS REWARD. RAN away on Sunday night last, the following slaves, viz. ZACK, a bright Mulatto, about 6 feet high, slim made, has a surly way of speaking, is about 24 years of age: He had on a new felt hat, osnaburg shirt, country cloth breeches and waistcoat.--NAT, a dark Mulatto, rather fleshy, about 5 feet 10 inches high, and apt to frown: He had on and took with him a mixed wool and cotton country cloth coat, a Kendal cotton coat dyed brown, a pair of blue breeches lined with brown linen, osnaburg shirt marked N in the bosom, and is about 24 or 25 years of age.--WILL, a tawny fellow, small made, about 5 feet 8 inches high, about 21 years of age, a carpenter by trade: He took with him a waistcoat and breeches made of country cloth, a hat and part of his tools: This is the second trip he has made. When he went away before, he took some of his tools which served him to travel by, as he told those that questioned him he belonged to me, and was going to work at my back quarters. Whoever will bring the said slaves to me, or secure them in gaol, so that I get them again, shall have the above reward, or TEN DOLLARS for either of them. JOHN TURBERVILLE, Westmoreland County, Virginia, July 6, 1785. ■ TEN DOLLARS REWARD. RAN away from the Subscriber about two and a half weeks ago, a Negro Wench, named NELLY, and was conveyed from this place to ALX, where she now is, in a flat belonging to the estate of Mr. Thomas Chapman, deceased.--She is middle sized, likely, has a small scar over one of her eyes, and has a variety of clothes, so that her dress cannot be described, but am informed she has, among other things, a hat and feather.--She was a few days ago in an out-house near Mr. Wales's, with a Negro man and woman.--Whoever will apprehend the said Wench, and have her confined in gaol until I can send for her, shall receive the above reward; and if delivered to me in this County, what is reasonable for their trouble and expences. CUTHBERT BULLITT, Prince-William County, July 8, 1785. ■ THE Subscriber has for sale, an undivided moiety of a valuable TRACT of LAND, called Paradise, lying in Gloucester County, in the State of Virginia, containing about 1200 acres.--Any person desirous of purchasing, may [know] the terms by applying to the Subscriber at his seat on Potomack, in Charles County, Maryland, either personally or by letter. RICHARD LEE, July 19, 1785. ■ To be RENTED, and may be entered on the first day of August, A GENTEEL three story BRICK HOUSE on Fairfax-street, next door to Messieurs Williams, Cary, and Company's store, suitable for a genteel family or a wholesale or retail store.--Its advantages are needless to mention.--For terms apply to Mr. ANDREW WALES in ALX, or the Subscriber in Dumfries. PHILIP DAWE, July 21, 1785. ■ **Williams, Cary and Co.**, Have received, in addition to their former assortment, A Variety of mattresses, porter in bottles, loaf sugar, Florence oil, &c.&c. They have also just received by the *Fanny*, Capt. Smith, from Bourdeaux, choice claret in bottles, chintzes, ribbons, gauzes, cambricks, laces, mens' and womens' silk hose, ditto gloves, a variety of perfumes, plain and scented hair-powder, umbrellas, &.&c. ALX, July 21, 1785. ■ DELIVERED to my hostler (by an unknown person) on the 9th day of June last, an iron grey NAG, about 6 years old, 13 hands and an inch high, marked on the near shoulder with the letter N, on the near buttock and on the off jaw with the letter O, has three saddle marks, a bald face, wall eyes, a switch tail, the end of which inclines to white, and a few white hairs on the fore part of the near hind foot.--Whoever proves property and pays expences may have said nag, otherwise he will be exposed to sale at Public Vendue by the Subscriber. WILLIAM WARD, ALX, July 16, 1785. ■ PROPOSALS, For Printing by Subscription, MISCELLANEOUS COLLECTIONS, From the PAPERS of the late Major-General CHARLES LEE; Consisting of:

I.--Pieces on various political and military subjects;

II.--Letters to the General from several Persons of the first Character, both in Europe and America;

III.--Letters from the General to his Friends in Europe, before the late War; and also to the principal American Characters, both civil and military, during his Command in the Continental Army. To which are prefixed MEMOIRS of his LIFE. The Whole will contain a great and useful Variety of military and political Knowledge, and in a striking Manner elucidate the Abilities and decisive Conduct of this great and experienced Officer: In Three Volumes [further details given]. GODDARD and LANGWORTHY, Baltimore, July 15, 1785. N.B. Subscriptions are taken in at the Printing Office in Baltimore; Mr. Frederick Green's, Printer, in Annapolis; and at Messrs. George Richards and Co's., ALX ■ **Thirty Dollars Reward**. RAN away from the Subscribers in Loudon County, Virginia, on the 16th inst. two young Irish servant Men, viz. JOHN KEILLY, who is well set, but rather under the middle stature, much pox-marked and has brown hair: He had on and took with him a short light grey Bath coating coat, with brass buttons, brown velveret waistcoat and breeches, white thread stockings, one or two pair of worsted ditto, new imported coarse shoes, brass carved buckles, a half-worn fine hat, the brim of which had been cut smaller, two pair of new osnaburg trousers, two osnaburg shirts, one ditto of fine brown sheeting, &c. ROBERT CALLAHAN, a barber by trade, about 5 feet 10 inches high, rather slender made, and has black hair: He had on and took with him an old blue broadcloth coat, light cloth waistcoat, brown Virginia cotton breeches, thread stockings, one pair of shoes, one pair of osnaburg trousers, an old felt hat, one white shirt, and two osnaburg ditto.--The above reward will be given for securing the above described Servants in any gaol, so that the owners may get them again, or Fifteen Dollars for either of them if brought home, all reasonable charges paid, and an allowance for so doing. JOHN CRAINE, LEVEN POWELL, July 19, 1785.

Page 4. Poetry. "On Angling." ■ WILLIAM LYLES and CO., is selling rum [see like ad Vol. II No. 68] ■ FOSTER SWIFT announces his practice as Physic [see like ad Vol. II No. 75] ■ HUIE, READ and CO. announce the sailing of the Ship *Ann* [see like ad Vol. II No. 75] ■ WILLIAM BAKER offers lot for sale [see like ad Vol. II No. 75] ■ WILLIAM WARDEN offers reward for return of runaway apprentice lad named JAMES LACEY [see like ad Vol. II No. 76] ■ WILLIAM HARTSHORNE has for sale a lot at the corner of Wolf and Washington streets, and one on Fairfax-street near the corner of Gibbon-street [see like ad Vol. II No. 75] ■ JAMES RUMSEY and NICHOLAS ORRICK, Bath, Berkeley County, have purchased houses for receiving genteel boarders [see like ad Vol. II No. 75] ■ JOSEPH ROBERTSON offers reward for runaway apprentice lad named JOHN GRIMES [see like ad Vol. II No. 75] ■ The Partnership between Lowry and M'Kenna is dissolved and request that accounts are settled; Lowry to soon leave for England [see like ads Vol. II No. 73] ■ EDWARD HARPER seeks return of books lent [see like ad Vol. II No. 76] ■ DAVID SHOAN seeks customers for wharf building [see like ad Vol. II No. 76] ■ JOHN AUGUSTINE WASHINGTON, has for sale tract near Snicker's-Gap, Loudon County [see like ad Vol. II No. 76] ■ Administrators of JOHN MILLS, deceased, seek settlement of accounts [see like ad Vol. II No. 76] ■ WILLIAM FITZHUGH offers for sale a valuable tract of land in Stafford County [see like ad Vol. II No. 70] ■ WILLIAM RAMSAY requests return of books belonging to the late WILLIAM RAMSAY [see like ad Vol. II No. 73] ■ LAWRENCE HOOFF offers reward for return of runaway Negro woman named WINNY [see like ad Vol. II No. 74] ■ THE Subscribers to M'MURRAY's Maps of the United States of America are requested to call at the Printing-Office for them. ■ ALX: Printed by GEORGE RICHARDS, and COMPANY, at their Printing-Office on Fairfax-street--by whom Advertisements, &c. are thankfully received for this Paper,--and where Printing is performed with Care and Expedition.

1785/07/28, Vol. II No. 78

Page 1. WILLIAM LYLES and CO., is selling rum [see like ad Vol. II No. 68] ■ WILLIAM HARTSHORNE has for sale a lot at the corner of Wolf and Washington streets, and one on Fairfax-street near the corner of Gibbon-street [see like ad Vol. II No. 75] ■ JOHN SUTTON has for sale a dwelling-house on Royal-street; intends to go to England this fall and wishes to settle accounts [see like ad Vol. II No. 76] ■ The Partnership between Lowry and M'Kenna is dissolved and request that accounts are settled; Lowry to soon leave for England [see like ads Vol. II No. 73] ■ RICHARD LEE has for sale tract of land called Paradise, in Gloucester County [see like ad Vol. II No. 77] ■ OLIVER PRICE, Clerk of Council, requests citizens to suspend improvements along Washington and Franklin streets [see like ad Vol. II No. 76] ■ EDWARD HARPER seeks return of books lent [see like ad Vol. II No. 76] ■ DAVID SHOAN seeks customers for wharf building [see like ad Vol. II No. 76] ■ JOHN GRAHAM has for sale two small lots on Queen-street, and a plantation in Fairfax County [see like ad Vol. II No. 76] ■ Reward for lost gold watch returned to the Printing-Office [see like ad Vol. II No. 76] ■ ROBERT PETER, George-Town, offers for sale twelve or fourteen valuable lots in George-Town [see like ad Vol. II No. 77] ■ WILLIAM WARD seeks owner of grey nag [see like ad Vol. II No. 77] ■ JOHN AUGUSTINE WASHINGTON, has for sale tract near Snicker's-Gap, Loudon County [see like ad Vol. II No. 76] ■ JOHN CRAINE, LEVEN POWELL, Loudon County, offer reward for return of Irish servant men [see like ad Vol. II No. 77].

Page 2.

LONDON, May 12. The Emperor has confirmed his favor in the Prince de Kaunitz. A few days after the Prince's 74th birthday, the Emperor sought him out at an early morning meeting at the menagerie, saying: "Happy be the day on which the Prince of Kaunitz was born." The Prince, surprised, wept with joy. The King added that he counted himself among the Prince's friends, and would be present when the Prince entertained them that day ... M. Le Comte de Peyrouse, the next Captain Cook of France, meets daily with the French King, about to depart for Rochefort, pause briefly at Buenos Ayres, thence round Cape Horn in the favorable season. His five year voyage will see him winter in the Sandwich islands for refitting, and to visit ports, bays and coasts of which Captain Cook made little or no mention. **May 16.** Letters from the **Hague** call peace a certainty; some predict Baron Woffenar to be appointed Ambassador to the Court of Vienna. By the same channel, we hear he Dutch East India company will pay no dividend this year ... One of the King's messengers arrived at Lord Carmarthen's office Friday, with despatches from the Earl of Torrington, his Majesty's Ambassador at the Court of Brussels.

These say accord has been reached between the Emperor and the Dutch, the latter having conceded all the Emperor's points except respecting the Duchy of Brabant; treaties should be signed at Brussels. The sum to be paid the Emperor for his expenses is mitigated by French mediation. **May 17.** Though the Imperialists were not marching when the last account came in from Vienna, the Emperor's troop disposition is such that he can collect 100,000 men in the Low Countries at very short notice, in case the treaty is broken off ... A **Toulon** letter says they are adding six ships of the line for merchant ship convoying--two for ships from Marseilles, two for those from Toulon, and two for Brest ships--into the Mediterranean. The ships of the line are in response to merchant complaints of trade being stopped in the Mediterranean by great numbers of Barbary corsairs daily cruising there. **May 20.** Extract of a letter from **Utrecht, May 12:** The States of Holland have responded to the Emperor's new claims, seemingly disposed to grant more than before; there are great hopes for an amicable conclusion. Some say, however, that concessions now to the Emperor will only trigger more demands, until the republic must either accept war or annihilation. This last has not be made public. Newly appointed Ambassadors to his Majesty, Comte de Woffenar, and the Baron of Leyden, have set off for Vienna ... A letter via a Maryland ship says "This Province and Virginia keep up their credit; but Massachusetts' public faith has been so much prostituted they can now get little on credit. If you ask them for cash, they suggest you look up to the clouds for it" ... Extract of a letter from **Naples, April 23:** His Catholic Majesty will resume the siege of Algiers this year, also employing the naval forces of the King of Naples, his son. The Neapolitan officers' skill and courage has won them the honor of being called out again against those pirates. And, as the Queen of Portugal's fleet is to join the combined fleets of Spain and Naples, the pirates will soon br obliged to respect the flag of the European powers ... **May 23.** The *Hendrick*, Clarke, from Philadelphia is arrived in the river. The *Bethia*, Elles; *William*, Pitt; and the *Union*, [Capt.] -----, from Charleston, South Carolina, are arrived in the Downs ... The *George*, Capt. Little, from Boston to Amsterdam, spoke with the *Neptune*, Callahan, in lat. 48 long. 38 on the first of May, all well. ■ **CHARLESTON, S.C., June 20.** The vulgar have an accounting for everything they do not understand, and had Blanchard and Jeffries crossed the Channel in a balloon three centuries ago, they would have been burned for riding the devil's back. An old book tells of a friar, an abbess, and several nuns who were said by locals to have been seen flying to and from the upper nunnery windows, like doves to a dovecote. They were all burned, for dealing with the devil. None of them would confess to the imputed carnality. But now we know they were secretly balloonists ... So eminent were Spaniards for temperance, they had a law, perhaps no longer in force, which decreed that gentlemen convicted of a capital crime could be pardoned on pleading intoxication--it being supposed that gentility would more rather suffer death than confess to so beastly a vice as drunkenness. ■ **BOSTON, July 4.** A navigation act will probably be proposed for the security of our carrying trade. It will immediately restrict foreign bottoms visiting our ports. We must discriminate between those who exact extra duties on us, or prohibit certain articles being carried in American bottoms, from those who accord us the same privileges as their own citizens. The King of Sweden grants us the privileges granted his own; we should afford the same to Swedes trading to America. ■ **PHILADELPHIA, July 9.** A letter from a gentleman in Charleston, South Carolina expounds snobbishly and at length [a full column - Eds.] on the Carolinians: dissipated and luxurious, with a great deal of natural, unimproved sagacity; hospitable to strangers; and placing the summit of their happiness in the ostentatious display of handsome equipages, and good living. **July 21.** An epidemical disorder, the natural consequence of the bad air from the stagnated lakes formed by the earthquakes in Calabria, continues to afflict and depopulate that unhappy province; nor is the earth there totally free from tremors. ■ **BALTIMORE, July 19.** The following is taken from the (Boston) ***Exchange Advertiser*, June 23, 1785.** We are going to the devil as fast as we can--our money is gone--our trade ruined--our countrymen no longer virtuous, our countrywomen no longer industrious--our gentlemen fit for nothing but to dress and to dance--our ladies as foolish and more extravagant than ever--our mechanics turned gentlemen--our army friends to monarchy--our religion subverted--our old staunch whigs and patriots abused as bigots and blockheads; in short our whole frame of State is diseased--well, what then is to be done, why I'll tell you what *ought* to be done--Do you, ye ladies, strip off your trash, and put it in the fire--feathers, muslin, gauze, silks, ribbons, and such expensive trumpery, consecrate to the flames, and ruin your husbands no more.--Get up [Continued on Page 3].

Page 3. [Boston Diatribe (*continued*)] at five in the morning, and instead of sauntering your time away in the mall with a parcel of idle young fellows, take the broom in your hand and sweep out the house--D'ye hear! Clothe yourselves and families in good homespun, of your own making; and instead of reading a parcel of nonsensical novels and romances, go in the kitchen and see about dinner, and don't sit at the parlour windows lolling in an armed chair, with a fan in your hand, complaining of the heat of the weather.--And as for you, ye gentlemen, I would advise you to alter your conduct; instead of opening your stores at nine o'clock, arise at the dawn of day, look over your books, and don't be so polite as to leave them entirely up to your clerks, you may now and then take up a newspaper, but you must not stop every body you meet, with "Any thing new today Sir!" And this gentlemen and ladies, is my advice, and if you don't like it, you may leave it; and so I am your humble servant, BLUNT ... **July 22.** Extract of a letter from a gentleman in **London** to his correspondent in this town, dated **May 7, 1785**, received by the last packet: There has been this day the greatest fire in the Horsely Down, that has been known since the great fire in London. Several vessels and other craft lying at the wharves were consumed. The India Company had two vessels and a warehouse of tea burnt. The loss in warehouses of hemp and corn, and other goods, with houses, &c. Is valued at £700,000 sterling ... On Saturday last sailed from New York, his Most Christian Majesty's packet, *La Martinique*, for l'Orient, in which went passengers, Mr. and Mrs. M'Cauley Graham, that learned, patriotic lady, and friend to America.■ **ALX, July 28**. Last Tuesday two Ships, said to be from Baltimore, passed by this Port for George-Town. ■ Died on the 24th of May, on his Passage from Lisbon to Boston, JOSEPH MAYO, jun., Esq., of Powhatan, in the County of Henrico, in the 29th Year of his Age, whose Death is an irreparable Loss to his Country.--His last Will and Testament shews he was the Friend of Universal Liberty, by giving Freedom to One Hundred and Fifty Souls, who by the Laws of this Country, were bound in Slavery to him. ■ NAVAL-OFFICE, ALX. *Inward Entries*. Sloop *Hero*, J. Humphreys, Schooner *Betsey*, J. Gautice, and Schooner *Nancy*, T. Robinson, from Baltimore; Sloop *Polly*, J. Child, Rhode-Island. *Cleared Outwards*. Sloop *Polly*, J. Child, and Sloop *Hero*, J. Humphreys, for Boston; Schooner *Adventure*, R. Sanderson, Barbadoes; Schooner *Betsey*, J. Gautice, Baltimore; Sloop *Polly*, W. Bartlett, Surinam; Brig *Ann-Maria*, J. Robertson, St. Eustatia; Brig *Hannah*, E. Perkinson, Amsterdam. ■ To be LET, on Ground-Rent in Fee-Simple, to the highest Bidder, on Monday the 3d Day of October next, **One Hundred LOTS of Ground**, Contiguous to the Town of ALX, each lot containing half an acre, fronting on two streets, on one 176 feet 6 inches, and on the other 123 feet 5 inches, some of which are water lots, and many of them fronting on a street 100 feet in width, leading from the extensive wharf now building by Captain Harper and others into the country, intersecting Washington street, which is likewise 100 feet in width; at the intersection of the two streets a space is left for a Market-House and other public buildings; the residue of the lots are adjoining the last mentioned lots, and the lots on the west side of Washington-street. WILLIAM ALEXANDER, WILLIAM GIBBONS STUART, Executors of John Alexander, deceased, July 26, 1785. ■ FOR SALE, A Genteel CHAIR, almost new, and two likely good young HORSES, sit for the saddle or gears. Inquire of the Printers. ALX, July 28, 1785. ■ ALL persons indebted to the estate of WILLIAM SOUTHARD, deceased, late of Loudon County, by bond, note, account or otherwise, are requested to make immediate payment; and those who have any legal demands against the said estate by bond, note, account or otherwise, are desired to bring them properly adjusted that they may be paid.--ANN PEYTON, daughter of John Smith and Margaret his wife, is desired to apply for Twenty Pounds, a legacy left her by the will of the said Southard. HARDAGE LANE, Acting Executor of William Southard, Loudon County, July 23, 1785. ■ For sale, at the store of **James Craik and Co.**, For cash, produce, or short credit if required, A LARGE and general assortment of choice DRUGS and MEDICINES, which they will dispose of by wholesale or retail, at such rates as cannot fail to suit the purchaser. ☞ Wanted, a quantity of SNAKEROOT of the best quality. ALX, July 17, 1785. ■ TO BE SOLD, **A complete WAGGON**, with a good Set of HORSES.--Inquire at WILLIAMS, CARY and COMPANY's Store. ALX, July 27, 1785. ■ To be sold for ready money on Friday the 5th day of August next, at the late dwelling-house of WILLIAM DOUGLASS, deceased, in Loudon County, about 7 miles from Leesburg, SIX likely NEGROES, the property of the deceased, consisting of three fellows, a wench and two children; also, three strong working horses belonging to the same estate.--The sale to begin at twelve o'clock. HUGH DOUGLASS, Executor, Loudon County, June 20, 1785. ■ WANTED TO HIRE, A Steady NEGRO WOMAN, that understands washing, ironing and dressing victuals in a plain way.--To such a person good wages will be given by PHILIP DALBY, ALX, July 26, 1785. ■ King George County, July 23, 1785. To be sold at Public Auction, on the second Wednesday in September next, if fair, if not the next fair day, TWO hundred acres of valuable LAND, situated upon the river Potomack, about half a mile from Hooe's-Ferry; this land is exceeding rich and level, about one half cleared, the rest well timbered. The situation of this place, is very beautiful, having an extensive view of the river Potomack, abounding with excellent fish and fowl.--One half the purchase-money will be expected on the day of sale, at which time a good and sufficient title will be made the purchaser, the other half to be paid on the 10th of September 1786, on giving bond and approved security to the Subscriber. ROBERT YATES. ■ ROBERT FERGUSSON, Port-Tobacco, offers reward for return of strayed or stolen horse [see like ad Vol. II No. 77] ■ JOHN TURBERVILLE, Westmoreland County, offers reward for return of runaway slaves ZACK, NAT and WILL [see like ad Vol. II No. 77] ■ WILLIAM WARDEN offers reward for return of runaway apprentice lad named JAMES LACEY [see like ad Vol. II No. 76].

On Saturday the 30th Instant, will be Sold at the Vendue Store, as usual,
A Variety of WET and DRY GOODS, among which are, Sugars of the first Quality, West-India and Continental Rum and a Quantity of common Flour.--Also, a Waggon and four Horses with Harness complete.
☞ To be sold at Private Sale, LOTS in different Part of the Town, and a HOUSE and LOT on Royal-street, near the Junction of that and King-street, well situated for Business.
S. ARELL, Vendue-Master.
ALX, July 28, 1785.

CUTHBERT BULLITT offers reward for return of runaway Negro wench named NELLY [see like ad Vol. II No. 77] ■ JOHN WISE has for rent the noted Public House so long kept by Mr. John Lomax [see like ad Vol. II No. 74] ■ PHILIP DAWE, Dumfries, offers for rent a genteel three-story brick house on Fairfax-street [see like ad Vol. II No. 77] ■ TWENTY DOLLARS REWARD. RAN away on Tuesday the 19th instant from the Subscriber, a likely Mulatto man, named JOE, about 5 feet 6 inches high, and about 22 years of age: He took with him a London brown coarse turned ratteen coat with white metal buttons, a blue cotton coat, a striped calico waistcoat, a striped and clouded worsted stocking pattern ditto, a parson's grey broadcloth ditto, a pair of spotted purple and white velveret breeches, a pair of figured brown corduroy ditto, a pair of blue cotton leggings, white yarn stockings, shoes half worn, two pair of large handsome plated buckles, a hat with a gold band, button and loop. He is very artful and has a very smooth tongue. He escaped once before, endeavoured to pass for a freeman, assumed the name of John Smith, and had taken his passage in some boat that was going down Potomack; and I suspect he will endeavour to fall on some such plan again to effect his escape. Whoever takes up the said runaway, and secures him so that I may get him again, shall receive EIGHT DOLLARS reward if 20 miles from home, SIXTEEN if 30, and if 40 or more the above reward, besides reasonable charges if brought home. DANIEL CARROLL, jun., Montgomery County, Maryland, July 25, 1785. ■ TWENTY POUNDS REWARD. WENT away from the Patuxent Iron-Works last night, the four following Irish indented servant men, viz. PATRICK RILEY, a lusty well-made fellow, about 5 feet 7 or 8 inches high, light hair and eyes: He had on and took with him, a felt hat, one osnaburg and one check shirt, brown roll trousers, a dark coloured short jacket, and coarse shoes with strings in them.--WILLIAM KEEFE, a likely well looking fellow, light hair and eyes, nearly the same height of Riley, and likewise in the same dress.--JOHN DELON, a slender made fellow, black hair and eyes, dark complexion, his dress nearly the same as the others.--JOHN HOGAN, a slender made fellow, about 5 feet 5 inches high, black hair and eyes, his dress also nearly the same. Whoever will take up the above servants, and deliver them to the Subscriber, shall receive the above reward, or FIVE POUNDS for either of them, and reasonable expences paid by THOMAS SNOWDEN, July 19, 1785.

Page 4. Poetry. "The Thunderstorm." ■ **Williams, Cary and Co.**, Have received, in addition to their former assortment, A Variety of mattresses, porter in bottles, etc. [see like ad Vol. II No. 77] ■ RICHARD CONWAY has for sale Barbadoes rum [see like ad Vol. II No. 76] ■ GODDARD and LANGWORTHY, Baltimore, propose to public works on Major-General Charles Lee [see like ad Vol. II No. 77] ■ WILLIAM FITZHUGH offers for sale a valuable tract of land in Stafford County [see like ad Vol. II No. 70] ■ Administrators of JOHN MILLS, deceased, seek settlement of accounts [see like ad Vol. II No. 76] ■ ALX: Printed by GEORGE RICHARDS, and COMPANY, at their Printing-Office on Fairfax-street--by whom Advertisements, &c. are thankfully received for this Paper,--and where Printing is performed with Care and Expedition.

1785/08/04, Vol. II No. 79

Page 1. JAMES CRAIK and CO. has for sale a large and general assortment of choice drugs and medicines [see like ad Vol. II No. 78] ■ HUGH DOUGLASS, Loudoun Co., Executor of William Douglass, dec., has for sale six likely Negroes [see like ad Vol. II No. 78] ■ The Partnership between Lowry and M'Kenna is dissolved and request that accounts are settled; Lowry to soon leave for England [see like ads Vol. II No. 73] ■ RICHARD LEE has for sale tract of land called Paradise, in Gloucester County [see like ad Vol. II No. 77] ■ JOHN TURBERVILLE, Westmoreland County, offers reward for return of runaway slaves ZACK, NAT and WILL [see like ad Vol. II No. 77] ■ WILLIAM WARDEN offers reward for return of runaway apprentice lad named JAMES LACEY [see like ad Vol. II No. 76] ■ ROBERT YATES, King George Co., has for sale 200 acres of valuable land situated on Potomack River, about a half a mile from Hooe's Ferry [see like ad Vol. II No. 78] ■ CUTHBERT BULLITT, Prince William Co., offers reward for return of runaway Nelly [see like ad Vol. II No. 77] ■ DANIEL CARROLL, jun., Montgomery Co., Md., offers reward for return of runaway named Joe [see like ad Vol. II No. 78] ■ WILLIAM WARD seeks owner of grey nag [see like ad Vol. II No. 77] ■ JOHN SUTTON has for sale a dwelling-house on Royal-street; intends to go to England this fall and wishes to settle accounts [see like ad Vol. II No. 76] ■ THOMAS SNOWDEN offers reward for return of Irish indented servants who went away from the Patuxent Iron Works [see like ad Vol. II No. 78] ■ RICHARD CONWAY has for sale Barbadoes rum [see like ad Vol. II No. 76] ■ EDWARD HARPER seeks return of books lent [see like ad Vol. II No. 76] ■ JOHN WISE has for rent the noted Public House so long kept by Mr. John Lomax [see like ad Vol. II No. 74] ■ PHILIP DAWE, Dumfries, offers for rent a genteel three-story brick house on Fairfax-street [see like ad Vol. II No. 77].

Page 2.

HAGUE, May 14. The Council of State have laid before the States General Baron von Sprengporten's plan to raise a regiment of dragoons--to be on the same footing as the other regiments in the State's service. Although the necessary forms are not yet gone through, there is no doubt the corps will soon be established ... Their High Mightinesses will take into the service of the Republic the Hessian brigade of the Prince of Hesse Darmstadt, being one light cavalry regiment and two battalions ... The concord and good harmony between the Prince Stadtholder and our new General daily increases: The Count de Maillebois has explained himself on that subject...Free from all party spirit, and impartial, that great general owned that he did not think to have found the Stadtholder so profoundly skilled in the theory of military art, particularly as he had never had the opportunity of experience to instruct him, and that plans laid down for the defence of these Provinces by his Serene Highness alone were astonishingly great. This honorable eulogium ought to shut the mouth of slander, which has been so long unjustly open against our Stadtholder. ■ **LONDON, May 12.** Last January at Old Calabar, on the windward coast of Africa, a large Guineaman from Cork took in a number of slaves. The crew mutinied, confined their officers, and put to sea, with an intent to sell the cargo at some of the Spanish settlements in the West Indies. Whilst debating the disposition of their late commanders, a strong S.W. wind drove them near the coast of Morocco, where two piratical corsairs took them, and carried them into Marmora. These wretches have paid dearly for this atrocious act, being all sent upcountry as slaves. The Captain and officers were released at the instance of the French Consul, Mr. Debilleneuve, who accepted bills on their owners, and advanced them money for their return at the first opportunity. This intelligence comes via a Portuguese brig from Madera, who on the 28th March spoke with a Dutchman, bound from Salee to Rotterdam with the unfortunate Captain and his officers on board ... **June 5.** On Wednesday last arrived from the United States of America, Colonel Smith (late Aid-de-camp to General Washington during the American war) as Secretary to an Ambassador from his country; and on the day following his Excellency John Adams (with his lady and daughter) as Plenipotentiary to the Court of Great Britain. We hear he has delivered his credentials in to the Marquis of Carmarthen. Yesterday his Excellency John Adams was introduced to and most graciously received by his Majesty. He is for the present residing at a hotel in Piccadilly ... Extract of a letter from an English gentleman at **Algiers, May 2.** A warm reception awaits the combined forces of the several powers designed against this city. The seaward batteries mount a great number of fine artillery, of a prodigious bore, the smallest being 42 pounders. Gun boats and floating batteries are all bomb proof, built on a new and masterly construction; their crews are also very desperate, and fear no danger. The garrison is well equipped, consisting of 25,000 regular troops within the walls, besides the Moors who bear the Spaniards an implacable hatred. These, plus the army of horse and foot, on the land side, can repel treble the force the Spaniards can muster against them ... The liberty the King of France gave Americans to trade to his West India islands has greatly disgusted many in his kingdom. Among others, the Parliament of Rouen has written a strong protest letter which applies to our own present situation. Herewith some abstracts. "Our colonists are consumers who belong to us; to give them up to a foreign power is to renounce the advantages we possess of the general balance of their trade, which we owe to our own colonies and to our manufacturers." Here the letter quotes a passage from Mr. Nekar which avers the King's edict will absolutely destroy the 70 million livres trade between France and her West Indies islands. The Parliament anticipates his Majesty's flag in those ports may be eclipsed by the Americans. The 1765 and 1775 system must be preserved. Why should the Americans complain of the exclusion which extends to all of France's allies? By what right can the Americans claim a share of the trade always exclusive to subjects of France? Is not the independence they enjoy, and which they owe principally to your Majesty's protection, a sufficient rich present to them? After sacrificing for them our treasure, fleets, and armies, are we to crown all by the sacrifice of our trade, the source of our future prosperity? Gratitude is a weak bond between nations. The United States can enrich themselves only by usurping the trade of our colonies, or that of the Spanish settlements. The proximity of the Antilles would facilitate the success of such an enterprize." Thus France begins to see the impolicy of the aid she gave to the Americans; and now trembles lest the United States, the creatures of her own hands, should strip her of her colonies, in return for their liberty ... **June 6:** As of the 28th of last month, they advise from Paris that accommodation between Holland and the Emperor is certain. The treaties are not to be signed for some time, as the Dutch deputies going to Vienna must work out the compensation for the Emperor's expences in making preparations in Germany and Flanders; and also for the danger sustained by his Majesty's subjects in Flanders, by breaking the dykes at Lillo, &c. ... **June 7:** The *Brisk*, Captain Buller, of 18 guns, and the *Weazle*, of 16 guns, Captain Cooper, are ordered to the Halifax station immediately, in addition to the squadron there, under the command of Commodore Sawyer ... **June 8:** A correspondent, who has good reason for what he suggests, recommends the Post Master General investigate the three-fold increase in letters passing between both France and Spain, and Ireland. The Comte de Vergennes has a happy talent for bringing about revolutions--changing the Swedish government from limited to an absolute monarchy, and severing America from the British Empire. Our Ministers should be watchful, for those who know him intimately say an object he has greatly at heart is severing Ireland from our empire, as well ... Extract of a letter from **Bombay, Jan. 4, 1785**: A recent event may be of the utmost consequence to the East India Company. Majee Scindia, one of the first men of India, a friend to the English, recently came into much power. Hearing of a quarrel between two of the chiefs or princes under the King of Delhi, he joined one of them. They agreed to attack the other in the morning, but that night the chief Scindia had joined was assassinated in his tent. Scindia had address enough to prevail on the officers belonging to the assassinated chief to continue with him, though it was supposed that he had been the cause of his death. In a few days he obliged the other to lay down his arms, and surrender all to him. Thus Scindia got possession of one of the largest countries in the east, and could be a most formidable enemy to the Company. He enjoys the support of the people; it is an action which they pride themselves upon, being able to deceive either friend or foe. They have neither ideas of honor or justice, so as they gain their end, the care not who they sacrifice. ■ **KINGSTON,** (Jamaica) **June 4.** A friend writes from Rio de la Hache, May 20, on the Spanish Main, that the Indians of the Kingdom of Santa Fee are in revolt against the Spanish Government. Several other Indian tribes have caught the spirit of insurrection; and it is supposed, that this business, so important to the whole world, and dreadful to the Spaniards, will be attended with the most interesting consequences. The public may rest assured, that the above intelligence is strictly true ... We hear several British vessels with Africa coast slaves put in at the Spanish Island of Trinidad, where they sold their cargoes for specie, thence proceeding to Barbadoes to purchase loading for their vessels. If permitted for a length of time, it will be highly beneficial to the owners, and in consequence many vessels will be diverted there otherwise intended for the British islands, or America ... A gentleman lately arrived from the Musquito Shore advises that whilst his Majesty's ships from hence lay off Truxillo, the Spaniards behaved remarkable courteous and friendly, daily sending off a number of fat bullocks for the use of the squadron ... By letters from St. Augustine, East Florida, a melancholy account of the few settlers now in that province ceded to Spain. The gloomy disposition of the Spaniards and their enthusiastic tenets, by no means accord with the sentiments of free men. The back settlement Indians are also highly incensed against the Spaniards, already having made several irruptions, and more fatal disasters seem to threaten. ■ **NEW YORK, July 22.** Colonel Jefferson, Minister Plenipotentiary from the United States of North America to the French Court, is arrived at Paris, and has had a private audience with the King, when he presented his credential letters. He was introduced to the King by the Sieur Lalive de la Briche, and to the Queen and the rest of the royal family, by the Sieur Sequeville ... **July 23:** Mr. Pitt has brought into the Commons House a proposition for a tax on bachelors, instead of that on maid servants, which had be scouted out of that Assembly ... Colonel Jefferson at present resides at Paris, as Minister Plenipotentiary from the Court of America to that of Versailles ... Mr. Pitt omitted from his budget a lottery, but on 3d June it was reported in Change alley there would be a lottery to benefit the American refugees ... **July 25:** By late arrivals at Boston from France, Holland, and Bristol we learn the dispute between the Dutch and the Emperor is being amicably adjusted, but that a war is almost inevitable between the Emperor and the King of Prussia ... Europe's drought is the severest in living memory: only five small showers from Christmas to the above vessels sailing ... **July 27:** On the arrival of the Bishop of Connecticut at his New London residence, the Presbyterians obligingly offered him the use of their meeting house, in which he preached to numerous audiences. The Episcopal Church had been burnt to the ground in the late calamitous war. The Parsonage escaped, and is now Bishop Seabury's residence ... The brig *George*, Captain Bernard from this port, and two other vessels from Nantucket, on a whaling voyage, touching at St. Lucia, were seized by order of the French government. ■ **PHILADELPHIA, July 29.** Extract of a letter from **Paris, May 17:** The great Duke de Choiseul is no more, his death an infinite loss to France and a benefit to England. Convinced France could give the law to Europe through dominion of the sea, he counseled risking everything to destroy England's marine power--the only such able to withstand Bourbon ambition. Although without office, he was the soul of the French cabinet during the war. He not only prevented powers most attached to England from declaring in her favor, but also set on foot the armed neutrality. [Continued on Page 3].

Page 3. [Duke de Choiseul Obituary (*continued*)] Through his friend, the Duke de la Vauguyon, he induced Holland to renounced her treaties of friendship with the best and oldest of her allies, and declare against her. Since quitting his ostensible situation of Minister, his only public step was in concert with his relation, the Duke of Praslin; they denied that France had promised England to keep up or build more than a certain fixed number of men of war. After making his last confession, The Duke de Choiseul in the presence of several noblemen declared, that though he had made it a point of duty to consult the personal satisfaction of his Sovereign (Louis XV), he was not conscious of having sacrificed to the Prince the interests of the State, or his own honor as a gentleman. He constantly opposed the extravagance of Madame de Barre, scoring to pay his Court to the King by flattering his mistress--and therefore refused to order that she should have the *honor* of being attended by a guard, whenever she went out. She obtained the order in spite of the Duke, and she did not fail to let him feel on a particular occasion, that he influence was greater than his. At a party of whist one evening with the King, she had the Duke for her partner. She already had got eight of the game, and held three honors in her own hand, and might consequently have laid down the game if it had so pleased her; but she wished to mortify the Duke for his refusal to let her have the guards to attend her. She therefore asked him if he could give her an *honor.* He answered in the negative; upon which she replied, "Well then, Monsieur le Duc, you see (said she, throwing down three) that I can get *honors* without *your* assistance." ■ **RICHMOND**. Yesterday was executed, at the gallows near this city, Reuben James, from Fauquier, for murder.■ **ALX, August 4**. The Commonwealth of Massachusetts have lately passed an Act, laying very heavy Duties on all Foreign Manufactures imported into that Commonwealth, by Land or Water, which is to continue in Force until the United States in Congress assembled, shall be invested with sufficient Powers to regulate the Commerce of these States. ■ Last Tuesday Evening died suddenly at Piscataway, Mr. JOHN BAYNES, formerly of Whitehaven. ■ DIED.] Mrs. WEST, Wife of GEORGE WEST, Esquire. ■ NAVAL-OFFICE, ALX. *Inward Entries.* Sloop *Polly*, J. Hale, from Providence; Sloop *Anchorsmith*, G. Jenkins, Maryland; Sloop *Polly*, J. Ellwood, Philadelphia; Schooner *Barbadoes*, W. Scott, Barbadoes. *Cleared Outwards.* Brig *Glory*, G. Richmond, for London.

PRICES CURRENT, ALX. / Tobacco, 26s. per Ct. / Fine Flour, 28s. per Barrel. / Wheat, 5s. per Bushel. / Jamaica Spirits, 4/6 per Gallon. / Windward Rum, 3s. per Ditto. / Continental Rum, 2s. per Ditto. / Molasses, 1/8 per Ditto. / Muscovado Sugar, 35s. to 42/6 per Ct. / Salt, 2/6 per Bushel, by Retail. / Corn, 3s. per Bushel / Exchange, 40.

☞ A MEETING of the ALX JOCKEY CLUB is requested on Wednesday the 10th inst., at Mr. REEDER's Tavern. ALX, August 1, 1785. ■ **Richard Conway,** HAS for sale, Barbadoes Rum and Spirits by the Hogshead, Muscovado and clayed Sugar in Barrels, and Lisbon Wine in Quarter-Casks. ALX, August 3, 1785. ■ **A CLERK wanted.** A YOUNG GENTLEMAN, who can give a close attention to business, writes a good hand, is correct in figures, and can come well recommended, will hear of a place, by applying to the Printers. ALX, August 3, 1785.

On Saturday the 6th Instant, will be Sold at the Vendue Store,

A Variety of Wet and Dry Goods, as Usual.

☞ To be sold at private sale, a number of LOTS on Washington and Duke streets, subjected to moderate ground-rents.--Also, some LOTS on Fairfax and Wilkes streets, and a few on Fairfax and Wolf streets.--A plan of these Lots may be seen at the Vendue Store.

**Also for sale, Soldiers Certificates.

S. ARELL, Vendue-Master.

ALX, August 4, 1785.

☞ BROADCLOTHS. **Jonathan Swift and Co.** Have for sale at their store on Capt. Harper's wharf, A General assortment of the most fashionable coloured broadcloths both fine and coarse, which they will dispose of for the sterling cost and charges, which were selected from the first manufactories in England, and are as low charged as any ever imported.--Also, a general assortment of DRY GOODS, suitable for the season, which they will dispose of at a very moderate advance for cash, bills, produce, or short credit with security.--They have on hand excellent London porter in small hampers, New-England rum, chocolate, pimento, hyson, souchong and bohea teas in chests and ½ chests. **They have just received a consignment of a few hogsheads of good MOLASSES, which they will dispose of cheap for cash. ☞ They discount 2½ per cent. for ready-money as usual. ALX, August 4, 1785. ■ **Thomas M. Savage,** Has for sale at his store, next door to Colonel Fitzgerald's, AN assortment of saleable GOODS, which he will sell off at prime cost and charges, for cash, or tobacco at the market price. ☞ Also, porter, port wine, and a small assortment of Irish linens, calamanco shoes, &c. ALX, August 4, 1785. ■ POTOMACK COMPANY. THE Directors of the Potomack Company observing by the lists handed them, that some of the Subscribers have not paid the first dividend of 5 per cent. (required to be paid the 15th ult.) request *those* gentlemen will immediately forward the same to me.--The dividend was laid as low as the nature of the business would permit, in order that the burden may be equal on the Subscribers, therefore a disappointment in receiving a part of the 5 per cent. may be attended with disagreeable consequences, as provision is now made for beginning to clear the navigation above the Great-Falls, and workmen are hired and hiring every day for that purpose.--The States of Virginia and Maryland, also many of the first characters in each, have forwarded their dividends to me, therefore I hope to be excused making personal application to such as have not paid. WILLIAM HARTSHORNE, Treasurer. ALX, August 2, 1785. ■ TEN DOLLARS REWARD. RAN away on Thursday night the 28th ult. an indented Irish servant man, named PATRICK GOGHERTY, about 5 feet 5 inches high, about 27 years of age, is hard of hearing, of a dark complexion, much pitted with the small-pox, round shouldered and rather clumsy: He had on and took with him, a round felt hat with a brass buckle in it, a blue surtout, a dark green coat without buttons or button-holes, a pair of corduroy breeches, a pair of black velvet and a pair of fustian ditto, a fustian waistcoat, three check and two white shirts, and two pair of shoes, with a pair of steel plated buckles.--He was seen last Friday going towards Leesburg.--Any person securing said servant so that his Master may get him again, shall receive the above reward and all reasonable charges paid, by applying to MICHAEL MADDEN. ALX, August 2, 1785. ■ RAN away from the Subscriber, living 5 miles from Bladensburg, a Negro Wench, about 22 years of age, named MARIA, about 5 feet high, well made, remarkable large legs and hips, when she went away gave suck, and had a small scar on one of her temples: She had on an old Negro cotton petticoat, and a coarse linen shift.--Whoever takes up the said Negro Wench, and secures her so that her owner may get her again, shall receive EIGHT DOLLARS reward from JOSEPH POPE, Prince-George's Co., July 29, 1785. ■ ☞ GOODS AT COST AND CHARGES. HAVING come to the final determination to decline the retail of goods, and having on hand a pretty general assortment, consisting of the following articles, viz. superfine and coarse broadcloths, coatings, linseys, baizes, shalloons, rattinets, calamancoes, stuffs, moreens, camblets, calicoes, chintzes, Irish linens, dimities, fustians, corduroys, king's cords, velvets, Marseilles quilting, princes stuff, black lastings, modes, satins, lustrings, sewing silk, threads, silk, thread and worsted stockings, buttons, buckram, twist, mohair, a good assortment of cutlery, an assortment of hardware, an assortment of saddlery, mens' leather shoes, womens' calamanco ditto, tin-ware, queen's ware, gauze, lawn, muslin, linen and cambrick handkerchiefs, paper, slates, gloves, stays, gunpowder, shot, teas, tea-kettles, stone jugs, iron pots, hoes, axes, hats, servants velvet and leather caps, japanned waiters, &c. &c.--Any person inclinable to take the whole, by making the payments agreeable, shall have them on satisfactory terms.--I have also for sale, two handsome black HORSES, which will answer very well for a match, with a Philadelphia-made dray nearly new, a cart and harness, all well fitted. HENRY LYLES. ALX, August 4, 1785. ■ NOTICE is hereby given to all whom it may concern, that a petition will be presented by the Common Council of the Town of ALX to the next General Assembly, praying that an act may be passed for preserving a perfect uniformity in the streets of the said town; and also, that the lands adjoining the said town, comprehended within the limits of the plan prepared by Robert Adam and John Allison, Esquires, bearing date the 27th day of last month, and now in the keeping of the Clerk of the said Council for the public inspection, may be improved and built upon in conformity to the beforementioned plan, whenever the proprietors or any of them shall be inclined to improve and to build upon the same, or any part thereof. ALX, August 4, 1785. ■ To be sold at Public Vendue, in fee-simple, on the premises, on Tuesday the 20th of September next, TWENTY-EIGHT LOTS, in the Town of ALX, late the property of THOMAS KIRKPATRICK, deceased, viz. one fronting on Water-street 60 feet by 123 feet 5 inches, on which is a large two-story BRICK HOUSE with three rooms on a floor, and a good cellar and kitchen under the house.--One fronting Queen-street 40 feet by 116 feet 6½ inches, with a good STORE, counting-room, cellar and kitchen.--One adjoining the above 36 feet front on Queen-street by 116 feet 6½ inches, with a large WAREHOUSE, the whole length of the front, now occupied in two tenements.--One fronting on Royal-street 27 feet 6½ inches by 99 feet 5 inches, on which is a neat framed HOUSE 20 by 16 feet, with two rooms on a floor and a good kitchen.--The remaining 24 unimproved LOTS front on several of the most principal streets in town, and are conveniently laid out so as to suit the purchasers.--Terms are, one-third of the purchase-money to be paid in six months, one-third in twelve months, and the other in eighteen months from the day of sale.--A plan of the whole may be seen by applying to JOHN ALLISON.--Bond and approved security will be required, and at the last payment, sufficient deeds will be given by ALEXANDER HENDERSON, ROBERT ADAM, JOHN MUIR, ROBERT M'CREA, JOHN GIBSON, WILLIAM HUNTER, jun., Executors. ALX, August 2, 1785. ■ WHEREAS Mr. DESKIN TEBBS, of Shenandoah Co., is in possession of a bond of mine for £.225, whereof £.75 was payable the first of May last, and the remainder the first of January 1786; which bond was obtained from me on account of the purchase of a tract of land shewed to me by the said Tebbs, previous to my entering into the bargain with him: And whereas it since appears that the said Deskin Tebbs is not himself possessed of the land he shewed me and which I bargained for, but of a small part of it only, and therefore has it not in his power to make me a conveyance according to the true intent of our agreement: I do therefore forewarn all persons from taking an assignment of my said bond, as I am determined not to pay it, because of Mr. Tebb's inability to convey to me the same land he shewed me at the time of our agreement, and for the purchase of which the said bond was given. ROBERT BROWN, Prince-William Co., August 4, 1785.

Page 4. Poetry. "Ode to Virtue." ■ WILLIAM LYLES and CO., is selling rum [see like ad Vol. II No. 68] ■ **Williams, Cary and Co.**, Have received, in addition to their former assortment, A Variety of mattresses, porter in bottles, etc. [see like ad Vol. II No. 77] ■ WILLIAM HARTSHORNE has for sale a lot at the corner of Wolf and Washington streets, and one on Fairfax-street near the corner of Gibbon-street [see like ad Vol. II No. 75] ■ FOR SALE, A Genteel CHAIR, almost new, and two likely good young HORSES, fit for the saddle or gears. Inquire of the Printers. ALX, July 28, 1785. ■ WILLIAM ALEXANDER and WILLIAM GIBBONS STUART, executors of John Alexander, dec., have for sale one hundred lots of ground contiguous to the Town of ALX [see like ad Vol. II No. 78] ■ WILLIAM FITZHUGH offers for sale a valuable tract of land in

Stafford County [see like ad Vol. II No. 70] ■ HARDAGE LANE, acting executor of William Southard, dec., requests settlement of outstanding accounts [see like ad Vol. II No. 78] ■ TO BE SOLD, A complete WAGGON, with a good Set of HORSES.--Inquire at WILLIAMS, CARY and COMPANY's Store. ALX, July 27, 1785. ■ ROBERT PETER, George-Town, offers for sale twelve or fourteen valuable lots in George-Town [see like ad Vol. II No. 77] ■ JOHN CRAINE, LEVEN POWELL, Loudon County, offer reward for return of Irish servant men [see like ad Vol. II No. 77] ■ PETER SAVARY offers reward for return of stolen or strayed mares in Prince-George's County, Maryland [see like ad Vol. II No. 76] ■ JOSEPH MITCHEL offers reward [text in prose] for return of runaway Negro fellow named CALEB [see like ad Vol. II No. 76] ■ PHILIP DALBY seeks to hire a steady Negro woman [see like ad Vol. II No. 78] ■ ALX: Printed by GEORGE RICHARDS, and COMPANY, at their Printing-Office on Fairfax-street--by whom Advertisements, &c. are thankfully received for this Paper,--and where Printing is performed with Care and Expedition.

1785/08/11, Vol. II No. 80

Page 1. **Jonathan Swift and Co.** have for sale at their store on Capt. Harper's wharf a general assortment of goods [see like ad Vol. II No. 79] ■ **Richard Conway,** has for sale, Barbadoes Rum and Spirits [see like ad Vol. II No. 79] ■ HENRY LYLES has for sale goods at cost and charges [see like ad Vol. II No. 79] ■ Directors of the Potomack Company seek outstanding subscriber payment of 5 per cent. [see like ad Vol. II No. 79] ■ **Thomas M. Savage,** has for sale at his store next door to Colonel Fitzgerald's an assortment of goods [see like ad Vol. II No. 79] ■ Notice is given that a petition will be filed for an act respecting uniformity of streets in the Town of ALX [see like ad Vol. II No. 79] ■ Executors of the estate of Thomas Kirkpatrick, dec., have for sale 28 Lots in the Town of ALX [see like ad Vol. II No. 79] ■ MICHAEL MADDEN offers reward for return of runaway indented Irish servant man, named Patrick Gogherty [see like ad Vol. II No. 79] ■ **Williams, Cary and Co.**, Have received, in addition to their former assortment, A Variety of mattresses, porter in bottles, etc. [see like ad Vol. II No. 77] ■ To be sold, at the Printing-Office, A Variety of Blank Books, consisting of Ledgers, Journals, Cash-Books, Letter-Books, &c.&c. Also, Stoughton's Bitters, Anderson's Pills, Daffy's Elixir, Balsam of Honey, Squire's Elixir, Bateman's Drops, Godfrey's Cordial, &c.&c. ■ ROBERT BROWN, Prince William Co., warns against taking assignment of a bond he executed with Deskin Tebbs [see like ad Vol. II No. 79] ■ JOSEPH POPE, Prince George's Co., Md., offers reward for runaway Negro wench named Maria [see like ad Vol. II No. 79] ■ The Partnership between Lowry and M'Kenna is dissolved and request that accounts are settled; Lowry to soon leave for England [see like ads Vol. II No. 73] ■ Chair and horses for sale, inquire of the Printers [see like ad Vol. II No. 79] ■ ☞ A great Variety of BLANKS, printed on good Paper, may be had at the Printing-Office.

Page 2.

VIENNA, May 4. A courier lately arrived from Petersburgh bears dispatches saying the Empress leaves it entirely to our Monarch whether to reach an accommodation with the Dutch, or resort to force of arms. In all cases his Imperial Majesty may be assured the Empress of all the Russias supports any solution he judges best for his subjects. She will render all services our alliances and most sincere friendship may require ... **May 8:** The Empress of all the Russias has established a Consul at Ragusa, new evidence she wishes to increase her influence in the Levant. It will not be surprising if the Republic of Ragusa claims Russian protection, if only to shake off the humiliating Turkish yoke, which compels the Ragusans to send deputies regularly to Constantinople, where they are obliged to appear at the audiences in a large peruke with an enormous beard, and an old hat on their head. ■ **VENICE, April 24.** The Senate is determined to augment our maritime armaments, which will require considerable sums. A decree last Saturday calls for opening a two million ducat loan, reimbursable in ten years, bearing an annual interest of three and a half per cent. ■ **LONDON, May 10.** A fire last Saturday morning near the end of Stony lane, at Horsley-Down, Southwark caused the heaviest losses in years. The first buildings destroyed were extensive turpentine, pitch and tar warehouses, built close together. Their melted contents were further scattered and splashed by the very water intended to douse the fire. The fine and extensive warehouses, and their contents, belonging to the Messrs. Davis are quite destroyed. Covering several acres, the ruins include several hundred edifices--dwellings, warehouses, stores, and outbuildings. Losses are estimated at more than three hundred thousand pounds ... Extract of a letter from **Mentz, April 12:** Our Elector is in a very desperate state, and the Comte de Laleyn or the Comte d'Alberg seem to have some chance for this electorate. Uniting under one head the three electorates, and abolishing the celibacy of priests will not easily be carried out, and may be postponed to a more propitious time ... The Baron de Herbert gives himself much trouble to no purpose, to engage the Porte to fix the territorial boundaries with the Court of Vienna. The Ottoman government as usual uses objections and delays to bury the affair. Only when the Court of Vienna is free to concentrate on the Porte will the affair be terminated. It does not want the deepest political penetration to discover that foreign Councils have no small influence in the Turkish Divan. **June 8:** By letters from Paris we learn that the merchants and parliaments in vain make representations for abrogating the arrêt of August, 1784, the constant answer is, that it was impossible to do otherwise. Probably the maritime towns will have to submit to its inconveniences. Seventy-five ships obliged by contrary winds to put into Spanish and Portuguese ports are expected at Bordeaux.. There are a great number whose fate is unknown; nor are the apprehensions less at other ports. No fewer than 200 vessels, which ought to have arrived, are missing. Five American vessels with sugar and coffee put into Hamburg to dispose of their cargoes there. All these incidents must considerably affect commerce. ■ **PORTSMOUTH, New Hampshire, June 22 & 23.** An Act to vest the United States Congress assembled, with full power to regulate trade, and enter into treaties of commerce [verbatim text given--Eds.], proceeds to discharge the public debt, to be in effect only fifteen years, and not to begin until all states have enacted like legislation. Signed for the House of Representatives by C. Toppan, Speaker, P.T.; and for the Senate by John Langdon, President. ■ **BOSTON, July 25.** By certain intelligence from Halifax we learn of the most flagrant treaty violation, under the direction of the British Commodore Douglas, on the Banks of Newfoundland. A high handed stretch of tyrannic power has driven our fishermen from their stations there, and destroyed or forced abandonment of their fish flakes, erected in places allowed them by treaty--by which outrageous exertions of arbitrary and vindictive power, our enemies reveal the most nefarious intention of resting from our hands that most invaluable staple and thus reducing us to a situation the most abject and dependent. Can you tamely indure this ye independent freemen and citizens of Massachusetts? Gracious God! How long shall that haughty nation be suffered to add revenge and cruelty to the most vile and opprobrious insults, and wantonly infringe the most solemn treaties, yet (we blush to name it) we are fostering in our bosoms the viper that stings us, and are tamely suffering them to insult and triumph over us in our own ports, by frustrating the salutary laws of our country.... We are credibly informed, that an attempt to ship sixty head of cattle for our enemies, will be made this day, which it is earnestly hoped the patriotic will frustrate. ■ **NEW YORK, August 1.** A nautical correspondent informs masters of vessels bound to the Northward of Cape Hatteras, and especially those that fish in about the Cape, and are in any wise short of provisions, that in lat. 35, 46, and about the longitude of the Cape, there is a large muscle bank, intermixed with cockles and small pebbles, lying in 50 fathom of water, and abounds with sundry fish, such as sea bass, sea trout, flounders, skate, tusk and dog fish. The sea bass are remarkable large, on average twenty to the hundred weight.... The water upon this bank differs very little in colour from the ocean, and in the very height of winter is very little colder. Also, in winter, by towing over this bank, one catches such as the ballaho, which they have generally in the West Indies, but for these strong 20-30 pound fish, the tackle must be strong. Some have been obliged to bend the dipping line to the inner end of the towing line, and luffing the vessel in the wind, to take the fish. No common towing will hold them, except using this method; they are supposed to be overgrown blue fish. ■ **PHILADELPHIA, July 27.** At St. George's, Bermuda, there was lately tried a very curious cause. Dr. F. Forbes inoculated a Negro belonging to a Mr. Fox, of the above island, without the consent or knowledge of the latter. The Negro died in the operation. Mr. Fox sued the doctor for the value of the Negro, which, with cost of suit, was awarded by the jury ... With the utmost pleasure we inform the public that the majority of tenants refuse to pay the exorbitant rents of the recent past. Many landlords have yielded to the storm and done with a good grace what others will find themselves compelled to do. A house in Second street, extremely well situated, which during the influenza that has prevailed since the peace, let for £230 now brings in but £120. And several houses let for one half their former rent. Some even for less ... Extract of a letter from the town of **Prosperous, in Ireland**: The following remarkable circumstance happened near here about three weeks ago. A poor woman owed her landlord fourteen pounds, and took part of that to him. He refused it, saying he would have all or nothing. He detained her in talk until the day was far spent; she then set out for home on a car. About a mile from her house she overtook a soldier, to whom she reluctantly gave a ride. Hearing the nearest lodging place was two miles off, he begged to sit by her fire until morning. She told him she was afraid to suffer it, as it was an isolated house, and nobody in it but her and her girl. At last she agreed, saying he should sleep in the girl's bed, and the girl with her. About midnight, two men with blacked faces broke in and demanded her money. After some pleading, she said let me fetch it. Going in the next room she told the soldier that he had rewarded her kindness by bringing accomplices to rob her. He started up, snatched his musquet, and ran into the next room; on which the two thieves made off with all speed; but he fired after, and shot one of them, who, when examined, proved to be the landlord. ■ **RICHMOND, July 30.** The schooner *Sally*, Captain Lunsford, belonging to Rappahannock, on her passage to Richmond, was on Saturday the 23rd instant, boarded by the pirates Butler, Moore and Slaughter, armed with guns and cutlasses, and plundered of goods to a considerable amount, property of Mr. Paine and Co. of this city. When informed of this, Commodore Baron dispatched one of his boats under Captain James, in pursuit of them, who fortunately overtook them at Nansemond, and conveyed them safely to Hampton gaol, where they remain in chains until their trials, Monday next ... Last Sunday evening fifteen prisoners broke out of the public gaol, eight of whom were apprehended the same night. The other seven remain at large, and it is much to be feared they will commit depredations on the honest and industrious citizens, as they were all seen mounted on horses. The Governor and Council of State offer a reward for their apprehension, twenty pounds for each of the above ... **August 6:** Extract of a letter from a gentleman in **Bayonne**, to his friend in Virginia, dated **March 20, 1785:** Your December 1st letter requested information on the freedom and exemptions granted our port and territory, now extending about ten leagues. We begin to feel the advantages of the new constitution effective 1st September, last. Long before your revolution we petitioned for freedom of commerce with the immunity and exemption of all duties. Our proximity to Spain promised advantages, and the glorious event of your independence made us conjecture the greatest increase in our trade. But behold, in more than six months, not a single American vessel has [Continued on Page 3].

Page 3. [The Bayonne Letter (*continued*)] visited our bay. We receive and despatch all kinds of wet and dry goods, without paying any duties, or conformable to any kind of formality. Our demands for tobacco and rice are considerable, and also much wanted by our neighbors the Spaniards. Trash tobacco has not been sold under sixty livres tournois per hundred; what I mean by trash, is such as is fit only for rappe. Rice commonly sells for 55-60 livres per hundred. Furs are priced according to quality, and fetch a very great price. Soon our port will be a general magazine, where all foreigners will bring in their commodities and purchase ours; particularly those from the north. Our manufactures are coarse cloths, blankets, thread, Bern handkerchiefs, shoes, &c, &c. Our merchants are always supplied with fine linens, cloths and all other kinds of goods, also plenty of fine iron, nails, anchors, &c. The English have already begun trading here. I have seen three of their ships loaded in the Thames, with a variety of cloths, stuff, &c. For this free port. They take in return wines and brandies, which articles we can furnish cheaper than Bourdeaux. Two able and knowledgeable American merchants, one the nephew of the famous General Greene, toured the ports of this kingdom and were much astonished when they saw ours--having far exceeded their expectations, finding in the dry docks ships from 3 to 400 tons burthen, and one of 800 tons. The greatest care is taken in conveying vessels into the harbour in safety, pilots being provided who go some distance to sea in order to meet and convey them in ... Last Monday as the Elizabeth City sheriff was conveying Butler, Moore and Slaughter (the three pirates) to Warwick County for a magistrate's examination, Butler escaped even though he was handcuffed ... Last Wednesday the Cumberland sheriff brought to the public gaol Susanna and Sarah Bauham, mother and daughter, for the murder of Sarah's male, bastard child. The infant was found in the bushes with a black silk handkerchief round his neck; by which it was supposed he was strangled. The mother is charged with aiding and abetting in this cruel and unnatural murder.■ **ALX, August 11**. The Ship *Triton*, Captain Claas Keeke, in 11 Weeks from Amsterdam, arrived at Philadelphia the 26th Ult., in which came Passenger the Daughter of his Excellency M. Van Berkel, Minister Plenipotentiary from the United Netherlands to the United States of America. ■ MARRIED.] Mr. JOHN MASON to Miss POLLY PARSONS. ■ NAVAL-OFFICE, ALX. *Inward Entries*. Sloop *Betsy*, J. Gutro, and Schooner *Olive-Branch*, J. M'Kenny, from Baltimore; Schooner *Fly*, D. Rollins, New-England; Sloop *Molly Beverly*, W. Wade, Charleston; Sloop *General Washington*, T.J. Lake, Philadelphia. *Cleared Outwards*. Sloop *Polly*, J. Child, and Sloop *Polly*, J. Hale, for Rhode-Island; Schooner *Lottery*, Z. Mann, Baltimore; Brig *Glory*, W. Jackson, Whitehaven; Schooner *Fly*, D. Rollins, West-Indies; Sloop *General Washington*, T.J. Lake, Port-Tobacco.

PRICES CURRENT, ALX. / Tobacco, 25s. per Ct. / Fine Flour, 28s. per Barrel. / Wheat, 5s. per Bushel. / Jamaica Spirits, 4/6 per Gallon. / Windward Rum, 3s. per Ditto. / Continental Rum, 2s. per Ditto. / Molasses, 1/8 per Ditto. / Muscovado Sugar, 35s. to 42/6 per Ct. / Salt, 2/6 per Bushel, by Retail. / Corn, 3s. per Bushel / Exchange, 40.

To be sold at Public Vendue, on the 25th of August next, at the house of Peter Catlett, in Frederick Co., near Col. Martin's, SUNDRY articles belonging to the estate of RICHARD RIGG, deceased, amongst which are a well chosen collection of BOOKS on various subjects, viz. divinity, science and history; likewise, a surveyor's compass, mathematical instruments, a spy-glass, microscope, hydrometer, barometer and many other articles too tedious to mention.--The sale to begin at 10 o'clock, where due attendance will be given by JOHN M'COOLE, Executor. July 20, 1785. N.B. All persons indebted to said estate are requested to come and discharge the same; and all that have unsettled accounts to come and settle them. ■ FOR SALE, MEDICINES in large or small assortments, suited for the supply of practising physicians, or of private families: To recommend the quality of which, as well as the moderate rates at which they are sold by the Subscriber, he relies on the experience of those who have heretofore had dealings with him in that way, since his supplies have been procured regularly by importation from Europe subsequent to the peace. WILLIAM BROWN, ALX, August 11, 1785. ■ THE Subscriber having entered into Partnership with JOHN DUNDAS, wishes to have all his private accounts settled as soon as possible, he therefore requests all those that are indebted to him to make immediate settlement of the same; and those who have any demands against him are desired to bring in their accounts and receive payment.--He returns his sincere thanks to those who have been pleased to favor him with their custom, and hopes his conduct will ever merit a continuance of their favors. WILLIAM HEPBURN, ALX, August 8, 1785. ■ **Hepburn and Dundas,** Have for sale, at the late store of the said Hepburn in King-street, a very general assortment of European GOODS suitable to the present and ensuing season, which they will sell reasonable, by wholesale or retail for cash, bills of exchange or country produce; among them are the following articles, viz. SUPERFINE and common broadcloths, Bath coatings, bearskins, duffils, Negro cottons of different colours, striped and rose blankets, rugs, printed velvets, corduroys, corded dimities, thicksets, jeans, fustians, shalloons, durants, tammies, calamancoes, an assortment of metal buttons and trimmings of various kinds, chintzes, stamped cottons and linens, scarlet cardinals, mens' and womens' silk, worsted, thread and cotton stockings, silk, kenting, lawn, gauze and check handkerchiefs, black modes, ribbons, sewing silk, silk mitts and gloves, mens' and womens' leather gloves, womens' stays, fine and coarse 3/4, 7/8 and yard-wide Irish linens, Russia sheetings, 6-4 and 7/8 checks, striped hollands, black and white silk and thread lace, black silk bonnets, ladies' fans, horn and ivory combs, stitching and Scotch threads, coloured ditto, bedtickings, bed-bunts, silver and common sleeve-buttons, 4, 4½ and 5 pound pins, mens' and boys' fine and coarse hats, spectacles, an assortment of religious and historical books, spelling-books, testaments, a very neat edition of Salmon's grammar and Bailey's dictionary, osnaburgs, bagging, brushes, sifters, mens' and womens' saddles, ditto whips, curb and snaffle bridles, saddle-cloths, girths, mens' and womens' leather shoes, childrens' red Morocco ditto, mens' fine and coarse boots, bed-cords, trace-ropes, Leiper's snuff in bottles, china, queen's ware, stone jugs, copper tea-kettles and coffee-pots, an assortment of pewter, pewter table and tea spoons, powder and shot, brass cocks, plated, pinchbeck and common shoe and knee buckles, candles in boxes with locks and keys, broad and narrow hoes, shovels, hammers, augers, gimblets, pinchers, 4d. 8d. 10d. 12d. and 20d. nails, spikes, steel plate and common handsaws, hand and whip saw files, locks and hinges of various kinds, and-irons, frying-pans, iron pots and Dutch ovens, a general assortment of cutlery, a few hogsheads of good Jamaica spirits, West-India rum, pepper, bohea tea, loaf sugar, bar-iron, and a few hampers of best London porter.--They expect to receive by the first vessels from Europe a very general assortment of goods suitable to the approaching season, which they will be enabled to sell on very reasonable terms. ☞ Said Hepburn has a few LOTS of GROUND on the Ferry-wharf, to let on ground-rent for ever. ** Said Dundas will rent the HOUSE and LOT now in the tenure of Mr. Patrick Murray, and the store thereunto adjoining with two neat back rooms, a good loft, a cellar under the whole, and has lately been completely repaired and painted, and possession will be given on the first of November.--Also, the Store in the house where he now lives, of which immediate possession will be given. ALX, August 8, 1785. ■ THE Subscriber has for sale, SEVEN LOTS of GROUND, situated on Queen and Washington streets, four of them are 20 feet front by 175 in depth, and three of 23 feet front and 83 feet deep.--A plan of them may be seen by applying to JOHN BRYCE, on Harper's wharf. ALX, August 8, 1785. ■ FOR SALE, A VERY valuable LOT, 20 feet front by 60 in depth, subject to small Ground-Rent, advantageously situated on Fairfax-street on which is a small convenient Store, now occupied by Messieurs PORTER and INGRAHAM.--For terms apply to Col. WILLIAM LYLES. ALX, August 11, 1785.

On Monday the 15th Instant, being Fairfax Court Day, will be Sold at the Vendue Store, A VARIETY of WET and DRY GOODS, among which are West-India and Continental rum, sugars, soap, candles, chocolate, &c.&c.--Also, three or four healthy young NEGROES. ** To be sold at private sale, a few LOTS on some of the most frequented streets in this Town.

S. ARELL, Vendue-Master.
ALX, August 11, 1785.

Randle Mitchell and Son, Have for sale at their store on Fairfax-street, opposite the Court-House, which they will sell low for cash or country produce, JAMAICA spirits, Antigua rum, best New-England ditto, molasses, Madera wine of the best quality, port wine, [Teneriffe] ditto, loaf sugar, brown sugar, green and bohea teas, pepper, allspice, china, glass and queen's ware, window glass, nails, steel, shot and gunpowder, with a general assortment of DRY GOODS. ALX, August 8, 1785. ■ ALL persons indebted to JOHN DUNDAS and COMPANY, either by bond, note, or book account, are desired to pay their respective debts to WILLIAM NICHOLS, or his order, who is fully authorised to receive the same; and all persons having claims against the said Company are desired to apply as above for payment. JOHN DUNDAS, ALX, August 3, 1785. ■ ALL persons indebted to JOHN DUNDAS and COMPANY, either by bond, note or book account are desired to pay their respective debts to JAMES HENDRICKS, Esq., and all persons having claims against the said JOHN DUNDAS and COMPANY, are desired to apply to Mr. HENDRICKS, for payment, who is fully authorised to adjust all matters belonging to the Company. WILLIAM NICHOLS, ALX, August 3, 1785. ■ SIX DOLLARS REWARD. STRAYED away from the Subscriber, living in Culpepper [sic] County near the Ridge, 6 miles from Snickers's-Gap, on the 8th of May last, a SORREL HORSE, about 13 hands 3 inches high, trots and gallops very well, has no brand, was shod before, has a narrow blaze in his face, and his mane and tail are mixed with white hairs.--Whoever secures the said horse, and gives information thereof, so that the owners may get him again, shall receive TWO DOLLARS, and if brought home the above reward and all reasonable charges paid by JOHN COOK, August 6, 1785. ■ ALL those indebted to Mr. JOHN KLEINHOFF, late of ALX, for dealings in his stores in Prince-William and this Town, are desired to pay their respective balances to the Subscribers, who are legally authorized to receive the same.--So little attention has been paid to former advertisements on this subject, we shall only now observe, that the necessity of finally closing this business will justify our putting it in the hands of a lawyer in one month from this date. JAMES HENDRICKS, DANIEL GRAY, Assignees. ALX, August 6, 1785. ■ STRAYED or stolen from the Subscriber, on the 29th of last July, a BAY MARE, nine years old, 14 hands and a half high, paces and trots, has a little white on one of the hind legs, a star in her forehead and is branded thus B2 on the shoulder, and B on the buttock.--Whosoever takes up said mare and brings her to me, shall have TEN DOLLARS reward, besides reasonable charges paid by BOSTON MARCH, Rockingham Co., August 1, 1785. ■ STRAYED or stolen from the commons of ALX, about the 16th of June last, a BLACK HORSE, about 14 hands high, 6 or 7 years old, no brand to be seen, with a little white under his foretop, newly shod, a small lump on his back hurt by a saddle, a natural pacer, heavy mane and tail, the hair cut on the top of his head, crooked hind legs, and he will not stand by the bridle.--Whoever takes up said horse and brings him to JACOB MOOR, Constable in ALX, shall receive ONE GUINEA reward, or the same reward if delivered to the Widow PRICE, paid by MARY EVANS, on Little-River, Loudon Co., August 8, 1785.

Page 4. Poetry. "The Summum Bonum, Or, Infallible Receipt for Happiness." ■ **James Craik and Co.**, has for sale a large and general assortment of choice drugs and medicines [see like ad Vol. II No. 78] ™ ROBERT YATES, King George Co., has for sale 200 acres of valuable land situated on Potomack River, about a half a mile from Hooe's Ferry [see like ad Vol. II No. 78] ■ THOMAS SNOWDEN offers reward for return of Irish indented servants who went away from the Patuxent Iron Works [see like ad Vol. II No. 78] ■ Employment offered to a young gentleman for clerk [see like ad Vol. II No. 79] ■ PHILIP DAWE, Dumfries, offers for rent a genteel three-story brick house on Fairfax-street [see like ad Vol. II No. 77] ■ WILLIAM LYLES and CO., is selling rum [see like ad Vol. II No. 68] ■ DANIEL CARROLL, jun., Montgomery Co., Md., offers reward for return of runaway named Joe [see like ad Vol. II No. 78] ■ WILLIAM FITZHUGH offers for sale a valuable tract of land in Stafford County [see like ad Vol. II No. 70] ■ RICHARD LEE has for sale tract of land called Paradise, in Gloucester County [see like ad Vol. II No. 77] ■ WILLIAM ALEXANDER and WILLIAM GIBBONS STUART, executors of John Alexander, dec., have for sale one hundred lots of ground contiguous to the Town of ALX [see like ad Vol. II No. 78] ■ WILLIAM HARTSHORNE has for sale a lot at the corner of Wolf and Washington streets, and one on Fairfax-street near the corner of Gibbon-street [see like ad Vol. II No. 75] ■ HARDAGE LANE, acting executor of William Southard, dec., requests settlement of outstanding accounts [see like ad Vol. II No. 78] ■ JOHN SUTTON has for sale a dwelling-house on Royal-street; intends to go to England this fall and wishes to settle accounts [see like ad Vol. II No. 76] ■ Complete waggon for sale by Williams, Cary and Company [see like ad Vol. II No. 79] ■ PHILIP DALBY seeks to hire a stead Negro woman [see like ad Vol. II No. 78] ■ ALX: Printed by GEORGE RICHARDS, and COMPANY, at their Printing-Office on Fairfax-street--by whom Advertisements, &c. are thankfully received for this Paper,--and where Printing is performed with Care and Expedition.

1785/08/18, Vol. II No. 81

Page 1. **Hepburn and Dundas,** have for sale at the late store of Hepburn in King-street a very general assortment of European goods [see like at Vol. II No. 80] ■ Reward offered by either Mary Evans or Jacob Moor for horse strayed or stolen from the commons of ALX [see like ad Vol. II No. 80] ■ WILLIAM LYLES and CO., is selling rum [see like ad Vol. II No. 68] ■ JAMES HENDRICKS and DANIEL seek settlement of accounts owed to John Kleinhoff, late of ALX [see like ad Vol. II No. 80] ■ WILLIAM HEPBURN seeks settlement of his private accounts [see like ad Vol. II No. 80] ■ ROBERT BROWN, Prince William Co., warns against taking assignment of a bond he executed with Deskin Tebbs [see like ad Vol. II No. 79] ■ JOSEPH POPE, Prince George's Co., Md., offers reward for runaway Negro wench named Maria [see like ad Vol. II No. 79] ■ JOHN DUNDAS seeks persons with outstanding accounts with John Dundas and Co. to settle with William Nichols; William Nichols seeks indebted persons to pay debts to James Hendricks [see like ad Vol. II No. 80] ■ WILLIAM BROWN, late physician of ALX, has medicines for sale [see like ad Vol. II No. 80] ■ **Randle Mitchell and Son**, have for sale at their store on Fairfax-street, Jamaica spirits, etc. [see like ad Vol. II No. 80] ■ JOHN M'COOLE, executor of Richard Rigg, dec., has for sale items at the house of Peter Catlett, in Frederick Co. [see like ad Vol. II No. 80] ■ The Partnership between Lowry and M'Kenna is dissolved and request that accounts are settled; Lowry to soon leave for England [see like ads Vol. II No. 73] ■ BOSTON MARCH, Rockingham Co., offers reward for return of bay mare [see like ad Vol. II No. 80],

Page 2.

LONDON, June 18. Notwithstanding the lack of recent information on the affair of the Scheldt, circumstantial evidence indicates it will be peaceably resolved ... The connections between the Courts of Spain and Portugal, by marriage, are favorably based on the two parties being virtually of the same country, differing only in district and dialect. Whether the marriage will lead to revolution or re-union between the two kingdoms is a remote consideration. Neither a remote nor improbable hope is that Portuguese policy favorably disposed toward us may be useful in our treaty now under negotiation with the court of Madrid ... In consequence of some disagreeable Indian behaviour on the Canadian frontiers, several forts will be erected on the heights where only a few fortifications existed heretofore. Previous to the American war, the natives were most steadfast friends to England ... Extract of a letter from **Dublin, June 1:** Yesterday Mr. Thomas Carey, supposed to be the Printer of the *Volunteer's Journal* in August last, was tried on two indictments, for high treason, in the Court of King's Bench, before Lord Earlsfort, the Chief Justice, and his brethren the Honorable Mr. Justice Robertson, Mr. Justice Henn, and Sir Samuel Bradstreet, Bart. The two indictments stated that Carey printed a letter signed H. Murray in the *Volunteer's Journal* of 25 August, and of 30 August. Counselor Hewit stated the indictment, and the Attorney General the case. The first prosecution witness was Bryan Rorke, one of the newspaper staff, and by his evidence it appeared the prisoner was in the County of Kilkenny several weeks before and after the two issues. The Court and the Jury were unanimously of the opinion that he should be acquitted. He was ordered to give bail for good behaviour for seven years, which he instantly did, and thereupon was discharged. [Another paper represents that Mr. Carey was fully and honorably acquitted ... Extract of a letter from **Belfast, June 5:** In my last I informed you Portugal had finally admitted the manufactures of Ireland on the same terms as the British. This will bring back the wines of Portugal to their former duties in this country--the additional duty of £30 per ton laid on Portugal and Madera wines this session by our Parliament having been conditional, till the Court of Portugal would receive our manufactures pursuant to treaties ... Extract of a letter from **Paris, June 3:** Dr. Franklin, having seen his successor installed, is preparing to return to Philadelphia. As he cannot bear the fatigue of a carriage, he will embark on the Seine, which runs before his house at Passy, and go to Rouen, and thence to Havre, where the ship is getting ready that is to carry him to America ... The following is said to be the cause of a sloop of war being stationed off Brest harbour. A few months ago there was a report some ships of war were equipping at Brest for the East Indies; the government sent to Paris to inquire the particulars. The answer to our Ambassador was France was not going to send any ships there. The ships, however, continued equipping and occasioned another inquiry which received no reply, in consequence of which the sloop remaining near Ushant ... Last Monday Lord George Gordon went to several tradesmen in the city, particularly Fleet street, and advised them to shut up their shops next day ... Yesterday Lord Derby rose in the House of Lords to say he was going to make a motion, in some degree of a personal nature, which he hoped their Lordships would excuse. He had received a petition from Manchester against the Irish measures, signed by 120,000 persons, the parchment therefore so extremely heavy and unwieldy he was unable to lift it, requesting a clerk to assist him to carry it into the House. His motive for such a motion was that it might remain on their journals as a monument to the zeal of the people of Manchester, in opposing the dangerous measure now going to be adopted. The Lord Chancellor replied the motion was useless inasmuch as without it the numbers of petitioners would be transmitted to posterity, and by the petition remaining on records of the house. As the noble Lord had made a personal motion, the Lord Chancellor personally requested its withdrawal. This was done, but Lord Derby still needed a clerk's assistance; together with great difficulty they brought the petition in, but were unable to lift it on the table. In that they were assisted by the Lords Carlisle, Storm[illegible]at, &c. &c. &c. ... A petition of tanners at Manchester, also one from clock makers there, were presented, read, and ordered referred to the committee on the Irish Commercial Propositions ... Extract of a letter from **Vienna, June 1:** An account from Inspruck says an extraordinary phenomenon happened in the country of Closter-Stein, attributed to the winter's severity. A sort of pestilential fog has spread over the fields, destroying the young corn which earlier promised an abundant harvest. We can only hope it does not spread to other countries ... Extract of a letter from **Dunkirk, June 7:** An American ship, the *Virginia Packet*, Steane, from Maryland is seized here for a contraband trade and, as customary, the crew imprisoned. The American Minister will probably be favored with release of the people, but the ship and cargo are forfeited ... Extract of a letter from **Ostend, June 8:** The two frigates fitted here are ordered directly to Gibraltar, thence to cruise the Mediterranean to protect the Imperial flag. The *Alexander*, which is to be the Commodore, mounts 34 guns, including eight carronades, is commanded by Pierre Gustavus Delleck; all other officers are English, Scotch or Irish, as is the crew. They will be joined at Gibraltar by to other ships ... By accounts from Yorkshire we learn of larger orders received at different ports for the woolen manufactory of that country, than have been known for years past; accordingly it is supposed all sorts of fine wool will be much higher than they have been, and the stock in the makers hands is so small, that the whole may be consumed before new wool can be obtained. Without a large quantity of Spanish wool recently imported, the foreign orders could not have been executed ... By the laws of Lycurgus, celibacy in men was held infamous, bachelors constrained to walk naked through the market place in winter, singing a disparaging song about himself, and forfeiting any honors normally accruing in old age. If a man did not marry by the time of life fixed for marriage, he was liable to an action ... By the laws of Solon, the giving of portions in marriage with young woman was totally abolished, unless they were only daughters. Solon further ordained the bride could carry to her husband no more than three suits of clothes, and a few household goods of little value. Solon held marriage ought not to be a mercenary business ... Formerly there was a tax in England upon widowers, repealed at the revolution ... The Emperor has lately published a law worth the British legislature adopting. In future no clergyman shall hold two benefices to which cure of souls is annexed, because one cannot be tended to without neglect of the other. This is extended to Bishops and Prebendaries of the metropolitan churches, so that those holding several rectories served by curates must resign all but one. Were his to take place in England, how many fat pluralists would become thinner; and how many half-starved curates turn rectors, and gather flesh? ■ **CHARLESTON, July 21.** Th riches discovered at Senora, in New Andalusia, South America, are immense. One gold mine has been discovered within 12 leagues of the presidency del Alter, from where 14 pits only 2 feet deep, with little labor, vast quantities of grains of gold have been found. Two other equally rich mines have been discovered in the neighbourhood. ■ **PORTSMOUTH, (N.H.) July 20.** A few days ago the lightning entered a school house at the southward, killing a number of scholars and much hurting many more. Ought not parents interest themselves so much for the safety of their offspring, as to have metallic conductors to all school houses? **July 29:** The Newbury paper reports that on Friday the 22d instant a boy about 7 years old, son of Mr. David Graves, of Southampton, was returning home from school, just as he was entering the door of his father's house, he was struck dead by a flash of lightning. ■ **SPRINGFIELD, July 12.** The legislature of the State of Vermont at their last session passed an act granting to Reub[e]n Hamon, jun. Esq; a right of coining copper and regulating the same. ■ **NEW YORK, August 5.** In the chest of a miser, in the northern district of this State, lately deceased, was a written screed directed to his heir: *Farthings* are the seeds of guineas, growing by gentle gradations into pence, shillings, pounds, thousands, tens of thousands, and millions. They are the *semina* of wealth, and may be compared to *seconds* of time, which generate years, centuries, and even eternity itself. ■ **PHILADELPHIA, August 4.** Extract of a letter from **Roseau**, in **Dominica**, dated **July 2:** Last Thursday about 8 a.m. after a few days of rain, particularly in the mountains, the river Roseau came down suddenly in such a torrent as to threaten destruction to the lower town; in 20 minutes it rose 15 feet above normal, washing away several small houses and damaged larger one. No lives were lost, but many lost sugar and dry goods in flooded cellars, totaling several thousand pounds. Had not the rain then ceased, there would have been greater destruction and hundreds drowned. Had it happened at night, many must have perished attempting their escape ... Extract of a letter from **St. John's, Antigua,** dated **July 13**: Last Monday at 3:00 a.m. earth tremors began and increased in violence for almost a minute, when there was the most tremendous concussion of the earth ever remembered in this island. It filled every soul with consternation and terror. There are no reports yet of material hurt ... **August 6.** Extract of a letter from **Cadiz, April 29.** The grand armament destined to go against Algiers cannot be completed before the end of July, as the floating batteries and gun boats are of an entirely new construction, much superior to anything ever before invented. The ships of war are almost ready, and the transports will soon take in stores and provisions. A great number of fine pieces of artillery, some of surprising bore, are already shipped, as also a large quantity of camp equipage. Although not announced, the command will probably be either Comte O'Reilly, or Don Antonio Barcelo, most preferring the former. Many distinguished foreign officers have arrived, and have permission to go as volunteers, among them some Americans of great military courage. The Portuguese are ordered to hold themselves in readiness, and form a junction by mid-July at farthest. These, together, will make an armament of a prodigious force. Notwithstanding this vast equipment, the Algerines will make a vigorous resistance. They have been strengthening and augmenting their fortifications since the last bombardment, and are in a formidable state, served by an innumerable multitude of desperate persons ... Extract of a letter from a gentleman in **Washington**, to his friend in this city: The executive of the State of Frankland has lately concluded a treaty of amity and perpetual [Continued on Page 3].

Page 3. [Letter From a Gentleman in Washington (*continued*)] friendship with the Cherokee Indians, and a negotiation is now on foot to give them representation in the new legislation. The predatory excursions of some western tribes and the Creek Indians has given some alarms here and in Kentucky, but it is hoped the U.S. Commissioners will so conciliate the tribes this summer that before the year's end a thorough peace will prevail on all our borders. The people of Kentucky have lately held a convention and adopted decided measure for a separation. They name their new society *the Commonwealth of Kentucky;* this will occasion another deputation to Congress next winter ... *The London Universal Register, of the 14th of June, has the following article:--* "See'st thou a man diligent in business (said Solomon) he shall stand before princes and great men," &c.--A la mode John Adams, the American Plenipo--formerly, it is said, a disinterested composer of differences, under the name of an attorney; but now laying his head together with Cabinet Ministers, and holding familiar tete-a-tetes for the public welfare. What exquisitely fine feelings must have pervaded royal and noble breasts, on seeing a quondam declared rebel in an elevated independent station? But the time is now come when "the wolf shall dwell with the lamb, when the calf and the young lion, and the fatling shall herd together." It is whispered that the celebrated Dr. Price is political father confessor to the new Plenipo, and has already given him absolution." ■ **BALTIMORE, August 12.** Last Tuesday evening arrived here, directly from China, the ship *Pallas*, commanded by its owner, Capt. O'Donnell. She has on board a valuable cargo, consisting of an extensive variety of teas, china, silks, satins, nankeens, &c. &c. We are extremely happy o find the commercial reputation of this town so far increased as to attract the attention of gentlemen engaged in this distant but beneficial trade. It is no unpleasing sight to see the crew, Chinese, Malays, Japanese, and Moors, with a few Europeans, all habited according to their different countries, and employed together as brethren. Thus commerce binds and unites all nations of the globe with a golden chain ... **August 16:** The Assembly of the State of Georgia have generously offered the Connecticut line of the late Continental army to locate their bounty lands within that State, with other benefits and privileges, on certain conditions. ■ **ALX, August 18**. A large Barn, belonging to Mr. George Nixon near Leesburg, was lately set on Fire by Lightning, which, with a large Quantity of Grain, was entirely consumed.--The Loss is said to amount to 300l. ■ Last Week a laboring Man drank a large Quantity of Rum, and died in a short Time afterwards. ■ A Correspondent says, he is much surprised to see the Dancing-School, encouraged here for the Instruction of Children, so much crouded by grown Practitioners.--*Query*, Whether it would not be more prudent for them to employ the Master to teach in the Evenings, when their Awkwardness would be less conspicuous?-- ■ The Brig *Marquis de la Fayette*, Capt. Dunham, and Ship *Hazard*, Capt. New, from this Port, are arrived at Gravesend. The Brig *Betsey*, Capt. Perkins, from this Port, is arrived at Liverpool. The *Iris*, Capt. Cole, from this Port, is arrived at Lisbon. The *York*, [Capt.] Outram, and *Betsey*, [Capt.] Clarke, from Virginia, are arrived in the English Channel. The *Minerva*, Capt. Bright, from London, is arrived in James River. The *Tweed*, Capt. Grame, from London, is arrived in Rappahannock. Last Monday Evening the Brig *Nancy*, Capt. Brown, arrived here in 23 Days from Port-au-Prince. — Capt. Brown left the following Vessels at that Port: Schooner *Sally*, Capt. Mitchemore, from Rhode-Island; Brig —, Capt. Smith, from New-Haven; and Sloop —, Capt. Baynes, from Wilmington. ■ DIED.] Dr. SHUBAEL PRATT, formerly of Connecticut. — At Providence, Rhode-Island, in the 79th Year of his Age, the Honorable STEPHEN HOPKINS, Esq., formerly Governor of that State. ■ NAVAL-OFFICE, ALX. *Inward Entries*. Sloop *Hero*, J. Humphries, and Schooner *Greyhound*, R. Thompson, from Baltimore; Sloop *Lark*, S. Brown, Cape-Francois; Sloop *Night Ramble*, A. Etherige, and Sloop *Goodluck*, M. Everige, North-Carolina; Sloop *Judith*, S. Martin, Providence. *Cleared Outwards*. Ship *Fortune*, T. Halden, for London; Sloop *Hero*, J. Humphries, Baltimore; Sloop *Molly Beverly*, W. Wade, St. Eustatia. ■ Extracts from Mr. Neckar's Observations on Finance. IT is a just cause of surprise certainly, to find one nation in the actual habit of acquiring by its commerce, a credit superior to one half the gold and silver which the rest of Europe receives annually. On this view of the prosperity of France, one cannot forbear exclaiming, what can she want more? Yet, in attending to a state of the exportations and importations of the kingdom, one truth will appear whose consequences cannot be a matter of indifference: It is, that the advantage of the exchange in favor of France, rests on two great foundations; the exterior commerce of her manufactures, and the various articles imported from her islands. — It is known in general, but I doubt if Administration ever had the time, or inclination to collect just ideas on the subject. The commerce of her manufactures, and importations from her islands, make up three fourths of the exportations of the kingdom. — The knowledge of this ought to alarm Government; for both the one and the other of these branches of trade, is subject to events. —The great vent of manufactures, though favored by the indefatigable industry of France, and the habit of other nations, is still liable to unforseen diminutions; the productions of workmanship do not resemble the privileged gifts of the soil and climate. —Men may every where learn to do the same work—the different countries of Europe may all learn to manufacture themselves, what at present they seek from foreigners: Or it may be the fashion to do without those things; or prohibitions may be more rigorous.—In short, the industry which is nourished and established in the midst of political liberty, and territorial fertility, will in time, make great progress in the vast republic formed on the American continent; and this new power will one day, in some manner, have her share in furnishing the West-Indies, with commodities.—It belongs to the French Administration to watch over the sources of the present national prosperity; and to be more uneasy about treaties of commerce, and navigation, than the extension of the empire. The United States will not come to Europe for the production of a country, so near to them; and from the greater or less freedom of access, we may one day be obliged to give them to our Colonies; who can pretend to assign the part they will have in the exchange, which enriches France? But I am averse to entering deeply on points so nearly allied, at this moment, to political connections and treaties.

PRICES CURRENT, ALX. / Tobacco, 25s. per Ct. / Fine Flour, 28s. per Barrel. / Wheat, 5s. per Bushel. / Jamaica Spirits, 4/6 per Gallon. / Windward Rum, 3s. per Ditto. / Continental Rum, 2s. per Ditto. / Molasses, 1/8 per Ditto. / Muscovado Sugar, 35s. to 42/6 per Ct. / Salt, 3s. per Bushel, by Retail. / Corn, 3s. per Bushel / Exchange, 40.

On Saturday the 20th Instant, will be Sold at the Vendue-Store,

A VARIETY of WET and DRY GOODS, consisting of West-India and Continental rum, brandy, gin, sugar, tea, chocolate, soap, candles, &c. Irish linens, calicoes, muslins, cloths, gauzes, osnaburgs, canvas, nankeens, and an assortment of jewelry — Also, a likely Negro fellow and two young wenches, one of which has a fine child. ** Likewise to be sold, a number of LOTS situated in different parts of the town.

S. ARELL, Vendue-Master.

ALX, August 18, 1785.

JOHN COOK, Culpeper Co., offers reward for return of strayed sorrel horse [see like ad Vol. II No. 80] ■ RICHARD LEE has for sale tract of land called *Paradise*, in Gloucester County [see like ad Vol. II No. 77] ■ Mount-Vernon, August 15, 1785: THE Subscriber wants a HOUSE-KEEPER, or HOUSEHOLD STEWARD, who is competent to the charge of a large family, and attending on a good deal of company.—One who has been in the practice of these, and can produce testimonials of his (for a man would be preferred) or her abilities, sobriety, honesty and industry, will receive good wages and find a comfortable birth.--Without such testimonials it will be useless to apply. G. WASHINGTON ■ **D. and I. M'Pherson**, Have for sale on the most reasonable terms, for cash or country produce, MADERA wine by the pipe, hogshead and quarter-cask, rum by the hogshead and barrel, loaf and brown sugar, rice, tar, pitch, turpentine, nails, train oil, sail duck, cordage and a few gross of bottles. ALX, August 17, 1785 ■ **Richard Conway,** has for sale, Barbadoes Rum and Spirits [see like ad Vol. II No. 79] ■ **ALX Races.** On Thursday the 20th of October next, will be run for over the course near this Town, the ALX JOCKEY CLUB PURSE of ONE HUNDRED GUINEAS, free only for the Members of the Club, the best two in three four mile heats. Aged horses carrying ten stone; six year old, nine stone four pounds; five years old, eight stone four pounds; four years old, seven stone six pounds; three years old, six stone six pounds. On Friday the 21st, the JOCKEY CLUB purse of FIFTY GUINEAS, by four and three years old, and free only for Members of the Club. Four years old, carrying seven stone six pounds; and three years old, six stone six pounds; the best two in three two mile heats. The horses to start precisely at 12 o'clock each day. No horse will be allowed to start whose rider is not dressed in a silk jacket, jockey cap, and half boots. Judges are appointed who will determine all disputes. The Members to dine together at Mr. LYLES'S on the first day of the races.--Dinner to be on the table at 3 o'clock. ☞ This is to give notice, that the names of the members will certainly be published in this paper that do not pay up their arrears by the tenth day of October next. August 18, 1785 ■ THE FALMOUTH RACES will commence on the fourth Monday in October next, free for any horse, mare or gelding whatever. The first day's race for ONE HUNDRED POUNDS, four mile heats; and on Tuesday for FIFTY POUNDS, three mile heats. The weights and regulations to be agreeable to the Fredericksburg Jockey Club. And on Wednesday a give and take purse for THIRTY POUNDS.--Ten stone to be the standard. DANIEL TRIPLETT, Secretary and Treasurer. Falmouth, August 15, 1785. ■ *Salisbury*, August 15, 1785. A WHITE man, who called himself JOSEPH LODGE, came to my plantation on the 6th instant, when I was from home, and swopped a horse with a slave of mine; and I have reason to believe the horse he let my Negro have is a stolen one. He is a bay about 14 hands high, not more than 5 or 6 years old, slender made, has a large head, is very low in flesh, branded on the near shoulder [reverse capital B] and has a small imperfect brand on his off buttock. Any person having a legal title to said horse, may have him by applying to the Subscriber in one month from the date hereof, unavoidable accidents excepted. If no owner appears within that time I shall allow the present possessor to dispose of him. SAMUEL LOVE, jun. ■ TO BE SOLD, A VERY valuable LOT on Pitt-street, in an advantageous part of this flourishing town, suitable situated for any kind of business, containing 22 feet 6 inches in front, and 123 feet back.--Terms may be known by applying to RICHARD CONWAY, Esq., ALX, August 18, 1785. ■ RAN away from the Subscriber, living within 8 miles of Winchester, on the 8th inst., a Negro fellow named NED, about 5 feet 7 inches high, walks as though lame, turns his feet out very much, and is about 18 years of age: He had on and took with him a white coat, jacket and breeches, a ruffled shirt, a gray great coat, and baggage consisting of books, writing-paper, and may attempt to forge a pass.--Whoever will take up said fellow and secure him so that his Master may get him again, shall receive, if taken within the County FOUR DOLLARS, and if out of the State FOURTEEN DOLLARS, and all reasonable charges, paid by JOSEPH HOLMES, August 9, 1785.

Page 4. Poetry. From the *Weekly Magazine*, "Verses Written on a Blank Leaf of Pope's Moral Essays." ■ WILLIAM ALEXANDER and WILLIAM GIBBONS STUART, executors of John Alexander, dec., have for sale one hundred lots of ground contiguous to the Town of ALX [see like ad Vol. II No. 78] ■ WILLIAM HARTSHORNE has for sale a lot at the corner of Wolf and Washington streets, and one on Fairfax-street near the corner of Gibbon-street [see like ad Vol. II No. 75] ■ **Thomas M. Savage,** has for sale at his store next door to Colonel Fitzgerald's, an assortment of saleable goods [see like ad Vol. II No. 80] ■ Notice is given that a petition will be filed for an act respecting uniformity of streets in the Town of ALX [see like ad Vol. II No. 79] ■ FOR SALE, A VERY valuable LOT, 20 feet front by 60 in depth, subject to a small Ground-Rent, advantageously situated on Fairfax-street, on which is a small convenient Store, now occupied by Messieurs Porter and Ingraham.--For terms apply to Col. WILLIAM LYLES, ALX, August 11, 1785. ■ Executors of the estate of Thomas Kirkpatrick, dec., have for sale 28 Lots in the Town of ALX [see like ad Vol. II No. 79] ■ WILLIAM FITZHUGH offers for sale a valuable tract of land in Stafford County [see like ad Vol. II No. 70] ■ JOHN BRYCE has for sale seven lots situated on Queen and Washington streets [see like ad Vol. II No. 80] ■ ☞ A great Variety of BLANKS, printed on good Paper, may be had at the Printing-Office. ■ **Jonathan Swift and Co.,** have for sale at their store on Capt. Harper's wharf a general assortment of goods [see like ad Vol. II No. 79] ■ HENRY LYLES has for sale goods at cost and charges [see like ad Vol. II No. 79] ■ Directors of the Potomack Company seek outstanding subscriber payment of 5 per cent. [see like ad Vol. II No. 79] ■ MICHAEL MADDEN offers reward for return of runaway intended Irish servant man, named Patrick Gogherty [see like ad Vol. II No. 79] ■ To be sold, at the Printing-Office, A Variety of Blank Books, consisting of Ledgers, Journals, Cash-Books, Letter-Books, &c.&c. Also, Stoughton's Bitters, Anderson's Pills, Daffy's Elixir, Balsam of Honey, Squire's Elixir, Bateman's Drops, Godfrey's Cordial, &c.&c. ■ ALX: Printed by GEORGE RICHARDS, and COMPANY, at their Printing-Office on Fairfax-street--by whom Advertisements, &c. are thankfully received for this Paper,--and where Printing is performed with Care and Expedition.

1785/08/25, Vol. II No. 82

Page 1. G. WASHINGTON seeks house-keeper or household steward [see like ad Vol. II No. 81] ■ Races of the ALX Jockey Club Purse announced [see like ad Vol. II No. 81] ■ WILLIAM LYLES has a lot for sale on Fairfax-street [see like ad Vol. II No. 81] ■ The Fredericksburg Jockey Club announces horse races at Falmouth, Va. [see like ad Vol. II No. 81] ■ SAMUEL LOVE, jun., Salisbury, Va., seeks owner of horse feared stolen he received in trade [see like ad Vol. II No. 81] ■ ☞ A great Variety of BLANKS, printed on good Paper, may be had at the Printing-Office. ■ **D. and I. M'Pherson,** have for sale Madera wine, etc. [see like ad Vol. II No. 81] ■ RICHARD CONWAY advertises for sale a lot on Pitt-street [see like ad Vol. II No. 81] ■ JOHN COOK, Culpeper Co., offers reward for return of strayed sorrel horse [see like ad Vol. II No. 80] ■ WILLIAM ALEXANDER and WILLIAM GIBBONS STUART, executors of John Alexander, dec., have for sale one hundred lots of ground contiguous to the Town of ALX [see like ad Vol. II No. 78] ■ Directors of the Potomack Company seek outstanding subscriber payment of 5 per cent. [see like ad Vol. II No. 79].

LONDON, June 4. The eloquence of Sir Gregory Page Turner has indeed a little astonished Parliament, but there is no wonder in his applause of the shop tax, and his deep knowledge of the luxuries of the trade. He married a St. James street milliner, and attests from examining her books that the profit margin is wide. Thus he concludes that the tax is a good one ... **June 11:** John Adams (commonly called his Excellency John Adams, Ambassador of America) and George Gordon (commonly called Lord George Gordon, President of the Protestant Association) were quite cordial and sincere at their meeting at the Dutch Ambassador's, after an absence of 17 years without ever turning their coats, their coats being spun of that incombustible hero the Asbeston of the Ancients; and which old cloaths were found so admirable for their wear and other good qualities, that the fires which devoured Boston, consumed Esopus, destroyed Norfolk, and endangered London, only served to cleanse and purge them, in like manner as we read of the fiery furnaces of King Nebuchadnezzar, which tended only to add lustre to the true blue garments of Shadrach, Meshach, and Abednego, of whom Daniel says "And the Princes, Governors, and Captains, and the King's Counselors, being gathered together, saw these men, upon whose bodies the fire had no power, nor was an hair of their head singed, neither were their coats changed" ... **June 18:** A Correspondent, who mostly resides in the Country, cannot help remarking the revolutions that are constantly happening in kingdoms, from reading in the public prints of Mr. Adams, the American Envoy, being introduced at Court, and that his Secretary was the principal Aid-de-Camp to General Washington. It is a pity (says the same correspondent) that Lord North was not the master of the ceremonies of the occasion; and that brave General an assistant, who so generously published a proclamation of mercy to those deluded Americans who threw themselves at his feet, "Excepting only one Hancock and Adams, whose offences were too atrocious to be forgiven." It might seem strange that Mr. Adams, who bore such an active hand in the late rebellion, should of all others, be the man pitched upon by the Thirteen States as their legate in this country. This is looked upon as no great mark of delicacy or politeness of Congress; but, when the matter is duly attended to, it will appear they could not get well past it. Who could have such a claim, as Mr.. Adams, to be the representative of the body he was so instrumental in creating? And how could *his* or *their* triumph be complete, unless that representation was to be in Great Britain? Gratitude required no less from them; and the boldness of *his* patriotism could no otherwise have been so well manifested. As to any umbrage we might [Continued on Page 2].

Page 2. [Commentary on John Adams (*continued*)] take at such an appointment, there was no occasion to think much about it. The last dozen of years has so far mollified our natural hardiness of spirit, that they knew we would easily dispense with much ceremony ... Our rulers, it is *said*, are not a little puzzled about finding a proper person to be wafted over the Atlantic, by way of excambium for the American *Plenipo*. The Minister, it seems, made the first offer to a Welch gentleman, whom he was under some obligation to serve. But the ancient Briton...fired at the proposal, sputtered out something, with so much vehemence, about the affront offered, by such a barter, to *hur known* pedigree and descent, that our young *Palinurus* thought it prudent to sheer off immediately, to save his slim bark from the hazard of being brought to blows with an adversary of far superior weight of metal. To what quarter he next steered for traffic, we have not heard; but it is not thought he will find this *commutation* job more easy than a former one. Few of any note will choose, in all probability, to be balanced against a man, whose origin they know not, and whose chief personal distinction is the mischief he has done. ■ **St. GEORGE's** (Bermuda) **July 2.** We hear from Nassau, in the island of Providence, of continued differences between the loyalists and the old residents. Since Governor Maxwell sailed for London they have been in continued broils; like true Englishmen, for want of a foreign enemy they quarrel among themselves. The assembly are so divided that the Lieutenant Governor James Edward Powell issued a proclamation proroguing the General Assembly until Wednesday the 20th ... By West Indian accounts, two regiments of British troops are just arrived at Barbadoes, one for Domina, one for St. Vincent. Also, that our cruisers and men of war have not suffered any American vessels to go into any of the islands unless in distress. Several had been seized and condemned at St. Kitt's, and elsewhere, having two sets of papers on board. ■ **BOSTON, August 3.** Extract of a letter from **Paris, May 9:** A balloon for the Royal family is to be launched here early next month. The King and Queen (under the direction of the famous Montgolfier) intend an aerial excursion of the metropolis and its environs. The Queen is so determined that she lately told her illustrious consort that she would go up even if he would not accompany her: "I will be the first of the blood Royal (said her Majesty with great good humour) that visited the celestials, if I perish in the attempt." ■ **PHILADELPHIA, August 13.** Recent accounts from Kentucky confirm the SIX NATIONS are greatly dissatisfied with the late treaty, alleging British officers at Niagara and Detroit told them our commissioners imposed on the Indians in asserting those lands were ceded to us by the British, and that we were to take possession of the abovementioned posts; that the celebrated Brant had arrived from England and sided with them, in consequence of which several tribes besides the SIX NATIONS held a council at the Shawanese town--the result of which we are unable to learn. But as two chiefs--Cornplanter and another--have since been at Fort Pitt and presented to Colonel Harmar (our commander there) papers exchanged at the treaty, it is reasonably conjectured their intentions are hostile and unfriendly. The Colonel, after talking with them, refused to accept the papers; he observed that those who gave the Indians such information with a view to excite their jealousy and make them uneasy, were enemies both to them and to us. The Indians said they always understood the lands contracted for by the Pennsylvania Commissioners were to be set apart as hunting grounds for both parties--not to be surveyed and the trees spotted for the purposes of settlement and cultivation. Also, that as only a few of their chiefs were at the treaty, they had not been fully and regularly represented. In their drunken frolics they have declared they had never been conquered, and would not give up their lands. They seem more inclined to believe British emissaries and incendiaries because we had taken possession of Niagara and Detroit. These are the main grounds for the Indians' non-compliance with the treaty. We hear an express has been sent with this intelligence from Fort Pitt to Congress ... *An useful Hint.* Rising at 6 instead of 8 daily, for 40 years, amounts to 29,200 hours: 3 years, 121 days, 16 hours. This affords 8 hours per day for ten years--the same as adding ten years to one's life, for the cultivation of our minds or the despatch of business. This calculation is made without any regard to Bissextile [leap year--Eds.] ■ **BALTIMORE, August 19.** The old American Company of Comedians are landed at Annapolis, from Jamaica where they have performed the last ten years with great reputation. At the beginning of the late contest, Messrs. Hallam and Henry, their managers, were desired by the then President of Congress to remove from the continent until American independence was secured and acknowledged. They are said to be a very respectable company, both for the propriety of their conduct and the excellency of their performances. Mr.. Henry, who is arrived with them, has been a pupil of Mr. Sheridan--so remarkable in Europe for his readings for the instruction and amusement of the nobility and gentry in London. Mr. Henry, well qualified to teach eloquence in the Sheridonian manner may, after the State Theatre is opened in Maryland, make tender of his abilities to the public in this useful and much wanted branch of science and entertainment .. Died, a few days since, at the seat of the late Richard Croxall, Esq., Mr. ARCHIBALD BUCHANAN, for many years an eminent and respected merchant in this town. ■ **RICHMOND, August 20.** Thursday last, being the day appointed for laying the first stone of the foundation for the capitol of this State, the ancient and honorable society of Free and Accepted Masons, and the Hon. Archibald Cary, Speaker of the senate, went in procession from the lodge room to the ground allotted for the purpose, and having deposited the medals for the occasion in the foundation stone, they laid the same in the sight of a numerous concourse of ladies and gentlemen. After which they returned to the lodge room, and, in the afternoon went to the capitol for an elegant dinner with members of the Privy Council, the Common Hall, the commissioners of the public buildings, and many other gentlemen. The evening was spent in the most festive harmony and good order ... By a letter from the Sweet Springs we learn that the Shawanese Indians are out on the frontiers in great force, united with the Six Nations. At Point Pleasant they killed Col. Thomas Lewis, a Major, and 3 Captains. Colonel Lewis and his party were killed at a place called Racoon Bottom, to which the Indians invited them to hold treaty talks. This bloody treachery is said to be revenge for a recent murder of an old Indian hunter by a party of whites going down the Ohio. The fort at Point Pleasant is in great distress, and the inhabitants of Green Briar, stimulated by Col. Samuel Lewis, brother to Thomas, are in motion to its relief. ■ **ALX, August 25.** The Sloop *Phebe*, Capt. Cartwright, of this Port, was lately seized and condemned at St. Lucia, with 12 S[illegible] of other American Vessels; amongst which were three Whalemen that had put into an out Port of the Island for the sole Purpose of obtaining a Supply of Wood and Water. Several American Vessels have also been seized at the British Islands. Yesterday Morning the Schooner *Molly*, Capt. Cox, arrived here, in 21 Days from St. Kitt's. — A Brig from Baltimore arrived at that Island a few Days before, Capt. Cox left it. ■ Yesterday Morning, Mr. JOHN LORDAN, a promising young Gentleman, a Native of Ireland, died here, deservedly regretted by his Acquaintance. His Death was occasioned by a Mortification of one of his Legs, which he broke, a few Days ago, in riding an unruly Horse. ■ A few Days ago a labouring Man was crushed to Death in this Town, by the sudden falling of a Bank of Earth, under which he was digging. ■ From a late European Publication, "Anecdotes of his Excellency John Adams, late Minister Plenipotentiary, from the United States of North-America, to their High Mightinesses the States-General of the United Provinces;—now representing the said States at the Court of St. James's." Mr. Adams is descended from one of the first families which founded the colony of Massachusetts-Bay [in] 1630. He applied himself early to the study of the laws of his country; and no sooner entered upon the practice thereof, but he drew the attention, admiration, and esteem of his country-men, on account of his eminent abilities and probity of character. Not satisfied with barely maintaining the rights of individuals, he soon signalized himself in the defence of his country, and mankind at large, by writing his admirable dissertation on the Canon and Feudal Laws; a work well worthy the attention of every man who is an enemy to ecclesiastical and civil tyranny. [Article discusses the political ideals of Mr. Adams; continues to Page 3].

Page 3. Public Vendue by S. Arell, Vendue-Master [see like ad Vol. II No. 81] ■ On Monday the 19th of September next, on the premises, the Subscribers will let on ground-rent for ever, with the liberty of purchasing out the annuity; SOME LOTS of GROUND, well situated on Fairfax and Water streets, in this town.--A plan of the Lots may be seen at any time, on application to the Subscribers.--They have also for sale, on the most reasonable terms, a good assortment of MERCHANDISE. M'CREA and MEASE, ALX, August 25, 1785. ■ CAME to the Subscriber's farm, in the vicinity of this town, on Sunday last, a small gray MARE, with abundance of small brown spots, (commonly called flea-bitten) cropt in the left ear, no brand, about 8 or 9 years old, about 13 hands high, shod all round, a natural pacer.--The owner is desired to prove property, pay charges, and take her away. PETER DOW, ALX, August 25, 1785. ■ WHEREAS one RICHARD EVEREST, an Englishman, by trade a black or white smith, and about ten years ago lived with Mr. Hough, storekeeper in Loudon, Virginia, has lately had [sic] left him a considerable legacy.--If he will apply to the Subscriber in Annapolis, Maryland, he will be further informed respecting said legacy.--Any person giving information of the above Richard Everest, will render an essential service to his wife and children, and if required, be rewarded for their trouble by EDWARD VIDLER, Annapolis, August 12, 1785. ■ **Fresh Hyson and Gunpowder Teas**, Received by the *Empress of China*, directly from Canton, and to be sold by **Porter and Ingraham**, Who have for sale a general assortment of EUROPEAN GOODS, on very reasonable terms, for cash or tobacco: Amongst which are, A Variety of low-priced broadcloths, Coatings, duffils, baizes, Shalloons, calamancoes, Durants, [cambleteens], Lastings, mens' worsted and thread hose, Ladies cotton ditto, Mens' coloured beaver and lamb gloves, Ladies ditto, Boys and maids ditto, Checked handkerchiefs, Nankeens, Irish linens, Tablecloths, Lawns, gauzes, Dowlas, Holland duck, Calicoes, Russia sheetings, Irish ditto, Ticklenburgs and sewing twine, Mould candles by the box, Black pepper, Bohea tea by the chest or dozen, Sugar in barrels, 4d. and 20d. nails, German steel, Bar-iron, shot and lead, Tinplates. ☞ A large assortment of HARDWARE, and a variety of other articles. ALX, August 25, 1785. ■ To be LET, and immediate possession given, THREE UPPER STORIES of a large commodious BRICK STORE, situated on Capt. Harper's wharf, which is well calculated for a wholesale store and very convenient for the reception of produce of every kind.--For terms, apply to Capt. HARPER, or JONATHAN SWIFT and CO., ALX, August 25, 1785. ■ To be sold, to the highest bidder, at Urbanna, on Monday the 24th of October next, being Middlesex Court-Day, THE LOTS, STORE and WAREHOUSES belonging to JAMES MILLS and COMPANY, which are as commodious and convenient as any in the State. — Also, a valuable NEGRO WATERMAN. — Twelve-months credit, on bond, with security. — The property not to be altered till the terms are complied with. ■ FIVE GUINEAS REWARD. RAN away, from the Subscriber living on Piscataway-Creek, on the 13th inst., two Irish servants, coopers by trade, viz. JOHN BLAKE, a short well set fellow, about 5 feet 7 or 8 inches high, round faced, fair complexion, pitted with the small-pox, short light-coloured hair, and white eyes: He had on, and took with him, two osnaburg shirts, two pair of osnaburg trousers, dyed country cotton coat, a reddish coloured cloth waistcoat and a coarse felt hat.--The other named WILLIAM HUMPHREYS, is a spare fellow, nearly the height of Blake, has a long face, thick visage, pretty much pitted with the small-pox, brown skin, short black hair, which he sometimes ties, and black eyes: He had on, and took with him, two osnaburg shirts, one white linen ditto about half worn, two pair of osnaburg trousers, a blue double-breasted cloth waistcoat, a coarse felt hat, and a pair of coarse shoes.--They probably may change their names and clothes, and write a false pass, as one of them is a tolerable good scholar.--It is supposed they stole a small boat and went down the river in her.--Whoever takes up said servants, and returns them home to me, or secures them in any gaol, so that I can get them again, shall receive the above reward. JOHN CAWOOD, Prince-George's Co., Maryland, August 18, 1785. ■ TWENTY-FIVE DOLLARS REWARD. RAN away last night, from the Subscriber, living in ALX, an indented servant man, named STEPHEN BOWDEN, a bricklayer by trade, about 22 years of age, 5 feet 10 inches high, dark complexion, light brown hair, full eyed, has a bold look, a large gap in his upper jaw, from the loss of three or four teeth, a remarkable scar in his forehead just under his hat occasioned by a fall, and a rolling gait in walking. He has had a sore on one of his shins, the mark of which may be seen on examination, though it may be healed: He had on and took with him, a pretty good new felt hat, an osnaburg shirt and trousers, a cotton coat of a nankeen colour, a calico jacket the stamp resembling shells, with fustian back, coarse shoes, plain buckles, and some other clothes.--It is supposed he has a black Barcelona silk handkerchief on his heck.--Being pretty talkative, and an artful, sly, impudent villain, he may probably change his name, attempt to pass for a freeman, and, if taken up, to escape from custody, as he did on a former trip, two months ago, at Fredericksburg.--It is supposed he is making for Baltimore or Philadelphia.--Whoever will take him up, and convey him to me in ALX, shall receive the above reward; and all reasonable charges. WILLIAM WRIGHT, Bricklayer, ALX, August 22, 1785.

Page 4. Poetry. "The sure way to gain Esteem." ■ **Hepburn and Dundas,** have for sale at the late store of Hepburn in King-street a very general assortment of European goods [see like at Vol. II No. 80] ■ JOHN BRYCE has for sale seven lots situated on Queen and Washington streets [see like ad Vol. II No. 80] ■ WILLIAM LYLES and CO., is selling rum [see like ad Vol. II No. 68] ■ JAMES HENDRICKS and DANIEL seek settlement of accounts owed to John Kleinhoff, late of ALX [see like ad Vol. II No. 80] ■ WILLIAM FITZHUGH offers for sale a valuable tract of land in Stafford County [see like ad Vol. II No. 70] ■ WILLIAM HARTSHORNE has for sale a lot at the corner of Wolf and Washington streets, and one on Fairfax-street near the corner of Gibbon-street [see like ad Vol. II No. 75] ■ **Randle Mitchell and Son,** have for sale at their store on Fairfax-street, Jamaica spirits, etc. [see like ad Vol. II No. 80] ■ WILLIAM BROWN, late physician of ALX, has medicines for sale [see like ad Vol. II No. 80] ■ WILLIAM HEPBURN seeks settlement of his private accounts [see like ad Vol. II No. 80] ■ Reward offered by either Mary Evans or Jacob Moor for horse strayed or stolen from the commons of ALX [see like ad Vol. II No. 80] ■ The Partnership between Lowry and M'Kenna is dissolved and request that accounts are settled; Lowry to soon leave for England [see like ads Vol. II No. 73] ■ BOSTON MARCH, Rockingham Co., offers reward for return of bay mare [see like ad Vol. II No. 80] ■ RICHARD LEE has for sale tract of land called Paradise, in Gloucester County [see like ad Vol. II No. 77] ■ To be sold, at the Printing-Office, A Variety of Blank Books, consisting of Ledgers, Journals, Cash-Books, Letter-Books, &c.&c. Also, Stoughton's Bitters, Anderson's Pills, Daffy's Elixir, Balsam of Honey, Squire's Elixir, Bateman's Drops, Godfrey's Cordial, &c.&c. ■ ALX: Printed by GEORGE RICHARDS, and COMPANY, at their Printing-Office on Fairfax-street--by whom Advertisements, &c. are thankfully received for this Paper,--and where Printing is performed with Care and Expedition.

1785/09/01, Vol. II No. 83

Page 1. **Porter and Ingraham**, have for sale a general assortment of European Goods [see like ad Vol. II No. 82] ■ Races of the ALX Jockey Club Purse announced [see like ad Vol. II No. 81] ■ JONATHAN SWIFT and CO. has for lease three upper stories of a brick store on Capt. Harper's wharf [see like ad Vol. II No. 82] ■ Lots, store and warehouses of James Mills and Co. to be sold in Urbanna [see like ad Vol. II No. 82] ■ M'CREA and MEASE to sell some lots on Fairfax and Water streets [see like ad Vol. II No. 82] ■ PETER DOW seeks owner of stray gray mare [see like ad Vol. II No. 82] ■ JOHN CAWOOD, Prince George's Co., Md., offers reward for return of runaways JOHN BLAKE and WILLIAM HUMPHREYS [see like ad Vol. II No. 82] ■ WILLIAM WRIGHT, bricklayer, offers reward for return of runaway indented servant man named STEPHEN BOWDEN [see like ad Vol. II No. 82].

LONDON, June 18. A correspondent has sent the substance (obtained by way of France) of the Empress of Russia's answer to the King of Prussia upon his remonstrance on the bartering project between the Emperor of Germany and the Elector of Bavaria. The Empress saw this project as the only sure way of preventing a war, and seriously wished for its immediate execution. This she conveyed in her letter to the Duke of Deux Ponts, inviting him to join in. However, she was so ill requited by him she declares to the King she has no intention to push the bartering project unless both parties immediately concerned shall have fully agreed on it ... Digging a slope on a pond's edge near the paper mill, workers cast up in Portuguese and other gold, money to amount to £800, and a rough diamond of considerable value. It is supposed that a women of property, who drowned herself in that pond, buried her money before doing so ... Paris is talking about a nobleman of the first distinction who, having lost much at the Queen's parties, needed to dispose of an extensive and valuable collection of pictures to get funds. On learning this, her Majesty made a party among the nobility, attended the sale, and the pictures were soon sold for near double what they originally cost, or were intrinsically worth ... Extract of a letter from **Dublin, June 4, 1785**: Judging the politics of this country by the public prints would be fallacious. The voice of the people appears against the commercial alterations in their present state; those who were friends to them in their original state charge the English Minister with pusillanimity and deception; those who have always opposed them charge him with design to overturn the independency of the Irish Legislature--so that he is now unpopular with all parties. A remonstrance against those altered propositions has certainly been voted in the Privy Council here, and despatched to St. James's, and it is openly asserted and no where contradicted that Mr. Forster, who may be termed the Irish Minister, has strenuously opposed the alteration of the old, and introduction of the new propositions, and that his Grace of Rutland is equally displeased. While this contention rages in politics, improvements in the arts and manufactures increase with astonishing avidity, no where more rapid than in Dublin, where several magnificent edifices are erecting, many old streets widening, and new avenues making from various parts of the city to a wide convenient road which encircled it. The spirit of volunteering still subsists, of late materially increased in ardor, but their military principle is strictly defensive, and his Majesty is everywhere revered, beloved, and respected [Continued on Page 2].

Page 2. [The Dublin Letter (*continued*)] Indeed, such is the loyalty of these people that I am convinced the most effectual means of increasing aristocratic influence would be to permit some branch of the royal family to reside among them in an official capacity; it is what I heard often wished ... There is an uncommon amount of specie here now. Most of the guineas sent to America are back, and the balance of exchange send in great quantities of money from other quarters ... Mons. Buffy's death, in a political view, is much regretted in France, he being particularly well qualified for his India post. As a man of address and insinuation he knew how to manage the country powers, and had an implacable enmity towards this country ... A country gentleman paid his first visit to town, and went to the Drury lane theatre. A man seated next to him identified Mrs. Siddons, the King and Queen, and their beauteous progeny. "Pray, who are those ladies attending on her Majesty?" "Maids of honor," replied the other. "And I suppose those gentlemen attending on the King are men of honor?" "Oh, no! They are Lords of the bed chamber." ... It is not less remarkable than true, that a cause [case] was a few days ago closed in one of the lower Courts which had commenced in the reign of King William. The Solicitor General was one of the Council ... **June 21:** Yesterday's mail brought letters from the continent saying great preparations are being made in France for the Emperor's reception, who will visit his royal Sister on his return from Italy; from the same sources: the August Prince intends visiting this country, also ... The two Dutch Ambassadors who are to make public concession at the Court of Vienna for insulting the Imperial flag, are actually set out from the Hague. ■ **KINGSTON, (Jamaica) June 18.** It must touch the feelings of the most inhuman of our species, says a correspondent, to behold those sable wretches who have, from long confinement on board of vessels from the African coast, been reduced to horrid spectacles of misery and want, in that state sent to public vendue, and there sold to the highest and best bidder! When the return of the sales can scarcely average half a johannes for each--of the many public offences complained of (says our correspondent) this must necessarily appear, to the disinterested, as one of the first which requires to be remedied. ■ **SHELBURNE,** (Nova Scotia) **July 21.** Extract of a letter from a gentleman at **Beaver Harbour**, to his friend here, dated **July 15, 1785**: A fire here about 8 days ago was so dreadful it nearly accomplished total ruin of the settlement, destroying 21 houses and damaging a number of others. Few escaped without losing something; nearly every garden in this place is ruined. ■ **Charleston,** (S.C.) **August 4.** Last Friday arrived the schooner *Matilda*, Capt. George Wanton, from New Providence. Sailing from Baltimore July 3 with a cargo of flour, corn &c. for the Bahamas. On arrival there she was not permitted to land any part of her cargo, ordered immediately to put to sea again. Captain Wanton reports that a vessel of Portsmouth, Virginia, had been seized there by the collector, notwithstanding oath having been made of her being in distress. Several other American vessels were ordered out in 24 hours, under pain of like seizure ... **August 12:** In consequence of a Chamber of Commerce advertisement calling attention to circular letters from the New York Chamber, and the Boston Committee of merchants, traders and citizens, there was a numerous and respectable meeting at the City Exchange yesterday. Mr. Dessauser chaired, Col. Gervais presented several papers which were then read by Mr. Legare. Col. Gervais presented a Charleston Chamber of Commerce report which expressed the highest approbation of those States as have already stood forth to rescue the U.S. commercial interests from impending ruin, so much in danger from the British restrictions. The report's purpose was to propose that the citizens present a memorial to the next meeting of their legislature praying their speedy interposition in such manner as may seem most effectual. This idea meeting general approbation, a Committee was named for that purpose: John Matthews, Esq; Col. Gervais, Dr.Budd, William H. Gibbes, Esq; Mr. W. Logan, Mr. Edward Darrell, Mr. Dessausure, Mr. Thomas Morris, Mr. John Blake. ■ **BOSTON, August 8.** Our advertising customers need not regard the duty of six pence on an advertisement under 96 words, as the conspicuous manner in which they will be set off, will compensate for it ... **August 11:** While the selfish politics of the *Butean faction* are hurrying on to destruction an infatuated nation, with whom, if we consult our *real interest*, we shall never have any future *commercial* or other connection; it cannot but afford the most heart felt satisfaction to every American and Frenchman that the bonds of union will only improve between this country and France. We have an authentic and indisputable account that that most excellent nobleman and warm friend to America, the New England States in particular, the Marquis de la Fayette, has so worked on our behalf that he has procured our great and magnanimous ALLY totally to remit the 20 per cent duty on foreign oil, from all sent from any of the United States to France. The provider of oil for lighting Paris and all other French cities, as well as the royal navy, has sent via the Marquis proposals for receiving at Nantz, Bourdeaux and Havre de Grace 16,000 quintals, or 8000 barrels, of our spermaceti oil, the next year--to be paid in any commodity of growth, manufacture or produce of France, at the current price, of which weekly bills are published. Any difference arising will be settled by six arbitrators, three each French and American, who may call a seventh in case of disagreement. A company of very respectable merchants in this State are now forming to accept these proposals, and carry out the plan, whereby France can furnish us with her manufactures on terms infinitely superior to any from our old rancorous step-mother, Great Britain ... **August 15:** Yesterday se'nnight the *Mercury* British transport of 36 guns, owned in London, sailed from Nantasket Road for Shelburne, laden with hay, sheep and cattle for our dearly beloved brethren, the refugees of that place. *If our enemies hunger, feed them.* Who she was freighted by we could not learn. She was commanded by one Stanhope, who it is said when Captain of a British frigate and had taken any prize, would even rip open the prisoner's waistband of their trousers for small plunder. ■ **NEW YORK, August 16.** It is strange, says a correspondent, that every person we meet are complaining of hard times, that they are in want, &c. Where I live, says he, they do have some few wants, but judge their unreasonableness as I list them: the hungry want food; the sick, health; the naked, cloaths; the rich to grind the face of the poor, and the poor to plunder the property of the rich. [The list continues in this vein.] Two other trifles came to our correspondent's mind, of which he believes they are in want: good sense, and good manners ... It is believed the treaty proposed for October 1st at the mouth of the great Miami will close all business with the natives for the present. A great additional cession of lands is expected. Congress have appointed Major General Robert Howe, one of the Indian Affairs Commissioners, to attend ... At an Episcopal Clergy convention, at Middletown, Connecticut, a number of gentlemen received ordination from the hands of Bishop Seabury. ■ **PHILADELPHIA, August 18.** The expected arrival of that great philosopher, that great politician and to add a wreath of glory of more immortal texture, that truly benevolent citizen of the world, Dr. Franklin, in this State cannot fail to produce a most sensible effect on the weal public. To doubt his being chosen President, when that office is vacated, would be to call in question not only the honor and gratitude, but even the common sense of Pennsylvania ... **August 25:** A few days since Thomas Hutchins, Esquire, Geographer to the United States, and Surveyor General of lands ceded by Great Britain to the U.S., set out for Fort Pitt, from whence he proceeds with his deputies to survey and lay off those lands, as instructed by Congress ... From the MASSACHUSETTS SPY: At a meeting of the proprietors, purchasers and settlers of lands on the river **SUSQUEHANNA,** under the countenance and title of the State of Connecticut, at Hartford, on the 13th of July, 1785, taking into consideration the circumstances of their claims, the large sums of money expended in their purchase, settlement and defence of the same, and the justice of their claims to said lands, do resolve [summarized]: that the purchase from the Indian proprietors was fair; at the time of purchase the right of Connecticut to the jurisdiction and pre-emption of that territory was never in doubt, being based on the charter and letters patent to Connecticut 18 years prior to those to Sir William Penn; that in confidence of this, they made the purchases and thereafter with much blood and treasure defended their possessions against the common enemy, to the great emolument and security of the United States; that although the Court constituted to determine the right of jurisdiction between Connecticut and Pennsylvania have astonished the world with a decision for Pennsylvania, yet we maintain the validity of our land purchases, and will not surrender them; that the conduct of the state and people of Pennsylvania towards the proprietors of the lands on the river Susquehanna, in consequence of the decree at Trenton, A.D. 1782, was impolitic, unjust and tyrannical, and a tendency to interrupt the harmony of these States. ■ **BALTIMORE, August 16.** A London letter says last May the Humane Society (for the purpose of recovering persons apparently drowned) dined together, on the anniversary of their institution, at the London Tavern, the Earl of Stamford in the Chair. After dinner, the fruits of their noble charter were introduced--a procession of men, women and children, whom they had rescued from a premature grave, offered a spectacle which cannot be equaled, among them two gentlemen who have made themselves Governors. The day was spent in the finest luxury of the heart. ■ **ALX, September 1.** From the *Halifax Journal*, dated July 1, we learn, That they had received an Account of the Resolutions of several of the United States, in Consequence of Great-Britain's Adherence to her Navigation Act, and considering the Merchants and Traders of North-America as other Foreigners, which had occasioned heavy Imposts on British Bottoms, quoting an Extract of a Letter from Boston, dated June 17, as follows: "After August, a British Vessel arriving here will be obliged to pay 5l. per Ton, and 25 per Cent. on all Goods on board, so that you will govern yourself accordingly." Extract of a Letter from a Gentleman in Botetourt County, dated August 23, to his Friend in this Town. "Col. Lewis, who was supposed to be killed by the Indians, has lately been brought in, escorted by Ten Shawanese Chiefs, who rescued him from the Mingoes and Cherokees, who were the Indians that fired on him and his Party as they were going to treat with the Shawanese at the Salt Lick. — The (*to be continued*).

Page 3. (*continued*) following is the Speech, delivered in Council at Musquisack Town, on the 29th of July last: 'Brothers, You have seen all our head Men Yesterday; but they are not all here now.--Brothers, When your People settled this Side of the big River, it made us very uneasy.--We are glad you have ordered them away.--Peace we are wishing for.--Brothers, We are happy, young and old, that you have called all the People off our Lands, which we hope may be the Means of promoting Peace and Harmony between us.--Brother Colonel Lewis, We have brought you and one more out of that bad Man's Hand (the Wolf.)--We all wish you well, and safe home.--Brothers the Virginians, We hope you have nothing to study but Peace, and let us hold fast our Chains of Friendship; you must not mind the bad People amongst us.--Peace is the Height of our Desire.--It is only one Man (the Wolf) who has done all the Mischief, and will not mind any Good that is said to him.--Brother Colonel Lewis, We hope you will be strong to acquaint our American Brethren, that our Wishes are Peace.--We shall send Ten of our principal Men for to escort you home, having appointed one out of every Town, to convince you that all our People are of one Sentiment, and unanimously desirous to reunite the former Friendship which so happily subsisted between us.--Brothers the Virginians, Listen to your younger Brothers; the great Spirit has allowed us now happily to meet, and to inform you that we are very sorry for what has past.--Brother Colonel Lewis, When you were coming off to meet your youngest Brothers, and when you were jovial and happy, expecting to see them, a Storm darkened your Joys.--When you arrived here at the Houses of your Brothers, they took you by the Hand, and wiped the Tears from your Eyes; now your Eyes are cleared and the Tears wiped away, you can see if your youngest Brothers treat you with Friendship. 'For the loss of the great Man that set off along with you we are all sorry; but we hope you will bury all Remembrance of eternal Oblivion.--The Reason that we request of you to forget what is past is because our most earnest Wishes are to live with you in Unity and Friendship.--In respect to your Trade, we are glad to hear that you mean to be reasonable in exchanging your Goods for Furr.--We hope Brother, that you now see plain that the Fault ought not to be laid on us the Shawanese.--We have Orders to be at Peace from all Nations, white and red; but the Cherokees and one trading Man of the Mingoes are endeavouring to do all the Hurt they can, and to set us at Variance. You see the Mischief is not committed by us; and those that do it, it is out of our Power to prevent. 'From your youngest Brothers the Shawanese, with three Strings of Wampum. 'Signed by Ten Chiefs.'" ■ NAVAL-OFFICE, ALX. *Inward Entries*. Sloop *Dove*, S. Packard, from Providence; Sloop *Dolphin*, A. Steuart, Philadelphia; Schooner *Lottery*, Z. Mann, Baltimore; Schooner *Polly*, W. Cox, St. Christopher's. *Cleared Outwards*. Schooner *Barbadoes*, W. Scott, for Barbadoes; Schooner *Lottery*, Z. Mann, Baltimore; Schooner *St. George*, C. Finley, West-Indies; Sloop *Lark*, S. Brown, Massachusetts; Brig *Fanny*, W.B. Smith, Bourdeaux; Sloop *Dolphin*, A. Steuart, Philadelphia; Sloop *Dove*, S. Packard, Turk's-Island.

On Saturday the third Instant, will be Sold at the Vendue-Store,

A VARIETY of WET and DRY GOODS, consisting of a few hogsheads of Barbadoes spirits, West-India and Continental rum, brandy, gin, a quantity of the best muscovado sugar, tea, chocolate, soap, candles, &c. Irish linens, calicoes, muslins, cloths, gauzes, osnaburgs, canvas, nankeens, and an assortment of jewelry.--Also, a kiln, containing about 50,000 well burnt bricks.--Likewise, a likely Negro fellow and two young wenches, one of which has a fine child. ** Likewise to be sold, a number of LOTS situated in different parts of the town.

S. ARELL, Vendue-Master.

ALX, Sept. 1, 1785.

EDWARD VIDLER seeks Englishman RICHARD EVEREST to resolve legacy [see like ad Vol. II No. 82] ■ **Robert Allison,** Has for sale, at his Store in King-street, for Cash, or Country Produce, by Wholesale and Retail, the following GOODS, viz. SUPERFINE and second broadcloths, with trimmings to match, cassimers, coatings, bearskins, kerseys, duffils, fearnoughts, linseys, flannels, rugs, Yorkshire coverlets, a large assortment of Negro cottons, yarn stockings, mens' and womens' worsted hose, coarse hats, calamancoes, durants, tammies, camblets and cambleteens, chintzes, calicoes, stamped cottons, corduroys and spotted velvets, black everlastings and russels, cotton denims, fustians and jeans, pillow and bed tick, Marseilles quilting, yard-wide shirting, 7/8 and yard-wide Irish linens, brown and white Irish sheetings, brown Holland, Dutch Silesias, brown and white drillings, osnaburgs and brown rolls, bibles and testaments, writing-paper, ink-powder and sealing-wax, osnaburg thread, taylors' ditto, nuns' ditto, stitching ditto, tapes and garterings, cambricks, kentings, black and white gauzes, ribbons, ladies' black silk bonnets, check and cotton handkerchiefs, wove, death-head and campaign buttons, mohair, silk and twist, gilt and plated coat and vest buttons, shirt buttons, shoe and knee buckles, sleeve buttons, London pins, scissors, rasors, kirby fish-hooks, shoe tacks and knives, awl blades and lasts, cutteau and pen knives, knives and forks, knitting pins, snuff and tobacco boxes, stock, chest, pad and saddle-bag locks, cut, whip and hand-saw files, drawing-knives, butchers' knives, spike gimblets, augers, chisels and gouges, marking-irons, steel compasses, sad-irons, iron pots and Dutch ovens, 4d. 6d. 8d. 10d. 12d. and 20d. nails, shovels and tongs, curry combs and horse-brushes, brass tea-kettles and candlesticks, beer-cocks, warming-pans, tea-trays and servers, quart and pint jacks, sweeping, scrubbing and hearth brooms, an assortment of glass and queen's ware, mens' saddles and bridles, girths, surcingles, stirrup-leathers and coat-straps, saddle cloths and housings, mens' and boys' leather breeches, slates, powder and lead, pewter spoons, plates, dishes and basons, mens' and womens' coarse and fine leather shoes, ladies' stuff ditto, hair sieves, pimento, soap, window-glass, &c. ALX, September 1, 1785. ■ THE Subscriber returns his grateful acknowledgments to his former customers, for their past favors, and desires to inform them, and the public in general, that he has removed from the corner of Fairfax and Princess streets, to his house near the corner of King and Royal streets, where he carries on the Taylors' business as usual, and earnestly solicits the continuation of the favors of his friends, and the encouragement of the public, who may depend on having their commands executed with despatch and care. JOHN LONGDEN. ☞ He has to rent a convenient store and counting-room, with a commodious cellar. ALX, September 1, 1785. ■ DANIEL CARROLL, jun., Montgomery Co., Md., offers reward for return of runaway named Joe [see like ad Vol. II No. 78] ■ IF Mr. JAMES BARKER, of or near Birmingham, in Warwickshire, England, who has been some time in North-America, and is supposed to have lived in New-York, in the mercantile line, *is now living*, he is earnestly requested to write immediately to the Subscriber, in St. Paul's Lane, Baltimore, and inform him where he now lives, and he will then hear of something greatly to his advantage, no less than a handsome sum of money, left to him by his relations in England. JOHN RAWLINS, Baltimore, August 4, 1785. ■ **Crocketts and Harris,** Have just imported, in the Ship *Batavia*, Capt. Carsten Haufman, from Bremen, and for Sale, at their Store, in Second-street, A QUANTITY of German Osnaburgs, Ticklenburgs, Tow Linen, Hessians, and ready made Bags. Baltimore, August 25, 1785. ■ To be Sold at private sale, any time before the first day of October ensuing, TWO hundred acres of good LAND, lying within four miles of ALX, on which is a Dwelling-House with two rooms on a floor, a Meat-House, Stable, Negro Quarter, and good Barn, there is a good apple, peach and cherry Orchard, and a good Spring of Water near the house. About 8 acres of the above land is good Meadow, now in Timothy, but more easily be made and watered; there is also a sufficiency of Timber and

Fire-Wood on the premises.--It is a pleasant situation, is on a good road to ALX, and within half a mile of a merchant-mill.--Any person inclinable to purchase, may view the land, and know the terms, by applying to the Subscriber, living on the premises. RICHARD SANFORD, September 1, 1785. ■ **Winchester Races.** ON Thursday, the 27th day of October next, will be run for over the course near this place, a PURSE of FORTY POUNDS, free for any horse, mare, or gelding, carrying one hundred and twenty pounds weight, the best two in three three mile heats. On Friday, the 28th, will be run for over the same ground, a PURSE of TWENTY POUNDS, free for any horse, mare, or gelding (the winning horse the preceding day excepted) same weight, and the best two in three three mile heats. Horses of both days to start precisely at twelve o'clock, and to be entered with Mr. JAMES G. DOWDALL one day before the race, subscribers paying four dollars, entrance money, for the first purse, or double at the post; and non-subscribers five dollars and an half, or double at the post; and for the second day's purse, subscribers paying two dollars entrance, or double at the post; and non-subscribers three, or double at the post. And on Saturday, the 29th, will be run for over the same ground, at the same hour, the ENTRANCE MONEY of both days, free for any horse, mare, or gelding (the winning horses the two preceeding days excepted) same weight, the best two in three three mile heats. All disputes to be determined by Managers appointed for that purpose. Three horses at least to start on each day, or no race. Winchester, August 23, 1785. ■ TO BE RENTED. THE Subscriber has to rent, in the vicinity of ALX, Va., the four following PLANTATIONS, viz. One of 200 acres, one of 166 acres, one of 130 acres, and one of 106 acres.--Likewise, a small PLANTATION, near the Upper Falls of Potomack, Maryland side, containing between 70 and 80 acres. Possession of the above plantations may be had at Christmas next.--Also, to lease on ground-rent, for ninety-nine years, renewable for ever, three LOTS, situate on Falls-street, in George-Town. Dimensions 22 by 70 feet. For further particulars, apply to HENRY TOWNSEND, George-Town, Maryland, September 1, 1785. ■ STRAYED or stolen from ALX, the 21st instant, a light bay GELDING, full 15 hands high, black switch tail, with a white spot close to the back, dark brown mane, his two hind-feet white above the fetlocks, his fore hoofs a little cracked, his off eye white or walled, his near eye brown, a blaze in his face, which on the lower part goes entirely to his off nostril, and a little white reaching to the lower lip on the off side, has no perceivable brand.--ONE GUINEA reward will be given to any person who will deliver said horse to the Subscriber in ALX, with reasonable charges if found out of the county. JOHN SUTTON, August 30, 1785. ■ TWENTY DOLLARS REWARD. RAN AWAY from the Subscriber, on the 19th instant, a TAWNY WOMAN, about twenty years of age, of a middle size, long curly hair, had on and took with her a variety of cloathing. It is suspected that she will be carried off or concealed by a white man, who has been very intimate with her for some years.--Whoever takes up said woman, and delivers her to the Subscriber, shall have the above reward, if taken 50 miles from home, and out of the State, if that distance, and within the State, the one half thereof; and if a longer or shorter distance, a proportionable reward, and all charges, paid by RAPHAEL BOARMAN, Cornwallis's-Neck, Charles County, Maryland, August 25, 1785.

Page 4. Poetry. "Poetical Rondeau, Said to be Written by Mr. Gray." ■ WILLIAM LYLES and CO., is selling rum [see like ad Vol. II No. 68] ■ Directors of the Potomack Company seek outstanding subscriber payment of 5 per cent. [see like ad Vol. II No. 79] ■ SAMUEL LOVE, jun., Salisbury, Va., seeks owner of horse feared stolen he received in trade [see like ad Vol. II No. 81] ■ ☞ A great Variety of BLANKS, printed on good Paper, may be had at the Printing-Office. ■ D. and I. M'PHERSON have for sale Madera wine, etc. [see like ad Vol. II No. 81] ■ Executors of the estate of Thomas Kirkpatrick, dec., have for sale 28 Lots in the Town of ALX [see like ad Vol. II No. 79] ■ WILLIAM ALEXANDER and WILLIAM GIBBONS STUART, executors of John Alexander, dec., have for sale one hundred lots of ground contiguous to the Town of ALX [see like ad Vol. II No. 78] ■ The Partnership between Lowry and M'Kenna is dissolved and request that accounts are settled; Lowry to soon leave for England [see like ads Vol. II No. 73] ■ WILLIAM HARTSHORNE has for sale a lot at the corner of Wolf and Washington streets, and one on Fairfax-street near the corner of Gibbon-street [see like ad Vol. II No. 75] ■ G. WASHINGTON seeks house-keeper or household steward [see like ad Vol. II No. 81] ■ RICHARD CONWAY advertises for sale a lot on Pitt-street [see like ad Vol. II No. 81] ■ WILLIAM FITZHUGH offers for sale a valuable tract of land in Stafford County [see like ad Vol. II No. 70] ■ The Fredericksburg Jockey Club announces horse races at Falmouth, Va. [see like ad Vol. II No. 81] ■ To be sold, at the Printing-Office, A Variety of Blank Books, consisting of Ledgers, Journals, Cash-Books, Letter-Books, &c.&c. Also, Stoughton's Bitters, Anderson's Pills, Daffy's Elixir, Balsam of Honey, Squire's Elixir, Bateman's Drops, Godfrey's Cordial, &c.&c. ■ ALX:

Printed by GEORGE RICHARDS, and COMPANY, at their Printing-Office on Fairfax-street--by whom Advertisements, &c. are thankfully received for this Paper,--and where Printing is performed with Care and Expedition.

1785/09/08, Vol. II No. 84

Page 1. ROBERT ALLISON has goods for sale at his Store in King-street [see like ad Vol. II No. 83] ■ HENRY TOWNSEND, George-Town, Maryland, has for rent four plantations [see like ad Vol. II No. 83] ■ John Sutton offers reward for return of strayed or stolen gelding [see like ad Vol. II No. 83] ■ CROCKETTS and HARRIS have just imported in the Ship *Batavia* a quantity of osnaburgs, etc. [see like ad Vol. II No. 83] ■ JOHN LONGDEN has moved his business to his house near the corner of King and Royal streets [see like ad Vol. II No. 83] ■ RICHARD SANFORD offers for sale 200 acres of land lying within 4 miles of ALX [see like ad Vol. II No. 83] ■ JONATHAN SWIFT and CO. has for lease three upper stories of a brick store on Capt. Harper's wharf [see like ad Vol. II No. 82] ■ WILLIAM WRIGHT, bricklayer, offers reward for return of runaway indented servant man named STEPHEN BOWDEN [see like ad Vol. II No. 82] ■ The Winchester Races are announced [see like ad Vol. II No. 83] ■ DANIEL CARROLL, jun., Montgomery Co., Md., offers reward for return of runaway named Joe [see like ad Vol. II No. 78] ■ RAPHAEL BOARMAN, Cornwallis's-Neck, Charles Co., Md., offers reward for return of runaway woman [see like ad Vol. II No. 83].

Page 2.

LONDON, June 20. HOUSE of COMMONS: *LOYALISTS.* Mr. Pitt proposed some relief for the Loyalists. Claims have amounted to between 4 and 500,000 pounds, (divided into different classes), about 471,000 pounds of which adjudged fair and equitable, some with a higher priority than others. His intention is to allow the whole claims, but pay only part this year. He proposed to pay 150,000 pounds this year, to raise that sum *by way of a lottery*, and pay it in proportion, thus: 40 per cent to the two classes of greatest merit, and 30 per cent to the three others ... **June 21:** Last week four young gentlemen, one of elevated rank, were interrupted by the watch in a tipsy midnight frolic, and after a scuffle overpowered and taken to the Mount street watch house. One of them, being rather violent to the constable, was without ceremony committed to the black hole. The group was obliged to send for one of their tradesmen who, on entering, started at seeing the young gentlemen. The constable and watchman, now finding who they had in custody, pressed around him and hoped his Royal Highness would not be offended at their having detained him .Upon which the Prince, who was only in high spirits by the wine he had drunk, exclaimed, "Offended my good fellows! By no means. Thank God! The laws of this country are superior to rank--and when men of high station forget the decorums of the community, it is fit that no distinction should be made with respect to them. It should make an Englishman proud to see the Prince of Wales forced to send for a taylor to bail him." We do not scruple to say that the people of England will find more satisfaction in this sentiment of his Royal highness, than they could possibly enjoy from the report of his having a heart so cold and cautionary as never to have committed a debauch ... Extract of a letter from **New York, May 9**: The Dutch Consul, Mr. Valkhamecht has petitioned Congress to establish a Dutch colony at Four Indians Pass on the North River, about 40 miles from this city, where they propose building a town of about 100 houses, with a place of worship and other public buildings, for the purposes of trade. As the government of the States General seconds this by letters under the seal of the Republic, it is imagined Congress will find it in U.S. interests to comply in the fullest latitude, as the Dutch, like the Jews, are known to bring and force a trade wherever they go to settle. Several Dutch families with effects to no small amount have lately come over to reside in this city. The Congress now contemplates a variety of imposts to recommend to the several States for concurrence, all on articles of luxury. Provisions are cheaper in this city by one third than two years ago, as the farms begin to flourish ... **June 24:** America has experienced a peculiar advantage over all other countries. Greece, Rome and Britain approached by degrees to magnificence and independence; their aborigines were barbarians, but the first settlers in America were masters of arts and sciences. If we may judge of the body of the people from those who reside among us, they must possess fertile invention, extensive genius, and strong judgement. Mr. Adams, their Ambassador, has been successful in every negotiation he has undertaken; the loan he obtained in Holland astonished the most refined politicians and subtle financiers in Europe. In our schools, universities, and inns of court, are any American youths of the first rate genius. In the polite arts they are not behind the Europeans. West, Copley, Stewart, and Browne are from America. The works of the latter two artists are well known: their performances exhibited at Somerset House do them infinite credit. Mr. West, we understand, is finishing a picture of the celebrated American treaty, in which he has introduced the portraits of Messrs. Adams, Jay, Franklin and Lawrence, as also Mr. Oswald. Mrs. and Miss Adams, wife and daughter to the Ambassador from the United states, are as accomplished women as any in England ... In consequence of Mr. Pitt's successful motions in favor of the American loyalists, a state lottery is to take effect in Great Britain, the profits to be applied to gentlemen under that description ... According to letters from Harwich of Sunday evening, the packet had just arrived from Helvoetsluys. At her sailing Friday the public report was that affairs between the Emperor and the States are settled; only the treaty signing remains. The following are handed about as some of the treaty conditions: free navigation of the Scheldt for Imperial vessels, not exceeding a certain size, from the sea to Antwerp; demolishing some of the forts on the Scheldt's shores; the Ambassadors at Vienna to make some concessions for the affront offered the Imperial flag on the river Scheldt; the Republic to pay ten millions of florins towards compensating the Emperor's expence of sending troops, ammunition, &c. into the Austrian Netherlands. ■ **KINGSTON,** (Jamaica) **June 20.** The celebrated Dr. Price, who formerly employed his pen so nobly in favor of the American cause, has, we find, lately sent a legacy to the States, entitled, '*Observations on the importance of the American revolution.*' Among other advices, he recommend them 'to attend to their best interests by laying heavy duties on the importation of foreign commodities.' A writer in last March's Political Magazine makes this remark on that part of Price's legacy: "The Americans are too fond of getting English goods *without paying for them....* Importing goods without ever paying for them is the heaviest of all duties. The disciples therefore have arrived at complete perfection *in the art of taxing the English*, unless by heavy duties [Price] means *never paying at all" ...* When triumphant General Wolfe was battering down Quebec's walls, the Marquis de Montcalm wrote the Parliament of Paris that although he probably would not survive the loss of the place, he could console himself on his defeat--in that it would one day serve his country more than a victory. French policy, it is evident, saw at that time the approaching independence of the English Colonies. ■ **NEW YORK, August 24.** By letters from the island of Grenada we learn that on Monday, 6th June, put in there in consequence of having spring a leak, the American ship *Grand Turk,* Jonathan Ingersol, Master, from the Cape of Good Hope ... **August 27:** Last week his Excellency Richard Henry Lee, Esq; President of Congress set out from here for Pennsylvania. His health and constitution seriously weakened and impaired from his public duties, his physicians recommend the waters of Harrowgate, near Philadelphia. Strongly impregnated with minerals, the Faculty deems the waters great restoratives, though initially operating as emetics. As soon as his Excellency has recovered, he will return to his duties. Meanwhile, Commonwealth of Massachusetts delegate Samuel Holton, Esq; will fill the Presidential Chair, and officiate. ■ **PHILADELPHIA, August 20.** Extract of a letter from **London, May 6:** In America I perceive no improved system of government, nor increase in commerce. Here, in this country, we see the reverse, thanks to the not yet 25 year old Minister, Mr. Pitt. He will restore this fallen empire to former splendor ... Respecting the productions of the Philadelphia Bank, much depends on the Legislature, and closing subscriptions. Capital already is too large for the city, for I believe it already in decline. I can only hope for the prudent management of so many respectable men are deeply concerned in its welfare ... **A PROCLAMATION** of the U.S. Congress, June 15, 1785 [verbatim text given--Eds.] condemns the acts of several disorderly persons crossing the Ohio and settling on the unappropriated lands. As this is premature, disrespectful to federal authority and illegally preempts the rights of others, such persons are ordered immediately to decamp, with their families. **RICHARD HENRY LEE**, President. Charles Thomson, Sec'ry. ... **August 22:** Last week several companies of infantry and one of artillery marched through Reading on their way westward, being the quota of troops from New York ordered raised by Congress for the defence of the frontiers ... It must give every friend to American manufactures great pleasure to hear that Mr. John Baird, lately from North Britain, has constructed near Wilmington a barley shelling mill, the milled barley to be seen at Mr. John Morton's store. It is judged equally prepared and preferable in taste to the best Scotch barley ... **August 31:** Mr. Marbois, Charge des Affaires of France, has delivered to Congress a letter from his most Christian Majesty, concerning the Marquis de la Fayette. It contains expressions of that monarch's friendship for the United States, and assurances that the King wishes for opportunities to let the young General experience farther marks of the satisfaction he has in his zeal and ability ... A vessel with freight for Newfoundland has returned denied entering, or landing any cargo, being an American bottom. The captain found a brig from this port had been seized there, and was to be sold in a few days--not being owned by *British* subjects, manned by *British* seamen, and navigated according to *British* laws ... The Massachusetts impost law which took effect on the 1st instant is aimed at "the root of the evil" affecting the commerce of this country since the establishment of the peace. This law will prevent foreigners from becoming carriers to us. Immediately on its taking place, his Britannic Majesty's frigate *Mercury*, Capt. Stanhope, and several other British vessels left the port of Boston, one of which, the *Three Brothers*, Capt. Boothby, from Liverpool, has since arrived at New York. It is to be hoped other Legislatures in the U.S. will pass laws for the better regulation of commerce and navigation, and for the encouragement of the manufactures and mechanics of America. Our own friends and artisans ought most certainly to have the preference. A peculiar attention to their interest will undoubtedly promote the welfare of our own country.

Page 3. **BALTIMORE, September 2.** Captain Making, of the brig *Jane*, which arrived at Philadelphia last Thursday, the 25th, reports the following. On Tuesday he spoke a brig from Virginia bound to London, the Captain of which informed him that, about half an hour before, there had been alongside a boat, with six persons on board, who told him they had been taken four days before by a pirate schooner, off Cape Henry. The wind blowing hard, Capt. Making could not understand what vessel they belonged to, but the Captain of the brig said the boat was about 5 miles distant, in search of a vessel bound in ... Monday, the 22d ult. Arrived at New York in 8 weeks from London, the brigantine *Mercury*, Capt. Innis, by whom we learn that the insurance on remittances from New York, by the *Antelope* packet, Capt. Kempthorne, were in general saved to the shippers, from the safe arrival of the specie at the Bank of England ... The *Courier de la L'Orient*, his Most Christian Majesty's packet, is arrived at New York in 52 days from L'Orient ... Lately died in Lebanon, Connecticut, that distinguished patriot Jonathan Trumbull, Esq; late Governor of that State, at an advanced age ... The following estimate, taken from a May 23rd London paper, gives us an idea of the amazing expence of the late American war to Great Britain; it may serve as a lesson to future princes, as well as impress an horror of every tyrannic system among mankind: "Ye Gods! What havock does ambition make among your works!" Money expended in the late American war: £146,859,632. Added by it to the national debt, inclusive of the winding up accounts: £117,842,563. Soldiers, sailors, &c. Killed, died, lost, or missing in the war: 432,840. Widows and orphans left, by a moderate computation: 1,000,000. Lives of all nations, lost in the dispute: 1,382,000. Reckoning the value of the men lost, of the deprivation and preservation of industry, of the losses of trade, ships &c. Money expended the public, and loss by individuals, it is probable the war has cost, in all its branches: £400,000,000. And the loss of territory may be estimated at: £100,000,000. ■ **ALX, September 8.** By Accounts from the West-Indies, we learn, That scarcely a Day passed, at either the French or English Islands, without some American Vessels being seized. The French Officers in particular are so strict, that no American, except in the greatest Distress, can even procure a Puncheon of Water (the free Ports excepted) and then not without Officers till they returned on board. ■ Tuesday last passed this Port, for the Eastern Branch, the Ship *Thetis*, Capt. Ramsay, after a Passage of 11 Weeks, from the Clyde. ■ DIED.] Mr. JAMES CUNNINGHAM HOLMES, Accomptant. —Mr. WILLIAM LAMELY, Skinner, lately from England. —In Prince George's County, Maryland, Mrs. CASEY. ■ NAVAL-OFFICE, ALX. *Inward Entries*. Ship *Paragon*, H. Hughes, from the Isle of May; Brig *Martha*, G. Slacum, and Schooner *Mary*, D. Johnston, St. Eustatia; Schooner *Nancy*, N. Spooner, Barbadoes; Sloop *Hero*, J. Humphries, Baltimore; Sloop *Speedwell*, W. Scott, Philadelphia; Sloop *William*, R. Torge, Baltimore. *Cleared Outwards*. Sloop *Hero*, J. Humphries, for Baltimore; Sloop *Judith,* S. Martin, Rhode-Island.

On Saturday the tenth Instant, will be Sold at the Vendue-Store,

A VARIETY of WET and DRY GOODS, consisting of a few hogsheads of Barbadoes spirits, West-India and Continental rum, brandy, gin, a few hogsheads of porter, a quantity of the best muscovado sugar, tea, chocolate, soap, candles &c. Irish linens, calicoes, muslins, cloths, gauzes, osnaburgs, canvas, nankeens, and an assortment of jewelry.-- Also a likely Negro fellow and two young wenches, one of which has a fine child. **Likewise to be sold, a number of LOTS situated in different parts of the town.

S. ARELL, Vendue-Master.

ALX, Sept. 8, 1785.

John Murray and Co. HAVE FOR SALE, **A** QUANTITY of spirits, Windward-Island and country rum, Coniac brandy, Teneriffe wine, molasses, loaf and brown sugar, coffee, chocolate, allspice, pepper, and fine Liverpool salt.--Also, a good assortment of European Goods suitable for the approaching season.--The above articles will be disposed of on a very reasonable terms for cash, or tobacco, flour, wheat, hemp, or flaxseed at the current prices when delivered, either at this place, or if more agreeable, at their store in Dumfries. ALX, Sept. 7, 1785. ■ Just arrived from Barbadoes, and now landing on Colonel Hooe's Wharf, **A** SMALL cargo of Rum and Sugar in hogsheads and barrels, and a few hogsheads of choice Demarara Spirits fit for gentlemens use. Wanted in barter--flour, Indian corn, and canvases.--Part money will be given in the exchange.--Apply to Colonel Hooe's warehouse. ALX, Sept. 7, 1785. ■ WHEREAS I gave my bond to Mr. Henry M'Cabe, of Leesburg, for £.111 2s. 6d. payable in money, on the 4th day of August last; and also for the further sum of £.222 4s. 6d. payable in goods, on the first day of November next; which bonds were given to the said M'Cabe on account of the purchase of a house and lot in the town of ALX, and greater part of which still remains due; but having been lately informed that Messieurs Kirk and Bowdon of this place are in possession of a power of attorney from the said M'Cabe's mother, authorising and directing them to sue for the recover her dower of said house and lot, which suit I understand is about to be brought accordingly:--I therefore hereby forewarn all persons from taking an assignment of said bonds, as I am determined not to pay any part thereof until the said M'Cabe obtains for mee [sic] his mother's relinquishment of her dower of said house and lot. WILLIAM HEPBURN, ALX, Sept. 5, 1785. ■ FOR SALE OR CHARTER. THE BRIG *MARTHA*, burthen 158 tons, almost new, having only made two voyages, is well found, and has two suits of sails.--For terms, apply to RICHARD CONWAY, Who has for Sale, Barbadoes rum and spirits, by the hogshead, Grenada ditto, molasses, muscovado and clayed sugars, salt, Lisbon wine in quarter casks, hyson, souchong and bohea teas, in quarter chests, pepper in bags, and a few pieces of superfine broadcloths. ALX, Sept. 5, 1785 ■ THE Subscriber begs leave to inform the public in general, that he has opened TAVERN in the house lately occupied by Mr. JOHN LOMAX, where he flatters himself he will be able to entertain those gentlemen who please to favour him with their custom to their satisfaction; as he has furnished himself with good liquors of all kinds, and every other thing necessary for the accommodation of gentlemen. He has also good stabling, and plenty of hay and oats of the best quality. ALEXANDER THOMAS. ☞ Said Thomas will take in boarders on the most reasonable terms. ALX, Sept. 7, 1785. ■ TO BE SOLD, A NEGRO WENCH that is well used to house work, can cook, wash, &c. She has two children, a boy and a girl.--A short credit will be given for part of the pay.--Enquire of ROBERT ADAM. ALX, Sept. 7, 1785. ■ THE Subscriber has for sale, a likely NEGRO WENCH, with a fine Child; she is young and healthy, is a good cook, and understands house work well.--She will be sold cheap for cash or tobacco. JOHN LOMAX. ☞ Said Lomax has also for sale, military officers Certificates, bearing interest since May last.--Likewise, a quantity of empty Bottles. ALX, Sept. 7, 1785. ■ EIGHT DOLLARS REWARD. STOLEN out of a pasture adjoining the Burough of Winchester, on the night of the 28th instant, a dark bay HORSE, 15½ or 16 hands high, no visible brand or mark, a natural pacer, about 8 years old, a remarkable bag of skin hangs to the back of each fore leg, a very heavy mane, and will not let his ears be turned.--Whoever takes up said horse, and secures the thief, so that he may be prosecuted, shall receive the above reward, or Four Dollars for the horse only. JOHN KEAN, Winchester, August 30, 1785. ■ Just imported, and to be Sold by **Philip Poyer and Co.**, At the Store of Mr. ANDREW WALES, BARBADOES RUM and Spirits, in hogsheads and barrels; also, a quantity of Sugar of the best quality. ☞ Flour or Indian Corn, at the current price, will be taken in exchange. ALX, Sept. 7, 1785. ■ NOTICE is hereby given, to all persons interested in 51,302 acres of land, situate on the Ohio river, granted to George Mull, Adam Stephens, Andrew Lewis, Peter Hogg, John West, John Polson, and Andrew Waggoner, by patent, bearing date the 15th day of December 1772, that a petition will be prefered to the next General Assembly, praying that titles may be granted to each claimant for his individual share, agreeable to surveys of partition, made in the year 1773, in presence of a number of the proprietors, in consequence of and in obedience to articles of agreement entered into by the parties for that purpose. September 7, 1785. ■ CAME to the plantation of the Subscriber, in Frederick County, Virginia, the 23d instant, a dark bay HORSE, six years old, about fourteen hands and an half high, had on an old saddle and bridle, has been lately shod round, but the foreshoes are worn off, branded under the mane, on the off side of his neck, D. He is supposed to have been stolen from some of the upper counties by a Mulatto fellow. The owner is desired to come, prove his property, pay charges, and taken him away. CONRADE CRYTSINGER, August 27, 1785. ■ TEN DOLLARS REWARD.

STOLEN from the Subscriber, living in Winchester, on the 25th instant, a likely bay HORSE, about 14 hands high, 8 or 9 years old, a large tail, a very small mane, paces, trots and canters, lively, and has a good carriage, has the spavin, but is very little lame.--Whoever takes up said horse, and delivers him to the Subscriber, shall have the above reward, and all reasonable charges, paid by CHRISTIAN STREIT, Minister Lutheran Congregation, August 29, 1785. ■ M'CREA and MEASE to sell some lots on Fairfax and Water streets [see like ad Vol. II No. 82] ■ Lots, store and warehouses of James Mills and Co. to be sold in Urbanna [see like ad Vol. II No. 82] ■ JOHN RAWLINS seeks whereabouts of Mr. James Barker to receive a handsome sum of money [see like ad Vol. II No. 83] ■ EDWARD VIDLER seeks Englishman RICHARD EVEREST to resolve legacy [see like ad Vol. II No. 82].

Page 4. Poetry. "Jeu d'Esprit on the Word Idea." ■ Executors of the estate of Thomas Kirkpatrick, dec., have for sale 28 Lots in the Town of ALX [see like ad Vol. II No. 79] ■ WILLIAM ALEXANDER and WILLIAM GIBBONS STUART, executors of John Alexander, dec., have for sale one hundred lots of ground contiguous to the Town of ALX [see like ad Vol. II No. 78] ■ The Partnership between Lowry and M'Kenna is dissolved and request that accounts are settled; Lowry to soon leave for England [see like ads Vol. II No. 73] ■ G. WASHINGTON seeks house-keeper or household steward [see like ad Vol. II No. 81] ■ RICHARD CONWAY advertises for sale a lot on Pitt-street [see like ad Vol. II No. 81] ■ WILLIAM FITZHUGH offers for sale a valuable tract of land in Stafford County [see like ad Vol. II No. 70] ■ WILLIAM HARTSHORNE has for sale a lot at the corner of Wolf and Washington streets, and one on Fairfax-street near the corner of Gibbon-street [see like ad Vol. II No. 75] ■ **Porter and Ingraham**, have for sale a general assortment of European Goods [see like ad Vol. II No. 82] ■ Races of the ALX Jockey Club Purse announced [see like ad Vol. II No. 81] ■ PETER DOW seeks owner of stray gray mare [see like ad Vol. II No. 82] ■ JOHN CAWOOD, Prince George's Co., Md., offers reward for return of runaways JOHN BLAKE and WILLIAM HUMPHREYS [see like ad Vol. II No. 82] ■ ALX: Printed by GEORGE RICHARDS, and COMPANY, at their Printing-Office on Fairfax-street--by whom Advertisements, &c. are thankfully received for this Paper,--and where Printing is performed with Care and Expedition.

1785/09/15, Vol. II No. 85

Page 1. **Philip Poyer and Co.**, has just imported goods to be sold at the store of Andrew Wales [see like ad Vol. II No. 84] ■ Patentees of a 51,302-acre tract of land on the Ohio river seek petition to the General Assembly for titles agreeable to survey of partition [see like ad Vol. II No. 84] ■ CONRADE CRYTSINGER seeks owner of stray horse to collect property [see like ad Vol. II No. 84] ■ CHRISTIAN STREIT, Winchester, offers reward for return of stolen horse [see like ad Vol. II No. 84] ■ JOHN KEAN, Winchester, offers reward for return of stolen horse [see like ad Vol. II No. 84] ■ M'CREA and MEASE to sell some lots on Fairfax and Water streets [see like ad Vol. II No. 82] ■ **John Murray and Co.**, have for sale a quantity of spirits, etc. [see like ad Vol. II No. 84] ■ Colonel Hooe's warehouse has for sale Barbadoes rum, etc. [see like ad Vol. II No. 84] ■ WILLIAM HEPBURN warns others from taking assignment of bonds of Henry M'Cabe of Leesburg [see like ad Vol. II No. 84] ■ RICHARD CONWAY offers for sale the Brig *Martha*, and Barbadoes rum, etc. [see like ad Vol. II No. 84] ■ JOHN LOMAX has for sale a likely Negro wench [see like ad Vol. II No. 84] ■ ROBERT ADAM has for sale a Negro wench [see like ad Vol. II No. 84] ■ ALEXANDER THOMAS announces opening of a tavern in the house lately occupied by Mr. John Lomax [see like ad Vol. II No. 84] ■ The Winchester Races are announced [see like ad Vol. II No. 83] ■ JOHN LONGDEN has moved his business to his house near the corner of King and Royal streets [see like ad Vol. II No. 83] ■ RICHARD SANFORD offers for sale 200 acres of land lying within 4 miles of ALX [see like ad Vol. II No. 83].

Page 2.

VIENNA, (Germany) **June 1**. The Emperor has sentenced the Aulic Counsellor, Van Kreutznacht, to sweep the streets of Vienna for six years. His Majesty discovered that he has been guilty of great oppression and peculation. His hair has already been cut off, and he begins street sweeping next Monday ... An association of 12 ladies has been appointed to regulate the dress of the fair sex, so as to be clad at one third the present expence, and yet preserve a smarter and more captivating appearance ... A Prelate whose diocese is in Upper Austria sought the Emperor's permission to make a pilgrimage to Rome, to visit the tombs of St. Peter and St. Paul. His Imperial Majesty sent word he ought rather to visit his own bishopric; *and I will answer for it* (says the Emperor) *that St. Peter and St. Paul will be much the better pleased.* ■ **LONDON, June 23.** Mr. Pitt's American loyalist bill is characteristic of his being actuated by a sense of justice, and will win him the approbation of all parties, while also providing some relief for widows, orphans and others having large families to provide for. However, one hopes for two amendments. 1- As the bill says only those who *fought* in the army shall be entitled to rank in the second and third classes, and recover 40 per cent of their losses, it omits the many who from the nature of things could not *take up the musket*, yet whose defence of British sovereignty and consequent property losses not only equal but exceed those who did. For instance, Rev. J. Duche, former rector of Christ's church in Philadelphia, lost above ten thousand pounds, and has a large family to support. Many such could not enlist as soldiers, and an amendment allowing them 40 per cent recovery is highly worthy of Mr. Pitt's liberality of sentiment. 2-It is highly probable many such have, believing their relief doubtful in the nation's present embarrassed state, neglected to give in specification of their losses. A few weeks notice should be allowed them to register their claims. If these be attended to, Mr. Pitt's endeavour to relieve the real sufferer must be acknowledged complete ... Most of the letters from Jamaica in the last packet agree in a very melancholy account of its declining state of commerce from the heavy restrictions lately laid on sugars and rums. Further worsening may be expected by the emancipation of Ireland; no longer bound to submit to the English monopolies, Ireland will be at liberty to resort to any market for rums and sugars, instead of to the British plantations--the dearest upon the face of the globe. **June 24:** The port of Malaga was almost blocked up for 3 days by Algerine corsairs. Two King's frigates, however, dispersed them, and took *El Mustapha Douhora,* a new built corsair, put on the stocks just after the capture of another by the same name which had been most successful against the Spaniards ... Some ships are fitting for a voyage to the southern ocean, chiefly to observe French ships fitting for the same quarter ... Ireland may do a little smuggling trade with the West Indies, but it is ridiculous to talk of an interference with the trade of this country, when the greater part of all the islands are absolutely private property, either purchased by or mortgaged to the merchants of England. This is a fact ... A few days ago a duel was fought in Culvers, near Marlborough, between two itinerant theatrical gentlemen--Hevein, and Whitlock--over a glass of beer the night before. The next morning about 9 o'clock they met with pistols, seconds and about 40 towns people. Mr. Whitlock seemed to devote about 10 minutes to prayer, then turned and bid Mr. Hevein fire. (Hevein had won a toss for first-to-fire.) He did, without injury. Mr. Whitlock then fired, also without injury. The seconds intervened, and reconciled the two. It then came out that although the seconds had shown pistol balls to the combatants, they had loaded the pistols with wheat ... The tax on bachelors raises many risible possibilities [listed wittily, at length-Eds.], such as enhancing the worth of unmarried ladies; requiring rules to determine rates, ages, qualifications, property, &c; the lessening of illicit commerce may require pensioning ladies of easy virtue, or securing employment for them ... The Duke of Bedford realizes in his parsimony all that we read of Gray, Bencraft, Gresham and Cutler; nay, Sir John, with his darned stockings converted from silk to worsted by mending, was the most liberal man alive in comparison. His Grace lives retired at *Nancy*, secluded from all the world but *Nancy Parsons*; no English travelers are ever introduced to him, for his grace affects not to be popular! ... Lord Effingham certainly will go to America as Ambassador. His lordship, from his well known intrepidity, may bid defiance to *tarring and feathering!* ... Commercial negotiations between Great Britain and America are demurred by our court refusing American ships in East Indies ports, under any conditions different than those for other nations. Soon after American Ambassador Adams presented his credentials, he secured an appointment for business at Lord Caermarthen's office. Mr. Adams unexpectedly made a sort of demand that American ships be permitted to trade in British oriental ports. The Secretary demurred giving an answer until after consultation with the rest of the Cabinet., which agreed that to admit any power whatever to a participation of the India rights would be prejudicial to the interests of Great Britain, and the chartered rights of the East India Company. Unfortunately for the Minister, Mr. Adams has first stumbled on the only ground our minister holds sacred and hallowed. He would freely give up everything else belonging to Englishmen, but this SACRUM SACRORUM, this Mexico and Peru of England, he cannot give up to insatiable American malcontents. Such would oblige him to break with his East India friends in Leadenhall Street! Even worse, he would have his beloved Ireland on his back, which he is now so strenuously parrying off from meddling with that oriental, inexhaustible treasure. For if he admits America, he must admit Ireland, sister Ireland; what a blessed tripartite partnership that would make of India ... The Court of Spain have not, as reported, given up the intended attack against Algiers, but only postponed it on account of the plague raging among the Moors. It still appears to be the firm resolution of all the Mediterranean powers to humble those pirates by the total destruction of Algiers ... We hear it is a certain truth that Mr. Pitt's Irish propositions are well received in Ireland, and that his Majesty and his Minister are extremely popular with the people at large in the kingdom. The penal laws against the Roman Catholics being repealed, and their arming themselves being encouraged and countenanced by his Majesty's servants, even when the Scotch were refused that privilege, have done away with their prejudices against the House of Hanover, and indispensably bound them to the support of the present Administration. The Protestant landholders, however, begin to express great uneasiness, and many of them, who are now in London, declare publicly, that their Roman Catholic tenants hold a very unusual and dictatorial language on the subject of renewing their leases. ■ **BOSTON, August 29.** Friday morning died, much lamented, Captain JOHN GILL, for many years a printer in this metropolis, aged 54. A friend to his country and mankind, whose integrity and industry were equally conspicuous, and not to be unnoticed, though in the vehicle of a newspaper. ■ **NEW YORK, August 30.** [Here begins an unusually detailed, almost hour by hour account of a mutiny, and the fate of the cast-away ship's complement, running over a column and a half. The bare details follow.--Eds.] James Duncanson, Master and part owner of the schooner *Amity* belonging to St. Kitt's; Robert Watson, mate; and John Brewer, boatswain of said schooner arrived here last Saturday and reported: on August 10, 1785, in company with the schooner *Industry*, they left Norfolk, Virginia for the coast of Africa, and continued in company until the 15th, in lat. 36,50. N. long. 68 W. of London. At 10:00 p.m. Richard Squire, John Matthew, Alexander Evans, and the mulatto Stuart took possession of the *Amity*. They put the captain, mate, boatswain, and one John Boadman in irons, below. Boadman had taken an oath with them to turn pirate, but had neither assisted them nor given information about their designs. Having now all secure, they wore ship and stood to the westward. On the 18th they spoke a sloop from Rhode Island with horses, bound to Cape Francois, asking its Captain for some provisions, saying they were from Jamaica, had passengers aboard, and were making for Norfolk. Their design was to put the prisoners aboard the sloop if she had been bound to any part of the continent. On the 19th, abut 8:00 p.m. they hoisted out the long boat, fitted it with mast and sails, put in a cask of water and a barrel of bread, a compass, a quadrant, some rum, and beef, the Captain, mate, boatswain and 3 black boys, and turned them adrift. They reckoned themselves 80 leagues from land. The 21st at 4:00 p.m. they saw a sail westward, rowed through the calm to it, and went on board the ship *Three Friends*, Capt. Alexander Browne, from Jamaica, for Boston, remaining that night and next day. However, at 4:00 p.m., desirous of getting to Virginia, and with a fine breeze from the S.E., they left the ship [Continued on Page 3].

Page 3. [The *Amity* Mutiny (*continued*)] Because of strong winds they were forced to lay to much of the following morning and afternoon. In the morning they did speak a Virginia brig who said they were about 60 leagues from the Capes. In the late afternoon they were able to sail and intercept a ship, the *Atlantic*, Capt. William Tresenthen [possibly Trefenthen--Eds.] bound from Grenada to New York who took them aboard, and hoisted their boat in. [There follows a detailed description of each pirate: nationality, age, physique, personalities--as well as of the *Amity*, as detailed as a ship builder would give.] Those last seen aboard the *Amity*: Squire, Matthew, Evans, Stuart, Boadman, and the black boys Dick and Will (taken last April in the *Amity* from off the Africa coast.) ... **Sept. 5:** Congress on the 25th of last month resolve that the early, unsolicited and continued labours of Mr. Thomas Paine, in explaining and enforcing the principles of the late revolution, by ingenious and timely publications on the nature of liberty and civil government, have been well received by the citizens of these States; and that in consideration of those services and the benefits produced thereby, Mr. Paine is entitled to a liberal gratification from the United States. ■ **PHILADELPHIA, September 3.** Extract of a letter from **Paris, June 17.** The Marquis of Luzerne, late Ambassador to the United States of America, is appointed Governor of the Windward islands. His Majesty has also granted to M. De Marbois, Charge des Affairs of France in the U.S. the intendancy of St. Domingo. His Most Christian Majesty has also prohibited sale of the 31st volume of Voltaire's works, being a publication dangerous to the morals and religion of his subjects ... A French gentleman now at New York, educated at the Academy of Sciences at Paris, is desirous of being employed in raising and conducting a China and Earthenware Manufactory. He is said to be well skilled in them, and has directed a principal manufactory of them in France ... Wednesday last arrived in this port, the ship *Favourite*, Capt. Vallance, from Amsterdam, and brought 300 passengers. The ship *Adolph*, Capt. Clarkson, arrived here last week, brought about 200 passengers from the same place. **Sept. 6:** Yesterday arrived here in five weeks from London, the ship *Harmony*, Capt. Willet. In her came passengers, Messrs. Nicholas Waln, John Townsend, Thomas Colles, John Scorer, Edward Shippen, jun., Alexander Scott, and William Delaplain; Captain Barnet and his lady; Major Marrice and his lady; and Captain Cook ... The arrival of that justly celebrated and revered patriot, Dr. BENJAMIN FRANKLIN, may be hourly expected in this city, as he has taken passage on board the ship *London Packet*, Captain Truxton, which sailed from England about the same time the *Harmony* left Gravesend. ■ **BALTIMORE, September 9.** The latest papers from London advise that his Excellency John Adams had pressed the Marquis of Caermarthen to open a negotiation for the payment of the Negroes taken from the subjects of the American States during the war. The Marquis had refused, declaring that the American States had in no one instance complied with the Definitive Treaty of Peace, and until that should be fulfilled, he must decline entering into that or any other negotiation. **Sept. 13:** On August 13th the ship *United States,* Capt. Bell, arrived at [Barbadoes], from Pondicherry, and is hourly expected at Philadelphia. ■ **ALX, September 15**. On Wednesday, the 7th Instant, the Worshipful Master of Lodge No. 39, attended by the Brethren in Procession, laid the Foundation-Stone of the Alexandria Academy, and affixed thereon a Plate, with the following Inscription:

"The Foundation of the
ALEXANDRIA ACADEMY
Was laid the 7th of September, 1785, in the ninth Year of the Independence of the United States of
NORTH-AMERICA,
By Robert Adam, Esq; Master of Lodge No. 39; Antient York Masons, attended by the Brethren; and as a Monument of the Generosity of the Inhabitants, stands dedicated to them and all Lovers of Literature."

By Accounts from Antigua, we learn, that most of the Windward Islands have sent over Memorials to the British Government, through the Hands of their different Agents in London, couched in very strong and spirited Terms, complaining of the great Injury the sustain for want of a proper commercial Intercourse being established between Great-Britain and America. ■ Last Tuesday passed this Port, for the Eastern Branch, the Ship *Philadelphia*, Captain Towers, from Baltimore. Same Day, a Labourer, on Messieurs Harper and Keith's Wharf, lost his Life, by Falling [off] the Bank. Same Night, the store of Dr. David Jones, of this Town, was broke open, and robbed of Goods to a considerable Amount. ■ DIED.] Miss PANCAS, late from Philadelphia. ■ NAVAL-OFFICE, ALX. *Inward Entries*. Schooner *Governor Parr*, J. Leath, and Schooner *Nepa*, J. Bishop, from Barbadoes; Schooner *Lottery*, Z. Mann, Baltimore; Sloop *Charming Polly*, J. Ellwood, Philadelphia; Sloop *Industry*, J. Webb, Boston. *Cleared Outwards.* Brig *Britannia*, W. Lambert, from London; Schooner *Lottery*, Z. Mann, Baltimore. ■ ☞ NOTICE is hereby given to the Subscribers for building a School-House in Alexandria, that a general Meeting of them is appointed to be held at the Court-House *to-morrow Evening*, at Four o'Clock; where and when it is requested that all the Proprietors will attend. The Materials for the Building are all procured, and laid on the Spot, and the Work going on briskly; so as in all Probability to be ready for opening the Schools at Christmas next. It will consist of three spacious Rooms, intended for a Grammar-School, an English Reading-School, and a School for teaching Writing and Arithmetic, with other practical Branches of Mathematics: But it is necessary that the Subscribers should meet, and determine on several Points of great Importance in this Business, before the Scheme can be carried into full Execution, or any Provision be made for instituting the Schools, when the Building shall be read.--For such essential Purposes is the Meeting *to-morrow* appointed; the therefore it is hoped all the Gentlemen concerned will be punctual in attending. ALX, Sept. 15, 1785.

PRICES CURRENT, ALX. / Tobacco, 25s. per Ct. / Fine Flour, 28s. per Barrel. / Wheat, 5s. per Bushel. / Jamaica Spirits, 4/6 per Gallon. / Windward Rum, 3s. per Ditto. / Continental Rum, 2s. per Ditto. / Molasses, 1/8 per Ditto. / Muscovado Sugar, 35s. to 42/6 per Ct. / Salt, 3s. per Bushel, by Retail. / Corn, 3s. per Bushel / Exchange, 40.

On Monday the nineteenth Instant, will be Sold at
The Vendue-Store,

A VARIETY of WET and DRY GOODS, consisting of West-India and Continental rum in hogsheads and barrels, muscovado sugar, wine in bottles, soap, chocolate, porter in puncheons, cloths in patterns of various colours, chintzes, cambricks, linens, queen's ware, &c. &c.--Also, two or three likely Virginia born Slaves, and a single Chair.

S. ARELL, Vendue-Master.

ALX, Sept. 15, 1785.

To be SOLD at the Printing-Office, **Webster's Grammatical Institute** in THREE PARTS, Being a Spelling-Book a Grammar, and an Art of Reading and Speaking, recommended by many Gentlemen of Literature, as far preferable to Dilworth's, Fennings's, Lowth's, or any other foreign School-Book. It contains many Improvements in the English Language, and is the Production of an American Genius. ■ THE Subscriber has now finished a large and commodious LIVERY STABLE, and is ready to take in gentlemens' horses.--Those that are pleased to favor him with their custom, may depend that good usage and attendance will be given. PATRICK MURRAY. ALX, Sept. 15, 1785. 85-89. ■ THE Subscriber is empowered to lease for five years, commencing from next January, the elegant House, with the Offices, Garden and Plantation, opposite ALX, in Maryland, commonly called OXEN HILL.--The superior quality of the land, and the uncommon conveniences in the house itself, as well as every other improvement, has justly ranked it among the first seats in Maryland, and is so generally known, that a particular description is unnecessary. WILLIAM BAKER. ☞ The Subscriber will rent the House he now lives in for seven months, and give possession of the first of October next.--It is a very excellent stand for a store, and will also accommodate a family. ALX, Sept. 15, 1785. ■ To be Sold to the highest Bidder, on Tuesday, the Eighteenth of October next, at Newgate, PART of a PLANTATION formerly advertised by the Subscriber. It is well watered, and may be conveniently divided into several small farms.--One half the purchase money to be paid down, the residue on long credit, the bonds bearing interest from their date.--Fifteen per cent. discount will be allowed for ready money in the second payment.--Any person who wishes to see the above land, will be shewn the same by Mr. Samuel Love, jun. living near the premises. JOHN MONROE, Croyden, Westmoreland Co., September 14, 1785. ■ EIGHT DOLLARS REWARD. STRAYED or STOLEN, from a pasture, near Bath, in Berkley County, on the 26th of August last, TWO HORSES--one a chestnut sorrel, about 14½ hands high, 6 years old, a small star in his forehead, no brand, his tail drawn short, and appears to have been docked, though he is not. The other, a black, about 14 hands and an inch high, 6 hears old, docked, and branded B.M. on the left buttock.--Any person delivering said Horses to Col. Joseph Mitchel, of Martinsburg; Dr. Daniel Norton, Winchester; Mr. Robert Throckmorton, jun. Bath; or the Subscriber, in Fairfax County, shall receive the above Reward. THOMSON MASON, September 14, 1785. ■ THIRTY DOLLARS REWARD. BROKE GAOL, on the night of the 4th of August last, a MULATTO MAN, named THOMAS VALENTINE, about 5 feet 10 or 11 inches high, a very down, Indian look; had on when he made his escape, an Irish linen shirt, a short brown jacket, striped holland trousers, London made shoes, silver buckles, and a tolerable good hat; but he may change his cloaths, as he has many. I have heard that he was taken up in ALX since he broke gaol, but made his escape.--Whoever will take up said fellow, and secure him in any gaol, or deliver him to the Subscriber, shall receive the above Reward, and reasonable charges, paid by SAMUEL ABELL, Sheriff of Saint Mary's County, Maryland, September 14, 1785. ■ TEN DOLLARS REWARD. RAN AWAY from the Subscriber, living in Fairfax County, Virginia, on the 5th instant, a NEGRO MAN, named GEORGE, about 5 feet 7 inches high, 40 years old, thick and well set; had on and took with him, a Negro cotton jacket, tow linen shirt, and a pair of sacking trousers; has some scars upon his breast and other parts of his body.--Whoever will deliver said Negro to his master, shall receive the above Reward. EDWARD BLACKBURN, September 14, 1785. ■ HENRY TOWNSEND, George-Town, Maryland, has for rent four plantations [see like ad Vol. II No. 83] ■ ☞ A great Variety of BLANKS, printed on good Paper, may be had at the Printing-Office.

Page 4. Poetry. "Thoughts on the Seasons." ■ WILLIAM ALEXANDER and WILLIAM GIBBONS STUART, executors of John Alexander, dec., have for sale one hundred lots of ground contiguous to the Town of ALX [see like ad Vol. II No. 78] ■ The Partnership between Lowry and M'Kenna is dissolved and they request that accounts are settled; Lowry to soon leave for England [see like ads Vol. II No. 73] ■ Executors of the estate of Thomas Kirkpatrick, dec., have for sale 28 Lots in the Town of ALX [see like ad Vol. II No. 79] ■ RICHARD CONWAY advertises for sale a lot on Pitt-street [see like ad Vol. II No. 81] ■ ROBERT ALLISON has goods for sale at his Store in King-street [see like ad Vol. II No. 83] ■ CROCKETTS and HARRIS have just imported in the Ship *Batavia* a quantity of osnaburgs, etc. [see like ad Vol. II No. 83] ■ DANIEL CARROLL, jun., Montgomery Co., Md., offers reward for return of runaway named Joe [see like ad Vol. II No. 78] ■ RAPHAEL BOARMAN, Cornwallis's-Neck, Charles Co., Md., offers reward for return of runaway woman [see like ad Vol. II No. 83] ■ **Porter and Ingraham**, have for sale a general assortment of European Goods [see like ad Vol. II No. 82] ■ WILLIAM FITZHUGH offers for sale a valuable tract of land in Stafford County [see like ad Vol. II No. 70] ■ To be sold, at the Printing-Office, A Variety of Blank Books, consisting of Ledgers, Journals, Cash-Books, Letter-Books, &c.&c. Also, Stoughton's Bitters, Anderson's Pills, Daffy's Elixir, Balsam of Honey, Squire's Elixir, Bateman's Drops, Godfrey's Cordial, &c.&c. ■ ALX: Printed by GEORGE RICHARDS, and COMPANY, at their Printing-Office on Fairfax-street--by whom Advertisements, &c. are thankfully received for this Paper,--and where Printing is performed with Care and Expedition.

1785/09/22, Vol. II No. 86

Page 1. WILLIAM BAKER offers for sale the Oxen Hill plantation [see like ad Vol. II No. 85] ■ JOHN MONROE, Croyden, Westmoreland Co., Va., offers for sale part of a plantation [see like ad Vol. II No. 85] ■ THOMSON MASON offers reward for return of strayed or stolen horses [see like ad Vol. II No. 85] ■ SAMUEL ABELL, Sheriff of St. Mary's Co., Md., offers reward for return of Thomas Valentine who broke gaol [see like ad Vol. II No. 85] ■ JOHN LOMAX has for sale a likely Negro wench [see like ad Vol. II No. 84] ■ **John Murray and Co.**, have for sale a quantity of spirits, etc. [see like ad Vol. II No. 84] ■ Colonel Hooe's warehouse has for sale Barbadoes rum, etc. [see like ad Vol. II No. 84] ■ RICHARD CONWAY offers for sale the Brig *Martha*, and Barbadoes rum, etc. [see like ad Vol. II No. 84] ■ PATRICK MURRAY announces his newly finished livery stable [see like ad Vol. II No. 85] ■ WILLIAM HEPBURN warns others from taking assignment of bonds of Henry M'Cabe of Leesburg [see like ad Vol. II No. 84] ■ EDWARD BLACKBURN offers reward for return of runaway Negro man named George [see like ad Vol. II No. 85].

VIENNA, June 4. Although the dispute with Holland is likely to be brought to an amicable issue, a general peace is not to be expected. There are considerable movements on the frontiers of Turkey. The recent change in the Ottoman Ministry will probably occasion some alterations in the political systems of other countries. In that regard, the Cabinet of Versailles continues to render very effective services to our court. It is said the Count de Choiseul-Gouiffier, the French Ambassador at Constantinople, has received orders to act in concert with the Imperial Internuncio to press for a decision with regard to the limits of the two empires, on which the Divan has not come to any resolution. The advices received by the Marquis de Noailles from Paris are said to be the subject of this affair ... A Convention is said to be negotiating with the Court of Madrid, according to which the Spaniards are annually to supply us, for ten years, nine thousand quintals of quick silver. **Petersburg, June 8.** The British Minister set out last Wednesday, on his return to London, as did the Imperial Minister for Vienna. Some are of the opinion that the departure of these Ambassadors is preparatory to measures for settling the famous affair between the two Imperial Courts and the Sublime Porte, and some say it is to negotiate a league with some of the German Princes. ■ **LONDON, June 30.** Thursday died at his house at Cranham Hall in Essex, General James Oglethorpe, aged 102 years. He was the oldest General in England. In the year 1706 he marched with a party of guards, as Ensign at the proclamation of peace ... A certain Ambassador is come over for the express purpose of getting oils from Rhode Island and Nantucket imported here on the old duties. This is not the declared pretence, but it is well known that his countrymen are almost ruined by the prohibition of the new duties ... The late General Oglethorpe was foremost amongst those spirited gentlemen who founded the colony of Georgia in North America, in 1732. He watched its infancy with solicitude, and observed its increasing spirit with pleasure. He founded Savannah, and when the Spaniards attempted invasion, he beat them from the fort they took possession of, and rescued the province ... The last letters from Paris mention that the 40,000 man camp ordered formed in French Flanders has been countermanded by the ministry, and the troops are to return to their former quarters ... This morning advice was received that 50 sail of ships from the West Indies and America were safe arrived in the channel ... Advices from Gibraltar inform us that a stranger, French by extraction, settled there ever since the peace, has invented a new snuff for such delicate consumers as take it merely to shew their fine boxes. Much the same colour as the Spanish, it is made from burnt coffee and cream, and will cure the vapours, particularly in the fair sex ... Letters from Cadiz dated June 4 mention authentic accounts from the [Havanna] of an epidemical dysentery breaking out there last March and April; upwards of 1000 inhabitants have been carried off.

Page 2. [**London** News (*continued*)] **July 16.** A discovery has lately been made of infidelity in the family of a person of high rank, and depositions of a great number of witnesses respecting the licentious conduct of the lady will speedily be filed in the Ecclesiastical Court, containing a narrative of circumstances hitherto unparalleled in the annals of ancient or modern gallantry ... Two of the Commissions appointed to inquire into loyalist claims will go on an especial commission to Nova Scotia, for the more perfect scrutiny. Mr. Pitt will introduce a bill for this purpose. The commissioners will take a secretary clerks with them. **July 18:** There was much good policy in ceding Florida to Spain, as it must lay the foundation of a future rupture between the New States and that country, especially as the Georgians and the Carolinians are by much the most lawless and licentious people in America, and disposed for every kind of mischief that poverty and internal discontent can lead to ... The American Ambassador, who knows nothing of trade, affects a superior information on all commercial points, and always sets the mistaken merchant to rights, who ventures to consult his opinion. There is much pomp, vast solemnity, and a good share of little greatness in his manners, which is apt to move the muscles of those who talk with him; he seems to feel more than is necessary for the dignity of the New States, and conceits that whatever he demands must be complied with ... Extract of a letter from **Barcelona, June 1:** The 14th of last month, a fine new ship from Brest, bound for this port, was captured by an Algerine [xebec], after a very desperate and bloody engagement of near two hours, in which the Algerines lost 60 killed and many wounded. The captain of the ship and six of the people escaped in a small boat, and got on shore. The remainder of the crew and eight passengers were all carried to Algiers, and sent up the country into slavery ... The following writing was placed below the head of the late Grand Vizier, which was fixed on the gates of the Seraglio: "This is the head of Hamil Mamed Pacha, late Grand Vizier, who deservedly incurred his punishment for betraying the interests of the State and religion, by managing affairs contrary to the sovereign will of the *Great Master of the Universe*; he acted like a tyrant, having, from his sordid avarice, been guilty of frequent and public oppressions of the people of God." ■ **KINGSTON,** (Jamaica) **July 27.** A large body of planters intend to petition the legislature to stop importation of American corn. "*Charity begins at home*," is a maxim requiring no reinforcement. There is ample fine land here to furnish corn in abundance, but--without the encouragement of a fixed and sure market, it will only be cultivated hand to mouth by each farmer according to his own need, and never rise into an article of trade as it should do. Every dollar paid for American corn, or American anything else that we can raise or make ourselves, is a robbery of so much committed against the island at large. **August 3:** Monday morning, soon after 9 o'clock, Benjamin, alias William Johnson, under sentence of death for piracy and murder, was put into a cart at the gaol, and conducted to the Ordnance Wharf, Mr. Simpson, Marshall of the Court of Admiralty, walking before the cart with the silver oar, and a party of the town constables attending; from the wharf he was conveyed to Cuckold's Point, the place of execution, and about eleven o'clock was launched into eternity, without shewing the smallest sign of contrition for the bloody and inhuman tragedy in which he had been a principal actor. Having hung seventeen minutes, he was cut down, his body put in irons, and gibbeted at the distance of about twenty yards from his associate Keating. Previous to his quitting the gaol he ate a very hearty breakfast, and on being brought to the cart it was not without great reluctance and some opposition that he would submit to be haltered; he objected to the executioner's going with him, and on being told it was a custom that could not be dispensed with, he insisted on his sitting with his back towards him, saying he would not keep such kind of company. At the Ordnance Wharf he in an audible voice said, "What do you all do here? I suppose you think you have got a prize." He had a prayer book with him, but made no use of it. It is said that some of the constables having carried rum into the wherry, unnoticed by Mr. Simpson's deputy, repeatedly furnished the prisoner with grog, so that when he reached Cuckold's Point he was so much intoxicated as to be obliged to be carried on shore by Negroes; he however made shift to walk or rather stagger from the sea side to the gallows, where he was accosted by Kelly, desiring to take leave of him; but this the obdurate Johnson obstinately refused, saying he had sworn away his life, well knowing that he only threw the people overboard. After standing a few minutes under the gallows, in a state of hardened insensibility, he mounted the ladder, and was observed to tremble; but this probably was only the effect of liquor. Several officers from the men of war at Port Royal being present at the execution made a small collection for poor Kelly, and we hear that a subscription is now handing about this town, and which it is to be ardently hoped will amply recompense him for crossing the Atlantic, at the expence of time and money, for the sole purpose of bringing an atrocious miscreant to justice. *Few public spirited instances equal to it are to be met with ...*

Montego Bay, July 30. We hear from the Windward Islands that since the beginning of last March upwards of 30 sail of Americans have been seized and condemned in Martinique and Guadaloupe. So very strict is the French government to keep American flour out of their islands that every store in Guadaloupe was searched; 30,000 barrels were found and condemned. This extreme rigor complies with express orders from the French Ministry, citing the ruinous consequences to the agriculture, trade and marine of France by allowing the American States free intercourse with the West Indies islands. This may serve as a useful lesson to Great Britain. ■ **SHELBURNE,** (Nova Scotia) **August 24.** By letters of the 16th from Halifax we learn a brig arrived there from London with the advice that his Majesty had been graciously pleased to continue his bounty of provisions to the loyalists in these provinces, for two years ... Extract of a letter from **Boston, August 14**: The *Mercury* has sailed a week since for your port and Halifax. I have no doubt you have seen the letters that passed between Captain Stanhope and our Governor. However, in case you should not, I send you copies, which you may depend are genuine. [The letters' content follows, summarized.--Eds.] On August 1, from the Mercury, off Boston Harbour, Stanhope requests the Governor discover and punish the ringleaders of those who, of late, have subjected him and his officers to public insults, to illiberal and indecent language in the newspapers, and recently took life threatening mob action against him and an officer. On the same day the Governor mildly notes the difficulties of post-war life, and suggests the captain may seek redress through the courts. Stanhope replies the next day that the Governor's reply is nothing less than evasive and insulting. The Governor terms Stanhope's language insolent and abusive, and vows appropriate action. Stanhope responds his correspondence has been neither abusive nor insolent "which is more than I can venture to say of yours." ■ **PHILADELPHIA, September 1.** A gentleman who was passenger on board gives an account of the disaster which befell the ship *Faithful Steward,* Conolloy M'Causland, master, from Londonderry bound to this port. The vessel sailed on 9th July with 249 passengers, who had with them property to a very considerable amount. At 10 o'clock the night of Thursday, 1st September, soundings were taken. Although no land had been seen at nightfall, to their great surprise they sounded in four fathoms of water. In a few minutes she struck ground, and they found it necessary to cut masts &c. All of which went overboard. At daylight they found themselves on Mohoba Bank, near Indian River, about 4 leagues south of Cape Henlopen. All hands remained on the wreck during the night, and every effort was made to get people ashore, about 100 yards away. However, by evening she was beat to pieces. The high seas swept the boats ashore, unmanned. Only by swimming or clinging to pieces of the wreck could one get ashore. Only 68 survived, among them the master, his mates and 10 seamen. During the day nearby inhabitants lined the shore, trying to help. Of 100 women aboard, only 7 survived. Several who made it ashore are since dead of their wounds, and others miserably bruised. We learn with great pleasure that several humane and public spirited gentlemen of this city are about raising a subscription for the relief of the unhappy people saved from the wreck. There can be no doubt of their meeting with great success from the benevolent inhabitants, who have never been backward in affording assistance to the distress.

Page 3. **ALX, September 22**. On Wednesday the 14th Instant, arrived at Philadelphia, in the ship *London Packet*, Captain Truxton, His Excellency Doctor FRANKLIN, late Minister Plenipotentiary from the United States of America to the Court of France, after an absence of near nine Years. ■ We hear from Berkeley County, that a Boy, by the Fright of a Horse which he rode, was forced against a Tree and instantly killed. ■ NAVAL-OFFICE, ALX. *Inward Entries*. Ship *Carolina*, J. Clarke, from Charleston; Ship *Peggy*, J. Tyndal, Whitehaven; Ship *St. Ann*, V. Caneva, Philadelphia; Schooner *Jesse*, S. Davis, Jamaica. *Cleared Outwards*. Sloop *Charming Polly*, J. Ellwood, for Philadelphia.

On Saturday the 24th Instant, will be Sold at the Vendue-Store,

A VARIETY of WET and DRY GOODS, consisting of West-India and Continental rum in hogsheads and barrels, muscovado sugar, wine in bottles, soap, chocolate, porter in puncheons, cloths in patterns of various colours, chintzes, cambricks, linens, queen's ware, &c. &c.--Also, two or three likely Virginia-born Slaves, and a single Chair.

☞ At 5 o'clock in the afternoon will be sold the SLOOP *INDUSTRY*, now lying at Capt. Harper's wharf, burthen about 60 tons, with all her materials as she came from sea. She is a strong built vessel, but 3 years old, and is well calculated to coast in the river, bay, or for the West-India trade.--An inventory will be exhibited at the time and place of sale, and may be seen at the Vendue-Store.

**I want a CLERK for the Vendue-Store.

S. ARELL, Vendue-Master.

ALX, Sept. 22, 1785.

Jonathan Swift and Company, Take the earliest opportunity to inform their friends and customers in town and country, that they have removed from Captain Harper's Wharf, to a store on the south side of Fairfax-street, where they have now open and ready for sale, A GENERAL assortment of WINTER GOODS, which they will dispose of by wholesale and retail, on the most reasonable terms, for cash, produce, or good bills of exchange on any part of Europe.--They return their grateful thanks to those gentlemen in the town and country who have favored them with their custom, and flatter themselves that the moderate prices of their goods, and their endeavours to give satisfaction, will induce them to continue their favors.--They have now on hand, excellent hyson, souchong and bohea tea, London porter, soap in boxes, chocolate, pimento, New-England rum, molasses, Liverpool ware, well assorted, and a few casks of nails of different sizes, which they will dispose of very low. ☞ Wanted, a Negro Woman, who has served in a decent family, who can cook in a plain way, and wash and iron.--None need apply but those who can be well recommended for their honesty, industry and sobriety. ALX, Sept. 22, 1785. ■ RAN AWAY, the 9th of June last, from David Ashton's, a free Mulatto man, in Westmoreland County, a yellow NEGRO SLAVE, son to the said Ashton, the property of the Subscriber; he is about 5 feet 10 or 11 inches high, and is blind of his right eye. Said fellow, since his elopement, has broke open a store in ALX, was pursued, and taken up at Falmouth, when he was ordered to be committed to Stafford gaol; but on his way had the daring resolution to attack his guard, which he robbed, and made his escape from. Whoever will secure said fellow, and send him to the Subscriber, living in the lower end of Westmoreland County, shall receive THIRTY DOLLARS reward, and travelling expences, paid by F. COX, sen., September 22, 1785. ■ WHEREAS a BOX, marked J.T. No. 1, was shipped on board by schooner at Hobb's-Hole, directed to Mr. James Thrashill, ALX--this is to request the owner would apply immediately for it, and take it away. THOMAS CONNOLY, Master, ALX, Sept. 22, 1785. ■ ☞ Advertisements omitted will be in our next. ■ **Herbert and Potts,** Have for SALE, at their STORE, on the Corner of Fairfax and Queen Streets, an Assortment of seasonable MERCHANDISE, among which are the following Articles: SUPERFINE, second and coarse broadcloths, forest ditto, duffils and kerseys, of a variety of colours, Negro cottons, scarlet, red and white flannels, striped linseys, beaver coating, swanskins, camblets, durants, halfthicks, fine cloth serges, shalloons, plains, plaids, yarn, worsted, cotton, thread and silk hose, osnaburgs, striped and rose blankets, carpets, cotton and wool cards, fine and coarse hats of all sizes, death-head and metal buttons, scarf and leger twist, sewing-silk, button moulds, sackings, green and mottled rugs, Marseilles quilting, satinets, fustians and jeans, plain and corded dimities, cotton counterpanes from 8-4 to 11-4, striped hollands, bed ticks and bunts, furniture check, queen's cords, velverets, apron and yard-wide checks, striped and plain lawns, plain, figured, tamboured and striped muslins, printed linens and cottons, Irish linens of all prices, printed and Barcelona handkerchiefs, Manchester gown patterns, black and white gauzes, German linen, osnaburg, tailors', stitching and nuns' threads, broad and narrow tapes, garterings, lustrings, persians and sarsenets, black and white satins, ribbons of every kind, velvet bindings, mens' and womens' gloves, writing-paper, horn and ivory combs, gimped and saddlers' fringe, silk laces and gloves, stays, ivory, buck, stag and bone handle knives and forks, cutteau and pen knives, tailors' shears and scissors, rasors, spectacles with steel and paper cases, mill, hand, and pit saw files, shoemakers' tools, H and HL hinges, tobacco and snuff boxes, carpenters' hammers, squares and handsaws, augers, spike and small gimlets, stock, pad, desk, chest, drawer and cupboard locks, knob ditto, steelyards, pins and needles, shoe and knee buckles, sleave-buttons, desk furniture, candlesticks and snuffers, copper tea-kettles and coffee-pots, bell-metal skillets, mortars and pestles, spades and shovels, pit and cross-cut saws, tailors' and womens' thimbles, steel and plated spurs, sealing-wax, wafers, quills, black-lead pencils, watch chains, strings, seals and keys, horse bells, 3d. 4d. 6d. 8d. 10d. 12d. and 20d. nails, flooring brads, crates of queen's, earthen and stone ware, white-lead, ground logwood, allum and copperas, shot, slates and pencils, blank and ruled books, sweeping, scrubbing, dusting, hearth, clothes, carriage and comb brushes, curry-combs and brushes, coffee, pepper and Indian-corn mills, wire and hair sifters, warming-pans, pipes, hyson tea, an invoice of medicines, and a collection of medical books, boxes of glass ware, and sets of china, marble chimney-pieces and side-board slabs, and a number of other articles. ALX, Sept. 22, 1785. ■ **William Hartshorne and Company,** Have removed their Store to Fairfax-street, opposite to Joseph Janney's, where they have for Sale, on reasonable Terms, for Cash or country Produce, JAMAICA and New-England rum, molasses sugar, and a variety of Dry Goods, besides a cargo of FALL GOODS, just arrived at Baltimore, and may be expected here in a few days, which, with what they have on hand, will make up a very good assortment.--Being obliged to quit the retail business, in order to settle their affairs, they propose to sell by wholesale only. ☞ Those indebted to them more than three months, will oblige them by paying as soon as convenient.--Such as have it not in their power to pay shortly, it is hoped will be so obliging as to settle accounts, and pass their notes for the balance. ALX, Sept. 22, 1785. ■ To be Let on Lease, for the Term of Ten Years, TWO thousand six hundred acres of LAND, in the county of Frederick, of as good quality as any of the same number in one body in said country, which will be laid off in lots or parcels as follow, viz. Three unimproved lots of 400 acres each, one improved of 400, and one other improved of 800. On the two last have been worked several hands many years, and they are in such order, and there is such a proportion of woodland now to be cleared, that twenty-eight or thirty hands may be worked to advantage on them.--The terms of the leases may be known by applying to Capt. William Ball, on the premises, who will also shew the land. The stocks of horses, cattle, hogs, corn, fodder and plantation utensils, may be had. There are fifty Negroes on the plantations, all of whom or a part may be purchased, and the remainder be had on hire for one year, by private bargain.--Ready cash will be required for one half of the purchase, and six months credit allowed for the other, on bond and security. HUGH NELSON, York, Sept. 15, 1785. ■ FALL GOODS. **Robinson, Sanderson and Rumney,** Are just now landing, from on board the Ship *Peggy*, Capt. Tyndal, from Whitehaven, A LARGE and well-assorted cargo of European Goods, suitable for the present and approaching season, which will be sold on the lowest terms, by wholesale only, at their store on Fairfax-street. N.B. They will give the highest cash price for good tobacco, as usual. ALX, Sept. 22, 1785.

For L O N D O N,

THE new ship *MARY*, JOHN STEWART, Master, burthen 400 hogsheads. She is now loading at George-Town, and will take in (with liberty of consignment) 150 hogsheads, at £.7 sterling per ton.-- She will positively sail by the middle of next month, nearly two-thirds of her cargo being as present engaged. For freight or passage, apply to the Master on board, or

MATTHEWS and ORME.

George-Town, Sept. 20, 1785.

To be Sold, on Saturday the 29th of October next, to the highest Bidder, by Public Auction, on the Premises, A MOIETY of an undivided TRACT of LAND, lying on Cedar-Run, in Prince-William County, about 15 miles from Dumfries, containing about 200 acres. This land was held as tenants in common by the late Rev. John Moncure and the late Rev. James Scott; the part belonging to the latter is directed by his will to be sold for the payment of his debts, and the benefit of residuary legatees.--The land will be divided before the day of sale, and a good title made to the purchaser. There is a tenant on said land, who has sowed some small grain, and if the purchaser should remove him, he must allow him a proper compensation for the grain sowed. The terms are, twelve months credit, with bond and approved security, to bear interest from the date if not punctually paid. T. BLACKBURN, Administrator of J. Scott, deceased. Prince-William County, Sept. 20, 1785. ■ AGREEABLE to the last will of Philip Noland, jun. deceased, will be sold to the highest bidder on the premises, about two miles and an half above Noland's Ferry, on the fifteenth day of October next, if fair, if not the next fair day, the said Noland's dwelling Plantation, containing at least 213 acres. This plantation, as to soil, water, meadow, and orchard, is equal to any land of the quantity on Potomack river; the orchard has made 3000 gallons of cyder a year. Said land lies on the river about three quarters of a mile, on which is a dwelling-house, kitchen, meat-house, and a new barn. The situation of the place is very beautiful and healthy.--The money must be paid as the children come of age; that is in give years one hundred pounds, and one fourth part of the balance in nine years, one fourth in ten years, one fourth in eleven years, and one fourth in thirteen years. The purchaser must give bond, with approved security, for the payment of the money and interest. The interest must be paid annually, for the support of the children, otherwise the bonds shall be liable to be put in suit, for the recovery of the principal and interest.--On the above land is a fine limestone quarry, within 400 yards of the river, where a large quantity of lime might be made, and if the river should be made navigable, in a little time pay for the land.--On the same day, at the aforesaid place, will be sold some cattle, horses and hogs; also, some corn, fodder and wheat, on one years credit, giving bond and approved security. THOMAS NOLAND, Executor, September 20, 1785. ■ IN order that my dower may not be prejudicial to the sale of the above land, and my children might not be injured by me, I oblige myself to take for and in lieu of my right of dower, two hundred pounds, one years credit, on giving bond and approved security. MARY NOLAND, Widow, September 20, 1785. ■ The Printing-Office to sell Webster's Grammatical Institute in Three Parts [see like ad Vol. II No. 85].

Page 4. Poetry. "Night." ■ **Porter and Ingraham**, have for sale a general assortment of European Goods [see like ad Vol. II No. 82] ■ WILLIAM ALEXANDER and WILLIAM GIBBONS STUART, executors of John Alexander, dec., have for sale one hundred lots of ground contiguous to the Town of ALX [see like ad Vol. II No. 78] ■ The Partnership between Lowry and M'Kenna is dissolved and request that accounts are settled; Lowry to soon leave for England [see like ads Vol. II No. 73] ■ **Philip Poyer and Co.**, has just imported goods to be sold at the store of Andrew Wales [see like ad Vol. II No. 84] ■ Patentees of a 51,302-acre tract of land on the Ohio river seek petition to the General Assembly for titles agreeable to survey of partition [see like ad Vol. II No. 84] ■ CONRADE CRYTSINGER seeks owner of stray horse to collect property [see like ad Vol. II No. 84] ■ CHRISTIAN STREIT, Winchester, offers reward for return of stolen horse [see like ad Vol. II No. 84] ■ JOHN KEAN, Winchester, offers reward for return of stolen horse [see like ad Vol. II No. 84] ■ ROBERT ADAM has for sale a Negro wench [see like ad Vol. II No. 84] ■ DANIEL CARROLL, jun., Montgomery Co., Md., offers reward for return of runaway named Joe [see like ad Vol. II No. 78] ■ Races of the ALX Jockey Club Purse announced [see like ad Vol. II No. 81] ■ The Winchester Races are announced [see like ad Vol. II No. 83] ■ WILLIAM LYLES and CO., is selling rum [see like ad Vol. II No. 68] ■ WILLIAM HARTSHORNE has for sale a lot at the corner of Wolf and Washington streets, and one on Fairfax-street near the corner of Gibbon-street [see like ad Vol. II No. 75] ■ To be sold, at the Printing-Office, A Variety of Blank Books, consisting of Ledgers, Journals, Cash-Books, Letter-Books, &c.&c. Also, Stoughton's Bitters, Anderson's Pills, Daffy's Elixir, Balsam of Honey, Squire's Elixir, Bateman's Drops, Godfrey's Cordial, &c.&c. ■ ALX: Printed by GEORGE RICHARDS, and COMPANY, at their Printing-Office on Fairfax-street--by whom Advertisements, &c. are thankfully received for this Paper,--and where Printing is performed with Care and Expedition.

1785/09/29, Vol. II No. 87

Page 1. **Jonathan Swift and Company,** has for sale a general assortment of winter goods [see like ad Vol. II No. 86] ■ **William Hartshorne and Company,** Have removed their Store to Fairfax-street, opposite to Joseph Janney's, where they have for Sale, on reasonable Terms, for Cash or country Produce, JAMAICA and New-England rum, molasses, sugar, and a variety of Dry Goods, besides a cargo of FALL GOODS, just arrived from Baltimore, and may be expected here in a few days, which, with what they have on hand, will make up a very good assortment.--Being obliged to quit the retail business, in order to settle their affairs, they propose to sell by wholesale only. ☞ Those indebted to them more than three months, will oblige them by paying as soon as convenient.--Such as have it not in their power to pay shortly, it is hoped will be so obliging as to settle accounts, and pass their notes for the balance. ALX, Sept. 22, 1785. ■ HUGH NELSON, York, offers for lease 2,600 acres of land in the county of Frederick [see like ad Vol. II No. 86] ■ **Herbert and Potts,** offer for sale at their store on the corner of Fairfax and Queen streets, an assortment of seasonable merchandise [see like ad Vol. II No. 86] ■ **Robinson, Sanderson and Rumney,** have fall goods for sale just arrived on the Ship *Peggy* [see like ad Vol. II No. 86] ■ ☞ A great Variety of BLANKS, printed on good Paper, may be had at the Printing-Office. ■ The Ship *Mary*, John Stewart, Master, takes on tobacco and sets sail from George-Town [see like ad Vol. II No. 86] ■ T. BLACKBURN, Administrator of J. Scott, deceased, offers for sale a moiety of an undivided tract of land on Cedar-Run, Prince William Co. [see like ad Vol. II No. 86] ■ THOMAS NOLAND, Executor of Phillip Noland, jun., deceased, offers for sale plantation above Noland's Ferry; widow Mary Noland releases dower [see like ads Vol. II No. 86].

Page 2.

LONDON, July 19. Extract of a letter from **Cadiz, June 28.** On the 22d of this month an 18 gun Algerine corsair was sunk off Mahon by two Spanish frigates, and all on board perished. Those fierce and vindictive plunderers kept an incessant firing from their tops into the King's ships, the very time their vessel was going down, which killed and wounded upwards of 20 men. The same corsair, two days before, took a large ship from Amsterdam for Leghorn, which they manned and sent to Algiers. All the Dutch prisoners, except the Captain, were on board the rover at the time of the engagement, and perished with the Barbarians ... The project of a league between the several Princes of Germany, to maintain the balance of power in the Empire, is not longer a mystery. As the King of Prussia is to be the head of it, or the centre of the union, these Princes are sending Ministers to Berlin for conferences on the confederation conditions and objects. M. Beulwitz, Minister of State of the Electorate of Hanover is already there, and with the Count de Finkenstein went to Potsdam to open negotiations. Naturally, the Emperor is not indifferent to these movements, which seem to indicate some dissidence respecting him, in quality as head of the Germanic body. To express how far he is from a design of aggrandizing himself at the expence of other members of that body--and how sincerely he has at heart those objects for which the confederation is formed -- his Imperial Majesty offers to put himself at the head of the United Provinces and States. Further, to destroy the suspicion and trust which the rumours respecting an exchange of Bavaria have given rise to, he makes the strongest reassurances that such reports are totally baseless. This was the commission the Count de Trautmansdorff, Minister from the Emperor to the Electorate Court of Mentz, and the circle of the Upper Rhine, was charged with at different Courts in that part of Germany. He there declared, "That the rumours of exchange and secularization had the more sensibly affected his Majesty, as he wished nothing more than to preserve the constitution of the Germanic body in all its integrity, and to see the States of the Empire maintained in the quiet possession of the countries that now belong to them: Paternal views, into which his Imperial Majesty was disposed to enter with the said States, by closer connexions, to guarantee mutually their respective possessions." ... Extract of a letter from an English gentleman in **New York, June 2**, to his friend in England: [An unusually long, and florid article on the significance of the *Empress of China*'s spectacularly successful first voyage, here much summarized.--Eds.] The ship, and American East Indiaman, took furs, gensang, cordage, and Spanish dollars, of which the gensang alone more than purchased her returns, a considerable balance left behind, and the dollars brought back to America. This plainly threatens Europe's East India trade, adding to America's prospects to the wealthy regions of the South, and to the West Indies--all of which could be a dangerous source of opulence ... **July 20:** The death of the Prince Bishop of Lubeck, announced in last Saturday's Gazette, will be a considerable loss to the Protestant interest in Germany (though his highness did not exercise any sovereign authority, that being delegated to the Archbishop of Bremen.) His hospitality, temperance and universal benevolence made him one of the chiefest ornaments of the Lutheran church ... Lord Sackville in his House of Lords speech on the commercial resolutions relative to Ireland (the speech admired both for its content and its delivery), strongly marked the distinction between a real union (such as that with Scotland) and the present patchwork attempt with Ireland. After a comparing the Scottish and Irish plans, point by point [text given--Eds.], Lord Sackville observed that no one could believe that the plan for Ireland be either final or conclusive ... The Dutch city of Rotterdam is so well policed its doors and windows are seldom fastened, robberies hardly ever heard of. One contributing factor: on discovery, vagrants are taken into custody, sent to the Rasp House, kept to hard labour there for a time, then sent out of the country. **July 21:** The poor laws of this country are execrable, the folio of corruption, and--aggravating their malignity--low, illiterate tradesmen whose obvious interest is to huddle into each poor house as many paupers as they can. Such tradesmen, therefore, as cheesemongers, coalmen, tallowchandlers, bakers, &c. &c. Should never be suffered in the governing part of any parish ... Extract of a letter from **Dublin, July 15:** Nothing can be more pleasing than to see with what spirit the several counties and cities throughout this island stand forward to express their sentiments relative to the commercial propositions, now pending in the British Parliament; among these, the freeholders and freemen of the county of Tipperary, at a meeting in Cashel, have voted an address, not only to Henry Prettie and Daniel Foley, Esquires, representing the county in Parliament, but also to Richard Pennefather, and William Pennefather, Esquires, burgesses for Cashel; Thomas Barton, Esq, ditto for Fe??rd; and the Hon. William Moore and Stephen Moore, Esquires, ditto for Clonmell in Parliament;

instructing them to postpone the discussion of those propositions until the next session. ■ **NEW YORK, September 10.** Congress have directed the Board of Treasury to report an ordinance for fixing the standard of weights and measures throughout the United States of America ... On a report from the Secretary for Foreign Affairs, together with a letter of the 10th ult. from the Hon. Minister Plenipotentiary of the United Netherlands, and a commission from their High Mightinesses the Lords the States General, to Daturic Larder, appointing him their Consul for New Hampshire and Massachusetts, to reside at Boston, the Congress have resolved that the said commission be registered, and notification thereof be issued to the states, that the Consul may take up his duties ... On the 17th ult. Congress resolved that, despite many recommendations, many states still have but two representatives, a situation derogatory and dangerous to the public welfare. Accordingly the Secretary of Congress will monthly published a list of the unrepresented states, or represented on by two, that remedial measures may be taken ... On a report of the board of Treasury, Congress resolved that lost certificates of the United States, payable to the bearer, may not be replaced without proof of their having been destroyed ... On the 20th ult Congress resolved that the Secretary for Foreign Affairs draft an act recommending the States pass legislation punishing for infractions of the laws of nations, and to secure the privileges and immunities of public Ministers from foreign powers ... The 7th inst Congress resolved that the Post Master General is authorized and instructed, under the Board of Treasury, to contract--under good and sufficient security--conveyance of mail by the stage carriages, from Portsmouth, N.H. to Savannah, Georgia; and from New York city to Albany, N.Y., according to the accustomed route. **Sept. 15:** A principal reason *Bachelors* do not marry is the excessive folly of the times. An ignorant blockhead of a mechanic, and his still more stupid wife, bring their daughters up such fine ladies, that men are afraid to venture on them. Dress and a fine person may captivate fools; but there must be something superior to these to attract men of sense. Marrying a woman for her beauty is like eating a bird for its singing. ■ **PHILADELPHIA, Sept. 17.** A committee from a respectable meeting of citizens held at Byrne's tavern, having waited on Doctor Franklin to propose him a seat in the Executive Council at the ensuing election. It is with the greatest pleasure the committee announce to the public his accession to their proposal; to which they do not apprehend there will be a dissenting voice in the city. ■ **ALX, Sept. 29.** At an Examination Court, held here on Tuesday last, Joseph Miner, for Burglary and Felony, was ordered by said Court to Richmond for further Trial. ■ The *Minerva*, Capt. Hewson, is arrived in James-River, from London. The *Glasgow*, [Capt.] Patrick, from Virginia, and *Potomack Planter*, [Capt.] Johns, from Maryland, are arrived at Dover. ■ MARRIED.] Mr. JONATHAN SWIFT, Merchant, to the amiable Miss NANCY ROBERDEAU, elder Daughter to General ROBERDEAU, of this Town.

Page 3. NAVAL-OFFICE, ALX. *Inward Entries.* Sloop *Hero*, J. Humphries, from Baltimore. *Cleared Outwards.* Sloop *Hero*, J. Humphries, for Baltimore.

PRICES CURRENT, ALX. / Tobacco, 25s. per Ct. / Fine Flour, 28s. per Barrel. / Wheat, 5s. per Bushel. / Jamaica Spirits, 4/6 per Gallon. / Windward Rum, 3s. per Ditto. / Continental Rum, 2s. per Ditto. / Molasses, 1/8 per Ditto. / Muscovado Sugar, 35s. to 42/6 per Ct. / Salt, 3s. per Bushel, by Retail. / Corn, 3s. per Bushel / Exchange, 40.

On Saturday the first of October, will be Sold at the Vendue-Store,

A VARIETY of WET and DRY GOODS, consisting of West-India and Continental rum in hogsheads and barrels, muscovado sugar, wine in bottles, soap, chocolate, chintzes, cambricks, linens, cloths, paints of various colours, glass and queen's ware, &c. &c.--Also, Specie Certificates.

☞ And on Monday the third of October, will be rented, a number of LOTS, on Water-street, between Prince and King Streets, on ground-rent, for ever, with the privilege of purchasing out in ten or twenty years.

S. ARELL, Vendue-Master.

ALX, Sept. 29, 1785.

The Alexandria Inn and Coffee-House, Is now open, and ready for the Reception of Travellers and others:

THE house is large, and well calculated for the above purpose, with the convenience of a large and commodious stable, where horses are taken in at livery, on the most reasonable terms, by the year or month.--I have in this house several very convenient private rooms, with fire-places, where gentlemen may be most comfortably accommodated.--It will continue to be furnished with most kinds of liquors of the best quality, and such varieties of the seasons as our markets will afford, accompanied with such attendance as, I hope, will not fail to please. HENRY LYLES, ALX, Sept. 29, 1785.

To be Sold to the highest Bidder, on Wednesday, the 23d of November, at my Farm, on Potomack River, if fair, otherwise the next fair Day,

THAT valuable TRACT of LAND, containing between six and seven hundred acres, bounded by the Potomack on one side, and Rosier's-Creek on the other, with navigation at the door, situated within two miles of the Roundhill Church, Washington's Mill, and Machodick Warehouses, and nearly opposite Cedar-Point, on the Maryland side.--The soil is good for corn, wheat, or tobacco, and the place noted for fish, crabs, wild fowl and oysters. It has every advantage for farming, having salt marshes and meadow ground, that may be reclaimed at a small expence. A good dwelling-house, with four rooms below stairs and two above; a large barn, tobacco-house, corn-houses, and Negro quarters.--The land will be surveyed, and sold by the acre. It will be shewn to any one inclinable to purchase, by Mason Bennett, who lives on the premises.--One-third of the purchase-money to be paid on the day of sale, in specie, tobacco, or officers and soldier's certificates at specie value. The remainder to be paid in eight years, by equal annual payments. The purchaser to give bonds with approved security, to carry interest from the day of sale. Possession to be given the first day of January 1786.

At the same time and place will be sold, a few Negroes, the Stock of Horses, Cattle, Sheep and Hogs, with the Fodder, Hay, Straw, plantation Utensils, and 100 barrels of Corn.--Half the purchase-money to be paid down in specie, tobacco, or certificates, as above; the other half in twelve months. The purchasers to give bond with approved security, to carry interest from the date, if not punctually paid.--Five per cent. discount will be allowed for any of the credited property, paid for on the day of sale.

G. WEEDON.

September 28, 1786.

THOMAS CONNOLY, master of a schooner at Hobb's-Hole, seeks owner of box marked J.T. No. 1 [see like ad Vol. II No. 86] ■ **Gurden Chapin and Co.**, Have for Sale at their store (lately occupied by Messrs. William Hartshorne and Co.) in King-street, near the Corner of Fairfax-street, the following Articles, which they will sell on reasonable Terms, for Cash, Wheat, Corn, Flour, or Tobacco: SUPERFINE, second and coarse broadcloths, coatings, duffils, fearn[o]ughts, serges, striped linseys, red, white and yellow flannels, swanskins, Kendal cottons, plaids, yarn and worsted hose, mens' and womens' cotton, thread and [?] ditto, corduroys, cotton and silk velvets, satinets, royal ribs, jeans, jeanets, pillow fustian, plain and corded dimities, bordered and plain Marseilles quilting, drawboys, diaper and Denmark tablecloths, clouting diaper, lustrings, padesoys, Egyptian prunes, white, black and blue satins, black modes, pelongs, sarsenets, silk serges, silk quilts, shalloons, durants, calamancoes, camblets, hairbines, rattinets, tammies, moreens, duroys, sagathees, bombazines, black lasting, mourning crapes, calamanco, leather and Morocco shoes, mens' shoes and boots, yellow canvas, crewels for marking, twist, mohair, sewing silks, Irish and French linens, Irish, Russia and Flanders sheetings, ravens duck, sailcloth, osnaburgs, brown rolls, dowlas, dark and light [ground?] chintzes, calicoes, printed cottons and linens striped, plain and spotted lawns, cambricks, plain, corded and sprigged muslins, tiffany, gauze, Bandano, Barcelona, lawn, printed and check handkerchiefs, souffle gauze and tiffany aprons, plain, striped and spotted black gauzes, cyprus, figured, and striped white gauzes, catgut, skeleton and stick wire, thread laces and edgings, blond and black laces, plain, coloured, painted and black ribbons, tastes, womens' leather and silk gloves and mitts, mens' leather and silk gloves, 2d. 4d. and 6d. ferrets, thread, silk and cotton laces, fine and coarse hats, ladies riding ditto, cotton and linen checks, striped hollands, Scotch, osnaburg and tailors' threads, buckram, Bibles, testaments, prayer-books, spelling-books, psalters, London vocabularies, Clark's Corderius, Nepos[?], Shallust, Ovid, Horace, Virgil, Justin, Kennett's Antiquities, *Selectae e Veteri*, Rudiman's Rudiments, Vettenhal's and Christie's Latin Grammars, Clark's and Christie's Introductions, Clark's Homer, 2 vols. *Eutropius*, Milton's *Paradise lost*, Greek testements, Young Man's Companion, blank books and alphabets, tapes and bobbins, ivory and horn combs, a large assortment of twist, metal and fashionable buttons, pins, sewing and sail needles, sealing-wax, wafers, ink-powder, paper, slates, slate and lead pencils, fiddle strings, camel's hair pencils, painting, shoe, clothes and sweeping brushes, drum-lines, bed-cords, traces, leading-lines, calfskins, foal and neat's leather, shovels and tongs, rat-traps, chafingdishes, coffee-mills, copper tea-kettles and coffee pots, gun-locks, stock, door, cupboard, chest, pad and bag locks, nail and spike gimlets, augers, H, HL, T, chest, dovetail, mortise, strap and box hinges, lemon squeezers, thumb-latches, stone, smiths' sledge, claw and saddlers' hammers, carpenters' braces and collars, glue, vices, seale-beams, knives and forks, oyster, cutteau and pen knives, rasors, shoe-knives, awl-blades, tacks, lasts, curriers' knives, scissors, tailors' and sheep shears, shoemakers' and carpenters' pincers, nippers, bricklayers' and plasterers' trowels, butchers' and table steels, brass cocks, candlesticks and snuffers, window and wood screws, steel and plated spurs, pinking-irons, round and flat bolts, bullet-moulds, plane-irons, sugar-nippers, marking-irons, chisels, gouges, chimney-hooks, sconces, brass kettles, temple and common spectacles, tailors' thimbles, womens' brass and silver ditto, an assortment of files and rasps, tobacco and snuff boxes, round, oval and square waiters, rules and size-sticks, bottle-stands, table-ketches, screw and window pullies, coopers' compasses, sleeve-buttons, brass, steel, white-metal and plated shoe and knee buckles, watch chains and keys, fish-hooks, hooks and eyes, escutcheons and handles, sets of desk-mounting, hoes, axes, spades, shovels, coopers' and carpenters' adzes, Turky oil-stones, spice mortars, bar-iron, steel, nail-rods, 4d. 6d. 8d. 10d. 12d. 20d. and 24d. nails, 10d. 12d. and 20d. brads, springs, 12 oz. 14oz. 16oz. and 18 oz. tacks, pump-tacks, castings, flat-irons, frying-pans, pit, hand and mill saws, soap, candles, cheese, porter, saddles, bridles, stirrup-irons, bridle-bits, girths, girth-web, window-glass, an assortment of glass, china, tin, and queen's ware, pewter, horse and chair whips, powder, shot, lead, wine, Jamaica spirits, West-India and Continental rum, molasses, loaf and brown sugar, bohea, souchong, congo, green and hyson teas, coffee, chocolate, pimento, pepper, nutmegs, cloves, mace, cinnamon, cotton, brimstone, indigo, copperas, saltpetre, corks, mustard, Leiper's snuff in bottles, stone jugs and butter-pots. &c. &c. &c. ALX, Sept. 29, 1785. ■ ☞ The Obligation given by Mr. William Hepburn to Mr. Henry M'Cabe, is but one Bond, and not Bonds, as mentioned in this Paper. ■ **For BOSTON,** THE Sloop *INDUSTRY*, James Rob, Master; will sail in eight days.--For freight or passage, apply to the Master on board, at Harper's Wharf, or to PORTER and INGRAHAM. Who have for sale, best Swedish iron in bars, a few barrels of choice mackerel, New-England rum in barrels, &c.&c. ALX, Sept. 29, 1785. ■ TO BE SOLD, In Fee Simple, A VERY valuable LOT, advantageously situated on Prince-street.--Inquire at the Printing-Office. Sept. 29, 1785.

FOR SALE,

ONE thousand three hundred acres of LAND, suitable for cropping and farming, conveniently situated to the trade of ALX and Dumfries, lying on Bull-Run, in Loudon.--For terms, apply to Mr. Richards, on the premises, or Mr. John Chapman, in the neighbourhood.--The horses, stock and crops may be had with the land, or may be purchased separately. JOHN PAGE.
Rosewell, Gloucester, Sept. 27, 1785.

Berkeley, September 13, 1785.

THE LANDS in this county, contiguous to those of James Wormeley, Esq; at the Rocks, formerly advertised for sale, are now to be rented.--They will be laid off in lots, in such a manner, that every lot shall comprehend some meadow ground, or low grounds, which in fact are meadow. Mr. Wormeley, jun. will be up by the 14th of November, and grant leases to those who may wish to become tenants, provided terms mutually agreeable can be adopted. There are two thousand seven hundred and odd acres.--Any person disposed to purchase seven hundred acres may be accommodated with that quantity.--Application may be made, between this period and November, to Mr. James Wormeley, or Mr. Nicholas Roper, who will shew the land, either to those who mean to rent it, or to any who would choose to purchase, and who are empowered to make engagements in my absence. RALPH WORMELEY, jun.

On Tuesday, the 15th of November next, in the Borough of Winchester and County of Frederick, will be sold to the highest Bidder, for ready money,

FORTY valuable SLAVES, the property of the late Robert Burwell, deceased, in order to discharge the debts of that estate. The sale will be conducted in the absence of the Executors by,
SAMUEL BAKER.
September 28, 1785.

WHEREAS the bonds given at the sale of the personal estate of James Nourse, Esq; deceased, become payable the first and twenty-sixth days of November.--Notice is hereby given, that the Subscriber will attend on said days, at Charlestown, in Berkeley County, to receive all such sum or sums of money as will on those days be due, and expressed in the bonds aforesaid. WILLIAM NOURSE. ☞ A young Negro Fellow, and a Negro Boy, together with the Plate, Linen, Books, &c., the remainder of the personal effects of the said James Nourse, Esq; will be offered for sale, at Captain Cherry's tavern, in Charlestown, on Thursday the tenth day of November next.--The conditions will be made known on the day of sale, September 26, 1785. ■ TWENTY DOLLARS REWARD. RAN AWAY from the Subscriber, living near Bath, in Berkeley County, on the 7th instant, a SERVANT MAN, named WILLIAM KELLY, about 5 feet 8 or 9 inches high, and has dark hair and eyes: He had on and took with him, a blue cloth coat, spotted velvet jacket, corduroy breeches, and light coloured worsted stockings.--He took his bag-pipes with him, on which he plays tolerably.--Whoever will take up said Servant, and secure him, so that his master may get him again, shall receive the above Reward, paid by JOHN STEED, September 27, 1785. ■ RAN AWAY from the Subscriber, on the 21st of last month, a MULATTO WOMAN, named MOLLY, of a middle size. She took with her two Virginia cloth jackets and petticoats, one brown and one green baize ditto, with sundry other things.--As she can read, and is handy at her needle, it is probable she will endeavour to pass for a free woman. She is very artful, and capable of inventing a falsehood.--Whoever delivers said woman to me, in Culpepper or Fredericksburg, or secures her in any gaol, so that I may get her again, shall be handsomely rewarded. JAMES DUNCANSON, Fredericksburg, Sept. 26, 1786.

Page 4. Poetry. "The Boy's Choice of a School-Master." ■ WILLIAM BAKER offers for sale the Oxen Hill plantation [see like ad Vol. II No. 85] ■ JOHN MONROE, Croyden, Westmoreland Co., Va., offers for sale part of a plantation [see like ad Vol. II No. 85] ■ THOMSON MASON offers reward for return of strayed or stolen horses [see like ad Vol. II No. 85] ■ EDWARD BLACKBURN offers reward for return of runaway Negro man named George [see like ad Vol. II No. 85] ■ **Porter and Ingraham**, have for sale a general assortment of European Goods [see like ad Vol. II No. 82] ■ WILLIAM ALEXANDER and WILLIAM GIBBONS STUART, executors of John Alexander, dec., have for sale one hundred lots of ground contiguous to the Town of ALX [see like ad Vol. II No. 78] ■ The Printing-Office to sell *Webster's Grammatical Institute* in Three Parts [see like ad Vol. II No. 85] ■ WILLIAM LYLES and CO., is selling rum [see like ad Vol. II No. 68] ■ DANIEL CARROLL, jun., Montgomery Co., Md., offers reward for return of runaway named Joe [see like ad Vol. II No. 78] ■ To be sold, at the Printing-Office, A Variety of Blank Books, consisting of Ledgers, Journals, Cash-Books, Letter-Books, &c.&c. Also, Stoughton's Bitters, Anderson's Pills, Daffy's Elixir, Balsam of Honey, Squire's Elixir, Bateman's Drops, Godfrey's Cordial, &c.&c. ■ PATRICK MURRAY announces his newly finished livery stable [see like ad Vol. II No. 85] ■ ALEXANDER THOMAS announces opening of a tavern in the house lately occupied by Mr. John Lomax [see like ad Vol. II No. 84] ■ WILLIAM HARTSHORNE has for sale a lot at the corner of Wolf and Washington streets, and one on Fairfax-street near the corner of Gibbon-street [see like ad Vol. II No. 75] ■ SAMUEL ABELL, Sheriff of St. Mary's Co., Md., offers reward for return of Thomas Valentine who broke gaol [see like ad Vol. II No. 85] ■ F. Cox, sen., offers reward for return of runaway from David Ashton's, Westmoreland County [see like ad Vol. II No. 86] ■ RAPHAEL BOARMAN, Cornwallis's-Neck, Charles Co., Md., offers reward for return of runaway woman [see like ad Vol. II No. 83] ■ ALX: Printed by GEORGE RICHARDS, and COMPANY, at their Printing-Office on *Fairfax-street*--by whom *Advertisements*, &c. are thankfully received for this Paper,--and where Printing is performed with Care and Expedition.

1785/10/06, Vol. II No. 88

Page 1. HENRY LYLES announces opening of the Alexandria Inn and Coffee-House [see like ad Vol. II No. 87] ■ **Herbert and Potts,** offer for sale at their store on the corner of Fairfax and Queen streets, an assortment of seasonable merchandise [see like ad Vol. II No. 86] ■ **Robinson, Sanderson and Rumney,** have fall goods for sale just arrived on the Ship *Peggy* [see like ad Vol. II No. 86] ■ The Ship *Mary*, John Stewart, Master, takes on tobacco and sets sail from George-Town [see like ad Vol. II No. 86] ■ G. WEEDON has for sale a tract of land two miles of the Roundhill Church, Washington's Mill and Machodick Warehouses [see like ad Vol. II No. 87] ■ TO BE SOLD, In Fee Simple, A VERY valuable LOT, advantageously situated on Prince-street.--Inquire at the Printing-Office. Sept. 29, 1785. ■ The Sloop *Industry*, James Rob, Master, is to sail for Boston [see like ad Vol. II No. 87] ■ RALPH WORMELEY, jun., Berkeley Co., has lands for sale [see like ad Vol. II No. 87] ■ JOHN PAGE has 1,000 acres for sale on Bull-Run in Loudon Co. [see like ad Vol. II No. 87] ■ SAMUEL BAKER has for sale in Winchester, Va., 40 valuable slaves of the property of the late Robert Burwell, deceased [see like ad Vol. II No. 87] ■ WILLIAM NOURSE seeks to settle accounts of James Nourse, Esq., deceased [see like ad Vol. II No. 87] ■ THOMAS CONNOLY, master of a schooner at Hobb's-Hole, seeks owner of box marked J.T. No. 1 [see like ad Vol. II No. 86].

Page 2.

COPENHAGEN, June 28. At the request of the West India Company, who are the farmers of the St. Thomas custom house, his Majesty has suppressed all the royal officers who were employed there, except the weigher. Each of them, however, has a pension settled on him proportioned to his salary. **Trieste, June 20:** All vessels coming hither from the Levant are obliged to remain outside the port 48 days, since the report of the plague breaking out in Smyrna. The outbreak was the fault of some people who opened a tomb holding several of last year's plague victims. However, recent reports say only those workmen were affected, most of them dying from it. Ships which had fled some distance at the first alarm are now returned, and taking in cargo. **Paris, July 8:** On May 29th a treaty of confederation was signed by the King of Prussia, the King of Sweden, the Electors of Saxony and Treves, the Margrave of Anspach, and the Duke of Deux Ponts. Its purport is preserving the invisibility of the empire. France and Holland are invited to sign as guarantees, interested for their own tranquility, in the maintenance of the present constitution of the Germanic body. ■ **LONDON, July 21.** It is a fact that General George Washington, late Commander in Chief of the American Army, has actually hired a house at Walworth, within two miles of the metropolis, for the purpose of his residence ... Extract of a letter from **Dublin, July 14**: Mr. Sheridan's printed remark, that instead of Ireland's being a jewel in the British crown, that she had an imperial diadem of her own, deserves to be written in letters of gold, or rather perpetual adamant, and deeply imprinted on the breast of every Irishman. We have our own Parliament, the right to make our own laws for internal and external affairs, and consequently to export our own manufactures without any restriction, as well as import such merchandize and raw materials as other nations permit. That the British Legislature should once again impose shackles of illegal restraint, and wrest every essential of a free and independent people, is a matter of the most ruinous and alarming consideration. Can they suppose that Irishmen are so desirous of "the onions and garlic of Egypt" as to wish again to return to their captivity, and to forsake those happy prospects which were almost within their grasp? It will be found that have not deviated from these principles that hitherto actuated them in their various pursuits, and will make use of every constitutional effort to retain and preserve inviolate, those invaluable acquisitions. **July 22:** An extract of a letter from **Philadelphia, June 5th**: The Spanish Ambassador is just arrived here en route from Cuba to New York, where Congress are now sitting. He brings near two hundred thousand hard dollars, and forty thousand pounds sterling, to clear off debts to individuals. As foreign nations favor us much more than Great Britain seems to do, it is believed the English ships and goods will soon be excluded here, and we now are no longer in her power, but can easily bring her to reason. Meetings in Boston and here, &c. are holding for that purpose. Peace is more and more confirmed among us, surprisingly so, considering the great confusions of the late war. The new crops promise well ... General Washington, so it is asserted, has taken a house at Walworth; if so, it is rather a remarkable circumstance that he should think of residing in a village which takes its name from Sir William Walworth, so famous in history for having quelled a rebellion by striking its leader dead ... Corn crops in Poland, Russia and adjoining countries are more promising this year than for some years past ... MARRIED, a few days ago, the Rev. Mr. Blewit to the wealthy landlady of the Castle Inn, at Chesterfield. Preferring the sound of the bar bell to the solemn toll of the parish tenor, he philosophically relinquishes the ambitious pursuit after church preferment, consoles himself with the enjoyment of domestic comforts, and a well stocked cellar, and bids fair to be one of the most respectable landlords in the county. ■ **SALEM, September 13.** On Saturday last, the ship *Atlantic*, commanded by Captain Tresethen [possibly Trefenthen], but having on board as freighter and supercargo Captain Jonathan [Ingersol], of this town, arrived here from New York. On their passage to that place from Grenada, on the 23rd ult. They met with a boat, having on board Captain Duncanson, his mate, boatswain, and three black boys, as related in our last week's paper. He informed that the next day after leaving the ship *Three Cranes*, Capt. Brown, by whom he and his mate &c. Were first taken up, they spoke with a brig from Virginia, bound to London, who informed them that they were then 60 leagues from the capes of Virginia, which being their object, though in a hazardous situation, the declined going on board the brig. At four P.M. the same day, the wind blowing hard, the *Atlantic* hove in sight, when their situation was so alarming as induced them gladly to embrace this opportunity of saving themselves. They accordingly made for the ship, were taken on board, their boat was hoisted in, and they arrived at New York as above.

While Captain Ingersoll was at New York, a pilot boat arrived, which fell in with, near Sandy Hook, a schooner answering the description of the *Amity* (piratically taken possession of by Richard Squire and others) on which an armed vessel, manned with a number of volunteers, accompanied by Captain Duncanson, his mate and boatswain, sailed in quest of her. Though this exertion for recovering the vessel, and capturing the villains, proved unsuccessful, we have the pleasure of informing the public, that the said schooner *Amity* is now at anchor in our harbour, and that the piratical crew are safely lodged in the public gaol of this town, of which event we have collected the following particulars, viz.

Captain Ingersol, on his passage from New York, was three days successively in sight of the *Amity*, which, from the particular he had received of her, he well knew; but circumstances did not admit of her being captured. Just before he got in, he spoke with a fisherman in the Bay, who informed, that he had been alongside the schooner, and sold the people some fish, for which they paid the money; but that he knew not who they were. Captain Ingersoll, on the day of his arrival, saw the *Amity* near Cape Ann, and concluded from her appearance that the crew intended to make a harbour. Immediately on his landing, and giving the above intelligence, a fast-sailing brig belonging to E.H. Darby, Esq. was fitted and armed in order to go in quest of her; and at 3 o'clock P.M. she was under sail, with 50 or 60 respectable volunteers on board. Very soon after quitting the harbour, they saw the schooner standing in; and, that their design might not be suspected, inclined to the eastward till, finding themselves several leagues without her, they tacked, and came in after her. They discovered her at anchor a mile or two from Marblehead harbour; and, on coming up with her, several gentlemen from the brig boarded her, when they found only three white men and a Negro; Squire, Matthews, the Mulatto, and a Negro having gone on shore at Marblehead. The schooner was brought into the harbour, and the men taken in her committed to prison. Squire, and those ashore with him, were found at a tavern, taken before a magistrate, examined, and brought over the next morning, and the whole properly secured in gaol.

On board the schooner one man, said to be Wise, or Wiseman, was found in irons. It is said he was taken on board at the Vineyard, as a passenger for Newburyport, whither the Pirates told him they were bound; but having displeased them, they thought proper to confine him. The remainder consisted of some persons who were on board when Captain Duncanson was turned adrift. They had two pieces of cannon, and were armed, besides, with pistols, cutlasses, &c.

The following writing was found on board the above schooner, and there is scarcely a doubt of the several names and marks subscribed being the real signatures of the villains now imprisoned for piracy.

August the 21 = 1785

This Is to Certyfy that the Scooner Sweet Belonging to the Seamen and Officers of the Said Scooner have Taken In hand to Persue on a Cruce In Defence of Our Selvs and Against all Other Nation and Nations or Power Powers as We on Oath Volentearly Do a Gre to Stick and Obay our Officers Com In any that that he or We Shall a Grea to Gether In any Way or Ways to Chais or Give Chais to any Vessell or Vessells What So Ever, and Like Wise that no man Shall Get Drunk Or Be Rangellsum In any Ocations What So Ever--And Who Ever Boards any Vessell or Vessells Shall Do the In Dever to Secure all Property that thay Shall Get for our one Use and that thay Who Ever Is found Keeping any Goods Clothing Cash or Jeuels of any Kind Shall forfite there Share of All Such Goods or Goodse that Shall be Capyvated By us In the Said Scooner--And he or any of us Shall Dis Close or Give any Information or Disvols any agreements that we Shall Be on Othe upon either Wile We Be Long to the said Scooner or at Our Departure Shall Be Put to Deth or any Punishment that the Rest Shall think thay Justly Deserve as We this 21 Day of August In the Year of our lord 1785 Do take a Volentary Oathe to the Said Articles as our hands Below mentions as Seald Oppysit to our Respective Names.

Names —	*Stations*
Rich'd Squire	*Capt.*
John Mathews	*Lieut.*
Alex Evens	
John Rogers	*his* + *mark*
George Stewart	*his* + *mark*

[With a seal affixed to each name.]

N.B. The person who signed John Rogers is supposed to be the same whom Captain Duncanson mentioned by the name of John Boadman.

NEW YORK, September 20. Last Friday the sloop *Unity*, Capt. Nicholas Bailey, arrived here from New Providence, where the Captain, having sprung a leak, had put in distress, and immediately waited on the Governor, who ordered him to the Collector; and notwithstanding he was short of water, and in a leaky condition, the Collector told him he could not repair until he went to the Judge of the Admiralty, and got a warrant of survey of 3 mariners and two ship-carpenters; which he obtained, and the surveyors judged her not fit for sea, yet he was allowed only one day to refit, and informed that if he did not depart in 48 hours he should be seized, and vessel and cargo confiscated. This severe injunction compelled him to return here again with the whole of his cargo, except so much as was necessary to defray expences, which were 70 pieces of eight to the Judge of the Admiralty and Surveyors; 21 to the governor; to his Secretary (*a puppy who damn'd him and all the Americans, for a rebellious set of rascals*) 15. ■ **PHILADELPHIA, September 23.** Tuesday last being the day appointed for the *consecration* of the *Sublime* Lodge of Philadelphia, for conferring the *superior* degrees of Masonry, the brethren assembled at the Lodge room, in Lodge alley, and walked in procession to the New Lodge, in Black Horse alley, attended by a band of music. The Thrice Puissant then opened the Lodge, and introduced the business with a suitable prayer, when the constitution and bye-laws were read. After which was delivered, an elegant oration, composed by brother Vannost, and a beautiful ode set to music, composed by brother Smith, of the Sublime Lodge.

Form of Procession
The Master of Ceremonies or Sword Bearer
Brother Orator and Clergy
The Treasurer with the Bible and velvet Cushion
The Thrice Puissant, with the Worshipfuls Deputy Grand Master and Grand Warden of Pennsylvania at his right and left
Brother Inspector
The Senior and Junior Sublime Wardens
The Sublime Secretary
The Brethren of the Sublime Lodge two and two
The Brethren of the Royal Arch
Past Masters; Officers of Lodge No. 2
Officers of Lodge No. 3
Officers of Lodge No. 4
Officers of Lodge No. 8
Officers of Lodge No. 9
Invited Brethren two and two
Tyler.

There has been no instance of a masonic procession which exhibited a more respectable appearance, and the solemnities used in consecrating the Lodge were very striking. A pretty collation was prepared by the Sublime Lodge, for the visiting brethren; and in the afternoon the brethren dined together, at the City Tavern, and spent the day in the greatest harmony. The following toasts were drank:

1. The Sublime Lodge of Perfection this day consecrated.
2. Our illustrious Brother King of Prussia.
3. Our beloved Brother George Washington, the intended Grand Master of America.
4. That dignified Philosopher and Friend to Mankind, Brother Benjamin Franklin.
5. The Grand Lodge of Pennsylvania.
6. May the rust of discord never corrode the present polished chain of Masonic Fellowship [Continued on Page 3].

Page 3. [Masonic Event (*continued*)]

7. May *health*, *stability* and *power* be ever the supporters of our Lodge.
8. May Beauty and Merit be the reward of Virtue and Secrecy.
9. The Land we live in.
10. Our worthy Brethren round the Globe.
11. Increase, Love and Unanimity to the antient Craft.
12. All Masons who honor the Order by conforming to its Rules.
13. The Memory of old.

RICHMOND, October 1. Extract of a letter from **Norfolk**, dated Sunday morning, **September 25, 1785:** A higher tide and severer storm were never known at this place than happened yesterday; the damages sustained thereby are immense--almost all the ships in the harbour were drove from their moorings, and many warehouses entirely carried away--vast quantities of salt, sugar, corn, lumber, and other merchandise were totally lost--the lower stories of many buildings were filled with water. ■ **ALX, October 6.** On Saturday Evening last arrived here the Sloop *Phebe*, Capt. Cartwright, from St. Lucia, where she was seized and condemned, and the Vessel and Cargo bought in by the Captain. Capt. Cartwright informs, that on the 24th Ult. near the Capes of Virginia, in a violent Gale of Wind, he shipped a heavy Sea, which carried away his Bowsprit, stove about 30 Casks of Rum and Molasses, swept every Thing off the Deck, and laid the Sloop on her Beam-Ends; but fortunately she soon righted.--During the Gale Capt. Cartwright saw five dismasted Ships, apparently in great Distress.--

After the Gale had abated, he boarded a large Ship, entirely dismasted, loaded with Wheat, and without any Person on board, which, by her Papers and some Windsor Chairs he took out of her, he supposes to be a Dutch Ship from Philadelphia.--He spoke the ----, Capt. Savage, from Machapungo, bound to Philadelphia, dismasted. On Sunday last arrived here the Ship *Grandbourg*, Capt. LeJoyille, in 52 Days from Cadiz, with whom came Passengers Capt. Ervin and his Crew, who sailed from Cadiz in October last for this Port, but were unfortunately taken and carried into Tangiers.--Capt. Ervin informs, that neither he or any of his People were put to Service, but, on the contrary, treated in the most humane Manner. Capt. LeJoyille informs, that he met with heavy Gales of Wind; and, from the Number of Wrecks he saw, it is to be feared great Damage had been done. Yesterday Morning passed this Port for George-Town, the Ship *Washington*, Capt. ----, from London.--She had a long Passage; and, since the late Gale, rolled away the Heads of her Fore and Main Masts. ■ NAVAL-OFFICE, ALX. *Inward Entries*. Schooner *Lottery*, Z. Mann, from Baltimore; Sloop *Washington*, J. Thompson, Philadelphia; Sloop *Ranger*, N. Stowe, Turk's-Island; Ship *Grandbourg*, [Capt.] LeJoyille, Cadiz. *Cleared Outwards*. Brig *Charles*, S. Makins, for Morlaix.

On Saturday the eighth Instant, will be Sold at the Vendue-Store,

A Variety of Merchandise, as usual.

S. ARELL, Vendue-Master.

October 6, 1785.

THE Executors of JOHN ALEXANDER, deceased, were prevented from disposing of the LOTS lately advertised by them on the day appointed, by the badness of the weather, but they will proceed on Thursday the Twentieth of the present month, to let the said lots, on the terms mentioned in their former advertisement. ALX, October 5, 1785. ■ To be Sold for Cash, Produce, or a short Credit, ALL the STOCK in TRADE belonging to JOHN SUTTON, consisting of a variety of DRY-GOODS, suited to the present season.--Any person wanting to purchase the whole of the Stock, will be treated with on very advantageous terms, by applying at the Subscriber's store in ALX. JOHN SUTTON, October 6, 1785.

To be Sold at private Sale, any Time before the first Day of December next, when Possession will be given.

ONE hundred and fifty acres of LAND, lying in Loudon County, State of Virginia, on Little River, within forty-five miles of ALX, and about forty from Dumfries, on which is a very elegant stone house, with five comfortable rooms, four of which have fire-places, a good cellar under the whole house, a convenient kitchen and other necessary out-houses, together with a young apple and cherry orchard nearly come to perfection. The land is well watered with springs. There are on the premises a good grist and merchant mill, with a very good stone mill-house; the mill has been rebuilt this last summer, and now in good repair, with all necessary bolts for merchant-work, and is equal to any in this part of the country for grinding. There is also adjoining said mill, a good saw-mill, built last spring; and fronting the same, a convenient stone storehouse, with a counting-room, and a good cellar under the whole. There is also a large still-house, well finished, built but two years, with two stills, one 110, the other 60 gallons, which will also be sold. It is well situated for trade, and may suit a person of that turn. There is a public road leads by the mill to both the abovementioned navigable towns, and to different part of the country.--The Subscriber has also for sale, three hundred and ten acres or leased land, nearly all tillable, about one hundred acres of which is cleared and under good fence; it is of a good quality, and will suit for planting or farming, being in good order for both.--The terms for the whole are as follow: One half ready cash, the other half payable in twelve months, the purchaser giving bond, with approved security, bearing interest from the date.--Fifteen per cent. will be allowed for ready cash in the last payment.--Any person inclinable to purchase, may apply to the Subscriber on the premises.

NATHANIEL WEEDON.

October 4, 1785.

RAN AWAY early in the morning of the 25th instant, from the Subscriber, near Upper-Marlborough, in Prince-George's County, Maryland, a very likely, well-made, young NEGRO FELLOW, named MICHAEL, about five feet ten inches high, about twenty years of age, rather of a yellow complexion: He had on when he went away, a green cotton coat, striped blue and white linen jacket, osnaburg breeches, white cotton stockings, and shoes and buckles. He also took with him three or four fine linen shirts, three pair of brown thread stockings, a white broadcloth coat, and several other things. He broke open my desk, and stole three guineas and a silver watch, the maker's name and number of which is forgot, and went off on a likely bay horse, about seven years old, fourteen hands one or two inches high, very well made, paces slow, trots and gallops, one hind-foot white, a very small star in his forehead, hardley perceivable, branded C.H. on the near buttock, has been used to run in a carriage, and shews the marks of the harness on his breast. He was seen in ALX a little before sun-down, the evening of the day on which he went off, and told his brother, who lives with Colonel Fitzgerald, that he was sent by me down to Mrs. Eleanor Brent's, near Dumfries, in Stafford County, Va., where it is probable he will be harboured.--Whoever will apprehend and secure him and the horse, so that I get both again, shall be entitled to a reward of FIVE POUNDS, current money or Four Dollars for the horse alone, with reasonable charges is brought home. CLEMENT HILL. N.B. When he went through ALX, he had on the white cloth coat, green cotton jacket, nankeen breeches, white shirt, a black ribbon about his neck, and boots, and it is probable had a forged pass, as, I am informed, on a former trip which he made, he had one. September 30, 1785. ■ T. BLACKBURN, Administrator of J. Scott, deceased, offers for sale a moiety of an undivided tract of land on Cedar-Run, Prince William Co. [see like ad Vol. II No. 86] ■ TO BE SOLD, On Monday the 24th Instant, at my Farm, near the Lower Falls of Potomack, **S**UNDRY blooded HORSES, of different ages. Twelve months credit will be allowed, on giving bond with approved security, to bear interest from the date, if not punctually paid.--Also, to be sold at the same time and place, some LANDS, in Fayette County, on the waters of Kentucky river. WILLIAM SCOTT, October 5, 1785. ■ THOMAS NOLAND, Executor of Phillip Noland, jun., deceased, offers for sale plantation above Noland's Ferry; widow Mary Noland releases dower [see like ads Vol. II No. 86] ■ F. Cox, sen., offers reward for return of runaway from David Ashton's, Westmoreland County [see like ad Vol. II No. 86] ■ RAPHAEL BOARMAN, Cornwallis's-Neck, Charles Co., Md., offers reward for return of runaway woman [see like ad Vol. II No. 83] ■ JAMES DUNCANSON, Fredericksburg, offers reward for return of runaway mulatto woman named Molly [see like ad Vol. II No. 87].

Page 4. Poetry. "The Cot." ■ PATRICK MURRAY announces his newly finished livery stable [see like ad Vol. II No. 85] ■ WILLIAM HARTSHORNE has for sale a lot at the corner of Wolf and Washington streets, and one on Fairfax-street near the corner of Gibbon-street [see like ad Vol. II No. 75] ■ WILLIAM LYLES and CO., is selling rum [see like ad Vol. II No. 68] ■ DANIEL CARROLL, jun., Montgomery Co., Md., offers reward for return of runaway named Joe [see like ad Vol. II No. 78] ■ To be sold, at the Printing-Office, A Variety of Blank Books, consisting of Ledgers, Journals, Cash-Books, Letter-Books, &c.&c. Also, Stoughton's Bitters, Anderson's Pills, Daffy's Elixir, Balsam of Honey, Squire's Elixir, Bateman's Drops, Godfrey's Cordial, &c.&c.&c. ■ **Gurden Chapin and Company,** have for sale at their Store (lately occupied by Messrs. William Hartshorne and Co.) in King-street, an assortment of articles [see like ad Vol. II No. 87] ■ ☞ A great Variety of BLANKS, printed on good Paper, may be had at the Printing-Office. ■ **Jonathan Swift and Company,** Take the earliest opportunity to inform their friends and customers in town and country, that they have removed from Captain Harper's Wharf, to a store on the south side of Fairfax-street, where they have now open and ready for sale, **A** GENERAL assortment of WINTER GOODS [see like ad Vol. II No. 86] ■ **William Hartshorne and Company,** Have removed their Store to Fairfax-street, opposite to Joseph Janney's, where they have for Sale, on reasonable Terms, for Cash or country Produce [see like ad Vol. II No. 87] ■ HUGH NELSON, York, offers for lease 2,600 acres of land in the county of Frederick [see like ad Vol. II No. 86] ■ SAMUEL ABELL, Sheriff of St. Mary's Co., Md., offers reward for return of Thomas Valentine who broke gaol [see like ad Vol. II No. 85] ■ ALX: Printed by GEORGE RICHARDS, and COMPANY, at their Printing-Office on *Fairfax-street*--by whom *Advertisements*, &c. are thankfully received for this Paper,--and where Printing is performed with Care and Expedition.

1785/10/13, Vol. II No. 89

Page 1. NATHANIEL WEEDON has for sale 150 acres of land in Loudon County [see like ad Vol. II No. 88] ■ WILLIAM SCOTT offers for sale sundry blooded horses [see like ad Vol. II No. 88] ■ The executors of JOHN ALEXANDER, deceased, reschedule sale of lots [see like ad Vol. II No. 88] ■ JOHN SUTTON has for sale all stock in trade belonging to John Sutton [see like ad Vol. II No. 88] ■ ☞ A great Variety of BLANKS, printed on Good Paper, may be had at the Printing-Office. ■ HENRY LYLES announces opening of the Alexandria Inn and Coffee-House [see like ad Vol. II No. 87] ■

CLEMENT HILL, near Upper-Marlborough, seeks return of runaway horse [see like ad Vol. II No. 88] ■ SAMUEL ABELL, Sheriff of St. Mary's Co., Md., offers reward for return of Thomas Valentine who broke gaol [see like ad Vol. II No. 85]

ALGIERS, June 27. On the 5th a French ship from Cadiz entered this port with M. Le Compte D'Espily, charged with full power from the King of Spain to treat for peace. On the 7th, the Compte had an audience with the Dey, who received him in a very friendly manner. On the 12th, two Spanish men of war of 74 guns, a frigate of 36, and a brigantine of 18, under command of Rear Admiral Don J. Massorado, came into the Roads near the Castle, displaying the white flag. Next morning the Dey sent out a boat, bearing also a white flag, in which were the French Consul, his Chancellor, and the Captain of the port, who remained on board until three in the afternoon; on their departure the Spanish Commander saluted with 7 guns. The Consul reported to the Dey that the Commander had come expressly, by order of the King, to conclude a peace, to which the Dey answered that "it was well," and he was pleased with his intention. **Vienna, July 16:** It is reported the Empress of Russia will furnish the Emperor with 30,000 Tartar cavalry, completely equipped for war, at 30 florins per head. It is said the Emperor set out to Petersburg on September 1st. **Rotterdam, July 30:** Last Monday morning at 6, an extraordinary courier arrived from Vienna with news the commissioners of the Republic had experienced a most gracious reception from his Imperial Majesty, who assured them he would immediately issue orders for the pacific negotiation to be resumed at Paris, between his Minister and those of the Republic, mediated by his Most Christian Majesty. ■ **LONDON, August 6.** Admitting the French prohibitary edict will in some degree affect the consumption of British goods in that country, we may expect new demand in other markets--as the proudest nation on earth thus publicly declares to the world that English manufactures are superior ... Great preparations have been making for some months for a grand naval review at Portsmouth, at which his Majesty will be present. The friends of anarchy conceive these preparations are for more serious work. However, the above is the fact ... The East India Company have given leave to a Company of private adventurers to fit out two ships on a trading voyage to Kamtchatka, and environs, which--with the quality of furs abounding there--may be a very advantageous undertaking. One of the *Resolution*'s officers, the vessel last there, purchased furs for 15-20 pounds of European goods which netted him upwards of £250 in London ... The fleet at Spithead is designed for only a short cruise--perhaps only to maneuver the ships, perhaps to observe French moves--but at any rate not to bring on any question with our rival nation. Those who know our condition are sensible we cannot covet war, and intelligent men are sensible there is a very good reason why France will not push us to one. The Prince will continue afloat during the cruise, and be made a Post Captain after his arrival ... A gentleman who came from New Brunswick a short time since declares that in a few years [Continued on Page 2].

Page 2. [New Brunswick News (*continued*)] the new settlers will be able to supply the West India Islands with everything formerly gotten from New England. The number of settlers increases rapidly, and progress in land clearing is astonishing. ■ **BASSETERRE, (St. Kitt's) August 27.** On the 24th at half after eleven at night, there commenced the most severe hurricane since the fatal one of 1772. Damage in town is trifling, but the country has suffered considerably, although we have yet but few particulars. The estate of Anthony Somersall, sen.,Esq., St. Ann Parish, has lost all buildings but the residence. The dwelling house of John St. Ledger Douglass, Esq. In St. Peter Parish, Basseterre, is partly unroofed.

When the gale began, there were only 6 sail of vessels in the road who all put to sea. The *Spooner*, Capt. Loran, since drove on shore and lost, crew saved. The *Thomas*, Capt. Purber [Furber?], gone ashore, cargo and crew saved. The brig *Venus*, Capt. Clarkson; Mr. Priddie's schooner *Hazard*, Capt. Gadderer; Messrs. Stack and M'Namara's schooner *Jane*, Capt. Lodwick; were drove out and not since heard of. Mr. Tyson's schooner *Betsey*, Capt. Ridstrum, is ashore below Old Road.

We have just been informed from Deep Bay that five vessels are run on shore and lost there, three the property of Mrs. Woods and Capt. Richard Basden, one of Mr. Patrick Burke's, and the other of Mr. Forbes--and that houses and estates in that parish have suffered considerably.

As far as we can judge by the injury the canes have suffered in this Parish, we may venture to assert that one half of the next year's crop is lost, the forward pieces are entirely ruined, and the young sprouts so whipped and twisted they will not recover, even by moderate and seasonable weather, so as to make near as much sugar as was expected from them a few days ago. ■ **St. JOHN's,** (Antigua)

August 26. Wednesday night around ten began a north east gale which turned violent about twelve, and continued so until morning. The vessels in the harbour rode it out tolerably well, except an American brig and some small craft which went on shore. Three of the latter (droughers) were totally lost, viz. A sloop of Mr. John Smith coming round from Willoughby Bay with sugars, went on shore at the Hawksbill and bilged. A sloop of Mr. William Smith went to pieces, and another of Mr. Michael Pratt, with no hands on board, drove to sea and overset. We have not heard of any lives lost. Many trees are torn up by the roots, others rent almost to pieces, a great deal of damage to the stand-over canes, and a large quantity of Indian corn nearly ready to reap is destroyed. Fortunately the ensuing crop was very backward, by which means it sustained no very material injury. The sky still wears a gloomy and unsettled aspect, and we fear that all is not yet over ... **Sept. 2:** From the appearance of the weather after the gale, until Tuesday morning, most people were apprehensive we should have another storm--especially as the 1772 hurricane was preceded by similar threatenings. Yesterday and today the wind has been variable, both days remarkably sultry. A small schooner belonging to this port, Capt. Dapwell, out in the gale, has since put into St. Bartholomew's. Several vessels in the harbour ran on shore, and a brig, schooner and sloop lost. An elegant house lately erected for the Swedish Governor was blown down, and much damage done in the country. From Dominica we hear the government sloop was run on shore with 4 small craft, and all lost. The vessel which brings the account was at a distant part from the capitol (Rosseau) and does not speak very particularly as to these circumstances, or the loss in buildings and plantations ... **CUSTOM HOUSE, St. JOHN's,** August 26, 1785: To be sold at this office on Thursday the 1st of September next, at 12 o'clock precisely, the brigantines *Hazard* and *Little Tom*, with their tackle, apparel and furniture, condemned in the Vice Admiralty Court of this island. At the same time will be sold the cargoes of the said vessels, consisting of staves, shingles, flour, hickory hoops, &c. Also condemned in the said Court. ■ **PORTSMOUTH,** (N.H.) **September 16.** It is with pleasure we report that a military spirit is beginning to spread itself in several parts of this State; one regiment will be completely uniformed completely in American homespun. We hope the spirit spreads throughout New Hampshire, and that--at the expected review--the first regiment in this State will not be the last for *martial* appearance and *proficiency* in military discipline. ■ **SALEM, Sept. 20.** Four women now living in a town in this State, being daughter, mother, grandmother, and great grandmother were so lately brought to bed that they all now suckle their respective infants. ■ **BOSTON, September 22.** Extract of a letter from a gentleman in **London of July 1, 1785**, to his friend in this town: Mr. ----- accompanied Mr. Adams to the King's levee, after which according to custom Mr. Adams was introduced to the King's closet where (as is usual for foreign Ministers) he made a speech to his Majesty, in performing which he was somewhat affected. The King replied: the whole of this business is so extraordinary that the feelings you discover upon the occasion appear to me just and proper. I wish to be clearly understood before replying to the obliging sentiments you have expressed in behalf of the United States of America. I was the last person in England to consent to the empire's dismemberment, and accordingly prosecuted the war to the utmost. But I consented to their independence, ratified by treaty. I receive you as minister Plenipotentiary, and you shall receive all respect and protection granted others here. Just as I was the last to consent, so I would be the last to disturb things. I hope and trust from blood, religion, manners, habits of intercourse, and almost every other consideration, that the two nations will continue for ages in friendship and confidence with each other. (Lord Carmarthen, Secretary of State, who was the only other person present, repeated all to Mr. ----- the day after; and which, for its manliness and propriety, deserves to be written in letters of gold.) Mr. Adams as then presented to the Queen, to whom he made a speech (as is customary.) She thanked him for his friendly expressions toward her and her family, and was very happy to see him in England. ■ **NEW HAVEN, September 1.** The following are the officers appointed in this State in May last, to command the troops raised for the defence of our frontiers: Major John P. Wyllys; Captains Jonathan Hart, David Strong; Lieutenants Jacob Wilcox, John Pratt, ----- Forthingham; Ensigns Jacob Kingsbury, David Bissell. On the 27th ultimo, 60 of the above troops marched to West Point, under command of Capt. Hart. Several smaller detachments have since marched, amounting in the whole to about 90 ... **Sept. 21:** On Friday the 16th, *Holy Orders* were administered in Trinity Church here, by the Right Reverend Bishop Seabury, when three gentlemen were admitted *Deacons*, and three ordered *Priests*--and on Sunday the 18th four were *promoted* to the same *Holy Order* in *Christ's Church*. The solemnity of the offices, and the devout behaviour of the candidates, impressed the minds of those present with sensations of reverence and delight, more easily to be imagined than described. ■ **NEW YORK,**

Sept. 30. The master of a ship from Nova Scotia reports the French have sent an armament of four sail of the line, and some lighter ships, to Cape Breton, to prevent the English from erecting any military works in that part of the world. ■ **PHILADELPHIA, October 1.** Last Monday evening DOCTOR FRANKLIN attended the meeting of the *Union Fire Company,* which he founded here in 1736. There are only four now living who composed it at its first formation. The present members are chiefly descendants of his colleagues, and felt greatly honored by his presence. He signed the new articles, and said he would have his buckets, &c. In good order by the next meeting.

The proposed measure of conveying the mail holds advantages: expedition, regularity of communication, and saving the public nearly 5000 guineas *per annum.* For the stage proprietors propose not only to carry the mail for half that now given post riders, but the numerous way-letters which generally pass through that channel subject to no postage whatever, will of course come into the mail ... **Oct. 4:** The intendants and wardens of Charleston, S.C., in city council convened, have passed an ordinance to suppress E.O. tables within that city. The fine for opening or setting up any such table is one hundred pounds ... We hear an American vessel from Boston, with a British Register, has been seized and confiscated at Antigua ... By the Spanish packet just arrived from Vera Cruz and Havanna we learn the frigate *Agneda* was arrived at the latter port with three millions of dollars, to pay off the last debts of that government; and that the frigate *Matilda* from Philadelphia also arrived there. ■ **RICHMOND, October 1.** *Abridgement of politics in the Western Country, March, 1785*: In the new State called FRANKLAND, the General Assembly met for the first time, passed several laws to promote their internal interests, and appointed a Commissioner to carry a representation to Congress, expressing their desire to be under the protection of the Federal Government. *April:* Governor Martin published a long manifesto, opposed, and using some threats in case the new authority was not given up. *May*: The people of Kentucky met in convention debated the question of their separation, and set another meeting for August. About this same time similar measures were taken in Washington County, drawing the Virginia Government's attention, and it is thought by means of misrepresentation, excited it to adopt wrong measures. *June:* Gov. Martin's manifesto circulated in the western Country, was ingeniously answered by two different hands, and was afterward held in much derision. The annual election of Assemblymen for the new State took place, generally demonstrating the good sense and independence of the electors. Also, the Commissioner from Congress returned greatly satisfied with his reception. *July:* the Executive of Virginia took extraordinary measures against the friends for new States. This produced a spirited remonstrance and general alarm over the infringement of constitutional privileges. *August:* The new Assembly of Frankland met, set a time for a Convention to amend the constitution, and chose a Commissioner to the North Carolina Assembly, as a very friendly overture was made by the present Governor Caswell, and some others, the first characters of that State ... In Kentucky the new Convention met and appointed two Committees--one to report objections, the other reasons for separation; being reported and debated in a Committee of the whole, all opposition subsided and a separation was unanimously resolved on. In Washington the measures of Government operate so as to increase the number of friends for a new State. ■ **ANNAPOLIS, October 6.** The following letter to a gentleman in Philadelphia from the celebrated Dr. Price is worthy of the attention of every friend to America; an author whose writings are so important and valuable, and whose endeavours for the prosperity of this country have been so clearly demonstrated, merits our highest esteem. It is therefore to be wished that every state in the Union would adopt the sentiments [Continued on Page 3].

Page 3. [The Dr. Price Letter (*continued*)] of the venerable Doctor in this letter; such conduct will reflect a glory on our republican governments, and render them respectable to every free country. He feels that Pennsylvania's test law is contrary to every principle of justice and good policy. Although the test is so expressed that real friends to the American cause (and particularly Quakers) might scruple to take it, it deprives two fifths of the people of the rights of citizenship. The Doctor's "Observations upon the American Revolution" moved one critic to accuse him of utopianism, but Doctor price still hopes the American revolution will prove an introduction to a better state of human affairs. [Signed: RICHARD PRICE, Newington Green, July 22, 1785.]

ALX, October 13. The following is extracted from a particular Account of the Treatment of Capt. Ervin and his People, whose Arrival here from Morocco, via Cadiz, we mentioned in our last: --"Capt. Ervin, being ordered before the Emperor at Morocco, among other Things, was asked what Religion he professed, and whether the Americans worshipped the Sun, Moon and Stars?--On his informing him the

Americans worshipped one God who ruled in Heaven, he replied, then I am at Peace with your Nation; but ordered him and his People to Moggadore, where they were put under the Care of a Jew, who supplied the Captain with Money weekly, taking an Account of the same, to furnish him and his People with Provision.--Some Time afterwards the Emperor arrived at Moggadore, where the Captain and Crew were ordered before him, when he informed them, that he did not consider them as Slaves, and that they were at Liberty to go about the Country without Molestation, but that they must not attempt an Escape from his Dominions, until some Person appeared to release them; and that he considered the Americans as free a People as Englishmen, and ought to pay him the same Respect as other Christian Nations did.--After some Stay at Moggadore, they were all ordered again before the Emperor at Morocco, who told them they were given up to the Spanish Ambassador; and that they were to be sent to Cadiz, where they were to be delivered to Mr. Harrison, the American Consul.--He then asked them if they had been well used, and if they had had sufficient Supply of Provisions during their Stay in his Dominions, to which they replied in the Affirmative.--He then said that he should send Orders to his Bashaw to restore them every Thing which belonged to them.--From Morocco they were ordered to Tangiers, where they embarked on board a Spanish Ship for Cadiz." ■ The General Assembly of Pennsylvania have lately passed an Act, laying additional Duties on certain Manufactures imported into that State, whether in foreign Vessels of those of any other State, for the Encouragement of their own Manufactures. ■ The Sloop *Experiment*, Capt.Stewart Dean, arrived at Madera, on the 20th of August, in 30 Days from New-York. ■ DIED.] Mrs.SARAH MANLEY, Relict of JOHN MANLEY, Esq; -- At Dumfries, Mrs. NANCY WEST, Wife of Mr.ROGER WEST. ■ NAVAL-OFFICE, ALX. *Inward Entries*. Sloop *Phebe*, J. [Cartwright], from St. Lucia; Brig *Industry*, P. Moore, Madera; Sloop *Favorite*, A. Banks, Tortola; Schooner *Hopewell*, B. Rig, and Sloop *Sally Moore*, J. Cooper, George-Town. *Cleared Outwards*. Schooner *Lottery*, Z. Mann, for Baltimore; Schooner *Nepa*, J. Bishop, Barbadoes.

PRICES CURRENT, ALX. / Tobacco, 25s. per Ct. / Fine Flour, 28s. per Barrel. / Wheat, 5s. per Bushel. / Jamaica Spirits, 4/6 per Gallon. / Windward Rum, 3s. per Ditto. / Continental Rum, 2s. per Ditto. / Molasses, 1/6 per Ditto. / Muscovado Sugar, 35s. to 42/6 per Ct. / Salt, 3s. per Bushel, by Retail. / Corn, 3s. per Bushel. / Exchange, 40.

On Saturday the 15th Instant, will be Sold at the Vendue-Store, said to be for the Benefit of Underwriters,

AN elegant collection of books, a bale of blankets, cloths, and coarse and fine linens. And on Monday the 17th, being Fairfax Court day, will be sold, a variety of WET and DRY GOODS, consisting of rum in hogsheads and barrels, sugars, chocolate, hyson and green teas, &c. a likely young Negro woman well acquainted with house-work, and a healthy boy about 8 years of age; also, a waggon and four good horses. And on Tuesday the 18th, on Harper and Watson's wharf, will be sold about thirty hogsheads of Barbadoes spirits, and a quantity of muscovado sugar of the first quality.

☞ To be sold at private sale, a dray and two good horses, or will be exchanged for a good road horse.

S. ARELL, Vendue-Master.

October 13, 1785.

Hooe and Harrison, HAVE FOR SALE, ALUM, and Cadiz salt, Madera wine, French Brandy, Bottled claret, Sailcloth, Cordage, Anchors, German steel, Hyson tea, Hampers of stone ware, &c.&c., ALX, October 13, 1785.

THE Ship *UNION*, commanded by Capt. GILES SULLIVAN, now lying in this port, will take tobacco on freight, for London, with liberty of consignment, at £.7 sterling per ton, and will be ready to begin her lading in a few days.--The *Union* is perhaps as fine a merchantman as has been built in Virginia; and has good accommodations for passengers.--For terms, apply to the Captain on board, or

HOOE and HARRISON.

ALX, October 13, 1785.

William Wilson, Has for Sale, at his Store, on Fairfax-Street, A GENERAL assortment of FALL GOODS, which he will dispose of on very low terms, for cash or produce.--He has also for sale, Lisbon salt, a few pipes of old Madera wine, Barbadoes spirits, dipped and mould candles, canvas No. 6 and

7, and cordage. ALX, October 13, 1785. ■ **D. and I. M'Pherson,** Have for Sale, at their Store, A Quantity of choice West-India rum, muscovado sugar and Madera wine.--They give ready-money and a good price for wheat, flour and Indian-corn. ALX, October 13, 1785. ■ **William Taylor and Co.**, Have for Sale, at their Store on Fairfax-Street, formerly occupied by Messrs. Lowry and M'Kenna, and next Door but one to Col. Dennis Ramsay's Store, A LARGE assortment of EUROPEAN GOODS, suitable to the season, which they will sell on reasonable terms, by wholesale or retail, for cash or country produce. ALX, October 13, 1785. ■ **Wanted, to wait on a Lady,** A GIRL, about 12 years of age; she must be of creditable parents, of a good disposition, and active, and know something of plain needlework, in which she will be further instructed.--A person answering the above description, may hear of an agreeable situation, by applying to the Printers. October 13, 1785. ■ General Post-Office, September 17, 1785. THE United States in Congress assembled, having resolved, "That the Post-Master-General be authorised and instructed, under the direction of the Board of Treasury, to enter into contracts, under good and sufficient security, for the conveyance of the different mails, by the stage carriages, from Portsmouth, in the State of New-Hampshire, to the town of Savannah, in the State of Georgia, and from the city of New-York, to the city of Albany, in the State of New-York, according to the accustomed route: NOTICE is hereby given (pursuant to directions from the Honorable the Commissioners of the Treasury) That the Post-Master-General is ready to receive proposals for contracts for the aforesaid purpose.--And that the proprietors of the stage carriages already erected, as well as those persons who may incline to erect new ones between the places specified in the resolution of Congress, may be enabled to make their proposals with greater precision, they are informed, that the following will be considered as essential articles of the contract, viz. The mail to be carried (both going and returning) to every post-office in the route, three times in every week, except between the cities of New-York and Albany, and between the city of New-York and the town of Portsmouth, in New-Hampshire; on which route it will be expected only twice in each week *during the winter season*. The mail to be taken from and delivered at each post-office, by the proprietors of the stages or their agents at stated hours; and a reasonable time (after the receipt of the mail by the Post-Master) allowed for receiving letters, and making up another mail to be forwarded: This time not to exceed one quarter of an hour at small offices, nor two hours at capital ones. In case of accidents happening to the stage, the mail to be forwarded, so as to reach each office at the stated hour, at the expence of the proprietors of the stage. A secure and convenient place in each carriage, to be set apart for the reception of the mail, and appropriated solely to that purpose: This place to be lined and covered with painted canvas, so as to keep out rain and snow, and to have a good lock and key. The proprietors of the stages to be answerable for the care and fidelity of the persons employed in carrying and delivering the mail. The proprietors and their drivers to be under oath not to carry, or suffer to be carried in their stages, any letters or newspapers, but what they shall deliver into a post-office. Bond with two sufficient sureties, to be given for the fulfilment of the contract. Portmanteaus and gabs for containing the letters, to be furnished at the expence of the United States. The sums agreed upon for carrying the mails, to be paid by the Post-Master-General, in four equal quarterly payments; each payment to be made punctually at the expiration of each quarter. The contract to continue for one year. Any person willing to contract for the carriage of the mails, or either of them, are desired to send their proposals (by post) to the Post-Master-General, at his office, No. 55, Queen-street, New-York, on or before the 17th of October next, after which no proposals will be received. By order of the Post-Master-General, JAMES BRYSON, Assistant. ■ Richmond, October 7, 1785. THE President and Directors for opening and extending the navigation of James river, give this public notice, that they are desirous of employing a proper person to superintend the hiring and management of a large number of labouring hands to be engaged in said work. No person need apply without producing to the Directors proper credentials of his capacity and fitness for conducting the said business, JOHN HARVIE, EDMUND RANDOLPH, DAVID ROSS, WILLIAM CABELL. ■ To be Let on Ground-Rent, for Ninety-nine Years, TWO LOTS, on Duke-street, near Colonel Hooe's warehouse, and three adjoining my wharf, very convenient to the river either for stores, warehouses or dwelling-houses.--The Subscriber has likewise a DWELLING-HOUSE to rent, by the year, which has three rooms on the lower floor and four above, with a back yard, suitable for a garden or other conveniencies.--The plat of the lots may be seen, and the terms of the whole made known, by applying to THOMAS FLEMING. ALX, October 13, 1785. ■ THE FALMOUTH RACES, formerly advertised to commence on the Fourth Monday in October, is postponed till the Fifth Monday of the same month, on account of its interfering with the Alexandria Races. DANIEL TRIPLETT, Secretary and Treasurer, September 27, 1785.

Page 4. Poetry. From the *Edinburgh Weekly Magazine*, "Epitaph on Hogarth, in Chiswick Church-Yard'." ■ G. WEEDON has for sale a tract of land two miles of the Roundhill Church, Washington's Mill and Machodick Warehouses [see like ad Vol. II No. 87] ■ WILLIAM LYLES and CO., is selling rum [see like ad Vol. II No. 68] ■ DANIEL CARROLL, jun., Montgomery Co., Md., offers reward for return of runaway named Joe [see like ad Vol. II No. 78] ■ The Sloop *Industry*, James Rob, Master, is to sail for Boston [see like ad Vol. II No. 87] ■ RALPH WORMELEY, jun., Berkeley Co., has lands for sale [see like ad Vol. II No. 87] ■ WILLIAM HARTSHORNE has for sale a lot at the corner of Wolf and Washington streets, and one on Fairfax-street near the corner of Gibbon-street [see like ad Vol. II No. 75] ■ JOHN PAGE has 1,000 acres for sale on Bull-Run in Loudon Co. [see like ad Vol. II No. 87] ■ SAMUEL BAKER has for sale in Winchester, Va., 40 valuable slaves of the property of the late Robert Burwell, deceased [see like ad Vol. II No. 87] ■ RAPHAEL BOARMAN, Cornwallis's-Neck, Charles Co., Md., offers reward for return of runaway woman [see like ad Vol. II No. 83] ■ To be sold, at the Printing-Office, A Variety of Blank Books, consisting of Ledgers, Journals, Cash-Books, Letter-Books, &c.&c. Also, Stoughton's Bitters, Anderson's Pills, Daffy's Elixir, Balsam of Honey, Squire's Elixir, Bateman's Drops, Godfrey's Cordial, &c.&c.&c. ■ **Robinson, Sanderson and Rumney,** have fall goods for sale just arrived on the Ship *Peggy* [see like ad Vol. II No. 86] ■ Lot for sale on Prince-street [see like ad Vol. II No. 88] ■ PATRICK MURRAY announces his newly finished livery stable [see like ad Vol. II No. 85] ■ WILLIAM NOURSE seeks to settle accounts of James Nourse, Esq., deceased [see like ad Vol. II No. 87] ■ JOHN STEED, living near Bath, Berkeley Co., offers reward for return of runaway servant man named William Kelly [see like ad Vol. II No. 88] ■ JAMES DUNCANSON, Fredericksburg, offers reward for return of runaway mulatto woman named Molly [see like ad Vol. II No. 87] ■ F. Cox, sen., offers reward for return of runaway from David Ashton's, Westmoreland County [see like ad Vol. II No. 86] ■ ALX: Printed by GEORGE RICHARDS, and COMPANY, at their Printing-Office on *Fairfax-street*--by whom *Advertisements*, &c. are thankfully received for this Paper,--and where Printing is performed with Care and Expedition.

1785/10/20, Vol. II No. 90

Page 1. HENRY LYLES announces opening of the Alexandria Inn and Coffee-House [see like ad Vol. II No. 87] ■ **The ALX Town-Purse. O**N Saturday the 22d instant, will be run for, the TOWN-PURSE of FIFTY GUINEAS, free for any horse, mare, or gelding (the winning horses the two preceding days excepted.) Aged horses carrying nine stone; six years old, eight stone, seven pounds; five years old, seven stone ten pounds; four years old, seven stone; and three years old, a feather; the best two in three four mile heats. On no account will two horses belonging to the interest of any one man, be allowed to start for the purse. Three horses to start, or no race. ALX, October 20, 1785. ■ WILLIAM LYLES and CO., is selling rum [see like ad Vol. II No. 68] ■ Lot for sale on Prince-street [see like ad Vol. II No. 88] ■ WILLIAM HARTSHORNE has for sale a lot at the corner of Wolf and Washington streets, and one on Fairfax-street near the corner of Gibbon-street [see like ad Vol. II No. 75] ■ WANTED TO HIRE, **A** Smart active Negro WENCH, who understands cooking, washing and ironing, and who can be well recommended for her honesty and sobriety.--Inquire at the Printing-Office. October 20, 1785.

From the ENGLISH CHRONICLE: *As every circumstance which can in the least elucidate the terrible catastrophe of M. Pilatre de Rozier, cannot but interest those who were honored with his acquaintance, or informed of his virtues, we trust it will be unnecessary to apologize to our readers for inserting a letter from one of his most intimate friends, particularly as it will tend to present us with the cause of his destruction in a very striking point of view, and all the accounts hitherto published, have been imperfect.*

Bologna, June 25, 1785: [The writer, one **DURIEZ**, gives a detailed, eye witness account of the accident in which the world famous balloonist, Rozier, died. The narrative, which ends with hypotheses as to causes, is as complete as one from the Federal Aviation Administration, and the National Transportation Safety Board. Here we give only a summary.--Eds.] After six months preparation, the Montgolfier was launched at 7:05 a.m., and rose to 3600 feet. Observers then saw M. De Rozier and M. De Romain under much agitation in their gallery.

Rozier valved-off some of the balloon's inflammable air. The balloon descended a little, but then a light vapor issued from the upper part of it, from that a two foot flame which mushroomed to a ball of fire twice the balloon's size. All fell to earth, the men crushed on impact. The writer believes the cause to have been an electrical charge passing from one cloud to another, through the inflammable gas.

Page 2. . **LONDON, August 6.** SOME politicians offer considerable wagers that the new States are divided among the different powers of Europe in the course of five years. This is certain, that if the Europeans could agree about the division--the boasted dominion of the new States would be sunk into separate dependencies in a hurry.

The sinking fund, prior to the American war, produced more than two millions three hundred thousands pounds in the course of one year; Mr. Pitt expects such again before Ladyday, 1787. So fortunate it is for this country that we now have an honest man at the Helm. As to the last Ministry, Faro and Hazard, and cocks and horses, and girls, would have sunk all surpluses, and left the Treasury--like Falstaff--purse-drained to the utmost farthing.

The Chancellor was right, that nobleman has a manliness of mind, which will not stoop to the disguise of any honest sentiments that occur to him. That France has spies and emissaries in Ireland is beyond question; that she may have them here, too, and that they may watch the debates of both houses, is equally probable. It was indeed observed at the time the learned Lord made the remark, that a well dressed foreigner, who is a constant attendant, walked off soon after.

Lord North is so heartily sick of his new connexions, as hardly ever to be seen by any of them; his orders to the porter are, let in the old set who came here during the war, but as to Blue and Buffs, shut, shut the door, good John--on Charles and Ned, tie up the knocker, swear I'm sick, I'm dead.

By an antient ordinance of Spain, still in force, the Captains of ships of war are commanded to *perish* rather than lower the Royal flag when once hung out! Surely, then, an English Captain will not suffer the flag of his country to be insulted. Even the Roman fleet--mere boats compared to the modern British--maintained a Sovereignty in its own seas! ■ **CHARLESTON,** (S.C.) **Sept. 15.** From the Intelligence Office we learn the rice exported from the 3rd December, 1784, to the 30th July, 1785, 52,286 whole barrels, 5,750 half barrels. Negroes imported from Africa, the West Indies, and different parts of the continent, from March 17, 1785 to September, 1786, 2,445 ... Our *good* friends the British prophesy America cannot much longer exist as a sovereign and independent nation, under the pressure of her many difficulties: distracted state of commerce, lack of a circulating medium, distrust of Congress, a want of public faith, &c. &c. These, say the ministerial scribblers, cannot fail to sap and undermine the glorious fabric we have spent so much blood and treasure to erect. But we trust that the great guardian of the rights of mankind, will encircle the fair frame of liberty with his myriads of angels, and inspire every true American with virtue to defend it--dispel those clouds that intercept its rays--and thereby render the above predictions abortive. ■ **BOSTON, September 12.** The English Papers mention that the unfortunate Col. Palfrey, of this town, who was taken on his passage to France where he was to be U.S. Consul General and Commercial Agent, is yet in existence, in Algiers. Why is he not ransomed? His official character alone ought certainly to induce Congress to endeavour his redemption. We have too great an opinion of the justice and philanthropy of that August body to suppose they have not, and if they have, why has not his family been acquainted with it? ■ **NEW YORK, Oct. 3.** The Irish propositions having undergone great alterations, disgustful in the highest degree to the Irish Parliament, as well as the whole manufacturing interest of Great Britain, a number of principal personages from both houses presented an address to his Britannic Majesty on July 27: For an advantageous and permanent commercial settlement between his Majesty's kingdoms of Great Britain and Ireland, we have proceeded on the foundation of the rights of the Parliament of Ireland. An advantageous and lasting commercial agreement must be just and equitable; Ireland's subjects, ships and mariners must enjoy the same privileges with those of Great Britain, and secured by legislation of the Parliament of Ireland in order to be in valid for Irish citizens. ■ **PHILADELPHIA, October 1**. An act to encourage and protect the manufactures of this State, by laying additional duties on the importation of certain manufactures which interfere with them. Enacted September 20, and seal affixed. *The following are the articles enumerated in this act, and subject to the duties annexed.* Upon any coach, chariot or landau or other carriage, having four wheels, the sum of *twenty pounds*. Upon every chaise, chair, kittereen, curricle or other carriage, having two wheels, *ten pounds*; and in the same proportion for any part of such carriage. Upon every clock, *thirty shillings*. Upon every dozen packs of playing cards, *seven shillings and sixpence*. Upon every dozen reaping hooks and sickles, *twelve shillings and sixpence*. Upon every dozen scythes, except Dutch and

German, *fifteen shillings*. Upon every hundred weight of refined sugar, *eight shillings and fourpence*. Upon every gallon of beer, ale, porter, and cyder, *sixpence*. Upon every dozen bottles of beer, porter or cyder, *four shillings*. Upon all malted barley, or other malted grain, *five per centum ad valorem*. Upon all salted or dried fish, *seven shillings and sixpence*, for every hundred weight thereof. Upon every hundred weight of cheese and butter, *eight shillings and fourpence*. Upon all beef, *two per centum ad valorum*. Upon all pork, *five per centum ad valorum*. Upon every pound of soap, except Castile soap, *one penny*. Upon every pound of chocolate, *fourpence*. Upon every pound of candles, tallow or wax, *one penny*. Upon every pound of glue, *twopence*. Upon every pound of starch and of hair powder, *one penny*. Upon all hulled barley, dried peas, and mustard, *ten per centum ad valorem*. Upon all manufactured tobacco, other than snuff, *sixpence* for every pound thereof. Upon every pound of snuff, including the bottles, canister, or other package, *one shilling*. Upon all lampblack, cotton and wool cards, manufactured leather, pasteboards, parchment, writing, printing, wrapping and sheathing paper, and paper hangings, *ten percentum ad valorem*. Upon every pair of mens' and womens' leather shoes, *two shillings*. Upon every pair of womens' stuft shoes or slippers, *one shilling*. Upon every pair of boots, *five shillings*. Upon every saddle, for mens' or womens' use, *twelve shillings and sixpence*. Upon every ounce of wrought gold, *twenty shillings*. Upon every ounce of wrought silver, *two shillings*. Upon all utensils and vessels of pewter, tin or lead, upon all wrought copper, brass, bellmetal and cast iron, *ten per centum ad valorum*. Upon all British steel, *ten per centum ad valorum*. Upon all slit-iron, nail-rods, and sheet-iron, *ten per centum ad valorum*. Upon all garments ready-made, for mens' and womens' wear, including castor and wool hats, *ten per centum ad valorum*. Upon every beaver hat, *seven shillings and sixpence*. Upon all blank books, bound and unbound, *ten per centum ad valorem*. Upon all tarred cordage, yarns of fixed rigging, *eight shillings and fourpence* for every hundred weight thereof. Upon all white ropes, log-lines, twine and seines, *twelve shillings and sixpence* for every hundred weight thereof. Upon all polished or cut stones, in imitation of jewelry, chimney pieces, and tables, and other polished marble; upon all cabinet and joiners' work, horsemens' whips, carriage whips, walking canes, musical instruments and instruments used in surveying, *ten per centum ad valorem*. Upon all teas imported from Europe or the West Indies, viz. Upon every pound of hyson tea, *sixpence*; upon every pound of other tea, *twopence*. Upon all rum imported in any vessel belonging to any foreign state or kingdom, *sixpence* for every gallon thereof, and the like sum for all rum imported into this state by land or water, from any of the United States, except it should be made to appear by the oath of the exporter, certified by the collector of the port whence it may be last shipped, that it was distilled in the State from whence it be imported, or that it has been imported into that State by vessels belonging to the United States. Upon all wines and fruit, being of the growth of the kingdom of Portugal, or of the territories thereunto belonging, viz. Upon all wines, *one shilling* for every gallon thereof; upon every box of lemons, *five shillings*; upon every hundred weight of raisins, or other fruit, *seven shillings and sixpence*; the said duties to continue as long as the flour of America, is prohibited from being imported into the kingdom and territories aforesaid. Upon every ton of shipping, belonging in whole or in part to any foreign nations or state whatever, except as the honorable the Congress of the United states have entered into treaties of commerce with, *seven shillings and sixpence* for every ton thereof, carpenters' measure for each and every voyage. Upon all ready made nails, *ten per centum ad valorum*. Upon all testaments, psalters, spelling books and primers, in the English and German languages; upon all romances, novels and plays, *fifteen per centum ad valorem*. Upon all horn and tortoiseshell combs, *five per centum ad valorum*. Upon all saddle-trees, *ten per centum ad valorum*. Upon all linens made of flax, *two and a half per centum ad valorum* ... **Oct.7:** Monday last there arrived the sloop *Delaware*, Capt. Warner, from Turk's Island; in lat. 36, 30, in 25 fathoms of water, met the gale on the 24th ult. And was laid on her beam ends about 9 A.M. but by cutting away the mast, got her righted by seven in the evening, but lost everything off the deck; stove all the water, and were reduced to the greatest distress. The Tuesday following, spoke the ship *Nancy*, Capt. Welch, from New York for Charleston, who had rode out the gale under Cape May, from whom they got some supplies. The next day went ashore at Currituck to get supplies, but the gale had been so severe that the sea had made a breach in the sound, and laid the country under water for 2 or 3 miles; washed away many houses, together with almost all their cattle and ground stock; the inhabitants being obliged to take to the trees for safety, notwithstanding which, many lives were lost. The shore for many miles was covered with cattle, household goods, &c. A Virginia built sloop drove ashore in the gale, without any person on board, neither sails, spars or cargo. On the 29th, off Cape Henry, spoke a sloop from Providence, Rhode Island, for Baltimore, Capt. James Pettis, from whom they got a supply of water and other necessaries; the Captain informed, that he saw that day a schooner about 80 tons burthen bottom upwards. Last Friday, spoke a sloop from Washington for this port, that had lost her anchors and cables at Ocracock Bar. On Saturday they met a New England schooner who kindly took them in tow, till they got within our Capes; they could not learn the Captain's name, but acknowledged the favor with gratitude ...

Page 3. Requisitions upon the United States for the year 1785, being an extract from a report of the Grand Committee of Congress on supplies. The Committee have not been able to obtain information on how many States have complied with the resolution of February 17th, or that of April 18th, 1783, relative to a rule for quota ing federal. They are therefore of the opinion, that the several States which have not decided on that subject, be again solicited to come to a decision thereon, and to send forward the same, as a measure necessary to enable Congress to effect a settlement of accounts with the several States, and to apportion to each a just quota of the public expenses; but in the mean time, as the public faith renders it the duty of Congress to continue their annual demand for money, the Committee are of the opinion, that in the appointment thereof, the several States should be quotaed agreeable to justice, on the best information Congress may from time to time have upon the subject. And upon this principle recommend to Congress, that the said sum of three millions of dollars, be quotaed upon the several states, as follow, viz.

	Dollars
New Hampshire	$ 105,416
Massachusetts	448,854
Rhode Island and Providence Plantations	64,636
Connecticut	264,182
New York	256,486
New Jersey	166,716
Pennsylvania	410,378
Delaware	44,886
Maryland	283,034
Virginia	512,974
North Carolina	218,012
South Carolina	192,366
Georgia	32,060
	$3,000,000

Which sums, when paid, shall be passed to the credit of the States respectively, on the terms prescribed by the resolution of Congress of 6th October, 1779, and together with the monies relied on to discharge he aforesaid deduction of 708, 452 dollars, be applied in conformity with the several appropriations in the preceding part of this report, giving preference according to the order in which they are stated in the estimate.

As more than two thirds of the sum called for is to be applied to the payment of interest on the domestic debt, the committee are of the opinion that the several Legislatures may so model the collection of sums called for, that one third of any sum being paid in actual money, the other two thirds may be discharged by the interest due upon loan office certificates, and upon other certificates of the liquidated debts of the U.S. and, to ascertain the evidences of interest due upon loan certificates, the holders thereof respectively shall be at liberty to carry them to the office from which they were issued, and the holders of other certificates of liquidated debts of the U.S., to carry the same to the loan office of the state wherein they are inhabitants, or if a foreigner, to any loan office within the U.S., and to have the interest due thereon settled and certified to the last day of the year 1784. ■ **ANNAPOLIS, October 13.** On Thursday last the Jockey Club Purse of 100 guineas was run over the course near this city, and won by Mr. Pearce's horse, Hotspur. On Friday the Subscription Purse of £75 was won by Mr. Hammersley's horse Spry. Yesterday afternoon a match was run over the course near this city for 100 guineas, by Mr. Hammersley's brown horse Spry, and Mr. Pearce's gray horse Hotspur, which was won hollow by Spry.

Page 3. **ALX, October 20**. Extract of a Letter from a Gentleman in Cadiz to his Friend in this Town, dated August 4, 1785. "We have at length the unexpected Pleasure to inform you, that Captain Ervin and his People have been set at Liberty by the Mediation of his Catholic Majesty, and now return Home by the French Ship *Grandbourg*, Captain LeJoyille.--The Money we have been obliged to advance for their Support whilst detained in Barbary, and to get them Home, we place in your Account.--The Brig is gone to wreck at Tangiers.--We are sorry to find our Navigation exposed to so much Danger in these Seas.--The Moors are still to be feared, and the Algerines, having lately concluded a Truce with Spain, are more formidable than ever, crusing without restraint and spreading their Ravages all along the Coast of Portugal.--They have captured several Vessels belonging to the Portuguese, who, however, are fitting out Frigates, and, we hope, will at least curb their Depredations.--We have often heard that some one was to come on the Part of Congress to settle a Treaty with these Free-Booters, but none has appeared.--If this Master is not attended to, the Consequence will be more sensibly felt than People in general may be aware of." ■ "At a public Examination of the ALX Latin School, held in the Court-House on Friday last, it was agreed to give a Prize to the best Scholar in each Class, in which there more than two Boys.--The First could have none, as it contained only two.--The Judges, after examining the Second for above four Hours, could not determine who was entitled to the Prize.--The Trustees are to attend on a future Day to determine the Matter.--In the Third it was adjudged to Master *Samuel Love*.--And that of the Fourth to Master *William Brown*.--The Fifth and Sixth, as falling under the Description of the First, were not entitled to any. After the Classical Examination was finished, there was a Competition in Speaking English Orations, which each of the Boys had previously prepared.--Master *Samuel Baker*, Master *Thomas Wilson*, Master *Samuel Love*, Master *John Parsons* and Master *James Watson*, were unanimously judged to be the best Speakers.--The Orations being finished, the Company, which was splendid and numerous, were entertained with Music by the Orphean Society, until a few of the Youths prepared to act a Part of the Comedy called the *Miser*--in which Master *Wilson*, personated Scrapely--Master *James Watson*, Justice Nosewell--Master *John M'Crea*, James the Cook--Master *Samuel Love*, the Clerk--Master *Archibald Taylor*, Smoothly--Master *George Thomson*, Mariana--Master *Benjamin Dulany*, Sagely.--In short, the Boys in general acquitted themselves in such a Manner as to answer the most sanguine Expectations of the Judges and Spectators." ■ ☞ The Subscribers to the TOWN-PURSE, to be run for on Saturday next, have thought proper to alter the Heats from Four to Three Miles. ■ NAVAL-OFFICE, ALX. *Inward Entries*. Sloop *Hero*, J. Humphries, Schooner *Pilgrim*, H. Travers, and Schooner *Charlotte*, C. Dukes, from Baltimore; Sloop *Dolphin*, A. Steward, Philadelphia. *Cleared Outwards*. Brig *Christiana*, S. Barnard, for France; Sloop *Washington*, J. Thompson, Philadelphia.

PRICES CURRENT, ALX. / Tobacco, 24s. per Ct. / Fine Flour, 30s. per Barrel. / Wheat, 5s. per Bushel. / Jamaica Spirits, 4/6 per Gallon. / Windward Rum, 3s. per Ditto. / Continental Rum, 2s. per Ditto. / Molasses, 1/6 per Ditto. / Muscovado Sugar, 35s. to 42/6 per Ct. / Salt, 3s. per Bushel, by Retail. / Corn, 3s. per Bushel. / Exchange, 40.

PORTRAIT of a BACHELOR [commentary on the life of a bachelor].

On Saturday the 22d Instant, will be Sold at the Vendue-Store,

A Variety of Merchandise, as usual.

S. ARELL, Vendue-Master.

October 20, 1785.

ALX, October 20, 1785. Ready for the Press, And will be published in a few Months, In One Volume Octavo, LOWE's MASONIC SERMONS, Occasional SPEECHES, And Funeral ORATIONS: As formerly delivered by himself before the Right Worshipful MASTER, the Worshipful WARDENS, and other MEMBERS of St. JOHN's LODGE of FREE and ACCEPTED MASONS, in FREDERICKSBURG. CONDITIONS. The Book will be printed on good Paper, and with an elegant Type. The Price to Subscribers will be One Dollar, One Half paid down at Subscription, and the other Half when the Book is delivered to the Subscribers. As soon as a sufficient Number of Subscribers is acquired, to defray the Expence of the Press Only, the Book will be immediately published. Such Gentlemen as may choose to encourage the Publication, will please to give in their Names to Mr. Charles Elliot, Bookseller, Fredericksburg; Messrs. Goddard and Langworthy, Printers, Baltimore; Mr. Dobson and Mr. Oswald, Printers, Philadelphia; or George Richards and Company, Printers, ALX. ■ **Washington, Butler and Nivison,** Have for sale, at their store in Leed's-Town, on Rappahanock [sic] River, A LARGE assortment of European GOODS, suitable for the season, which they will sell on the most reasonable terms for cash, bills of exchange, country produce, or short credit, upon giving bond with approved security. Leed's-Town, October 19, 1785. ■ WE have several LOTS of GROUND, on different streets in this town, to let on ground-rent--Also, a Piece of Ground, within the south side of our wharf, to let for a term of years. HOOE and HARRISON, ALX, October 20, 1785. ■ **Windsor Chairs**, Of all sorts, made and sold by EPHRAIM EVANS, Late from Philadelphia, at his house at the upper end of Prince-street, ALX. N.B. Any person having good yellow poplar Plank, of two inches thick, and from seventeen to nineteen inches wide, may hear of a purchaser by applying as above. October 20, 1785.

THE Ship *PARAGON*, Capt. HENRY HUGHES, now lying ready in this harbour, will take tobacco on freight, to the address of Messieurs John B. Berard and Company, L'Orient, at forty livres per hogshead.--Those who may be inclinable to ship to the above port, and have not an acquaintance with Messieurs Berard and Company, may be guarantied by applying to us.--The *Paragon* is a fine fast-sailing ship, and has good accommodations for passengers.--For freight or passage, apply to the Captain on board, or

HOOE and HARRISON.

ALX, October 20, 1785.

STRAYED from the Commons of ALX, about nine or ten days ago, a black COW, with a white face, has a few white spots under her belly, of a middling size, and is about 5 years old. Whoever will return said Cow to the Subscriber, shall receive FOUR DOLLARS Reward, and reasonable charges. MICHAEL MADDEN, ALX, October 20, 1785. ■ ☞ A great Variety of BLANKS, printed on good Paper, may be had at the Printing-Office.

Page 4. Poetry. "An Apostrophe to Dame Fortune." ■ NATHANIEL WEEDON has for sale 150 acres of land in Loudon County [see like ad Vol. II No. 88] ■ DANIEL CARROLL, jun., Montgomery Co., Md., offers reward for return of runaway named Joe [see like ad Vol. II No. 78] ■ **Hooe and Harrison** have for sale items [see like ad Vol. II No. 89] ■ HOOE and HARRISON announce the Ship *Union*, Capt. Giles Sullivan, will take on tobacco, and sets sail for London [see like ad Vol. II No. 89] ■ WILLIAM SCOTT offers for sale sundry blooded horses [see like ad Vol. II No. 88] ■ The executors of JOHN ALEXANDER, deceased, reschedule sale of lots [see like ad Vol. II No. 88] ■ JOHN SUTTON has for sale all stock in trade belonging to John Sutton [see like ad Vol. II No. 88] ■ CLEMENT HILL, near Upper-Marlborough, seeks return of runaway horse [see like ad Vol. II No. 88] ■ To be sold, at the Printing-Office, A Variety of Blank Books, consisting of Ledgers, Journals, Cash-Books, Letter-Books, &c.&c. Also, Stoughton's Bitters, Anderson's Pills, Daffy's Elixir, Balsam of Honey, Squire's Elixir, Bateman's Drops, Godfrey's Cordial, &c.&c.&c. ■ **William Wilson** has for sale a general assortment of fall goods [see like ad Vol. II No. 89] ■ **D. and I. M'Pherson** have for sale a quantity of choice West-India rum, etc. [see like ad Vol. II No. 89] ■ **William Taylor and Co.** have for sale at their store on Fairfax-street, a large assortment of European goods [see like ad Vol. II No. 89] ■ Employment for a girl to wait on a Lady, apply to Printing-Office [see like ad Vol. II No. 89] ■ The President and Directors for opening and extending navigation of James river seek superintendent [see like ad Vol. II No. 89] ■ THOMAS FLEMING has for 99-year ground-rent two lots on Duke-street [see like ad Vol. II No. 89] ■ DANIEL TRIPLETT, Secretary and Treasurer of the Falmouth Races, announces one week delay of the race [see like ad Vol. II No. 89] ■ RAPHAEL BOARMAN, Cornwallis's-Neck, Charles Co., Md., offers reward for return of runaway woman [see like ad Vol. II No. 83] ■ ALX: Printed by GEORGE RICHARDS, and COMPANY, at their Printing-Office on *Fairfax-street*--by whom *Advertisements*, &c. are thankfully received for this Paper,--and where Printing is performed with Care and Expedition.

1785/10/27, Vol. II No. 91

Page 1. Messieurs Richard and Company, It seems there has been a great deal of political Scribbling in the Maryland Papers, respecting their Delegates for the General Assembly--One of them, Mr. M'Mechen, has been attacked with particular Severity; and his voting for the Potomack-Bill furnished his Antagonists with a Pretence that he had been acting contrary to the Interests of his Constituents--He was obliged at length to come forward with an Address, in Defence of himself, which, as it displays a Liberality of Sentiment, and the Dictates of an honest Mind, I request you will insert in your next Paper. Yours, &c. A CUSTOMER.

To the **ELECTORS** of **BALTIMORE TOWN**.

Gentlemen, many reports, replete with misrepresentation and falsehood, and injurious to my public character, have lately been circulated in a variety of anonymous publications. [The letter writer here begins his defense--a full page and a third of the four-page paper--which we here only summarize.--Eds.] The duties of my legislative station have been performed with integrity, zeal, and a warm attachment to your interests. I have been slandered over my handling of three subjects: a College on the Western Shore, for opening the Potomack, and laying duties on imports and exports. The Eastern Shore College Bill passed, authorizing an allowance of £1250 per annum; I thought the Western Shore entitled to an equal share. I am charged both with voting for the Potomack Bill, not having *firmness enough to withstand the great personage from Virginia.* Connexion with the Western Country would be an immense source of wealth to this State, and I deemed it a *local prejudice*, in the extreme, to dissent to a scheme for the improvement of these natural advantages, which a number of respectable counties in this State enjoy, and who, as members of the body politic, were entitled to the countenance of the Legislature. Finally, my enemies assert this industrious commercial town is "tottering on its base," intimating the present deplorable situation is occasioned by the weakness and impolicy of your Delegate. The want of a circulating medium is one great cause of our distress; our imports so far exceed our exports as to occasion a constant drain of our specie. I hear no objection to a tax on imports, and I voted only for a *small* duty on exports. I have also heard clandestine insinuations against me as voting for a bill to relieve nonjurors. I confess myself an advocate for obliterating all odious distinctions [Continued on Page 2].

Page 2. [Letter to Baltimore Electors (*continued*)] Since I have been in office, the *local* business of Baltimore Town has been nearly equal to the business of the rest of the State. I do not fear open and manly attacks, but stabbing in the dark is a line of conduct to which a liberal mind can never stoop. Let my enemies present us with their names, and I shall be ever ready to confront them. I beg leave to return my warmest thanks for your confidence. I subscribe myself, Gentlemen, Your most obliged Humble Servant, **DAVID M'MECHEN** Baltimore, 1785. ■ **LONDON, August 5.** On Wednesday Sir Archibald Campbell was at the levee, and took leave of the King on his going to be Governor of Madras, in the room of Lord Macartney ... The speculative politicians seem to concur that the ships preparing for sea are intended for the East Indies, where it is said the French have sent out a very considerable force ... His Majesty's most gracious Answer to the address on the Irish Resolutions [verbatim text printed] expresses his pleasure with the Commercial Settlement worked out, based on full and equal participation of both kingdoms ... A peace hath been concluded between the King of Spain and the Dey of Algiers, with condition that the King give the Regency of Algiers:

Pieces of eight	1,000,000
Brass cannon	25
Iron	ditto
Mortars	4
Bombs	4,000
Bullets	10,000
Quintals of gunpowder	2,000
Quintals of musket shot	5,000
Ditto of cordage	500
Ditto of strong ropes	15
Cables	30
Masts	100
Oars	500
Oak plank for gun carriages	2,000
Pieces of sailcloth	400

Besides these there are certain presents that must be given to the Dey and his ministers. The city of Oran will be as formerly engaged on the land side, and all those who shall be taken prisoners, shall be made slaves.

A new Superintendant is appointed to the port of Brest, and the whole business of the marine and naval department is carrying on with unremitting vigor ... If the Parliament of Ireland retain any idea of their own dignity, or the least regard for the interests or rights of their country, we think it impossible that they should ever assent to the propositions; but even supposing that ministerial influence should carry them through, the time will come when the people of Ireland will disclaim them, and deny them to have been their act ... Extract of a letter from **Paris, July 24:** Last Friday before over 100 persons a man walked across the Seine, beyond the Neuilly bridge, opposite Surrene. He had on his feet a sort of cork buskins, stopped three or four times in the middle of the river, never sank lower than mid-leg, and completed the trip in 61 minutes ... The 4000 Brittany peasants who revolted dispersed at the sight of a regiment; many, taken into custody, are to be tried in Rennes ... According to a recent count in Amsterdam there are 13,861 *widows* now living there! ... **Aug. 8:** A letter from **Madrid, July 2,** says the Infant Don Luis is at the last extremity at Arenas, his usual residence ... The last accounts from America mention that about 20,000 Indians of Buenos Ayres approached the Spanish settlements; the Governor sent 200 foot and 50 horse against them who were nearly cut to pieces. M. De la Peitra, the Intendant, was so struck with this catastrophe he was seized with a fit of apoplexy, and died on the spot ... A vessel from the Havanna arrived at Cadiz with the report the arsenal there burned to the ground, the damage done not ascertainable ... Several couriers from Barcelona with despatches from Count d'Assalto, Commandant there, with an account that the number of French troops in Rousillon and Navarre increase daily. No doubt we shall soon know why. ■ **EDINBURGH, August 1.** This day the foundation stone of the South bridge was laid with great solemnity by the Right

Honorable Lord Haddo, Grand Master Mason of Scotland, in presence of the Right Honorable the Lord Provost and Magistrates, a number of nobility and gentry, and the Masters, Officers, and Brethren of all the Lodges of Free Masons in this city and neighbourhood, besides an innumerable crowd of spectators. The Grand Master at laying the foundation stone, was supported on the right hand by the Duke of Buccleugh, and on the left by the Earl of Belcarras. We have not, upon any occasion, seen a procession so numerous, there being about 800 Brethren, and very properly conducted. ■ **CHARLESTON,** (S.C.) **Aug. 30.** A post will shortly be established to ride from this city to Augusta, via Savannah--of great utility to merchants and others who transact business in the two places, and the public in general. A printing office has recently been established in the town of Augusta by Mr. G. Hughes, who publishes a weekly paper there, and, we are told, meets with very liberal encouragement. A college and a church will speedily be erected, and building is carried on with great rapidity, so that, from its flourishing state (being now the seat of government) we may reasonably presage, it will shortly vie with the capitol of that State ... **Sept. 13:** The North West fur trade is of very great importance to the Americans. The export of peltries last year from Canada was £130,000 sterling. This season a 150 and a 200 man party of Canadians are, with very valuable goods, will explore the N.W. until they reach the S.E. part of America; they do not expect to return in less than 5 years. Ten large vessels are expected in Canada this summer, some of them 600 tons burthen ... The Portuguese discoveries on Africa's west coast are a remarkable instance of the slow progress of arts. In the beginning of the 15th century they were totally ignorant of that coast beyond Cape Non, 28 deg. North latitude. In 1410 Prince Henry fitted out a fleet for discoveries; he proceeded along the coast to Cape Bajadore, in 20 deg. But had not the courage to double it. In 1418, Tristane Vaz discovered the island Porto Santo; and the year after the island of Madera was discovered. In 1439 a Portuguese Captain doubled Cape Bajadore; the next year the Portuguese reach Cape Blanco, lat. 20 deg. In 1446 Nuna Tristan doubled Cape Verd, lat. 14 deg. 40 min. In 1448 Don Gonzallo Valle took possession of the Azores. In 1449, the islands Cape Verd were discovered by Don Henry. In 1471 Pedro d'Escovar discovered the island of St. Thomas, and Prince's Island. In 1486, Bartholomew Diaz, employed by John II of Portugal, doubled the Cape of Good Hope, which he called Cabo Termites, from the tempestuous weather he found in the passage. ■ **PHILADELPHIA, Oct. 13.** Humanity will, no doubt, prompt Americans to give whatever assistance lays in their power to relieve the distresses of the West Indies, occasioned by the late hurricane; but *sound policy* dictates any supplies they can afford should be in American bottoms, as the British have for some time endeavoured to destroy the usefulness of American vessels. A correspondent proposes an immediate embargo on all British bottoms, as least for their loading lumber and provisions. This no doubt is in the power of the Executive Councils of the various States, and this no doubt they will do ... **Oct. 14:** The Honorable James Irvine, Esq. Monday last resigned his appointment of Vice President, when the Honorable Charles Biddle, Esq. Was unanimously chosen to supply the vacancy ... Extract of a letter from **l'Orient, Aug, 5:** A few days ago we heard the Algerines declared war against the United States. The enclosed translation is a faithful copy of a letter written our Consuls, and by them communicated to us. Please to advise thereof any of your friends concerned in the shipping trade. We do not doubt Congress will soon adopt some vigorous measures to quell those troublesome pirates. "Copy of a letter from the Consuls of Nantz, to the Consuls of l'Orient, Gentlemen: we annex to this a copy of a letter we have just received from M. De Soulange, by which he informs us the Algerines have declared war against the United States of America, and that they are fitting out eight ships to take the American vessels.... We have the honor to be, &c." "Copy of M. De Soulange's letter to the Consuls at Nantz: Toulon, 14th July, 1785. Gentlemen, Commodore de Ligondes, who arrived from Algiers, on board the *Minerva* frigate, of which he has the command, has brought me intelligence that said state was fitting out eight ships, both xebecs and barques, from 18 to 36 guns, designed to cruise from Cape St. Vincent's to the Western islands, in order to take Americans, against whom they have declared war. I send you immediate advice thereof, gentlemen, both for your own interest [Continued on Page 3].

Page 3. [Ligonde's Warning Letter (*continued*)] and to request that you will instantly give advice of this to the American Captains. The Algerines have another division of four vessels, but too small to occasion any uneasiness. I am, &c." ... **Oct. 19:** A letter from **Providence, Rhode Island,** says the ship from Nova Scotia that was refused provisions at Boston came here. Our merchants supplied her, which stripped this place to that degree, that flour rose from 34 shillings to 40. Corn so scarce we cannot get any, without an unreasonable price. Rye the same. The ship sailed in the last severe storm we had, she stove to pieces, lost 800 barrels of flour, several hundred bushels of corn, oxen, &c. So that the wind and sea, as well as acts of British Parliament, seem to threaten the *tories* with starving. ■ **BALTIMORE, October 18.** The last advices from Jamaica inform us of a most dreadful hurricane which happened there the 27th of August last. The injury sustained by the town of Kingston is very considerable, and the plantations in the country have experienced a similar fate. Mr. Edie, of the Custom House, has with much industry collected the following particulars done to shipping in the harbour, and on the neighboring coast. "Brig *Swift*, Dove; a ship and a sloop, name unknown, sunk; ships *Hornet*, Campbell; *Amity's Production*, Dale; *Alexander*, Rosiere; brigs *Neptune*, Thompson; *Washington*, Kean; *Philadelphia*, M'Cann; *Adventure*, Brand; schooners *Holland*, Erman; *Favorite*, Camplin; and sloop *Sally*, Patterson, are on shore on the Palisadoes. The packet boat *Swallow*, White, and the ship *Molly*, Arpinal, on shore near Greenwich; ship *Henry*, Dennison; brigs *Hope*, Penlerick; *Success*, Dare; *Mary*, Cortam; and schooner *General Campbell*, Morgan, on shore on the west end and totally wrecked. Several other vessels, names unknown, lost, and some on shore dismasted.

A ship, two brigs, two schooners, and four sloops were dashed to pieces on the Chain of Rocky Keys. The ships *Mary and Ann*, and *Jamaica*, are said to be lost at Annotto Bay. In this dreadful calamity many lives have been lost; several drowned bodies and the mangled fragments of others were hastily interred in the strangers burying place, immediately on their being found ... A letter from a master of a ship to a gentleman in Philadelphia, dated **Cadiz, August 6:** I cannot close this without relating the impediments I met on my passage from England, by the Algerine cruisers. The first was near the Rock of Lisbon, who after a strict scrutiny of my pass and some detention, permitted me to proceed; the next I fell in with off Cape St. Vincent; a large ship then in company with me, drew the attention of the Algerine xebec, who despatched her boat after me, and pursued the ship. Fortunately a breeze sprung up, and gave me the advantage of the boat, who declined her chase, and joined the xebec, who by this time had commenced a running fight with the ship, that was obliged to take shelter under a Spanish fort. The next I fell in with off Cape St. Mary's, who made me hoist my boat out and send my pass on board him, who after a deal of examination, and strict scrutiny into the reality of my pass, suffered me to go on. At 12 o'clock of the night, not being the 10 leagues from Cadiz, was brought to by two more, who served me as before, and the next morning I was joyfully anchored here, where I am told they have extended themselves to the westward of the Western islands in search of American and Portuguese vessels. At present there is a truce subsisting between them and Spain, but it is conjectured it will not terminate in a permanent peace ... Yesterday arrived here, after a passage of eight weeks from Liverpool, the ship *Olive Branch*, Capt. Thomas Patten. ■ **ALX, October 27**. Extract of a Letter from a Gentleman in New-York to another in this Town, dated October 13, 1785. "There is the greatest Reason to apprehend an existing War upon our Trade by Algiers.--The Secretary for Foreign Affairs has been ordered by Congress to send these Communications to the Executives of the different States, that our Commercial People may be on their Guard.--It is certain that Spain has made a Truce with Algiers, so that at present the Trade of Portugal and of the United States of America, seem to be the only Objects left for these People to War upon." ■ His Britannic Majesty's Packet *Carteret*, Capt. Newman, will sail with the Mail from New-York for Falmouth, on Wednesday, the 2d of November. ■ On Monday the 17th Instant, died at New-York, the Honorable SAMUEL HARDY, Esq; a Delegate from this Commonwealth to Congress; and the next Day his Remains were interred in St. Paul's Church-Yard, in that City. The Procession, which was solemn and splendid, was composed of all the Members of Congress, public Officers both Continental and State, and foreign Ambassadors, and a prodigious Concourse of Citizens. Minute Guns were fired on the mournful Occasion, and every other Funeral Honor and Respect was paid to the Remains of that amiable and distinguished Statesman and Senator.

On Friday last was run for over the ALX Course, the ALX Jockey Club Purse of One Hundred Guineas, and was won by Capt. Snickers's Horse *Careless*.

The first Four Mile Heat in 9 Minutes. . . . . Careless, 1st
William Fitzhugh, Esquire's *Targuin*, ... 2d
The second Head in 8M. 54 Sec. . . . . Careless, 1st
. . . . Tarquin, 2d

On the Afternoon of the same Day, the ALX Jockey Club Purse of Fifty Guineas was won by Mr. Hammersley's bay Colt *Spry*.

First Two Mile Heat in 4M. 20 Sec. . . . . Spry, 1st
William Fitzhugh, Esquire's sorrel }
Horse } . . . . . Ironsides, 2d
Mr. Darnal's bay Colt 3d
Gen. Spotswood's gray Colt 4th
The second Heat in 4M. 16 Sec. . . . . Spry, 1st
. . . . Ironsides, 2d
Mr. Darnal's and Gen. Spotswood's Colts . . . . dr.

And on Saturday following, the Town-Purse of Fifty Guineas was won by Gen. Spotswood's *Cumberland*. The first Four Mile Heat in 8M. 35 Sec.

Mr. Hutchings's	*Polydore*, 1st
Mr. Pearce's	*Hotspur*, 2d
Gen. Spotswood's	*Cumberland*, 3d
William Fitzhugh, Esquire's	*Paul Jones*, 4th
Mr. Hammersley's	*Bet Bouncer*, 5th
Second Heat in 9M.	*Cumberland*, 1st
	Polydore, 2d
	Paul Jones, dist.
	Bet Bouncer, dist.
	Hotspur, dr.

The third Head *Cumberland* galloped round alone.

The Ship *Grange*, Captain Roberts, is arrived at Philadelphia, after a remarkable short Passage of 27 Days from Liverpool. The *Active*, *Messenger*, and *Mary-Ann*, [Capt.] Priestman, from Virginia, are arrived at Liverpool. The *Marquis de la Fayette*, Capt. Dunham, sailed from Gravesend for this Port on the 24th of July. The *Alexandria*, ----, for Virginia, sailed from Liverpool on the 23d of August. ■ NAVAL-OFFICE, ALX. *Inward Entries*. Sloop *Betsy*, R. Stonehouse, from Boston; Sloop *Betsy*, P. Duncan, New-York; Sloop *Charming Polly*, J. Ellwood, Philadelphia; Ship *Charming Peggy*, C.H. Ruther, London. *Cleared Outwards*. Schooner *Jesse*, S. Davis, for Jamaica; Schooner *Mary*, D. Johnston, St. Croix; Ship *Grandbourg*, [Capt.] LeJoyille, Cadiz; Sloop *Sally*, P. Godfrey, Antigua; Sloop *Industry*, J. Rob, Boston.

On Saturday the 29th instant, will be sold at the Vendue-Store,

A VARIETY of merchandise, consisting of rum and sugars, cloths, blanketing, linens, &c.

And on Monday the 10th of November, will be sold to the highest bidder, a number of LOTS on Fairfax and Wilkes streets, some subject to no rent, and others to a very small one; also a LOT on Water-street, between Wolf and Wilkes streets, beautifully and conveniently situated; also some LOTS on Washington and Oronoko streets; and the same day will be rented a number of LOTS on Cameron and Pitt streets, near the Market-House.

☞ For private sale, a few valuable LOTS, a likely Negro boy, warranted sound, a dray and two good horses and a second hand chariot, which if not sold before Saturday, will then be exposed to public sale. S. ARELL, Vendue-Master.

RAN away on the 8th inst., from Goose-Cree[k], JACOB SHEETS, a Dutchman, who is about 5 feet 8 inches high, of a dark complexion, and has short black hair: He had on when he went away, a red great-coat, a blue waistcoat, white linen overalls, a pair of black grained shoes, with plated shoe-buckles, and a new wool hat.--Said Sheets took with him a black Mare, the property of the Subscriber, about 14 hands high, branded on the near shoulder R, and under the mane with the same letter, a small star in her forehead, a switch tail and shod all round.--Whoever takes up said Sheets and secures him and the Mare, shall receive THIRTY DOLLARS Reward, or Twelve Dollars for the Mare only, paid by JOHN WIMMER, Charles-Town, Berkeley County, October 21, 1785. ■ Employment for a smart active Negro WENCH, inquire at the Printing-Office [see like ad Vol. II No. 90] ■ **Jonathan Swift and Co.** Have for sale at their store on Fairfax-street, A GENERAL assortment of FALL and WINTER GOODS, which they will dispose of on moderate terms for cash, bills of exchange or produce; among their assortment they have a few pieces of elegant shag, which they will dispose of by the piece or pattern. **They give the highest market price for flour, wheat or corn. ☞ They have an excellent brass stove for sale. ALX, October 27, 1785. ■ **Randle Mitchell and Son,** Have removed their store from Fairfax-street to King-street, the sixth door from the corner of Fairfax-street, nearly opposite to the alley which leads from King-street to the Court-House, where they have for sale, either by wholesale or retail, at the very lowest prices, for cash or country produce, A LARGE and general assortment of most kinds of DRY-GOODS, linens, woollens, stuffs, cutlery, ironmongery, hosiery and haberdashery suitable for the season, also, rums, sugars, wines, molasses, teas, dying stuffs, window-glass, soap, coffee, pepper, ginger, allspice, China, queen's, glass, and earthen ware, saddlery, &c. ALX, October 27, 1785. ■ **Wanted Immediately,** As a Bar-Keeper, A Genteel young MAN, who is smart, active, and sober, and who can be well recommended.--To such a one the most generous wages will be given by HENRY LYLES, ALX, October 27, 1785. ■ TO BE SOLD, On very moderate terms, for CASH or COUNTRY PRODUCE, **Two Lots of Ground, in** fee-simple, beautifully situated on Prince-street, with many advantages, which, with the terms, may be known, by inquiring at the Printing-Office. October 27, 1785. ■ TO BE RENTED, For one or more Years, A Large and convenient Dwelling-House, with four rooms on the lower floor, with a fire-place to each, and three rooms above: It has also an excellent kitchen, and a room adjoining well finished, which was intended for a house-keeper or white servants, a meat-house, dairy and stable, a good garden and grass-lot adjoining, and all well enclosed.--For terms apply to W. THOMPSON, Colchester, October 22, 1785. N.B. A good Storehouse may be likewise had by applying to W.T. ■ BY virtue of a decree of the County Court of Berkeley to me directed, will be exposed to public sale on the second Tuesday in November next, a valuable TRACT of LAND, formerly the property of Mr. JAMES CUNNINGHAM, deceased, lying on Mill-Creek, containing about 300 acres, with the incumberance of two widows thirds.--Three annual payments will be allowed the purchaser, on bond and approved security, with interest from the date.--Due attendance will be given on the premises by W. HENSHAW, Executor, October 15, 1785. ■ THE Subscriber gives notice, that he will locate Lands on the northwest side of the Ohio River, where the Virginia military claims are to be laid, for one-third of the lands, to be divided according to its quality, and will be at the expence of the chain carriers and markers. He will also attend to the surveying and seeing the said lands clear of disputes. Any person that inclines to employ him may lodge their warrants with Col. Anderson, with a line directed to me or whosoever superintends that business. If their warrants have not been entered with Col. Anderson, and he not convenient, may direct them to the subscriber living in Washington county, Pennsylvania, to the care of Mr. Donaldson in Winchester. He flatters himself, that from his extensive knowledge of the western country and his attention to that business, it will be in his power to execute every gentleman's business much to their advantage and satisfaction. JOHN HARDIN, October 10, 1785. ■ WAS taken up in the Borough of Winchester on the 2d inst. a Negro Man, named MICHAEL, who is now confined in gaol; also a dark bay horse which was found in his custody. They answer the description of a man and horse advertised in the ALX paper on the 13th inst. by Clement Hill. The owner is desired to come or send for him and the horse, pay charges, and take them away. JOHN DONALDSON, Winchester, October 18, 1785.

Page 4. Poetry. From the *Hibernian Magazine*: "To a Friend who pressed the Author to marry for sake of a great Fortune." ■ **Hooe and Harrison** have for sale items [see like ad Vol. II No. 89] ■ **D. and I. M'Pherson** have for sale a quantity of choice West-India rum, etc. [see like ad Vol. II No. 89] ■ **William Taylor and Co.** have for sale at their store on Fairfax-street, a large assortment of European goods [see like ad Vol. II No. 89] ■ HOOE and HARRISON announce the Ship *Union*, Capt. Giles Sullivan, will take on tobacco, and sets sail for London [see like ad Vol. II No. 89] ■ The President and Directors for opening and extending navigation of James river seek superintendent [see like ad Vol. II No. 89] ■ ☞ A great Variety of BLANKS, printed on good Paper, may be had at the Printing-Office. ■ THOMAS FLEMING has for 99-year ground-rent two lots on Duke-street [see like ad Vol. II No. 89] ■ Employment for a girl to wait on a Lady, apply to Printing-Office [see like ad Vol. II No. 89] ■ NATHANIEL WEEDON has for sale 150 acres of land in Loudon County [see like ad Vol. II No. 88] ■ CLEMENT HILL offers reward for return of runaway Negro fellow named MICHAEL, from Upper Marlborough [see like ad Vol. II No. 88] ■ Printers solicit subscriptions for printing of Lowe's Masonic Sermons [see like ad Vol. II No. 90] ■ **Washington, Butler and Nivison** have goods for sale at their store in Leed's-Town [see like ad Vol. II No. 90] ■ WE have several LOTS of GROUND, on different streets in this town, to let on ground-rent--Also, a Piece of Ground, within the south side of our wharf, to let for term of years. HOOE and HARRISON, ALX, October 20, 1785. ■ EPHRAIM EVANS has Windsor Chairs for sale [see like ad Vol. II No. 90] ■ HOOE and HARRISON announce sail of the Ship *Paragon*, Capt. Henry Hughes; *ready* to take tobacco on freight [see like ad Vol. II No. 90] ■ MICHAEL MADDEN offers reward for return of strayed horse [see like ad Vol. II No. 90] ■ To be sold, at the Printing-Office, A Variety of Blank Books, consisting of Ledgers, Journals, Cash-Books, Letter-Books, &c.&c. Also, Stoughton's Bitters, Anderson's Pills, Daffy's Elixir, Balsam of Honey, Squire's Elixir, Bateman's Drops, Godfrey's Cordial, &c.&c.&c. ■ ALX: Printed by GEORGE RICHARDS, and COMPANY, at their Printing-Office on Fairfax-street--by whom Advertisements, &c. are thankfully received for this Paper,--and where Printing is performed with Care and Expedition.

1785/11/03, Vol. II No. 92

Page 1.

CONSTANTINOPLE, July 9.

The Divan has told the Republic of Venice it was its desire they make peace with the Tunisians, or else it would assist the latter with all its forces. Their Ambassador with difficulty obtained a 75 day delay. The Bashaw of Scutari is thought involved. The Venetians have entered into a treaty with Russia, which may engender another war with the Ottoman empire. ■ **MALAGA, July 24.** They write from Gibraltar that two Barbary corsairs captured and took to Ceuta and Tangiers four Portuguese vessels laden with coals, and a Portuguese brig with a valuable cargo. ■ **NAPLES, August 2.** A few days ago 14 boxes of consecrated silver were brought here from Calabria and taken to the royal mint to be made into money. The same vessel carried a large sum of money to be deposited in the sacred chest of Calabria, arising from the sale of possessions and effects of suppressed convents. ■ **l'ORIENT, August 20.** Paul Jones is arrived here from Paris to fit out 3 ships, on his own account it is said, of which he will take command, on an expedition to Kamtchatka to purchase furs, and establish a factory. This he is enabled to do by lately having received four hundred thousand livres for the prizes he took in the war. ■ **LONDON, August 31.** Extract of a letter from **Minden, August 18:** The articles of the confederacy, lately concluded at Berlin, are to be published at large by order of his Prussian Majesty, when all the German Princes will be invited to accede to it, as likewise every foreign power that wishes to preserve the Germanic body inviolate, and to secure it from the encroachments the Emperor aims at. It will therefore become the strongest league or alliance that ever took place ... By a letter from **Cadiz, August 10** we learn the *Apollo*, Capt. Tate, from Philadelphia, with a valuable cargo, was stopped about 20 leagues from that place by two Algerine corsairs, who took out six barrels of beef and other provisions; but finding the Captain an Englishman, and the ship under English colours, they suffered him to proceed ... Extract of a letter from **Amsterdam, August 24:** The Deputies from the States of Groningen and Utrecht, having made it known that the Lords the States of those provinces had not only entered into a solemn league, but were resolved at all events to support every article of the general confederacy, which exempts a subject of France, &c. from becoming Veldt Marshal in the armies of the United Provinces, the States General have appointed mediators to wait on those assemblies, to confer with them ... Extract of a letter from the **Hague, August 19:** We have not yet heard how the Paris negotiations are going between the Emperor and this Republic; the points are under deliberation in the different provinces, so not much progress can be made at Paris. In the meantime, the people in Austrian Netherlands do not greatly credit a long peace in view of warlike preparations: fortresses being repaired, magazines being filled, troops on a warlike footing, and furloughs denied both officers and men ... The honorable Mr. Temple, his Majesty's Envoy to the American States, attended a levee at St. James on Friday, and Saturday morning set out with his lady and family for Portsmouth, thence to New York, the present residence of the American Congress. **Sept. 3:** The new source of commerce likely to be opened by the present commercial expedition to the South Seas and the North West coast of America bids fair to be productive of the best consequences to this nation. The extent of the coast is immense; that part, discovered by our famous navigator, Capt. Cook, on his third and last voyage, reaches from Cape Blanco in lat. 42 to the extreme point of the continent, about 72 North, a distance of 30 degrees, or 1800 miles, all of which is inhabited, and many parts very full of people. In the course of a very few years there is every probability of immense quantities of our manufactures being consumed there (especially hardware and woollens), the inhabitants being at present totally destitute of every European commodity. They clothe themselves with the skins of various land and marine animals, many of which are of the most valuable kinds, especially the sea otter, the fur of which is most exquisitely fine, all of which they part with for the most trifling toys and trinkets. The furs find an excellent market at Canton, Japan, and other parts of India, selling at enormous profits ... By a letter from **Tunis, July 9**: The Venetian fleet, commanded by the Chevalier Emo, is expected every day before our port, to begin hostilities again; but far from being disposed to peace, our Regency authorizes the captures which continue to be made on the subjects of the Republic. One of the corsairs has again lately taken a ship laden with corn. The third of this month as large English ship from Constantinople arrived at Port Farina with the following presents for our regency, viz. 30 brass cannon, 20 iron cannon, 4 mortars, 150 bombs, 100 barrels of gun powder, 30 tons of pitch, a quantity of cordage, sails, &c. Also on board were four skillful bombardiers, or engineers. It is singular this ship could escape the Venetian squadron. The pestilence abates here every day; but at Tripoli it has redoubled its ravages, and that city is in the greatest desolation ... Extract of a letter from the **Hague, August 24:** It is in vain to attempt to conceal it, that notwithstanding the efforts of the friends of the House of Orange, the affairs of the Stadtholder, instead of mending, grow every day worse and worse. His Serene highness's orders for the troops to march to Amersfort, at the sole request of four Deputies of Utrecht, without the sanction of the majority of the States of that province, gives general offence; the letter written by his Highness on that occasion has been severely and bitterly criticized. The burghers of Utrecht, on their part, persist in their resolution of defending themselves and shutting their gates. This resolution is strengthened by several towns in the province of Holland, who have determined to lodge a complaint before the states against the Stadtholder, for issuing those orders, and at the same time to propose depriving his Highness of the power of granting patents without the consent of the provinces. It is not easy to foresee how his Highness will extricate himself from this dilemma, if the other towns should adopt this plan, which it is more than probable they will ... Extract of a letter from **Lisbon, August 18:** The situation in which the Spaniards have left our court by the truce they have patched up with the infidel Algerines is far from pleasing; and, considering the family connexions that have lately taken place, rather unexpected. Her most faithful Majesty is resolved, however, to protect her trade. The *Algarve* of 30, and *San Josef* of 24 guns are for this purpose ordered to Sacre Bay to convoy and protect the home trade from the mouth of the Straits. There are also in the Mediterranean a ship of 60 guns, and three others, cruising against the barbarian flag, with orders not to spare them wherever they meet them ... Extract of a letter from **Elsineur, August 13:** A Russian squadron of nine ships of war has just saluted the Castle, and cast anchor in our roads, the Admiral's ship, a two-decker mounting 76 guns. Their stay here will be but short, their destination being to the southward. There only business is probably fresh provisions, having been out 18 days only from Cronstadt. **Sept. 6:** The Court of France has issued an order which strongly suggests their pacific intentions. The persons under obligation to hold in readiness and maintain the artillery horses, have received permission to dispose of them, if they think fit, on condition that only once a year they shall on given notice be able to muster a number of horses equal to that which they received into their custody. Until the war office notice, artillery horses taken up in the last war were kept in constant pay and liable for monthly musters ... We hear that despite the Irish triumph over Ministry in regard to the propositions, Mr. Flood still intends to bring forward his motion declaratory of the legislative independence and omnipotent authority of the Irish Parliament ... We hear also, and with considerable astonishment, that Mr. Curry is to be Chancellor of the Exchequer, in the room of Mr. Foster, on his advancement to the chair ... Sir A.S. Hammond has succeeded Commodore Bowyer in the command of his Majesty's ships in the river Medway, and hoisted his broad pennant in the *Irresistable*, 74 guns, at Sheerness ... Two pilot boats are now cruising off the mouth of the Humber, to conduct the Russian fleet, daily expected from the north, into that river ... Advices from Madrid mention the death of Don Louis, youngest brother of the King of Spain, a few days ago, [in] the 58th year of his age ... Yesterday some despatches were received from New York via the *Greyhound* packet, Capt. Dunn. Trade has been very slack there for some time, and few English ships were at that port when the packet sailed ... Extract of a letter from **Copenhagen, August 10:** The Oriental Company's ship *Achilles*, from China, which is the fifth this year, is safe arrived, and brought a very valuable cargo, the majority of which is disposed of already. The Prince Royal, who set off on a tour to Germany the 25th of last month, is said to go to pay a visit to one of the courts, with whom a matrimonial alliance is certainly intended ... Extract of a letter from **Brussels, August 23:** Today's Dutch post brings an account of a dangerous insurrection in Utrecht, and that troops are marching to quell the insurgents who, when the post came away, had formed themselves into [Continued on Page 2].

Page 2. [Utrecht Insurrection (*continued*)] military positions, as if determined to face all opposition. The cause of these commotions is related variously here. The Prince de Ligne, Governor of Antwerp, arrived here this day ... Extract of a letter from **Paris, August 23:** You surprise me that in England you apprehend a war with this country. Nothing is more improbable than the supposed grounds on which your apprehensions are raised--an armament at Brest. Such may give alarm in England, but here it is a non-entity. Merchants here are at rest, and none are more skillful in snuffing a storm. The affairs of Ireland are not as much talked of. I don't know about in the cabinet, but in the political world here they make less noise than the Westminster election. You may speculate commercially without fear of being disturbed by war ... Thursday three capital houses in the city were obliged to stop payment, on account of remittances from America not arriving as promised, for goods sent there. Several other houses are in the same line; if their remittances arrive late they must experience the same fate. The change wore a gloomy appearance on this occasion, and each merchant returned to his counting house to discover how far his name was involved.

The present situation of Europe and America is turbulent. Men are impatient for they know not what, and become restless in attempting to obtain it. The Dutch army weakened by desertion--their Civil Government tottering under certain cabals and tumults--the Stadtholder finding it difficult to keep the balance even--the Emperor harassing them by the peremptory demand of unreasonable terms--the newly acquired Russian dominions in the Crimea already tired of their masters--the Emperor and the Porte, barely civil to each other--the whole Turkish Empire a scene of anarchy, tyranny, cruelty and dissipation--the Spaniards vamping up a catch-penny peace with a nest of pirates--secret alliances forming by the northern Powers--at home, many distractions of party--Ireland refusing a commercial treaty, the most advantageous ever made, and talking of sending ships out to India--the Philosopher can see an indication in all this; a finger pointing out *this is Man!* Such has been the case ere now, and such will be the case again to the end of the volume of time ... Extract of a letter from **Tripoli, June 25:** This city is involved with miseries too afflicting to be described--the calamities of the plague and famine. Four ships are leaving for Europe, filled with refugees, among them the only professor of medicine here. This calamity will be the more fatal as the methods of the Levant for repressing its shocking effect are unknown here. Our grain and provisions are scanty, with little prospect of relief as those disposed to help will fear infection. Great numbers perishing from the famine are seen through the streets, trying to survive by gnawing bones, and greedily devouring vegetable refuse thrown on the dunghills ... An act ought as speedily in the next session as possible to be brought forward, enacting, "that all women, of whatever age, rank, profession, or degree, whether virgins, maids or widows, that shall, from and after the passing of such act, impose upon, seduce and betray into matrimony, and of his Majesty's liege subjects, by the contrivance, help, means and use of perfumes, scents, paint, cosmetic washes, artificial teeth, false hair, Spanish wool, iron stays, hoops, high heel'd shoes, bolstered hips, or cork rumps, shall incur the penalty of the laws now in force against *witchcraft, sorcery*, and such like misdemeanors; and that the marriage, upon conviction do stand null and void," such deceptions being now the rage of the town. ■

NEWCASTLE, July 22. On Sunday last Mr. John Joseph Heideck preached in High Bridge and Groat Market meeting houses here. This gentleman is a German by birth, and was a Jewish rabbi, or preacher, six years among the descendants of Israel; and he embraced the Christian faith about two years ago. He was professor of Oriental languages in the University of Dublin, for some time before his conversion. Animated with an uncommon zeal, he is on his way to preach the gospel throughout Germany. In London he is to publish a letter written in Hebrew, addressed to the Jews, containing the reasons and grounds of his conviction. It is scarce fourteen months since he could speak the English language in public; his discourses are delivered in a warmth peculiar to a mind lately opened to, and impressed with the importance of divine truth. He can preach in five languages, and understands nine. As he is a master of all the learning of the Jews, and of their prejudices against the gospel, he promises to be a useful instrument in converting and strengthening his brethren. ■ **NEW YORK, October 21.** The French are very industrious in erecting new fortifications and repairing old ones in all their West India islands, and the English Ambassador's absenting himself at the Court of Versailles, makes things put on an equivocal appearance ... Notwithstanding the late disastrous hurricane has been so lately and severely felt at Jamaica, yet we find them, by late papers, so absorbed in vice, that instead of thanks offerings to the deity for their preservation from the most imminent danger, horse racing, &c. fill the catalogue of their amusements. ■ **PHILADELPHIA, October 21.** Extract of a letter from a gentleman at **Fort Pitt**, to his friend in **Carlisle**, dated **Sept. 25:** I am just going on board the boat for the Miami river. I have heard the gentlemen gone as messengers are at Sanduski, all well and going on with their business. The surveyors with Captain Hutchins are gone down the river, and I believe will meet no interruption. Mr. Cunningham, one of the State surveyors, has met with no hindrance, and has got well forward with his business, laughing at some who went off in a hurry. The people find that Congress are determined to carry their resolutions into effect, and will acquiesce in the measure.

There have been several rumours of Indians; some few are true, the mischief that has happened I believe done by a banditti of different nations, viz. Cherokee, Shawanese, Mingos and some Delawares, who have joined contrary to the opinion of their nations, to steal horses and plague the poor people on the frontiers, some few lives have been lost, but less than reported, I have the greatest reason to believe that affairs with the Indians are going on as well as can be expected, until we get possession of the western posts ... The determined resolution of the two Imperial Courts to ascertain the proper limits betwixt their dominions and those of the Porte, together with the confusions at present raging all over the Turkish dominions, seem to portend the destruction of that despotic Empire, nor can this be regretted, when we consider in what misery the Turkish common people are kept by their tyrants, whose Government is founded on bloodshed, and continued acts of cruelty. **October 22:** The Commonwealth of Massachusetts, have laid the following duties on the articles herein after enumerated. An impost of five per centum, at the time and place of importation, on all wrought pewter, not made or manufactured in any of the United States, and an impost of seven and a half per centum, at the time and place of importation, on all beef, pork, butter and cheese not raised or made in any of the United States, and an impost of ten per centum, on all soal leather, tanned calfskins, bound psalters, psalm books, spelling books, and primers, and on all account and other blank books, and nails of all sorts; and an impost of twelve and a half per centum, on all boots, bootlegs, shoes, shoe vamps, goloshoes and slippers, and all kinds of plated ware, hard soap and candles, and glue, and on all coaches, riding chairs, sulkeys, and on all parts of riding carriages, horse harness, saddles, saddle cloths, bridles, whips and canes; and on all girthweb, livery lace, coach and chaise lace, carpets of all kinds, copperplate furniture, umbrellas, muffs, tippits, and all kinds of combs; and an impost of twenty-two and a half per centum, at the time and place of importation, on all beer, ale, and porter, every kind of ready made clothes or apparel, except such as are made of leather; and all kinds of cabinetmakers work, and ready made wooden household furniture; and an impost of two and a half per centum, on all woolen and linen cloths and woolen stockings: For all anchors, twopence per pound; for every axe, hatchets, scythe, carpenter's or cooper's adze, two shillings; for every bit for boring of pumps, sixpence per pound; for all carriage hoops and attire, twopence per pound; for every mill saw, twelve shillings; for every scale beam, fourpence per pound; for every pair of steelyards, for each pound they are capable of weighing, one penny per pound; for every spade or shovel, one shilling; for every hoe, one shilling; for every pair of wrought iron andirons, fourpence per pound; for all kinds of cast iron ware, one penny per pound; for every pair of iron shovel and tongs, one shilling; for all sorts of iron crows, spikes, tackle and other hooks, thimbles, scrapers and marline spikes, twopence per pound; for all kinds of pump and whaling geer, sixpence per pound; for all wrought copper (sheet copper excepted) including worms for stills, ninepence per pound; for every hat other than beaver, beaveret and castor hats, sixpence; for every pound of loaf sugar, fourpence; for every hundred pounds weight of British cordage, seven shillings; for every hundred pounds weight of every other foreign cordage, cables and yarns, three shillings; for every ounce of wrought gold, ten shillings; for every ounce of wrought silver, two shillings; for every pair of wool or cotton cards, one shilling; for every pair of buckskin breeches, nine shillings; for every pair of other leather breeches, four shillings; for every pair of leather gloves and mitts, one shilling; for every pound of wash leather, three shillings; for every pound of painter's colours, ground in oil, twopence; for every pack of playing cards, two shillings; for every pound of manufactured tobacco, fourpence; for every yard of paper hangings, one penny; for every clock, twenty-four shillings; for every house jack, twelve shillings; for every gallon of New England rum, one penny; for every gallon of foreign rum, sixpence; for every gallon of every other foreign distilled spirits, sixpence; for every gallon of Madera wine, eightpence; for every gallon of every other kind of wine, sixpence; and the duty and excise of ten per centum, on all gold and silver watches, all kinds of jewelry and paste work; gauzes, lawns, cambricks, muslins, silks of all kinds, flowers and feathers, usually worn for ornament, silk hose, mitts and gloves, silk and gauze handkerchiefs, silk velvet, shawls, ribbons, sarsenet; all kinds of wigs, cushions, and other hair manufactures; tin ware, seamen's compasses, starch, hair powder, children's toys, marble and china tile, raisins, citron, almonds, nuts and cordials, mustard and lindseed oil.

The **Hon. Benjamin Franklin**, Esq; Counsellor elect for the city of Philadelphia, on Monday last took his seat in the Supreme Executive Council, and was this day unanimously chosen President thereof, under the 20th section of the Constitution, which provides that they (the President, or, in his absence, the Vice President and Council) "shall supply every vacancy in any office, occasioned by death, resignation, removal, or disqualification, until the office can be filled in the time and manner directed by law or this Constitution." ... **October 25.** We the judge, and all other officers of the Town Hall, of this village of Orta, Island of Fayal [declare] we and the adjoining islands in the Azores are in very great distress for provisions, particularly Indian corn and flour, the crop failure such as obliges publication in all newspapers, to make it known to all in America, to encourage their coming with eatables, absolutely duty free. The kindness always shown American vessels merits in some degree that Americans would attend to our distress with immediate supplies. [Signed and sealed by] the judge, the 30th August, 1785: **JOSEPH FELIPPE FERREIRA CABRAL.** ■ **RICHMOND, October 29**. Last Monday the Honorable General Assembly elected as Speaker, Benjamin Harrison, Esq., who, on taking the chair, allowed he was at a loss for words [Continued on Page 3].

Page 3. [Benjamin Harrison's Speech of Acceptance (*continued*)] He felt his election, and the post to be an honor, he might from time to time need the members' assistance, he would not be a slave to rule and order; the peace, happiness and safety of the Commonwealth depends on what we do here, so let us be diligent. Being as we all are, fallible, he may make some errors, but assures they will not be the work of design [&c.] ■ **BALTIMORE, October 28.** Copy of a letter [summarized below--Eds.] from the manufacturers and gentlemen of Frederick Town, directed to the Committee of the association of tradesmen and manufacturers of Baltimore. Frederick Town, October —, 1785. We received your letter transmitting that of the tradesmen and manufacturers of Boston, on the subject of our trade, and its ruinous and alarming state. At a town meeting it was agreed immediate exertions are necessary, and to this end the below-signed were appointed a Committee of correspondence to coordinate with you and others. A petition is being circulated for signatures. We are, &c. Thomas John, Philip Thomas, Jacob Steiner, Elijah Evans, Michael Bayer, Nicholas White, Joshua Dorsey. ■ **ALX, November 3**. A late Letter from Belfast to a Gentleman in Philadelphia says, "Two Saddles of very extraordinary Workmanship (the Manufacture of Mr. Michael Harrison, Saddler of this Place) are shipped in the *Irish Volunteer*, Capt. Wallace, for the Use of General Washington." ■ DIED.] In Berkeley County, WILLIAM DREW, Esquire, late Clerk to the Senate. ■ NAVAL-OFFICE, ALX. *Inward Entries*. None. *Cleared Outwards*. Sloop *Dolphin*, A. Steward, for Philadelphia; Ship *Carolina*, J. Clarke, Bremen; Sloop *Charming Polly*, J. Ellwood, Philadelphia. ■ ANECDOTE, **A** YOUNG Frenchman... [text continues].

PRICES CURRENT, ALX. / Tobacco, 24s. per Ct. / Fine Flour, 29s. per Barrel. / Wheat, 5/6s. per Bushel. / Jamaica Spirits, 4/6 per Gallon. / Windward Rum, 3s. per Ditto. / Continental Rum, 2s. per Ditto. / Molasses, 1/6 per Ditto. / Muscovado Sugar, 35s. to 42/6 per Ct. / Salt, 3s. per Bushel, by Retail. / Corn, 4s. per Bushel. / Exchange, 40.

Ellicott's ALMANACK, For 1785, to be sold by the Printers hereof. ■ **I** WILL sell on low terms, for cash, produce, or a short credit, the LOT and STORE on Fairfax-street which I at present occupy.--Also, a valuable LOT in Dumfries, on which is a large brick HOUSE with other improvements. WILLIAM WILSON, ALX, November 3, 1785. ■ TO BE SOLD, **A House and Lot, situated** on Prince-street, near Capt. Harper's Wharf.--The house is new and was intended as a store, and is a most excellent stand for a retailer.--The lot is 20 feet front and 88 feet back.--For terms apply to THOMAS TOBIN, ALX, Nov. 1, 1785. ■ **One Hundred Negroes are** wanted on hire for the use of the Potomack Company, for each of whom there will be an allowance of twenty pounds, Virginia currency, per ann. also clothe them, pay their levies and furnish them with rations, viz. one pound of salt pork, one pound and a quarter of salt beef, or one pound and a half of fresh beef or mutton and a sufficiency of bread each day; and also a reasonable quantity of spirits when necessary.--It is expected the Negroes will be good and able working hands, and that they will come well clothed, or to be supplied with what may be deficient, which is to be stopped out of the next year's clothing.--Application is to be made to Mr. WILLIAM HARTSHORNE in ALX, or to Mr. JAMES RUMSEY, the principal superintendent of the work, who are authorised to contract for them. By order of the Board of President and Directors, JOHN POTTS, jun. Secretary, ALX, Nov. 1, 1785. ■ TO BE SOLD, In Fee-Simple, A VERY valuable LOT, advantageously situated on Prince-street--Inquire at the Printing-Office, ALX, Nov. 2, 1785. ■ To be sold to the highest bidder, at the plantation of the Subscriber opposite to ALX, on Monday the 28th inst. if fair, if not the next fair day, ALL the personal estate of GEORGE FRASER HAWKINS, Esq; deceased, consisting of Negroes of different ages and sexes, cattle, sheep, hogs, horses, a variety of household furniture, and one half of a new flat, between 30 and 40 hogsheads burthen.--Six months credit will be allowed the purchasers for all sums above 25s. upon their giving bond and good security.--All persons will have claims against the estate, are requested to bring them in legally proved; and all those who are indebted to the same, will, by discharging their accounts, much oblige their humble servant, SUSANNA T. HAWKINS, Executrix, Prince-George's County, Maryland, Nov. 1, 1785. ■ TO BE SOLD, On very moderate terms, for CASH or COUNTRY PRODUCE, **Two Lots of Ground, in** fee-simple, beautifully situated on Pitt-street, with many advantages, which, with the terms, may be known, by inquiring at the Printing-Office, October 27, 1785.

On Saturday the 5th instant, will be sold at the Vendue-Store,

A VARIETY of merchandise, consisting of rum and sugars, cloths, blanketing, linens, &c. And on Monday the 7th instant, will be sold to the highest bidder, a number of LOTS on Fairfax and Wilkes streets, some subject to no rent, and others to a very small one; also a LOT on Water-street, between Wolf and Wilkes streets, beautifully and conveniently situated; also some LOTS on Washington and Oronoko streets; and the same day will be rented a number of LOTS on Cameron and Pitt streets, near the Market-House.

☞ For private sale, a few valuable LOTS, a likely Negro boy, warranted found, a dray and two good horses and a second hand chariot, which if not sold before Saturday, will then be exposed to public sale. S. ARELL, Vendue-Master.

☞ WANTED, an able fellow to drive a dray, to whom good wages will be given.

ALX, Nov. 3, 1785.

I have for sale 2000 acres of LAND, on Clifty-Creek in Kentucky, within five miles of a station, the quality of which I have certified by some of the most respectable characters in that country, who are well acquainted with it.--It has been patented near twelve months.--I will exchange it for Negroes or any saleable property.--My terms are ONE DOLLAR per acre. ALEXANDER SKINNER, ALX, Nov. 1, 1785. ■ TO BE SOLD, **By ROBERT ALLISON,** A few Barrels of choice HERRINGS. ALX, October 2, 1785. ■ TO BE SOLD, A HOUSE and LOT, situated on Market and King streets in the town of Leesburg and near the Court-House.--The Lot contains 211 feet front on Market-street, and 105 feet front on King-street.--The house is two stories, 40 feet by 30 feet, has two rooms and a parlour on the lower floor, and four lodging rooms on the second floor, with fire-places to each, a kitchen, stable and other out-houses. The situation is equal to any in the town of Leesburg for either a retail store or any kind of business.--Any person inclining to become a purchaser, may, if not agreeable to take the whole of the Lot, have it divided. For terms apply to WILLIAM HEREFORD, ALX, November 3, 1785. ■ George-Town, October 25, 1785. THIS is to forewarn all persons from purchasing any bonds of mine which I passed to HENRY YOST for a brick house he sold to me in this town last spring, having understood since he had made it over to Mr. Ninian Beall Magruder before he sold it to me, I being determined to pay no more until my title to the house is made good by said Yost. ALEXANDER DOYLE. ■ On Tuesday the 13th day of December next, will be sold to the highest bidder on the premises, A LEASE for four years of that beautiful and excellent place called Gisborough, lying in Prince-George's County, at the mouth of the Eastern-Branch of Potomack, 3 miles from ALX, 6 from George-Town and 10 from Bladensburg, with ten working Negroes for the said term of four years, with stock of every kind, and corn and fodder sufficient for the maintenance of the said Negroes and stock for one year. There is about 200 bushels of wheat sowed on the land, the soil of the first quality, either for farming or planting, a good fishery, and the greatest plenty of wild fowl. At the same time and place will be exposed to public sale, about fifteen Negroes, consisting of men, women, children, boys and girls, a waggon and team, several horses, amongst which are some valuable mares and colts, one of which is full blooded, 4 years old next spring, and upwards of 15 hands high, got by the Arabian. One year's credit will be given for the Lease, three months credit for one-third of the purchase-money of the Negroes and horses, and one year for the other two-thirds. Ten per cent. will be deducted for ready-money for the last payment, and all kinds of certificates will be taken at their passing value. ☞ I have about 3 or 400 barrels of Indian-corn which I will sell for ready-money only. WILLIAM BAYLY, George-Town, October 28, 1785. ■ On Tuesday the 20th of December next, will be sold at public sale at Mattox-Bridge, Westmoreland County, SUNDRY valuable SLAVES, amongst whom are several house-carpenters; also, men, women, boys and girls. Six months credit, on bond and approved security, will be given the purchasers, CATHARINE JETT, October 27, 1785.

Page 4. Poetry. "On taking the BARK, By a LADY." ■ **Jonathan Swift and Co.** Have for sale a general assortment of Fall and Winter Goods [see like ad Vol. II No. 91] ■ **Randle Mitchell and Son,** Have removed their store from Fairfax to King-street and have a large and general assortment of dry-goods [see like ad Vol. II No. 91] ■ HENRY LYLES seeks employment of a bar-keeper [see like ad Vol. II No. 91] ■ **Washington, Butler and Nivison** have goods for sale at their store in Leed's-Town [see like ad Vol. II No. 90] ■ Printers solicit subscriptions for printing of Lowe's Masonic Sermons [see like ad Vol. II No. 90] ■ **Hooe and Harrison** have for sale items [see like ad Vol. II No. 89] ■ **William Wilson** has for sale a general assortment of fall goods [see like ad Vol. II No. 89] ■ W. THOMPSON, Colchester, has for rent a large and convenient dwelling-house [see like ad Vol. II No. 91] ■ W. HENSHAW, Executor of James Cunningham, deceased, has for sale a tract of land on Mill-Creek, Berkeley Co. [see like ad Vol. II No. 91] ■ HOOE and HARRISON announce sail of the Ship *Paragon*, Capt. Henry Hughes; ready to take tobacco on freight [see like ad Vol. II No. 90] ■ JOHN HARDIN offers to locate lands on the northwest side of the Ohio River [see like ad Vol. II No. 91] ■ EPHRAIM EVANS has Windsor Chairs for sale [see like ad Vol. II No. 90] ■ MICHAEL MADDEN offers reward for return of strayed horse [see like ad Vol. II No. 90] ■ **D. and I. M'Pherson** have for sale a quantity of choice West-India rum, etc. [see like ad Vol. II No. 89] ■ **William Taylor and Co.** have for sale at their store on Fairfax-street, a large assortment of European goods [see like ad Vol. II No. 89] ■ HOOE and HARRISON announce the Ship *Union*, Capt. Giles Sullivan, will take on tobacco, and sets sail for London [see like ad Vol. II No. 89] ■ HOOE and HARRISON have for sale several lots of ground on ground-rent [see like ad Vol. II No. 91] ■ The President and Directors for opening and extending navigation of James river seek superintendent [see like ad Vol. II No. 89] ■ JOHN WIMMER, Charles-Town, Berkeley Co., offers reward for return of runaway JACOB SHEETS [see like ad Vol. II No. 81] ■ JOHN DONALDSON, Winchester, has taken up Negro man Michael and confined in gaol; answers description sought by Clement Hill [see like ad Vol. II No. 91] ■ Employment for a smart active Negro WENCH, inquire at the Printing-Office [see like ad Vol. II No. 90] ■ To be sold, at the Printing-Office, A Variety of Blank Books, consisting of Ledgers, Journals, Cash-Books, Letter-Books, &c.&c. Also, Stoughton's Bitters, Anderson's Pills, Daffy's Elixir, Balsam of Honey, Squire's Elixir, Bateman's Drops, Godfrey's Cordial, &c.&c.&c. ■ ☞ A great Variety of BLANKS, printed on good Paper, may be had at the Printing-Office. ■ ALX: Printed by GEORGE RICHARDS, and COMPANY, at their Printing-Office on Fairfax-street--by whom Advertisements, &c. are thankfully received for this Paper,--and where Printing is performed with Care and Expedition.

1785/11/10, Vol. II No. 93

Page 1. From the London MORNING POST

THOUGHTS *on a* **NEWSPAPER**

It has been observed that there is not so inconsistent, so incoherent, so heterogeneous, although so useful and agreeable thing as a public newspaper; the very ludicrous contrast in advertisements, the contradictory substance of foreign and domestic paragraphs, the opposite opinions and observations of contending essayists, with premature deaths, spurious marriages, births, bankruptcies, &c. Form a fund of entertainment for a world, which is in itself no bad epitome.

Abstracted from politics, the general tenor of our domestic situation is not a little curious; whether it arises from accident or design I know not, but I have frequently seen after a paragraph reciting the elegance of an entertainment, a commission of bankruptcy has immediately followed; after a city feast I have seen a melancholy account of the sudden death of an Alderman, by an apoplectic fit; after an advertisement of the art of fencing taught by Monsieur Longsword, the circumstances of a duel followed, wherein one of the combattants have been run through the body; after a marriage, a divorce; and thus I have seen these paragraphs naturally follow, in the same uniform order in a newspaper, as their consequences do in real life.

Our curiosity may be extended by observing the various effects the different articles of intelligence have on different persons. Thus a marriage will mortify the breast of an old maid, hurt the pride of a young one, while it gives consolation to many a poor dejected husband, who reads that another has fallen into his situation. A death, if it is a wife, will make husbands envy the widower: Wives and widows pity the deceased, and, hurt at the husband's good fortune, exclaim against the monster for not shewing a proper degree of sorrow on the occasion; while one of them, perhaps, marries him a month after. Indeed all the passions incident to the human frame are elated and put in motion by a newspaper. It is a bill of fare, containing all the luxuries as well as the necessaries of life. Politics are now the roast beef of the times, and a dish equally sumptuous to the king and the cobbler; poetry is plumb pudding, and palatable only to lovers of the muse; there are others that act as vegetables to complete the course; while our mails from France and Spain serve up nothing but kickshaws and fricassees.

It is a caricature, happily calculated to hit the ordinary and unbounded prejudices of society. One person's affections lie in the price of stock, and the arrival of our East and West India fleets; another in a dreadful battle, either by sea or land, in which he solaces himself he can read the account free from its dangers; a third places his delight in a curious anecdote; a fourth in a tale of scandal; a fifth in horse races; a sixth in theatrical intelligence; and a seventh in a poet's corner. Thus is a newspaper a magazine, or toy shop, where every one has his hobby horse; and thus all capacities and descriptions are periodically furnished with instruction, amusement, and information. ■ **UTRECHT, August 18.** Today this whole city has been in confusion from a morning report that a body of troops were on their march hither, and at no great distance. Several citizens ascended the Dom tower to see whether they could discover the troops, but when the post came away in the evening, nothing had occurred. The committee of citizens have, by public advertisement in the *Gazette* of this city have requested all the free armed corps of the Republic, especially those of Guelders, Overyssel, and Holland, to pass immediate word of the march, their origin and destination, order of battle, strength, weaponry &c., so that timely measures can be taken. In the meantime, we hear his Serene Highness wrote the Deputies of the States of this Province on August 14: In reluctant accord with your wish that a regiment, possibly of a Utrecht division, be sent to quell the anarchy and confusion now reigning at Amersfort, have ordered out an 80 man detachment of Major General Vander Hoop's regiment of cavalry, and the 2nd battalion of the Prince of Hesse Darmstadt's infantry regiment, to march from Nimuegen to Amersfort, under General Vander Hoop. They will march the 16th, towards Ede on Weluwe, arriving Amersfort the next day. We flatter ourselves that your Lordships will see the troops properly quartered, and strenuously recommend they not be employed against the inhabitants unless in absolute necessity, no other means effectual to maintain the peace and support the magistrates. We sincerely hope that it may please God to prevent all mischief, and that every thing might be peaceably adjusted. We are, &c. ■ **LONDON, August 16.** Extract of a letter from **Halifax, in Yorkshire, August 10:** Mr. Joseph Binns, of this town, with a natural genius for sciences, assisted by years of intense study and application, has discovered a certain method in the steerage of balloons, which will astonish the scientific part of the world. Yesterday this gentleman, accompanied by Messrs. Newmarch and Frobisher of the same place, eminent for their mathematical knowledge and calculations, ascended from the Beacon Hill, a prodigious eminence in this neighbourhood; and to the pleasure of some thousands of spectators, he conducted the balloon for twenty miles, in a horizontal direction, against the wind. This philosophical phenomenon ascertains the steerage from the immediate and remote powers of electric repulsion; and from the same machinery, Mr. Binns can supply the exhausted gaz, and raise it high and lower at pleasure ... **August 17:** They write from Vienna, on the 2nd, that vast quantities of artillery and martial stores continue to be delivered to the Imperial magazines of that city, and sent down the Danube to the fortresses on the frontiers of the Turkish provinces, where the garrisons are all augmented, in particular the towns of Helfintche Zouchte and Donetgtchle are full of troops ready to file off upon the shortest notice. These advices conclude that this looks like war, but the two Imperial courts understand each other ... **August 20:** One of the principal reasons which broke off the commercial negotiations, at Paris, between Great Britain and France, was over French West Indies produce being admitted into the British dominions on a small duty--which would materially have injured the British West India islands; from the low price of their lands, &c. The French would be able to undersell our rum, sugar, coffee, cotton, indigo, and drugs. America has made a demand of the same natures, which under proper restrictions (intended to prevent the smuggling any articles not professedly the growth and nature of North America) has been offered to be complied with ... A merchant in the city has received a **letter from Amsterdam**, which says their trade to Spain is almost at a stand on account of the number of armed Barbary vessels cruising the Mediterranean. The last two ships which sailed from thence are both taken and carried into Algiers; their crews were not sent up to the country, but employed immediately to work on some new fortifications erecting at the mouth of the harbour ... Extract of a letter from **Versailles, August 3:** The confederation under the auspices of the court of Berlin daily gains strength, and puts on a serious appearance. The light in which the Emperor sees this league renders it more worthy of attention. His sentiments are clearly expressed in Count Kaunitz's June 11 letter to the Emperor's ministers at different courts in the empire: **Vienna, June 11, 1785**: My April 13 letter informed you of the steps taken by the court of Prussia which, under the most odious pretences, seeks to form a league with the greater part of the States of the empire, in which--though his Imperial Majesty is not directly mentioned--it is evidently aimed at him. That letter also gave our reasons which at first induced us to consider it impossible that those measures could be countenanced anywhere. To our great surprise, the contrary has happened, and several of the principal States have voluntarily acceded to the confederation proposed at Berlin. But to convince those States by *facts*, His Majesty invites the States to form immediately a solemn confederation, with himself as head of the empire. His Majesty cannot give a more unequivocal proof of his real sentiments, and desire to maintain the legal constitution of Germany: It therefore cannot be doubted, that those states, who, notwithstanding this declaration should, contrary to every expectation, enter into a foreign league, must, in the opinion of every unbiased person, appear to be actuated by motives widely different from those which they openly profess [Continued on Page 2].

Page 2. [The Count Kaunitz Letter of June 11 (*continued*)] You will be pleased instantaneously to communicate the answers you may receive to this declaration, which I charge you to make in his Majesty's name ... Extract of a letter from **Leghorn, July 21:** We just now learn of a remarkable convulsion in the State of Venice. The Doge has been seized in his Palace; several members of the lower senators imprisoned, and all at the instigation of the spiritual council. Such a shock has not visited that Republic for four score years, and it is difficult to say how it will end ... Extract of a letter from **Utrecht, August 7:** We are in hopes that harmony will be restored between the people and the magistrates. This desirable event will be the result of the zeal of the six regents nominated at the Amsterdam meting, to prevail on our magistrates to endeavour to regain the confidence of their fellow citizens ... By a recently published list, it appears the navy of this Republic has 64 ships, exclusive of six now fitting out, their crews numbering 11,520 men ... Extract of a letter from on board his Catholic Majesty's ship of war, *St. Ildephonso,* Vice Admiral Don Joseph [Massoredo]: The commission, or business (as we supposed) when we left Carthagena with the *St. Ildephonso*, *St. John Nepomuceno*, and frigates *Santa Brigida*, and *Santa Casilda,* was reduced to try the sailing of the new ship of 74 guns, *St. Ildephonso.* Despite continual Levant winds, we kept close to the wind, outsailing all the squadron, and on the 12th of last month we got in sight of Algiers at 7:00 p.m., very contrary to our expectations. We presented ourselves before the fort, hoisting a flag of truce, but it being late, we were not surprised that no answer was given our signal. We were visited by a Moorish envoy, and the French and Swedish Consuls, and all went calmly, a number of gun salutes being given and received in the following days. At length there came a Turk with a letter from Ignacio Alava, saying preliminary peace negotiations had been concluded. On the 19th the armed brig *Atocha* sailed with despatches to Alicant for the court, and we took aboard eight large boatloads of live stock, vegetables, and refreshments for the squadron. On the 21st the French frigate *Minerva* arrived to retrieve French subjects captured by the Algerines on neutral vessels. On the 26th the Admiral and his officers paid a farewell call on the Dey, ending with 21-gun salutes given and received. We weighed anchor on the coast of Spain, having earlier sent the *Santa Casilda* to the Captain General at Mahon, to suspend the port's weapons from acting against the States of Algiers. The latter have 9 armed vessels from 22 to 36 guns, which sailed for the ocean the 6th July, besides several smaller ones. These had until that day been prevented from going out to make reprisals against the powers at war with them. The have also 75 gun and mortar boats, the former armed with a brass 24-pounder, as they supposed the expedition at Mahon was intended against them as before. Don Joseph Massaredo and his squadron has been cruising on the two coasts, and this day, the 17th came to anchor in the Bay of Alicant, bringing a ratification of the treaties to our Sovereign. A Catalan vessel bound for the West Indies was intimidated in her way down the Straits and the crew took to their boat; but she was restored to the Spanish Admiral, who manned her with some of his people, and brought her from Algiers to the bay of Alicant; the Captain was severely punished for going near the Spanish ship, and frightening the crew, who were ignorant that a treaty of peace as then on foot. On the 15th of this month came to anchor in this bay a small Algerine corsair who, after being furnished with oars and other necessities, which she had been obliged to throw overboard in a violent squall of wind, sailed out of the bay, and the next morning captured three Neapolitan vessels, two of them laden with ship timber and hemp, for the arsenal at Carthagena, the crews of which abandoned their vessels, fleeing ashore in their boats. We fear almost every ship that comes within the Straits will be visited and plundered. We have three vessels under 40 days quarantine; those of Naples, Portugal and Genoa must suffer severely; in course the Algerines will declare war against some northern powers to keep their cruisers fully employed ... Extracts of a letter from **Nantucket, March 16:** The islanders have held two town meetings, and [are] drafting a memorial to the government and Boston, requesting independence, in order to contract with England to carry on the whale fishery free from duty. I doubt not it will be granted as they are unable to pay their taxes by reason of the duty on oil, and the rapid depopulation of monied men; the whale fishery will be carried into Nova Scotia, and the island left desolate. Contracting with England would employ at least 100 square rigged vessels from this state, and give every man a chance of adventuring under the cloak of Nantucket property. It will employ hundreds of men from the U.S., and thousands within. The annual profit from their produce would bring double or treble the amount of their present tax, make a fund for remittance, and check the growth and interest of Nova Scotia. William Rotch sails for England in May as an embassy to lay the matter before King and Parliament (provided it succeeds at the court of Boston.) ... An Englishman, who has the welfare both of his native and of its Sister Island entirely at heart, asks the following questions: If separated from England, can Ireland preserve her freedom, raise and support a naval force to protect her own commerce render secure her happiness and general prosperity? Are not emissaries of our perfidious neighbours exciting the utmost artifice, using gold to foment discord? Do they not consider separation of Ireland and Great Britain the only circumstance by which they can hope to subdue if not destroy the commerce of both? Are they not augmenting their land and sea forces to fall upon us? Can anything be more desirable to the enemies of Ireland and Great Britain than separation? Can any friend of either think on this without horror? Will either island be so infatuated as to be ensnared by enemies of both? Is it not in their interest to throw off every prejudice, divest themselves of all passion? Having done so, will they not see that firm union is absolutely necessary to preserve them from the projected attacks of artful and powerful enemies, who are watching every opportunity to deceive, and, if possible, to subjugate them both? Do not these questions deserve the most serious consideration? ... **September 6:** Extract of a letter from **Constantinople, June 20:** The Sublime Porte continues the most general and complete revolution ever, in the Ottoman Empire, by bloody executions, banishments, and exiles. Although somewhat accustomed to the barbarous sight exhibited on the gates of the Seraglio, they now border on discontent. The deposition of Ibrahim Effendi, newly raised to Mufti, and now banished to his country house, has been followed by that of Tefderdar Faizi Ismael. The former, to whom the Grand Seignior has given for successor Arabzade Attulah Effendi, is reproached with having been the cause of the late Grand Vizier's misfortune, and the Bashaw of Belgrade, Soleiman Effendi, has been appointed Tefderdar in the room of Faizi Ismael. In these delicate circumstances the Bashaw, who enjoys all the confidence of the Sultan, has not left the city; he stays mostly at Ostokoi, a house near the castle, lately occupied by his Highness. ■ **SALEM, October 18.** We are desired to insert (as worthy of public notice) an account of two operations in surgery, viz. On the 15th of June last, the wife of Mr. Benjamin Stoddard, of Scituate, a woman in her 73rd year, had her leg amputated by Dr. Thomas Thaxter, of Hingham, for a cancerous excrescence which weighed two pounds and seven ounces. Though it was of 17 years growth, had become ulcerous, and the woman much emaciated, it is now healed, and she very well for one of her years. About two years since, in July, Dr. Thaxter extirpated from the breast of Mrs. Turner a like excrescence, which weighed 17 ounces, and which, it was judged, would have opened in three weeks. She entirely recovered, though more than 70 years of age. ■ **BOSTON, October 20.** While *our people* complain of the scarcity of money and high taxes, let them attend to the following extract of a letter from a gentleman in Great Britain, whose eldest son--an officer in the British army--was killed at the time General Howe forced his way into Philadelphia; which letter was received last Saturday night, and came by the last British packet from New York. After reading it let any of us say which is the country suffering most? And upon reflection, we shall find we have reason to bless God that *our* lot is cast in this good land. The letter is dated **July 23:** The oldest men living do not remember such a dry season; few have been able to cut a tenth of their usual quantity of hay. The corn, however, is in general fine, particularly the wheat and barley. I am afraid the *tenants* will be ruined, and of course the landlords also; for as there is no grass, nobody will buy *cattle*. Money is become very scarce, and taxes are as high as plenty. I am obliged to pay for the liberty of using a four wheeled carriage, an annual duty or tax to Government of above £10 viz. £7 a year for the carriage only, £2.5 for the driver or postilion, and a guinea a year for using two horses. Indeed *our taxes* that people of *middling fortune* must continually experience great difficulties. The *American war* hath ruined *England*. You should think yourself happy in living under another Government. ■ **NEW YORK, October 20.** Extract of a letter from **London, July 29:** The people of Jamaica are strenuously seeking to be supplied from the U.S., the distance from your country and the infancy of the new settlements render them unable to supply their wants. At first general, lately they qualified it to include provisions and livestock, in vessels of dimensions and crew strength to preclude smuggling, but this lies dormant and unnoticed. I wonder much that some of you don't exert to the utmost to secure exclusive resupply rights, without which I do not see how you succeed or flourish. I enclose a pamphlet distributed to both houses of Parliament by which you may see the Jamaicans' view is not much different than your colonies' before the war. It might give you the grounds to urge the most respectable among you to use the same endeavors to exist, as the West India islands are to ease themselves and suit their convenience. By the pamphlet (which is taken from the Nova Scotia Packet of the 21st ult.) we find a very respectable part of Jamaica are in favor of the American trade, by the very ardent and unremitting addresses and petitions to government for a repeal, or at least a revisal of the navigation act, so far as it respects the West India islands, setting forth their opinion of the incapacity of the *Royal Refugee woods*, of supplying them, &c. Government, it seems, has not, nor will it in any manner grant their requests.

It is, and ought to be, one of the first studies of a *Prime Minister*, or of a *government in general,* of every independent nation, to create and to circulate PREJUDICES against all nations that are their *sworn*, or *natural enemies*. The most latent spark being once introduced it is esteemed a general policy gently to fan the fire until the whole constituent body becomes impregnated with this venomous principle, and the breasts of all men beat high *to arms!* Then, only *rank* and *file* them and they will *fight like bull dogs!* The dullest observer, let him but travel, and attain to the most trifling knowledge of the men and manners of different nations, and he will discover this: He will see that national prejudice in general is not confined to the *nation* only, but is extended to its *individuals*, to its *manners*, and to *all it produces* [Continued on Page 3].

Page 3. [Thoughts on Prejudice (*continued*)] For an instance, let us examine the *prejudices* that exist between *France* and *England*: England is a natural enemy to France, therefore natural policy dictates that a prejudice be inculcated. A number of articles of French manufactures were prohibited, as were also in France of English manufactures, in order to encourage their own: This augmented the prejudice on both sides, and among the vulgar in England (it has even become a ministerial idea) French goods of every kind were regarded as *poor trash!*

It was natural for Americans to imbibe the same sentiment while they were subject to great Britain; but, that is happily no longer the case. France is now our *great friend* and *ally*. We have experienced so many striking and never to be forgotten acts of philanthropy and nobleness in the ever to be revered LOUIS XVI, LA FAYETTE, and many other patriots and heroes of that nation; we have seen many proofs of heroism and magnanimity in her troops when interposed in our behalf, and an amiableness of disposition in the French in general; we have seen for ourselves, that no nation can outvie them in profound researches into the polite arts and sciences, such as natural philosophy, metaphysics, mathematics, &c. And finally, we know that their *manufactures* are *superior* to the English, even if those articles which necessity obliges us to import (for those who have visited the French manufactories, who are judges of goods, give them the preference) and shall we, notwithstanding all these very forcible considerations, prove ourselves incapable of every sentiment of gratitude or benevolence, by suffering these *illegitimate prejudices* still to exist? It is certainly high time we *turn the scale*; let us divest ourselves entirely of all those prepossessions in favor of *Britain* and her *manufactures*, and prohibit the latter, except in our own bottoms, for the encouragement of our manufactures and those of our friends; and, taking our perspective through a true mirror, let us view *France* in its fair light, and I doubt not that we shall properly attend to her loud invitations and turn our *commerce* to that country, to the detriment of those who are striving to ruin us as a *commercial nation* ... **Oct. 26:** By letters received last Friday from London, we are informed the King and Council of Great Britain have exhibited an instance of commercial amity towards America, encouraging the ship building and advantageous to the navigation of this country. By this order, the produce of the U.S. continues exempt from foreign duties all other powers pay, provided it shall be imported in ships built and owned in America, and navigated by three-fourths American seamen, or in British ships navigated according to law. Vessels not American built, although American owned, and under American colours, are to pay foreign duty. The built to be ascertained by inspection, and the property and crew by the Captain's affidavit. The advantages from this are evident; the exemption from foreign duty, granted to imports in our own ships into the ports of Great Britain, will be the means of promoting a more extensive navigation from America, and by excluding foreign-built ships, sailing under American colours, from being our carriers, we shall be prompted to extend the scale of our marine, under the certainty of profitable employment and exclusive advantage. ■ **PHILADELPHIA, October 29.** Extract of a letter from **Nashville, July 21:** We have enjoyed almost an uninterrupted quiet from the Indians this summer, the inhabitants are moving out of their forts, and settling on their plantations through the country, so that we hope shortly our settlements will be flourishing. The Chicasa profess inviolable friendship, provided we do not intrude on their hunting ground, which they have described very minutely. We hear commissioners are appointed by Congress to treat with the southern tribes, and establish permanent boundaries; the present disposition of the Indians bids fair for that business to be carried on with success, if not marred by the clashing scheme of the Georgia company, of purchasing the great bent of Tenasee, and its is said Mr. Martin, one of the commissioners, is of that company ... Extract of a letter dated **Sullivan county, State of Frankland, August 20:** Last month I suppose you heard that the principal Chief of the Chicasas was as high up as the Great Island; he seems to be a very intelligent and noble spirited man; he has a surprising knowledge of the cause of the late revolution, and the nature of the American government, and talks very feelingly of our growing power, and the danger his people are in of having this country wrested from them. He is urgent in soliciting trade down the Tenasee, and says he will protect it from the plundering Cherokees. A small essay will be made, if it succeeds well, it will be an inducement for the merchants on James river to embark largely, as it is certain, that the Tenasee is the nearest and best communication between the eastern navigation and the Mississippi. One matter I am doubtful will interrupt our pleasing prospect of trade, a private company of gentlemen seem to be driving at a project to purchase the great bent of Tenasee, that is to say, what may fall out to be south of the claim of North Carolina; the Chicasas and Creek Indians are said to be much averse to this proposal; but we are told the Georgian Assembly countenance it, and the principal men in both North Carolina and Virginia, are members of the company. How unfortunate it is for America, that neither her treasury can be supplied, nor the bulk of her citizens benefited, by the fruits of the labour of her patriot sons ... **November 1:** Capt. Robertson, who arrived at Savannah, Georgia, September 15 in a sloop from New Providence, informs that on his passage from Baltimore to that island he was chased the greatest part of the day by a brig and a sloop, which he supposed were pirates; and at Nassau he was told that a yellow sided schooner, with 3 white men and 2 Negroes on board, had sailed from Abaco about six months ago on a cruise to the continent ... From the LONDON MORNING CHRONICLE of Aug. 15: Extract of a letter from **Alicant, July 22:** The first of this month a large American ship, from Boston, bound hither with a valuable cargo, was captured by an Algerine corsair, within 3 leagues of this port, and carried to Algiers. The ship and cargo were condemned, and the Captain and crew sent up the country into slavery. ■ **BALTIMORE, November 4.** The Association of tradesmen and manufacturers of Boston, being greatly interested in the late act of the Commonwealth of Massachusetts Bay, for the encouragement of the manufacturers of that State, have voted they do consider all persons who in any manner counteract, or endeavour to weaken the operation of the act aforesaid, **ENEMIES TO THE MANUFACTURING INTEREST OF THAT STATE.** ■ **ALX, November 10**. Extract of a Letter from St. Eustatia to a Gentleman in this Town, dated October 8, 1785. "Captain Robertson, in the Brig *Ann-Maria* from your Port, arrived here on the 22d of August, and put out to Sea in the dreadful Night of the 24th, when she unfortunately ran foul of a large Sloop, belonging to St. Kitt's, that put out also from this Road the same Night.--Some Time afterwards the Brig's Sails blew loose and she overset, when every Soul perished, except a Negro Boy who belonged to the Sloop, and had got on board the Brig at the Time they were entangled, who was taken off the Wreck some Days afterwards, and from whom we have the above Particulars." ■ Last Monday Evening the Tobacco Warehouse in this Town, was broke open by some Villains, and a large Quantity of loose Tobacco stolen therefrom. ■ ☞ The Gentlemen of ALX, who are desirous to become Subscribers to the Assemblies for the approaching Season, are requested to meet at the Coffee-House this Evening at 6 o'Clock, to form Regulations for the same.--It is intended that the Assemblies commence on Thursday the 17th Instant, at Mr. Wise's new Room.--Subscribers are to enter their names with Mr. George Richards.--Country Gentlemen who wish to subscribe, will please to apply to the Managers. ■ NAVAL-OFFICE, ALX. *Inward Entries*. Sloop *Molly Beverly*, W. Wade, from St. [Eustatia]. *Cleared Outwards*. Sloop *Nancy*, N. Spooner, for Demarara. ■ THE Subscriber has for sale in the town of Fredericksburg, THREE LOTS (lately enclosed) on which are a good house with four rooms on a floor, a kitchen, meat-house, a large stable.--They are agreeably situated for a private family: For business none more so, as they have a great command of the back grade.--They are so situated as to admit of divisions, and will be disposed of as it may be most convenient.--He has also a small TRACT of LAND, about three miles from the said town, containing between 160 and 200 acres, which he will dispose of likewise.--Its situation renders it valuable to a resident in the town, being well watered and wooded, and adapted for farming.--Twelve months credit will be allowed without interest, if the money is punctually paid when it becomes due, if not, it is to bear interest from the date.--A mortgage of the premises, with bond and approved security, will be required.--The price will be made known by the Subscriber at Mount-Vernon.--An exchange for land in the County of Fairfax will be prefered. GEORGE WASHINGTON, Nov. 9, 1785.

On Saturday the 12th instant, will be sold at the Vendue-Store,

A VARIETY of WET and DRY GOODS, consisting of rum in hogsheads and barrels, sugars, cloths, linens, calamancoes, coarse stockings, calicoes, hats, womens' shoes, a quantity of cordage, and green, hyson and bohea teas. And on Monday the 21st instant, will be sold, and rented, several LOTS of GROUND on Queen and Washington streets, six LOTS on Oronoko and Alfred streets, some on Prince-street, between Water and Union streets, some on Fairfax-street, beautifully situated, and a few on Wilkes-street.

S. ARELL, Vendue-Master.

ALX, Nov. 10, 1785.

☞ For private sale, very low, a chariot, a Negro boy, a dray and two horses, and a quantity of stone.

**Wanted, a man to drive a dray, to whom good wages will be given.

THE public are hereby most respectfully informed, that Mr. GEORGE M'CANDLESS'S well known tavern, in Gay-street, will be resigned by him in the course of this week, and on Monday the 7th day of November instant, will be opened by the Subscriber, who takes the earliest opportunity of acquainting them, as well as the gentlemen, in particular, who used that house, that he is determined to conduct the same in a manner which (he humbly hopes) cannot possibly fail of obtaining their approbation. Having been for the last four years employed in the business of the above tavern, induced many of its principal customers to solicit his undertaking it on his own account, which he means to do, and continue the same well-provided table and accommodations, in all respects, as they were used to in that noted house. JAMES STUART, Baltimore, Nov. 1, 1785. ■ Just imported in the *Alexandria*, Captain Watkins, from Liverpool, and the *Johanna Florentina*, Captain Norwood, from Dublin, by **Jesse Taylor**, A LARGE assortment of Manchester goods, Irish linens, stamped ditto, and cottons, which, with those goods he has on hand, he will sell on reasonable terms, by wholesale or retail, for cash, tobacco, wheat, flour or flaxseed. ALX, Nov. 10, 1785. ■ TO BE LET, THE STORE, Cellar and Counting-room, lately occupied by Messrs. Randle Mitchell and Son, on Fairfax-street, opposite the Court-House, it is an excellent stand for business, either in the wholesale or retail line.--The whole are in good order and may be entered upon immediately.--For terms apply to WILLIAM HERBERT, ALX, Nov. 10, 1785.

WANTED TO CHARTER,

For Lisbon and back again,

A GOOD vessel with a Mediterranean pass of the newest cut, that will carry from 4 to 5000 bushels. Her cargo is ready to be put on board immediately.

JESSE TAYLOR.

ALX, Nov. 10, 1785.

Just arrived in the Brigantine *Alexandria*, John Watkins, Master, from Liverpool, A Quantity of SALT, COALS and DRY-GOODS, which are to be sold by WILLIAM BUDDICOM, at Mr. Andrew Wales's.--The said vessel is to be CHARTERED to any port in Europe, but would give a preference to Liverpool, she being fully intended for a constant trader to that port. — She is a new British built vessel with a Mediterranean pass of the newest cut.--For terms apply to said Buddicom. ALX, Nov. 10, 1785. ■ To be sold to the highest bidder, on Monday the 21st instant, at Addison's Ferry, opposite ALX, SEVERAL valuable mares, horses, fillies and colts, most of them blooded, amongst which are a full blooded mare in foal by Mr. Hall's *Eclipse*, a colt three years old by the Arabian, one ditto two years old by Col. Loyd's *Traveller*, one ditto one year old by *Union*, all out of the above mare; a filly three years old by General Cadwallader's *Bajazet*, a genteel saddle-horse four years old, and a pair of well matched carriage horses; there will be 25 or 30 in all; also a chariot with harness for four horses.--Three years credit will be given, bond and security required, and the interest regularly to be paid, or the indulgence to be forfeited. HENRY ROZER, Notley-Hall, Nov. 9, 1785.

Page 4. Poetry. "Epitaph on a Blacksmith." ■ **Jonathan Swift and Co.** Have for sale a general assortment of Fall and Winter Goods [see like ad Vol. II No. 91] ■ **Randle Mitchell and Son,** Have removed their store from Fairfax to King-street and have a large and general assortment of dry-goods [see like ad Vol. II No. 91] ■ HENRY LYLES seeks employment of a bar-keeper [see like ad Vol. II No. 91] ■ W. THOMPSON, Colchester, has for rent a large and convenient dwelling-house [see like ad Vol. II No. 91] ■ WILLIAM HEREFORD has for sale a house and lot on Market and King streets in Leesburg [see like ad Vol. II No. 92] ■ JOHN HARDIN offers to locate lands on the northwest side of the Ohio River [see like ad Vol. II No. 91] ■ TO BE SOLD, **By ROBERT ALLISON,** A few Barrels of choice HERRINGS, ALX, November 2, 1786. ■ WILLIAM WILSON has for sale a lot and store on Fairfax-street, and a lot in Dumfries [see like ad Vol. II No. 92] ■ THOMAS TOBIN has for sale a house and lot on Prince-street near Capt. Harper's wharf [see like ad Vol. II No. 92] ■ ALEXANDER SKINNER has for sale 2000 acres on Clifty-Creek, Kentucky [see like ad Vol. II No. 92] ■ **Washington, Butler and Nivison** have goods for sale at their store in Leed's-Town [see like ad Vol. II No. 90] ■ ALEXANDER DOYLE warns others against taking bonds he passed to Henry Yost [see like ad Vol. II No. 92] ■ WILLIAM BAYLY has for 4-years lease place called Gisborough, Prince-George's County [see like ad Vol. II No. 92] ■ JOHN WIMMER, Charles-Town, Berkeley Co., offers reward for return of runaway JACOB SHEETS [see like ad Vol. II No. 81] ■ **Ellicott's ALMANACK,** For 1786, to be sold by the Printers hereof. ■ JOHN POTTS, jun., Secretary of the Potomack Company, seeks 100 Negroes for hire [see like ad Vol. II No. 92] ■ TO BE SOLD, In Fee-Simple, A VERY valuable LOT, advantageously situated on Prince-Street--Inquire at the Printing-Office. ALX, Nov. 2, 1785. ■ SUSANNA T. HAWKINS, Executrix of George Fraser Hawkins, Esq; deceased, seeks to sell estate in Prince-George's County [see like ad Vol. II No. 92] ■ Two lots of ground for sale on Pitt-street; inquire at the Printing-Office [see like ad Vol. II No. 92] ■ CATHARINE JETT offers for sale at Mattox-Bridge, Westmoreland County, sundry valuable slaves [see like ad Vol. II No. 92] ■ JOHN DONALDSON, Winchester, has taken up Negro man Michael and confined in gaol; answers description sought by Clement Hill [see like ad Vol. II No. 91] ■ To be sold, at the Printing-Office, A Variety of Blank Books, consisting of Ledgers, Journals, Cash-Books, Letter-Books, &c.&c. Also, Stoughton's Bitters, Anderson's Pills, Daffy's Elixir, Balsam of Honey, Squire's Elixir, Bateman's Drops, Godfrey's Cordial, &c.&c.&c. ■ ☞ A great Variety of BLANKS, printed on good Paper, may be had at the Printing-Office. ■ ALX: Printed by GEORGE RICHARDS, and COMPANY, at their Printing-Office on Fairfax-street--by whom Advertisements, &c. are thankfully received for this Paper,--and where Printing is performed with Care and Expedition.

1785/11/17, Vol. II No. 94

Page 1. Messieurs RICHARDS and COMPANY,

Please to insert the following Copy of a Memorial and Remonstrance, lately presented to the General Assembly of this Commonwealth, now sitting, and you will much oblige many of your Readers, particularly your humble Servant, J.J.

To the Honorable the GENERAL ASSEMBLY *of the* COMMONWEALTH *of* **VIRGINIA.**

[James Madison's famous *Memorial and Remonstrance* addressing religious freedom is printed, verbatim, including his citations from the *Declaration Rights*: its Preamble, Articles 1 and 16. The text uses the entire first page, and carries over onto the next page.--Eds.]

Page 2. [Following the Conclusion of the *Memorial and Remonstrance*.] **LONDON, August 4.** The Danish court has set the visit of the Prince Royal of Denmark to England. It is certain his Highness's object is to pay his devoirs to one of our illustrious Princesses ... **August 16:** Copy of a letter from the right Honorable George Gordon, President of the Protestant Association, to Joseph Benedict Augustus, Emperor of Germany, and King of the Romans. **SIR, IF** you had paid attention to the remarks I made on your ordinance against the Jews, on the 14th of March, 1782, and reversed that ordinance accordingly, you and your subjects would not have been in such a state of distraction and plague as at this hour. I observed much meekness and forbearance towards you from that period till the 18th of September, 1783. (Notwithstanding your hereditary Arch Treasurer's domestics at the Court of London loaded me continually with reproaches, insults and injuries, because I loved the Jews.) A year and a half was sufficient time for a man of your character, as to abilities and discernment, to make yourself master of the consequences of those remarks. I then had the honor to address three different letters to Elias Lindo, Esquire, and the Spanish and Portuguese, and Nathan Saloman, Esquire, and the German and Dutch Jews, requesting those rulers to submit my best intended endeavours to the consideration of Judah and the tribes of Israel, whithersoever dispersed over the whole world. In a very few days after, Providence, without any expence, brought two Greek gentlemen to my service, between whom and me an Italian friend negociated, and they, at the time in Turkish habits, took solemn and kind charge of two large packets of politics, under my hand and seal, directed to **ACHMET IV**, Grand Seignior, the present wise Sultan on the throne of Turkey, who was recommended to me by a Scots Chieftain. The Greeks undertook to deliver my letter into the Sultan's own hands. These letters contained my sentiments and advice concerning the governments and characters of the leading men in Europe and America, and stirring up Constantinople, Egypt and all Judea, against the Spanish and Portuguese inquisitions, and the Italian religion, and against your tyrannical aggressions in Holland, and against the Empress of Russia's uncivilized depredations in Turkey. Yesterday I had the honor to communicate these circumstances to Monsieur de Lyden, Envoy Extraordinary, de leurs Hautes Puissances, at the Dutch hotel, in Hereford street, and to press his Excellency, in the most endearing expressions that occurred to me, to take especial care that as advantageous terms of peace with Amsterdam shall be obtained by you, as Algiers have accepted from the King of Spain. I am, indeed, truly sorry I can say nothing more agreeable and comfortable to you at present; but if you will turn to me, I will turn to you. I am under vows to the Protestant Association, who chose me for their President, and am indispensably bound to be honest to them, and no human power can dissolve the obligation. If it is true what we hear of you, that you are afraid of being poisoned by the Italian Priests in your own house, fly to the hotel of Comte Wassenar, and Baron Van Leiden, the Dutch Deputies, and lodge with them, and you will be as safe and happy as Rahab was with Joshua's spies in Jericho. I find the Dutch Ambassador here a very good sort of man--and I may also dare venture to assure your Imperial Highness that the Republic has also sent agreeable and right hearted men to Vienna, to lead your Majesty into the ways of peace. Praying that the living God, the King of the Jews, may open your eyes to see the truth. I am, Sir, With due estimation, Your sincere friend, And Humble Servant, **G. GORDON**, Welbeck street, London, Aug. 10, 1785. ■ **NEW YORK, November 4.** The late requisition from Congress, connected with two former ones, makes complete provision for the payment of the whole of the interest of the domestic debt of the U.S. It is therefor to be hoped that these provisions, together with that of the land ordinance, will enhance the credit of public securities, as they certainly rest on substantial funds.

The poverty of the general treasury, the reluctance with which the legislatures levy, and the unwillingness of the people to pay taxes, together with an unusual urgency, in the domestic creditors to recover their public debts, seem to precipitate us to a novelty of measures, the consequences of which are to be dreaded, because they are altogether unknown.

When the subject of extending American manufactures is suggested to our legislatures, many persons approve it, but with a serious shake of the head, have replied, 'we are yet too young.' This was another argument made use of when we fist opposed Great Britain; we were then 'too young to resist'--Their armies and navy were held forth as too terrible for the young Americans to encounter--and if the virtuous sons of America had then been influenced by such suggestions, we might now have been shackled by Great Britain, and strippling, as we were, to have been long since grey in misery. If we are 'too young' for manufactures, we are too young for our independence; for an independent nation, to depend wholly on the supplies of others, for their cloathing and every other manufacture, is quite a political solecism; such a people may please themselves with sounds, and their independence like a child's rattle, may tickle their fancy. 'We must grow more numerous before we can manufacture,' cries another. Let such persons consider, that our wants are only in proportion to our numbers. 'Population produces manufactures,' cries another. But this is a mistaken hypothesis. I rather suppose that manufactures will increase population. When manufacturers are encouraged in America, emigration from Europe will increase; and numberless manufacturers would be induced to come among us. But what encouragement has the industrious mechanic to leave his business in Europe to starve in this country, while he is waiting for us to 'become more populous?' Encourage our manufactures, and we shall soon find ourselves sufficiently populous. All nations but the Americans know the value and abilities of America; we have those resources within ourselves which no other nation can boast. But crampt by our own humiliating ideas, we totter about like infants, afraid to venture beyond the length of our leading strings. If heaven had not blessed us with every advantage collectively, we should become, by pusillanimity and irresolution, the most contemptible people on earth. But bountiful Nature has put us above those misfortunes, into which our own folly would involve us, and in spite of ourselves, yields spontaneously every natural resource we can ask for or even think of. How have other nations flourished? Not by folding up their arms, and crying out with disponding voice, we cannot help ourselves! Or backwarding every attempt by saying, stop till we grow older. No, youth is the time for exertion and enterprise, in the political as well as natural constitution. The seeds must be sown in infancy, and they will be rooted in age. Pray when are we to begin our manufactures? Some say, 'not till time shall have rolled, perhaps many centuries over our dust, and that of our posterity.' For this reason, because the poor manufacturers of Europe are obliged to live upon what our brutes would scarcely taste. If such abject poverty must be the portion of a manufacturing people, America must rue the day when they are in a situation to begin them. But I would rather query, whether such numbers of miserable beings, 'immersed in the deadly shades of manufacturing houses,' if they could find employ in America, would not readily come over into a country, where brutes were more sumptuously fed than themselves, in their present situation? America, thus luxurious and bountiful, would intice such emigrants. Upon the whole, the commerce, manufactures, and agriculture of America, are objects of the greatest moment. They require every attention to promote them. We hope the several States will deliberate with firmness. We in this State can safely trust the weighty concerns of our Government with our political fathers: Knowing, that in all their proceedings, the public good will be the standard of their decisions. ■ **PHILADELPHIA, November 4.** The ship *Rambler*, Capt. M'Comb, arrived at Beverly, N.E. the 22 ult. In 54 days from Cadiz. As he was going into the last mentioned port, on his outbound passage from Beverly, he was met by two Algerine galiots, from one of which he was hailed, and asked where he was from, and what was his cargo? He answered, from Cork, and laden with Newfoundland fish. The Algerines then told him to shew his colours, when, having English ones, he immediately hoisted them. This proving satisfactory to the pirates, they suffered him to proceed, without boarding him ... Extract of a letter (received by Capt. M'Comb) from a merchant in **Cadiz, August 25**, to a gentleman in Beverly: You have no doubt hard of the havock done upon our coasts, by the Algerines, since the truce between them and the Spaniards. A brig from Boston, to this place, laden with flour and lumber, has been carried into Algiers--and a ship belonging to New York, homeward bound from Lisbon with salt, and taken off the western Islands, has likewise been sent here, a prize to one of their cruisers. Capt. M'Comb I hope may be fortunate enough in not falling in with any of them, particularly as he goes so far under the protection of a Portuguese man of war and a frigate, which have come here to convoy some of their ships, detained here ... We are informed that the New York ship, mentioned in the above extract, was drove on shore by the Algerines, on a small island, at the entrance of the Straits, where they left her. She was afterwards taken possession of by a number of Spaniards, got off, and by them carried into Cadiz. The information thereof, of her being sent into that port [Continued on Page 3].

Page 3. [The Fate of a New York Ship (*continued*)] as a prize to an Algerine cruiser, is supposed to be a mistake ... An English vessel, carried into Algiers on suspicion of being an American, and there released, arrived at Cadiz the day before Capt. M'Comb sailed. The Captain informed that a schooner, Capt. Smith, from Boston, and a brig from some other port on the continent, were carried into Algiers, and the crews sold at auction, before he sailed ... **November 5:** Extract of a letter from **Malaga, July 29:** Last week, as a Portuguese armed vessel was convoying several ships from Lisbon, bound up the Mediterranean, she was attacked in the Straits of Gibraltar by an Algerine frigate of 28 guns, and full of men. After a desperate and bloody engagement of nine glasses, the Portuguese vessel was forced to strike to the barbarians, who--though victorious--had above 100 men killed, besides a vast number wounded, 19 of whom died the next day. All the ships in the convoy made their escape during the conflict, and got clear off. The Portuguese captain was unfortunately killed in the heat of the action as he was making a stroke against an Algerine Lieutenant, who was coming up the ship's side, at the head of 60 men. Notwithstanding this fatal accident, the Portuguese cleared the decks of the enemy, who were killed, as also their fierce and daring leader; yet this horrid carnage did not prevent a second boarding, which was received with equal bravery by the gallant crew, who being at last overpowered were compelled to submit to these terrible marauders ... **Nov. 7:** The great variety of accounts from the different parts of the new settled country westward, says a correspondent, demonstrate the many perils and dangers which the adventurers have and are continually experiencing. The savages seem not even to hint at a declared opposition to the new settlers, but appear to be in general of a peaceful disposition; they are, however, as deceitful as barbarous, for the very party that professes the greatest friendship today, will burn your house and murder you tomorrow. It is thought upon the whole, that as their numbers increase, they will be able to defy the plundering parties; and by their laudable industry in cultivating the rich and fertile soil of the western hemisphere, will change its prospect from a savage wilderness, to a civilized field that shall blossom like the rose ... **November 8:** Extract of a letter from a gentleman in **Cadiz Aug. 22** to a merchant in New York: Two American ships have been taken by the Algerines within this 12-14 days. One of them a ship from St. Ubes for Boston, taken well to the westward; the other a ship from Boston for this port, captured on this coast. The former of which the Turks a few nights ago ran on shore, a few leagues from this place; the latter having three men that proved themselves to be British subjects, by having proper certificates, claimed the protection of the English Consul, who procured their enlargement; the fate of the others are much to be pitied, more so than if they had fallen into the hands of the Moors, who are counted far more civilized. ■ **ALX, November 17**. On Saturday the 5th Instant, was read in the Pennsylvania Assembly, a Message from the President and Supreme Executive Council, stating that they had received a Petition from thirty-five Natives of China and Bengal, setting forth, that they had been compelled by Force of Arms to assist in navigating from Batavia to Baltimore the *Pallas*, Capt. O'Donnel; that they had been unjustly and severely treated on the Voyage; that they had come to this City, in hopes of being able to return to their native Country with Capt. Truxton; that they have been disappointed in their Expectations: They therefore pray such Relief may be granted them as shall be seen fit.--The President and Council, remarking on the above, observe, that it is highly necessary, these People may not have cause to conceive a well-founded Prejudice against this County: They had, therefore, come to two Resolutions on the Subject: Of which one was, to transmit their Petition to the Governor of Maryland, with a request to make Inquiry into the Charges contained in it, and if it should appear, that they had been aggrieved, to order that Justice be done them: The other Resolution was, that the General Assembly of this State be applied to, to make in the Interim such provision of Food and Clothing for them, ad Circumstances might require. ■ His Excellency William Livingston, Esq; is re-elected Governor of the State of New-Jersey.--And the Hon. Lambert [Cadwallader], John Cleves Symmes, and Josiah Hornblower, Esquires, are chosen Delegates to represent that State in Congress the ensuing Year. ■ Yesterday Morning a Fire broke out in Mr. Adam's Bake-House, which burnt with great violence; but by the timely and active Exertions of the Inhabitants, it was with Difficulty extinguished. ■ NAVAL-OFFICE, ALX. *Inward Entries*. Brig *Alexandria*, J. Watkins, from Liverpool; Schooner *Eagle*, B. Bowers, Jamaica; Sloop *Surprise*, J.T. Brooks, Surinam; Brig *Jane*, M. Turner, Turk's-Island; Sloop *Betsy*, S. Jackson, Providence; Schooner *Lottery*, Z. [Mann], Baltimore. *Cleared Outwards*. None. ■ **COFFEE-HOUSE and TAVERN.** MRS. BALL, begs leave to inform the PUBLIC in general, and her FRIENDS in particular, that she has removed from Annapolis to this town [Baltimore], and has taken that elegant and convenient house, fronting on Market and South streets, which was lately occupied by Major Brown, where she has opened a COFFEE-HOUSE and TAVERN. As she is desirous to obtain the approbation and encouragement of her friends, she has made such additions and regulations as will render her Coffee-house extremely convenient to all Mercantile Gentlemen, while Travellers may be accommodated in the best manner, she having provided excellent stabling and a good hostler. She returns her sincere thanks to those gentlemen who were so good as to favor her with their company, when she formerly resided here, and hopes they will indulge her with a continuance of their custom, assuring both them and the public at large, that every endeavour shall be used to give general satisfaction. Baltimore, November 11, 1785. ■ AS several of the Subscribers to the ALX Academy have neglected to settle with the Treasurer, the demands on him are now so pressing that there is a necessity for all delinquents to call on him without delay and settle their respective balances; and as it may not be generally understood that by a late regulation, considerable privileges is expected to attend every five pounds subscribed, those who have not qualified themselves for the advantage alluded to, ought by all means to call on the Treasurer and augment their subscription.--In the mean time the subscription will continue open in the hands of the Treasurer, for all those who wish to encourage this useful and generous undertaking, until the first of January next, when the building will be finished and the different tutors open their schools. ALX, Nov. 15, 1785. ■ **Ewan M'Lean**, Taylor from Edinburgh, BEGS leave to inform the public, that he carries on his business in its different branches at the house of Mrs. Shaw, on Royal and Queen streets, where any gentlemen who may please to employ him, may depend on their work being done in the best manner, in the newest fashion, and on the most reasonable terms. ALX, Nov. 17, 1785. ■ ALL persons indebted to the estate of the Hon. JOHN TAYLOE, Esq; deceased, for dealings at Neubro and Occoquan furnaces, are requested to settle their respective accounts by the first day of January next, those who do not attend to this notice will be sued immediately after that date. ROBERT HAMILTON, Neubro, Nov. 15, 1785. ■ WHEREAS I was compelled in the month of August last to give a bond to Mr. JOHN DUNDAS, payable on the 13th day of July next, for three hundred pounds, Virginia currency, with two gentlemen of this place as security, in order to obtain a valuable property then in his hands: I therefore forewarn all persons not to take an assignment of the same, as it was fraudulently obtained, and will not be paid unless recovered by a due course of law. WILLIAM NICHOLS, ALX, Nov. 9, 1785. ■ FOR SALE, A NEGRO WOMAN and child; also to be let on ground-rent forever, a LOT of ground on King-street, between Fairfax and Water streets, with a south front.--For terms inquire of ROBERT ALLISON, ALX, Nov. 17, 1785. ■ Found this morning in the Commons near this town, A MAN's SADDLE.--The owner is desired to apply to the Subscriber, pay expences and take it away. JOHN THOMAS, ALX, Nov. 14, 1785. ■ TEN DOLLARS REWARD. STOLEN from the Subscriber's store last week, a piece of yard-wide Irish linen, marked as follows, trunk 33--60, 2/10 sterling. Any person who will give information of the thief, shall receive the above reward. JONATHAN SWIFT and CO., ALX, Nov. 17, 1785.

On Saturday the 19th instant, will be sold at the Vendue-Store,

A VARIETY of WET and DRY GOODS, consisting of rum in hogsheads and barrels, sugars, cloths, linens, calamancoes, coarse stockings, calicoes, hats, womens' shoes, a quantity of cordage, and green, hyson and bohea teas; also a bale of damaged coatings, said to be sold for the benefit of underwriters. And on Monday the 21st instant, will be sold, and rented, several LOTS of GROUND on Queen and Washington streets, six LOTS on Oronoko and Alfred streets, some on Prince-street, between Water and Union streets, some on Fairfax-street, beautifully situated, and a few on Wilkes-street.

S. ARELL, Vendue-Master.

ALX, Nov. 17, 1785.

☞ For private sale, very low, a chariot, a Negro boy, and a quantity of stone.

FOR L'ORIENT.

THE Ship *UNION*, commanded by Capt. GILES SULLIVAN, now lying in this port, will take tobacco on freight for L'Orient at 40 livres per hogshead, to the address of Messrs. J.J. Berard and Co.--The ship is perfectly ready to take in, is a fine new strong vessel, with good accommodations for passengers.

HOOE and HARRISON.

ALX, Nov. 15, 1785.

FOR St. EUSTATIUS.

THE Brig *MARTHA*, SAMUEL HARPER, Master, now in this harbour, will sail for St. Eustatia about the 6th of December, and to return here again. She has good accommodations for passengers, and would take in freight for that Island, with liberty of consignment, and bring back the neat proceeds. For terms apply to RICHARD CONWAY. ALX, Nov. 15, 1785.

FOR LONDON,

THE Ship *HAZARD*, Capt. THOMAS NEW, burthen 450 hogsheads of tobacco, upon liberty of consignment, and will sail by the middle of December, one half of her cargo being engaged. The *Hazard* is a new British-built ship, with a Mediterranean pass.--For freight, or passage, apply to the Captain on board, Messrs. SMITH, YOUNG and HYDE, Fredericksburg, Mr. HUGH CAMPBELL, Hobb's-Hole, Mr. JAMES DUNLAP, Port-Royal, or JOSIAH WATSON, Esq; ALX.

For sale on board the said ship, a quantity of CORDAGE assorted, two TOP-CHAIRS and a PHAETON, HARDWARE, and sundry other goods, for which good crop-tobacco will be taken in payment.

Port-Royal, Virginia, October 26, 1785.

TO BE SOLD, **Jamaica spirits, ditto** Mahogany, brandy, pimento, fine table salt of the best kind, and a few barrels of limes.--Inquire of DANIEL ROBERDEAU, at his warehouse. ALX, Nov. 15, 1785. ■ FOR SALE, A LIKELY NEGRO BOY, about 17 years of age, is very active, and has been brought up to wait and tend on a table.--He is very honest and sold for no fault.--The terms may be known by applying to the Printers hereof. ALX, Nov. 17, 1785. ■ TO BE RENTED, For one year, or longer, as may be agreed on, ONE large lower ROOM of a three-story brick house, accommodated with a fire-place, and well calculated for a wholesale or retail store. Also, the two upper stories of the same house, containing FOUR ROOMS with a fire-place in each, well calculated for an extensive mercantile concern.---The house is on the same general plan, and under the same range and roof as Mr. Watson's store and warehouse.--With these apartments is to be rented one-half of Harper and Watson's commodious WHARF, to the pier-head.--For terms, which will be found reasonable, apply to ISAAC RAWLINGS, ALX, Nov. 17, 1785. ■ RAN away from the Ship *Charming Peggy* at George-Town, on the 12th instant, the two following sailors: PETER GEAL, a stout well-made fellow, about 5 feet 8 inches high, and GEORGE DICK, a short well-made fellow.--They took, with them a chest and bed.--Whoever will take up the said fellows and secure them in gaol, or deliver them on board the said ship, shall have EIGHT DOLLARS reward, or FOUR DOLLARS for either. CHRISTIAN HENRY RUTHER, George-Town, Nov. 16, 1785.

Page 4. Poetry. "On Seeing a Rose in October." ■ JAMES STUART, Baltimore, notifies the public he is opening the tavern on Gay-street formerly of George M'Candless [see like ad Vol. II No. 93] ■ **Jesse Taylor** has for sale items just imported in the Brigantine *Alexandria* and ship *Johanna Florentina* [see like ad Vol. II No. 93] ■ WILLIAM HERBERT has for lease a store, cellar and counting-room lately occupied by Messrs. Randle Mitchell and Son [see like ad Vol. II No. 93] ■ WILLIAM BUDDICOM has for sale at Mr. Andrew Wales's goods just arrived in the Brigantine *Alexandria* [see like ad Vol. II No. 93] ■ HENRY ROZER, Notley-Hall, will sell at Addison's Ferry, several horses [see like ad Vol. II No. 93] ■ **Randle Mitchell and Son,** Have removed their store from Fairfax to King-street and have a large and general assortment of dry-goods [see like ad Vol. II No. 91] ■ JESSE TAYLOR seeks charters for vessel to Lisbon and back [see like ad Vol. II No. 93] ■ ROBERT ALLISON has for sale herrings [see like ad Vol. II No. 93] ■ WILLIAM WILSON has for sale a lot and store on Fairfax-street, and a lot in Dumfries [see like ad Vol. II No. 92] ■ THOMAS TOBIN has for sale a house and lot on Prince-street near Capt. Harper's wharf [see like ad Vol. II No. 92] ■ ALEXANDER SKINNER has for sale 2000 acres on Clifty-Creek, Kentucky [see like ad Vol. II No. 92] ■ ALEXANDER DOYLE warns others against taking bonds he passed to Henry Yost [see like ad Vol. II No. 92] ■ WILLIAM BAYLY has for 4-years lease place called Gisborough, Prince-George's County [see like ad Vol. II No. 92] ■ ☞ A great Variety of BLANKS, printed on good Paper, may be had at the Printing-Office. ■ JOHN POTTS, jun., Secretary of the Potomack Company, seeks 100 Negroes for hire [see like ad Vol. II No. 92] ■ TO BE SOLD, In Fee-Simple, A VERY valuable LOT, advantageously situated on Prince-Street--Inquire at the Printing-Office. ALX, Nov. 2, 1785. ■ SUSANNA T. HAWKINS, Executrix of George Fraser Hawkins, Esq; deceased, seeks to sell estate in Prince-George's County [see like ad Vol. II No. 92] ■ Two lots of ground for sale on Pitt-street; inquire at the Printing-Office [see like ad Vol. II No. 92] ■ WILLIAM HEREFORD has for sale a house and lot on Market and King streets in Leesburg [see like ad Vol. II No. 92] ■ CATHARINE JETT offers for sale at Mattox-Bridge, Westmoreland County, sundry valuable slaves [see like ad Vol. II No. 92] ■ JOHN DONALDSON, Winchester, has taken up Negro man Michael and confined in gaol; answers description sought by Clement Hill [see like ad Vol. II No. 91] ■ To be sold, at the Printing-Office, A Variety of Blank Books, consisting of Ledgers, Journals, Cash-Books, Letter-Books, &c.&c. Also, Stoughton's Bitters, Anderson's Pills, Daffy's Elixir, Balsam of Honey, Squire's Elixir, Bateman's Drops, Godfrey's Cordial, &c.&c.&c. ■ ALX: Printed by GEORGE RICHARDS, and COMPANY, at their Printing-Office on Fairfax-street--by whom Advertisements, &c. are thankfully received for this Paper,--and where Printing is performed with Care and Expedition.

1785/11/24, Vol. II No. 95

Page 1. JAMES STUART, Baltimore, notifies the public he is opening the tavern on Gay-street formerly of George M'Candless [see like ad Vol. II No. 93] ■ Mrs. BALL, Baltimore, gives notice she has moved from Annapolis to Baltimore where she has opened a coffee-house and tavern [see like ad Vol. II No. 94] ■ The Treasurer of the ALX Academy seeks to settle outstanding subscriptions [see like ad Vol. II No. 94] ■ HENRY ROZER, Notley-Hall, will sell at Addison's Ferry, several horses [see like ad Vol. II No. 93].

HAGUE, September 7.

SEVERAL of the ringleaders of the late tumults in this city have been taken into custody, in order for exemplary punishment being inflicted on them. Such government measures are hoped will disappoint the views of the malcontents who have been endeavouring to bring abut a revolution in the United Provinces government. ■ **PARIS, August 29.** The assembly of the clergy have nominated four Bishops to wait upon the King and submit their representations on the subject of Cardinal de Rohan's imprisonment. ■ **LONDON, August 23.** Extract of a letter from **Bengal, dated Camp, near Ferochabad, in the Duab, Dec. 16, 1784:** A great dearth has desolated the upper provinces of this beautiful country. Hardly any rain has fallen during four years. In consequence, the crops have failed, and the poor starved. The scarcity was also in Bengal; but its being under better government preserved it from monopolists and ruin. Thanks to the Almighty! A plentiful crop promises this year, plenty of rain having fallen. From my inquiries, I find half of the inhabitants of the Duab and Robileund have perished. Every ditch, road, brook, pond and street of these countries were strewed with the dead bodies of men, women and children. As there is no police in this country, where the wretch expires, there he lies, till his flesh is stripped off by the dogs, which is generally done in two days. No one buries him--for who are friends to a starved wretch? Besides, the Hindoos do not bury their dead, but burn them, if they have the money to buy fuel. We have often been obliged to shift our camp, on account of the stench arising from the putrefaction of so many bodies. When you reflect that the people of Hindostan are the most abstemious in the world; that their daily food is never flesh; hardly anything else than about a seer (not quite two pounds weight) of wheat or barley made into cakes, and baked over a few lighted sticks; when you understand that such is their food, and simple water their drink, you may form some judgement of the rage of this famine, which could deprive them of even this little. Men and women, with their children in their hands, flocked to camp, offering themselves for sale, for a quart of corn. Mothers sold their children for four annas each (or about the fourth part of a rupee or half crown.) I could have purchased a thousand children at this price, from four to ten years of age. I actually did purchase three very fine children between seven and eight, for three rupees or half-crowns. I might have had them for a third of the sum, together with their mothers. I have them now. I had writings delivered with them; properly attested by the cutwal (or magistrate.) But as I shudder at the thought of one human creature being a slave to another, and fearing, should any accident happen to me, my executors might sell them, I have destroyed the writings, and declared them free. My sole motive for purchasing them was to preserve them from death.

But the most shocking instance of the effect of famine ever recorded, is what I am going to relate; and which happened half a quarter of a mile from me. A poor woman at this place had not tasted food for five days. In this extremity she was delivered of a live child. Hunger was so extreme, that she cut of the head of the infant, and threw it away; the body she put into an oven of hot sand, which the people of this country parch their corn. When it was something roasted, she drew it forth, and had actually eaten the arm and shoulder before she was discovered. I understand she perished the next day. History informs us of a mother devouring her child during the siege of Jerusalem, but then the whole city was starving. This poor wretch was reduced to this hard alternative in a British camp, where many, I am sorry to say, Europeans (oh the partial distribution of fortune!) were sick with repletion. You, in England, who are so accustomed to cherish dogs, and receive the fondest submission from them, are no doubt astonished to hear of these creatures devouring dead bodies of men in India. But I must set you right, by informing you that dogs are not private property here in this country as in England. A native would no more call a parrier (dog) his, than he would the jackal of the field. Wise nature has so ordered that this country, in which flesh putrefies almost as soon as life leaves it, abounds with those dogs called parriers. They are in shape like the fox-dog in England, but longer legged. Every village and town has many of them; they go up and down the streets seeking dead carcases, which they devour, whether of horses, bullocks, sheep or men. Nothing comes amiss to them; no one offends them. They are considered of essential service, and they are really so, preserving the land from pestilence, which animal corruption would certainly bring on without them. The sagacity of these animals is astonishing; they have been seen to walk by a famished wretch, in expectation of his sinking with weakness, every now and then looking in his face, as if to inquire how long he should be kept from his prey. So soon as the unhappy man falls, the dog seizes the part next him, which is generally the bowels, and tears them out before the wretch's face. It is observable that although the poor victim is unable to defend himself long before he falls, yet the dog never attacks him while he walks or stands. I have seen hundreds of bodies with two or three dogs tugging the limbs to pieces ... **Aug. 24:** *Bella, borrida bella!* It is now the universal cry. Agents are now sent down to the different port towns for the purpose of raising rendezvouses, for raising seamen to man the fleet, now fitting out at Spithead; and tenders are also placed in the river to convey such seamen as may be enlisted here; and for whom drums are daily beat, and handsome bounties given ... Great numbers of officers of rank in the naval service are pretty constant in their attendance at the Admiralty office, with the humble tender of their services ... Ministry are said to foreseen the storm approaching, that at present clouds the political atmosphere, and threatens to involve all Europe in a general war; and it is now said owing to this, and not to the Irish propositions, that Parliament has been adjourned only till October next. **Sept. 14:** Letters from **Paris of Sept. 3** declare the charges against Cardinal de Rohan were in general thought to be ill founded, and that the present Pope, Pius the 6th, wrote the King on his behalf and gave instructions to his Nuncio at Paris to insist on the Cardinal's being tried before the Conclave of the Holy See ... Extract of a letter from **Manchester, Sept. 10:** The Captain of the *Kitty and Polly* (belonging to Messrs. Brosler and Richardson of Liverpool, which vessel arrived here last Wednesday) saw off Cape Finistere, in lat. 42,5 long. 10,5 eleven sail of French vessels, five of which were of the line, and the rest frigates. One of them hailed him and ordered him to strike his flag. To which he replied, "That was what he could not possibly do; and if they persisted in having it struck, they must come and do it themselves." He reports that from their course there is no doubt they were bound [Continued on Page 2].

Page 2. [The Manchester Letter (*continued*)] for Cadiz. We have this from a passenger in the above vessel, who arrived here yesterday ... A gentleman arrived from India assures us General Mathews and his officers suffered death as follows: they were ordered to swallow poison, but manfully refused to be accessory to their own deaths, upon which they were tied together two and two, by the arms and legs, and thrown in couples upon the ground, in which situation scalding oil was poured upon them till they died. ■ **NEW YORK, Nov. 8.** Extract of a letter from **Vienna, Aug. 24:** The cold, not to say affronting manner in which the Dutch Ministers have been treated at our court is no longer an enigma. Pecuniary interest continues to be the stumbling block in our disputes with Holland. At their first audience the Excellencies Messrs. De Waffenaar and Van Leyden declared readiness to pay the sum stipulated for the Maestricht indemnity, but not in ready money. They meant to set it off against sums long due by the House of Austria to the Republic; especially the loan negociated by Charles VI who expressly promised to mortgage Silesia to the Dutch. Our Sovereign is by no means of the opinion this is a fit time to urge such claims. His Majesty wants cash, and is greatly offended by the proposition, the more so because he has never been in the full enjoyment of Silesia--the King of Prussia being in actual possession of the best and wealthiest part. Their Dutch Excellencies have asked the French Ambassador here to intervene, but if he has done so, it hath proved unavailing. The Deputies requested a second audience with the Emperor, which he flatly denied--sending word with great coolness by the State Chancellor: "That once for all he repeated to them, that he had abandoned his interest to the King of France, and was determined to hear no more on the subject but what might come through the mediation of his Most Christian Majesty."The Emperor granted the Dutch Deputies 30 days to get from their principals instructions to pay the Maestricht indemnity sums. They daily consult with the French Ambassador, and have sent an express to Paris, and one to the Hague to acquaint their High Mightinesses with the heavy tidings--and inform them of the means now taking under their very eye to compel the Republic to fulfill the conditions of the preliminaries. The fact is, orders have been despatched to reenforce the Austrian army in the Netherlands with five regiments ... **Nov. 10:** Last Thursday, the 3rd, Mr. John Lowe, a gentleman from Virginia, received *holy orders* from the hands of the Right Reverend Samuel Seabury, Bishop of the Episcopal Protestant Church, at Hampstead, on Long Island. As this is the first instance of an ordinance of the church which has ever taken place in this state, the solemnity of the occasion was almost beyond description--the excellent sermon delivered by the Bishop--the prayers, and tears of himself, his Presbyters, and the numerous assembly, for the success of this gentleman in his ministry, will be long had in remembrance by every spectator. ■ **PHILADELPHIA, Nov. 12.** On the 7th day of September last, Alured Clarke, Esq; Governor of Jamaica, laid a general embargo on all vessels within the several ports and harbours of that island, to continue for six weeks from that date ... The Honorable the General Assembly yesterday appointed John Bard, Charles Pettit, William Henry, Arthur St. Clair, and James Wilson, Esquires, to represent this State in the Congress of the United States. ■ **ALX, November 24.** Extract of a Letter from a Gentleman in Richmond to another in this Town, dated Nov. 16, 1785. "Last Evening three Algerines were brought to the Governor's from Norfolk, where they had arrived in a Vessel from England.--They were apprehended by Order of the Executive, on Suspicion of their being Spies--What Account they give of themselves I have not yet been able to learn." ■ By the United States in Congress assembled, New-York, November 2, 1785. On a Report of the Board of Treasury, to whom was referred a Letter of the 24th of October, from John Pierce, Esquire, Commissioner of Army Accounts, *Resolved,* That all Persons having Claims for Services performed in the Military Department, be directed to exhibit the same for Liquidation to the Commissioner of Army Accounts, on or before the first Day of August ensuing the Date hereof, and that all Claims under the Description abovementioned, which may be exhibited after that period, shall forever hereafter be precluded from Adjustment or Allowance; and that the Commissioner of Army Accounts give public Notice of this Resolve in all the States, for the Space of six Months. CHARLES THOMPSON, Secretary. ■ Copy of a Letter from the Committee of Merchants at New-York, to the Committee of Merchants in this Town, dated September 30, 1785. Gentlemen, AS a Committee of Correspondence of the City of New-York, we beg Leave to address ourselves through you to the State of which you are Members, and take the Liberty of enclosing you a Memorial from the Chamber of Commerce of this City; which, in our humble Opinion, contains Matter worthy of your serious Consideration. Among the Blessings of our late Revolution, it is not the least that the Laws and Constitutions which we have established are Creatures of the public Will, and may be altered and modified by that Power from which their Existence was derived. The general Sense therefore of any Defect in them will naturally and easily operate a Cure. But this general Sense is not always to be effected with the requisite Celerity. For although nothing can be more evident to Reason than this Proposition, that whatever injures a Part is detrimental to the Whole, yet a long Time may elapse before the Feelings of a Community can be excited by the Ills which afflict any particular Order of Citizens. When we see the Landholder and Merchant seduced into a false Idea that their real Interests are different, it is not to be wondered at (though it must be lamented) that one State should suppose it can derive Advantage or may escape Danger from Circumstances of Injury, or Oppression to another. But if Reason will not suffice to shew the Falacy of such Opinions, a happy but severe Experience past, and we apprehend a future Experience less happy and more severe will evince, that our Union is the Basis of our Grandeur and Power. That Foundation once removed, the Superstructure of national Felicity must crumble into Dust. You cannot but perceive, that although the late Treaty with Britain has given the Name of Peace, yet we in fact are called on to wage a variegated War. And unfortunately for us as the Enmity is less open, so the Enemies are more numerous.--All Europe did indeed desire to see us independent; but now that we are become so, each separate Power is equally desirous of rendering our Interests subservient to their Commercial Polity. We may, and perhaps we ought to except those Powers who (closely allied to us in Peace and War) find their political Interests connected with those of the United States. But alas, how frail is the Tenure of national Prosperity, when it hangs on the Ties of political Interests. Interests which perpetually change. Whatever then may be the internal Discussion between particular Citizens or between the several States, one Truth results to Reason, and has been sanctified by long Experience, that the Prosperity of our Country and the Affluence of every Order of Citizens in it, has kept equal Pace with our foreign Trade. The Extension of the one, invariably has, and we may venture to pronounce that it necessarily must produce an increase of the other. Our Commerce, foreign and domestic, forms also the only Source of a Marine, and hence the Commercial War, which we complain of, for we are so far removed from the ancient World, that by a Marine alone we can be respected as a Nation; and unless the Nation be respected, its Citizens will be despised; unless the Nation hath Power to exact, the Citizen will in vain demand his Right. The Injury and the Insult may, and in the first Instance, must affect the Interests and the Feelings of the Merchant, but in the Event every Citizen will suffer from the Wrongs which his Fellow-Citizen has endured, and so with respect to the States themselves; those most commercial, those most dependent on the Sea, will feel most sensibly the Attempts of foreign Nations, to restrict our Trade in general, and the carrying Trade in particular. But when Revenue is to be obtained, and when Fleets are required, the States least commercial will in vain regret that the Commerce of their Sister States is decayed, and their Seamen destroyed. It is the Part of Wisdom to foresee, and of Prudence to avoid those Things, which we may else want the Patience and the Power to repel or endure. We request you therefore, to use the inestimable Privileges of which we are possessed, and from that elevated Station on which Freedom has placed every American Citizen, calmly and deliberately to examine the Conduct of foreign Powers, with Relation to

America, and if, from mature Reflection, you shall be convinced that the Right of Regulating Commerce, or any other Authority ought to be vested in the United States in Congress, additional to those which they now possess, we invite you to correspond with us on the important Subject, and to take such Measures with your own Legislature, as may be most effectual for giving to the Sovereign Representation of our Union, that Consistency, Efficiency and Respectability, which are necessary to the Safety, Prosperity and Happiness of those over whom they preside. We are, Gentlemen, &c. (signed). ■ The Honorable Richard Henry Lee, William Grayson, James Monroe, Edward Carrington, and Henry Lee, jun. Esquires, are chosen to represent this Commonwealth in the Congress of the United States for the ensuing Year. ■ Last Monday William Wall, a Sailor belonging to the Ship *Mary*, lying in this Harbour, fell overboard and was drowned. ■ The Schooner *Tryal*, Capt. Bell, from Virginia for the West-Indies, put into Bermuda for fresh Hands on the 2d of October, Part of her Crew being sick. ■ MARRIED.] Col. DENNIS RAMSAY, Merchant, to Miss JENNY TAYLOR, Daughter of Capt. JESSE TAYLOR, Merchant. -- Mr. ROBERT LYLE, Merchant, to Miss MARTHA HEWITT, of Bladensburg. --In Frederick County, FRANCIS GILDART, Esq; to Miss ANN MARTIN, of Greenway Court. ■ Last Friday Night departed this Life, after a short Illness, the amiable Miss SALLY DOUGLASS RAMSAY.--Her refined Manners and benevolent Disposition, render her Death regretted by her Acquaintance, and irreparable to her Relations. ■ NAVAL-OFFICE, ALX. *Inward Entries*. None. *Cleared Outwards*. Schooner *Lottery*, Z. Mann, for Baltimore; Sloop *Ranger*, N. Stowe, Bermuda.

Messrs. RICHARDS and COMPANY,
Please to insert the following Lines on the Death of the much esteemed Miss [RAMSAY], and you will oblige. G.H.

HOW vain, alas! are all the Joys of Time,
Fleeting at best, and like the Meteor's Blaze;
O would Mankind secure those Joys sublime,
That shine in Heav'n with never fading Rays.

Esteem sincere bewails the early Doom,
Of blooming Virtue snatch'd in haste away,
She pours Complaints upon her youthful Tomb,
And mourns that such a Heart e'er felt Decay.

And well she may, for sure a better Heart,
Ne'er had a Mansion in the human Breast,
The Soul immortal, her far better Part,
Is gone to taste immortal Joys and Rest.

Ye weeping Friends, who clad in Mourning go,
Relations dear, with Grief and Woe opprest;
Permit a Stranger's Tears with yours to flow
Upon her Tomb, and mingle with her Dust.

With bitter Grief let Hope be intermixt,
You've lost a Friend on whom a Crown's bestow'd,
Torn from your Arms her Soul above is fixt,
Gone from this vain World to a blest abode.
ALX, Nov. 18, 1785.

Messrs. RICHARDS and COMPANY, GENTLEMEN,
HAVING seen an advertisement in your last paper signed *William Nichols*, forewarning all persons from taking an assignment on a bond which he have to me the fifth day of August last, for Three Hundred Pounds, Virginia currency, payable on the 13th day of July next, with Col. JAMES HENDRICKS and Capt. JESSE TAYLOR, as securities for the punctual payment thereof, and which Mr. Nichols has asserted was obtained from him in a fraudulent manner, it may therefore not be improper for me, in order to convince the public of the falsity of this declaration, to give a short account of the manner in which it was obtained, and for what it was given. On the 13th day of July, 1784, I entered into an agreement with Mr. Nichols as agent for MAR[K] BIRD and JAMES WILSON, Esquires, of Philadelphia, to take the management of a store to be established in this town, in consequence of which he became obligated to me for *Six Hundred Pounds*, Virginia Currency, Three Hundred Pounds of which remain yet unpaid, and for which the abovementioned bond was given.--Shortly after the failure of Mr. Nichols, he came to ALX, with an order from Messrs. BIRD and WILSON, to receive the goods out of my possession in order to close the business, as he said "it would enable him to close a dozen more" (his interest in the store having been made over to them the day before his failure) but as there were several debts owing by me, as agent for the company, besides this debt of mine, I refused to give up the property till I was first secured. On his finding this to be the case, and that I would not take *him* for the payment of these debts, he prevailed on Col. HENDRICKS and Capt. TAYLOR to be his securities for the payment of Six Hundred Pounds to Mr. [Page 3] GEORGE HUNTER, and Three Hundred Pounds to me which were the principal debts of the company; the others, being trifling ones, were settled in another manner. This is a short and true state of the matter; and I now publicly call on

Mr. Nichols and the gentlemen who are his securities, to shew in what manner the bond was fraudulently obtained. JOHN DUNDAS, ALX, Nov. 21, 1785.

On Saturday the 26th instant, will be sold at the Vendue-Store,

A VARIETY of WET and DRY GOODS, consisting of rum in hogsheads and barrels, sugars, cloths, linens, calamancoes, coarse stockings, calicoes, hats, womens' shoes, a quantity of cordage, and green, hyson and bohea teas.

S. ARELL, Vendue-Master.

ALX, Nov. 24, 1785.

☞ For private sale, very low, a chariot, a Negro boy, and a quantity of stone.

WANTED immediately, to attend a store of dry-goods, a smart active LAD, of 15 or 16 years of age, who can write a good hand, and is acquainted with figures; one who has served in a store would be preferred.--None need apply but those who can be well recommended. Inquire of the Printers. ALX, Nov. 24, 1785. ■ TO BE SOLD, **One hundred acres of** excellent pecoson land, equal to any in this State, lying on the Potomack, within two miles of ALX, and which, at a small expence, may be reclaimed. There is on said land a large range of wood.--The terms are one half cash, one quarter in six months, and the other in six months more. Apply to ROGER WEST, Nov. 24, 1785. ■ To be sold at Fredericksburg, on Wednesday the 14th of December next, to the highest Bidder, for Ready-Money, or Country Produce at cash price, ALL the household and kitchen furniture, belonging to the Stage-Office, consisting of twenty-seven beds, with furniture complete, mahogany tables, black walnut ditto, mahogany and Windsor chairs, a neat case of drawers, and a great variety of other valuable articles.--At the same time, and on the same terms will be sold a four-horse waggon. NATHANIEL TWINING, Nov. 24, 1785. N.B. Articles purchased at the sale, if not taken away in four days afterwards, will be again sold at the risk of the first purchaser. ☞ All persons indebted to the said tavern, are requested to make immediate payment, as no longer indulgence can be given. ■ SIX POUNDS REWARD. RAN away from the Subscriber in the month of November, 1784, an Irish servant, named PATRICK CONDON; he appears to be about 23 years old, six feet high, smooth faced, long visaged, brown hair, very forward and talkative when in liquor which he is very fond of, had a cut of an ax near one of his ancles, which was not healed when he went away, and I am well informed he was in Dumfries gaol, and turned out last month, no one appearing to claim him: He had on an old blue jacket, his other clothing was very ragged, and went by the name of WILLIAM PETRE. He went from Dumfries towards Falmouth, and it is very probable he is now loitering between these parts. Whoever brings him home, shall have the above reward paid by J.G. DOWDALL, Winchester, Nov. 1, 1785. ■ Loudon County, September, 1785. FARLING BALL, Gentleman, returned a certificate, that Timothy Hixon had taken up as a stray, a MARE, about 13 hands and a half high, of a brown colour, a small star in her forehead, branded on the near shoulder ID, appraised by Charles Bennett, William Hixon and John Hanby, to Three Pounds Ten Shillings, currency. (Copy) Teste, CHARLES BINNS, D. Clerk. ■ STRAYED or stolen from the Subscriber on the night of the 20th inst. a black horse COLT, three years old, neither docked nor branded, shod before, his near hind foot white, the white part scared as if scalded, is about 14½ hands high, and has a hanging mane and full eyes.--If taken up 20 miles from home and brought to me, I will give Three Dollars, if a shorter distance two, and reasonable charges. JOSEPH JANNEY, ALX, Nov. 23, 1785. ■ **Joseph Allison**, Has imported in the *Alexandria*, Captain Watkins, from Liverpool, a neat and general assortment of Manchester GOODS, among which are the following articles: POCKET and pillow fustians, thicksets, satinets, olive, light, blue and black beavers, corduroys, printed velverets, rich silk velvet waistcoat patterns, striped holland, yard, 3-8 and 7-8 cotton checks, elegant furniture ditto, with cord, tassels and fringe to match, 10-4 and 11-4 counterpanes neatly fringed and scolloped, new fashioned printed quiltings, &c. He has likewise on hand an assortment of coarse woollens, such as Negro cottons, duffils, rose blankets, worsted, yarn and plaid hose, all which he will sell on the most reasonable terms for cash or country produce. ALX, Nov. 24, 1785. ■ I WILL sell that beautiful and healthy plantation, commonly called the LODGE, situated in Prince-George's County, about two and a half miles from the ALX ferry.--This tract contains 323 acres, about 120 of which are cleared upland and nearly 60 acres of meadow ground of the first quality, about 30 are cleared and well set with timothy, which yields a larger crop than any meadow I ever saw.--Both the upland and meadow are laid off in divisions, and are in fine order for grazing. The improvements are a good dwelling-house, a fine garden, and every necessary building.--Taking in all its advantages it has ever been considered among the first forest plantations in the State. WILLIAM BAKER. ☞ Military Land-Warrants for 4000 acres for sale very cheap. ALX, Nov. 24, 1785. ■ GEORGE WASHINGTON, Mount Vernon, has for sale three lots in Fredericksburg, and a tract of land about 3 miles from said town [see like ad Vol. II No. 94] ■ FOR SALE, NEAR two thousand acres of LAND on Buck-Creek, in Lincoln County, which has been located near three years, by one of the first characters in that County, and who informed me that it was the best land that was then to be got. I will dispose of it for cash, Negroes, dry or wet goods, and all kinds of certificates will be taken at their passing value; but an exchange of land in this county would be prefered. TO BE LET, for one or more years, and possession given the first day of January next, the house near the Falls-Church, ten miles from ALX, on the main road leading through Leesburg to Winchester, seven miles from George-Town, and on the main road leading from thence by Newgate to North and South Carolina, which makes it a convenient stand for a tavern or store, as there is one at present kept in it.--Also, a house about two miles higher up the road to Leesburg, convenient for a tavern; there will be let more or less land with this as may be agreed on.--Also a plantation, about half a mile from the last mentioned place.--The two last mentioned places have exceeding fine never failing springs.--Also, a farm in Loudon County, near Sugarland-Run; the land is of a good quality, well watered, upwards of fifty acres of land cleared, some improved meadow, and more may be made.--The terms may be known by applying to OPIE LINDSAY, Colchester, Nov. 21, 1785. ■ THE Subscriber begs leave in the most respectful manner, to return his grateful acknowledgments, to his friends and kind customers, who favored him with their custom, during his residence in Fairfax-street, and informs them he has now removed to Royal-street, near the corner of King-street, where he carries on the Tallow-Chandler and Soap-Boiling business as usual, and will use his utmost exertions to give general satisfaction. ☞ He gives ready-money for tallow, tow or cotton candle wick. WILLIAM HAYCOCK, ALX, Nov. 24, 1785. ■ **William Taylor and Co.**, Have for sale, at their store on Fairfax-street, formerly occupied by Messrs. Lowry and M'Kenna, and next door but one to Col. Dennis Ramsay's Store, DOUBLE milled drabs; Superfine and second cloths of various colours; Blue, buff and light cassimers; Blue and red duffils; Gray and mixt coatings; Rugs and blankets; Swanskins; Scarlet, red, white and yellow flannels; Striped linseys and embossed serges; Red and light baizes; Fine green and white plushes; Shalloons and rattinets; Pink, blue and green tammies; Striped and plain blue and green calamancoes; Blue, green and light durants; Blue and green camblets; Corduroys and queen's cord; Honeycomb and Rodney's cord; Spotted and plain velvets; Pillow fustians; Figured jeans and jeanets; Blue, green, pink, black and red moreens; Superfine black bombazeens; Black and light crapes; Mens' plain and ribbed yarn and worsted hose; Thread, cotton and silk ditto; Childrens' spotted ditto; Ladies' silk gloves and mitts; Lamb, kid and best white ditto; Shammy gloves and mitts; Linen and cotton checks; Haerlem and furniture ditto; Cambricks, clear and long lawns; Black and white gauzes; Needle worked lawn aprons; Kentings and kenting handkerchiefs; Common, souflee and white catgut; Manchester cottons and printed linens; Light and dark ground French and Dutch calicoes; Satins and modes; Green, pink and black persians; Black Barcelona neckcloths and handkerchiefs; Dove and changeable ditto; Common silk ditto; Ladies' silk cardinals trimmed with ermine; Satin, Persian and durant quilts; 7/8 and yard-wide Irish linens; British osnaburgs' Hessian rolls', Fine Flanders bedticking; Common and ell-wide ditto; 6, 7 and 8-4 bed-bunts; Linen and cotton handkerchiefs; Stamped, spotted, and bordered souflee ditto; Diaper toweling and tablecloths; Mens' castor and felt hats; Wool and cotton cards; Bar-lead and shot; Mens' Morocco slippers and childrens' Morocco shoes; Ladies' best calamanco and common ditto; Scarf and common twist; French and English sewing silk; Scotch and coloured threads; Common and best writing-paper; Bonnet pasteboards; Bibles, testaments and psalters; Spelling-books; Sealing-wax and Dutch quills; Best London playing cards; Inkpowder; 3½, 4 and 4½ pins; Temple and common spectacles; Hatter's trimmings; Ivory, tortoishell and horn combs; Shaving boxes, soap and brushes; Tooth and buckle brushes; Hair pins and hair-powder; Washballs and pomatum; Silk and swan powdering puffs; Toupee and pinching irons; Plated spurs and spring snuffers; polished bridle bits with bridons; Common snaffle ditto; Polished and common stirrup irons; Surcingle and strainweb; Shoemakers' and saddlers' tools; Mill and handsaw files; Brass and iron candlesticks; Warming-pans and copper tea-kettles; Pewter quarts and padlocks; Brass cocks with keys; Common and best rasors; Large and small scissors; Barlow and common penknives; A large assortment of knives and forks with carvers; Oyster knives; Lettered, plain and tully gartering; Cap and apron tapes; Nonsopretty and [bobbing]; Mens' silk caps; Common and Whitechapel needles; Mens' thimbles; Womens' ditto; Silk, thread and beggars lace; Common and Bristol sleeve buttons; Gilt and silvered watch chains; Watch seals and keys; Paste, stock and knee buckles; Common shoe and knee ditto; Gilt and common coat and jacket buttons; Horse brushes and mane combs; Carpenters' planes, bits and chisels; Bottled snuff and Durham mustard; Slates and pencils; A variety of glass ware &c.&c. ALX, Nov. 24, 1785.

Page 4. Poetry. "Advice to a Young Lady, on seeing her Dance." ■ **Randle Mitchell and Son,** Have removed their store from Fairfax to King-street and have a large and general assortment of dry-goods [see like ad Vol. II No. 91] ■ JESSE TAYLOR seeks charters for vessel to Lisbon and back [see like ad Vol. II No. 93] ■ **Ewan M'Lean**, taylor from Edinburgh, had opened his business at the house of Mrs. Shaw [see like ad Vol. II No. 94] ■ ROBERT HAMILTON, Neubro, seeks to settle debts to the estate of JOHN TAYLOR, Esq; deceased [see like ad Vol. II No. 94] ■ WILLIAM NICHOLS warns public of taking assignment of bond from John Dundas [see like ad Vol. II No. 94] ■ ROBERT ALLISON has for sale a Negro woman and a lease on ground-rent [see like ad Vol. II No. 94] ■ WILLIAM HERBERT has for lease a store, cellar and counting-room lately occupied by Messrs. Randle Mitchell and Son [see like ad Vol. II No. 93] ■ JONATHAN SWIFT and CO. offer reward for stolen Irish linen [see like ad Vol. II No. 94] ■ HOOE and HARRISON note departure of the Ship *Union* for L'Orient, and taking tobacco as freight [see like ad Vol. II No. 94] ■ RICHARD CONWAY notes departure of the Brig *Martha*, Samuel Harper, Master, for St. Eustatius [see like ad Vol. II No. 94] ■ The Ship *Hazard*, Capt. Thomas New, departs by middle of December for London [see like ad Vol. II No. 94] ■ JESSE TAYLOR seeks charters for vessel to Lisbon and back [see like ad Vol. II No. 93] ■ DANIEL ROBERDEAU has for sale Jamaica spirits, etc. [see like ad Vol. II No. 94] ■ Employment for a likely Negro boy saught; apply at the Printers [see like ad Vol. II No. 94] ■ ISAAC RAWLINGS has for rent rooms in house under the same range and roof as Mr. Watson's store [see like ad Vol. II No. 94] ■ CHRISTIAN HENRY RUTHER, George-Town, offers reward for return of runaways from Ship *Charming Peggy* [see like ad Vol. No. II No. 94] ■ Found this morning in the Commons near this town, A MAN's SADDLE.--The owner is desired to apply to the Subscriber, pay expences and take it away. JOHN THOMAS, ALX, Nov. 14, 1785. ■ JOHN POTTS, jun., Secretary of the Potomack Company, seeks 100 Negroes for hire [see like ad Vol. II No. 92] ■ TO BE SOLD, In Fee-Simple, A VERY valuable LOT, advantageously situated on Prince-Street--Inquire at the Printing-Office. ALX, Nov. 2, 1785. ■ WILLIAM BUDDICOM has for sale at Mr. Andrew Wales's goods just arrived in the Brigantine *Alexandria* [see like ad Vol. II No. 93] ■ WILLIAM BAYLY has for 4-years lease place called Gisborough, Prince-George's County [see like ad Vol. II No. 92] ■ CATHARINE JETT offers for sale at Mattox-Bridge, Westmoreland County, sundry valuable slaves [see like ad Vol. II No. 92] ■ WILLIAM HEREFORD has for sale a house and lot on Market and King streets in Leesburg [see like ad Vol. II No. 92] ■ ALX: Printed by GEORGE RICHARDS, and COMPANY, at their Printing-Office on Fairfax-street--by whom Advertisements, &c. are thankfully received for this Paper,--and where Printing is performed with Care and Expedition.

1785/12/01, Vol. II No. 96

Page 1. Mrs. BALL, Baltimore, gives notice she has moved from Annapolis to Baltimore where she has opened a coffee-house and tavern [see like ad Vol. II No. 94] ■ A smart active lad wanted to attend a dry-goods store [see like ad Vol. II No. 95] ■ ROGER WEST has for sale 100 acres of excellent pecoson land [see like ad Vol. II No. 95] ■ NATHANIEL TWINING, Fredericksburg, has for sale household and kitchen furniture belonging to the Stage-Office [see like ad Vol. II No. 95] ■ WILLIAM HAYCOCK has removed his store to Royal-street [see like ad Vol. II No. 95] ■ **John Allison**, has imported in the Brigantine *Alexandria*, a neat and general assortment of Manchester goods [see like ad Vol. II No. 95] ■ WILLIAM BAKER offers for sale a beautiful and healthy plantation commonly called the LODGE, situated in Prince-George's Co., Md. [see like ad Vol. II No. 95] ■ OPIE LINDSAY, Colchester, has for sale nearly 2,000 acres of land on Buck Creek in Lincoln Co., and offers lease on a house near the Falls-Church [see like ads Vol. II No. 95] ■ CHARLES BINNS announces that Timothy Hixon has taken up a stray mare [see like ad Vol. II No. 95] ■ TO BE SOLD, In Fee-Simple, A VERY valuable LOT, advantageously situated on Prince-Street--Inquire at the Printing-Office. ALX, Nov. 2, 1785. ■ JOSEPH JANNEY offers reward for strayed or stolen colt [see like ad Vol. II No. 95] ■ J.G. DOWDALL, Winchester, offers reward for return of runaway Irish servant named Patrick Condon or William Petre [see like ad Vol. II No. 95] ■ CHRISTIAN HENRY RUTHER, George-Town, offers reward for return of runaways from Ship *Charming Peggy* [see like ad Vol. No. II No. 94] ■ Found this morning in the Commons near this town, A MAN's SADDLE.--The owner is desired to apply to the Subscriber, pay expences and take it away. JOHN THOMAS, ALX, Nov. 14, 1785.

Page 2. **LONDON, August 10.**

The peasant at Zevenhuysen, against whom an action had been brought for damages done to Mr. Blanchard's balloon, proved he understood Logic better than Aerostatics, saying" "Gentlemen, it is an established point in law , that whatever falls from the clouds becomes the property of the owner of the land on which it falls. Mr. Blanchard and his balloon fell in my field. Ergo, Mr. Blanchard and his balloon both became my property, which I permitted him to repurchase for ten ducats, to which I am justly entitled." This curious syllogism, which appears irrefragable, diverted the court exceedingly; and Mr. Blanchard was one of the first to join in the laugh ... **September 14:** The following are said to be the resolutions proposed for the Counties and Boroughs of Scotland, previous to the meeting of Parliament.

I. That there is no good reason why Scotland should be treated with insolent contempt, while Ireland has a due deference paid to it.

II. That they who have advised withholding for some time past from Scotland, one of the fifteen judges of the court of session, the number solemnly stipulated by the articles of Union, have not due regard for their country.

III. That with the calm but firm spirit of men determined to maintain their constitutional privileges, we will oppose the insidious attempt to infringe on our agreement with England in 1707, by changing our supreme court of justice "as then constituted."

On Saturday died Lord Abergavenny, at his house in Grosvenor Place; the title and estate devolves to his son, Lord Neville ... Extract of a letter from **Algiers, Aug. 29:** A few days ago five Jews were strangled in this city by order of the Dey for defrauding a Christian merchant of much money and merchandise. They had visited most of the cities and capitol towns of Europe--particularly London, Bristol, Liverpool, Amsterdam, Bourdeaux and Port l'Orient--where their frauds totally ruined many, bringing families to the greatest distress and misery. Their two clerks were seized the next day, but were not in possession of any of the property. Nonetheless they were each given 100 bastinado blows on the soles of their feet, and sentenced to perpetual slavery, from not reporting either the villainy or their masters as notorious imposters. Their scheme to defraud the merchant was very artfully contrived, exactly the same as used to defraud unwary London tradesmen ... His Majesty is going to turn all the deer out of the Little Park at Windsor, and fill it with oxen, sheep, &c. For his own use; thus, the King is going to be his own butcher. An Oxford market butcher, from whom this comes, says if his Majesty had seen the slaughter houses which his German butchers made in America, to feed the politics of Lord North, Messieurs Jenkinson, Ellis, and Dundas, it would have satiated the most carnivorous passion.

Comte de Guichen has been singularly unhappy in the untimely end of both his sons. A nobleman of considerable merit, he is no less distinguished for his bravery than his humanity. Seamen aboard his ship think the measure of their satisfaction in serving with him; they call him *le pere des matelots,* or the father of the sailors. When he received his blue ribbon at l'Orient from the court, he assembled all the naval officers of his fleet: "Gentlemen, his Majesty has thought proper to recompence the service of his naval officers by a blue ribbon; he does me the honor to think me worthy of representing that corps, and orders me to wear this unequivocal mark of his approbation." The Vicomte de Roquefeuille, who perished with M. De Guichen, distinguished himself last war in the cutter *Levrier*, in company with the *Hussard*, when he fought an English frigate for upwards of an hour and a half, and only fled when he saw that he must certainly yield to superior force if he continued the combat ... Extract of a letter from **Amiens, Aug. 23:** The arrêt prohibiting importation of English goods except under such heavy duties as little short of prohibition, is nearly as unpopular in France as England. These people cannot equal the English in any manufacture which the latter have brought to perfection; the arrêt will deprive the French of many luxuries and even necessaries of Life hitherto imported from England. Above all, it is unpopular with shop keepers, who got the principal part of their livelihood selling English goods. I know a man in the neighbourhood of this city who dealt in second hand English carriages, selling fourscore yearly, clearing near £4000 yearly. The cuts his trade up by the roots, reducing him from opulence to distress. However, although this may check a trade in English articles too bulky to be smuggled, as long as there are free ports in France you may be assured your manufactures will, as usual, find their way here--under the eyes and even in sight of the most vigilant custom house officers. One of them told how it might be done without any danger from the laws. There was a great England-Dunkirk trade in new and old clothes. As the latter is a free port, English clothes will of course be landed there as before. The difficulty will be to get them out of town by land; but this is circumvented by people employed for that purpose, dressing themselves in the clothes and thus carry them out before the face of the officers, selling them in the country. They sometimes put on two or three waistcoats, and as many coats, and when stopped at the gate, say they are absolutely necessary to preserve them from the cold. The arrêt, therefore--to cut off trade with England--is incomplete while free ports are suffered in France. Till you hear, therefore, that the free ports are stripped of their privileges, you may look on the arrêt as a *brutum fulmen*--it will make a noise and no more ... **Sept. 15:** We should notice something going forward in France. They are equipping their fleets, augmenting their armies, and Spain is reinforcing Minorca, and brushing up the old fortifications. The dissensions in this country, and the determination of preserving the administration, against the will of the people, not one of which administration are capable of conducting a war, even against the Irish potato boats, have induced the French to make preparations for a war. There is nothing so easy as for the natural enemy to pick a quarrel. Phedrus has finely delineated that truth in his beautiful fable of the Lion and the Lamb ... We hear from Scotland that the shopkeepers in Edinburgh, Canongate and Leith, have determined to resist the shop tax ... **September 19:** Extract of a letter from **Brussels, Sept. 13:** We are all in agitation here, all is war and rumors of war. Last Friday morning, marched to the frontiers of Holland upwards of 3000 men of the Bender regiment by order of the Emperor, and double that quantity of dragoons, &c. Are preparing to follow them. There is to be an immediate encampment near Antwerp of about 20,000 men in all; and last night (Sunday) a courier arrived at the court of Brussels to the Arch Duke's, but his despatches are still secret. The general speculation is that the requisition made by the Emperor is acceded to by the Dutch; but others differ, concluding this military pageantry will produce very serious consequences; meantime the amusements and levities of this gay town go on as usual, and the grim visaged war has by no means "smoothed his wrinkled front;" the Brabantins, or rather the anglicised Flemings, "dance to the lascivious pleasings of a lute." ... Extract of a letter from the **Hague, Sept. 6:** Matters here, both domestic and foreign, are coming to the most disagreeable extremities. Nor are our affairs abroad in a better situation; the States are continually assembled without knowing what to determine upon--the Emperor having allowed them till the 15th to determine whether they accept his conditions; and in the meantime is making the most alarming preparations. The seizure of contraband goods in the mail of the Ambassador's messenger is an additional, embarrassing stroke. Messrs. De Waffenaar and De Leyden are certainly recalled from Vienna ... By a Nobleman just arrived from Germany we are told that preparations are making for a war between the Emperor and the Republic, all hopes of accommodation being nearly at an end ... Extract of a letter from the **Hague, Sept. 12:** News from Germany and the Austrian Netherlands convince us the Emperor's intentions are hostile. Letters from Deutz of the 5th confirm this alarming intelligence, saying they hear the Paris negotiations are stopped. The Emperor, worn out by difficulties the Republic raises about the sum to be paid, has signified to the States General they must immediately and finally resolve that matter. In other words--comply with his terms, or he will attack them ... Letters received Friday from the Hague say the Prince of Ligne was ordered to attack the fortresses on the banks of the Scheldt, and that when the post set out 6000 men were on the march to execute the enterprise ... Extract of a letter from **Madrid, Aug. 8:** We cannot imagine the motive for the warlike preparations making in this kingdom; the conferences of our Cabinet are more frequent than usual; several regiments have received orders to march to Catalonia; a fleet of eight sail of men of war are fitting out at Carthagena, to be increased to 16. These are said to be destined to guard the straits of Gibraltar, as the most pressing orders are sent to Cadiz for 12 sail of men of war as soon as possible. ■ **KINGSTON, (Jamaica) Sept. 28.** By a gentleman of veracity, lately from Cape Francois, we are assured it was confidently reported in every polite circle there, that 10,000 regular troops were under orders in Old France to embark for Hispaniola, whose arrival was daily expected ... Ordinances have lately been published throughout the French West India islands, to suppress and prohibit all foreign trade, under pain of confiscation of goods and imprisonment of persons. The Americans are particularly pointed at in these restrictive edicts, which has given rise to various conjectures. ■ **NEW YORK, Nov. 18.** We have been informed by private gentlemen from London, in the late ships, that that Court do not intend to conform to the articles of the late treaty of peace with America any further than they can be insured of its good consequences to their country--*The* **WESTERN POSTS** *in America they are determined not to relinquish!* ■ **PHILADELPHIA, Nov. 19.** The following is a copy of a letter wrote by three American Captains, who are captives at

Algiers, which was forwarded by the British Consul, to Richard Harrison, Esq; Consul for the United States at Cadiz. It is of so interesting a nature, that the Printers are all requested to publish it.

Algiers, Aug. 27, 1785
Richard Harrison, Esq; **SIR, WE** the subjects of the United States of America, have had the misfortune to be captured by the Algerines, brought into this port, and made slaves of. We were stript of all our wearing apparel, and brought to a state of bondage and misery.--The severities we endure are beyond your imagination. The British Consul, Charles Logil, Esq; has taken us into his house. We hope you will take our grievances into consideration, and make some extra provision for us: For no man can exist on the provisions which are dealt out by the king of this place, who may truly be called the King of cruelties.--Inform Congress and the different States of our situation. All nations, who have subjects in the hands of those infidels, exert themselves to relieve them--and while captives make them some extra allowance. We hope you will write to the British Consul on this head; he will give you every information respecting us, and how matters may be accommodated with America. If we do not make some terms, our trade will be ruined. The Algerines are at present fitting out cruisers with all possible expedition: Two will cruise off the Western Isles, and the rest off Portugal.

Americans beware! Let nothing tempt you to come in the way of those people, for they are worse than can be imagined. The ship *Dauphin*, Richard Obryan, commander, belonging to Messrs. Mathew and Thomas Irwin, of Philadelphia; was taken the 30th of July, 80 leagues to the N.W. of St. Ubes; and the schooner *Maria*, Richard Stephens, master, owned by Messrs. William Foster & Co. Of Boston, and consigned to you at Cadiz, was taken the 24th of July. We Americans are 24 in number, Captain Obryan's crew are at the Marine, where [Continued on Page 3].

Page 3. [The Algerines' American Captives' Letter (*continued*)] they experience all the miseries of slavery. Captain Stephens's crew are at the King's house. The Spaniards have made peace with those people; in consequence of which, they will be all over the Atlantic. They talk of ransoming us as high as from £400 to £600 sterling; however, you perhaps may know our price, and the customs of these heathens, in that particular, better than we do. We hope you will write to Charles Logil, Esq; and to us miserable sufferers, and advertise our situation to our brethren in America.

RICHARD OBRYAN,
ISAAC STEPHENS,
ZACARIAH COFFIN

Nov. 21: Last week 70 men of the first American regiment, under Major Haintrammach, marched through Carlisle on their way to Fort Pitt, where they go to do duty; and we hear that a large party have gone through York County, for the same place and purpose ... **Nov. 22:** The General Assembly of South Carolina on the 12th ult. Passed an act, entitled "An act for regulating sales under executions, and for other purposes herein mentioned," which obliges plaintiffs to receive in satisfaction of debts the property of the defendants upon appraisement; the said act to continue and be in force until the end of the next session, and no longer ... We hear the General Court of the State of New Hampshire, at the session lately begun at Concord, have passed an act for making many kinds of personal property a tender in the discharge of debts payable within that State ... By a gentleman just arrived from the westward, we learn the treaty with the Indians was going on at the Great Miami, much to the satisfaction of the Commissioners, and bears much with them as to its permanency. The Indians are signifying every mark of approbation. ■ **ALX, December 1**. The House of Delegates of Maryland on the 19th Ult. took into Consideration "a Bill for the Support of Ministers of the Gospel of all Denominations or Societies of Christians within that State," when there appeared for the Bill 21; against the Bill 41. On Monday the 21st Ult. was read in the House of Delegates now sitting at Richmond, an engrossed Bill to postpone the Collection of the Tax for the Year 1785, when the Question being put, there appeared for it 48; against it 50. ■ Late London Papers mention, that the King of Prussia means to take a decided Part against the Emperor, in favor of the Dutch. ■ DIED.] In this Town, on his way to Mount-Vernon, JAMES MACKAY, Esq; of the State of Georgia, a Native of Scotland. --In New-Hampshire, in an Apoplectic Fit, the Hon. JOHN SULLIVAN, Esq; Speaker of the House of Representatives, and Major-General of the Militia of that State, and late a Major-General in the Continental Army. ■ NAVAL-OFFICE, ALX. *Inward Entries*. Sloop *Washington*, D. Peoples, and Sloop *Dolphin*, A. Steward, from Philadelphia; Brig *Mary*, C. Briggs, and Schooner *Adams*, B. Witham, Rhode-Island; Sloop *Hero*, J. Humphries, Baltimore; Schooner *Judith*, E. Cook, Boston; Schooner *Barbadoes*, S. Fell, Barbadoes. *Cleared Outwards*. Ship *Peggy*, J. Tyndal, for Whitehaven; Brig *Industry*, J. Gibson, Madera. ■ From the MASSACHUSETTS CENTINEL. George Manly was executed at Wicklow in Ireland, pursuant to his sentence, for the murder of

Mr. Williams: At the gallows he made the following speech: MY FRIENDS, YOU are assembled to see--what? A man take a leap into the abyss of death. Look and you shall see me go with as much courage as *Curtius*, when he leapt in the gulph to save his country from destruction. What will you say of me? You say that no man without virtue can be courageous.--You'll say I have killed a man--*Marlborough* killed his thousands, and *Alexander* destroyed millions: Marlborough and Alexander, and many others who have done the like, are famous in history for great men--But I killed one solitary man. I am a little murderer, and must be hanged. Marlborough and Alexander plundered countries--they were great men--I ran in debt with the alewife, she becomes a witness against me, and I must be hanged. Now, my friends, I have drawn a parallel between two of the greatest men that ever lived and myself; but these were men of former days. Now I'll speak a word of some of the present day. How many men were lost in the American war, both sides could not have been in the right, yet Lord North is a great man, and I am but a little fellow. The King of France takes our ships, plunders our merchants, kills and tortures our men, but what of all that? What he does is good! He is a great man! He is clothed in purple, his instruments of murder are bright, and shining, mine was a rusty gun, and so much for comparison. Now I would fain know that what authority there is in scripture for a rich man to murder, to plunder, to torture, to ravage whole countries, and what law is it that condemns a poor man to death for killing a solitary sheep to fed his family? But bring the matter closer to our country--What is the difference between running in a poor man's debt, and by the power of gold, or any other privilege, preventing him from obtaining his right, and clapping a pistol to a man's breast, and taking from him his purse? Yet the one shall thereby obtain a coach, and honors, and titles. The other, what? A cart and a rope. From what I have said, my [brethren], you may, perhaps, imagine I am hardened, but believe me, I am fully convinced of my follies, and acknowledge the judgement of GOD has overtaken me. I have no hopes but from the merits of my Redeemer, who I hope will have mercy on me, and he knows that murder was far from my heart, and what I did was through rage and passion, being provoked thereto by the deceased. Take warning my dear comrades; think, O! think! What would I now give that I had lived another Life!

PRICES CURRENT, ALX. / Tobacco, 22s. per Ct. / Fine Flour, 29s. per Barrel. / Wheat, 5/6s. per Bushel. / Jamaica Spirits, 4/6 per Gallon. / Windward Rum, 3s. per Ditto. / Continental Rum, 2s. per Ditto. / Molasses, 1/6 per Ditto. / Muscovado Sugar, 35s. to 42/6 per Ct. / Salt, 3s. per Bushel, by Retail. / Corn, 4s. per Bushel. / Exchange, 40.

On Saturday the 3d instant, will be sold at the Vendue-Store,

A VARIETY of WET and DRY GOODS, consisting of rum in hogsheads and barrels, sugars, cloths, linens, calamancoes, coarse stockings, calicoes, hats, womens' shoes, a quantity of cordage, green, hyson and bohea teas, a number of 6, 8 and 10 plate stoves, and a quantity of bar-iron.

S. ARELL, Vendue-Master.

ALX, Dec. 1, 1785.

☞ For private sale, very low, a chariot, a Negro boy, and a quantity of stone.--Also, a waggon and four horses, and geers complete with two lock chains, on credit for six months with bond and approved security.

TO BE LET, A WAREHOUSE on the wharf, completely fitted for the reception of all kinds of country and West-India produce.--For terms apply to WILLIAM HERBERT, ALX, Nov. 30, 1785. ■ WHEREAS the Subscriber took a certain Edward Jones with a bay HORSE, his two hind feet white, is a natural trotter, branded on the near buttock with a swivel stirrup; this is to give notice to the owner to prove his property to the said horse, pay charges and take him away. JACOB MOORE, ALX, Nov. 30, 1785.

For HAVRE-DE-GRACE, in France,

THE Ship *MARY,* NASH GOODWIN, Commander, and will be ready to sail by the 10th inst.--For passage apply to WILLIAM HUNTER, jun. and CO., JOSIAH WATSON, or the Master on board.

Dec. 1, 1785.

I hereby forewarn all persons from taking an assignment of a BOND of mine in the possession of WILLIAM STONE, as he has acted contrary to his agreement with me. JOHN MURTLAND, ALX, Nov.

29, 1785. ■ THIS is to give notice to whom it may concern, that we intend to apply to the present General Assembly, for an act to enable the executors of James Nourse, deceased, to sell a certain tract of land in Berkely County, Virginia, on the head of Worthington's-Run, containing near 1000 acres, belonging to the estate of the deceased, that the intent of the will may be fully complied with. JOSEPH NOURSE, JAMES NOURSE, WILLIAM NOURSE, Executors, Nov. 30, 1785. ■ Just received, and to be sold by **D. and I. M'Pherson,** At their store the third door above Gilpin's wharf, A Quantity of woollens, consisting of blankets, duffils, long-ells, plaid and Shetland hose, white plains, flannels, &c.--They have also for sale, Grenada, Barbadoes and St. Croix rum by the hogshead and barrel, sugar, molasses, pork, tar, pitch, turpentine, Madera wine, salt, cordage and sail canvas; also, a ship's anchor, weight 1400lb. with a variety of other articles. ☞ They want to purchase a quantity of flour and Indian-corn. ALX, Nov. 30, 1785.

Montgomery County, Maryland, Nov. 29, 1785.

To be sold by public vendue, on Thursday the 16th day of March next, if fair, if not the next fair day, (if not sold before at private sale) the following lands, lying in the County aforesaid, viz.

ABERDEEN, with two small tracts nearly adjoining, making in the whole about 180 acres of level fertile land, whereon are the following valuable improvements: A commodious two-story brick dwelling-house, 42 by 30 feet, four rooms, a passage and bar well finished, on the lower floor, and four rooms on the upper, not quite finished, a cellar underneath the whole with convenient divisions, a large and convenient kitchen with a good brick chimney, another house with a brick chimney, which, with a small expence, might be converted into a storehouse, a good tobacco-house 32 by 22 feet, a large and well constructed stable divided into stalls, and several other convenient and necessary out-houses; a large garden with a stone wall round it, and adjoining the dwelling-house, a well of excellent water within a few steps of the kitchen door, about nine acres of excellent meadow now in Timothy, and an orchard of apple trees of the best kind of fruit.--About 70 acres of this land are yet to clear, the rest under good and sufficient fencing, and the whole adapted to farming or planting.--Through this tract and close to the dwelling-house runs the road from George-Town to Frederick-Town, is about 13 miles from the former and 30 from the latter, and less than a mile from the Court-House of this County.--This stand is justly esteemed one of the best in the County for a tavern, and has been occupied as such for several years.--If this tract is not sold at or before the abovementioned time, I propose to rent it with the house thereon, for a term of years.--Also, 500 acres of LAND, being part of a tract called Leakins's Lot, lying on the waters of Seneca, about 20 miles from George-Town and 35 from Baltimore.--The soil of this land is well adapted to the cultivation of fine tobacco, it lies level and abounds with springs of excellent water, and a large quantity of beautiful watered meadow might be made thereon at a very small expence.--There are about 40 or 50 acres of this land cleared, which rents for 2000lb. of crop tobacco yearly, and the assessment of 200 acres paid by the tenants yearly.--The improvements are a small log dwelling-house, a few out-houses, and a young orchard of apple trees.--Also, 250 acres of LAND, being part of a tract called Exchange and New Exchange Enlarged, lying within a mile of Aberdeen. — This land lies level, abounds in springs of good water, and is suitable for either planting or farming.--There are about 30 acres of very valuable meadow ground belonging to it, 40 or 50 acres fresh cleared, under good fence, and in good order for cropping.--The rest of the improvements are a Negro quarter and new log tobacco house 52 by 22 feet, and covered with shingles.--Also a tract called Addition to Discovery, containing 90 acres.--This land lies about 15 miles from George-Town, is remarkably strong and rich, abounding in heavy timber and springs of excellent water.--There are about 30 acres of it cleared and under a good fence, and about 3 acres of beautiful meadow now in grass.--The improvements are a small log dwelling-house, kitchen, a good framed tobacco-house, and 200 bearing apple trees of the very best kind of fruit.--The title to these lands is indisputable, and the terms of payment will be made very easy to the purchasers.

JAMES SUTER.

STOP THE THIEF! STOLEN from my waggon at the White-Oak Spring on the 20th instant, a strawberry roan MARE, 13½ hands high, heavy made, 12 years old, branded with a three barred woman's stirrup-iron, half ridged mane, and a short docked tail.--Whoever takes up said mare and secures the thief, shall receive SIXTEEN DOLLARS, and EIGHT DOLLARS for the mare only, if brought to Mr. RICHARD SIMPSON, near the White-Oak Spring, Fairfax County, or to the Subscriber living in Frederick County, Virginia, near Col. Zane's iron-works, with all reasonable charges. JAMES WILSON, Nov. 30, 1785.

Page 4. Poetry. From the *Hibernian Magazine*; "Verses presented by a Gentleman to his Wife, on the Anniversary of their Wedding Day." ■ **Randle Mitchell and Son,** Have removed their store from Fairfax to King-street and have a large and general assortment of dry-goods [see like ad Vol. II No. 91] ■ WILLIAM BUDDICOM has for sale at Mr. Andrew Wales's goods just arrived in the Brigantine *Alexandria* [see like ad Vol. II No. 93] ■ **Ewan M'Lean**, taylor from Edinburgh, had opened his business at the house of Mrs. Shaw [see like ad Vol. II No. 94] ■ ROBERT HAMILTON, Neubro, seeks to settle debts to the estate of JOHN TAYLOR, Esq; deceased [see like ad Vol. II No. 94] ■ WILLIAM NICHOLS warns public of taking assignment of bond from John Dundas [see like ad Vol. II No. 94] ■ **William Taylor and Co.** have for sale at their store on Fairfax-street a list of goods [see like ad Vol. II No. 95] ■ DANIEL ROBERDEAU has for sale Jamaica spirits, etc. [see like ad Vol. II No. 94] ■ JESSE TAYLOR seeks charters for vessel to Lisbon and back [see like ad Vol. II No. 93] ■ HOOE and HARRISON note departure of the Ship *Union* for l'Orient, and taking tobacco as freight [see like ad Vol. II No. 94] ■ RICHARD CONWAY notes departure of the Brig *Martha*, Samuel Harper, Master, for St. Eustatius [see like ad Vol. II No. 94] ■ The Ship *Hazard*, Capt. Thomas New, departs by middle of December for London [see like ad Vol. II No. 94] ■ A likely Negro boy, about 17 years of age, for sale [see like ad Vol. II No. 94] ■ ISAAC RAWLINGS has for rent rooms in house under the same range and roof as Mr. Watson's store [see like ad Vol. II No. 94] ■ ROBERT ALLISON has for sale a Negro woman and a lease on ground-rent [see like ad Vol. II No. 94] ■ CATHARINE JETT offers for sale at Mattox-Bridge, Westmoreland County, sundry valuable slaves [see like ad Vol. II No. 92] ■ ALX: Printed by GEORGE RICHARDS, and COMPANY, at their Printing-Office on Fairfax-street--by whom Advertisements, &c. are thankfully received for this Paper,--and where Printing is performed with Care and Expedition.

1785/12/08, Vol. II No. 97

Page 1. **D. and I. M'Pherson** have for sale at their store the third door above Gilpin's wharf, a quantity of woollens, etc. [see like ad Vol. II No. 96] ■ The Ship *Mary*, Nathaniel Goodwin, Commander, to sail for Havre-de-Grace, France [see like ad Vol. II No. 96] ■ JACOB MOORE seeks owner of horse found of Edward Jones [see like ad Vol. II No. 96] ■ Executors of James Nourse seek of the General Assembly an act to permit sale of land in Berkeley Co., Va. [see like ad Vol. II No. 96] ■ J.G. DOWDALL, Winchester, offers reward for return of runaway Irish servant named Patrick Condon or William Petre [see like ad Vol. II No. 95] ■ JAMES WILSON offers reward for return of mare stolen from his waggon at the White-Oak Spring, Fairfax Co., Va. [see like ad Vol. II No. 96] ■ WILLIAM HERBERT has warehouse for lease on the wharf [see like ad Vol. II No. 96] ■ JAMES SUTER, Montgomery Co., Md., has for sale several tracts of land, including one called Aberdeen [see like ad Vol. II No. 96]

LISBON, August 9.

Our merchants are greatly alarmed at the repeated captures made by the Algerines. Some letters received here a few days ago bring the advice that those Barbarians have now at sea not less than 17 ships, mounting 20-36 guns, and 250-300 men each. The largest of them are constantly cruising off Cape St. Vincent, the others at the mouth of the Straits. In the province of Algarve, one of those pirates landed his crew, who carried off several heads of cattle, and also a man, woman and a child. The Governor has taken every possible care to prevent repetition of such misfortunes. In the midst of our anxiety, we have been greatly relieved by the safe arrival of four East Indiamen, very richly laden. ■ **HAGUE, Sept. 30.** We have received the agreeable news that the preliminary articles of peace between the Emperor and this Republic were concluded upon at Paris, on the 20th of this month, of which the following are the principal:

That their High Mightinesses are to pay 9,500,000 florins, Dutch money, as a compensation for the fortress at Maestricht and its dependencies, and 500,000 florins each for the damage done by the inundations. The above is to be paid by installments of 1,250,000 florins each, the first payment to be made 3 months after the treaty ratification, into the treasury at Brussels. The second is to be made six months later, and so on until full payment.

Their Mightinesses cede the town and castle of Dahlem, with all its appurtenances, except Oost and Cadier, to the Emperor, on condition of having a compensation made them in exchanges that may be thought necessary in the country called Over Maeze.

The boundaries of Flanders shall remain as they were settled in 1664, and if there be any points time may have rendered obscure, Commissioners shall be appointed to settle them.

The High Mightinesses acknowledge the Sovereignty of the Emperor on the Scheldt, from Antwerp to the end of the land of Sastingen, conformably to the line drawn in 1664, which is agreed to be cut through, as is fully explained in the map signed by the respective Ambassadors, and the States General entirely give up the right of demanding any toll or duty whatever in that district, nor shall the trade of his Imperial Majesty's subjects be in the least molested, provided no greater extension is granted to it than is agreed by the treaty of Munster of the 30th of January, 1648, which shall in this respect remain in full force.

Their High Mightinesses to evacuate and demolish the forts of Kruischans and Frederik Henrik, and cede the ground to his Imperial Majesty.

Their High Mightinesses, to give fresh proof how willing they are to facilitate a permanent good standing between the Republic and the Emperor, agree to cede forts Lillo and Leiskenshoek, with all that belongs to them, in their present state, to his Imperial Majesty, except the artillery and ammunition.

His Imperial Majesty gives up all pretensions to the villages of Bladel and Reussel.

All money pretensions between Sovereign and Sovereign to be entirely annulled, and commissioners appointed to settle those of individuals.

The above articles were drawn up in the presence of the Comte de Vergennes, appointed to act as [Continued on Page 2].

Page 2. [Peace Treaty (*continued*)] mediator by his most Christian Majesty, and underwrote by the signing Ambassadors, "With the approbation of the Emperor and the States General." ■ **LONDON, Sept. 9.** Extract of a letter from Bourbon Lanci, in **Burgundy, August 28:** The Marechal Duke Fitz-James is here, and takes the waters; he is worn to a mere skeleton, and according to physicians cannot live a month; and, what is strange, both his sons are in an agonizing state, one (the Duke) has lost the use of his limbs by the palsy, and is pronounced incurable by the faculty; the younger son (the Chevalier, Colonel of Berwick's regiment) is in a decline, and little or no hopes are conceived of his recovery; so, were it not for the younger Duke's children, there would be an end to the offspring of King James in France ... **Sept. 15:** Mr. Pitt was much abused at Horsham on his way to Brighton. The populace assembled as soon as was known, and broke the windows of the coach. The Minister at first laughed; but as soon as he found stones entering the windows, and the cry of, No shop tax, no Irish propositions, he squatted down in the bottom of the carriage, and the post boys galloped through the croud as fast as the horses could draw their Right Honorable luggage ... **Sept. 16:** The French go beyond us in everything--in their extension of commerce--in their cultivation of science--and in their liberal institutions for every species of distress. A recent instance of the attention and humanity of Paris we recommend to the city of London. The chamber of the city of Paris have erected 12 baths, hot and cold, for the use of the poor, where they are to be permitted to bathe gratis, and have every accommodation furnished them, of attendants, linen, &c. ... According to letters from **Marseilles**, no fewer than 29 vessels of and for that port, with very valuable cargoes, had been taken by the Algerine corsairs, in the course of the last six months, and carried into Algiers, where their crews were all made slaves of ... **Sept. 20:** Extract of a letter from **Constantinople, Aug. 12:** We are all in motion here. The castles and forts on the Black Sea are all filled with artillery and troops, and intrenchments are making to defend the approach to them. Three thousand men are constantly employed on the new works at the mouth of the Danube. The plan of the French engineers on the banks of the canal between Burgudore and the entrance to the Black Sea is carrying on with the greatest alacrity. Plainly, the Turks do not rely on promises of friendship and moderation made by the neighbouring powers. The ancient Bashaw of Belgrade, whose head has been in such danger, is just appointed Governor of Salina ... **Sept. 21:** The -----, Capt. Folger, is safe arrived at Dover from Boston, with despatches to their Ambassador at our court. It is said in consequence of some intelligence received at Boston from the court of London respecting trade, the act will be repealed that lays a heavy duty of British ships, and trade established on a more equal footing ... A gentleman just arrived from Gibraltar in the *Bacchus*, Prouting, reports they met with 6 stout frigates and one line of battle ship, of the Portuguese nation, between Cape St. Vincent and Cape Spartel, part of a 12 sail squadron cruising to protect there trade from the Algerines. These pirates are said to be now gone farther to the westward, to pick up vessels from Brazil and America ...

Oct. 1: The following are some of the momentous objects Mr. Pitt is expected to adjust before the next meeting of Parliament, viz.

1. A commercial and constitutional arrangement between Great Britain and Ireland.

2. A federal treaty with the Germanic Powers.

3. To enforce an immediate surrender of the English settlements of the coast of Africa, which the French have wrested from us, and fortified, and to demand satisfaction for so daring a violation of a positive article of the late peace.

4. To require an apology from the Court of Versailles for the late insult offered to the British flag, even in the British channel.

Oct. 7: A letter from **Paris, Sept. 22,** says that two English frigates and a sloop appeared every day at five o'clock in the evening hovering before the road of Cherbourgh, to observe what is going forward there, and they are not hindered from approaching as near as they can. During the last campaign three millions were expended in paying 5000 workmen. All the timber with which the Conick Caissons are constructed is brought in Hamburg, Danish, and Swedish vessels. The Duke de Harcourt presides over this undertaking, which he often visits, and encourages workmen, with whom he passed the spring and summer ... Extract of a letter from **Leghorn, Sept. 11:** Commerce with the United States of America to the ports in the Mediterranean is almost annihilated at present, owing to the number of Algerine vessels, which infest the seas, and are very active after the thirteen stripes [word missing] several American vessels have lately escaped the vigilance of those freebooters, under English colours, and got safe to their destined ports. These [word missing] pillagers have, within these few days, taken three vessels belonging to the Pope's dominions, bound here, and sent to Algiers, where the crews are put into captivity, which causes great unease. These pirates do not confine themselves to the Mediterranean, but now cruise between two and three hundred leagues farther to the westward than at any former period, in which latitude they have lately taken several valuable prizes from different nations ... **Oct. 8:** Yesterday Baron Linden, the Dutch Ambassador, notified to his Majesty, in official form, the signing of the preliminaries at Paris for final settlement of the differences between the Republic of the States General and the Emperor of Germany; and afterwards had a private conference with the King ... A letter from **Nantz, Sept. 24** says the ingenious M. Pierre Barb[letters missing] with 8-10 other gentlemen, took passage to Charleston, South Carolina, in the *Courier de l'Amerique*, which sailed a few days since, in order to try silk culture in that province. They are patronized by the King, and have encouragement from the American government ... **Oct. 11:** The following substance of the resolution of the States of Zeeland is proof the provinces are from unanimously approving the preliminaries signed with the Emperor. The States of that Province complain loudly of his Imperial Majesty's demand for an exchange of the district of Dahlem inclosed in the Duchy of Lembourg for somewhat equivalent. They consider the steps taken by the Republic, not only useless, but humiliating and derogatory to the dignity of the Republic. The offer of five millions of florins was more than sufficient to convince all Europe of the Republic's earnest wish for peace. That it was trifling with its honor and dignity to suppose the expences of the march of the Austrian troops amounted to that sum--that as to the additional demand of seven millions and a half made by Count de Mercy, they felt the Republic had already made too great sacrifices for peace, and therefore ought resolutely to oppose any further concessions. That the confidence the Republic placed in the powerful intercession and formidable support of France, had hitherto prevented their taking the necessary security precautions; but that if all the steps the Republic took towards pacification proved unavailing, and it should be obliged to defend its rights and dignity by force of arms, that Province would not be wanting to contribute to the utmost of its power towards the preservation of the liberty and independence of the State, as became a faithful branch of the confederacy ... By letters from **Paris** we learn France is making every possible effort for putting its navy on a footing as respectable as the most formidable of its neighbours; and further, it is in agitation to add 32 men to each of the regiments of cavalry, previous to a general review of these corps in the ensuing spring ... The preliminary articles fixed by the High and Mighty States and the Emperor is thought will by no means allay the discontent and turbulence long brooding on the Continent. The Dutch are very far from unanimity in making the concessions; his Prussian Majesty looks with a jealous eye on the extension of the Imperial Dominions; nor is it at all probable that the Emperor, who has even shewn an active spirit, and hitherto found he had merely to ask to obtain, will find his ambition amply gratified, and sit quietly down with his present acquisitions. ■ **PORTSMOUTH,** (N.H.) **Nov. 11.** The Great and General Court of this State finish their sessions this week. We have not been able to obtain the result of their deliberations! Only that paper money, after a judicious hearing, was thrown out as a member not worthy of the honors of citizenship. ■ **FALMOUTH, Nov. 5.** About 12 months ago a number of Bostonians attempted to get that town incorporated with city privileges; but that true spirit of republicanism which has ever characterized Bostonians crushed in embryo the bastard of aristocracy. However, by the late papers it seems that a hankering still exists in the noddles of a designing few to wrest from the commonalty, as some are pleased to stile the very best class of inhabitants, the government of the town, and vest it in the hands of those whose business it will be totally to destroy the remaining privileges of the people; but we fondly hope the bulk of the inhabitants have still too much virtue--too high sense of their own importance, to be this duped by those enemies to their liberties--those foes to their dignity as men. ■ **PROVIDENCE, Nov. 12.** The Honorable General Assembly of this State is adjourned to Monday the 27th of February next, then to be convened in this town ... In their last session, an Act was passed with the requisitions of Congress of the 27th September last; and the sum of £19,390 1 6 9 [sic] being this State's proportion of three millions of dollars) is by said Act to be paid into the Continental Loan Office, out of the £20,000 tax ordered at the previous session. ■ **NEW YORK, Nov. 23.** Yesterday morning arrived at Sandy Hook in 12 weeks from London, the ship *Union*, Capt. Johnston; on board of which is the Hon. Mr. Temple, the British Consul, together with his lady (daughter of Governor Bowdoin, of Massachusetts) and family ... **Nov. 25:** On Wednesday last, Congress elected the Hon. John Hancock, Esq; of Massachusetts, President of that August body. He not being present, they proceeded to the choice of a Chairman, when the Hon. David Ramsay, Esq; of South Carolina was elected. ■ **PHILADELPHIA, Nov. 25.** Extract of a letter, received by the *Astrea*, from a gentleman at **l'Orient, Sept. 7**, to a merchant in Salem: I hope this will find you safe out of the reach of the Algerines. We have had no news more than what was current when you left; but there are hopes the Algerines are not so formidable an enemy as people have made us fear. From the account Mr. Jefferson gives, he thinks three ships of 40 guns would entirely protect our trade, by sending them on their coasts, so that they dare not send a rover to sea. ■ **RICHMOND, Dec. 3.** On Saturday last, between four and five o'clock in the afternoon, Mr. Busselot, a French gentleman, raised a Balloon from the capitol square on Shockoe Hill, in this city, which ascended to a great height. The wind setting Northeast, it took that course, and descended before night ten miles distant from the city, on the plantation of Captain John Austin, in Hanover. ■ **BALTIMORE, Nov. 29.** It is with pleasure we inform the public that the account of the death of General SULLIVAN, which was taken from a northern paper, is now contradicted; for the General still lives--emphatically and politically lives ... **Dec. 2.** The wardens office at Philadelphia hath given notice that the *floating beacon* on the *Brown* will be removed therefrom, on the 1st day of December next, and a large buoy placed in its stead, during the winter season ... We hear a petition, praying for an emission of a paper currency, hath been presented to the General Assembly of this state, signed by 910 inhabitants of Baltimore County, among whom are said to be many respectable names; and that next Thursday is the day appointed to take it under consideration ... The petition of tradesmen, manufacturers, and others, from the town of Baltimore, and a similar one from Frederick Town, are referred by the General Assembly to the Committee of Manufactures, who are now employed in draughting a bill on the important matters therein contained. ■ **ALX, December 8.** His Excellency PATRICK HENRY, Esq; is re-elected Governor of this Commonwealth. The Hon. WILLIAM SMALLWOOD, Esq; is chosen Governor of the State of Maryland. The Honorable John Henry, William Hindman, William Harrison, Richard Ridgely, and Nathaniel Ramsay, Esquires, are elected Delegates to represent the State of Maryland in Congress for the ensuing Year. ■ NAVAL-OFFICE, ALX. *Inward Entries.* Ship *Merchant*, R. Brill, from Falmouth; Sloop *Three Sisters*, J. M'Clenachan, Philadelphia; Schooner *Cynthia*, S. Thornton, Providence; Brig *Betsy*, P. Brown, Glasgow. *Cleared Outwards.* Sloop *Vulcan*, J. Christie, for St. Croix; Sloop *Washington*, D. Peoples, and Sloop *Dolphin*, A. Steward, Philadelphia; Sloop *Betsy*, J. Welch, North-Carolina; Sloop *Betsy*, S. Jackson, Providence; Brig *Mary*, C. Briggs, Rhode-Island; Sloop *Little Tom*, J. Cartwright, Demarara.

Page 3. "The Ring," story of Frederick, Lord Carlisle, who was enamoured of Evelina; possession of a ring. ■ Anecdote of a Gentleman coming out of Westminster Hall and a boy who stole his snuff-box.

PRICES CURRENT, ALX. / Tobacco, 22s. per Ct. / Fine Flour, 29s. per Barrel. / Wheat, 5/6s. per Bushel. / Jamaica Spirits, 4/6 per Gallon. / Windward Rum, 3s. per Ditto. / Continental Rum, 2s. per Ditto. / Molasses, 1/6 per Ditto. / Muscovado Sugar, 35s. to 42/6 per Ct. / Salt, 3s. per Bushel, by Retail. / Corn, 4s. per Bushel. / Exchange, 40.

Hooe and Harrison, Have for sale, MADERA wine of London, New-York and Virginia quality, Sherry of

2, 3, 4, 5, and 11 years old, a few quarter casks of Pajarate wine, claret in boxes, French brandy, Jamaica spirits, Geneva in cases, Cadiz salt, alum ditto, and sundry other goods. ALX, Dec. 7, 1785. ■ To be rented until the first day of November, 1786, THE HOUSE and LOT lately occupied by Mr. THOMAS REEDER.--The conveniencies and situation of this tenement for a publican, are inferior to none in ALX. Terms may be known by applying as early as possible to SAMUEL ARELL. ALX, Dec. 8, 1785. ■ To be sold on Saturday the 17th instant, at public vendue, A HOUSE and LOT, situated on King-street, opposite to Mr. John Gretter's, containing 15 feet in front and 92 feet back. For particulars inquire of VALENTINE UHLER, ALX, Dec. 7, 1785. ■ JONATHAN SWIFT and CO. offer reward for stolen Irish linen [see like ad Vol. II No. 94] ■ **Robinson, Sanderson and Rumney,** Are now landing from on board the *Hope*, Captain Cragg, from Whitehaven, a fresh assortment of European GOODS, suitable for the present season, which they will dispose of on the lowest terms, at their store on Fairfax-street, by wholesale only. Also the following articles: IRISH mess beef in tierces; Ditto in barrels; Irish mess pork in ditto; Best rose butter in sirkins; Barley in cags; Single refined sugar; Best Durham mustard; Candles; Soap; Red port in bottles; London porter in ditto; Strong beer in ditto; Pipes; Stone and earthen ware; Lisbon and Liverpool salt; Two neat sets of Mahogany chairs, 1 dozen each. ☞ They will give the best cash price for Tobacco as usual. ALX, Dec. 7, 1785. ■ FOR SALE, For cash or country produce, TENERIFFE wine in pipes, Fayal ditto in ditto, Port ditto in hogsheads, Claret ditto in boxes, and Pimento by the bag, a variety of dry goods, and a few tons of best Swedish iron. For charter to any port in Europe, a vessel of about 600 hogsheads burthen, British built, with a Mediterranean pass. WILLIAM HUNTER, jun., Dec. 7, 1785.

FOR LONDON,

THE ship *FRIENDS*, JOHN MUIR, Master, is now taking in tobacco consigned to Mr. Thomas Blane.--All his friends, who wish to ship, will please to advise the quantity and the time they can have it ready, either to John Ballantine, Westmoreland, William Hunter, jun. or the Master on board.--In order to get her off quick, one hundred hogsheads will be taken on liberty.

☞ Captain Muir has an elegant CHAISE with harness complete to dispose of.

ALX, Dec. 7, 1785.

FOR SALE, THE SLOOP *THREE SISTERS*, now lying at Col. Hooe's wharf, Philadelphia built, and well calculated for the river business.--Any person desirous of purchasing may know the terms and see the inventory, by applying to the Subscriber near said wharf.--Who has for sale a few pipes, half pipes, and quarter casks of Teneriffe wine, old Jamaica spirits, by the hogshead or smaller quantity, Liverpool china, and queen's ware in crates. JOHN M'CLENACHAN, ALX, Dec. 8, 1785. ■ To be sold cheap, and the payments made easy, AN exceeding valuable well improved farm, containing 376 acres, situate about four miles from Winchester, in the County of Frederick and State of Virginia, adjacent to the road leading from thence to Staunton, convenient to several merchant mills, and to places of worship of various denominations. It is remarkable well timbered and watered, and has a good proportion of meadow made, and to be made. There are on the premises about 90 acres of land clear, a good dwelling-house, kitchen, barn and other necessary buildings.--A more particular description may be unnecessary; but the subscriber takes the liberty of assuring the public, that in his opinion, it is the most valuable farm of its extent in that part of the country, of which there is any prospect of the sale. For terms apply to SAMUEL PLEASANTS, merchant in Philadelphia, or to the Subscriber near Winchester. ALEXANDER WHITE, Dec. 7, 1785. ■ On Friday the 16th instant, will be sold by public vendue at the Subscriber's plantation, FOUR valuable TRACTS of LAND in Fairfax County, conveniently situated for trade, lying on the main roads leading from the back country to ALX, and all on different courses. Also, another TRACT, on the Sugar Lands, equal in quality to any in that place.--The titles are indisputable, and the lands will be shewn on application. The same day will likewise be sold, three LOTS of GROUND in ALX, one 31 feet 4 inches fronting Pitt-street, and 84 feet back, on which is an unfinished brick house; another on Duke-street, 16 feet front and 57 feet back, on which is a tolerable good framed house; the third is on Prince-street, unimproved, 31 feet, and advantageously situated for business. At the same time and place will be sold, all the stock of horses, cows, five waggons and gears, and some farming utensils. Eighteen months credit will be given the purchasers, on bond and unquestionable security, and interest from the day of sale if not punctually paid.--Certificates at their passing value will be received in payment, and the usual discount for ready cash. GERRARD T. CONN, Dec. 7, 1785. ■ **Philip Dalby**, Has received by the ship *Potomack* from London, AN assortment of cloth and silk cloaks and cardinals, stuff and silk petticoats, with a variety of low-priced printed calicoes, and a few articles of millenary, which, with other goods he has on hand, he will dispose of for cash, certificates, or short credit. ALX, Dec. 7, 1785. ■ **B.A. HAMP,** Has imported in the *Potomack*, Capt. Bradstreet, from London, a general assortment of European GOODS, which he will sell cheap for cash or produce, at his store on Fairfax-street, three doors below Messrs. Robinson, Sanderson and Rumney's store, consisting of the following articles, viz. WOOLLENS, Shalloons, Durants and tammies, Calicoes, Linens, Sheetings, Printed cottons, Haberdashery, Hosiery, Mens' and boys' hats, Men's shoes and boots, Womens' stuff and satin shoes, Window glass, Powder and shot, Saddlery, Ironmongery, Hardware, Jewelry, An elegant assortment of China, &c. ALX, Dec. 1785. ■ On Tuesday the 13th instant, will be sold to the highest bidder at Gisborough, in Prince George's County, at the mouth of the Eastern-Branch of Potomack river, THE LEASE of Gisborough, Negroes, horses &c. as formerly advertised in this paper; also, two or three valuable Negro women who have been used to cooking, washing, ironing and working in the house; likewise, a servant man and his wife, the man is an excellent stone and brick mason. The terms of sale are, one-third of the purchase money to be paid in three months, and the other two-thirds in twelve, and if the first payment is not punctually made, the indulgence on the last payment to be forfeited. Bond and security will be required. WILLIAM BAYLY, George-Town, Dec. 6, 1785. ■ TWENTY DOLLARS REWARD. RAN away from the Subscriber a few days ago, an Irish indented servant man, named WILLIAM SMITH, by trade a carpenter, is about 5 feet 8 or 9 inches high, of a yellow complexion, has grey eyes, a down look, and has just recovered from a long spell of sickness: He had on when he went off an old brown coat, a white double-breasted flannel waistcoat with black horn buttons, coarse blue cloth breeches with black buttons, a check shirt, grey stockings, tolerable good shoes, round iron buckles, and a hat covered with pitch and tar.--Whoever will take up and secure said servant, or return him to his master, shall receive the above reward, and reasonable charges. JOHN EVANS, ALX, Dec. 1, 1785. ■ GEORGE WASHINGTON, Mount Vernon, has for sale three lots in Fredericksburg, and a tract of land about 3 miles from said town [see like ad Vol. II No. 94] ■ CHRISTIAN HENRY RUTHER, George-Town, offers reward for return of runaways from Ship *Charming Peggy* [see like ad Vol. No. II No. 94].

Page 4. Poetry. "The Muses Ode; From Mr. Pratt's last Publication called *Landscapes in Verse*." ■ **John Allison**, has imported in the Brigantine *Alexandria*, a neat and general assortment of Manchester goods [see like ad Vol. II No. 95] ■ TO BE SOLD, In Fee-Simple, **A** VERY valuable LOT, advantageously situated on Prince-Street--Inquire at the Printing-Office. ALX, Nov. 2, 1785. ■ A smart active lad wanted to attend a dry-goods store [see like ad Vol. II No. 95] ■ ROGER WEST has for sale 100 acres of excellent pecoson land [see like ad Vol. II No. 95] ■ JOHN MURTLAND warns others from taking assignment of a bond of his in the possession of WILLIAM STONE [see like ad Vol. II No. 96] ■ **William Taylor and Co.** have for sale at their store on Fairfax-street a list of goods [see like ad Vol. II No. 95] ■**Randle Mitchell and Son,** Have removed their store from Fairfax to King-street and have a large and general assortment of dry-goods [see like ad Vol. II No. 91] ■ OPIE LINDSAY, Colchester, has for sale nearly 2,000 acres of land on Buck Creek in Lincoln Co., and offers lease on a house near the Falls-Church [see like ads Vol. II No. 95] ■ WILLIAM BAKER offers for sale a beautiful and healthy plantation commonly called the LODGE, situated in Prince-George's Co., Md. [see like ad Vol. II No. 95] ■ CHARLES BINNS announces that Timothy Hixon has taken up a stray mare [see like ad Vol. II No. 95] ■ WILLIAM HAYCOCK has removed his store to Royal-street [see like ad Vol. II No. 95] ■ JOSEPH JANNEY offers reward for strayed or stolen colt [see like ad Vol. II No. 95] ■ ALX: Printed by GEORGE RICHARDS, and COMPANY, at their Printing-Office on Fairfax-street--by whom Advertisements, &c. are thankfully received for this Paper,--and where Printing is performed with Care and Expedition.

1785/12/15, Vol. II No. 98

Page 1. **Hooe and Harrison**, Have for sale MADERA wine of London, New-York and Virginia quality, etc. [see like ad Vol. II No. 97] ■ **Robinson, Sanderson and Rumney,** have goods for sale now landing from on board the *Hope*, Captain Cragg, from Whitehaven [see like ad Vol. II No. 97] ■ **Philip Dalby,** has for sale an assortment received by the ship *Potomack* from London [see like ad Vol. II No. 97] ■ WILLIAM HUNTER, jun. has for sale Teneriffe, etc. [see like ad Vol. II No. 97] ■ SAMUEL ARELL has for rent the house and lot lately occupied by Mr. Thomas Reeder [see like ad Vol. II No. 97] ■ The Ship *Friends*, John Muir, Master, is now taking in tobacco consigned to Mr. Thomas Blane, and will soon sail for London [see like ad Vol. II No. 97] ■ **B.A. HAMP**, has imported in the ship *Potomack*,

Capt. Bradstreet, from London, a general assortment of European Goods [see like ad Vol. II No. 97] ■ WILLIAM HERBERT has warehouse for lease on the wharf [see like ad Vol. II No. 96] ■ VALENTINE UHLER has for sale a house and lot situated on King-street, opposite to Mr. John Gretter's [see like ad Vol. II No. 97] ■ GERRARD T. CONN has for sale four valuable tracts of land in Fairfax Co., Va. [see like ad Vol. II No. 97] ■ JOHN EVANS offers reward for return of runaway Irish indented servant man named WILLIAM SMITH [see like ad Vol. II No. 97].

LEGHORN, August 26.

According the letters from different parts, the Algerine pirates are now more annoying than they have been at any former time to the commerce in the Mediterranean. Of the several gangs of pirates now at sea, four or five are so barbarous as to murder the crews of all the vessels they capture. ■ **LONDON, Sept. 12.** Last week copies of the late resolutions of his Majesty respecting deserters were sent to commanding officers of all British and Irish regiments, in every part of the globe. The punishment (whipping and death) for desertion is diametrically opposed to the thinking of leading military figures, and also by no means has the desired effect. It is therefore his Majesty's will, by and with the advice of the Privy Council, that deserters shall be sent to the Africa coast, or the East Indies, for Life, without any alleviation of the sentence, branded and badged as criminals, under perpetual stoppages, cloathing, &c. Being only provided them as at present ... **Sept. 21:** We hear a treaty of marriage is on foot between the Duke of York and Princess Frederica of Prussia, daughter of the Prince of Prussia; great preparations are making for entertainments and festivities at the palace of her aunt, opposite the arsenal in Berlin ... The following original papers from the *Edinburgh Courant* will give some ideas how fortunes are made in India. (Part of a letter from the Nabob of Arcot to the Directors of the India Company.) Inclosed you have a translation of an Arzee from the Killadar of Vellore. *I have thousands of them;* this will give you some idea of the miseries brought on this devoted country and the wretched inhabitants by the oppressive hand of Lord Macartney's management, nor will the *embezzlements* of *collectors* thus obtained appear less extraordinary.

The Arzee says: I have represented to your Highness the violences and oppressions under Lord Macartney's collector of revenue, &c. Such of the inhabitants as had escaped the sword and pillage of Hyder by taking refuge in the woods, &c. On the arrival of the collector, returned to the villages, set about the cultivation of the lands, and rebuilt their cottages. But now the collector has imprisoned the inhabitants' wives and children, seized the few jewels they had, and, before the faces of their husbands, flogged them to make them produce other jewels, &c.

Terrified with flagellation, some of them produced their jewels, &c. The collector flogged the women severely, tore the children from their teats, tied cords around their breasts, and exposed them to the scorching heat of the sun. Some of the large children he exposed to sale. The women who intended to return to their habitations have fled for refuge into Hyder's country. Every day is ushered in with fresh violence--I have no power to do any [Continued on Page 2].

Page 2. [Lord Macartney's Collectors (*continued*)] thing. Who will hear what I have to say? My business is to inform you who are my masters.

The present Governor is not like the former Governors; here is a very great man in Europe; and all the great men in Europe are obliged to him for accepting the Government of this place; it is his custom when he makes friendship with anyone, to continue always; and if he is an enemy to any one he will never desist till he has worked his destruction — he is now exceedingly displeased with the Nabob, and you will understand by and by, that the Nabob's business cannot be carried on. He (the Nabob) will have no power to do anything in his own affairs: You have therefore no right to fear him. You sent ten mangoes for my master and two for me, all of which I have delivered to my master, thinking ten not sufficient to present him with ... **Sept. 27:** A letter from **Venice, Aug. 25:** Chevalier Emo advises that his fleet again bombarded Sufa; the attack lasted 3 nights, during which 400 shells were thrown, of which 58 burst in the air, and 258 fell in the town, and did much damage by destroying 150 houses. The enemy fired 600 cannon balls, which did no further damage than wounding two soldiers. The fleet after this left the coast on the 6th of this month ... **Oct. 11:** The Emperor is said to be preparing a reply to the King of Prussia's declaration about the Germanic league. Prince Kaunitz is going immediately to Ratisbon. ■ **NEW YORK, November 29.** A duel on September 5th in South Carolina by Colonel Maurice Simons of Charleston and Mr. William Clay Snipes, of the Round O, left the former dead--depriving the State of a useful member, a wife of the best of husbands, and his children of an affectionate father. One of the most indelible stains that Christianity suffers, and the highest affront to the author thereof, is dueling. The wise Legislature of Pennsylvania, viewing this as an enormity too prevalent in this country, have introduce a bill to suppress such by severely penalizing both parties. Such, and so absurd, are the modern ideas of honor, that it is impossible for a good Christian to be a man of honor. Can the man who is both a husband and father dispense with his grand obligation to protect his wife and educate his children, to gratify the ambition of facing death, or humoring the caprice of a desperado. Where is the person upon earth, though ever so remote from the sunshine of fortune, who makes not a link to the great chain of nature, and is not, therefore necessary therein. True courage is a perfection of nature which is born therewith; and the man who possesses it has no necessity to form schemes for distinguishing himself therein, nor should he be solicitous to shew that extraordinary quality of every trifling occasion, which only appears in an amiable light when exerted for the public good; there the advantages resulting therefrom are truly noble; public applause and honest fame; there, if death be the consequence, how great the catastrophe! The glorious reputation of dying in your country's cause! How poignant must be the reflections of the surviving duelist. What have I done? Torn from an happy family an indulgent father; robbed the community of a useful member; or sent an unprepared soul into eternity.

Without these republican virtues, industry and frugality, our boasted independence and liberty will soon sicken and languish, and bring us under the subjection to some other power.

There seems to be no necessity, says a correspondent, for pocketing the insults, and tamely bearing Britain's encroachments and her perfidious conduct, in not delivering up the frontier posts agreeable to a solemn treaty. Notwithstanding all our encumbrances, we can, if necessity requires it, find men and money enough to compel. Experience teaches us Britain can not be trusted; that she is our mortal enemy and inimical to our welfare; that after such flagrant proofs of British perfidy, if they persist in retaining our frontier posts, is repel them by force. Our procrastination can answer no salutary end; let the demand for a fulfillment of the treaty be peremptory, and not wait until she recovers from the bruises sustained by American prowess ... Extract of a letter from **Fort Pitt, Oct. 13**, to a gentleman in Middletown: We marched from West Point the 7th of September, with a full company of 70 men, completely equipped with arms, clothing, and camp equipage. The clothing was very good, the coats excepted, which are coarse. We arrived here yesterday after a 36-day march, with as little trouble as could be expected on so long a march, and with recruits.

The company is healthy and in good spirits, except two men left en route because of their sickness. Eight deserted us during our march, none retaken---We shall remain here but one or two days. Col. Harmer met us before our arrival, on his route to New York. He says our destination is down the Ohio as far as Muskingum--170 miles distant--where we are to build a stockade fort, to prevent our being insulted by the Indians, and huts for the winter. Major Doughty, with a company of New York troops, is now at Fort M'Intosh, awaiting our arrival, when we shall go down river together. Major Hamtrach was at West Point when we departed, with a company nearly complete, and is expected to march on in a few days. Col. Harmer expects to send on two companies more from the State of Pennsylvania this fall. One company that he enlisted from the year's men has gone down to the Miami with the commissioners, on the treaty. The whole force here will then consist of 6 companies. Col. Harmer will exert himself to have a respectable garrison in the Indian country this winter. We flatter ourselves we shall spend the winter very agreeably, as it is excellent hunting and fishing where we are to quarter. The commissioners departed from Fort M'Intosh the 20th ult. to go down to the treaty. The surveyors are some of them at this place. We had the pleasure to meet Col. Sherman here, who has been down the Ohio about 40 miles. Captain Hutchins with some of the surveyors began to run the east and west line; but have not proceeded more than three miles, they apprehend it unsafe at present. The Surveyor General is determined not to proceed till he has the protection of some of the Indian chiefs; for which he has sent a messenger among them, who has not yet returned. If this measure is unattended with success, he will set off instantly for Congress.

There is a Delaware warrior detained a prisoner in this fort, who, in a frolic here some months hence, killed two men and wounded two more. His trial comes on next week, and it is not doubted he will be sentenced to suffer death; he is one of the principal warriors of his nation, and occasioned us much mischief in the late war.

I make just mention of the agreeable surprise I met with today. We happened to arrive here the day before a grand horse racing was to take place, and continue for three days, and instead of being in an uninhabited country, I found myself one among a thousand spectators, and principally from the country adjacent.

Pittsburg is very pleasantly situated, and consists of upwards of an hundred buildings near the fort.

Here are goods in the greatest plenty; but they bear a high price. Provisions are remarkably cheap; flour is at two dollars per cwt. And beef at twenty shillings; venison is sold for a copper a pound. ■ **PHILADELPHIA, Dec. 6.** Extract of a letter from **Washington, North Carolina, Oct. 20:** Last Tuesday arrived here the brig *Betsy*, Capt. Loughead, after a very distressing voyage. On Saturday at 4 o'clock P.M. she overset, when the people were obliged to cut away her masts; by which means the vessel righted ... Whatever opinion men may form of the Emperor of Germany in point of politics, we do not inquire into, but that his reign is daily marked with acts of wisdom and moral prudence, cannot be denied; for whilst with one hand he stabs that hydra, superstition, the other is employed in the services of humanity, and to forward the welfare of his subjects. An edict published the 22d of September, in favor of the peasantry, and other vassals of his Kingdom of Hungary, is proof. It is as follows:

WE, Joseph II &c. &c. Since our accession to the Sovereignty, we have not been sparing of our parental cares; but on the contrary, have by unwearied application, endeavoured to effect and establish on the most permanent foundation, the welfare and happiness of our subjects, without any distinction of state, nation or religion; wherefore, being convinced that the improvements of agriculture and the encouraging of industry are the best means to obtain so advantageous and desirable an end, and that this cannot be effected, but in as much as personal liberty, which by the civil and natural right, belongs to every individual in particular, whatever rank or class he may belong to, be firmly and generally established, and the sole and full enjoyment of the property they hold, under the protection of the laws, be to them irrevocably secured and confirmed; we are graciously pleased to order and command (that no one may pretend ignorance of our intentions) and that all those whom it may concern, may strictly conform to our supreme will and pleasure, that it may be universally published within every part of our dominions in Hungaria, that we have suppressed and do hereby entirely and for ever abolish the condition of state of servitude, known in Hungaria by the name of *Jobbagyonal-stand*. It is hereby also ordered that the word *Jobbagy*, which in the Hungarian language, signifies *subject*, be never employed in future to convey the same meaning as it did before. On the contrary, it is our will and pleasure, that all our subjects within the said kingdom, without any distinction of nation or religion, be, in what regards their persons, considered, held, and looked upon throughout our dominions, as men absolutely free, as we do declare them by these presents, as the right of nature, and the general good and welfare require it.

[After the above preamble follow five articles, explanatory of the edict.--Eds.] By the first, every man hitherto called vassal or subject, is at liberty to marry without consent of his Lord, to give himself up to the study of arts and sciences, learn any trade, &c. And carry it on wherever he may think proper. The second provides that no vassal, nor his son or daughter, be compelled into the service of his Lord; but that such a condition be at his or their own choice, and upon a proper salary, and for such wages as he or they may agree for with the said Lord. By the third it is declared lawful for every man of any description whatsoever, to sell, mortgage, or give or exchange his goods and chattels, subject nevertheless to the just and perpetual fee, due annually to the Lord of the manor, wherever such a fee is duly established by law. The fourth and fifth are to give authority to the heads of tribunals and other judges, to put the edict in full force, to prevent any disobedience from the Lords, and maintain the aforesaid subjects in the full and perfect enjoyment of personal freedom, without any hinderance or restriction. ■ **ALX, December 15**. A Meeting of a Number of Gentlemen has been lately held at Charleston, South Carolina, for the Purpose of taking into Consideration the proposed Plan of opening a Communication, by Locks, between Cooper and Santee Rivers.--The Result of the Meeting was to Petition the Legislature at their next Sitting for a Charter.--That the Company should consist of a Thousand Shares, at 100l. Sterling each Share, Three Guineas to be paid down at subscribing, the Remainder as soon as shall be agreed upon when the Charter is obtained.--The Plan is so highly approved of that one Gentleman has subscribed his Name for Three Hundred Shares. ■ A few Days since, a Sailor belonging to a French Ship lying in this Port, was drowned in attempting to desert. ■ Last Thursday a Carpenter fell from a high Scaffold on which he was at Work, and though much bruised, there are Hopes he will recover. ■ MARRIED.] Mr. EDWARD HARPER, Merchant, to Miss ----- HIGGINSON. ■ NAVAL-OFFICE, ALX. *Inward Entries*. Brig *Richmond*, J. Green, from Newport; Schooner *Lottery*, Z. Mann, Baltimore. *Cleared Outwards*. Brig *Martha*, S. Harper, for St. Eustatius; Schooner *Judith*, E. Cook, New-England; Schooner *Eagle*, B. Bowers, Jamaica; Ship *Paragon*, H. Hughes, l'Orient; Ship *St. Ann*, V. Caneva, Cadiz. ■ An act to prevent distress being made by the Sheriffs of this Commonwealth for the taxes due for the present year, until March next, and admitting facilities in payment thereof [full text of bill given].

Page 3. [Tax Bill (*continued*)] Nothing to affect the collection of the taxes for Rockingham County, for the years 1784 and 1785. Dec. 2d, 1785, passed the House of Delegates, and Dec. 3d, 1785, passed the Senate. ■ A List of Letters remaining in the Post-Office at ALX, which will be sent to the General Post-Office as dead letters if not taken up before the 5th of January next, JOHN ADAMS; Samuel Adams, care of William Bushby; Joseph Broders, 2; Joshua Birks, 2; Stephen Bowden, care of William Wright; John Bryce; Nicholas Bryce; Samuel M. Brown; John Balentine; Stiebel Baker; Richard Browning care of Joseph Caverly; Mr. Brown; Capt. William Brown; Capt. Thomas Connoly, 3; Richard Clark, 2; William Carling; John Christie; Mathias Conrad; William Cunningham, 3; Cornelius Cunningham; Jonathan Cartwright; Henry Carberry; Francis Coffin; Mr. Coalman; George Chapman, 2; Robert Dunn; Sarah Darrell; John Duffield; Mungo Dyk, care of R. Lyle; John Dogherty; Peter Daggin, care of P. Jiles; Daniel Dymond, care of Hugh Lyle, Berkeley; Robert Evans; George Evans, care of William Duvall; William Fitzhugh; Matthew Fitzgubon; Joseph Fulmore; Ignatius Fenwick; Sarah Flaker, care of John Jolly; Mr. Fleming; Robert Ferguson; Robert Fulton; James Fletcher; Bryan Fairfax; Thomas Fitzhugh, care of Col. Gilpin; Birket Falcon, 2; William Fenner; Rev. David Griffith; Capt. Moses Griffing, care of William Hartshorne; John Gregor; John Graham; James Gibson and Samuel Donaldson; Samuel Gormly; John Hanson; William H. Hamon; Stephen Holmes, care of Thomas Glover; Elizabeth Hunter; Doctor Peter Hoak; Joseph W. Harrison; Mrs. Hannah; Alexander Hannah, care of Josiah Watson; James Holiday; Richard Hollinsbury; Andrew Jamieson; William Johnston; Henry Jenningham, care of Joseph Caverly; James Irwin, care of James Lownes; Charles Jones; James Keith; Doctor James Kirby; Charles Gay, alias George Knox; John Kleinhoff; James Kelly, care of Josiah Watson; William Lowry; Henry Leigh; Robert Latham; Arthur Lind; Richard Lane; George R. Leiper; Charles Lee; John M'Kinney, 4; Jeremiah Mahony, 2; Maurice Morarty; John W. Miller; Hugh M'Cahen; John M'Clay; Alexander M'Dugal, care of William Hunter, jun.; James M'Cready, care of John Hunter; Philip Marsteller; Robert Omond; Michael Osburne, care of William Bushby; Charles Polk; Thomas Pilkington; Philip Poyer; Shubael Pratt, 2; Oliver Price; Capt. Richard Quirk, care of Jesse Taylor; Benjamin Russell, care of Thomas Clementson; Thomas Read, care of William Bushby; John Remnant, care of John Chew; John Ryan, care of Cumberland Ferguson; John Royston; Thomas M. Savage; Thomas Swan; William Scott; Doctor David Stewart; James Sinclair, care of Mr. Holliday; William Sool, care of Chevalier Barber; William Shakespeare; Jacob Sloates, care of George Carrell; Capt. William Baxter Smith, and Skinner and Ramsay, care of Col. John Fitzgerald; Michael Swope; Mr. Thomas; Michael Thorne, 2; Peter Tail, care of Thomas Kirkpatrick; Thomas Tobin; Ebenezer Watson; Thomas Wharton; Leven Wales; William Wright. ALX, Dec. 12, 1785.

A CHARTER WANTED,

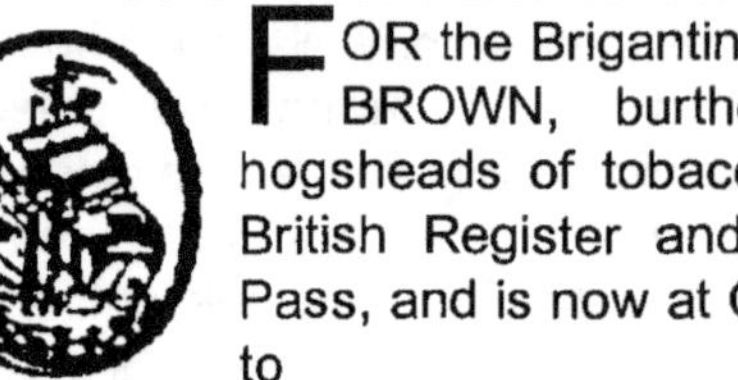

FOR the Brigantine *BETSY*, Capt. BROWN, burthen about 270 hogsheads of tobacco. She has a British Register and Mediterranean Pass, and is now at Quantico. Apply to

HUIE, REID and CO.

Dumfries, Dec. 14, 1785.

LOTS to be let on Ground-Rent in this town, by Hooe and Harrison, ALX, Dec. 15, 1785. ■ TO BE SOLD, In Fee-Simple, A VERY valuable LOT, advantageously situated on Prince-Street--Inquire at the Printing-Office. ALX, Nov. 2, 1785. ■ JOHN MURTLAND warns others from taking assignment of a bond of his in the possession of WILLIAM STONE [see like ad Vol. II No. 96].

On Saturday the 17th instant, will be sold at the Vendue-Store,

A VARIETY of WET and DRY GOODS, consisting of twenty hogsheads of excellent Barbadoes rum, sugar in hogsheads and barrels, cloths, linens, calamancoes, coarse stockings, calicoes, hats, womens' shoes, green, hyson and bohea teas, osnaburgs, blankets, coatings, linseys, jeans, &c.&c.

☞ To be sold at private sale, a Negro Boy about 9 years of age, warranted sound

**Those who have received indulgence, are desired to settle their accounts. Should they not do so before Saturday, the like indulgence will not again be given them.

S. ARELL, Vendue-Master.

ALX, Dec. 15, 1785.

Andrew Jamieson and Co., Biscuit-Bakers, opposite the Printing-Office, BEG leave to inform their friends and the public, that they have lately begun the biscuit-baking business, which they intend carrying on in all its branches. They have for sale common ship bread, fine ditto, small fine ditto, equal to the Philadelphia small cag bread. They can furnish biscuit for ship stores and for exportation on the shortest notice; and they hope to merit the approbation of all who may please to favor them with their orders. ☞ An [Apprentice] or two are wanted for the above business. **A generous price will be given for ship-stuff and middlings. ALX, Dec. 15, 1785. ■ LOTS and HOUSES to RENT in ALX, SUNDRY LOTS on Water and Wolf streets, now in the tenure of Michael Madden.--A large STORE having three floors, on Union-street near Prince-street, now in the tenure of William Hartshorne and Co. and may be had on a very short notice. The above are part of the estate of Jonathan Hall, deceased.--The terms may be known by applying to Col. George Gilpin, or the Subscriber. A HOUSE and LOT on Fairfax-street, about the length of a square below the Presbyterian Meeting-House, now in the tenure of John Harper, Taylor, and may be entered in a few days.--A large three story brick HOUSE on Fairfax-street, opposite to Joseph Janney's, where William Hartshorne and Co. keep their store, this may be entered on the first of February next and perhaps sooner.--A BRICK-YARD about a mile from the Court-House; it has a case or wall built for burning bricks, the clay and situation of the ground are very suitable for the purpose, and there is a log [cabin] that may answer for a dwelling.--I have GROUND to rent for ever on different streets; also, some about a mile from the Court-House near the river, at one shilling per foot; or I will sell ground in fee-simple to any person that will find all materials and build me a house, if we can agree on the terms.--A title shall be made when the building is finished agreeable to contract. WILLIAM HARTSHORNE, ALX, Dec. 15, 1785. ■ TO BE LET, A Very convenient three story brick STORE, on the north-east corner of Prince and Union streets, lately occupied by Jonathan Swift and Co., the lower story of which is now in the tenure of Edward Harper. The situation of the store for any kind of business is superior to any in this town. The terms may be known by applying to JOHN HARPER or to said EDWARD HARPER. ALX, Dec. 15, 1785. ■ FOR SALE, ONE hundred acres of LAND in Fairfax County, 9 miles from ALX and 7 from George-Town; it lies one mile from the Falls-Church, and adjoins the plantation lately occupied and owned by Mr. John Hunter; upwards of 20 acres may be made into good meadow, being well watered by Four-Mile-Run, and several excellent springs. For terms apply to Mr. WILLIAM BUSHBY in ALX, or the Subscriber in Baltimore, by whom an indisputable title will be given, as the contest at law respecting this land is now ended in his favor. ADAM FONERDEN, Dec. 15, 1785. ■ To be sold by public sale at Greenhead, in Machodick-Neck, Westmoreland County, on Tuesday the 20th instant, if fair, if not the next fair day, UPWARDS of twenty valuable SLAVES, with a quantity of corn, fodder and household furniture, belonging to the estate of Thomas Rowand, deceased.--Part will be sold for cash and part for crop tobacco and casks.--Credit will be given until the first of May, 1786, giving bond with approved security, bearing interest from the date if not punctually paid. JOHN ROWAND, Administrator, Dec. 13, 1785.

Page 4. Poetry. "The Incurable, To Doctor ----." ■ **D. and I. M'Pherson** have for sale at their store the third door above Gilpin's wharf, a quantity of woollens, etc. [see like ad Vol. II No. 96] ■ The Ship *Mary*, Nathaniel Goodwin, Commander, to sale for Havre-de-Grace, France [see like ad Vol. II No. 96] ■ JOHN M'CLENACHAN offers for sale the sloop *Three Sisters* [see like ad Vol. II No. 97] ■ JACOB MOORE seeks owner of horse found of Edward Jones [see like ad Vol. II No. 96] ■ Executors of James Nourse seek of the General Assembly an act to permit sale of land in Berkeley Co., Va. [see like ad Vol. II No. 96] ■ JAMES WILSON offers reward for return of mare stolen from his waggon at the White-Oak Spring, Fairfax Co., Va. [see like ad Vol. II No. 96] ■ **William Taylor and Co.** have for sale at their store on Fairfax-street a list of goods [see like ad Vol. II No. 95] ■ ALEXANDER WHITE offers for sale an exceeding valuable well improved 376-acre farm, situate about 4 miles from Winchester, Frederick Co., Va. [see like ad Vol. II No. 97] ■ JAMES SUTER, Montgomery Co., Md., has for sale several tracts of land, including one called Aberdeen [see like ad Vol. II No. 96] ■ ALX: Printed by GEORGE RICHARDS, and COMPANY, at their Printing-Office on Fairfax-street--by whom Advertisements, &c. are thankfully received for this Paper,--and where Printing is performed with Care and Expedition.

1785/12/22, Vol. II No. 99

Page 1. **Robinson, Sanderson and Rumney**, have goods for sale now landing from on board the *Hope*, Captain Cragg, from Whitehaven [see like ad Vol. II

No. 97] ■ WILLIAM HUNTER, jun. has for sale Teneriffe, etc. [see like ad Vol. II No. 97] ■ HUIE, REID and CO. seek charter for Brigantine *Betsy*, Capt. Brown [see like ad Vol. II No. 98] ■ Hooe and Harrison have lots to rent on ground-rent [see like ad Vol. II No. 98] ■ SAMUEL ARELL has for rent the house and lot lately occupied by Mr. Thomas Reeder [see like ad Vol. II No. 97] ■ **Andrew Jamieson and Co.**, announce opening of a biscuit-baking business opposite the Printing-Office [see like ad Vol. II No. 98] ■ **Philip Dalby**, has for sale an assortment received by the ship *Potomack* from London [see like ad Vol. II No. 97] ■ WILLIAM HARTSHORNE offers for sale sundry lots and houses to rent in ALX [see like ad with details Vol. II No. 98] ■ GEORGE WASHINGTON, Mount Vernon, has for sale three lots in Fredericksburg, and a tract of land about 3 miles from said town [see like ad Vol. II No. 94] ■ ADAM FONERDEN offers for sale 100 acres in Fairfax Co., Va. [see like ad Vol. II No. 98] ■ A List of Letters remaining at the Post-Office [see list printed Vol. II No. 98] ■ TO BE SOLD, In Fee-Simple, **A** VERY valuable LOT, advantageously situated on Prince-Street--Inquire at the Printing-Office. ALX, Nov. 2, 1785. ■ EDWARD and JOHN HARPER offer for rent a three-story brick store on the north-east corner of Prince and Union streets, lately occupied by Jonathan Swift and Co. [see like ad Vol. II No. 98].

Page 2. Messrs RICHARDS and COMPANY,

I have enclosed you two late Acts of the British Parliament, respecting Tools and Tobacco, which I hope you will publish in your paper, not doubting but they will be very acceptable to most of your Readers, especially those of Virginia and Maryland. Yours, &c. **CORRESPONDENT.**

An Act to prohibit the Exportation to foreign parts, of Tools and Utensils made use of in the Iron and Steel Manufactures of this Kingdom; And to prevent the seducing of Artificers or Work-Men employed in those Manufactures, to go into Parts beyond the Seas.

WHEREAS the exportation of the several tools and utensils made use of in preparing, working up, and finishing the iron and steel manufactures of this Kingdom, or either of them, will enable foreigners to work up such manufactures, and thereby greatly diminish the exportation of the same from this Kingdom; [The act first enumerates the types of tools and utensils that shall not be exported beyond the seas, except to Ireland]: hand stamps, dog head stamps, pulley stamps, stamps of all sorts, hammers and anvils for stamps, screws for stamps, iron rods for stamps, presses of all sorts in iron, steel or other metal, which are used for giving impressions to metal, or any parts thereof; presses of all sorts called cutting out presses, beds and punches to be used therewith; piercing presses of all sorts, beds and punches to be used therewith, either in parts or pieces, or fitted together; iron or steel dies to be used in stamps or presses either with or without impressions on them; rollers of cast iron, wrought iron, or steel, for rolling of metal, and frames for the same; flasks or casting moulds, and boards used therewith; lathes of all sorts for turning, burnish, polishing, either the whole together, or separate parts thereof; lathe strings, polishing brushes, scoring or shading engines, presses for horn buttons, dies for horn buttons, sheers for cutting of metal, rolled steel, rolled metal with silver thereon, parts of buttons not fitted up into buttons, or in any finished state; engines for chasing, stocks for casting buckles, buttons, and rings; cast iron anvils and hammers for forging mills for iron and copper; roles, slitters, beds, pillars and frames for slitting mills; die-sinking tools of all sorts, drilling engines, tools for punching of glass, engines for covering of whips, polishing brushes, bars of metal covered with gold, or silver, iron or steel screw plates, pins and stocks for making screws, or any other tool or utensil whatever, which now are, is, or at any time or times hereafter shall or may be used in, or proper for the preparing, working, finishing, or completing of the iron or steel manufactures of this kingdom, or either of them, by what name or names soever the same shall be called or known, or any model or plan, or models or plans, of any such tool, utensil, or implement, or any part or parts thereof; [those disobeying this are subject to the items being seized, and they themselves after judicial process, may be fined two hundred pounds, and imprisoned.]

II. [This section authorizes his Majesty's customs officers to search for, seize, and secure any of the enumerated items above, both ashore and on board ships, vessels and boats. Any such items shall be legally condemned, then sold at auction, proceeds of which go half to his Majesty's use, and half to the officer seizing, and prosecuting the case.]

III. [This section applies to any captain or Master who knowingly permits or allows any of the enumerated items to be put on board his ship, on and after August 1st, 1785. The fine will be two hundred pounds for each offense, and in the case of those commanding vessels belonging to his Majesty, the culprit will not only incur the fine, but forfeit his employment, and be incapable of holding any government office under his Majesty, his heirs or successors.

IV. [This section applies to any employee of customs found guilty of knowing or permitting export of an enumerated item; he shall be fined two hundred pounds, forfeit his employment, and be incapable of any further government employ--as the Captains and Masters, above. *[To be continued.]* ■ **LONDON, Sept. 2.** Lord Viscount Sackville has left his estate in perfect condition. Seeing his approaching end with firmness and resignation, he deliberately arranged all his affairs, called his household to his side, and took the most affectionate farewell of his son and relations. By his death, his Life estate of Stoneland, worth £2000 a year goes to his nephew, the Duke; but the improvements he has made, the house he has built and furnished, the inclosures he has made, &c. Gives his son a very considerable claim. The borough of East Grinstead is now divided between the Duke of Dorset and Lord Sackville: and the young Lord, now 18, enters into possession of a clear £7000 a year, after paying his sisters their dowers and the several legacies.

In few occurrences do we feel ourselves more interested in the dying scenes of those who have figured in the higher departments of Life. The following particulars are from unquestionable authority. When Sir John Ellicot had been called in and consulted, his Lordship asked him if everything proper had been done? The doctor answering in the affirmative, his lordship, with firmness replied, "I am aware of my state, and am perfectly resigned." He then wished to know if there might be time to send for his attorney from London, for the purpose of making a codicil to his will; and expressed satisfaction on being told that there would. Some particulars relating to his youngest daughter's fortune, and other testamentary affairs, were soon after settled. After which he called his family about him, and desired to send for the clergyman of his parish, that they might receive the sacrament. He could have wished, he said to have seen his son at age; but adding, that he might in that case have lived to suffer additional ills, he acquiesced in his present lot, believing it to be for the best. This last act of his Life manifested a magnanimity rather uncommon; and afforded a circumstance that will be considered by some as curious. He called to the bed-side Mr. Cumberland. "You see (said his Lordship) the state I am in, and *I charge you* to mind what I now say to you.--I have seen much of Life, and experienced--its vicissitudes; but in no one situation of my Life did I ever feel a failure in my fortitude, any more than I do this present moment." Convulsions soon apprised him of the approach of death, when he calmly ordered his family to withdraw, and with unshaken composure, closed the awful scene.

Lord Sackville had been afflicted with the stone, and was supposed to have injured the intestines by dissolvents that had been prescribed for that disorder. The complaint in his bowels that brought on an inflammation, was thought to be owing to indigestion from eating fruit.

His Lordship has remembered in his will many friends, and all his servants. To those out of livery he has left annuities of £20 a year ... **Sept. 16:** One of the first electors of Germany is the very first potentate that has held out the terrors of persecution against the body of free-masons; this ancient and honorable order has been held in such esteem and veneration, that the first men in almost every kingdom in Europe have considered it a mark of dignity and true honor to be admitted as members of some particular lodge, and even crowned heads, revered for their wisdom, penetration, and magnanimity, at present add an additional lustre to such societies. Surely so many good, pious, and learned men would not have encouraged other persons to enter such assemblies (even supposing they had been deceived themselves) if they thought it would tend in the least to the injury of mankind. It is therefore illiberal to the utmost degree, and seems to border on the gloomy dictates of Gothic barbarism, to endeavour to prejudice an institution that almost seemed to bid defiance to the tooth of time ... **Oct. 1:** Yesterday the Marquis of Carmarthen, and several other of the ministerial nobility, dined with Mr. Adams, the American Plenipotentiary, at his house in Grosvenor Square ... **Oct. 5:** A gentleman just arrived from Bourdeaux relates that on August 14th, on his passage from Martinico to that place, the body of a man was seen floating about 50 yards from the vessel. The Captain immediately ordered out the boat and four hands, who soon brought the seeming dead carcase on board, but what was their surprise on finding the unhappy person breath[ing] and manifest[ing] every symptom of returning sense and Life! The surgeon bled him and chafed his temples with volatile spirits, and in less than half an hour he opened his eyes, and exclaimed in the English tongue,"O Lord where am I?" On taking off his clothes in order to put him to bed, they discovered a cork jacket and a sort of trousers of the same kind. The next day being a good deal recovered, the miserable man told them he sailed from the port of Salem, in New England, in a brig bound for Madera, and about 3 days before they were attacked by a Saletine rover, who boarded and took them; that, pretending to be lame, he was neglected by the Moors, and about eleven at night took an opportunity of slipping on his cork apparatus, and let himself down as easily as possible from the fore chains, totally unobserved. That he floated some distance and then pushed himself forward with his hands, willing to perish in the water than be carried into slavery. In this condition, sometimes on his back, [Continued on Page 3].

Page 3. [The Salem Sailor Story (*continued*)] and sometimes on his belly, he drove about the ocean and at last sunk into a kind of trance, in which state he was discovered by the French ship. On their arrival at Bourdeaux, the Chamber of Commerce presented the brave American with a purse of 300 crowns, and he is now waiting an opportunity of returning in the packet, which sails from Port l'Orient to New York every month ... **Oct. 14:** Advices from **Brussels, October 2** mention great rejoicings made in that city, upon the opening of the Scheldt, and the prospect of Antwerp being restored to her ancient commerce and splendor ... This being the season of the year that fleets usually sail with annual supplies for Jamaica, &c. the West India merchants are in the greatest dilemma how to act, for to despatch the ships without necessary utensils, would be despatching them to no purpose; and the penalty for shipping them is forfeiture of the goods, and all others with which they may be packed, a fine of £200 and one year's imprisonment in the common gaol; the fine and imprisonment extending to masters of vessels, and officers of the customs, who may receive or permit such utensils to be laden on any ship or vessel whatever. The house of Messrs. Long, Drake and Long, petitioned the Chancellor of the Exchequer to issue an order of Council, for dispensing with the above act, but nothing has been done. Thus are our foreign possessions in danger of being ruined by the folly of a puny minister, who mistake arrogance and obstinacy, for spirit and resolution, and a pitiful ambition, for genius to govern ... The Regency of Tuscany has issued orders for fifteen gallies to be added to those already in commission for the protection of their trade against the Algerines. ■ **CHARLESTON, Nov. 22.** When the Captain of the *Peace and Plenty* lay at Cadiz, an American ship was brought in there by the Algerines, and the Captain was offered on payment of £500 for himself, £300 for his Mate, and £100 for each sailor as ransom, to be liberated, yet being unable to deposit the money, the unfortunate captives were all carried to Algiers, where they expected to be made slaves. ■ **BOSTON, Nov. 30.** A friend to the marine department observes that the treatment from the commander of a ship late from Europe, to the pilot of this harbour, has been such, as if passed over in silence will tend to destroy all the decorum necessary to be observed to a person holding that important office, as all vessels that go from, and come to this place, are under his immediate trust. ■ **NEW YORK, Dec. 12.** A letter from **Dublin, Sept. 29** says Captain Cauzier, in one of his Majesty's revenue cutters, ordered round to the western coast of Ireland to stop the smuggling tobacco and India goods, which is now practiced by the Americans to a degree considerably injurious to the revenue of this country, a few days since fell in with an American brig, well armed and manned, which he attacked for near an hour, but had the misfortune to lose the cutter, by an unlucky shot, which took place between wind and water, and sunk her in a few minutes. The crew happily were saved in the boat, after having suffered some hardships on one of the Skelig islands. The above is one among many other arguments for the reduction of the tobacco duty, which now amounts to near one shilling per pound, on an article not originally worth 3d. It is the opinion of everyone conversant in the trade, that if the tobacco duty were fixed at so low a rate as 3d. per lb. The revenue would benefit in three-fold proportion to what it does now, for then the temptation to smuggle would cease; whereas at present, not 10 hogsheads of tobacco in 500 imported into this country are regularly entered. The American cargo above alluded to is a strong proof. This vessel, after sinking the revenue cutter, landed 200 hogsheads of tobacco, of 1000 lb. Each, which cost the merchant in Virginia under 4d. per lb. in all about £25,000. By smuggling this tobacco on shores, the concerned saved, at one shilling per lb. Duty, near £9000 which together with the after sale of it, which is generally disposed of at 6d. per lb. Will make a clear profit of a great many thousand pounds to the ship. ■ **PHILADELPHIA, Dec., 9.** A Halifax paper of the 8th ultimo informs that the commissioners ascertaining the losses and services of such persons who have suffered their rights, properties and possessions, during the late *unhappy dissentions* in America, in consequence of their loyalty to his Majesty, and attachment to the British government, arrived there a few days since. This event lightens up the gloomy visage of our quondam friends, and the commissioners are almost smothered with '*loyalty*' and 'addresses.' ... **Dec. 10:** The General Assembly of New Jersey, at their last session, passed an act to authorise the U.S. Congress assembled to regulate foreign trade; and an act to raise 110 men in that State to serve for three years, unless sooner discharged. ■ **RICHMOND, Dec. 17.** Yesterday the Honorable General Court passed sentence on the following criminals, viz. John Fowler and William Presto, for robbing Captain Jones's store in ALX; John Wyatt, alias Reuben Purcell, for stealing a Negro belonging to Mr. Benjamin Robinson, of King and Queen, were all capitally convicted, and received sentence of death. Nicholas Wood, stealing two sheep, the property of Mr. John Baird of Prince George; and Katey Burcher, a free mulatto, for stealing some silk twist out of the store of Mr. Ebenezer M'Nair, of this city: both were burnt in the hand ... Lately died at Portsmouth, Mr. GOODRICH WILSON, Vendue Master at that place. ■ **ALX, December 22.** Extract of a Letter from a Gentleman in Cadiz to his Friend in this Town, dated September 15, 1785. "The Algerines have lately taken two American Vessels, the one the Schooner *Mary*, Captain Stephens, from Boston, the other the Ship *Dauphin*, Captain O'Brian, from St. Ubes for Philadelphia.--Report says that have captured three others.--The Crews of the two first I know with certainty have been publicly sold at Algiers; and unless Measures are adopted for the Protection of our Trade, there is no saying where the Mischief may end.--We must at last renounce all Intercourse with these Parts." ■ Another Letter of the 5th of October says, "The Spaniards, I believe, will effect their Peace with the Algerines and other Pirates of Barbary.--This Circumstance will render the Danger greater for our Vessels.--I understand Mr. Jefferson and Mr. Adams have Power to treat for us, but nothing is yet done, nor is it a Work so easily accomplished, but at the Expence of much Time and Money." ■ We hear that last Saturday Se'nnight, a Tavern-Keeper, near the Mouth of Conecocheague, murdered a Man who was drinking at his Door, by giving him a severe Blow on the Head with a large Club, which killed him instantly.--As soon as the Tavern-Keeper had committed this rash Action he made off, and has not since been heard of. ■ DIED.] Mr. SAMUEL COLLARD. --Mr. MARTIN SHUGARS, Tavern-Keeper. ■ NAVAL-OFFICE, ALX. *Inward Entries*. Brig *Ceres*, G. Bray, from Philadelphia; Schooner *Henrietta*, B. Paviett, Baltimore; Sloop *Polly*, W. [Bartlett], Surinam; Sloop *Fitz William*, C. Gardner, Gloucester; Schooner *Industry*, J. Foster, Beverly. *Cleared Outwards*. Ship *Mary*, N. Goodwin, for Havre-de-Grace; Sloop *Polly*, J. Martin, Providence.

PRICES CURRENT, ALX. / Tobacco, 22s. per Ct. / Fine Flour, 29s. per Barrel. / Wheat, 5/6s. per Bushel. / Jamaica Spirits, 4/6 per Gallon. / Windward Rum, 3s. per Ditto. / Continental Rum, 2s. per Ditto. / Molasses, 1/6 per Ditto. / Muscovado Sugar, 35s. to 42/6 per Ct. / Salt, 3s. per Bushel, by Retail. / Corn, 4s. per Bushel. / Exchange, 40.

THE Subscribers to the ALX Academy are requested to meet at the Court-House on Friday next, at twelve o'clock, to take into consideration a proposal for appointing an additional number of Trustees, and for enabling a less number than a majority of the whole to act in execution of the trust committed to them. By order of the Trustees, CHARLES LEE, Clerk. ALX, Dec. 22, 1785.

For FREIGHT or CHARTER to Cadiz, Lisbon, or any of the West-India islands,

THE ship *FRIENDS*, JOHN MUIR, Master. The *Friends* is a British ship of about 300 hogsheads burthen, completely fitted, with a Mediterranean pass of the newest cut. Apply to the Captain on board at Hooe's wharf, or WILLIAM HUNTER, jun.
ALX, Dec. 22, 1785.

WANTS employment as a CLERK, a middle aged man.--Any gentleman in want of such, by directing a letter to Captain MUIR, will be immediately waited on. ALX, Dec. 22, 1785. ■ **James M'Kenna**, Hath opened store on Fairfax-street, next door to Col. Fitzgerald's, where he sells by wholesale and retail, for cash and all kinds of country produce, BEST Jamaica spirits, West-India rum, New-England ditto, superfine and second cloths, coatings, Bath rugs, duffils, linseys, flannels, corduroys, mens' and boys' worsted hose, printed linens and calicoes, dyed plains, ladies' cardinal cloaks, Irish 7-8 and yard wide linens, mens' and womens' leather shoes and gloves, shalloons, gauzes, tammies, calamancoes, osnaburgs, checks of all breadths, shoe thread, white sewing ditto, silk, ribbons and taste, writing-paper, quills, wafers, mustard, snuff in bottles, hair-powder, hyson, souchong and bohea teas, mould candles, nails, powder and shot, Negro cottons, indigo, mens' and boys' hats, twist, playing cards, smoaking tobacco, carpenters' rules, brass and iron candlesticks, check handkerchiefs, blankets, sleeve-buttons, watch keys, seals, chains, springs and crystals, best alum salt and a variety of delf and queen's ware. ALX, Dec. 22, 1785. ■ **Dr. Ebenezer Richmond**, RESPECTFULLY offers his services to the inhabitants of this town [Leesburg] and the country adjacent, in all cases of physic and surgery. Those who may think proper to employ him may depend upon being attended with expedition, assiduity and fidelity. The recommendations he has in his possession, which he is ready to shew to any person who will take the trouble to peruse them, from physicians of eminence and gentlemen of public character, will, he flatters himself, induce those who may stand in need of medical assistance, to make trial of his abilities to serve them: And a Life devoted to the pursuit of scientific knowledge in general, and to the study of the healing art in particular, together with several years successful practice in the army and navy of the United States, and in a domestic line, emboldens him to believe that those who may venture to confide in him will not be disappointed in their expectations. **He may be spoke with at Mr. Roper's tavern. Leesburg, Loudon County, Dec. 18, 1785.

FOR L'ORIENT,

THE brig *SOPHIA*, E. ROBERTS, Master, now lying at Baltimore, and will sail by the 29th instant.--She has elegant accommodations for eight passengers.--For passage apply to Mr. SETH BARTON, Baltimore, or JONATHAN SWIFT and CO. Who have for sale a general assortment of WINTER GOODS; also, a few bags of allspice, which they will dispose of on the lowest terms for cash or produce. ALX, Dec. 22, 1785.

MR. WILLIAM LOWRY, being gone for England, intending to return early in the season with a large and elegant assortment of Spring and Summer GOODS, and having appointed Messieurs JESSE TAYLOR and JAMES M'KENNA his attornies during his absence, to collect, receive, sue for and recover, all the remaining debts due to the late partnership, under the firm of LOWRY and M'KENNA, whether by bond note or otherwise; it is therefore earnestly requested that speedy payments may be made to either of his attornies, or consequences must ensue disagreeable to both parties. ALX, Dec. 22, 1785. ■ TO BE SOLD, At the Printing-Office, A SERMON on the RELATIONS of the CHRISTIAN MINISTRY.--Preached at St. Peter's and Christ-Church, in the City of Philadelphia, the 2d day of October, 1785, and published at the Request of the Episcopal Convention.--By CHARLES H. WHARTON, D.D. Also, a SERMON preached in Christ-Church, Philadelphia, on Friday, October 7th, 1785, before the General Convention of the Protestant Episcopal Church, in the States of New-York, New-Jersey, Pennsylvania, Delaware, Maryland, Virginia, and South-Carolina. On Occasion of the first Introduction of the LITURGY and Public Service of the said Church, as *altered* and recommended to future Use, by the Convention.--By WILLIAM SMITH, D.D., Principal of Washington-College, and Rector of Chester Parish, in the State of Maryland. Likewise, a Journal of a Convention of the Protestant Episcopal Church in the States of New-York, New-Jersey, Pennsylvania, Delaware, Maryland, Virginia, and South-Carolina, held in Christ-Church, in the City of Philadelphia, from September 27th to October 7th, 1785. ALX, Dec. 22, 1785.

Page 4. Poetry. "The MAIDEN's WISH." ■ **Hooe and Harrison**, Have for sale MADERA wine of London, New-York and Virginia quality, etc. [see like ad Vol. II No. 97] ■ **B.A. HAMP**, has imported in the ship *Potomack*, Capt. Bradstreet, from London, a general assortment of European Goods [see like ad Vol. II No. 97] ■ JOHN ROWAND, Administrator of the estate of Thomas Rowand, deceased, has for sale upwards of twenty valuable slaves [see like ad Vol. II No. 98] ■ JOHN M'CLENACHAN offers for sale the sloop *Three Sisters* [see like ad Vol. II No. 97] ■ JOHN EVANS offers reward for return of runaway Irish indented servant man named WILLIAM SMITH [see like ad Vol. II No. 97] ■ **William Taylor and Co.** have for sale at their store on Fairfax-street a list of goods [see like ad Vol. II No. 95] ■ ALEXANDER WHITE offers for sale an exceeding valuable well improved 376-acre farm, situate about 4 miles from Winchester, Frederick Co., Va. [see like ad Vol. II No. 97] ■ JAMES SUTER, Montgomery Co., Md., has for sale several tracts of land, including one called Aberdeen [see like ad Vol. II No. 96] ■ ALX: Printed by GEORGE RICHARDS, and COMPANY, at their Printing-Office on Fairfax-street--by whom Advertisements, &c. are thankfully received for this Paper,--and where Printing is performed with Care and Expedition.

1785/12/29, Vol. II No. 100

Page 1. **James M'Kenna**, Hath opened store on Fairfax-street, next door to Col. Fitzgerald's [see like ad Vol. II No. 99] ■ Messrs. Jesse Taylor and James M'Kenna, attornies for William Lowry, being gone to England, seek to settle outstanding accounts [see like ad Vol. II No. 99] ■ WILLIAM HUNTER, jun. seeks freight or charter for the ship *Friends*, John Muir, Master, to sail to Cadiz, Lisbon, or any of the West-India islands [see like ad Vol. II No. 99] ■ Capt. MUIR seeks employment of a clerk [see like ad Vol. II No. 99] ■ Printed Sermons to be sold at the

Printing-Office [see description Vol. II No. 99] ■ *Conclusion of the Tool Act begun in our last.*

V. [This section treats of those in possession of the enumerated articles, and who are believed to have the intent illegally to export the same. After due process, those convicted are liable for a two hundred pound fine, and imprisoned twelve months, or until the fine is paid.]

VI. [This section speaks to artificers--and others employed in the iron and steel processing of Great Britain--from leaving therefrom, as well as persons attempting to recruit artificers &c. into leaving. Those convicted shall be fined 500 pounds, and imprisoned 12 months or until the fine is paid.]

VII. Provided always, That no person shall be prosecuted for any of these offenses, unless such prosecution be commenced within 12 months after the commission of the offence.

VIII. [This section names the judicial systems in which such cases shall be tried. Half the proceeds from such prosecutions shall be applied to the use of his Majesty, the other to the customs officer(s) prosecuting, after deducting the charges of prosecution from the whole.]

IX. And it be further enacted by the authority aforesaid, That if any suit or action shall be commenced any person for what he shall do in pursuance of this act, such suit or action shall be commenced within three months next after the fact committed; and the person so sued may file common bail, or enter a common appearance, and plead the general issue not guilty, and may give this act and the special matter in evidence; and if the plaintiff or prosecutor shall become nonsuit, or suffer [Continued on Page 2].

Page 2. [The Tool Act (*continued*)] discontinuance, or if a verdict pass against him or her, or if, upon demurrer, judgement shall be given the plaintiff, the defendant shall recover treble costs. ■ **PERA, (near Constantinople) Aug. 25.** The Russian marine in the Black Sea becomes every day more formidable, and the Porte seems not to be without inquietude. A squadron of one ship of the line and 12 frigates has been cruising along the coasts, and approached so near as to be distinctly seen to pass before Synope. It is thought that, on its entrance into the Port of Sebastonopolis, in the Crimea, they will find the Admiral's ship now building there and near completion, and that as soon as it is ready to put to sea, the squadron will make a second cruise under the command of a Vice Admiral. Advices from the Crimea mention, that the Russian Black Sea naval force is 3 ships of the line of 74 guns, two others of the same rate which are in the docks at Cherson, 15 frigates of 36-50 guns, and four or five cutters. ■ **HAGUE, Oct. 3.** Their High and Mightinesses the States of Holland and West Friesland will this day resume their usual deliberations ... The Court will go into mourning on Sunday next for the late Queen of Sardinia ... The States of Zeeland have consented to the raising of an additional artillery company, and to augmenting the corps of miners, &c. ... Letters from Nimeguen say the Prussian troops at Wesel and in the neighbourhood have orders to hold themselves in readiness to march on the first notice. Our politicians, who delight in forming conjectures say, this regards the Emperor. ■ **MIDDLEBURGH, Sept. 30.** Their High Mightinesses the States of this Province have come to the following resolution relating to the ratification of the Preliminary Articles of accommodation between the Emperor and the Republic. They in the first place approve the conduct of the Deputy of the Province, who was present at the meeting on foreign affairs, especially with regard to annotations made against the resolution of their High Mightinesses, reserving the rights and free deliberation of this Province; and it was further determined to write the Deputy, and direct him to declare.

That their High Mightinesses the States of this Province in declarations of 14th May and 12th September, with every necessary degree of prudence, but cordially and frankly expressed their fears on the dangerous and trifling mode in which the negociations were carried on; and had seriously insisted that the Court of France, whose advice the Republic followed, should be requested finally to declare, at a time when the condescension of the Republic was nearly exhausted, how far His Most Christian Majesty intended to support the Republic; and at the same time this Province offered every assistance in its power for the defence and preservation of the liberty and independence of the State:

That notwithstanding this, a majority of States (if three Provinces in such a deliberation can be called a majority) neglecting all these just observations, had thought it proper to give other instructions to the Ambassadors at Paris, against which the Deputy of this Province was obliged to protest:

But that even these instructions, when compared with the Preliminary Articles as signed, appear to differ widely; from which they are obliged to conclude, that either the Ambassadors went beyond their orders, or received some secret ones unknown to their High Mightinesses:

That without entering into particulars, they only observe, that the States General left the determination of the differences between the sum demanded and that offered, to the arbitration of his Most Christian Majesty, on a supposition that that sum--once settled--should be in full of every claim of the Emperor on the Republic; and that in consequence of such their condescension, the Emperor would not erect any fresh batteries near the forts of the Republic, and would demolish those already erected; at the same time ultimately acknowledge the sovereignty of the Republic over the Scheldt, and without reserve renounce all pretensions in general to any of the domains of the Republic; that the trade to India should be stopped conformable to the 5th article of the treaty at Vienna; and that the Scheldt, and the canals of Sas, the Swin, &c. Should be kept shut by the Republic, according to the 14th article of the treaty of Muenster:

That nevertheless none of these articles, which induced their High Mightinesses to make these concessions, are to be found in the preliminary articles, but even the reverse of them is there stipulated:

That, therefore, the States of this Province, declared they would in no wise be concerned in the ratification of those Preliminaries, but totally left them, and the consequences which must ensue to the detriment of the State, to those Provinces who, by their direction, suffered such oppressive stipulations to be introduced into the negociation, and think they ought to be admitted. ■ **LONDON, Oct. 14.** The following was written by the King of Prussia to the States General of the United Provinces of the Low Countries: High and Mighty Lords, and particularly good friends and neighbours, &c. We, Frederick, by the Grace of god, King of Prussia, Margrave of Brandenbourg, &c. &c. &c. After communicating to you the 29th February our uneasiness on the disagreeable situation of the Lord hereditary Stadtholder Prince of Orange and Nassau, and having received your 31st August reply--assurances so agreeable respecting that affair, we hopes there would be no more such circumstances, and that the Lord Hereditary Stadtholder would have been left in the quiet exercise of his incontestably Stadtholder prerogatives. But since we learn the contrary, and even some unfavorable advices from some of your provinces, this has excited us to despatch to the Lower States of the Province of Holland and West Friesland a letter, a copy of which is enclosed. Convinced of your love of equity, and your affection for the House of Orange and Nassau, we pray your interposition in order that the Lord Hereditary Stadtholder may peaceably enjoy the rights belonging to him hereditarily; that those taken from him may be restored, and that a perfect harmony may be established. Thus we recommend in the most serious manner to your High Mightinesses the welfare and interests of the lord Hereditary Stadtholder, of our dear niece, and of their family, which gives so much hopes, that you and the Lords of their respective States consider that we cannot be indifferent respecting the cruel and unmerited fate of persons so nearly related to us; but, on the contrary, we watch over the welfare due to them, and to which we ought to contribute by every possible means. To that effect, we equally present our impartial mediation, in quality of fiend and neighbour, and with the best of intentions. We hope to see, in consequence, that our wishes will be fulfilled in that respect; and in this expectation we remain at all times affectionate to your high Mightinesses as a friend and neighbour. [signed] **FREDERICK**, Berlin, Sept.18, 1785. [and underneath:] **FINCKENSTEIN.** ... **Oct. 15:** The following is a dependable explanation of the account in last Saturday's papers, relating to a dispute between an American Governor and an English Captain: By private letters from Nova Scotia, we are informed that a number of small vessels were sent by Commodore Sawyer, under the convoy of the *Mercury* frigate, from Halifax to Boston for cattle and livestock; that Captain Stanhope waited on Governor Bowdoin at Boston, attended by his officers, in their uniforms, and immediately after the Captain and his officers left the Government House they were insulted and stoned by the populace, who desired them to leave off their uniforms, d___d the K___ their master, and nearly killed Captain Stanhope and two of his boat's crew with stones. Captain Stanhope, in a very gallant manner, went through the mob to the Government house, and made his complaint to Governor Bowdoin, who assured the Captain that he and his people should have satisfaction, and not be offended in future; but in returning to his boat again he was mobbed, and the following day the Boston newspapers were filed with low and scurrilous abuse on the K___g of G.B. his Ministers and servants. The Captain therefore wrote the Governor, desiring him to correct the scandalous libels published in the newspapers; but the governor having given an evasive answer, Captain Stanhope, in a very spirited and becoming manner, went on shore again and remonstrated with Governor Bowdoin, and assured his Excellency, that if any further insult was offered to the King's flag, or his officers, he would lay that part of town about his ears; and accordingly had placed his ship in a situation proper for that purpose when the last advices left Boston ... Miss Ann Frankland, daughter of the Rev. William Frankland, sometime rector of Oswaldkirk, near Malston, in the North Riding of York county, while fondling a little dog was bitten on the lip. The dog was not perceived to be mad. A maid servant doing the laundry heard the crying out, and in taking the dog away was herself severely bitten on the arm. She continued washing, her arm several hours in the soap suds. Miss Frankland was seized with the hydrophobia, and died with all its dreadful symptoms. The maid escaped them, whence it was concluded that the searching quality of the soap had secured her from the fatal effect of such an accident. Whether the like experiment may be preventative of the evils attending the bite of mad animals in other subjects may be worth the trial ... Extract of a letter from **Warsaw, Sept. 22:** M. Buchols, his Prussian Majesty's Minister at this Court, has delivered to the King of Poland, the already known declaration of the conclusion of the Germanic League. There is not the least appearance his Polish Majesty will enter into that confederation. The influence of the two Imperial Courts of Vienna and Petersburg is too considerable for any attempt to be made contrary to those powers' interests ... The Court of Madrid sent M. D'Expilly to Algiers to negociate a peace; a gentleman of first rate abilities: But according to a letter received last week, to a merchant in town, M. D'Expilly returned to Madrid accompanied by two Algerines, without effecting any more than a temporary cessation of hostilities; though this indeed cannot be said to be effected absolutely, for some Spanish traders as well as Genoese have been recently captured. The terms of the Dey are imperious in the extreme.

A letter from **Gibraltar** says a French ship called the *Duke de la March*, being chased by two Barbary corsairs, had run under the guns of the fortress for protection; that one of the corsairs had run in after her, on which the Governor sent an officer to acquaint the Captain of the corsair, that if he offered to take possession of the French ship he would sink him, and desired he would put to sea immediately, which order was complied with, and every mark of respect was shewn by the Governor to the French Captain, and a sloop of war sent to see him safe to Toulon.

According to letters from **Lisbon of the 29th ult**. One of the Portuguese vessels cruising off the mouth of the Mediterranean to protect their trade to the coast of Africa, had taken a large Algerine corsair of 24 guns, including pattararoes. The Moors held a very obstinate engagement of near five hours, when their captain was killed, and she immediately struck. The Portuguese carried her into Sacre Bay. Her most Faithful Majesty, in consideration of the services rendered by this capture, and to encourage similar ardor in others, had immediately given orders for the Captain, officers, and crew of her frigate to be rewarded.

A letter from the **Hague, Oct. 6** says the States General are again sitting. A very particular thing has happened for the first time in a century: on the first day of the meeting, the Deputies of the province of Utrecht, after a solemn protest against the articles preliminary to peace with the Emperor, took their leaves and set off for their own country, and it is whispered that the Deputies of Zealand, and Groningen, are about to follow their example: Warm contentions are expected in debating this business.

A poor crazy man begging from house to house, asked charity of the late Duke of Newcastle, pretending to be a relation, as they were all brothers and sisters from *Adam.* The Duke acknowledged the relationship and said: "Here is a penny for you; and if all your brothers and sisters give you as much, you will be a much richer man than I." ... A real repartee of a pretty red-headed boy, under five years of age, made to the King, in a natural, honest and innocent manner: Their Majesties returning from London lately to Windsor Castle, in their post chaise, at their being set down, a number of children surrounded the carriage to see the King [Continued on Page 3].

Page 3. [The Red-Headed Boy Story (*continued*)] and Queen: amongst them was a very fine boy, that morning put in breeches for the first time. His Majesty instantly fixed his eye on the chearful countenance of the child, and asked him, "Whose boy he was?" The lad replied, "My father is the king's beef-eater;" then said the King, "down on your knees, and you shall have the honor to kiss the Queen's hand;" to which the boy replied, "No, I won't kneel down, because I shall dirt my new breeches." This extempore repartee had such a pleasing effect on their Majesties, that they made the boy a present of five guineas, ■ **KINGSTON, Nov. 19.** His Honor the Lieut. Governor, by Proclamation 11th November, has appointed Friday the 9th of December, for a day of fasting, prayer and humiliation, to deprecate the wrath of Almighty God, manifested in the late dreadful calamities with which this island has been so frequently visited ... The great increase of the French navigation and trade is owing to their underselling most West India commodities, especially sugars, cotton, indigo, and all West India goods, by which France is now become the greatest market in the world, which is not to be wondered at, says our correspondent, when we consider their outbound cargoes cost them 20 per cent less, upon an average, than ours cost us; consequently the can afford to undersell of in all their returns ... **Nov. 23:** A gentleman of veracity lately arrived from Savannah, assures us the Georgians (who are a bold desperate people) are firmly bent on wresting the Floridas out of the hands of the Spaniards; so that we may soon expect to hear of the Dons having ample employment for their troops in that quarter of the globe ... Last Thursday morning, about 20 paces out of the road, near Dr. Spalding's pen in Liguanea, two gentlemen whose curiosity led them to examine the spot--from the hovering of a great number of *carrion crows*--discovered a human skeleton. Very little flesh pertained to the bone, though a lock of black wool was observed on the under part of the skull, next the ground. This induced the gentlemen to conclude it was a Negro who had hanged *himself*, if we may make use of the *masculine gender* upon this indeterminate occasion, as they observed the end of a rope tied to the branch of a small tree, close to the place, and a pail at a few yards distance. ■ **CHARLESTON, Oct. 8.** On Thursday last the Hon. M.E. Rutledge made his promised motion in the House of Representatives, to bring in a bill for prohibiting the importation of Negroes into this State for the term of three years. After a lengthy debate, it was negatived by 65 to 48. ■ **BOSTON, Dec. 5.** We are assured that the General Court have taken off, in part, the restrictions laid upon foreign vessels in the navigation act (British excepted) and we trust the Legislature will be ever impressed with the necessity of giving the commerce of the U.S. a preference to any other nation on the face of the whole earth. ■ **NEW YORK, Dec. 13.** By the latest accounts from Ireland, the troubles of that unhappy kingdom still wear a gloomy aspect.--Groaning under the weight of the iron hand of oppression, its inhabitants pant for the cooling streams of liberty. Several of the peaceable inhabitants of Dublin, have been shockingly wounded, by a number of British officers, as they were passing the streets, merely because they supposed them to belong to corps of Volunteers. O Britain! When shall thy insatiate thirst for blood be at an end! ... **Dec. 14:** The General Assembly of Massachusetts have resolved that a bounty be paid out of their Public Treasury, of five pounds for every ton of spermaceti oil,--three pounds per ton for brown and yellow ditto,--and forty shillings for all whale oil (so called) that may be taken by any vessel owned and manned wholly by the inhabitants of that Commonwealth, and landed within the same, from and after the first day of January next, until further orders from the General Court. ■ **PHILADELPHIA, Dec. 16.** In **CONGRESS**, New York, Friday, December 2, 1785. The Secretary of the United States for the department of foreign affairs, to whom was referred his letter of the 24th of November, to his Excellency the President, with Mr. J. Temple's commission, having been reported, "THAT John Temple, Esq; has presented to the United States in Congress assembled, a commission in due form, bearing the date the 5th of February, last, from his Britannic Majesty, constituting and appointing him, the Consul General of his said Majesty to these States. That there is yet no commercial [this column's right edge is torn away, and the missing letters are signed by *** asterisks, regardless of the number of letters possibly torn away.--Eds] treaty of convention subsisting between *** -nic Majesty and the United States, wher*** have a perfect right to establish Consuls in*** -nions of the other, but that amicable n***for that and other reciprocal privileges a*** pending: That although the issue of tho***-tions is as yet uncertain, it will neverthe*** -per for the United States, on this and eve*** -casion to observe as great a degree of *** may consist with a due regard to the *** honor and welfare;" Therefore,

Resolved, That the said John Temp*** and he hereby is received and recogni*** -sul General of his Britannic Majesty th*** United States, and that his commission b*** in the Secretary's office.

Resolved, That all the privileges, pr*** and authority, which the laws of nation*** -land give to a Consul general received *** -ted States from any nation with whom t*** commercial treaty or convention, are du*** John Temple, Esq; and shall be enjoyed ***.

Ordered, That certified copies of the ***-lutions be transmitted to the Executive *** -ent States for their information. ■ BALTIMORE, Decem*** [These *** asterisks continue, as noted above, to signify whatever words or letters, in the right edge of this column, have been torn away.--Eds] Copy of a letter dated Paris, September *** by Mr. Barclay, Consul General of *** Mr. Zachariah L'Orieth, M*** l'Orient.

"I embrace the first opportunity o*** you, that the Algerines have commer*** -ties against the Americans, and have *** of their vessels, some of which are arrive*** with their cargoes and people on board *** -tised for public sale.--You will please *** known to such Commanders of vessels *** the United States as are in your port, th*** govern themselves accordingly.

"It is a considerable time since som*** taken to make a truce with the States of *** doubtless proper measures will be purs*** redemption of the people, and the pr*** such unfortunate incidents in future.--I *** ... **Dec. 23:** Early yesterday morning *** out in the dwelling house of Mr. Tho*** P*** in Water street, within one door of *** Light lane, which was entirely co*** nearly the whole of the two adjoining bu*** fire had made such progress in Mr. Dou*** before discovered, that he and fami*** time to save themselves, leaving eve*** perish in the flames. ■ [A portion of the second and nearly the entire third column are ripped away from microfilm copy.] **ALX, December 29**. On Tuesday the 27th Instant being [the anniver]sary of St. John the Evangelist, the [?] Lodge No. 39, Ancient York Masons, [?] Lodge-Room, from whence they mar[ched in pro?]cessional Order to the Presbyterian M[eeting House?] and after hearing a well adapted Disc[ourse?] [?]rity and general Benevolence among M[?] vered by the Rev. William M'W[hir, re]turned to Brother Lyles's Tavern, w[here they] [?] and spent the Evening in that social [?] Mirth so characteristic of the Anci[ent Bene]volent Craft. ■ A few Days since arrived here from [?] Schooner *Jesse*, Capt. Davis.--On the [?] 9th Instant, on his Passage here, a Mr. [?], Mate of the Schooner, was missing, a[?] posed he leaped overboard. We hear from Jamaica, that on Thu[rsday] 17th Ult. about 3 o'Clock in the Morning [?] Shock of an Earthquake was felt at Kingston [and] its Vicinity, which was immediately followed by Noise like that of distant Thunder. ■ A late Jamaica Paper says, "Spain bids fair to be suddenly disabled in her Power and Resources, by the alarming Troubles in South-America, which are daily gathering to a Head, and, without a speedy and effectual Cure, will inevitably rise to such a Pitch of Strength and Aggravation, as to bid Defiance to the most potent Efforts of the *Dons*. ■ "For the dearest and best Interests of Religion, Liberty, Virtue and Humanity, it is most ardently to be wished, that whenever the South-Americans enter heartily, and with the Energy becoming Men determined to be free, into the arduous Struggle above alluded to, it may be followed by complete Emancipation from the bigotted and cruel Tyranny of Spain." ■ The Schooner *Bumper*, Capt. M'Kellan, from Philadelphia, is arrived at Kingston, Jamaica. ■ MARRIED.] At Hayes's, Montgomery County, Maryland, on the 11th Instant, HENRY TOWNSEND, Esq; to the truly accomplished Miss REBECCA CHESLEY, the third Daughter of JOHN CHESLEY, Esq; of St. Mary's County. ■ "On Friday the 16th Instant, after a short Illness, departed this Life, at his House in Port-Tobacco, WALTER HANSON JENIFER, Doctor of Physic, a Gentleman eminent for his professional Abilities, and distinguished for all those Virtues which render Men useful to Society; a dutiful Son, [remainder ripped away].

Page 4. [Nearly the entire left and a portion of the second column are ripped away from the microfilm copy.] WILLIAM HARTSHORNE offers for sale sundry lots and houses to rent in ALX [see like ad with details Vol. II No. 98] ■ **Hooe and Harrison**, Have for sale MADERA wine of London, New-York and Virginia quality, etc. [see like ad Vol. II No. 97] ■ HUIE, REID and CO. seek charter for Brigantine *Betsy*, Capt. Brown [see like ad Vol. II No. 98] ■ Hooe and Harrison have lots to rent on ground-rent [see like ad Vol. II No. 98] ■ SAMUEL ARELL has for rent the house and lot lately occupied by Mr. Thomas Reeder [see like ad Vol. II No. 97] ■ TO BE SOLD, In Fee-Simple, **A** VERY valuable LOT, advantageously situated on Prince-Street--Inquire at the Printing-Office. ALX, Nov. 2, 1785. ■ **Ebenezer Richmond**, offers his services of physic and surgery to inhabitants of Leesburg, Va. [see like ad Vol. II No. 99] ■ EDWARD and JOHN HARPER offer for rent a three-story brick store on the north-east corner of Prince and Union streets, lately occupied by Jonathan Swift and Co. [see like ad Vol. II No. 98] ■ ADAM FONERDEN offers for sale 100 acres in Fairfax Co., Va. [see like ad Vol. II No. 98] ■ **Andrew Jamieson and Co.**, announce opening of a biscuit-baking business opposite the Printing-Office [see like ad Vol. II No. 98] ■ **Robinson, Sanderson and Rumney**, have goods for sale now landing from on board the *Hope*, Captain Cragg, from Whitehaven [see like ad Vol. II No. 97] ■ JAMES SUTER, Montgomery Co., Md., has for sale several tracts of land, including one called Aberdeen [see like ad Vol. II No. 96] ■ ALX: Printed by GEORGE RICHARDS, and COMPANY, at their Printing-Office on Fairfax-street--by whom Advertisements, &c. are thankfully received for this Paper,--and where Printing is performed with Care and Expedition.

1786/01/05, Vol. II No. 101

Page 1. An ACT for the better securing the DUTIES payable on TOBACCO [text completes entire page; summary follows]. *Whereas the many regulations already provided by law to prevent the fraudulent and cladestine importation of tobacco into the kingdom of Great-Britain, and to prevent the relanding of the same within the same kingdom, after it has been shipped for exportation, or exported from the said kingdom, have beren found ineffectual*; Effective January 1, 1786, (1) no tobacco brought into Great-Britain (except that of Spain and Portugal), other than from some ports within his Majesty's colonies, plantations, islands or territories in America or from some port or place within the United States of America, upon pain of forfeiture of the package, and also ship or vessel on board or in which the same shall be imported or brought, together with her guns, furniture, ammunition, tackle, and apparel; (2) no tobacco to be brought into Great-Britain, its colonies or America, after January 1, 1786, from any port within the United States of America, in any ship less burthen than seventy tons and which ship is either British built or belonging to the United States of America, with conditions given as to combinations of mariners on board and destination within Great-Britain; (3) no tobacco to be brought into Great-Britain otherwise than in hogsheads, casks, chests, or cases; each containing at least 450 pounds net weight of tobacco, or master upon such ship shall forfeit treble the value of the tobacco; (4) nothing in this act shall extend to loose tobacco for the use of the seamen then belonging on board; (5) nothing in this act shall extend to prevent evidence from being received in any suit brought for the forfeiture of any vessel or on account of any tobacco imported; (6) the collector and comptroller and two other chief officers employed in the management of customs at a port or other place where a ship or vessel shall have taken on board tobacco, shall upon clearing of ship by proper officers deliver to the master a manifest or content in writing under their hands and seals of office; said manifest to contain the name of the port or place where tobacco was taken on board, name of the ship or vessel so taking, and the tonnage thereof, with the number of hogsheads, casks, chests and cases containing the same and the particular weight of the tobacco therein contained; duplicate of manifest to be transmitted to commissioners of customs in Great-Britain, else for every forfeiture the sum of two hundred pounds; (7) no tobacco of the growth or production of the United States of America, except that waterborne before January 1st, 1786, shall be imported or brought into Great-Britain from the United States, in any ship or vessel whatsoever, unless the master in command shall have on board a manifest of contents in writing, made out and signed, on or before clearing of the ship, and at all ports or places within the United States where such tobacco shall be laden on board, containing names and weights, etc. [*To be continued*].

Page 2. **HAGUE, Oct. 26.** Friday last their High Mightinesses the States General appointed M. Le Comte de Maillebois, Governor of Breda. Tomorrow the General will take the usual oath, and set out Thursday for his post ... The last letters from Vienna advise the Emperor will shortly send a Minister to the Hague, as usual in times of peace. ■ **MADRID, Sept. 27.** The King our Sovereign willing to demonstrate to the Emperor of Morocco his sense of all the marks of friendship by which that Monarch has distinguished his Majesty and the Spanish nation, he having sent Mahomet Ben Osman as his Ambassador to Madrid, in consideration of which step the just resentment which he had conceived against the court of Morocco, since the 1774 siege of Mellile, his Majesty for that purpose has appointed Lieutenant Colonel Don Francisco Salinas y Moniho as his Envoy Extraordinary and Minister Plenipotentiary to Morocco, and to take with him some presents worthy both of donor and receiver. In consequence of which our Envoy embarked at Cadiz the 27th of April, on the frigate *St. Lucia*, and sailed to Mogador, in company with the brigantine *el Vivo*, carrying the King's presents with him and 12 Algerine slaves, set at liberty, to present to his Moroccan Majesty. The two ships anchored on the 30th ult. At Mogador, where the Envoy landed the same night and the two following days the presents were debarked. ■ **LONDON, Oct. 31.** An extraordinary circumstance worthy of the attention of the faculty in general. At Rye, in Sussex, lives 22-year old Margery Gascoigne who has been with child fours years at the end of this month; she has had labour pains every nine months. Her size is beyond description, and the movements of the embryo (if a child) are surprising, insomuch that she is forced to take great doses of opium that she may have some ease herself. This is from a letter written at her direction, for she is unable to write herself, having been confined to her bed this past 8 months, and her room for almost two years. Mr. Mackrell, at Rye, who attends her, knows the truth of the above ... Extract of a letter from **Lisbon, Oct. 16:** The vast sums of money yearly sent by Spain to Portugal for corn for its inhabitants long ago convinced the court to convert some lands into arable; but as the soil is exceedingly shallow in most parts of the kingdom, and the grain in dry seasons has been parched before it can be properly eared. Research, however, reveals several hundred acres of deep, moist soil in the valley of Algarve. The first trial in 1780 produced abundant wheat, and corn has since be sown all through the valley, from St. Juan to Breganzille. More tracts are being cleared, and it is expected in a few years to be both self sufficient and to supply neighbors in cases of necessity. Some vineyards are ploughed up and destroyed, but without any loss to individuals; the court had purchased the lands at fair value, and let them out to tillage. The Dutch and English methods of husbandry are introduced, and will probably have all the effect desires ... The Dutch are sending vast reinforcements to their settlements in the East Indies; the Dutch East Indiaman which lately passed through the Downs, was full of soldiers, numbers on deck and no doubt as many confined below, which last are obtained by *silver hopeng*, as they term it in Holland or in other terms, kidnaping; these, however are not Dutchmen, but natives of other countries whom the officers that are employed in raising recruits for the

Dutch Oriental Company at Amsterdam, inveigle into their music houses, and after running up a long score, (for the Dutch victualers know the art of chalking) without money to pay, they are hurried on board the ship, and confined to the hold till the ship gets to sea, at which period they are released to help in working the vessel. Two regiments have already been sent to the Cape of Good Hope, and two to Batavia, since the peace; those now going out are designed for the garrison at Trincomale on the Island of Ceylon, to which place they are also sending building materials for the repairs and augmentation of that place, so as if possible to make it impregnable against the future attempts of an enemy ... Extract of a letter from **Tangiers, Sept. 2:** According the letters from Morocco, the Emperor has sent the Jew Elikao Levi to Mogador, to communicate to the merchants his new regulation on the exportation of corn from his Empire. By it, none but the Spaniards, Portuguese, Genoese, and Tuscans are permitted to export grain in the ships of their own nations, and are bound to their respective ports, and paying a duty of 16 pezos for 20 fanegas (a measure of the country). All other nations pay 22 pezos for the same measure. The other duties remain of the ancient footing, viz. One pezo per fanegas; but all masters of ships, coming to take in a lading shall be obliged to apply to M. Giovanni Chiappo, brother to the Venetian Consul in this Kingdom, who has been appointed sole commissary for the corn trade ... There never was known so many different Indian nations to be confederated, as now have entered into an union against the United States of America. Deputies from all the tribes inhabiting the banks of the Ohio and Mississippi, the Creek, Mosghes [or, Mofghes--Eds.], and the others on the back of Georgia and Florida, have lately assembled at a grand council fire, and there is every reason to suppose they will commence hostilities in the spring. Joseph the Mohawk King has been the principal mover of this confederacy ... In consequence of the tax upon hackney coaches in Dublin, the proprietors of those leathern vehicles, refused to ply, and at present a hackney coach is not seen in the Dublin streets.--The following is a stanza from a ballad transmitted to us.

Pitt's found a cure for *sloth* and *dumps*,
While tax is heap'd on tax;
We now are forced to stir our *stumps*
None *ply* but castle *hacks*.

Nov. 4. Yesterday in polite circles it was reported the King made a proposal to the Prince of Wales of a very important kind: to settle £100,000 a year on his Royal Highness for his establishment--that £200,000 should be granted to pay his debts, and an adequate sum for completing the buildings at Carleton House--on condition the Prince consent to marriage; the Princess the King recommends is Frederica Louisa Wilhemina, daughter of the Prince of Orange, Stadtholder, born the 28th of November, 1770, and consequently now 15.

His Majesty desired his Royal Highness to take 3 days to consider the proposal. The Prince is reported to have answered he was sensible of his Majesty's paternal goodness in the proposal, and intreated him to believe that he was sincerely disposed to the marriage state. He had a high respect for the lady, of whose accomplishments he had heard the warmest commendations; but he trusted his majesty would excuse him from pledging his word to a Princess whom he had not seen.--Here we understand the matter rests.

The report so often propagated of a rupture on the eve of breaking out between Russia and the Porte, have been contradicted by the Russian Ambassador resident in London, who has told our court, by order of the Czarina, that the most perfect harmony subsists between the two empires.

According the letters from **Brussels of the 20th ult.** Lieutenant Colonel Hoilckte, with a detachment of troops, has been despatched to take possession of that part of Flanders added to the Emperor by the late preliminary treaty. They also add that his Imperial Majesty is expected at Brussels before Christmas, and the Governor is making ready to receive him.

The French are going to open three new ports as free ports for the Windward Islands, viz. One at St. Pierre for Martinique, one at Point au Petre for Guadaloupe and its dependencies, and one at Scarborough for Tobago also three for Hispaniola, one at Cape Francois, one at Port au Prince, and one at Cayet St. Louis.

The claims of the loyalists having been discussed, ministers have now transmitted from the treasury to the board of commissioners the memorial and claim of those persons who were within the British lines during the disputes, are were obliged to contribute to the necessities of the army. There are claims for very large sums for the rents of houses occupied by officers; for timber cut down and other damages; for craft; for provisions and other things furnished the army. The amount of these claims is enormous, but we suppose considerable deductions will be made on the scrutiny.

The venerable Frederick of Prussia is at length drawing near his final dissolution, being now confined with a most excruciating fit of the gout in his stomach, from which his physicians say it is next to an impossibility he will recover.

Earl Cornwallis and the Marquis de Fayette met at the late review of the Prussian troops at Potsdam, and had the honor of being introduced to each other, by the veteran Frederick himself.

Yesterday's post brought accounts of the greatest discontents which have shewn themselves for some years in Scotland, having broke out into acts of public outrage at Aberdeen. When the express left Aberdeen the prisoners who had been committed by the provost were liberated by force; the Council Chamber was nearly destroyed, and the magistrates obliged to fly for safety; the military were called in, but being found too few to encounter the vast numbers of the disaffected, no use was made of them. They are supposed to be encouraged and stimulated by the Jacobite and republican parties, who are both numerous there. ■ **QUEBEC, Nov. 3.** Yesterday about noon his Majesty's commission appointing Brigadier General Hope Lieutenant Governor and Commander in Chief of this Province, was published in the Castle of St. Louis, whereupon he took the usual oaths in Council, and received the seals, on which there was a royal salute fired from the ramparts. ■ **BOSTON, Dec. 16.** It is with great pleasure, says a correspondent, we behold the growth and population of the town Charlestown, which in 1775 was wantonly set on fire and burnt by the British troops. Such is the increase since, that a Printing Office has lately been set up by Messrs. Allen and Cushing, and a periodical paper published by them twice a week. Probably the great increase of passengers through town via the bridge now erecting across Charles River--said to be complete by the beginning of July next--will greatly advance the town in wealth and opulence; and Charlestown, so famous in the annals of America, will rise "like a Phoenix out of her ashes," and vie in a few years with any town in the New England States, such are its prospects, and such its delightful situation.

The proprietors of the bridge erecting across the Charles, having purchased the hull of the large prize ship *Lord Howe*, to sink her in the river so as to defend the bridge from the ice; in Wednesday the attempt was made when, by some mistake in the conductors, she was unfortunately sunk in the channel, where her stem and stern just appear at low water. She went down so unexpectedly and rapidly that two men, who were assisting, had not time to quit her, but being left in the water were saved by swimming, until taken up by the boats. ■ **NEW YORK, Dec. 19.** We hear agents have been sent to the piratical powers of Algiers and Morocco. Mr. Lamb, late a captain in the American army, is deputed to the [Continued on Page 3].

Page 3. [Agents to Algiers and Morocco (*continued*)] former; and Mr. Barclay to the latter. These gentlemen are now in Europe--and we have reason to hope the commerce of the U.S. will soon feel the good effects of their mission--in lowering the present exorbitant rates of insurance. ■ **PHILADELPHIA, Dec. 22.** Extract of a letter from **London, Nov. 2:** An extraordinary circumstance has just taken place, in which a Frenchman and a woman, under pretence of paying a creditor a sum of money due him, enticed him to a new house in Walworth hired for the purpose, and threatened to shoot him if he did not sign a check for £300. The man bound him and stayed there till the woman returned with the money, and tried to extort £200 more. The gentleman was resolute, declaring he would sooner die. They left him in possibly the most curious situation ever heard of.--A barrel of gun powder was placed near him in the room: a large horseman's pistol was pointed directly into it, loaded and primed; to the trigger was fastened a string which communicated with his hands, legs and body so that if he stirred the whole would blow up, and to this there were similar communications to the windows, that if they were thrown up the like effect would be produced. In this state he continued several hours and was thus found by a person that was prudent enough to listen to his advice, and breaking through the glass, carefully cut the strings before he opened the window ... **Dec. 24:** Extract of a letter from an American gentleman of high rank, on the other side of the Atlantic, to his friend in Massachusetts, dated **September, 1785**: This letter will be handed to you by -----. He will inform you in what manner the late navigation act of the Massachusetts has been received here: Some say it is a measure taken in a passion, and not well weighed in the scales of reason, and that we are ruining ourselves; that an act of Parliament will be passed to retaliate upon us, and prohibit our vessels from entering the ports of Great Britain; that the other States will not follow the example, &c. &c. On the contrary, I believe, that no measure was ever taken with more profound reflection; hat we are laying the foundation of wealth and power, and real independence; that no act of Parliament will be passed to retaliate; and that some of our different States will immediately follow the example, and all of them in time.

On Wednesday the 15th instant arrived at New York the British packet *Roebuck*, Capt. Britton, in 38 days from Falmouth. She brings an account that the Honorable Messieurs Adams and Jefferson had sent an Ambassador to the Dey of Algiers, respecting the hostilities lately commenced by his subjects against the commerce of the United States of America: Mr. Randall, son of Thomas Randall, Esq; of New York, appointed Secretary to the Embassy, was already arrived at Paris, on his way thither.

Capt. Britton, of the *Roebuck*, the 2d inst. In longitude 60,00, spoke the ship *Philadelphia*, Packet, Capt. Tucker, from St. Ubes, bound to New York, out 50 days. He had lost his mizzenmast and oars, had his forecastle stove in, and was in want of provisions and water, which Capt. Britton supplied him with. Capt. Tucker's distressed situation forced him to bear away for the West Indies.

Last week the Reverend Mr. Pilmore, arrived in this city from New York, and has since preached to several crouded auditories in St. Paul's Church. This gentleman has been for many years an indefatigable preacher among the Methodists, and has lately received ordination in the Episcopal Church. We hear there is a probability of his being settled in the neighbourhood of this city ... On the 3d instant, died, at his house in Providence, Rhode Island, the Hon. JOSEPH BROWN, Esquire. ■ **RICHMOND, Dec. 31.** Tuesday last being the anniversary of St. John the Evangelist, the ancient and honorable society of Free and Accepted Masons went in procession from the lodge to the church, where the Rev. John Buchanan, their Chaplain, preached a sermon suitable to the occasion: In the evening there was a ball at the capitol which was conducted with the greatest harmony and good order. ■ **ALX, January 5**. Late London Newspapers advise, That a large American Vessel, homeward bound, laden with Serges, Satinets, Muslins, Taffetas, Prunellas, Fustians, Moreens, &c. was the latter End of last Month chased by two Algerine Vessels, and sunk by a sudden Gale. It is not known whether the Crew were drowned or taken up by the Algerines.--Two Vessels from Capraya had been taken by them, as was learnt by the Master of the Vessel, who brought the Account of the Fate of the American Ship. These marine Plunderers have been considerably reenforced in the Mediterranean; the *John Baptist*, [Capt.] Cambiosa, richly laden on Account of the Republic of Genoa, fell a Sacrifice to them. ■ Yesterday departed this Life, in the 10th Year of his Age, Master HENRY CHEW, the only Child of Mr. ROGER CHEW.--He was a promising Youth, and "bid fair for Manhood."--His Death is an irreparable Loss to his bereaved Parents. ■ NAVAL-OFFICE, ALX. *Inward Entries*. Schooner *Abigail*, D. Leifkin, from New-England; Sloop *Betty*, P. Duncan, Baltimore. *Cleared Outwards*. Sloop *Surprise*, J.T. Brooks, for Guadaloupe. ■ TO THE PUBLIC, **As a citizen of the United** States, I deem it my duty to lay before the public the following circumstances--and though I cannot hope, by such means, to derive any satisfaction for the *personal injuries* I have experienced, yet I trust the exposition of a man, who I have found to be destitute of honor and honesty, may supply a caution (not altogether unserviceable) to the commercial interest of America. Having sailed, as Supercargo, on board the *Henry*, Captain Dennison, I arrived at Jamaica on the 29th of July, 1785.--A stranger in the country--equally unacquainted with its inhabitants and its customs, I thought it prudent to entrust the disposal of the cargo to more experienced hands, and, in the choice of Mr. JOEL EVANS, for that purpose, I flattered myself I had happily discharged my duty to all who were interested in the voyage: Apprized, however, of the dangers of the hurricane months, I did not neglect any precaution which could expedite the return of the ship; and expressly stipulated with Mr. Evans, that no credit should be given for any part of the cargo; and that rather than suffer a delay of more than three weeks, the whole should be offered for sale at public vendue. This limited time being expired, I anxiously reminded Mr. Evans of his engagement, and, once more, pressing the necessity of despatch, I declared a resolution to send the ship away even in ballast, rather than expose her to the storms of the approaching season. That a considerable part of the cargo, particularly the flour and lumber, was yet unsold, was, from day to day, the only excuse which Mr. Evans could furnish me; and on the very evening preceding the violent hurricane in which the *Henry* was lost, it was still the only reason he could give for his fatal proclamations. When, however, I called on Mr. Evans, the morning after the tempest had subsided, in hopes, in some degree, to retrieve the misfortunes of that event, by the enhanced price of the articles of flour and lumber, thus said to be unsold, my surprise and mortification were equally great, to hear from the same lips, that, except a small quantity of damaged fish, the whole property had long been disposed of! Such fallacy of conduct, added to the previous agitation of my mind and the natural inhospitality of the climate, produced a fever, which, for many weeks, confined me, in a desperate state, to my bed. During this tedious indisposition, I made frequent applications to Mr. Evans for the means of support, but as he had hitherto shewn his want of integrity as a merchant, he now evinced his want of feeling, as a man. My drafts were protested as often as they were presented; and, not satisfied with denying me the assistance that was due from him, he artfully endeavoured to depreciate my credit with others, by boldly asserting that he had fully paid the proceeds of the cargo with which he had been entrusted. My fever at length left me, but in so low and emaciated a state, that it was thought nothing but a change of climate could possibly restore my health and constitution. With this object in view, I waited on Mr. Evans for a settlement, and in order to accomplish it, I was obliged to allow 3 per cent. which he had charged for guarantying debts, when it must be remembered that I had particularly stipulated that no debts should be contracted. Upon this settlement, a sum of 360l. appeared to be due to me. Now let the public judge of this man's conduct (every trait of which I can prove) and let individuals beware of trusting him. He is well known in the city of Philadelphia, from which he withdrew during the war, and adds one of the many proofs of depravity exhibited by that class of Americans called REFUGEES. HENRY PRENTISS. ■ TO BE SOLD, On the most reasonable terms, A SMALL quantity of JAMAICA RUM, of the first quality, fit for immediate use, either by the quarter-cask or smaller quantity.--Also, a few white and black beaver hats of an excellent quality, Cayenne pepper, pimento, almonds, elegant plated castors, candlesticks, &c.&c.--Inquire of AARON HEWES, ALX, Jan. 4, 1786.

On Friday the 6th, and Saturday the 7th inst., will be sold at the Vendue-Store,

A VARIETY of WET and DRY GOODS, consisting of rum in hogsheads and barrels, brandy in barrels, sugar in ditto, gin in cases, Jamaica spirits, superfine cloths, coatings, kerseys, Negro cottons, worsted hose, linens, jeans, calicoes, teas, &c.&c.

**For private sale a Negro boy, a few hogsheads of choice old rum, and a few kegs of old Cogniac brandy.--Also a new BILLIARD-TABLE with necessary furniture, on three months credit.

☞ To be rented, a Store on Fairfax-street, near Col. Hooe's, well situated for business, with a counting-room, bed-room, loft, kitchen, cellar, and a stable.--Also, a two-story brick House on Water-street, near Col. Hooe's, with every necessary convenience for a merchant and his family.

S. ARELL, Vendue-Master.

ALX, Jan. 5, 1786.

☞ *THE Attendance of the Brethren of Lodge No. 39, is requested on Friday Evening the 20th Instant, being stated Lodge Night, there being Business of great Importance to come then before them.* By Order of the Master, SAMUEL ARELL, *Secretary.* ALX, Jan. 5, 1786.

For LONDON,

THE ship *FRIENDS*, JOHN MUIR, Master, now lying at this port, will take tobacco on board consigned to THOMAS BLANE.--As one-third of her cargo is engaged, she will sail in all February; and rather than detain her 100 hogsheads will be taken on liberty.--The *Friends* is a British ship, copper bottomed with a Mediterranean pass of the newest cut.--For freight or passage, apply to the Captain on board, at Hooe's Wharf, or WILLIAM HUNTER, jun.
ALX, Jan. 2, 1786.

Town of ALX, Jan. 2, 1786, **On Thursday next, at 3** o'clock in the afternoon, will be rented, by rooms, to the highest bidders, the PUBLIC WAREHOUSE on Point-West, for one year, as usual. OLIVER PRICE, *Council Clerk.* ■ TO BE LET on GROUND-RENT forever, **One Hundred LOTS of** GROUND, some of which are 40 by 176 feet 5 inches, situated on Queen, Princess and Oronoko streets, adjoining the property I rented to the Rev. Dr. Griffith, not more than 450 yards from the public Warehouses, Ferry and some of the most frequented wharves in ALX, and adjacent to the best water in or near this town.--The title is indisputable and clear of all incumbrances whatever, which circumstance must render said Lots more valuable than most of the property adjoining this town. Any person wanting to become an adventurer in this rising and flourishing place for the whole or any part of said property, will be treated with on the most advantageous terms by applying to the Subscriber, who will shew the plot and premises. BALDWIN DADE, ALX, Jan. 4, 1786. ■ FOR SALE, **A valuable Tract of** Land, containing about 275 acres, lying within four miles of ALX, about 120 of which are cleared and under tolerable good fencing, about 30 acres of good meadow, 10 of which are in order for Timothy.--The buildings are a dwelling-house with four fireplaces, kitchen, stable, storehouse, and a number of other convenient buildings.--The terms may be known of the Subscriber at Woodville, adjoining the premises. W. BIRD, Jan. 4, 1786. ■ **LOTS to be let on Ground-Rent in this town, by Hooe and Harrison**, ALX, Dec. 15, 1785. ■ Frederick County, Virginia,

Dec. 29, 1785. COMMITTED to this gaol, on suspicion of being a servant, but denies having a master, an Irishman, who calls himself LAWRENCE CASKIN, is about 6 feet high, of a dark complexion, by trade a tanner, and says he came into Baltimore last May, in a ship consigned to Messrs. Stewart and Plunket, Alexander Bell, Master.--His master is requested to come, prove property, pay charges, and take him away. JOHN WATERS, Gaoler.

Page 4. Poetry. "LINES addressed to AMBITION." ■ **William Buddicom,** At Mr. ANDREW WALES'S, near Captain Harper's Wharf, Has imported in the brig *Alexandria*, Capt. Watkins, from Liverpool, a variety of GOODS, which he will sel on the most reasonable terms for cash or country produce, viz. LIVERPOOL blown salt, candles by the box, spikes, all kinds of flooring nails, spriggs, perch hooks, broad and narrow hoes, ditto carpenters' axes, carpenters' tools in boxes assorted, grid-irons, flesh-forks, marline spikes, hooks and thimbles, shovels, spades, all kinds of nails, &c. suitable for a shipchandler, Dutch ovens, iron pots, stone jugs of 1, 2 and 3 gallons each, Scotch barley in jugs, oatmeal in ditto, hats by the box, woollens properly assorted, Manchester goods by the box assorted for small stores, seine and mullet twine, checks of all sorts, sail needles, Whitechapel ditto, shoes, romals, teas, a few crates of blue and queen's ware properly assorted, tarpaulin canvas, sail ditto from No. 1 to 8, a box containing 12 patterns of coats, a few patent medicines, six complete Hadley's Quadrants, with many other articles too tedious to mention. ALX, Dec. 29, 1785. ■ **James M'Kenna**, Hath opened store on Fairfax-street, next door to Col. Fitzgerald's [see like ad Vol. II No. 99] ■ Messrs. Jesse Taylor and James M'Kenna, attornies for William Lowry, being gone to England, seek to settle outstanding accounts [see like ad Vol. II No. 99] ■ SAMUEL ARELL has for rent the house and lot lately occupied by Mr. Thomas Reeder [see like ad Vol. II No. 97] ■ **Hooe and Harrison**, Have for sale MADERA wine of London, New-York and Virginia quality, etc. [see like ad Vol. II No. 97] ■ HUIE, REID and CO. seek charter for Brigantine *Betsy*, Capt. Brown [see like ad Vol. II No. 98] ■ For charter to St. EUSTATIUS or St. CROIX, **The schooner *MOLLY***, DENNIS JOHNSTON, Master, burthened 400 barrels, and will be ready to take in by the first of next month.--For terms apply to SAMUEL M. BROWN, or the said Master. ALX, Dec. 29, 1785. ■ **Ebenezer Richmond**, offers his services of physic and surgery to inhabitants of Leesburg, Va. [see like ad Vol. II No. 99] ■ **David Shaon**, WHARF-BUILDER, ADVERTISES the public that he is about to remove from hence to Baltimore, except persons desirous to improve their water-lots by building of wharves or piers next spring, will within four weeks contact him. He purposes to serve any such contract by bringing, at his own expence, to this town all suitable timber for the purpose, without any trouble or risque to the employer, and will do it and his work at the cheapest rates. DANIEL ROBERDEAU or JAMES KIRK, Esquires, can inform where he is to be treated with. ALX, Dec. 29, 1785. ■ WILLIAM HARTSHORNE offers for sale sundry lots and houses to rent in ALX [see like ad with details Vol. II No. 98] ■ Capt. MUIR seeks employment of a clerk [see like ad Vol. II No. 99] ■ Printed Sermons to be sold at the Printing-Office [see description Vol. II No. 99] ■ JAMES SUTER, Montgomery Co., Md., has for sale several tracts of land, including one called Aberdeen [see like ad Vol. II No. 96] ■ ALX: Printed by GEORGE RICHARDS, and COMPANY, at their Printing-Office on Fairfax-street--by whom Advertisements, &c. are thankfully received for this Paper,--and where Printing is performed with Care and Expedition.

1786/01/12, Vol. II No. 102

Page 1. (*Continuation* of the TOBACCO ACT). (8) If any tobacco is brought into Great-Britain without a manifest, all such tobacco so imported shall be liable to the same duties as tobacco of the growth of the Spanish or Portuguese plantations, and the master shall forfeit and lose the sum of one hundred pounds; (9) every master taking tobacco into Great-Britain as abovestated when asked shall produce the manifest, to have on board customs officers for inspection who will certify on the back of the manifest their examination; officers to receive certified copies of manifest; at customs house enter manifest information in a book to be kept for that purpose; officers to batten and lock down the main and other hatchways leading to the hold or place of stowage in ships, assisted by the master; (10) if the master of ship with imported tobacco shall not produce manifest or contents in writing to customs officers, and give copies as abovestated, all the tobacco on board the ship shall be subject and liable to same duties as tobacco of the growth of Spanish or Portuguese plantations, and the master shall forfeit the sum of one hundred pounds; (11) if any customs officer boarding a ship shall not demand manifest or not certify as abovestated, or neglects to certify receipt of manifest copy, or shall not in 24 hours after receiving enter copie in the book so directed, or neglect or omit to batten and lock down the hatchways as above said, such officer shall for each and every such offence respectively, forfeit and lose the sum of one hundred pounds; (12) the commissioners of his Majesty's customs shall fix and appoint at each port in England a certain place for mooring every ship laden with tobacco, from which place the ship shall not depart until their respective cargos of tobacco shall have been delivered from them in the manner herein after mentioned, and until cleared; commissioners in Scotland to follow same provisions; penalty for nonperformance is fifty pounds; (13) if after arrival of a ship laden with tobacco within the limits of any port of Great-Britain, or within four leagues of the coast thereof, bulk shall be broken, or any part of the cargo of such ship shall be unladen or unshipped, with intention to be laid on land, before such ship shall come to the place appointed for her discharge, and shall be there duly authorized by proper customs officers (unless in case of distress of weather, etc.), and master or other person having charge together with two or more mariners on board, shall make proof upon oath before collector of an accident, necessity, or distress each such ship or vessel together with her cargo, and her guns, furniture, ammunition, tackle, and apparel shall be forfeited and lost, and master shall forfeit the sum of one hundred pounds; or if fastenings or hatchway locks are broken before the ship's arrival at her moorings (unless like prove as above of unavoidable necessity), the master or other person having charge shall forfeit and lose the sum of one hundred pounds; (14) master upon arrival at moorings will make a just and true entry upon the burthen, contents, and lading of ship, with particular marks, numbers, qualities and contents of every parcel of goods then laden, to best of his knowledge, before the customs officer of the port, openly in the custom-house, as required by an act passed in the first year of the reign of her late Majesty Queen Elizabeth, intitled, An act for limiting the times for laying on land merchandise from beyond the seas, and touching customs for sweet wines; and by an act passed in the thirteenth and fourteenth years of the reign of his late Majesty King Charles the Second, intitled, An act for preventing frauds, and regulating abuses in his Majesty's customs, under the penalty of the forfeiture of one hundred pounds; the said master when making his report will deliver to the customs officer the manifest or contents in writing; for neglect or omission, refusal to deliver such manifest, the master to forfeit and lose the sum of one hundred pounds [*To be continued*].

Page 2. **LONDON, Oct. 31. A GENTLEMAN** who has read the April 14 *Calcutta Gazette* relates the famous *Tippo Saib* was poisoned in a dish of coffee by one of his concubines; but the dose either not being sufficiently strong, or working slow, this Prince had time to call in a Persian physician, who immediately administered an antidote which saved his Life. That the woman being discovered, she was placed on a pile of wood, so contrived as to admit the flame to one piece of timber at a time. This barbarous execution is said to have continued two hours before the wretched creature, who was consumed by inches, breathed her last ... **Nov. 3:** The idea adopted by his Majesty, of transporting for Life to Africa or India, all deserters, instead of shooting or whipping them, will have a much better effect than the former mode of punishment, and we trust it will in some measure put an end to that horrid custom practiced by the India Company of kidnaping young men, confining them in cellars, and transporting them for Life, without either law or justice to warrant such an outrage to the liberty of the subject. Hundreds of innocent young men are lost to their friends and to their country, and supposed to be drowned, who are thus trepanned by the India Company; and many a parent at this day bewails the loss of a child as dead, who is in perpetual slavery as a soldier on the burning plains of the eastern world. The Company never permits any of their soldiers to return, although they pretend to inlist them only for three years. The reason is obvious. They are afraid of prosecutions and heavy punishment for this daring breach of the laws. Indeed it is amazing that among other India enormities, this crime has not been brought before Parliament.

From **Stockholm** we learn that the beginning of this month the Swedish court received a courier from Constantinople, who brought the ratification of a treaty of commerce, which their King had just concluded with the Porte. The Swedish court has likewise concluded a new treaty with the Algerines, as well for the advantage as security of the Swedish ships in the Mediterranean, by virtue of which treaty the King of Sweden is to send a considerable present to the Dey, to consist of artillery, arms, ammunition and warlike stores.

The French artists who are gone to South Carolina, for the purpose of cultivating the silk of that colony, are said by a Parisian paper of the present month to have taken with them a new machine which performs all the work of the celebrated Piedmontese Reel, without any additional mechanism; and which gives stability and beauty to the silk. The French are vigorously promoting their own silk manufactories. The French, with all their art and ingenuity, cannot produce a silk machine equal to that which is used at Derby, and which winds 73,728 yards every time its water wheel goes round, which is three times every minute. It consists of 26,546 movements which are continually at work; one water wheel communicates motion to them all, one fire engine conveys air, and one regulator governs the whole apparatus ... **Nov. 6:** It is far from unpleasing to observe, that the Ministry have fully refuted many of the assertions of those who try to disappoint their endeavours, by their prudent and firm procedure with the court of Versailles. Ample concession and restitution are either already made on the African coast, or just about to be made. The outrages in that quarter have, upon inquiry, come far short of the excesses which some of our countrymen ascribed to them. They at length appear to be neither dishonorable nor disadvantageous to Britain: While they have occasioned some uneasiness to the French monarch and detracted not a little from the idea which we had entertained of the civilization, humanity and wisdom of the French nation. ■ **CHARLESTON,** (S.C.) **Dec. 15.** Extract of a letter from **Savanna, in Georgia, Nov. 24:** I mentioned in my former letter that the Commissioners from Congress had met the Indians at Golphinton, and that the Indians had returned satisfied; this was then the report:--Since that Mr. Telfair, one of the Commissioners appointed by this State, has arrived here from the treaty. It seems in the commission of Georgia Agents, they were directed to protest against any proceedings of the Congress Commissioners, that might militate against the rights, privileges and sovereignty of the State. Two Kings, or head men only met: In the articles of the treaty it was mentioned, that Congress claimed an exclusive right to the soil: That secondly, if a white man should trespass upon the Indians, the white man should be sent to Congress, who were to point out the mode of trying him. To these two articles the commissioners for the State of Georgia, made a protest, and broke up the Congress of the Continental Commissioners. A few days after seventeen Kings or head men, from the Upper and Lower Creeks, met the Agents of this State, who were empowered to treat with the Indians; they did so, and obtained a cession of country from them, in addition to what they had already granted, by running a temporary line from the Camouchie to the head of the southern branch of the St. Mary, giving a tract of about 60 miles by 40.--After this the Indians returned home, without entering into any treaty with the Commissioners from Congress. ■ **NEWBURYPORT, Dec. 14.** In the course of last week, a family removed with their effects into a newly finished house, and having considerable company, were necessitated to take up their lodgings in chambers lately plastered, and not sufficiently dried; in some of these chambers the company spent part of the evening, till at length a sister of the owner of the house complaining of being unwell, and a pain in her stomach, it was thought prudent that she retire to bed; but during her preparation therefore, her sister, wife to the house's owner, fainted, and on recovering herself, made the same complaints--their difficulties increasing, a doctor was sent for, who, when he came, found eight or nine of the company in much the same situation, among whom was the master of the house, who fainted and complained as the rest. The doctor ordered them out of the damp rooms, and they soon found relief.--This is inserted as a caution to others. ■ **BOSTON, Dec. 22.** At the last session of the General Court of the State of New Hampshire, a motion was made and seconded, to appoint a Committee to consider the expediency of altering the mode of punishment for petty crimes: And of obliging such as are convicted of them, to work out their salvation, not with fear and trembling, but with--*The Nail and Hammer.* ■ **NEW YORK, Dec. 26.** On the 18th instant the sloop *Experiment*, Stewart Dean, Esq; Commander, sailed from hence to Canton, China, this is the second adventure from the United States of America to so distant a point.--It cannot but give pleasure to every friend of his country, when it is considered there are men among us of judgement to plan, and souls of enterprise to execute what formerly would have been considered a hazardous and impracticable undertaking. Experience, however, has taught us that fancy often times paints danger in much stronger colours than what is found to exist in reality, and that by diligence and activity we are enabled to get over difficulties which, on a cursory view, are deemed insurmountable.--The *Empress of China* was considered a very small vessel to encounter the perils of so long a voyage, and yet she returned in perfect safety, though the navigation was novel to every to every person on board--a very small sloop, of not more than forty tons the property of an enterprising merchant, has twice, without the least loss, visited the Cape of Good Hope; and in the route to China, no part of the ocean teems with more danger than from hence to the Cape. It is reconcilable, therefore, both to the maxims of prudence and the probability of profit, that a sloop, built of the very best materials, fashioned according to the most approved model, navigated by so experienced a Commander, and loaded by citizens of approved judgement and competent fortune, should proceed on a voyage which, but a few years ago, was supposed impracticable.--We wish success to the undertaking; and we wish also that our legislative body, at their next meeting, may consider the importance of this branch of commerce, and make such regulations respecting it as may insure a certain as well as permanent advantage to this rising empire. To accomplish so desirable an end, it is only necessary to encourage the cultivation and proper curing of ginseng, to prevent its exportation to any other country than China (and that in our own vessels) and to impose a heavy duty of the produce of the east, unless imported directly from thence in ships which are the property of the citizens of the United States. By the *first* regulation, we shall soon be enabled without the aid of specie, to receive in return every *necessary* oriental commodity; and by the latter, the profits of this lucrative trade will rest entirely among ourselves. ■ **PHILADELPHIA, Jan. 2.** By Capt. Atkins, arrived at Boston, we are informed that the uneasiness respecting the capturing of American vessels by the Algerines had, in some measure, subsided;--few of their corsairs having for some time past ventured without the Straits, owing to the approach of winter and the vigilance of the Portuguese. No accounts of late captures by the Algerines had been received at Cadiz ... Capt. Smith, who is arrived at Boston from Martinico, informs that almost every house and store in Demarara has lately been consumed by fire ... **Jan. 6:** In November last two petitions were presented to the Assembly of New Jersey, from sundry inhabitants of the county of Sussex, praying an impost may be laid on all foreign merchandise imported into that State from the neighbouring States, which was read and ordered to lie on the table for a second reading. ■ **BALTIMORE, Jan. 6.** A writer on the situation of the affairs of Britain gives the following curious account of the national debt: "The national debt is above 272 millions, a sum which the human mind can hardly form an idea of. To give some assistance in forming a notion of it; were it to be paid down in guineas in a line, it would extend 4300 miles in length--were it to be paid in shillings, it would extend three and a half times and a half round the globe--and if paid in solid silver, require 60,400 horses to draw it, at the rate of 15 cwt. To each horse." ■ **ALX. January 12**. Late Boston Newspapers mention, that the new State of Vermont, from a State of Anarchy and Confusion, is softening down to a happier Condition.--That Courts of Law are regularly held there and Justice can be obtained through its proper Channel.--That the Policy of the State is managed with a Consistency and Energy that bids fair to transform that late dreary Wilderness into as fair a Republic as any in the Confederation.--That His Excellency Thomas Chittenden, Esq; was lately chosen Governor of that State, the Honorable Paul Spooner, Esq; Lieutenant-Governor, and the Honorable Moses Robinson, Ira Allen, and Stephen R. Bradley, Esquires, Agents to Congress.

Page 3. Lately DIED at Enfield, in England, Mr. TAYLOR, formerly a Butcher in London, worth 10,000l. in Trade, with which he retired.--He had often been heard to say, that he made his Money by two Maxims, viz.--*In selling to the Rich at his own Price, and to the Poor at theirs, by which he never had any Waste*. ■ The Honorable House of Assembly of the State of Pennsylvania stands adjourned to the Third Tuesday in February next. ■ MARRIED.] At Baltimore, Mr. JOHN HOLLINS, Merchant, to Miss SMITH, Daughter of the Hon. JOHN SMITH, Esquire. ■ NAVAL-OFFICE, ALX. *Inward Entries*. Schooner *Swallow*, S. Brown, from New-England. *Cleared Outwards*. Schooner *Cynthia*, S. Thornton, for Rhode-Island; Sloop *Ant*, J.C. Moran, Surinam; Schooner *Barbadoes*, S. Fell, Barbadoes. ■ BON MOT. **A** FEW mornings after the marriage of Miss Younge with Mr. Pope, a lady of her acquaintance met her, and after the usual compliments had passed, of congratulations on the marriage, "Pray," says the lady to the new bride, "how do you like Pope's Essay?" The new-married lady archly replied, "I find a similarity of sentiment in all those works perfectly consonant to *Younge's Night Thoughts*."

PRICES CURRENT, ALX. / Tobacco, 21s. per Ct. / Fine Flour, 30s. per Barrel. / Wheat, 5/6s. per Bushel. / Jamaica Spirits, 4/6 per Gallon. / Windward Rum, 3s. per Ditto. / Continental Rum, 2s. per Ditto. / Molasses, 1/6 per Ditto. / Muscovado Sugar, 45s. to 50s. per Ct. / Salt, 3s. per Bushel, by Retail. / Corn, 4s. per Bushel. / Exchange, 40.

On Saturday the 14th inst. will be sold at the Vendue-Store,

A VARIETY of WET and DRY GOODS, consisting of rum in hogsheads and barrels, brandy in barrels, sugar in ditto, gin in cases, Jamaica spirits, superfine cloths, coatings, kerseys, Negro cottons, worsted hose, linens, jeans, calicoes, teas, &c.&c.

**For private sale, a Negro boy, a few hogsheads of choice old rum, and a few kegs of old Cogniac brandy.--Also a new BILLIARD-TABLE with necessary furniture, on three months credit.

☞ To be rented, a Store on Fairfax-street, well situated for business, with a counting-room, bed-room, loft, kitchen, cellar, and a stable.--Also, a two-story brick House on Water-street, near Col. Hooe's, with every necessary convenience for a merchant and his family.

S. ARELL, Vendue-Master.

ALX, Jan. 12, 1786.

WANTED, IMMEDIATELY, **A Journeyman Printer**, Who can be recommended for Sobriety and Diligence. ALX, Jan. 12, 1786. ■ I HEREBY forewarn all persons from taking an assignment of a bond which I gave to ALEXANDER SMITH, for eighty pounds. JOSEPH GARDINER, January 6, 1786. ■ To be sold, at the Printing-Office, **A Variety of Blank Books,** consisting of Ledgers, Journals, Cash-Books, Letter-Books, &c.&c. Also, Stoughton's Bitters, Anderson's Pills, Daffy's Elixir, Balsam of Honey, Squire's Elixir, Bateman's Drops, Godfrey's Cordial, &c.&c.&c.

Just received, and to be sold by the Printers hereof,
Price *Half a Dollar*,
THE
Philadelphia Directory,
By FRANCIS WHITE,
Containing,

1. THE Names of the Citizens, their Occupations, and Places of Abode, in alphabetical Order.
2. The Members in Congress, and from what States.
3. Grand Departments of the United States, and by whom conducted.
4. Members of Council, from what Counties, and where residing in the City.
5. Members of Assembly, from what Counties, and their City Residence.
6. Judges and Justices of the Peace, with their Places of Abode.
7. Public State Offices, where, and by whom kept.
8. Counsellors at Law, and where residing.
9. Ministers of the Gospel, where residing, and what Church.
10. Physicians, Surgeons, and their Places of Abode.
11. President, Directors, Days and Hours of Businesses at the Bank.
12. Professors at the University.
13. Rates of Porterage, as established by Law.
14. Arrivals and Departures of all Posts and Stages.
15. The Society of Cincinnati, the Committee, their Places of Meeting, and Abode.
16. Omissions and Errors.

To which are annexed--A valuable, regular, and well calculated Table of Dollars, Crowns, French and English Guineas, with other Coins, suitable for any State; and digested in such Order, in one Line, as to render a Comparison between the States plain and easy.

Philip Dalby, Has for sale, at his store on the corner of Royal and Cameron streets, and next to the Vendue-Store, AN assortment of low priced coatings, which he will dispose of at a low advance, for final settlement certificates. He is also opening for sale a variety of ready-made clothes, consisting of knap, Negro cotton, swanskin, woollen lined, and printed velveret jackets; cloth, cotton, drab, and corduroy breeches; cloth coats, Bath surtout coats, loose great coats, ditto with velvet collars, sailors' jackets, trousers and check shirts; also, a beautiful assortment of printed calicoes, which, with the other goods he has on hand, he will dispose of on reasonable terms, for cash, flour or certificates. ALX, Jan. 9, 1786. ■ To be SOLD, for COST, THE STOCK of a well assorted STORE in George-Town.--There is not an article unsaleable.--The whole consists of MERCHANDISE well adapted for the situation of the store; and is laid in on terms the most advantageous.--The goods are all new, not having been purchased six months.--For particulars apply to JOHN FALLS and CO., George-Town, or RICHARD CATON and CO., Baltimore. **Tobacco, wheat, or other produce, would be received in payment--a part in certificates, or credit given with good security. December 20, 1785. ■ THIS is to certify, that HENRY YOST has satisfied John Yost, Peter Miller, and Frederick Wedzell, for their parts of a brick house in this town that said Henry Yost sold to me last spring, and has given them up the remaining bonds which I passed to him in part payment for said house; he also got them to make me a deed according to my first agreement with him; and, as I advertised the said bonds some time past, I do now agree that the said Yost has behaved as an honest man. ALEXANDER DOYLE, George-Town, Jan. 8, 1786. ■ I HEREBY forewarn any person or persons from taking any assignments of any bonds or notes granted by the Subscriber to GEORGE HAGELY of Berkeley County, Virginia, as I have fully paid him for the same. SAMUEL HARDISTY, Montgomery County, Maryland, Jan. 6, 1786. ■ To be sold at the plantation of Mrs. Sarah Monroe, in Fairfax County, for ready cash, on the 25th instant, if fair, if not, the next fair day, ALL the estate of John Monroe, deceased, consisting of six NEGROES, a man, a boy, two women, and two children, horses, cattle, household furniture, some carpenters' and joiners' tools, and sundry other things, for to discharge his debts, by EDWARD BLACKBURN, Executor, SARAH MONROE, Executrix, January 6, 1786. ■ **To the Friends of Literature in Alexandria and the Country adjacent.** THE Subscriber would beg Leave to solicit your kind Attention to the Institution of a CIRCULATING LIBRARY, which he is now establishing among you. He has long considered ALX as a Town daily growing in commercial Consequence, and increasing with a Number of valuable in intelligent Citizens--He therefore conceives, in such a thriving Place, his Proposals will meet with a general and hearty Approbation, as they evidently tend to the Amusement, Instruction and Welfare of the Community.--It would be needless and perhaps tedious to point out all the Advantages which must arise from a well regulated Circulating Library:--That it will promote the Cultivation of knowledge, the Refinement of Society, and the Happiness of Human Nature, will be readily granted by every enlightened Mind--Youth in a particular Manner will be benefited by it, as it will give them an Opportunity to extend their Inquiries in the Fields of Sciences, and lay before them a greater Number of excellent and instructive Authors than they probably could meet with in any private Library: Hence they may the better be enabled to prepare themselves to act on the great Theatre of Life, be better fitted for the Duties of Legislation and Civil Government, and to serve their Country with Satisfaction to themselves, and Honor to their Friends. As to those whose Fortunes are sufficient to indulge them in the Sweets of Leisure and Retirement, they may here find a Source of the most refined Pleasure, the Feast of Reason and the Flow of Soul; which is in no Way so well enjoyed as in the Perusal of the first Writers, both ancient and modern. Conscious then that nothing more need be said to a generous and candid Public, on the extensive Usefulness of this Institution, the Subscriber most cheerfully flatters himself with the Prospect of experience ing their kind Countenance and Encouragement:--And as it is his most ardent Wish to obtain the Patronage of those sentimental and liberal Hearts, who delight in Knowledge and Virtue, he is determined to make the greatest Exertions to render himself worth of their Favor, and will constantly endeavor to furnish his Collection with such new Publications as may merit their Attention, assuring them, that the Additions to his Circulating Library will be always adequate to the Encouragement he shall meet with from his worthy and learned Friends. WILLIAM MURPHY, ALX, Jan. 11, 1785.

☞ LADIES and GENTLEMEN may become Subscribers to the Circulating Library on the following moderate Terms, viz. One Year, Eight Dollars; Half Year, Five Ditto; Three Months, Three Ditto; One Month, Six Shillings and Eightpence.

**Said MURPHY has for Sale, a neat Assortment of Stationary, &c. which he will dispose of on the most reasonable Terms; among which are Bibles, Testaments, Spelling-Books, Primers, Ledgers and Journals, Letter, Invoice, Waste, Receipt and Memorandum Books; Quills, Penknives, Ink-Powder and Ink-Cake, Sealing-Wax and Wafers, Slates and Pencils, Black-Lead Pencils, Ink-Chests and Pots, Ladies' and Gentlemens' elegant Pocket-Books, with or without Instruments, Writing-Paper, Playing and Message Cards, a great variety of elegant Jewelry, Harpsichords, Piano Fortes, Spinets, Violins and Violincellos, Guitars, German-Flutes and Hautboys, &c. Instructions and easy Pieces of Music, for the above Instruments. ■ FOR SALE, and the Terms made easy, A Valuable TRACT or parcel of LAND, lying in Frederick County, Virginia, situated 16 miles below Winchester and 3 miles above Snickers's Ferry, containing 337 acres, well watered by three springs of excellent limestone water, and a fine stream running nearly through the middle of it. This land rents for 3000lb. of tobacco annually, and would rent for 4000lb. if let for a term of years.--I shall say nothing of the improvements, as I presume no person will purchase without first viewing the premises.--For terms apply to GEORGE NOBLE, Esq; who lives joining the said land, or to the Subscriber near Stephensburg. ELISHA WILLIAMS, January 6, 1786. ■ JOHN WATERS, Gaoler, Frederick Co., Va., seeks owner of Irishman Lawrence Caskin [see like ad Vol. II No. 101].

Page 4. Poetry. "On a GOOD CONSCIENCE." ■ **William Buddicom**, has for sale at Mr. Andrew Wales's, near Captain Harper's Wharf, goods just imported from Liverpool in the brig *Alexandria* [see like ad Vol. II No. 101] ■ **Hooe and Harrison**, Have for sale MADERA wine of London, New-York and Virginia quality, etc. [see like ad Vol. II No. 97] ■ HUIE, REID and CO. seek charter for Brigantine *Betsy*, Capt. Brown [see like ad Vol. II No. 98] ■ SAMUEL M. BROWN seeks charter to St. Eustatius or St. Croix for schooner *Molly*, Dennis Johnston, Master [see like ad Vol. II No. 101] ■ **David Shaon**, wharf-builder, advertises to the public that he is about to remove from ALX to Baltimore [see like ad Vol. II No. 101] ■ AARON HEWES has for sale a small quantity of Jamaica rum, etc. [see like ad Vol. II No.

101] ■ WILLIAM HUNTER, jun. seeks tobacco onboard the ship *Friends*, John Muir, Master, to sail in February for London [see like ad Vol. II No. 101] ■ SAMUEL ARELL, Secretary, Brethren Lodge No. 39, announces meeting [see like ad Vol. II No. 101] ■ BALDWIN DADE has for rent on ground-rent forever 100 lots situated on Queen, Princess and Oronoko streets adjoining the property rented to Rev. Dr. Griffith [see like ad Vo. II No. 101] ■ WILLIAM HARTSHORNE offers for sale sundry lots and houses to rent in ALX [see like ad with details Vol. II No. 98] ■ W. BIRD, Woodville, has for sale 275 acres within 4 miles of ALX [see like ad Vol. II No. 101] ■ Hooe and Harrison has lots to be let on ground-rent [see like ad Vol. II No. 101] ■ Printed Sermons to be sold at the Printing-Office [see description Vol. II No. 99] ■ JAMES SUTER, Montgomery Co., Md., has for sale several tracts of land, including one called Aberdeen [see like ad Vol. II No. 96] ■ ALX: Printed by GEORGE RICHARDS, and COMPANY, at their Printing-Office on Fairfax-street--by whom Advertisements, &c. are thankfully received for this Paper,--and where Printing is performed with Care and Expedition.

1786/01/19, Vol. II No. 103

Page 1. WILLIAM MURPHY announces the opening of a circulating library; gives subscription rates; has for sale stationary items [see like ads Vol. II No. 102] ■ (*Continuation of the* TOBACCO ACT). (15) all importers, proprietors, or consignees of any tobacco brought into Great-Britain as aforesaid shall within 10 days (for whole or major part) or 15 days (for lesser part), shall have made his report of entry with the customs officer at the port in Great-Britain where the ship arrived, an entry in writing by each of them agreeing of the manifest contents; paying to the customs officer the several subsidies, customs, duties and imposts due on the tobacco, and are hereby directed and required to become bound unto his Majesty to one or more bonds in penalty of double the amount of duties upon the tobacco so entered, within 18 months to commence at the expiration of 20 days after the report of the master or to commence from the entry of tobacco by them; (16) all tobacco so imported into Great-Britain shall, having been weighed, be forthwith deposited or lodged in, and secured at such particular warehouse or warehouses as shall be fixed upon, and from time to time appointed for that purpose, at the said several ports herein before enumerated within Great-Britain; (17) the customs commissioners (4 or more in England, and 3 or more in Scotland) are authorized out of any subsidies, customs, duties, or imposts paid by virtue or in pursuance of any act or acts of Parliament now in force, upon the importation of tobacco into Great-Britain, to provide as they deem requisite for the public service and for service of revenue, a warehouse or warehouses at each enumerated port, in which warehouse and no other all tobacco shall be deposited, lodged or secured; (18) the landing waiters appointed shall apply to the customs officers at such port of entry made of a ship with tobacco on board, or warrants of entry, ascertaining the duties to have been paid and for the manifest or contents accompanying the tobacco (who is hereby required and directed to deliver the same to such landing waiters), and such landing waiters are directed not to suffer any part of the tobacco on board such ship agreeably to the manifest, entered into their respective books (given to them by direction of his Majesty's customs officers) recording respective marks, numbers, weights, tares, and contents, of the several hogsheads, casks, chests and cases as described in the manifest, under penalty of forfeiture of fifty pounds; landing waiters directed to give to officers stationed on board ship, permitting them to make repairs on board in the presence of the officers, open the main and other hatchways leading to the hold, and bring upon deck the several hogsheads or other packages of tobacco particularly mentioned and described in orders so delivered by landing waiters, and affix to every such hogshead, cask, chest, or case of tobacco such mark or impression as the customs commissioners for the time being shall direct for that purpose, with the progressive number to each and every such hogshead, etc. so marked, the same required to be unshipped into proper craft and sent up under proper guards [Continued on Page 2].

Page 2. *(continued)* landing waiters required upon bringing containers to warehouses, and at or near the same, to cause the landing marks or other marks to be fixed and set upon every container; landing waiters required to enter marks in their respective books so given by the customs commissioners, with weights to be minutely and correctly taken as possible, giving the turn of the scale in favor of the Crown; (19) after containers are weighed, the several importers, proprietors or consignees shall be permitted in the presence of landing waiters, to draw or take for sample out of each container as much tobacco as they require not exceeding four pounds weight; (20) if it is necessary for merchants to take a second sample, permitted provided at the time of taking the first be returned to the respective hogshead, cask, chest or case, and provided such second sample is taken in the presence of the customs officer, not to exceed four pounds in weight; sample to be returned in order to be weighed [*To be continued*]. ■ **LONDON, Sept. 24.** It is well known that the family of Montague trace their descent from the remotest era of British history; but a circumstance, established by authentic records, still subsisting in the Duke of Manchester's line, worth remarking, is, that a female ancestor of the Duke's was mother to St. Patrick, who first preached Christianity to the natives of Ireland, and was claimed by them as the patron Saint; from hence, perhaps, might arise the attention which this respectable Peer has always shewn to the interests of the sister kingdom, and which he has endeavoured to unite with the mutual prosperity of both countries.

OLD BAILEY, Sept. 24. This day the court being again assembled, and much crouded, the capital convicts, twenty-five in number, were brought to the bar, and silence being proclaimed, Mr. Recorder addressed them in the following awful and pathetic speech:

Unhappy men! You have been convicted by the verdicts of most conscientious, merciful and attentive juries, of crimes which the laws of your country have wisely thought necessary to punish with death; you have broken the public peace; you have violated the laws of God and your country, disturbed the good order, tranquility and safety of that society, of which you all might once become useful and reputable members; had you walked in the fear of God and the paths of virtue, had you paid obedience to the laws of your country, the lowest among you might have maintained yourselves with honest industry, might have had the happiness of living respected and esteemed by your neighbours and friends, and of seeing families grow up around you in prosperity and peace; wretched as you are, you have suffered these opportunities to pass away, never more to return; you have finished your career of guilt, and have, for the crimes which you have committed, drawn down (as is most just) the deepest ruin and destruction on yourselves. The effects of your guilt have been such as ought to aggravate the horrors of your situation in no small degree, for most of you have involved the innocent with the guilty; you have drawn your innocent connexions and friends into a share of the consequence of your crimes. Some of you have afflicted parents and friends; others disconsolate wives and helpless children, whom you have reduced from a state of happiness and credit, to misery and disgrace. I fear, too, that many of you have the accumulated guilt of having contributed, by your evil counsel, in precipitating others into the same abyss of guilt and misery, into which you have fallen: In such a situation, all that can remain for you is, that the little time the law will allow you to live should be employed in reflecting on the crimes you have committed; for the deepest remorse and sorrow is necessary to atone for such crimes; in the hope, therefore, and earnest prayer, that God will grant you that repentance which alone can redeem you from the dreadful consequences of your guilt, it remains only for me to discharge the last and most painful part of m duty, in pronouncing upon you the dreadful sentence of the law, which is,

That you, and each of you, be taken to the place of execution, there to be hanged by the necks until you are dead, and the Lord have mercy upon your sinful souls.

■ **CHARLESTON, Dec. 20.** A number of uniform companies are now forming in this city, with great spirit and alacrity, and will soon, it is to be hoped make a very handsome appearance. This is a pleasing proof of that harmony and public spirit which gained us our freedom and independence, and we trust, will now guard and support them, together with our happiness ... Yesterday evening arrived here the sloop *Rising Sun*, Capt. Fellows, in 32 days from Connecticut.--The 28th ult., lat. 32, and long. 74, 28, was struck by lightning, which dismasted her, tore up her decks, cut away her rigging, and destroyed the compasses, quadrants, &c. on board. By the violence of the shock a leak was spring, but fortunately spoke a vessel the next morning, from which she received such friendly assistance as enabled her to gain this port. ■ **BOSTON, Dec. 28.** The spirit for perfection in the military art, with which the honor and respectability, the happiness and security of a State are essentially connected, we are happy in informing, shines with peculiar lustre and is making rapid improvement in our sister State of New Hampshire. Every exertion of the experienced and worthy Commander in Chief of that State is put in practice to make it as respectable and well disciplined as any troops in the world. The following are the uniforms of the several brigades of the militia of the State of New Hampshire:

	Colour	Facing
Gen. Bellows	white	deep crimson
Gen. Cilley	do.	deep blue
Gen. Moulton	do.	bright scarlet
Gen. Reed	do.	green
Gen. Dowe	do.	sky blue
Brigade, late Hale's	do.	b[illegible]
The Light-horse	green	scarlet
Artillery	blue	d[illegible]

A considerable shock of an earthquake was felt in several parts of the State of Connecticut a few days since ... While we boast a **WASHINGTON**, as the great Master of the Art of War--a **FRANKLIN**, the Chief of Philosophers--an **ADAMS**, and an infinitude of others, as statesmen and politicians, whose abilities have been acknowledged throughout the civilized world, America may pride herself in giving birth to the most celebrated artists of the present age. As an evidence of the abilities of the last mentioned, we insert the following extract from a late London print, which we are certain will be agreeable to our readers.

EXHIBITION *of the* **ROYAL ACADEMY**

"The President has called forth in his celebrated Venue, the magic powers of his pencil, and has added all the glow and brilliancy of colour, to the enchanting sweetness of the Cytherean character and expression; the Prince may be ranked as the finest portrait in the room. Loutherbourg has produced several wonderful landscapes. Copley has painted a capital group of the three youngest princesses--we could wish that the background had been more fully ordinate, and that his eye had been attentive to the greatness of distribution, which alone constitutes fine art. West has brought forward another of his suits of Windsor pictures. Indeed we must confess the exhibition much obliged, not only to those gentlemen, but to two other ingenious American artists, Stewart and Brown, who have this year distinguished themselves, and given great proofs of their promising abilities; Stewart sends three, amongst which the Naval Officer holds a conspicuous rank.--Brown exhibits six, some of which are the most pleasing female portraits in the room.

"Portraits of Sir William Pepperell's children, by Brown. A Charming composition, by an American artist; the trees seem unfinished and hard, but the figures are happily disposed, the characters beautiful, and the whole coloured true to nature.

"A lady, by Brown. The *Chief d'Oeuvre* of this young artist, the taste of disposition exquisite, and a charming imitation of a beautiful woman.

"A strong likeness of Sir William Pepperell, by Mr. Brown. The colour of the drapery is ill-chosen, but the picture has merit." ■ **NEW LONDON, Nov. 18.** We hear from East Hampton on Long Island, that on Wednesday the 9th inst. was married there, by the Rev. Mr. Williams of South Hampton, the Rev. Mr. Buell, to Miss Miller,--an amiable young lady of about 19, with superior accomplishments.

Let mortals subject to the waste of time,
Who part reluctant from their days of prime,
Be wise and good;
On scenes of future bliss regale the mind,
And, like the soaring eagle they shall find
Their youth renewed.

Mr. Buell was inducted into the pastoral care of the church of East Hampton, in 1746, at the age of 30.--since which time he has never been confined one day from the duties of his office, nor had an hour's sickness.--At the present he seldom preaches less than seven times a week; but often more. ■ **NEW YORK, Dec. 28.** The Anniversary of **ST. JOHN** the **EVANGELIST** was yesterday celebrated with the most respectful deference and splendor, by the brethren of every lodge of the Ancient and truly Honorable Society of the Free and Accepted Masons in this city, and by great numbers of very respectable gentlemen from the several European nations. A numerous and well conducted procession moved at about 12 o'clock, through the principal streets with the insignia of their several ranks, and a band of music, to St. George's Chapel in the following:

ORDER of PROCESSION

Tyler — Tyler

KNIGHTS TEMPLARS

Royal Arch Independent Lodge

Steward — Steward

Brethren out of Office

Treasurer — Secretary

Junior Warden — Senior Warden

J.D. — Past Master. — Master — S.D.

Lodge No. 2

Union Lodge

Lodge No. 5

Lodge No. 4

MUSIC

Lodge No. 210

Lodge No. 212

Lodge No. 169

Page 3. [St. John's Day Ceremonies by New York City Free Masonry (*continued*)]:

GRAND LODGE

Pursuivant

Grand Steward — Grand Steward

CHAPLAIN

Brethren invited by the Grand Lodge

Grand Treasurer — Grand Secretary

Grand Jun. Warden — Grand Sen. Warden

Deputy Grand Master — Past Grand Master

GRAND MASTER

Grand Steward Grand Steward

KNIGHTS TEMPLARS

Where the Reverend Mr. Beach preached an excellent sermon, adapted to the solemn occasion; after which the charity children performed a hymn with great influence on the passions of the audience. A very large collection succeeded; after which the brethren retired to their several lodges, dined, and passed the evening with that benevolence and affection which ever mark the **BRIGHT FREE** and **ACCEPTED MASONS.** ... **Jan. 3:** The late calamities of Jamaica might be made an affecting theme for the power of poetry.---This charming island, robbed of its beauty by the rude whirlwinds blast---chearful spring suddenly change to tempest and horror---verdure to devastation---paradise to chaos---would be an ample scope for imagination painting with lively imagery the variegated scenes of distress. This most valuable, but unfortunate island, contains upwards of 4,000,000 acres, and is divided by a ridge of hills running nearly from east to west, from sea to sea. The greatest part of the island is covered with woods which never lose their verdure. The trees in *gay confusion* adorn the hills; and the citron, and others, spread their beautiful leaves in the valleys.--In short, here would be *eternal spring*, were it not for the hurricanes!

Among the phenomena of the age, says a correspondent, the American revolution may justly be ranked, and the surrounding nations have viewed it with astonishment. They have been spectators of the first scene, have beheld us on the theatre, acting nobly the first part, fighting, bleeding, and conquering; establishing our independence, and taking rank among them; but the justice and rectitude of our laws, and policy of our measures, must finish our characters, and how the listening nations will suspend their opinions how far we deserve applause, until we act this second part, which is in good train, if the late requisitions of Congress are complied with: It will raise the expectations of the people, and even languid credit will begin to discover animation. Public creditors will wait with patience, when they see rulers and people pursuing just and equitable measures for paying their debts. Such conduct would tend to establish our nation, and render us respectable at home and abroad; while those who are sporting with public credit, and preying on the necessities of the unfortunate, would be driven to seek different employment.

Though poverty is viewed with such odium and contempt in these modern times, yet the wise republic of Rome, in their days of prosperity, when success attended all their enterprises, considered it as a virtue, the surest guardian of liberty; and it made it honorable, that it might be a barrier against luxury and ambition: But as soon as they swerved from these regulations, their decline was as rapid as their progress. What must have been the sensations of one of those primitive sages, had he beheld our modern ladies, in all the variegated and costly attire that art can invent or money procure, when the ladies of Rome were forbid, by an edict of the state, from wearing habits of several colours, or their ornaments exceed the value of half an ounce of gold? Surely if it was thought wise to banish luxury from among private families (in the infancy of that republic) which they viewed as inimical to the strength and safety of the commonwealth, it behooves us to improve the hint, and avoid the quicksands on which they foundered.--We set out upon the same economical plan that Rome did;--we have been as successful;--we have made equal progress in science;--and that we are verging on the same hapless precipice needs little sagacity to be convinced of. These are no chimeras, but melancholy facts, pregnant with horrors to this republic. We have plunged into luxury;--pleasure has succeeded temperance;--economy become obsolete;--dissipation the ton;--and excessive usury disgracing the government.--All omens of excessive slavery, and the annihilation of that fabric--which, with prudence, might rival the world.

On Wednesday the 28th ult. Congress resolved, "That the board of treasury be, and are declared to be vested with full authority to superintend and examine the conduct of all officers employed in the department of the treasury, and of the several commissioners appointed, or that hereafter may be appointed for the settlement of public accounts, as well those of the five great departments, as those authorized to adjust the accounts between the United States and the individual States. And in case any of the said officers, or commissioners, shall unnecessarily absent themselves from their respective offices, or shall engage in any business inconsistent with, or that may hinder a constant discharge of the duties of their several appointments, it shall be the duty of the board of treasury to make immediate report thereof to the Congress, that such measures be adopted thereon, as justice and public interest may require ... A gentleman of Westmeath, near Mullingar, in Ireland, made a rash promise when in liquor, of killing the first person he would meet, and unfortunately met a man of the name of Gallagher, in his hall, who was employed in the station of a horse rider, and shot him dead on the spot. The cook, who had seen the transaction, has lodged examinations against her master. This is one of those horrid consequences which proceed from such criminal excess ... Extract of a letter from **Seneca, Nov. 1785:** According to promise I write you the first opportunity after my return to Seneca. I saw the Cherokee Indians that had arrived when I left the place. My business would not permit me to tarry but two days, during which I had the time to hear the head warrior speak. He told the commissioners, that God made the red people of this earth, and placed them on the same to live, and we must know they were the first on this ground. They were the natives, who in former times could range about the country without restraint--it was not so now; but, however, he wished that those who now possessed what once was theirs would be united in friendship. He said the white people loved large corn fields, and they had been induced to give up much land; but that was not all, what was still their own was settled against their consent; but still they wished for peace. ■ **PHILADELPHIA, Jan. 10.** On Saturday morning last, departed this Life, aged 70 years, after a short but severe illness, which she sustained with true resignation, Mrs. **RUTH POTTS**, relict of JOHN POTTS, Esquire, of Potts Grove. If the tenderest performance of maternal duties, the most generous exercise of benevolence and charity to her fellow creatures, and the purest piety to her God, deserve to be lamented, then is the circle of her mourners numerous indeed. ■ **ALX, Jan. 19**. At a Meeting of the Directors of the Bank of North-America, held the 2d Instant at Philadelphia, a dividend of Three per Cent. was declared on the capital Stock, for the last Six Months. Extract of a late Letter from a Merchant at **Barbadoes** to a Gentleman in this Town. "We are much pleased with the Flour you last sent us, which was little inferior to the Philadelphia Superfine.--It was branded BEASON.--Whenever you ship more for this Island pray let it be of the same Kind, as it has so good a Character as to meet with a quick Market and great Price." ■ A few Days since was apprehended and committed to Gaol in this Town, Thomas Johnston, for Horse-Stealing.--Also, for Burglary, one William May, who has since his Commitment acknowledged himself to be the identical Person, lately under Sentence of Death in the State of Delaware, from whence he made his Escape by breaking Gaol, and for the apprehending of whom a Reward of One Hundred Pounds has been offered in the Philadelphia Papers. ■ MARRIED.] Mr. ROBERT SIM, to Miss ELIZABETH KING of Upper Marlborough. ■ INSURANCE *from* LONDON. To Jamaica, £.2 10s. per Cent.--To Quebec and Montreal--to Halifax or New-York, 2½ Guineas, warranted British Ships--To Charleston, James-River, and Annapolis, 2 Guineas, warranted British Ships--To Philadelphia, 2 Guineas, warranted British Ships. INSURANCE *from* DUBLIN. To Philadelphia, Boston, New-York, &c. 2½ Guineas. INSURANCE *from* LIVERPOOL, BRISTOL, GLASGOW, &c. To New-York, 2 to 2½ Guineas--To Quebec--To the West-Indies, 2 Guineas--To Jamaica, 2½ Guineas--To Boston, 2 to 2½ Guineas. ☞ American Ships pay from 5 to 7 Guineas per Cent. ■ NAVAL-OFFICE, ALX. *Inward Entries*. None. *Cleared Outwards*. Schooner *Industry*, J. Foster, for Beverly.

PRICES CURRENT, ALX. / Tobacco, 21s. per Ct. / Fine Flour, 28s. per Barrel. / Wheat, 5/6s. per Bushel. / Jamaica Spirits, 4/6 per Gallon. / Windward Rum, 3s. per Ditto. / Continental Rum, 2s. per Ditto. / Molasses, 1/6 per Ditto. / Muscovado Sugar, 45s. to 50s. per Ct. / Salt, 3s. per Bushel, by Retail. / Corn, 4s. per Bushel. / Exchange, 40.

Public Vendue to be held on Saturday the 21st ult. [see like ad Vol. II No. 102] ■ The Subscribers would sell upon the most reasonable Terms, **All their Stock of GOODS now on Hand**, Among which is a large Proportion of such as are suitable to the present Season. Six Months Credit will be given on Bond, with approved Security, if required. S. and T. HANSON. ALX, Jan. 14, 1786. ☞ Several Negroes to be hired either by the Month or Year. ■ Hooe and Harrison has lots to be let on ground-rent [see like ad Vol. II No. 101] ■ **Wanted**, By the Subscriber, a Quantity of good **HEMP**, For which the highest Price in CASH will be given. JAMES IRVINE, Ropewalk, ALX, Jan. 18, 1786. ■ ELISHA WILLIAMS offers for sale a valuable tract in Frederick Co., Va. [see like ad Vol. II No. 102] ■ **Twenty Dollars Reward. RAN** away from the Subscriber in June last, a very likely small Negro WOMAN, named SARAH, about 17 years old; she is blacker than common, has a very smooth skin, and had on when she went away coarse clothes, such as Negroes generally wear.--Whoever takes up the said Negro Woman and brings her home, shall receive Ten Dollars; and as I am apprehensive she is concealed by some ill-disposed free person, I will give Ten Dollars Reward to any person who will give just information of the same, so that the offender may be prosecuted. THOMAS NOBLE, Frederick County, Virginia, Jan. 9, 1786. ■ JOHN WATERS, Gaoler, Frederick Co., Va., seeks owner of Irishman Lawrence Caskin [see like ad Vol. II No. 101] ■ JOSEPH GARDINER warns others from taking bonds he gave to Alexander Smith [see like ad Vol. II No. 102].

Page 4. Poetry. From the *WEEKLY MISCELLANY*, "Verses addressed to a Gentleman, expressing some Fears of Death." ■ AARON HEWES has for sale a small quantity of Jamaica rum, etc. [see like ad Vol. II No. 101] ■ WILLIAM HUNTER, jun. seeks tobacco onboard the ship *Friends*, John Muir, Master, to sail in February for London [see like ad Vol. II No. 101] ■ Printed Sermons to be sold at the Printing-Office [see description Vol. II No. 99] ■ BALDWIN DADE has for rent on ground-rent forever 100 lots situated on Queen, Princess and Oronoko streets adjoining the property rented to Rev. Dr. Griffith [see like ad Vol. II No. 101] ■ SAMUEL ARELL, Secretary, Brethren Lodge No. 39, announces meeting [see like ad Vol. II No. 101] ■ WILLIAM HARTSHORNE offers for sale sundry lots and houses to rent in ALX [see like ad with details Vol. II No. 98] ■ W. BIRD, Woodville, has for sale 275 acres within 4 miles of ALX [see like ad Vol. II No. 101] ■ **Philip Dalby** has for sale at his store on the corner of Royal and Cameron streets, an assortment of low priced coatings [see like ad Vol. II No. 102] ■ Apply to JOHN FALLS and CO. or RICHARD CATON and CO. to purchase a stock of a well assorted store in George-Town [see like ad Vol. II No. 102] ■ ALEXANDER DOYLE certifies that Henry Yost has satisfied his former obligations [see like ad Vol. II No. 102] ■ SAMUEL HARDISTY, Montgomery Co., Md., warns others from taking bonds or assignments of him to George Hagely of Berkeley Co., Va. [see like ad Vol. II No. 102] ■ The Philadelphia Directory, by Francis White, for sale [see like ad Vol. II No. 102] ■ To be sold, at the Printing-Office, **A Variety of Blank Books,** consisting of Ledgers, Journals, Cash-Books, Letter-Books, &c.&c. Also, Stoughton's Bitters, Anderson's Pills, Daffy's Elixir, Balsam of Honey, Squire's Elixir, Bateman's Drops, Godfrey's Cordial, &c.&c.&c. ■ Employment offered for a journeyman printer [see like ad Vol. II No. 102] ■ **William Buddicom**, has for sale at Mr. Andrew Wales's, near Captain Harper's Wharf, goods just imported from Liverpool in the brig *Alexandria* [see like ad Vol. II No. 101] ■ EDWARD BLACKBURN and SARAH MONROE, Fairfax Co., have for sale Negroes and items from the estate of John Monroe, deceased [see like ad Vol. II No. 102] ■ ALX: Printed by GEORGE RICHARDS, and COMPANY, at their Printing-Office on Fairfax-street--by whom Advertisements, &c. are thankfully received for this Paper,--and where Printing is performed with Care and Expedition.

1786/01/26, Vol. II No. 104

Page 1. (*Continuation of the* TOBACCO ACT). (21) before weighing tobacco, landing waiters shall furnish the customs officer with a copy of the respective entries or warrants for the tobacco, and daily after they have weighed the same tobacco, to furnish such officers with landing numbers and weights of each hogshead, cask, chest or case so weighed on that day, which said warehouse officer are hereby directed to enter in proper books to be kept for that purpose; as soon as whole cargo of tobacco of one ship has been weighed and deposited in such warehouse, landing waiters to furnish warehouse officers with one of their books so kept, and after comparing the same with the accounts kept by them from the materials kept daily, sign the same book so left; if accounts correspond, return the same to landing waiter; (22) landing waiters shall, after weighing and depositing tobacco, deliver without fee or reward to each merchant having tobacco on board, an account from their books of the particular marks and number upon the hogsheads, casks, chests or cases, with weights, etc., and particulars of any damage cut off and separated from the tobacco; (23) no allowance at the scale or otherwise shall be made to the importers, proprietors or consignees for or in consideration for any imported tobacco that is damaged; merchant may refuse or separate out damaged tobacco; customs officers shall burn such tobacco without making any allowance to the importer, proprietor, or consignee for freight or other charges; (24) it shall not be lawful for any merchant or other person, nor shall they have liberty, to separate the stalk from the leaf, on pretence that the same is damaged or mean tobacco; (25) if any imported tobacco is damaged on board by stress of weather at sea or by such ship being forced on shore in any part of Great-Britain, or any unforseen accident, or by ship's bulging on an anchor or by the lighter in which the tobacco is put in order to be laid on land, or any such accident, customs officers may allow pay to the importer, proprietor or consignee at the rate of one halfpenny for each pound of such tobacco, not to exceed thirty shillings for all tobacco damaged; (26) upon examination of any unmanufactured tobacco imported into Great-Britain, that it is so much damaged is under the weight of 450 pounds, the importers, proprietors or consignees in presence of the landing waiter may deliver the same together in one hogshead, cask, chest or case and the landing waiters are directed to enter into their books the true and exact weight of all such found tobacco put into such containers; may be exported from the warehouse provided container amounts to 425 pounds weight or more; (27) persons entering tobacco into ports in Great-Britain shall finally discharged tobacco into the custody of the officers of the respective warehouses in order to be laden on board; indorse upon the ticket and bill to be delivered to searchers belonging to the customs, and appointed to examine the tobacco shipped for exportation, in a fair, distinct, and legible manner, the plantation or manifest mark and number which was upon each hogshead, cask, chest or case of tobacco at the time with is was first imported into Great-Britain, and also landing marks and numbers since placed, together with exact weight of tobacco contained; likewise endorse upon the same docket and bill, after weighing, in the presence of a customs officer, the tobacco so entered for exportation, the then weight, and the searchers shall not admit any docket unless marked as aforesaid; every exporter shall also write off the weight of each hogshead, cask, chest or case of unmanufactured tobacco; shall neglect or refuse to indorse upon the docket and bill shall forfeit and lose the sum of five pounds for every hogshead, cask, chest or case of such unmanufactured tobacco not indorsed upon the said docket and bill; (28) any importer or proprietor of tobacco that has given security for payment of duties in 18 months shall be desirous to discharge his bonds in ready-money sooner than the expiration date of 18 months, shall be abated upon such bonds so much as the discount at the rate of seven pounds per centum per annum, shall amount to in proportion to the time unexpired; (29) no debenture shall be made forth for any tobacco so imported into Great-Britain, or any drawback be paid or allowed for the same, when exported, or entered outwards for exportation, to any part or parts beyond the seas, unless the same be shipped and exported from the very same port or place at which such identical tobacco was originally imported into Great-Britain; [Page 2] any person causing such to be entered to forfeit and lose the sum of twenty pounds for every such hogshead, or other package of tobacco so exported; (30) any such tobacco warehoused as aforesaid shall be intended to be taken out of such warehouse for home trade, shall pay down in ready-money to the customs collector at the respective report where the tobacco is warehoused, the duties secured by bond and shall produce to and leave and deposit with the customs officer a clear, distinct, and proper voucher from the customs collector directed to such officer in whose custody such tobacco shall then be; customs collector is required without fee or reward to grant persons who have so paid duties a certificate that the duties have been so paid, describing therein by whom such duties were paid, when, and what ship or vessel on which imported, and also the marks and numbers of identical hogsheads, etc. in which tobacco shall be contained; (31) no unmanufactured tobacco shall be removed, carried or conveyed by land or by water within Great-Britain or shall be removed from any one place to another without a certificate from the customs officer; under penalty of the forfeiture of all such tobacco, the packages containing the same, and also the horses, cattle, carts, waggons and other carriages whatsoever employed or made use of in the removal; (32) before any unmanufactured tobacco shall be removed, the proprietor, factor or agent thereof shall describe and insert on the back of the certificate in a fair and legible manner the names of each particular package in which such tobacco is contained, with marks and numbers of each, exact weight, subscribe his name (*To be continued*). ■ **LONDON, Sept. 24. THURSDAY** morning Lord George Gordon waited upon Mr. Fraser, the under Secretary of State, at St. James's, and requested Mr. Fraser to acquaint him with what had been done with the letter on Irish affairs, including a note from Comte d'Adhemar, which he intrusted to his care to be delivered to the King on the 27th of August last, at night.--Mr. Fraser, with the greatest politeness, acquainted his Lordship that the letter had been immediately forwarded to Lord Sydney; but whether Lord Sydney had delivered it to the King or not, he could not inform his Lordship. The following is a copy of that letter.

To the **KING.**

SIR, The French Ambassador communicated something to me (in pursuance of the enclosed appointment*) that is of the greatest consequence to your Majesty to be informed of. It respects Ireland; and if your Majesty will condescend to direct me where you would be pleased to receive the information, I shall think it my duty to attend your Sovereign pleasure.

I am, Sir, with all due submission, may it please your Majesty, your unimpeachable humble servant,

G. GORDON

Welbeck Street, Saturday night

Aug. 26, 1785

*A note from the French Ambassador to Lord George Gordon:

Not thinking from what fell with Mr. Fraser, that Lord Sydney had delivered the letter to the King, Lord George Gordon went immediately to Buckingham House to intimate to their Majesties, that he intended to have the honour to come to the drawing room (Thursday) if it was agreeable to their Majesties. His Lordship was immediately conducted across the house to a room in the King's apartments, where one of the King's pages took his Lordship's message, and said he would carry it to the King. After sitting there about twenty minutes, the page came to his Lordship, and acquainted him that he was told to say, *'The name of Lord George Gordon was forbid to be mentioned at Buckingham House.'* Lord George asked the page if the King had returned him that answer?--The page said he had not seen the King.

Lord George Gordon then went home and dressed himself for the drawing room, and went down to the court at St. James's, and stood the whole time by Mr. Pitt, Lord Cambden, Lord Caermarthen, and Lord Sydney; but the King and Queen, and the Prince of Wales, all passed by without speaking to his Lordship. ■ **BOSTON, December 22.** Extract of a letter from **Bedford**,(in this Commonwealth) **Nov. 4**: This idle hour I will employ in giving you some account of a great discovery lately made in hydrostatics, by a Mr. Allen, from Martha's Vineyard--a man of good natural abilities, but who never had any advantage of philosophical studies, or other than common education. By accident he was led to attempt the trial of separating fresh from salt water, and has succeeded in a wonderful manner: He informs me that with his present machine he can separate 128 gallons in 24 hours: And that he is now constructing one on the same principle, capable of 700-800 gallons in that time.

How inconceivable its utility to mankind! Ships may be furnish with daily supplies of fresh water at a very small expence and trouble, and the freight of water in navigation, in the present mode, is enormous, particularly on long voyages, and in transporting live stock; ships to India are one third loaded with water. Destitute islands may be supplied by this method. And equal to either is the manufacture of salt, whereby we may supply ourselves without importing; as by this quick and easy process, the fresh water may be separated so effectually, that the remainder will cristalize almost immediately--and I dare prognosticate, that many other advantages will be derived from this and succeeding generations from this discovery.

He has communicated as much of the secret (reserving intricacies) as has convinced a learned Doctor West, of this parish, of its feasibility: He is to undertake for Mr. Allen, to lay it before the American Academy of Arts and Sciences at their next meeting: If they will secure him a premium, which he may think adequate to its importance, and his merits, he will divulge it to them; otherwise he purposes for Europe.

I am informed that Mr. Allen, when a boy, on a whaling voyage, approaching very near to a water spout, observed the circumfluous water to have the exact colour of fresh water, down to the very surface of the sea; and as the rain which poured down from the cloud was fresh, he had no doubt but that the separation took place at the surface before being drawn up: This first gave him the idea of his noble project, without having even one principle of the hydrostatic laws. The hypothesis, that salt water is drawn up the clouds in water spouts, and thereby a certain operation of air, while it is expanding and dispersing in the clouds, is separated from the saline particles, must be exploded, by this and several other new theories. From what I can gather, by he character and conversation of Mr. Allen, both his theory and machinery must be very simple.

I should conjecture, by some peculiar temperature, and the action of the air on the surface, he produces the effect to sink the grosser particles, while the pure and subtile float on top, to be received free from salt--Whatever may be the method, I am sure it must be simple, and therefor it will be much more useful to mankind--he assured me the apparatus may be made for a trifle, will wear (as his phrase is) "as long as stem, keel, and stern post of a ship," and be very little liable to derangement.

You have lately heard the lectures of the celebrated Dr. Moyes, on water spouts. I believe you will never be able to reconcile his darling theory to this discovery; although as yet we can only conjecture; but I dare say, Mr. Allen has as little knowledge of the laws of the electrical fluid, as of the doctrines of Confucious or Zoroaster. I hope the learned president of the Academy of Arts and Sciences will open a correspondence with Mr. Allen, and by some promises of reward to his heirs, induce him to commit the whole to writing, that in case he should die before the negociation is finished for the purchase of the secret, mankind may not even run the hazard of losing so valuable a discovery. ■ **PHILADELPHIA, Jan. 13.** Last week a poor woman having imprudently left her child, a boy of about three years old, alone in her room, in Fifth near Arch street, on her return found that he had miserably perished by his clothes catching fire, which, it is supposed, the child had been playing with. ■ **ALX, Jan. 26.** We hear that several Servants who had been purchased to work on the Potomack Navigation, lately ran away, but being soon after apprehended were sentenced to have their Heads and Eyebrows shaved, which Operation was immediately executed, and is to be continued every Week, during the Time of their Servitude, or until their Behaviour evinces that they are brought to a Sense of their Duty. This Notice, it is expected, will sufficiently apprize the Country should they again make a similar Attempt. ■ The

General Assembly of this Commonwealth adjourned on Saturday last to the last Day of March next. ■ DIED.] Mrs. ELIZABETH WILKINSON, aged 72 Years, late of Philadelphia, Relict of Mr. JOHN WILKINSON, formerly of that Place.

Page 3. ☞ The List of Acts passed at the late Sessions of the General Assembly were received too late for this Day's Publication, but will be inserted in our next. ■ *An ACT to provide for the POOR of the several Counties within this Commonwealth.* B*E it enacted by the General Assembly*, That the Court of every County within this Commonwealth, at their session to be held in the month of March next after the passing of this Act, shall cause their said County to be laid off into convenient districts, and shall direct the Sheriff of their County to cause publication to be made, that on some convenient day to be appointed by the said Court, an election will be held within each district, to consist of freeholders and house-keepers only, for the purpose of choosing three discreet, fit, and proper persons, being freeholders of and resident within the same, who shall be called and denominated Overseers of the Poor, and shall continue and be in office for and during the term of three years; at the expiration whereof other triennial elections shall be made in manner herein before directed; and the said Court shall, at the same time, appoint some person in each district, to superintend the election. And the said Overseers, upon notice to them respectively being given by the person appointed in their district to superintend the election of their being duly elected, they, or a majority of them shall meet together at some convenient place within their respective districts, between the first day of April, and the first day of August, in every year, and shall levy and assess upon the tithables within their said County (a copy of the list of which shall be furnished them by the Clerk of the County) competent sums of money, or tobacco in lieu thereof at a stated price, to be paid at the option of the party chargeable therewith, for the necessary relief and support of all such poor, lame, impotent, blind, and other inhabitants of their said County as are not able to maintain themselves. *And be it enacted*, That the Overseers of the poor in each district, shall monthly make returns to the Court of their County of the poor orphans in their district, and the said Court is hereby authorized to direct the said Overseers, or either of them, to bind out such poor orphans, apprentices to such person or persons as the Court on due inquiry shall approve of, and the indentures of such apprentices shall be filed in the office of the Clerk of the County, and not transferable to any person whatsoever, without the approbation of the Court. The said Overseers shall, on or before the tenth day of August annually, make up in a book to be kept for that purpose, an exact account of the persons to and for whom such monies are to be paid, the purpose for which, and the particular sums, a transcript of which, they shall once in every year return to the Court, to be there entered of record; a copy of which they shall also, on or before the same day, deliver to the Collector of the public taxes, who is hereby authorized and required to collect the same, together with the list of persons chargeable with the poor rates, and of the sum each person is liable to pay; which Collector shall give bond with good security to the Court for the faithful discharge of his duty herein, and shall have the same powers to collect the said poor rates, and have the same commission, and be subject to the same fines, forfeitures and prosecutions, as in the case of County levies. The said Collector shall pay the money or tobacco, as the case may be, to the several persons, or to their order, for whom it was levied, on or before the first day of October in every year; and in default thereof, it shall be lawful for the Court of the County to render judgment for the same with costs, on complaint of the party, or on motion by the Overseers; provided that the Collector has ten days previous notice of such motion. *And be it further enacted*, That the same power and authority given to, and vested in a Churchwarden, by an act entitled "An Act for the relief of Parishes from such charges as arise from bastard children born within the same," passed in the year of our Lord one thousand seven hundred and sixty-nine, is hereby given to the several Overseers of the Poor respectively, who shall perform the same duties as by that Act are required to be performed by a Churchwarden. And the said Overseers of the Poor in each County shall have power and authority to call on the late Churchwardens in their Counties or Parishes, for a settlement of their parochial accounts, and shall receive any money in their hands belonging to the Parish, heretofore levied for the support of the poor, to be applied to the debts contracted in support of the Parish poor. And in case any Churchwardens shall refuse to pay to the Overseers of the Poor in the County in which such Churchwardens acted, the balance which shall appear to be in their hands on settlement being made, as aforesaid, it shall be lawful for the County Court to render judgment for the same, with costs, on complaint of the said Overseers of the Poor, or their Attorney; provided such Churchwarden shall have ten days previous notice of such notion. And the court of every County within this Commonwealth shall be, and they are hereby authorized and required, whereof public notice shall be previously given by the Sheriff, to levy and assess upon the tithable persons in their respective Counties, all Parish charges which shall have accrued since the last laying of the levy of the Parishes within their respective Counties, and before the first of April next; and the Collector of the public taxes, shall collect and receive such levy, and pay the same to the person entitled thereto, shall have the same commission, and on refusal to pay, be liable to the same penalty and judgments as the Collector of the Poor Rates is entitled and made liable to. And to prevent vagrants and others, not betaking themselves to honest occupations, becoming burthensome to the industrious and useful part of the community, it is necessary that the Overseers in each district should be, and they are hereby empowered to compel and put all such to work, so long as such person or persons shall continue within their district and likely to become chargeable to the County. AND WHEREAS, by the dissolution of the Vestries, and abridging their future powers, no posssessioners of land can legally be appointed; *Be it enacted*, That the Overseers of the Poor, appointed by this Act, shall have the same powers, and are required to preform the same duty which was formerly prescribed for the different Vestries under the direction of the different County Courts, who are hereby empowered and required to make the like orders, and observe the same rules, as is directed by the Act, entitled "An Act for settling the titles and bounds of lands, and for preventing unlawful hunting and ranging." Dec. 23, 1785, Passed the House of Delegates, JOHN BECKLEY, C.H.D., Dec. 29, 1785, Passed the Senate, H. BROOKE, C.S.

On Saturday the 29th inst. will be sold at the Vendue-Store,

A VARIETY of WET and DRY GOODS, as usual, amongst which are a few barrels of Jamaica spirits.

☞ For private sale, a likely Negro Fellow, Woman and Child, a Dray and two good Horses, a valuable Lot on Prince-street, agreeably and conveniently situated, subject to a moderate ground-rent; this Lot will be sold very low for cash.--About 400 acres of Land, within five or six miles of ALX, 80 or 100 acres of which may be made good meadow, with no considerable expence.--An undivided moiety of a Water-Lot, some Lots adjoining this town, and several within it.--A Tobacconist's Utensils, in good order.

S. ARELL, Vendue-Master.

ALX, Jan. 26, 1786.

AT **Andrew Wales's** BREWERY, in ALX, May be had, on the most reasonable Terms, Excellent **BEER**, Of different Qualities. The Inhabitants of this Town and its Vicinity, Masters of Vessels and others, may be supplied with any Quantity and Quality of Beer on the shortest Notice. ☞ Yeast and Grains may be had at said Brewery, where the highest Price for BARLEY and HOPS will be given, as usual. Jan. 26, 1786. ■ **William Buddicom**, has for sale at Mr. Andrew Wales's, near Captain Harper's Wharf, goods just imported from Liverpool in the brig *Alexandria* [see like ad Vol. II No. 101] ■ **William Hunter, jun.** Has for sale, for Cash or Country Produce, FAYAL wine in pipes, Teneriffe do in do, Port in hogsheads, Claret in boxes of three dozen each, Best Swedish bar-iron by the ton, A variety of best cordage, A few crates of queen's ware, A variety of DRY-GOODS, &c., ALX, Jan. 25, 1786. ■ ALL persons indebted to the Subscribers, for dealings at their store in this place, are again requested to make payment, on or before the first day of April, to JOHN ALLISON, who is empowered to settle the same, for after that time no indulgence can be given.--Those to whom they may owe, will please to call and receive payment.--And those indebted to their store at Boyd's-Hole, will please to settle with Mr. JOHN DALRYMPLE, who is empowered to give final discharges, also to pay what may be due by them there. HUNTER, ALLISON and CO. **This is not to be repeated after the time above mentioned. ALX, Jan. 26, 1786. ■ **The Subscriber has LOTS** in this town to let on ground-rent, on Water, Union and Wolf streets, and on a fourth street to which no name is affixed; and a few rooms to let in his Warehouse for wet or dry goods, now well fitted for these purposes.--He has for sale, on the most moderate terms, JAMAICA SPIRITS in hogsheads or smaller casks, of the best quality; BLOWN SALT; ALLSPICE, and a few IRON HOOPS.--Inquire at my dwelling. DANIEL ROBERDEAU. ALX, Jan. 24, 1785. ■ TO BE RENTED For one year, or LEASED for a term of years, **A large commodious three-**story brick HOUSE, conveniently situated in the city of Richmond, with the following apartments: A cellar, 27 by 36 feet; upon the first floor, two rooms 17 feet 10, by 12 feet 4; two rooms, 13 feet 4, by 9 feet 4; one room, 25 feet 8, by 17 feet 6; one room, 19 feet 2, by 17 feet 6; one room, 17 feet 6 by 11 feet 8; with the necessary passages, and four fireplaces. Upon the second floor, one room, 26 feet by 18; one room, 20 feet by 18; two rooms, 14 feet by 10; two rooms, 14 feet by 13; with a passage through the house one way, 36 feet by 12; and another way, the whole length of 60 feet by 4, and with six fireplaces. Upon the third floor, two rooms, 14 by 10; two rooms, 14 by 13; three rooms, 20 by 24, with necessary entries, and these last rooms are so constructed that they may occasionally be thrown into one large Assembly room, 60 feet by 24, with a fire place in each end; there are besides, four other fire places on this floor. There are seven convenient lodging rooms in the garret, unconnected with each other, two of which have fire places; and the whole apartments are so contrived as to be independent of each other.--The house is planned, and intended for a Tavern, and will have every necessary appendage thereto; among which will be a stable, with stalls for 35 horses, and a garden, consisting of better than half an acre.--Inquire of Dr. J. CURRIE, Richmond, January 4, 1786. ■ **All persons are forewarned** from taking an assignment upon a bond which I passed to PETER GLASSCOCK in December, 1784, for ONE HUNDRED POUNDS, as I do not mean to pay it unless compelled thereto by law, he having not complied with the conditions for which the said bond was given. CHICHESTER CURTIS, Loudon County, Jan. 18, 1786. ■ TO BE SOLD, In FEE-SIMPLE, **Several valuable LOTS of** GROUND, conveniently and advantageously situated for Business, and the terms of Payment made easy.--Inquire of ANDREW WALES, Jan. 25, 1786. ■ **Notice is hereby given, that** for certain reasons, I forewarn all persons from crediting my wife Nelly Nelson, on my account, as I am determined to pay no debts of her contracting from the date hereof.--I also forbid any person from harbouring her. JOHN NELSON, Prince-William County, Jan. 20, 1786.

Page 4. Poetry. "The FARMER and the ROBIN-RED-BREAST. A FABLE." ■ S. and T. HANSON have for sale all their stock of goods on hand [see like ad Vol. II No. 103] ■ JAMES IRVINE wishes to purchase a quantity of good HEMP [see like ad Vol. II No. 103] ■ ELISHA WILLIAMS offers for sale a valuable tract in Frederick Co., Va. [see like ad Vol. II No. 102] ■ THOMAS NOBLE, Frederick Co., Va., offers reward for return of runaway small Negro woman named SARAH [see like ad Vol. II No. 103] ■ JOSEPH GARDINER warns others from taking bonds he gave to Alexander Smith [see like ad Vol. II No. 102] ■ SAMUEL HARDISTY, Montgomery Co., Md., warns others from taking bonds or assignments of him to George Hagely of Berkeley Co., Va. [see like ad Vol. II No. 102] ■ ALEXANDER DOYLE certifies that Henry Yost has satisfied his former obligations [see like ad Vol. II No. 102]. ■ WILLIAM MURPHY announces the opening of a circulating library; gives subscription rates; has for sale stationary items [see like ads Vol. II No. 102] ■ Printed Sermons to be sold at the Printing-Office [see description Vol. II No. 99] ■ The Philadelphia Directory, by Francis White, for sale [see like ad Vol. II No. 102] ■ **Philip Dalby** has for sale at his store on the corner of Royal and Cameron streets, an assortment of low priced coatings [see like ad Vol. II No. 102] ■ Apply to JOHN FALLS and CO. or RICHARD CATON and CO. to purchase a stock of a well assorted store in George-Town [see like ad Vol. II No. 102] ■ WILLIAM HUNTER, jun. seeks tobacco onboard the ship *Friends*, John Muir, Master, to sail in February for London [see like ad Vol. II No. 101] ■ Employment offered for a journeyman printer [see like ad Vol. II No. 102] ■ ALX: Printed by GEORGE RICHARDS, and COMPANY, at their Printing-Office on Fairfax-street--by whom Advertisements, &c. are thankfully received for this Paper,--and where Printing is performed with Care and Expedition.

End of Volume II.

Index

A

Abaco, 205
abbess, 125
Abednego, 144
Abell
  Samuel, 161, 162, 172, 177, 178
Aberdeen, 117, 224, 225, 235, 240, 245, 251, 257
  acts of public outrage, 248
  Council Chamber damaged, 248
  Jacobins, republicans suspected, 248
  magistrates fled, 248
  military outnumbered, 248
  prisoners liberated by force, 248
aborigines, 153
Aboville
  Chevalier, 4
Academy of Sciences
  Paris, 159
Accomptants, 155
account books, 7
accounting
  by the vulgar, fable, 125
accounts, 6, 12, 13, 22, 23, 26, 30, 35, 38, 39, 41, 48-50, 54, 55, 57-60, 63-65, 69, 70, 73, 74, 85, 91, 95, 100, 104, 109, 110, 116, 118, 120, 121, 124, 127, 128, 133, 136, 138, 147, 152, 155, 157, 160, 161, 166, 167, 173, 183, 198, 210, 215, 234, 240, 251, 262, 265
Achencrue, Scotland, 14
Achmet IV, 208
acting, 187
acts, 51, 52, 66, 83, 85, 87, 92, 113, 125, 134, 140, 143, 150, 169, 181, 184, 196, 205, 222, 226, 233, 235, 241, 245, 251, 257, 262, 266
  passed in the late sessions, 265
Acts of Assembly, 23, 24, 37, 53, 57, 113, 132, 133, 225
Adam, 122
  James, 40, 41, 49, 50
  Mr., 210
  Robert, 24-26, 35, 44, 45, 54, 60, 85, 107, 132, 156, 157, 160, 167
Adams, 144
  Mr., and Mr. Hancock, 144
  Mr., entertains Br. officials, 237
  Mr., Grosvenor Sq. house, 237
  Ambassador, 153, 158
  American Envoy, 144
  astonishing loan from Holland, 153
  John, 113, 145, 160, 179, 234, 239
  John, Am. Amb. to G.B., 128
  John, Am. Amb., and Lord Gordon, 143
  John, received by Queen, 179
  John, The Am. Plenipo, 140
  Mrs. & Miss, accomplished women, 154
  portrait of, West's, 154
  Samuel, 234
  statesman, politician, 258
Addison's Ferry, 206, 212
Addition to Discovery, 224
Addition to Georgetown, 40, 41, 49
Adjutant Generals, 107
Admiralty
  Judge of the, 24
Adventurers, 40
advertising, 28, 34
adzes, 11, 74, 80, 171
  carpenter's, 197
  cooper's, 197
Africa, 5, 101, 121, 128, 159
  Br. coast settlements, 227
  French fortifying sites, 227
  Portuguese discoveries, 190
African coast
  Br.-Fr. discussions, 253
  British outrages, 253
Agents, 84, 160, 182, 216, 254
agriculture, 164, 209, 233
  American, 209
  French, threatened, 164
  society formed (Phila.), 32
Aix La Chappelle, 65
alamodes, 15
Alava
  Ignacio, 202
Albany, 112
Albany boards, 34
Albany, N.Y., 182
  to, conveyance of mail, 169
Albemarle Co., 52
Aldermen, 14, 200
ale, 11, 64, 185, 197
Alexander, 223
  Charles, 2, 13
  John, 119, 126, 132, 138, 143, 152, 157, 161, 167, 172, 176, 177, 188
  William, 126, 132, 138, 143, 152, 157, 161, 167, 172
Alexandria
  Academy, 160, 210, 212, 239
  Common Council, 14, 45, 99, 119, 121, 124, 132, 250, 361
  court house, 8
  Inn and Coffee-House, 169, 172, 177, 183, 205
  Jockey Club, 131, 142, 143, 147, 157, 167, 191
  market house, 73, 126, 192, 199, 361
    building of, 99
  Post-Office, 7, 34, 234, 236
  Printing-Office, 1, 2, 7-9, 11, 12, 16-18, 21-23, 26, 29, 30, 35, 40, 45, 49, 54, 55, 60, 65, 68, 70, 75, 81, 82, 84, 86, 91, 95, 98-101, 105, 109, 110, 115, 116, 119, 120, 122, 124, 127, 133, 138, 143, 147, 152, 153, 157, 161, 162, 167, 171, 172, 177, 183, 188, 192, 193, 198-200, 207, 212, 219, 225, 230, 234-236, 240, 241, 245, 251, 255, 257, 262, 267, 361
  races, 142, 182, 183, 187
  warehouse, 69
Alexandria (Egypt), 75
Algarve
  1780 wheat experiment, 246
  corn growing successful, 246
  Dutch, English husbandry, 246
  pirates took cattle, people, 225
Algeria
  captured, enslaved U.S. Consul, 43
  Spain asks Porte's good offices, 47
Algerine bark
  pursues Bourdeaux ship , 111
Algerine corsairs, 51, 158, 194, 202
  24 guns, pattararoes, 243
  attempt seize snow off Madeira, 51
  block Malaga's port, 158
  captures 3 Neapolitan ships, 202
  enslave captured crews, 226
  stop English ship, 194
  sunk, all perished, 168
  take Venetian corn ship, 194
  taken by Portuguese ships, 243
  takes American ship, 205
  took 29 ships of/for Marseilles, 226
Algerine cruisers
  Cadiz, 191
  Cape St. Mary's, 191

Portuguese vessels, 191
Rock of Lisbon, 191
Western islands, 191
Algerine deterrent
3 Am. 40-gun ships, 228
close-in coastal patrol, 228
Algerine frigate, 28 guns
defeated Port. convoyer, 209
Algerine galiots
stop, waive ship Rambler, 209
Algerine pirates
Mediterranean commerce, 231
murder captured crews, 231
Algerine ransom rates
Captain-£500, 238
Mate-£300, 238
sailor-£100, 238
Algerine rover
fires on San Isadore fort, 112
Algerine slaves (12)
freed, gift to Morocco, 246
Algerine vessels
enslaved crews, 3 Pope ships, 227
halt U.S.-Mediterranean trade, 227
took 3 vessels of Pope, 227
Algerine xebec
Cape St. Vincent, 191
captures new Brest ship, 163
Algerines, 15, 186, 215, 239, 244, 249
alarm merchants, 225
Am. captives' letter, plea, 221
Am. ship, crew to Cadiz, 238
Americans' ransom £400-600, 222
blow up selves, Christian slaves, 111
capture 2 Br. ships, 111
captures by, 254
cruise off Western Isles, 222
cruise off Portugal, 222
declare war on U.S., 190
enslave captured crews, 238
fitting out 8 ships, 190
fitting out cruisers, 222
French subjects captured, 202
Jefferson's solution to, 228
pirates lose 60, 163
Portuguese measures, 254
put 24 Ams. into slavery, 222
seek Brazil, Am. vessels, 226
seize Dutch ships off Leghorn, 51
take Am. schooner, enslave crew, 222
take Am. ship, enslave crew, 222
take Boston brig, 209
take Boston ship, enslave crew, 209
take Eur. brig, enslave crew, 209
take Genoese traders, 243
take New York ship, 209
take Spanish traders, 243
take, release Eng.vessel, 209
Algiers, 66, 107, 178, 191, 208, 226, 239, 243
75 gun and mortar boats, 202
8 ships, 18-36 guns, 190
9 vessels, 22-36 guns, 202
Am. Amb. sent to Dey, 249
and Spain, 46
British Consul, 222
Captain of the port, 178
captives work on habour forts, 201
captured polacre taken to, 91
castle, 178
Chancellor, 178
defences described, 128
Devil's battery, 66
Dey of, 178, 189, 220, 202
Dey's terms very imperious, 243
English Consul at, 66
five Jews strangled, 220
French Consul, 178, 202
holds U.S. ConGen., 184
Jews defraud Christian, executed, 220
Lamb, Mr., sent as Agent, 248
Massorado, RAdm, Cmdr., seeks peace, 178
mole 500 toises long, 65
ready for Spanish assault, 66
roads, 178
Spain, Portug., Venice to attack, 56
Spain's assault on, 36
Spanish armament against, 140
Swedish Consul, 202
takes 2 Amsterdam ships, 201
Turks fitting out armed vessels, 55
two clerks to perpetual slavery, 220
two clerks' feet bastinadoed, 220
Algiers-Spain Peace, 189
terms, schedule of, 189
Algiers-Sweden
Swedish ship security, 252
Alicant, 202, 205
Allen
Charles, 17
Ira, 254
John, 31
Mr., hydrostatics, 264
alleys (see also "Streets"), 29, 79, 119, 192
alliances, 76, 111, 121, 133, 194
Barrier Treaty support, 9
matrimonial, 195
Russia-Austria, 4
secret, 196
Allison
John, 84, 132, 219, 230, 266
Joseph, 217
Robert, 15, 18, 23, 151, 153, 161, 199, 207, 211, 212, 219, 225
Thomas, 69
allspice, 28, 33, 49, 81, 137, 156, 240, 266
almanacks, 16, 22, 23, 198, 207
Massachusetts' tax on, 77
almonds, 197, 250
alms, 65
aloes, 29
Alsop
John, 78
Altena, 4
alum, 29, 81, 165, 181, 229, 239
alum salt, 15, 52
Alveres, 93
Ambassadors, 9, 10, 18, 24, 42, 46, 82, 110, 112, 124, 128, 139, 143, 153, 158, 159, 191, 194, 221, 226, 241, 246, 249
British, 55, 196
Dutch, 10, 18, 24, 117, 118, 143, 148, 208, 227
French, 117, 162, 214, 263
Prussian, 42, 43, 93
Russian, 247
Spanish, 117, 173, 181
Ambler
J., 20
Jaquelin, 11, 84
Ameling
John F., 84
America, 27
advantage over all others, 153
de Vergennes caused revolution, 129
leading men, 208
American Academy
Lord Gordon snubbed, 264
of Arts and Sciences, 264
American Company of Comedians, 145
American Consul, 181
American revolution [essay]
a rapturous appreciation, 260
Amersfort, 195, 201
ammoniac, 29
ammunition, 46, 226, 245, 252
Amsterdam, 10, 18, 37, 44, 49, 50, 56, 68, 77, 83, 105, 111, 113, 125, 126, 135, 194, 208, 220, 247
13,861 widows, 189
500 immigrants arrive Phila., 160
Barbary vessels block trade, 201
Mr. J. Mandrillon, Mcht., 19
Amsterdam Magistracy, 2

Anacreon, 16
Anamaboc, 116
anarchy, 254
anchors, 1, 135, 181, 197, 224, 262
and-irons, 15, 136
  wrought, 197
Anderson
  Bartlett, 31
  Col., 193
  Garland, 31
  William, 31, 34, 35, 45
Anderson's pills, 29, 84, 133, 143, 147, 152, 162, 167, 172, 177, 183, 188, 193, 200, 207, 212, 255, 262
Andre
  John, Maj., 107
Andrews
  Benjamin, 102
  Capt., 73
  J., 72
  Robert, 88
anecdotes, 88, 107, 121, 198, 228
  Alcibiades, 6
  King of Prussia, 21
angels, 122
Anhalt Zerbst soldiers
  died in Am. war: 126, 51
Annapolis, 12, 13, 16-18, 20, 23, 26, 30, 34, 40, 45, 56, 60, 64, 83, 123, 145, 146, 180, 210, 212, 219, 261
  horse race run, prize, 186
  Jockey Club races, 186
annuities, 237
Anspach
  Margrave of, 173
Anspachers
  died in Am. war: 461, 52
Antigua, 93, 140, 160, 192
  confiscates Am. ship, Br. register, 180
Antigua rum, 137
Antilles, 129
Antonio D'Acre
  Don, replaces Don Barcelo, 66
Antwerp, 3, 9, 13, 96, 154, 226
  20,000 man encampment, 221
  ancient commerce, splendor, 238
  Burgo-master, 3
  garrison, 3
  Key, or Quay, 3
  Prince de Ligne, Gov., 195
anvils, 94
Apedaile
  J., 34, 35, 45
Apostles, 41
apparel, 69, 79, 245, 252
  ready made, 197
apple orchards, 1, 2, 151, 176, 224
Apprentices, 1, 54, 55, 98, 101, 109, 110, 115, 116, 120, 124, 127, 128, 235, 265
apprenticeship indentures, 265
apron tapes, 218
aprons, 7, 15, 21, 58, 74, 99, 170, 218
Aquia, 60
Aquia Warehouse, 7, 90
Aquia-Run, 7, 12, 13, 26, 30, 90
Arabia, 66, 74
Arabic, 29
Arch Treasurer, 207
Archangel, 3
Archbishop of Bremen, 168
Architects, 107
Arcot
  nabob of, 71, 231
Arell
  David, 14, 54, 55, 64, 72
  Richard, 2, 6, 8, 12, 13, 22, 23, 30, 34, 40, 45, 103
  Samuel, 14, 98, 103, 108, 114, 115, 118, 119, 122, 127, 131, 137, 142, 146, 151, 155, 161, 165, 169, 176, 181, 187, 192, 199, 206, 211, 217, 223, 229, 230, 234, 236, 245, 250, 251, 255, 257, 262, 266
arithmetic, 90
armament
  at Brest, 195
arms, 43
army, 9, 13, 16, 20, 42, 43, 65, 66, 87, 93, 107, 125, 129, 158, 240, 247
  accounts, 215
  American, 16, 173, 248
  Austrian, 214
  British, 108, 203
  Continental, 123, 141, 222
  Dutch, 3, 196
  Imperial, 51
  Prussian, 76
  Russian, 93
  Spanish, 37
Arnheim
  Burgesses, 2
  garrison, 2
Arpinal
  Capt., 191
arrêt
  a brutum fulmen, 221
  of August 1784, abrogation asked, 134
arsenal, 42, 47, 202, 231
Artificers, 32
artillerists, 20
artillery, 9, 66, 201, 226
Artists
  American, 155
    in Gr. Britain, 154
  Ams., the most celebrated, 259
arts and sciences, 233
Arys
  H., 44
Arzee
  Killadar of Vellore, 231
Asbeston
  of the Ancients, 144
Ashton
  David, 165, 172, 177, 183
assafoetida, 29
assembly (social gathering), 121
astronomy
  new comet in Andromeda, 102
Athole Highlanders
  volunteer for Holland, 23
Atkins
  Capt., 254
Atkinson
  Mr., of Bank End, 51
  Capt., 73, 81, 82, 86
  J., 72, 107
Atkinson's iron forge
  opened at Lonningfoot, 51
attack
  by wolves, 57
attire, carriage, 197
Attorney General
  Connecticut's, in Georgia, 138
Attorneys, 45, 49, 50, 58, 61, 70, 71, 116, 237, 240, 251, 255, 265
Auditor's certificates, 25, 26, 30, 79, 86
Auditor's warrants, 21
augers, 11, 74, 80, 136, 151, 165, 171
Augusta
  college, church planned, 190
  printing office established, 190
  seat of government, 190
Augusta Co., 33
Augustus
  Joseph Benedict, 207
aurora borealis, 87
Austin
  John, Capt., 228
Austria, 3
  the spirited Joseph, 3
  3 proposed spring encampments, 76
  3000 to Holland frontiers, 221
  80,000 to assault Holland, 42
  80,000 troops march on Low Countries, 10
  accord with the Dutch, 125
  aggressions in Holland, 208
  alliance with Russia, 4
  Ambassador recalled, 10
  and Porte, uncivil, 196
  August Prince to visit England, 148

Austrian Netherlands, 154
buying 10,000 horses, 76
buying artillery Horses, London, 51
clergy limited to one benefice, 140
Court of Vienna, 10
De Reischach, Envoy Extr., 2
declares war on Holland, 5
demands religious order census, 65
dragoons to Holland frontiers, 221
Dutch affairs settled, 154
Dutch to apologize, 148
edict for Hungary, 233
Emperor, 2-4, 9, 13, 27, 31
Emperor and Prince de Kaunitz, 124
Emperor determined to annex Bavaria, 76
Emperor disposed to agree, 61
Emperor far from accommodation, 61
Emperor fears Italian Priests, 208
Emperor gives up Scheldt, 55
Emperor in Paris incognito, 42
Emperor quits negotiations, 61
Emperor receives Fr. King's letter, 76
Emperor refuses second audience, 214
Emperor rejects French mediation, 32
Emperor to Petersburg, 178
Emperor unlikely to rest, 227
Emperor views confederation, 201
Emperor's demands, 3
Emperor's demands on Holland, 96
Emperor's response, German League, 168
Emperor's forces, 3
Empress of Russia supports, 133
expects Hungarian tobacco, 116
flag insulted, 3, 13
France's proposals unacceptable, 51
Free Masons flourishing, 101
French King to mediate, 214
frontiers with Turkey, 201
German Electors side with, 42
gets 30,000 Tartar cavalry, 178
Governor General, 65
his Majesty wants cash, 214
Holland accommodation certain, 129
Holland, amicable adjustment, 130
Imperial flag insulted, 3
Imperial Internuncio, 162
Imperial Majesty, 2, 3, 13
Imperial Majesty's dignity wounded, 13
intends attack on Holland, 42
Low Countries forces, 61
Low Countries forces listed, 20
may war with Prussia, 130
new confederation, Emp. at head, 202
orders 5 regts. to Netherlands, 214
Paris negociations stopped, 221
peacetime land forces 290,000, 61
Prince de Ligne, 3
Prince of Kaunitz , 124
Prussia bans troops, 3
Prussia's Ger. league stand, 231
recalls Minister at the Hague, 4
regiments to turn back, 46
relgious reform hindered, 65
resumes Paris peace talks, 178
revenge upon, 13
rumored peace with Dutch, 96
Scheldt resolution, 138
State Chancellor, 214
supplies for 2000,000 man army, 65
Swiss officers, men made P.O.W.s, 46
troop disposition, 125
troops marched on Dutch lands, 77
troops take Fort Lillo, 4
troops toward Antwerp, 9
troops' march expence, 227
unreasonable terms for Dutch, 196
war with Dutch seems sure, 76
will war on Holland, 42
Austria-Holland
peace articles (list of), 225
prelim. peace articles signed, 225
preliminaries allow turbulence, 227
preliminaries [peace] signed, 227
Austrian artillery, 20
Austrian cavalry, dragoons
Cobourg regiment, 20
Tuscany regiment, 20
Warmser regiment, 20
Austrian Generals
Alton, Infantry, 20
Harrach, Cavalry, 20
Lelier, Cavalry, 20
Slade, Infantry, 20
Austrian infantry regiments
Dentmeister, Migazzi and Tillier, 20
Ligne, Kaunitz, Clairfayt, 20
Preyst, Latterman, 20
Vierset, Murry, Bonder, 20
Austrian infantry units
2 battalions Croats, Order of Battle, 20
4 militia battalions, 20
500 hussars, 20
600 Boulons, 20
Austrian Netherlanders
see warlike preparations, 194
Austrian Netherlands, 221
Austrian villages
barricaded, 9
Austrian-Dutch diplomacy, 32
Austrian-Dutch dispute
accommodation reached, 55
Authors, 193, 256
Aux Cayes, 33
awards, 105, 187
Awbrey
Thomas, 24
awl blades, 81, 151, 171
axes, 11, 74, 132, 171, 197, 217, 251
Azores, 190
asks Am. famine relief, 197
great distress for provisions, 197

B

Babadar
Tippoo Sultan, 66
Babson
S., 33, 63
bachelors, 187
non-marriage, reason, 169
back country, 48, 104, 229
Bacon
Chancellor, 101
bacon (food), 74
Baden-Dourlach
regiment, 2
badging, 231
Badinore, 18
bag buttons, 12, 100
bag pipes, 172
baggage, 143
bagging, 136
bags, 33, 58, 74, 151, 156, 240
Bahama, 112
assembly deemed illegal, 113
merchants, loyalists discontent, 113
Bahama Islands
discontent over Loyalists' treatment, 62

Bahamas, 52
drought, corn shortage, 4
permits Am. corn ships, 4
refuses Am. ship's landing, 148
seizes Am. ship, expells others, 148
Bailey
Nicholas, Capt., 175
William, 44
Bailey's dictionary, 136
Bailiffs, 54
Baird
John, barley shelling mill, 154
John, Prince George Co., 239
baizes, 6, 132, 146, 172, 218
bake houses, 29, 30, 40, 49, 55, 60, 210
Baker
Samuel, 171, 173, 183, 187
Stiebel, 234
Walter, 84
William, 88, 114, 120, 124, 161, 162, 172, 218, 219, 230
Bakers, 168
Baldwin
John, 118
Robert, 118
bale houses, 29
Balentine
John, 234
bales, 181, 211
Baley
William, 84
Ball
Burges, 94, 96, 104
Farling, 217
James, 31
Mrs., 210, 212, 219
Spencer, 95
William, Capt., 166
ballast, 249
balloon hats, 99
ballooning
a rage in Paris, 51
Balloonists, 183
Binns, Joseph, 201
Blanchard, Mr., 220
de Clermont, Swiss, 9
Frobisher, Mr., 201
Montgolfier, 144
Newmarch, Mr., 201
secret clericals, 125
balloons
Busselot, balloonist, 228
construction, ascension, journey, 9
cross Channel, 125
escaped incident, 51
for (Fr.) Royal family, 144
Joseph Binns, balloonist, 201
Montgolfier clock, 110
race, 3-heat, 14
Richmond-Hanover Co. flight, 228
steerage of, 201
steerage of, demonstrated, 201
suit against peasant fails, 220
balls, 37
balsam of honey, 85, 133, 143, 147, 152, 162, 167, 172, 177, 183, 188, 193, 200, 207, 212, 255, 262
Baltimore, Md., 4, 10, 14, 17, 20, 24, 25, 33, 37, 38, 43-45, 48, 50, 52, 53, 55, 56, 60, 62-65, 67, 70, 72, 75, 78, 88, 93, 97, 102, 103, 106, 112, 114, 115, 118, 119, 122, 123, 125-127, 135, 141, 145, 147, 148, 150, 151, 155, 160, 166, 167, 169, 176, 181, 185, 187, 188, 191, 198, 205, 206, 210, 212, 216, 219, 222, 224, 228, 233, 235, 239, 240, 244, 249, 251, 254-256
approval, Penna. paper money, 102
association, tradesmen, mfrs., letter to, 198
circulating medium, want of, 189
ginseng export figure, 62
imports exceed exports, 189
tradesmen, mfrs.' petition, 228
Baltimore Co.
inhabitants for paper currency, 228
Baltimore Furnace, 53
band of music, 175
bandano handkerchiefs, 49, 58, 81, 170
banishments, 203
Bank of England, 155
Bank of North America, 261
bank-head, 7
bankruptcy, 57, 200
banks, 3, 24, 52, 98, 145, 160, 255, 261
financial, 255, 261
Banks
A., 181
Baptists, 45
bar iron, 15, 136, 146, 171, 223, 266
bar lead, 7, 15, 52, 100, 218
Barb__
M. Pierre, silk culturist, 227
Barbadoes, 24, 44, 58, 63, 67, 69, 73, 83, 88, 93, 96, 103, 107, 114, 118, 126, 129, 150, 155, 156, 160, 181, 222, 254, 261
St. Vincent's, 96
Barbadoes rum, 44, 48, 55, 91, 94, 95, 100, 105, 118, 120, 127, 128, 131, 133, 142, 156, 157, 162, 224, 234
Barbadoes spirits, 142, 151, 155, 156, 181
Barbarian marauders
garda-costas fitting-out against, 112
barbarians, 153
cruising off Cape St. Vincent, 225
employ 17 ships, 225
mouth of the Straits, 225
ships: 20-36 guns each, 225
ships: 250-300 men each, 225
stop all nations' ships, 91
Barbary, 93, 186, 239
Dey forbids molesting Am. ships, 67
U.S. to buy off pirating, 56
Barbary coast
Spanish cruisers, 36
Barbary corsairs
Commodore's ensign: skull, battle axe, 106
Congress considers steps, 77
Genoese send Xebecs against, 106
light frigates cruise against, 105
masters of the Mediterranean, 51
seized Dutch ship, 105
stopping Mediterranean trade, 125
swarm seen in Corsican seas, 106
took Portuguese colliers, brig, 194
Barbary powers
27 sail at sea, 112
Barber
Chevalier, 234
Barbers, 123
Barbour
Philip, 31
Barcelo
Don Antonio, 140
Don., Lt. Gen., 36
Don, replaced by Don Antonio D'Acre, 66
Barcelona, 163, 189
Count d'Assalto, Cmdnt, 189
Barcelona handkerchiefs, 7, 79, 81, 147, 165, 170
Barclay
Mr., Cons.Gen. of _____, 244
Bard
John, 214
Barden
Joseph, 64
bark, 2, 29, 89
Barkeepers, 192, 199, 207

Barker
James, 151, 157
Barks
(unk) from Hierro island, 27
Algerine, 18 guns, 111
barley, 36, 203, 213, 229, 251, 266
hulled, 185
malted, 185
Scotch, 154
shelling mill shown, 154
Barlow knives, 218
Barnaby
John, 17
Barnard
S., 187
T., 38, 44, 49, 50, 83
Barnes
Abraham, 104, 109, 110, 116
Barnet
Capt., 160
barns, 1, 75, 89, 104, 141, 151, 166, 170, 229
barometers, 6, 136
Baron
Commodore, 135
Barques, 190
barrels, 6, 8, 11, 15, 21, 28, 33, 34, 38, 44, 52, 58, 63, 64, 69, 73, 75, 78, 79, 84, 86, 88-91, 94, 103, 108, 118, 122, 131, 136, 142, 146, 156, 159, 160, 164, 169-171, 181, 187, 198, 199, 206, 207, 211, 217, 223, 224, 228, 229, 234, 239, 250, 251, 254, 261
bars, 171, 224
bartering, 156
Bartlett
Capt., 114
W., 114, 126, 239
Barton
Seth, 240
Thomas, Fe??rd rep., 168
Basden
Richard, Capt., owns ships, 178
Bashaw of Belgrade
appointed Gov. of Salina, 226
bashaws, 181, 194, 203
basket buttons, 100
baskets, 6
basons, 15, 100, 151
Basseterre hurricane damage
2-year's cane crop , 178
Basseterre ship losses
Betsey, ashore, Old Road, 178
Hazard, drove out; no news, 178
Jane, drove out; no news, 178
Spooner, ashore, lost, crew saved, 178
Thomas, ashore, all saved, 178
Venus, drove out; no news, 178
Basseterre, St. Kitt's, 178
severest hurricane since 1772, 178
Batavia, 210
Bateman
Capt., 62
Bateman's drops, 29, 85, 133, 143, 147, 152, 162, 167, 172, 177, 183, 188, 193, 200, 207, 212, 255, 262
Bath, 19, 44, 107, 108, 115, 116, 120, 124, 161, 172, 183
Bath coating coat, 123
Bath coatings, 15, 136
Bath coats, 255
Bath Guide, 107
Bath rugs, 239
batteries, 3
floating, 140
Bauham
Susanna, Sarah; mother, daughter, 135
Bavaria
Austria seeks territory, 76
barter with Germany, 147
Elector of, 76
Bavaria peacetime
land forces: 24,000, 61
Baxter
Daniel, 43
Bay of Alicant, 202
Bay of Honduras, 93
Bayer
Michael, 198
Baylor
Col., 60
Bayly
William, 199, 207, 212, 219, 230
Baynes
Capt., 141
John, 130
Bayonne (Fr.)
trade situation described, 135
bays, 52, 124, 135, 174
Alicant, 202
Annotto, 191
Deep, 178
Gaspee, 5
Honduras, 93, 116
Hudson's, 4
Massachusetts, 19, 205
Montego, 164
Montenegro, 19
Sacre, 195, 243
Willoughby, 179
Beach
Mr., Rev., 260
beacon, floating
on the Brown, removal, 228
beacons, 52
bead planes, 11
Beale
T., Col., 104
Beall
George, 84
Thomas, 84
beards, 133
bearskins, 151
Beaty
Thomas, 84
Beaufort, 52
beaver coating, 165
Beaver Creek, 67
beaver gloves, 74, 146
Beaver Harbour
ruined by fire, 148
beaver hats, 7, 99, 250
beavers, 49, 58, 217
Beckley
John, 266
John, Clerk, 31
bed bunts, 7, 80, 88, 98, 136, 165, 218
bed cords, 81, 136, 171
bed rooms, 94
bed tickings, 15, 88, 136, 218
bed ticks, 80, 81, 151, 165
Bedford
Duke of, parsimony, 158
Bedford, Mass., 264
Bedinger
Henry, 84
beds, 212, 217
bedsteads, 16
beef, 8, 28, 49, 52, 58, 90, 103, 159, 185, 197, 198, 233
beef-eater, King's, 243
beer, 6, 158, 185, 197, 229, 266
beer-cocks, 151
Beeson
Edward, 84
beggars lace, 219
Beiler
Benjamin, 84
Beira
Prince of, 76
Belcarras
Earl of, 190
Belfast, 139, 198
Belgiojoso
Comte, 13
Belgrade
6000 Janissaries' cantonment, 93
Bashaw of: Soleiman Effendi, 203
garrison, 65
Bell
Alexander, 251
Capt., 56, 93, 97, 160, 216
bell hoops, 6
bell-metal, 185
skillets, 165
Bellows
Gen., 258

Belvoir, 25, 26, 34, 35
Bencraft
Mr., 158
Bengal, 210, 213
Bennett
Charles, 217
Mason, 170
Berard
J.J., 211
John B., 188
Bergen-op-Zoom, 3
Berkeley Co., 8, 21, 25, 26, 34, 35, 45, 50, 54, 59, 60, 69, 73, 82, 85, 90, 95, 108, 115, 116, 120, 124, 161, 164, 171-173, 183, 192, 193, 198, 200, 207, 224, 225, 234, 235, 255, 262, 267
Berkley
John, 11
Berlin, 43, 61, 76, 111, 168, 231
Court of, 9
French Minister at, 76
Jew Cerf, King's Commissary, 65
Bermuda, 5, 10, 73, 78, 216
Bern handkerchiefs, 135
Bernard
Capt., 130
Berne, 19
Berry
Mary, 70
Berstoff, 97
Berwick
Colonel of , 226
Besie
Marson, 19
Beulwitz
Hanover Minister of State, 168
Beverley, 10
Beverly, 239, 261
Beverly, N.E., 209
Bibb
Richard, 31
Bibles, 151, 170, 218, 256
Bicker
Henry, 32
Biddle
Charles, V.P. vice Irvine, 190
Clement, 4, 97
bilious disorder, 19
Bill of Rights, 50
billiard tables, 20, 250, 254
taxes on, 21
bills
Eastern Shore (Md.) College, 188
tea, 3
Teachers of the Christian Religion, 41
bills of exchange, 48, 49, 58, 90, 136, 165
bindings, 7, 12, 49, 74, 81, 165
Binns
Charles, 217, 219, 230
Bird
Mark, 216
W., 250, 257, 262
bird shot, 85
Birks
Joshua, 234
Birmingham, 20
Birmingham, Eng., 151
Biscuit Bakers, 235, 236, 245
biscuit baking, 49
Bishop
J., 160, 181
Bishop of Connecticut, 130
Bishops, 139, 213
Bissell
David, Ens., 179
Biterman
Mr., 34
bits, 80, 219
black
alamodes, 15
Barcelona neckcloths, 218
beaver hats, 250
beavers, 217
bombazeens, 218
bonnet silk, 28
brunellas, 58
crapes, 218
everlastings, 151
gauzes, 58, 74, 99, 151, 165, 170, 218
handkerchiefs, 79, 81, 218
hats, 88, 99
horn buttons, 230
laces, 7, 136, 170
lastings, 132, 170
modes, 58, 74, 81, 136, 170
pelongs, 81
pepper, 146
persians, 218
ribbons, 170, 177
saddle bags, 69, 70, 94, 100
satins, 79, 81, 165, 170
sealing-wax, 74
shoes, 192
silk bonnets, 136, 151
silk florentines, 15
silk handkerchiefs, 135
silks, 80
stockings, 69
stuff breeches, 89
taffetas, 81
velvets, 58
Black Sea castles, forts
filled with artillery, troops, 226
black walnut tables, 217
black-lead pencils, 165
blackball, 74
Blackburn
Edward, 161, 162, 172, 256, 262
T., 16, 18, 26, 166, 167, 177
Thomas, 84
Blacksmiths, 146, 206
Bladel, 226
Bladensburg, 48, 55, 60, 131, 199, 216
Blagrove
Benjamin, 23
Blair
A., 44
Blake
J., 114, 118, 122
John, 146, 147, 149, 157
Blanchard
Mr., 125
balloon racer, 14
cross channel ballonist, 125
Blane
T., 80, 82, 86
Thomas, 230, 250
blank books, 2, 12, 17, 59, 84, 86, 95, 100, 109, 115, 120, 133, 143, 147, 152, 162, 165, 167, 170, 172, 177, 183, 188, 193, 200, 207, 212, 255, 262
blank journals, 33
blanketing, 192, 199
blankets, 1, 135, 136, 165, 181, 217, 218, 224, 234, 239
blanks, 152, 161, 167, 177, 188, 193, 200, 207, 212
bleached sewing thread, 15
Blewit
Rev., 173
Blois, 10
blooded nags, 7
Bloomery, 95
blown salt, 266
blue, 6
Blue and Buffs, 184
blue ware, 251
BLUNT (pen name), 126
Boadman
John, 159, 175
Board of Treasury, 38, 63, 182, 215
boarders, 7, 115, 116, 124, 156
boarding houses, 108, 115, 120
Boarman
Leonard, 95, 100, 104
Raphael, 152, 153, 161, 172, 177, 183, 188
boat building, 59
boats, 146
Boatswains, 159
bobbing, 218
bobbins, 81, 170
Boggess
Robert, 104, 109, 110, 115
Bohea tea, 8, 33, 49, 64, 68, 73, 74, 81, 90, 103, 108, 109, 115, 120, 131, 136, 137, 146, 156,

165, 171, 206, 211, 217, 223, 234, 239
Bohemia, 76
Bois de Luc
garrison, 2
bolstered hips, 196
bolting cloths, 1
bolts, 171
Bombardiers, 194
Bombay, 129
bombazeens/zines, 170, 218
bombs, 189, 194
Bonder
infantry regiment of, 20
bonds, 132, 133, 138, 157, 170-172, 176, 187, 199, 207, 211, 212, 216, 219, 223, 225, 234, 262, 267
Judge of Probate, other, 77
bonnet pasteboards, 218
bonnets, 7, 15, 99, 151
Bonnyman
Capt., from Black River, 52
book-case locks, 80
Bookkeepers, 64
books, 7, 86, 95, 103, 109, 110, 119, 120, 124, 128, 136, 143, 161, 165, 167, 172, 181, 187, 193, 198, 200, 207, 240, 251, 256, 257, 262, 267
account, 197
blank (see "blank books"), 197
bound, unbound, 185
psalm, 197
spelling, 197
Booksellers, 17, 43, 187
Boorman
Raphael, 86, 91
boot legs, 98, 103, 197
Boothby
Capt., 155
boots, 7, 98, 99, 103, 136, 142, 170, 177, 197, 230
Bordeaux, 134
Boston, Mass., 4, 5, 10, 15, 16, 24, 28, 30, 35, 37, 49, 52, 56, 63, 66-68, 71, 83, 88, 107, 112, 114, 118, 121, 125, 126, 130, 134, 144, 150, 159, 160, 164, 169, 171, 172, 179, 180, 183, 184, 192, 222, 226, 238, 239, 242, 253, 254, 258, 261, 264
advertisement duty, offset, 149
British vessels depart, 155
Comm., mchts, traders, citizens, 148
Congress reponds to trade group, 102
Consul of France, 92
court of, 203
Eng. ship denied landing of goods, 77
Government House, 242
navigation act changes, 244
Nova Scotian refused provisions, 190
Stanhope-Bowdoin clash, 242
tradesmen, mfrs., letter by, 198
U.S. should bar Br. goods, 173
Boston Association
compliance, import duties act, 205
Boston harbour
ship captain-pilot protocol, 238
Boston's Foursold State, 2, 13, 17
Botetourt Co., 150
bottle corks, 74
bottle stands, 171
bottled snuff, 219
bottles, 1, 6, 15, 25, 26, 34, 64, 81, 89, 98, 100, 103, 108, 118, 122, 123, 127, 132, 133, 136, 156, 160, 164, 169, 171, 185, 229, 239
gross of, 142
Boucher
John, 84
Boulons, 20
bounties, 214
bounty lands
Connecticut's, in Georgia, 141
Bourbon
house of, 76
Bourbon ambition, 130
Bourbon Lanci, 226
Bourdeaux, Fra., 19, 123, 135, 149, 150, 220, 237
Chamber of Commerce, 238
Bowden
Stephen, 146, 147, 153, 234
Bowdoin
Gov., 228, 242
Bowdoin-Stanhope clash, 242
Br. to fire on Boston, 242
King's flag insulted, 242
bowels, 213, 237
Bowen
Jabez, elected LtGov., R.I., 87
Bowers
B., 210, 233
bowls, 49, 81
bowsprits, 63, 175
Bowyer
John, 31
boxes, 1, 2, 6, 8, 11, 15, 49, 63, 80, 89, 94, 119, 136, 146, 165, 218, 229, 251, 266
Boyd
Robert, Jr., 32
Boyd's Hole, 38, 266
Br. Royal Academy
Exhibition review, 259
Br. Tools Non-Export Act
1-year statute, limitations, 241
artificers may not leave, 241
customs' authority, duties, 236
defendants recovering costs, 241
enumerated articles, intent to export, 241
enumerated articles, possession of, 241
items covered, 236
not-guilty pleas, 241
penalties: customs' officers co-conspiracies, 237
penalties: customs' officers non-compliance, 237
petition to suspend, 238
prosecution proceeds, disbursement, 241
recruiting artificers prohibited, 241
ship captains' responsibilities, 236
trials, judicial systems for, 241
who may file bail, 241
Brabant, 9
Duchy of, 125
Duke of, and Austria, 14
Brabantins
dance to the lascivious flute, 221
Brace
Jan, Commodore, 4
braces, 171
Brackenridge
John, 31
Mr., 30
Braden
Joseph, 65, 75
Bradford
Capt., 45
Mr., Coffee House host, 117
William, Esq; AttyGen, Penna., 19
Bradhurst
B., 33
Benjamin, Capt., 39
Bradley
Stephen R., 254
brads, 165, 171
Bradstreet
Capt., 63, 230, 231, 240
Lyonel, 84
Samuel, Sir, Bart., 138
Brady
Capt., 22
Braganza family
extinction of, 76
Brand
Capt., 191
Brandenbourg
Margrave of, 242
branding, 231
branding for crimes, 239
brands, 142, 261

brandy, 8, 24, 81, 109, 142, 151, 155, 181, 211, 250, 254
Brant
  arrived from England, 144
brass andirons, 15
brass buckles, 59, 73, 123, 131, 171
brass buttons, 123
brass candlesticks, 80, 218, 239
brass chafingdishes, 16
brass cocks, 80, 136, 171, 218
brass inkpots, 80
brass kettles, 171
brass locks, 11
brass mariners' compasses, 74
brass sieves, 58
brass skillets, 80
brass stoves, 192
brass tea-kettles, 151
brass thimbles, 171
brass wire sieves, 58, 80
brass, wrought, 185
Bray
  G., 239
bread, 49, 198
Bready
  William, 84
breast buttons, 81
breast pins, 80
Breda, 2, 3
  Comte de Maillebois, Gov., 246
breeches, 22, 25, 34, 59, 69, 73, 89, 103, 120, 122, 123, 127, 131, 143, 151, 172, 176, 177, 230, 255
  buckskin, 197
  leather, 197
breeches patterns, 80
Breganzille, 246
Bremen, 151, 198
  Archbishop of, 168
Brent
  Daniel Carroll, 7, 12, 17, 22, 26, 30, 34, 40, 45
  Eleanor, 177
  William, 31, 59
  William, Col., 102
Brent-Town, 59
Brenton, 7, 22
Brenton-tract, 7, 12, 17, 22, 26, 30, 35, 40, 45
Brest, 47, 139
  8 war ships fitting out, 55
  armament at, 195
  new port superintendant, 189
Brewer
  John, boatswain, 159
breweries, 266
Brewers, 34
brick buildings, 118
brick houses, 2, 8, 28, 29, 57, 81, 86, 123, 127, 128, 132, 137, 198, 199, 212, 224, 229, 235, 250, 255, 266
brick prisons, 40
brick stores, 146, 147, 153, 235, 236, 245
brick-yard, 72, 235
Bricklayers, 16, 72, 85, 91, 146, 147, 153
Bricklayers' trowels, 171
Brickmasons, 230
bricks, 49, 151, 235
Bridge-Town, 114
bridges, vi, 69, 118
  construction mishap, 248
  Mattox, 199, 207, 212, 219, 225
bridle bits, 171, 218
bridles, 7, 74, 80, 94, 136, 137, 151, 156, 171, 197
bridons, 218
Brigantines (see also "Brigs")
  Alexandria, 206, 212, 219, 225, 230
  Betsy, 234, 236, 245, 251, 256
  Eglington, 85, 86, 95
  el Vivo, 246
  Fitzhugh, 15
  Hazard, 179
  Industry, 48, 55, 60
  Janet, 98, 109, 110
  Little Tom, 179
  Mercury, 155
  Spanish, 18 guns, 178
  Triton, 79
Briggs
  C., 222, 228
  John Howell, 31
Bright
  Capt., 141
Brighton, 226
Brigs (see also "Brigantines"), 141, 186, 238
  (unk) Am., Newfoundland seizes, 154
  (unk) from Antwerp, 37
  (unk) from Virginia, 155, 159, 173
  (unk) from Whitehaven, 27
  (unk) Halifax, from London, 164
  (unk) of E. H. Darby, 174
  (unk) Portuguese, 128
  (unk) Salem to Madera, 237
  (unk) supposed pirates', 205
  (unk), American, 179
  Active, 93, 112
  Adventure, 191
  Alexandria, 210, 251, 256, 262, 266
  Ann, 20
  Ann-Maria, 44, 58, 114, 118, 126, 205
  Apollo, 93
  Atocha (armed), 202
  Betsy/Betsey, 43, 52, 55, 63, 141, 228, 233
  Britannia, 160
  Ceres, 239
  Cesar, 72, 107
  Charles, 176
  Christiana, 187
  Commerce, 5
  Dolphin, 33-35, 41, 63
  Eglington, 83, 88, 91, 100
  Fanny, 122, 150
  Fitzhugh, 5, 38, 45, 49
  for sale, 65, 156, 157, 162
  Friendship, 19
  George, 130
  Glasgow, 83
  Glory, 78, 103, 130, 135
  government, 114
  Greenwich, 10
  Hannah, 126
  Hawk, 112
  Hope, 28, 191
  Industry, 15, 89, 91, 96, 103, 181, 222
  Jane, 155, 210
  Jane and Elizabeth, 93, 97, 100, 109, 114
  Janet, 122
  Jenny, 93, 118
  King Taminy, 43, 83
  Liberty, 28, 34, 40, 45, 52, 93
  Live Oak, 105
  Lovely Lass, 112
  Marquis de la Fayette, 33, 39, 44, 45, 63, 141
  Martha, 72, 73, 93, 155-157, 162, 211, 219, 225, 233
  Mary, 191, 222, 228
  May, 2, 5, 6, 9, 12, 13, 17, 20
  Nancy, 141
  Neptune, 191
  Patient Mary, 88, 107
  Patton, 24
  Peggy, 93
  Richmond, 24, 233
  Ruth, 113
  Sea-Horse, 24
  Sophia, 240
  Success, 191
  Swift, 191
  Triton, 58, 60, 64, 65, 75
  Union, 48
  Venus, 178
  Vry van Dwinglandy, 77
  Washington, 191
  William and Henry, 20, 44
  Zephyr, 5, 83
Brill
  R., 228
brimstone, 1, 171
brine, 33
Bristol, 5, 56, 93, 130, 220, 261

Bristol sleeve buttons, 219
Britain's Am. war costs
all dead: 1,382,000, 155
all losses: £400,000,000, 155
debt increase: £117,842,563, 155
KIA/WIA/MIA: 432,840, 155
money: £146,859,632, 155
widows, orphans: 1,000,000, 155
British, 67
British Agents, 71
British army, 108, 203
British Bottoms, 150
British claims, 35, 36
British Consul, 83
British Court, 63
British debts, 36
British Factors, 71
British goods, 67, 88
British government, 160
British Islands, 145
British merchants, 35, 71
British navy
armament, types, 252 ships, 42
ship types, arms, numbers, 42
British osnaburgs, 218
British vessels, 63, 80, 85, 88, 107, 150, 206, 211, 229, 234, 239, 246, 250, 261
Briton, 144
Brittany, 19
revolting peasants dispersed, 189
Britton
Capt., 248, 249
broaches, 11
broad axes, 1
broad hoes, 74
broadcloths, 6, 7, 11, 15, 44, 49, 74, 79, 81, 99, 108, 115, 120, 131, 132, 136, 146, 151, 156, 165, 170
brocades, 74
Broders
Joseph, 234
Brokers, 4
Broket
Robert, 85, 91
Brooke
Clement, 53, 55, 64, 70, 75
H., 266
Brooks
J.T., 103, 210, 249
brooms, 7, 125, 151
Brown
Capt., 141, 173, 234, 236, 245, 251, 256
Maj., 53, 210
Martin, 108, 115, 120
Mr., 234
P., 228
Robert, 132, 133, 138
S., 10, 141, 150, 254
Samuel M., 84, 234, 251, 256
W., 12, 13, 18, 23, 30, 35, 40
William, 8, 84, 118, 136, 138, 147, 187
William, Capt., 234
William, Maj., 17
Windsor, Maj., 93
brown sugar, 1, 89, 137, 142, 156, 171
Browne
Alexander, Capt., 159
Mr., artist, 153
Browning
Richard, 234
Brownlow
John, 17, 22, 29, 30, 40
Bruce
Mr., 94
Bruin
Peter B., 84
brunellas, 58
Brunswick peacetime
land forces: 16,000, 61
Brunswickers
died in Am. war: 3015, 52
brushes, 7, 74, 80, 81, 136, 151, 165, 171, 218, 219
Brussels, 3, 9, 13, 14, 46, 65, 76, 195, 225, 247
Counsellor of Commerce to U.S., 19
Court of, 4
Dutch Ministers at, 13
Emperor's Christmas visit, 247
rejoicings, Scheldt opening, 238
the Arch Duke's, 221
war and rumors of war, 221
Bryan
Samuel, Clerk, Penna. Gen. Ass'y, 97
Bryce
John, 137, 143, 147, 234
Nicholas, 234
Robert, 44, 50, 54
Bryson
James, 182
Buccleugh
Duke of, 190
Buchanan
John, Rev., 249
Buck Creek, 218, 219, 230
buckets, fire, 180
Buckingham House, 263
Gordon's name forbid in, 264
King's apartments, 264
King's pages, 264
buckle brushes, 218
buckles, 6, 7, 11, 28, 59, 73, 80, 81, 89, 123, 127, 131, 136, 147, 151, 161, 165, 171, 177, 192, 219, 230
Buckley
William, 107
Buckly
John, 89, 91, 105
buckram, 79, 99, 132, 170
buckskin boots, 99
buckskin breeches, 34
Budd
Dr., 149
Henry, 89, 91, 105
Buddicom
William, 206, 212, 219, 225, 251, 256, 262, 266
Buell
Rev., 259
Buenos Ayres, 124
Indians defeat Gov. troops, 189
Buffoon
Lord [Pitt], 66
Buffy
Mons., of India, 148
building stone, 28
buildings, 8, 66, 75, 118, 218, 229, 250
public, 2, 13
Bulkley
Rich., 87
Bull
John, delegate to Congress, 37
Bull Run, 99, 171, 173, 183
Buller
Capt., 129
bullet moulds, 171
bullets, 189
Bullitt
Cuthbert, 123, 127, 128
bullocks, 129, 213
bung borers, 80
buoys, 52
replaces floating beacon, 228
Burcher
Katey, 239
Burd
Edward, Esq.; Pa. Supreme Ct., 19
Burger
John, 32
burgessoise
Dutch captains using, 4
Burgo-master
Antwerp, 3
Burgudore, 226
Burgundy, 226
burials, 48
Burke
Patrick, 178
Burwell
Nathaniel, 8
Nathaniel, jr., 12, 17, 22
Robert, 171, 173, 183

Bush
  Philip, 50
  Theobald, Irishman, 19
Bushby
  William, 234, 235
bushels, 2, 104, 199, 206
businesses
  Allen and Cushing, Printers, 248
  Andrew Jamieson & Co., 235, 236, 245
  Brosler & Richardson, L'pool, 214
  Callender, Lewis & Co., 6, 9, 17, 22
  Clark & Nightingale, 4
  Colin MacIver & Co., 88, 91, 100
  Craik & Co., 29, 34, 35
  Crocketts & Harris, 151, 153, 161
  Daniel & Isaac M'Pherson, 1, 9, 13, 25, 26, 34, 81, 82, 86, 89, 91, 96, 104, 108, 109, 115, 120, 142, 143, 152, 182, 188, 193, 200, 224, 225, 235
  Davis, Messrs., 131, 133
  dissolved, 6, 9, 17, 59, 64, 70, 91, 100, 104, 109, 115, 120, 124, 133, 137, 138, 147, 152, 161, 167
  Dow, MacIver & Co., 88, 91, 100
  East-India Co. (see heading), 121
  Forrest & Stoddert, 8, 38, 79, 99, 100, 109
  George Richards & Co., 8, 13, 18, 23, 26, 30, 35, 40, 45, 50, 55, 60, 65, 70, 75, 82, 86, 91, 95, 100, 105, 110, 115, 120, 124, 127, 133, 138, 143, 147, 153, 157, 162, 167, 172, 177, 183, 187, 188, 193, 200, 207, 212, 216, 219, 225, 230, 235, 236, 240, 245, 251, 257, 262, 267
  Glassford & Henderson, 39, 41, 49
  Goddard & Langworthy, 44, 45, 55, 60, 65, 123, 127, 187
  Gurden Chapin & Co., 170, 177
  Harper & Fenner, 1, 12
  Hepburn & Dundas, 136, 138, 147
  Herbert & Potts, 79, 86, 165, 167, 172
  Hooe & Harrison, 1, 9, 22, 23, 30, 85, 89, 91, 96, 98, 105, 108, 181, 187, 188, 193, 200, 211, 219, 225, 228, 230, 234, 236, 240, 245, 250, 251, 256, 257, 261
  Huie, Reid & Co., 115, 116, 234, 236, 245, 251, 256
  Hunter, Allison & Co., 29, 266
  J.J. Berard & Co., 211
  James Craik & Co., 126, 128, 137
  James Hendricks & Co., 73, 81, 82
  James Hendricks & Daniel, 138, 147
  James Mills & Co., 146, 147, 157
  John B. Berard & Co., 188
  John Dundas & Co., 81, 86, 91, 94, 100, 104, 137
  John Falls & Co., 255, 262, 267
  John Mason & Co., 40, 41, 49
  John Murray & Co., 8, 24, 26, 35, 52, 55, 64, 156, 157, 162
  Jonathan Swift & Co., 7, 28, 30, 35, 49, 50, 58, 60, 65, 75, 90, 91, 100, 108, 115, 120, 131, 133, 143, 146, 147, 153, 165, 167, 177, 192, 199, 206, 211, 219, 229, 235, 236, 240, 245
  Jordan & Poyer, 88, 91, 100
  Kirk & Bowdon, 156
  Leertouwer, Huyman & Huiberts, 15, 18, 23, 85, 91, 95
  Lewis & Co., 6
  Long, Drake & Long, 238
  Lowry & M'Kenna, 104, 109, 115, 120, 124, 128, 133, 138, 147, 152, 157, 161, 167, 182, 218, 240
  M'Crea & Mease, 7, 12, 28, 30, 34, 35, 40, 45, 146, 147, 157
  Mathew & Thomas Irwin, Phila., 222
  Matthews & Orme, 166
  Oxley & Hancock, 39
  Paine & Co., 135
  Patuxent Iron Works, 127, 128, 137
  Philip Poyer & Co., 156, 157, 167
  Porter & Ingraham, 28, 30, 35, 143, 146, 147, 157, 162, 167, 171, 172
  Potomack Co., 84, 94, 96, 101, 131, 133, 143, 152, 198, 207, 212, 219
  Randle Mitchell & Son, 80, 86, 91, 137, 138, 147, 192, 199, 206, 212, 219, 225, 230
  Richard Caton & Co., 255, 262, 267
  Robinson, Sanderson & Rumney, 73, 81, 82, 166, 167, 172, 183, 229, 230, 235, 245
  S. & T. Hanson, 261, 267
  Shreve & Lawrason, 25, 26, 30
  Skinner & Ramsay, 234
  Stack & M'Namara, 178
  W. Mounsher & Co., 94, 100, 104
  Washington, Butler & Nivison, 187, 193, 199, 207
  Willams, Cary & Co., 100
  William Foster & Co., Boston, 222
  William Hartshorne & Co., 15, 18, 25, 29, 73, 81, 82, 86, 94, 95, 105, 165, 167, 170, 177, 235
  William Hunter, Jr. & Co., 223
  William Lowry & Co., 12, 13, 18, 58, 64, 65
  William Lyles & Co., 39, 44, 45, 79, 82, 86, 95, 100, 109, 110, 115, 124, 132, 138, 147, 152, 167, 172, 177, 183
  William Taylor & Co., 182, 188, 193, 200, 218, 225, 230, 235, 240
  Williams, Cary & Co., 6, 9, 13, 64, 89, 97, 98, 109, 123, 126, 127, 132, 133, 138
  Wright & Long, 25, 26, 35, 59, 65, 70
buskins, cork, 189
Busselot
  Mr., balloonist, 228
Butchers, 220, 254
Butchers' knives, 151
Butchers' steels, 171
Butean faction, 149
Butler
  a pirate, 135
  J., 24
  Joseph, 108, 115, 120
  Stephen, 95, 100, 104
butt soles, 98
butter, 1, 13, 28, 33, 49, 185, 197, 229
butter pots, 1, 171
button moulds, 165
buttons, 7, 12, 16, 25, 49, 59, 74, 80, 81, 100, 103, 123, 127, 131, 132, 136, 151, 165, 170, 171, 219, 230, 239
  parts of, or finished, 236

C

cabals, 196
Cabell
  Nicholas, 30
  William, 182
cabin boy, 19
cabinet work, 185
cable, 58, 189
  foreign, 197
Cabo Termites, 190

Cabral
 Joseph Felippe Ferreira, 198
Cadier, 225
Cadiz, 10, 44, 56, 66, 83, 105-107, 140, 162, 168, 176, 178, 180, 181, 186, 189, 191, 192, 194, 209, 214, 221, 222, 233, 238-240, 246
 Algerine cruisers, 191
 Am. Consul, 222
 arsenal, 66
 English Consul, 210
Cadiz salt, 89, 181, 229
Cadwallader
 Gen., 206
 Lambert, Hon., 210
Caen, Normandy, 32
Caermarthen
 Lord, East Indies policy, 158
 Marquis of, 160
cag bread, 235
cags, 24, 229
Cairo, 111
Calabria
 consecrated silver to Mint, 194
Calais, 4
calamanco shoes, 7, 28, 49, 74, 131, 132, 170, 218
calamancoes, 7, 12, 49, 59, 79, 81, 100, 108, 132, 136, 146, 151, 170, 206, 211, 217, 218, 223, 234, 239
Calderon
 Don Juan Briz, 27
Caldwell
 Capt., 43
calfskins, 171
 tanned, 197
Calhoun
 John Ewing, Hon., 37
calico gown, 86
calico waistcoats, 127
calicoes, 6, 7, 11, 12, 15, 28, 33, 49, 58, 74, 79-81, 98, 99, 103, 108, 132, 142, 146, 151, 155, 170, 206, 211, 217, 218, 223, 230, 234, 239, 250, 254, 255
Callahan
 Capt., 125
 Robert, 123
Callender
 Eleazer, 6, 9, 18, 22
calomel, 29
Calvert
 Benedict, 90, 95, 101
Cambiosa
 Capt., 249
cambleteens, 7, 146, 151
camblets, 7, 15, 81, 132, 151, 165, 170, 218
cambrick handkerchiefs, 74, 132
cambricks, 1, 6, 15, 58, 74, 80, 98, 99, 108, 123, 151, 160, 164, 169, 170, 197, 218
Cambridge
 sink of vice, profligacy, 5
Cambridge, Md., 17
Camden
 Lord, seated, 32
Camden, S.C., 92
camel's hair pencils, 170
camlets, 59
campaign buttons, 151
Campbell
 Adm., to Newfoundland as Gov., 110
 Alexander, 98, 109, 110, 120
 Archibald, Sir, 189
 Capt., 78, 113, 191
 Hugh, 211
 James, 84
Canada, 101, 121
 200 man exploration party, 190
 disagreeable Indian behaviour, 138
 French war expected, 62
 Jamaica seeks volunteers, 61
 needs more frontier forts, 138
 troops to 6 regiments, 61
Canada export
 peltries, £130,000 stg., 190
canals
 of Sas, 242
 of the Swin, 242
Canby
 Samuel, 59, 61, 70, 85, 91, 95, 104
candied sugar, 1
candle boxes, 74
candles, 1, 8, 15, 28, 33, 34, 49, 52, 63, 81, 94, 100, 136, 137, 142, 146, 151, 155, 171, 181, 197, 229, 239, 251
 spermaceti, 67
 tallow, 185
candlesticks, 11, 16, 80, 151, 165, 171, 218, 239, 250
 with handles, 15
candlewick, 218
cane (sugar), 101
canes, 197
 walking, 185
Caneva
 V., 164, 233
canister, 185
cannon, 46, 174
cannon balls, 231
cannon, brass, 189, 194
cannon, iron, 189, 194
Canongate
 shopkeepers resist shop tax, 221
cantharides, 29
Canton, 78, 87, 146, 194, 253
 fatal saluting incident, 92
 French assitance to Ams., 87
canvas, 7, 11, 15, 28, 68, 142, 151, 155, 156, 170, 181, 182, 224, 251
Cape
 Francois, 19
 Mr., 117
Cape ... (see "capes")
Cape de Verd islands, 43
capes, 25, 103, 134
 Ann, 24, 174
 Bajadore, 190
 Blanco, 190, 194
 Breton, 87, 180
 Cabo Termites, 190
 Clear, 105, 114
 Finistere, 214
 Francois, 19, 67, 116, 141, 159, 221, 247
 Good Hope, 56, 154, 190, 253
 Gratios a Dios, 47
 Hatteras, 134
 Henlopen, 164
 Henry, 155, 185
 Horn, 124
 in Virginia, 174, 175
 May, 185
 Nicola Mole, 66, 116
 Non, 190
 Spartel, 226
 St. Mary's, 191
 St. Vincent, 190, 191, 226
 Verd, de, 190
 Virginia, 174
Capraya, 249
caps, 85, 132, 218
Capus
 M., 93
Carberry
 Henry, 234
cardinals, 15, 136, 218, 229
cards, 74, 81, 100, 165, 218
 cotton, 185, 197
 playing, 184, 197
 wool, 185, 197
Carey, Thomas
 printer, Volunteer's Journal, 138
 tried for high treason, 138
cargo, 52, 67, 166, 167, 175, 185, 206, 211, 249, 250, 252
 loss causes suicide, 77
 sought, 28, 34, 39
Carling
 William, 234
Carlisle, 196, 222
 Lord, 39
Carlscrone
 magazines at, 9
Carmarthen
 Lord, 124

Lord, Br. Secretary of State, 179
Marquis of, 4, 128, 237
Carnan
John, 17
Carolina
tobacco price, London, 63
Carolinians
lawless and licentious, 163
Carpenters, 17, 90, 95, 121, 123, 199, 230, 233
ship, 175
Carpenters' adzes, 171
Carpenters' axes, 33, 251
Carpenters' braces, 171
carpenters' hammers, 80, 165
Carpenters' pincers, 171
Carpenters' planes, 219
Carpenters' rules, 239
carpenters' tools, 1, 11, 58, 80, 251, 256
carpetings, 7, 49
carpets, 49, 165, 197
Carr
William, 17
Carrell
George, 234
carriage attire, 197
carriage brushes, 80
carriage hoops, 197
carriages, 17, 177, 182, 220, 243, 263
4-wheeled, 203
riding, 197
taxes on, 20, 21
Carrington
Edward, 216
carrion crows
strip Negro suicide to bone, 244
Carroll
Daniel, 40, 41, 49, 78, 83, 84
Daniel, Jr., 127, 138, 151, 153, 161, 167, 172, 177, 183, 188
Carrollsburgh, 40, 41, 49
carronades, 139
Carson
John, Dr., Phila., 19
Carter
Edward, 30
Robert B., 69
Carter's Grove, 8
Carter's Run, 99
Carthagena
eight sail fitting out, 221
monstrous child born, 62
to send 2000 troops, 61
carts, 83, 263
Cartwright
Capt., 145, 175
J., 63, 83, 181, 228
Jonathan, 234
carvers, 218
Carwin
Thomas, 19
Cary
Archibald, Speaker, Va. Senate, 145
Thomas, 101
case of drawers, 217
cases, 1, 24, 85, 104, 165, 229, 246, 250, 254, 257, 262, 263
Casey
Mrs., 155
William, 16
cash books, 84, 133, 143, 147, 152, 162, 167, 172, 177, 183, 188, 193, 200, 207, 212, 255, 262
Cashel, 168
cask, 159
Caskin
Lawrence, 251, 256, 261
casks, 8, 34, 35, 41, 52, 58, 175, 235, 246, 257, 262, 263, 266
cassimers, 12, 49, 58, 74, 81, 98, 99, 151, 218
cassinets, 58
cast iron ware, 197
cast iron, wrought, 185
castaways
on Hierro, killed, 27
Castile soap, 100, 185
casting moulds
and boards for, 236
castings, 6, 49, 80, 171
castor hats, 7, 49, 81, 218
castors, 74, 250
Caswell
Gov., North Carolina, 180
Catalan vessel
intimidated in the Straits, 202
Catalonia
regiments march to, 221
catgut, 170, 218
Catherine the Great, of Russia, 47
Catholic religion, 26, 37, 46, 77, 84, 86, 95, 110, 116, 125, 159, 186, 202
Catlet
Alexander, 8
Catlett
Peter, 136, 138
Caton
Richard, 255, 262, 267
cattle, 33, 70, 73, 134, 149, 166, 167, 170, 185, 198, 203, 242, 256, 263
taxes on, 20
Cauzier
Capt., 238
Cavan
Patrick, 94, 96, 103
Caverly
Joseph, 98, 234
Phoebe, 72
Cawood
John, 146, 147, 157
cayenne pepper, 250
Cayet St. Louis, 247
Cecil Co, Md., 17
Cedar Point, 170
Cedar Run, 166, 167, 177
celibacy
laws of Lycurgus, 139
cellars, 2, 29, 44, 49, 69, 79, 94, 98, 99, 118, 132, 136, 151, 176, 206, 212, 219, 224, 250, 255, 266
certificate law, 21
Certificate to degree: Barrister at Law, 78
Certificate to practice as Attorney, 77
Certificate to practice as Attorney, Supreme Judicial Court--9£
Massachusetts' new tax on, 77
certificates, 38, 69, 217, 218, 229, 255
Ceuta, 112, 194
Ceylon, 247
chafing dishes, 15, 16, 80, 85, 171
Chain Carriers, 193
Chain of Rocky Keys, 191
chain spurs, 74
chains, 219, 223
chair whips, 171
Chairmen, 83, 84
chairs, 1, 13, 16, 126, 132, 133, 161, 164, 176, 187, 193, 200, 211, 217, 229
armed, 126
duties on, 184
riding, 197
Windsor, 176, 187, 193, 200, 217
chaise lace, 197
chaises, 94, 100, 104
duties on, 184
chalk, 34, 52
chalking, art of, 247
Chamber of Commerce, 73, 215
Charleston, 148
New York, 148
Chambermoney
crowns, 238
change [Exchange]
in Paris gloomy, 196
channel, British, 227
Chapin
Gurden, 170, 177
Chapline
Joseph, 84
Chapman
George, 234
John, 171
Thomas, 123

chariots, 44, 45, 54, 192, 199, 206, 211, 217, 223
duties on, 184
Charles Co., Md., 25, 26, 95, 100, 104, 123, 152, 153, 161, 172, 177, 183, 188
Charles River, 248
bridge building mishap, 248
Charles VI
loan negociated by, 214
to mortgage Silesia, 214
Charles-Town, 192, 200, 207
Charleston, 19, 20, 27, 31, 36, 37, 42, 44, 56, 62, 68, 77, 82, 92, 93, 103, 112, 121, 125, 135, 140, 148, 164, 185, 227, 238, 244, 253, 258, 261
Chamber of Commerce, 148
city council, 180
City Exchange, 148
Exchange, 56
extreme money shortage, 113
Indian treaty talks set, 62
intendants and wardens, 180
new theatre over Exchange, 56
St. Michael's church, 121
suppresses E.O. tables, 180
theatre: Am. Company opens, 56
U.S. commercial interests, 148
uniform companies forming, 258
Charleston exports
rice: 52,286 whole barrels, 184
rrice: 5,750 half barrels, 184
Charleston imports
Negroes: 2,445, 184
Charleston, S.C., 17, 52, 233
Charlestown, 172
Charlestown growth, signs:
Charles River bridge, 248
Printing Office, 248
twice-weekly newspaper, 248
charters, 85, 86, 95, 156, 206, 219, 225, 233, 234, 239, 240, 251, 256
Chase
Isaac, of Sutton, 37
J., 33
Thomas, Col., 16
Chasseurs, 20
4-horse, 46
checked muslins, 49
checks, 7, 12, 15, 58, 59, 73, 74, 79-81, 88, 98, 108, 136, 165, 170, 217
cheese, 1, 13, 22, 28, 33, 49, 64, 100, 171, 185, 197
Cheesemongers, 168
Cherbourgh
Eng. frigates, sloop hover, 227
Cherokee head warrior
account: white men, Indians, 261
Cherokees, 140, 150, 205, 261
Cherry
Capt., 172
cherry orchards, 151
Cherson, 111
docks, 2 ships, 74-guns, 241
Cheshire cheese, 64, 100
Chesley
John, 245
Rebecca, 245
Chester Parish, Md., 240
Chester-Town, Md., 17
Chesterfield
Earl of, Br. Ambassador, Madrid, 110
chests, 8, 49, 58, 68, 80, 90, 98, 108, 131, 146, 212, 246, 257, 262, 263
Chevalier de Marco Barbaro, 10
Chew
Betsy, 52
Henry, 249
John, 234
Roger, 25, 26, 35, 40, 249
Chiappo
Giovanni, corn commissary, 247
Chicamawga tribe
burned, left their towns, 37
Chicasas
principal Chief of, 205
soliciting Tenasee trade, 205
Chieftain
Scots, 208
Child
J., 126, 135
child's living relations
13 grandparents, 120 uncles, aunts, 37
Childs
Capt., 63
chimney hooks, 171
chimney pieces, 80, 85
marble, 185
chimneys, 1, 2, 80, 85, 165, 171, 224
China, 3, 56, 68, 146, 195, 210, 253
Am. trade ship reception, 87
excellent laws govern, 92
French Consul for, 87
valuable cargo from, 141
china ware, 6, 49, 80, 136, 137, 141, 159, 165, 171, 192, 230
chintz shawls, 49
chintzes, 15, 49, 58, 74, 79, 80, 99, 123, 132, 136, 151, 160, 164, 169, 170
chip hats, 99
chisels, 11, 74, 80, 81, 151, 171, 219
Chisholm
Capt., 93, 98
W., 122
Chiswick Church-Yard, 183
Chittenden
Thomas, 254
chocolate, 28, 33, 49, 52, 64, 108, 131, 137, 142, 151, 155, 156, 160, 164, 165, 169, 171, 181, 185
Chomel
Mr., 46
chopping knives, 15
Christ Church, 8
Philadelphia, 158
Christian faith, 196
Christian knowledge, 31
Christianity, 42, 45
stained by dueling, 232
Christianstadt
fortifications, 9
Christie
Capt., 93
J., 68, 93, 228
John, 234
Christmas, 130
churches, 8, 34, 42, 46, 69, 75, 85, 88, 107, 229, 255
building of gallery, 103
Chester Parish, 240
Chiswick, 183
Christ, 15, 240
Falls, 11, 218, 219, 230, 235
Lutheran, 157
Presbyterian Meeting House, 235, 245
Protestant Episcopal, 12, 23, 240
Roundhill, 170, 172, 183
St. Peter's, 240
Churchwardens, 12, 85, 90, 95, 187, 265
churchyard, 15, 183, 191
Cilley
Gen., 258
Cincinnati, Society of the
Independence Day toast, 117
Penna., new officers (list), 117
Penna., new standing committee (list), 117
cinnamon, 80, 81, 171
circulating library, 256, 257, 267
citron, 89, 197
civil list warrants, 21
claims, 8, 11, 16, 24, 35, 36, 39, 45, 48, 63, 85, 104, 109, 137, 193, 198, 215
Clairfayt
infantry regiment of, 20
claret, 2, 49, 81, 98, 103, 108, 114, 118, 122, 123, 181, 229, 266
Clark
John, 98, 101, 109
M., 68
Mark, Capt., 1, 13
Mr., 4

Richard, 234
Clark's and Christie's Introductions, 170
Clark's Corderius, 170
Clark's Homer, 170
Clarke
Alured, Gov. of Jamaica, 214
Capt., 125, 141
J., 164, 198
Clarksburgh, 104, 109, 115, 120
Clarkson
Capt., 160, 178
Matthew, 63
Thomas, 54
clasp knives, 7, 74
claw hammers, 171
clay, 235
clayed sugar, 118, 131, 156
Claypoole
A.G., 117
Mr., 17
Clearance, Vessel not wholly owned by citizen &c.--12/
Massachusetts' new tax on, 77
Cleared Outwards, 5, 10, 15, 20, 24, 28, 33, 38, 44, 48, 52, 58, 63, 68, 72, 78, 83, 88, 93, 103, 107, 114, 118, 122, 126, 130, 135, 141, 150, 155, 160, 164, 169, 176, 181, 187, 192, 198, 205, 210, 216, 222, 228, 233, 239, 249, 254, 261
Clement's Bay, Md., 69, 70
Clementson
Thomas, 234
Clendinnen
George, 30
Clergymen, 23, 41, 237
Clerks, 38, 53, 83, 84, 119, 121, 124, 126, 131, 132, 137, 165, 187, 198, 217, 239, 240, 250, 251, 265
Cleveland (Eng.)
great fall of snow, 36
Clifty Creek, 199, 207, 212
Clinton
Gen., 24
Gov., N.Y., 112
cloaks, 7, 98, 99, 229, 239
cloathing, 231
Clock makers, 40, 41, 49, 139
clocks, 40, 184, 197
hackney, tax, 247
Montgolfier, balloon, 110
Clonmell, 168
clothes, 43, 146, 255
clothes, old and new, 221
clothes, ready made, 197
clothing, 232
cloths, 7, 12, 58, 98, 103, 142, 151, 155, 160, 164, 169, 181, 192, 199, 206, 211, 217, 218, 223, 234, 239, 250, 254
coarse, 135
linen, 197
saddle, 197
woolen, 197
cloves, 80, 81, 171
Clyde, 43, 155
Clymer
George, 4, 97
coach lace, 197
coaches, 197, 223
duties on, 184
coal mine
at extremity of Gaspee Bay, 5
Coalman
Mr., 234
Coalmen, 168
coals, 47, 194, 206
coat buttons, 219
coat patterns, 251
coat straps, 151
coatings, 7, 12, 132, 146, 151, 165, 170, 211, 218, 234, 239, 250, 254, 255, 262
coats, 25, 33, 73, 89, 103, 120, 127, 131, 143, 146, 172, 176, 177, 221, 230, 232, 251, 255
Cobblers, 200
Cobelon the Lacedemonian, 121
cocks, 184
cocoa, 24
codfish, 34
codicil, 237
coffee, 8, 15, 24, 28, 29, 49, 52, 58, 64, 94, 98, 103, 156, 165, 171, 201, 252
coffee cups, 15
coffee houses, 17, 53, 77, 169, 172, 177, 183, 205, 210, 212, 219
New York, 117
coffee mills, 7, 11, 15, 80, 81, 171
coffee pots, 80, 136, 165, 171
Coffin
Francis, 234
Zachariah, 222
Cogniac brandy, 250, 254
coins, 255
Colchester, 1, 22, 83, 89, 99, 103, 193, 200, 207, 218, 219, 230
Cole
Capt., 141
T., 24
Collard
Samuel, 239
collars, 81, 171, 255
Collectors, 246, 252, 263, 265
embezzlements by, 231
College Hall (Phila.), 82
College of Nassau Hall
Vice Pres. S.S. Smith, 20
colleges (also see "schools"), 17
Colles
Thomas, 160
Collier
George, Sir, 92
Collington Meadows, 39
Collins
C., 10
Isaac, 17
M., 33
colours, painter's, ground in oil, 197
comb-brushes, 80
combs, 80, 165, 170, 197, 218, 219
horn, 185
tortoiseshell, 185
comedies
Miser, 187
Commanders, 223, 225, 235
commerce, 57, 141, 160, 215, 216
Great Britain - Ireland, 227
Jamaica-Spanish provinces, 101
laws for better regulation, 155
of America, 209
Commissaries, 38
Commissioners, 40, 41, 50, 60, 62, 63, 182, 252
Indian, 232, 261
Pennsylvanian, Indian affairs, 145
Common Sense
Thos. Payne, Author, 20
compasses, 33, 74, 136, 151, 159, 171, 258
compasses, seamen's, 197
Comptrollers, 246
Conclave of the Holy See, 214
concubines, 252
Condon
Patrick, 217, 219, 225
conestogoe-waggon, 17
confederacy (Berlin)
articles, 194
confederation (Berlin), 202
gains strength, 201
confederation of May 29
Duke of Deux Ponts, 173
Electors of Saxony, Treves, 173
France, Holland invited, 173
Kings of Prussia, Sweden, 173
Margrave of Anspach, 173
conferences
Brussels, 13
Confucious, doctrines of, 264
congo tea, 171
Congress (also see "U.S. Congress"), 38, 43, 48, 63, 78, 93, 130, 182, 186, 191, 210, 215, 216, 228, 254, 255
Livingston vice Adams, 113
Congressional Reps. (Penna.)
Bard, John, 214
Henry, William, 214
Pettit, Charles, 214

St. Clair, Arthur, 214
Wilson, James, 214
coniac, 8
coniac brandy, 24, 156
Conick Caissons
5000 workmen, 227
Duke de Harcourt presides over, 227
timber vessels for, 227
workmen paid 3 millions, 227
Conn
Gerrard T., 229, 231
Connecticut, 141, 149
Bishop of, 130
claims, Susquehanna River area, 149
earthquake, considerable shock, 259
Episcopal Church, Bishop Seabury, 117
permissive laws, villainy, 62
refuses court decree, Penna. lands, 149
Connecticut beef, 52
Connecticut frontier force
90 total to frontier, 179
Connecticut frontier force officers, 179
Bissell, Ens. David, 179
Pratt, Lt. John, 179
Strong, Capt. David, 179
Connecticut line
field officer volunteers for Holland, 23
of Continental army, 141
Connecticut pork, 52
Connicocheague valley, 2
Connoly
Thomas, 165, 170, 173
Thomas, Capt., 234
Conrad
Mathias, 234
Constables, 54, 137, 163
Constantinople, 46, 47, 75, 93, 133, 162, 194, 203, 208, 226, 241
all in motion, 226
plague in Galata, Pera, 75
Spanish, Swedish, Prussian hotels shut, 76
constellation
Andromeda, new comet, 102
constitution
arrangement, Br.-Ireland, 227
Consuls, 44
Continental Army, 123, 222
Connecticut line of, 141
Continental money, 69
Continental Officers, 25, 26, 40, 50, 60
Continental rum, 6, 11, 15, 21, 28, 38, 44, 52, 58, 63, 64, 78, 84, 88, 108, 122, 127, 131, 136, 137, 142, 151, 155, 160, 164, 169, 171, 181, 187, 198, 223, 228, 239, 254, 261
contraband trade, 139
conventions, 88
convents, 65
suppressed, effects sold, 194
convicts
marooned, killed by islanders, 43
Conway
Mr., 29, 34, 79
Richard, 14, 44, 48, 55, 69, 70, 73, 81, 82, 84, 94, 99, 100, 104, 118, 120, 127, 128, 131, 133, 142, 143, 152, 156, 157, 161, 162, 211, 219, 225
Cook
Capt., 124, 160, 194
E., 222, 233
Giles, Jr., 25, 26, 34
John, 137, 142, 143
Cook's Voyages, 119
cooking, 183, 230
Cooks, 187, 260
Cooper
Capt., 129
J., 181
coopering, 95
Coopers, 146
coopers' adzes, 80, 171
Coopers' compasses, 171
Coopers' tools, 11
Copenhagen, 173, 195
merchants stop payment, 110
Copenhagen, University of, 96
treatise, absolute government, 96
Copley
Mr., artist, 153
Copper
Cyrus, 6, 11, 24, 28, 30, 33, 35, 48, 54, 55, 58, 60, 65, 65, 69, 70, 73, 75, 75, 79, 88, 109, 110, 120
Elizabeth, 109, 110, 120
copper, 1
coining, regulating, Vermont, 140
sheet, 197
wrought, 197
copper bottom ship, 80, 82, 86
copper coffee-pots, 81
copper sauce pans, 81
copper scales, 6
copper tea-kettles, 6, 165, 74, 136, 171, 218
copper ware, 100
copper, wrought, 185
copperas, 81, 165, 171
copperplate furniture, 49, 197
Corbet
Thomas, High Bailiff, Westminster, 61
Corbin
Francis, 31
cordage, 1, 6, 7, 49, 68, 104, 113, 142, 168, 181, 182, 189, 194, 206, 211, 217, 223, 224, 266
British, 197
foreign, 197
tarred, 185
Cordell
John, 70, 71
cordelures, 49
cordials, 197
cords, 12, 58, 73, 109, 217, 218
cordureens, 58
cordurets, 58
corduroys, 6, 7, 11, 12, 15, 49, 58, 74, 79, 81, 98, 100, 132, 136, 151, 170, 217, 218, 239
Corfu, 110
Corinth, 121
Cork, 43, 107, 114, 209
cork apparatus, 238
cork rumps, 196
cork wood, 89
corks, 74, 171
corkscrews, 74
corn, 2, 7, 54, 103, 126, 139, 148, 163, 166, 167, 170, 175, 181, 187, 190-192, 194, 198, 199, 203, 235, 239, 246, 254, 261
crops good: Poland, Russia, 173
damage by storm, 118
Indian, 197
Morocco exports of, 247
corn houses, 2, 170
corn mills, 80
Cornet
Envoy Extr. from Palatine Elector, 105
Cornick
Capt., 77
Cornplanter
Chief, 144
Cornwallis's Neck, Md., 86, 91, 152, 153, 161, 172, 177, 183, 188
corporal punishment, 107
correspondence, Committee of Frederick Town, list of, 198
Cortam
Capt., 191
cosmetic washes, 196
cotton cards, 52, 185
cottons, 7, 58, 79-81, 151, 170, 171, 201, 206, 230, 243
Council
Supreme Executive, Phila., 197
Counsellor, Aulic
Van Kreutznacht, 157
Counsellors at Law, 255

Counselors, King's, 144
counterpanes, 7, 58, 80, 98, 109, 165, 217
counting rooms, 29, 44, 69, 79, 94, 132, 151, 176, 206, 212, 219, 250, 255
counting-house, 196
counting-house books, 12
Country Produce, 1, 2, 7, 22, 24, 48, 58, 68, 73, 79, 80, 82, 88, 94, 95, 100, 103, 104, 136, 137, 142, 151, 166, 167, 177, 182, 187, 192, 198, 217, 229, 239, 251, 266
country rum, 156
country stores, 81
County Clerk, 265
Courie
  Alley, Moorish King, 10
court days, 15, 33, 54, 58, 73, 118, 181
  Middlesex, 146
court houses, 8, 15, 99
  Alexandria, 8, 24, 28, 33, 48, 50, 55, 58, 64, 72, 73, 93, 99, 103, 119, 137, 160, 187, 192, 199, 206, 235, 239
  Fairfax, 15
  Fauquier, 22
  Frederick, 50
  Frederick Co., 60
  Montgomery Co., Md., 224
  old, 6
  Prince William, 40
Court of Bavaria, 10
Court of King's Bench
  Lord Earlsfort, Chief Justice, 138
court week, 40
Courtney
  John, 69, 71
courts, 35, 39
  Berkeley Co., 193
  British, 63
  chancery, 36, 39
  county, 38, 265, 266
  examination, 169
  Frederick Co., 50
  General, 38, 40, 52, 73
  records, 265
  St. James's, 145
  Superior, 40
  William, 74, 81, 85
Cove of Cork, 37
coverlets, 151
cows, 2, 116, 188, 229
Cox
  Capt., 145
  F., Sr., 165, 172, 177, 183
  Jacob, 81, 86
  Samuel, 65, 75
  Samuel, Maj., 64
  W., 150
Coxe
  Tench, 4, 97
crabs, 170
cradling, 45
Cragg
  Capt., 114, 229, 230, 235, 245
  T., 28
Craik
  James, 126, 128, 137
Craine
  John, 123, 124, 133
Cramphin
  Thomas, 84
cranberries, 1, 13
Cranham Hall, 162
crapes, 7, 48, 170, 218
crates, 7, 11, 49, 251, 266
cravats, 81
Crawford
  Adair, Dr., 19
  Capt., 24
Crayassi
  Chiaoux (secretary, 111
cream of tartar, 29
credit, 7
  Am., in England, gone, 71
  American, never so low, 27
Creek Indians, 140, 205
creeks
  Buck, 218, 219, 230
  Clifty, 199, 207, 212
  Goose, 64, 65, 75, 85, 103
  Great Hunting, 1
  Harris', 53
  Hunting, 119
  Mill, 193, 200
  Patterson's, 17
  Pawpaw, 59
  Piscataway, 146
  Powell's, 74
  Quantico, 73
  Rosier's, 170
crests, 54
crew, 10, 19, 46, 67, 106, 116, 129, 174, 176, 178, 181, 201-203, 205, 222, 225, 226, 243
  Chinese, 141
  drowned, 249
  Europeans, 141
  imprisoned, 139, 227
  in slavery, 163
  Indian, 3
  Japanese, 141
  Malays, 141
  Moors, 141
  murdered, 231
  mutiny, 128
  nearly killed with stones, 242
  saved, 238
  sick, 216
  sold at auction, 209
  with plague, 46
crewels, 170
crime, 83
Crimea, 111, 241
  hostile designs against, 92
  Russian dominions restive, 196
crimes, 258
  burglary, 169, 261
  horse stealing, 261
  murder, 88, 222, 239
  robbery, 83, 160, 165, 177, 205
  sentencing of, 238
  theft, 211
criminals convicted, 52
Croats
  20,000 march on Holland, 10
Crocket
  Benjamin, 33
  John, 33
Cromer, 36
Cromwell
  Oliver, 96
Crooks
  James, 64, 65, 75
Cropper
  John, 31
cropping, 171
crops, 78, 171, 217
crosscut saws, 11, 33, 74, 165
crows, iron, 197
Croxall
  Richard, Esq., 145
Croyden, 161, 162, 172
crude Antimony, 29
Cruisers, 5
Cruithanz, 9
cruppers, 74
Crytsinger
  Conrade, 156, 157, 167
Cuba, 173
  detachments drain island, 27
Cuba's governor
  confined, Moro Castle, 27
Cuckold's Point, 37, 163
Culpeper Co., 52, 94, 96, 137, 142, 143
Culpepper, 104, 172
Culvers, 158
Cumberland
  Mr., 237
  Mr, twits Sheridan, 71
  sheriff, 135
Cumberland Island, Ga., 77
Cunningham
  Cornelius, 234
  James, 193, 200
  Mr., State surveyor, 196
  William, 234
cupboard locks, 74, 80, 165, 171
cups, 81
cupula and gallery, 103
Curates, 140
currency, 97, 255

curricle, 184
Currie
J., Dr., 267
Curriers' knives, 171
Currituck, 185
sea breaches flooded country, 185
Curry
Mr., to Exchequer vice Foster, 195
curry combs, 7, 11, 80, 151, 165
Curry's-Bay, 74
curtain rings, 74
Curtis
Benjamin, Master (ship), 105
Chichester, 267
William, 31
Curtius, 223
cushions (hair manufactures), 197
customs, 246, 251, 252, 257, 258, 262, 263
Collectors of his Majesty's Customs, 87
customs house, 57, 220, 251
cut glass, 7, 49
cuteau knives, 81
cutlasses, 135, 174
Cutler
Manasseh, Rev., 19
Mr., 158
cutlery, 58, 73, 80, 100, 108, 132, 136, 192
cutters, 1
(Br.), off the Texel, 47
Dauphin, 9
Holland buys two, 37
Levrier, 220
of Holland, 3
Phoenix, 4
Cutters, revenue, H.M., 238
cutting-knives, 85
cutwal (magistrate), 213
cyder, 1, 13, 166, 185
Cylaeno, 14
cypress shingles, 108
cyprus, 170
Cyprus gauzes, 7

D

d'Adhemar
Comte, 263
d'Alberg
Comte, 134
D'Archarow
General, 116
D'Arcy
Mr., 9
d'Assalto
Count, Barcelona Cmdnt., 189
D'Auvergne
Capt., 20
d'Escovar
Pedro, finds St. Thomas, 190
D'Espily
M. Le Compte, mediator, 178
D'Expilly
M., Spain's peace negotiator, 243
d'Oels
Count, 13
D'Ordelin
Mons., Commodore, 87
Dade
Baldwin, 1, 11, 13, 17, 84, 250, 257, 262
Francis, 58, 61, 70, 71
Townshend, 58, 61, 70, 71
Daffy's Elixir, 84, 133, 143, 147, 152, 162, 167, 172, 177, 183, 188, 193, 200, 207, 212, 255, 262
Daggin
Peter, 234
Dahlem, 227
town and castle, 225
dairies, 193
Dalby
Philip, 73, 81, 82, 100, 104, 109, 126, 133, 138, 229, 230, 236, 255, 262, 267
Dale
Capt., 191
Dalrymple
John, 266
Damas
M., 101
Dance Teacher, 93
dancing, 141
dancing school, 12, 13
opens, 6
Dane
Nathan, 117
Daniel (Biblical), 144
Danish burying place
under Darby Square, Dublin, 66
Danube, 201, 226
Danville, Ky., 113
Dapwell
Capt., 179
Darby
E.H., Esq., 174
Darby Square
vaults, caverns, below pavement, 66
Darnal
Mr., 191
darning needles, 80
Darrell
Edward, 149
Sarah, 234
David
Richard, Col., 2
Davidson
Samuel, 84
Davis
Capt., 15
S., 15, 38, 93, 107, 164, 192
Simon, Capt., 24
Dawe
Philip, 123, 127, 128, 137
de Barre
Madame, extravagance of, 130
de Beelen Bertholff
Baron, 19
De Boiullie
M., commander, 31
M., Marischal de Broglio, 31
De Brantsen
M., 51
de Broglio
Comte and Comtesse, 4
De Chateaufort
M., Fr. Consul for the Carolinas, 56
de Choiseul
Duke, dies, 130
de Choiseul-Gouiffier
Count, Fr. Amb. to Turkey, 162
de Cisneros
Don Francisco, Admiral, 36
de Clermont
Mr. Henri, balloonist, 9
de Creutz
Baron, 9
de Crillon
M. L'Abbe, 13
de Damas
M. Le Vicomte, 101
de Dasas
Don Andrea, 14
de Fayette
Marquis, 248
de Finkenstein
Count, to Potsdam, 168
de Guichen
"le pere des matelots", 220
Comte, two sons lost, 220
Count, 19
de Guichen, Count
LtGen., French Naval Armies, 19
de Harcourt
Duke, 227
de Herbert
Baron, 134
de Kalatchow
M., Russian Envoy Extr. to Hague, 46
de la Briche
Sieur Lalive, 130
De la Peitra
M., Spanish Intendant, 189

de la Vauguyon
Duke, 130
de Laleyn, 134
de Lascy
Mareschal, 42
De Leyden
recalled from Vienna, 221
de Ligne
Prince, General, 3
Prince, Gov. of Antwerp, 195
de Ligondes
Commodore, 190
de Lyden
M., Envoy Extr., Rep. of Holland, 208
de Maillebois
Compte delays departure, 61
Comte, Breda Governor, 246
M., to command States General forces, 31
De Marbois
M., new Intendant, St. Domingo, 159
de Merci
Count, 31
de Mercy
Comte, 42
Count, 51, 227
de Montcalm
Marquis, letter from Quebec, 154
de Noailles
Marquis, 162
de Peyrouse
M. Le Comte, explorer, 124
De Reischach
Austria's Hague envoy, 14
Baron, recall of, 13
Envoy Extr., 2
De Rochambeau
M., van guard commander, 31
de Rohan
Cardinal, charges ill founded, 214
Cardinal, imprisoned, 213
De Romain
M., ballonist, 183
de Roquefeuille
Vicomte, 220
de Rozier
M. Pilatre, ballonist, 183
de Segur
Marquis, 51
De Soulange
M., 190
de Staremberg
M. De Wassenaar, Dutch Amb. to Russia, 46
de Steinfeld
Truber, Capt., 46
de Trautmansdorff
Count, Aust. Amb. to Mentz, 168
De Vergennes, 51
Comte, 226
Comte, revolutionary, 129
Count, 18
Mons., policies prevail, 31
De Waffenaar
Dutch Minister, Vienna, 214
recalled from Vienna, 221
De Zespedes
Excellency Don Vincent Emanuel, Gov. East Florida, 77
Deacons, 179
dead letters, 234
Deakins
William, 41, 49
William, Jr., 15, 18, 23, 40, 41, 50, 53, 84, 85
Dean
Stewart, 181
Stewart, Cmdr., 253
death, 82
death-head buttons, 49, 151, 165
deaths, 141, 145, 160, 164, 245
Abergavenny, Lord, 220
Andrews, Benjamin, 102
Bauham, S., male bastard child of, 135
Baxter, Daniel, 43
Baynes, John, 130
Bell, Capt., 93
Brent, William, 102
Brown, Joseph, 249
Brown, Windsor, 93
Buchanan, Archibald, 145
Buffy, Mon., 148
by drowning, 27, 63
by suicide, 77
Casey, Mrs., 155
Chew, Henry, 249
child, by fire, 264
Collard, Samuel, 239
Copper, Cyrus, 88
De la Pietra, M., 189
Drew, William, 198
Duke de Choiseul, 130
Ellis, John, 72
Frankland, Ann, 242
Frankland, Miss, 243
Gallagher, Mr., 260
Gibney, Hugh, 72
Gill, John, Capt., 159
Hardy, Samuel, Hon., 191
Holmes, James C., 155
Hopkins, Stephen, Hon., 141
Indian hunter, 145
James, Reuben, 130
Jenifer, Walter H., Dr., 245
Johnson, William, 163
Keaton, Maurice, 37
Lamely, William, 155
Lordan, John, 145
Louis, Don, 195
Mackay, James, 222
Malaysian, Robert, Maj., 19
Manley, Sarah, 181
Mayo, Joseph, 126
Moore, Mr., 114
Negro, by inoculation, 134
O'Rourke, Count, 96
officers of Col. Lewis, 145
Oglethorpe, James, Gen., 162
Oswald, Richard, 14
Pancas, Miss, 160
Parker, Mr., 112
Parsons, James, Capt., 5
Potts, Ruth, Mrs., 261
Pratt, Shubael, Dr., 141
Prince Bishop of Lubeck, 168
Queen of Sardinia, 241
Ramsay, Ann, 48
Ramsay, Sally Douglass, 216
Ramsay, William, 15
Rozier, Mr., balloonist, 183
Sackville, Lord Viscount, 237
Sawyer, T., 47
Selden, Miles, Rev., 48
Shugars, Martin, 239
Stevenson, John, Dr., 43
Sullivan, Gen., premature, 228
Sullivan, John, Hon., 222
Taylor, Mr., 254
Trumbull, Jonathan, 155
Twentyman, Thomas, 37
Wall, William, 216
West, Mrs., 130
West, Nancy, 181
Wilkinson, Elizabeth, 265
Wilson, Goodrich, 239
Woods, John, Capt., 58
Debilleneuve
French Consul, Marmora, 128
debts, 57, 63, 88, 90, 137, 138, 166, 171, 198, 210, 216, 219, 223, 225, 240, 250, 266, 267
American Continental or State, 27
continental, (U.S.) paying, 51
domestic, 208
public, 208
decanters, 81
deceased, 72
Alexander, John, 126, 132, 138, 143, 152, 157, 161, 167, 172, 176, 177, 188
Andre, John, 107
Barnes, Abraham, 104, 109, 110, 116
Brent, William, 59
Burwell, Robert, 171, 173, 183
Chapman, Thomas, 123
Copper, Cyrus, 109, 110, 120
Cunningham, James, 193, 200
Dade, Francis, 58

Douglass, William, 24, 126
Gibney, Hugh, 104, 109, 110
Hall, Jonathan, 235
Hawkins, George F., 198, 207, 212
Kirkpatrick, 95
Kirkpatrick, Thomas, 24, 85, 91, 100, 132, 133, 143, 152, 157, 161
Lowndes, Christopher, 48, 55, 60
Magruder, Thomas, 82
Mills, John, 118, 124, 127
Monroe, John, 256, 262
Noland, Philip, Jr., 166, 167, 177
Nourse, James, 172, 173, 183, 224
Ogle, Benjamin, 45, 54, 60, 64
Ramsay, William, 103
Reed, Joseph, 63
Richardson, Thomas, 122
Rigg, Richard, 136, 138
Rowand, Thomas, 235, 240
Rumney, William, Dr., 24
Scott, J., 166, 167, 177
Scott, James, 16
Southard, William, 126, 133, 138
Stubblefield, Thomas, 53
Tayloe, John, 210
Taylor, John, 219, 225
Tebbs, Foushee, 73, 86
Thornton, John, 8
Wood, John, 104, 109, 110
Deep Bay hurricane tally
5 ships on shore, lost, 178
houses, estates suffered much, 178
Deep Bay, St. Kitt's, 178
deepsea lines, 1
defendants, 222
Degeau
Charles, 59, 61, 70
Deity, 83
Dekay
Capt., 93
del Alter presidency
gold mine discovered, 140
Delafield
William, 52
Delaplain
William, 160
Delaware, 240, 261
abolished all fairs, 113
delegates, 210, 222, 228, 234, 266
delf bowls, 1
delf ware, 239
Delhi
King of, 129
Delleck
Pierre Gustavus, Cmdr., 139
Delon
John, 127
delures, 58
Demarara, 205, 228
houses, stores burned, 254
Demarara spirits, 156
demities, 12, 58, 59, 73, 74, 79, 81, 108
denims, 7, 49, 73, 109, 151
Denmark, 121
Flora Danica, 97
his Majesty, 173
Prince Royal , matrimony, 195
Prince Royal, Br. princess, 207
Prince Royal, England visit, 207
Denmark peacetime
land forces: 67,000, 61
Denmark tablecloths, 170
Dennison
Capt., 83, 191, 249
J., 83, 93
Denny
Capt., 63
W., 63
Dentmeister
infantry regiment of, 20
deputations, 84
Derby
Lord, 139
supreme silk machine, 252
deserts
Suez, 66
deserters, 252
badged as criminals, 231
branded, 231
life exile, Africa coast, 231
life exile, East Indies, 231
new Br. resolutions , 231
perpetual stoppages, 231
desertion, penalties for
cofining in cellars, 252
India Company's, 252
perpetual slavery, 252
shooting, 252
transporting, 252
Deshon
D., 68
desk furniture, 16, 80, 165
desk mountings, 171
desks, 175, 177
Dessausure
Mr., 149
Detroit, 91, 144, 145
Deutschmeister, 46
Deutz, 221
Deux Ponts
Duke of, 147, 173
Duke of, heir to Bavaria Elector, 76
Deveau
Mons., cmdg. Fr. packet, 56
devil, 125
DeWitt
T., 17
Diamond
James, 67
diamonds, 71
and gold coin dug up, 147
diapason
finger organ, 59
diaper tablecloths, 15, 28, 100
diapers, 11, 15, 33, 80, 170, 218
Diaz
Bartholomew, 190
dice, 121
Dick
Elisha C., 22, 26, 30, 40, 54, 55, 60, 69
George, 212
Dickinson
John, 117
dictionary, 136
die-sinking tools, 236
dies
for horn buttons, 236
Digges
George, 84
Dillon
Count, 76
Dilworth
Mr., 161
dimities, 28, 100, 132, 136, 165, 170
dipped candles, 181
directories, 255, 262, 267
Directors, 84, 94, 96, 101, 131, 133, 143, 152, 182, 188, 193, 198, 200, 255, 261
dishes, 15, 81
distichal panegyrics, 16
ditchers, 122
Divan, 162
Turkish, 134
dividends, 96
dividers, 33
divinity, 136
divorce, 200
Dobson
Mr., 187
Doctors (also see "Physicians"), 19, 20, 237, 253
Dogherty
John, 234
dogs, 213
dogskin gloves, 74
Dogwood-Plains, 44
Dolgorwsky
Prince, Russian Minister, Berlin, 111
dollars, Spanish, 168
Dom tower, 201
domestics
Arch Treasurer's, 207
Dominica storm losses
4 small craft run on shore, 179
5 vessels, all aboard lost, 179

gov. sloop run on shore, 179
Donaldson
John, 193, 200, 207, 212
Mr., 193
Robert, 108, 110, 120
Samuel, 234
Donetgtchle, 201
Dorset
Duke of, 56, 76, 237
Dorsey, 198
Joshua, 198
dorseys, 81
double-ironed planes, 11
Doughty
Major, 232
Douglas
Comm., 134
John, 54
Douglass
Hugh, 25, 26, 34, 126, 128
John St. Ledger, Esq., 178
William, 24-26, 34, 126, 128
Dove
Capt., 191
dovecote, 125
Dover, 5, 51, 169, 226
Dow
Peter, 146, 147, 157
Dowdall
James G., 152, 217, 219, 225
Dowe
Gen., 258
dowelling mills, 80
dower, 156, 167, 177
dowlas, 1, 6, 7, 11, 15, 49, 80, 98, 146, 170
Downs (the Downs), 105, 125, 246
Doyle
Alexander, 199, 207, 212, 255, 262, 267
drab hats, 88
drabs, 218, 255
dragoons, 3
drapery, 259
drawboys, 79, 170
drawer locks, 80
drawing knives, 11, 80, 151
drawings, 85
Draymen, 63
drays, 181, 192, 199, 206, 266
Drayton
Charles, Esq., 37
dress, ladies
association to regulate, 157
Dresser, 34
dressing, 126
Drew
William, 84, 198
drillings, 80, 151
Droughers
[West Indian coastal craft], 179
Droughers [droghers], 179
drownings, 114
drugs, 126, 128, 137, 201
drum lines, 171
Drummond
Lord Lewis, 26
drums, 214
dry goods, 1, 8, 15, 23, 24, 28, 48, 55, 64, 68-70, 73, 81-83, 94, 98, 99, 103, 105, 108, 109, 114, 115, 118, 122, 127, 131, 137, 142, 151, 155, 160, 164, 166, 167, 169, 176, 181, 192, 199, 206, 207, 211, 212, 217-219, 223, 225, 230, 234, 250, 254, 266
Duab
charnel house, described, 213
half the inhabitants dead, 213
Dublin, 9, 14, 18, 63, 66, 67, 93, 96, 101, 138, 148, 168, 173, 206, 238, 261
Attorney General, tyrant, 67
built environment improves, 148
Counselor Caldbeck, 19
Counselor Sheridan, 19
Danish burying place, 66
High Sheriff, 18
no hackney coaches, 247
Recorder Hussey, 19
the Castle Hacks, 19
Trinity College, 20
University of, 196
William Street conference, 9
ducal coronet, 54
Duche
J., Rev., 158
duck, 49
Dudley
Frances, 93
duels, 200, 231
account of, 121
non-fatal, wry account, 158
dueling
Penna. Legislature against, 232
stain on Christianity, 231
dueling (a moral tale), 71
Duffield
John, 234
duffils, 15, 146, 151, 170, 217, 218, 224, 239
Duke of Bedford
and Nancy Parsons, 158
lives retired at Nancy, 158
Dukes
C., 187
Dulany
Benjamin, 84, 187
Mary, 45, 50, 54, 60
Dulin
Edward, 24
Dumfries, 1, 7, 16, 17, 22, 29, 30, 39-41, 45, 49, 50, 54, 58, 60, 61, 64, 65, 70, 74, 75, 86, 89, 90, 98, 99, 104, 109, 110, 115, 120, 123, 127, 128, 137, 156, 166, 171, 176, 177, 181, 198, 207, 212, 217, 234
Dumoulin
Maj. Gen., 3
Duncan
P., 114, 192, 249
Duncanson
Capt., 173-175
James, 172, 177, 183
James, Master (ship's), 159
Dundas
John, 48, 81, 86, 91, 94, 100, 104, 136-138, 211, 217, 219, 225
Mr., 5
Mr., politics of, 220
dunghills, 196
Dunham
Capt., 141, 192
G., 24, 63
Dunkirk, 10, 139
seizes Am. ship, crew, 139
Dunlap
James, 211
Mr., 17
Dunmore
Lord, Gov. of Jamaica, 96
Dunn
Capt., 107, 195
Robert, 234
S., 20, 78
Dunstable hats, 99
durant quilts, 218
durants, 7, 12, 59, 81, 98, 100, 136, 146, 151, 165, 170, 218, 230
Durham mustard, 219, 229
Duriez
Mr., 183
Durisian
William, 107
duroys, 79, 81, 170
Dutch, 14, 21, 222
Dutch blankets, 11
Dutch calicoes, 218
Dutch captains
getting burgessoises, 4
Dutch cordage, 1
Dutch cords, 58
Dutch East India
company, no dividend, 124
Dutch fleet
at the Texel, suspect, 47
fitting out at Texel, 4
Dutch gin, 15
Dutch lace, 7
Dutch linens, 15
Dutch Oriental Company
recruits by kidnapping, 247
Dutch ovens, 52, 136, 151, 251

Dutch pictures, 68
Dutch Quills, 2, 12, 17, 218
Dutch ships, 176
Dutch skippers, 68
Dutchmen, 192
duties, 38, 154, 181
  foreign oil, 149
  import, Penna., schedule of, 184
  inland, 61
  luxury articles imposts, 153
  Maryland imports, exports, 188
  Massachusetts impost law, 155
  Massachusetts, on imports [list], 197
  oil, 203
  on advertisements, 149
  rum, 83
  tea, 83
Duvall
  William, 103, 234
dwelling houses, 1, 2, 24, 25, 54, 55, 60, 75, 80, 89, 94, 98, 104, 115, 151, 166, 170, 182, 218, 224, 229, 250
  for rent, 108, 118, 120, 193, 200, 207
  for sale, 120, 124, 126, 128, 138
  log, 224
Dyer
  Christopher, Capt., 102
Dyers, 34, 40, 45
dying stuffs, 192
Dyk
  Mungo, 234
Dymond
  Daniel, 234

E

E.O. tables, 180
Earl of Egremont, 104
Earle
  William, Jr., Capt., 20
Earlsfort
  Lord, 138
earrings, 74
earthen ware, 49, 80, 100, 159, 165, 192, 229
earthquakes, v, 245
East Florida
  Indians incensed at Spain, 130
  settlers discontent, 130
East Grinstead, 237
East Hampton, L.I., 259
East India , 201
East India Company, 56, 121, 129, 158, 178
  a puff Ministerial, 3
  British 'sacrum sancrorum', 158
  officers in service, 18
East Indiaman (Dutch)
  filled with soldiers, 246
East Indiaman (ship)
  (unk.) American, 168
East Indiamen
  4, richly laden, safe, 225
East Indies, 10, 56, 189
  American ships barred, 158
  French ships to, 189
East Indies (Fr.), 139
East-India Goods, 6, 33, 98, 101, 109
Eastern Shore (Md.) College bill, 188
Ecclesiastical Court
  to try lady's licentious conduct, 163
Ecluse, 3
Ede on Weluwe, 201
Eden
  Mr., 92
edge tools, 51
edgings, 7, 58, 170
Edie
  Mr., Kingston Custom Hse., 191
Edinburgh, 210, 219, 225
  civic, Masonic ceremony, 189
  Magistrates, 190
  Rt. Hon. the Lord Provost, 190
  shopkeepers resist shop tax, 221
  South bridge foundation stone, 189
Editors, 5
Edmonds
  Edmund, 90, 91, 98
  Thomas (of Sussex), 31
education, 5, 31, 80
Edwards
  Mr., 22
Effingham
  Lord, to Am. as Ambassador, 158
Egypt, 66, 208
  "onions and garlic of", 173
  banished nobles mount coup, 111
  tribute paid Grand Seignior, 75
Egyptian prunes, 170
Elbinge, 4
Elders, 31
elections, 14, 83, 265
  Westminster, 195
electrical fluid, 264
Elk-Ridge landing, 64, 70, 75
Elk-Run, 22, 23, 30
Elles
  Capt., 125
Ellicot
  Andrew, Esq., 19
  Sir John, 237
Ellicott's Almanack, 198, 207
Elliot
  Charles, 187
Elliot the immortal
  at Gibralter, 66
Elliot's stripes, 58
Elliott
  G.A., Sir, 111
Ellis
  John, 72
  Mr., politics of, 220
Ellwood
  J., 63, 130, 160, 164, 192, 198
Ellzey
  Lewis, 17, 18, 26, 30, 34, 35, 41, 49, 54
  William, 84
Elsineur, 110, 195
  Castle, 195
  Russian squadron arrives, 195
Elton
  Isabella, 25, 26
Elwell
  Capt., 66
Elwood
  J., 83, 103, 114
emancipation, 245
embezzlements
  by collectors, 231
emetic tartar, 2
emetics, 154
emigrants, 59
  saved at sea, 43
  tax upon, consequences, 66
emigration, 208
Emo
  Chevalier, 9, 18, 46, 47, 194
  Chevalier, bombards Sufa, 231
  Chevalier, Venetian fleet cmdr., 110
Emperors, 3, 5, 14, 93
Emperor at Morocco, 180, 181
Emperor of Morocco, 43, 83
employment, 12, 25, 28-30, 35, 40, 44, 55, 60, 64, 65, 70, 75, 91, 131, 137, 138, 142, 143, 152, 157, 182, 188, 192, 193, 199, 200, 207, 217, 230, 239, 240, 251, 267
Empress of China, 146
  Canton salute fatality, 92
Empress of Russia
  depredations in Turkey, 208
Enfield, Eng., 254
engineering
  military, 3
Engineers, 3, 195
engines
  covering of whips, 236
  drilling, 236
  fire, 253
  for chasing, 236
  scoring or shading, 236

England (also see "Great Britain"), 9, 12, 32, 33, 73, 74, 77, 104, 105, 108, 109, 115, 117, 118, 120, 121, 124, 128, 130, 131, 133, 138, 144, 147, 151, 152, 155, 157, 158, 161, 167, 168, 191, 204, 215, 240, 251, 252, 254
fleet to support Austria, 37
Parliament meets on trade, 14
peace Commissioner to Versailles, 14
repeal of navigation act, 14
St. James's, 10
English Channel, 141
English Chronicle, The, 183
English Cordage, 1
English Islands, 155
English Language, 1, 12, 22
English persians, 74
English servants, 16, 18, 23
English steel, 81
English sugar, 29
English thread, 49
engraving, 40
Enkhuysen
2 cavalry companies, 2
entertainments, 231
epigrams, 16
Episcopal
Clergy convention, ordinations at, 149
Episcopal Church, 249
burnt to the ground, 130
Connecticut, 117
Scotland, 117
Episcopal churchyard, 15
Episcopal Convention, 240
Episcopalians, 45
epitaphs, 16
epodes, 16, 22, 26
epsom salts, 2, 29
Erman
Capt., 191
ermine, 218
Ervin
Capt., 176, 180, 186
Ervine
James, Capt., 93
escutcheons, 171
Esopus, 144
Essex, 162
Etherige
A., 141
Euclidian principles, 67
Europe, 12, 35, 40, 45, 57, 70, 73, 78, 80, 86, 91, 123, 136, 141, 165, 206, 215, 220
general war threatens, 214
leading men, 208
peacetime land forces [list], 61
vessels to, 5
European continent
political fermentation (described), 91
European Goods, 6-8, 12, 13, 18, 22, 24, 28, 29, 49, 50, 52, 60, 73, 81, 82, 90, 91, 98-101, 109, 136, 138, 146, 147, 156, 157, 162, 166, 167, 172, 182, 187, 188, 193, 200, 229-231, 240
Eustace
John Skey, Col., 93
Eutropius, 170
Evans
Alexander, mutineer, 159
Elijah, 198
Ephraim, 187, 193, 200
George, 234
Joel, 249
John, 230, 231, 240
Mary, 137, 138, 147
Robert, 234
Evens
Alex, 174
Everest
Richard, 146, 151, 157
Everige
M., 141
everlastings, 151
Ewart
Robert, Capt., 37
exchange, 6, 11, 15, 21, 24, 28, 38, 40, 44, 48, 52, 54, 58, 59, 61, 63, 70, 78, 84, 85, 88, 90, 95, 104, 108, 122, 131, 136, 141, 142, 156, 160, 165, 169, 181, 187, 192, 198, 199, 206, 218, 223, 224, 228, 239, 254, 261
executions, 203, 252
for piracy and murder, 163
hanged by the neck, 258
exiles, 203
exports, 43, 57, 78, 101, 141, 173, 184, 185, 188, 190, 235, 236, 241, 245, 247, 254, 263
expresses, 3, 4
Eyre
Lyttleton, 31

F

fables, 16, 267
Fabrit
Francis, 6, 12, 13
faction, Butean, 149
Fairfax
Bryan, 234
Fairfax Co., 1, 6, 13, 15, 17, 22, 33, 35, 39, 53-55, 59, 64, 79, 99, 104, 109, 119, 121, 124, 161, 181, 206, 224, 225, 229, 231, 235, 236, 245, 255, 262
Fairfax Parish, 11
Falcon
Birket, 234
Fallen
Dr., 17
Falls
John, 255, 262, 267
falls (water), 10, 40, 41, 49, 53, 64, 94, 99, 131, 152, 177
Falls Church, 11, 218, 219, 230, 235
Falls of Potomack, 40, 41, 49
Falmouth, 20, 28, 43, 52, 107, 121, 142, 143, 152, 165, 191, 217, 227, 228, 248
incorporation, (discussed), 227
packets' free transport, Am. indigents, 37
Falmouth (N.E.), 102
Falmouth Races, 142, 182, 188
falsehoods, 12, 18, 26, 36, 44, 74, 82, 115, 216
Falstaff, 184
famine, 196
shocking consequences of, 213
fanegas, 247
Faneuil hall
Merchants, Traders, meeting, 72
fans, 6, 58, 81, 126, 136
Fanshaw
G., 20
Farmers, 10, 57, 173
farming, 7, 170, 171, 176, 199, 224
farming utensils, 2, 229
farms, 22, 53, 99, 146, 153, 161, 170, 177
for sale, 75, 81, 82, 89, 91, 94, 100, 235, 240
Faro, 184
Farris
Capt., 67
fashion, 68, 170
fast
appointed on Conn., 42
Fauquier Co., 22, 23, 30, 59, 99, 104, 109, 130
Faw
Abraham, 84
Fayal
asks Am. famine relief, 197
great distress for provisions, 197
Fayal wine, 266
Fayette
Marquis de la, 149, 154
Fayette Co., 177
Fe??rd
[Irish town, county, or district], 168
fearnoughts, 15, 151, 170
feathers, 22, 99, 125

worn as ornament, 197
Federal Court
adjudicates NY-Mass. controversy, 56
Fell
S., 222, 254
Fellows
Capt., 258
felt hats, 7, 49, 81, 103, 123, 131, 146, 218
fences, 1, 2, 103, 176, 224
fencing, 200, 224, 250
Fenner
William, 234
Fennings
Mr., 161
Fenwick
Ignatius, 234
Ferguson
Capt., 47
Cumberland, 234
Robert, 234
Fergusson
Robert, 122, 127
Ferochabad, 213
ferrets, 7, 81, 170
ferries, 250
Addison's, 206, 212
Alexandria, 119
Harper's, 73
Hawkins's, 75
Hooe's, 53, 126, 128, 137
Keys', 73
Noland's, 166, 167, 177
public, 79
Snickers's, 256
wharf, 136
ferry landings, 54
festivities, 231
fiddle strings, 170
fig-blue, 74
figs, 49
files, 80, 136, 151, 165, 171, 218
fillister planes, 11
Filson
John, 84, 86, 95
finance, 141
financiers, 153
finger organs, 59
Finley
C., 150
fire engine, 253
fire places, 2, 104, 169, 176, 193, 199, 212, 250, 266
fires, 141
Adam's bake house, 210
Horsely Down, Eng., 126
kills child, 264
fish, 24, 71, 127, 170, 174, 249
ballaho, 134
blue fish, 134
cockles, 134
dried, 185
flounders, 134
muscles (mussels), 134
Newfoundland, 209
salted, 185
sea bass, 134
sea trout, 134
skate, 134
tusk, 134
fish hooks, 74, 151, 170
fisheries, 14, 35, 71, 99, 199
for rent, 25, 26
whale, 203
Fishermen
Am., driven from Newfoundland, 134
fishing, 107, 232
Grand Bank of Newfoundland, 107
fishing seines, 98
Fitz-James
Duke, 226
Marechal Duke, 226
Fitzgerald
Col., 17, 29, 30, 40, 131, 133, 143, 177, 239, 240, 251
John, 11, 14, 53, 78, 84, 94
John, Col., 234
Fitzgubon
Matthew, 234
Fitzhugh
John T., 60, 65, 70
Mr., 60
Peregrine, 2, 9, 18, 25, 26, 35
Thomas, 234
William, 7, 12, 13, 26, 30, 90, 95, 96, 104, 109, 115, 120, 124, 127, 132, 138, 143, 147, 152, 157, 162, 191, 192, 234
Fitzsimons
Mr., 97
Thomas, 4
flagellation, 231
flags, 43
Flaker
Sarah, 234
Flanders, 3, 4, 9, 96, 129
boundaries of, 226
Count of, 14
Fr. 20,000 man camp, 76
newly Austrian troops dispatched, 247
troops for, victualling, 18
Flanders (Fr.), 82
40,000 man camp ended, 162
Flanders bedticking, 218
Flanders sheetings, 170
flannels, 1, 7, 11, 151, 165, 170, 218, 224, 239
Flannery
Jeremiah, 33, 35, 45
flasks
and boards for, 236
flat irons, 171
flats, 198
flaxseed, 93, 156, 206
fleets
East India, 201
Roman, 184
West India, 201
Fleming
Mr., 234
Thomas, 182, 188, 193
Flemings
dance to the lascivious flute, 221
flesh forks, 251
Fletcher
James, 234
Flood
Mr., 55, 195
flooring nails, 251
Florence, 18
Duchess of Albany's reception, 18
Grand Duke, Duchess, 18
Pretender's residence, 18
Florence oil, 123
florentines, 15, 49, 58, 99
Florida, 27
cedeing to Spain, benefits, 163
may rupture United States, 163
flour, 6, 8, 11, 15, 18, 21, 24, 28, 34, 38, 44, 49, 52, 58, 63, 67, 69, 71, 78, 84, 88, 108, 112, 122, 127, 131, 136, 142, 148, 156, 160, 169, 170, 179, 181, 182, 185, 187, 190, 192, 197, 198, 206, 209, 223, 224, 228, 233, 239, 249, 254, 255, 261
flower of sulphur, 29
flowers, 99
worn for ornament, 197
Floyd
Col., 113
fluid, electrical, 264
Flushing, 9
flutes, 256
fodder, 2, 166, 167, 170, 199, 235
Foley
Daniel, Tipperary rep., 168
Folger
Capt., 226
folly
of the times, excessive; results, 169
Fonerden
Adam, 236, 245
foolscap [paper], 59
Forbes
David, 58, 61, 65
F., Dr., 134
Mr., ship owner, 178

Ford
George, 51
fore chains, 238
fore planes, 11
Foreign Clearance--9d
Massachusetts' new tax on, 77
foreign rum, 197
Foreman
Benjamin, 8
forests, 5
forges, 3
forging mills for iron, copper
cast iron anvils, hammers for, 236
forks, 7, 15
Forman
John, 33, 40, 45, 86, 91, 95, 100, 104
Fornerden
Adam, 235
Forster
Mr., "Irish Minister", 148
fort (general)
Spanish, 191
Spanish, in No. Car., 43
Fort Cumberland, Md., 44, 104, 109
Forthingham
Mr., 179
fortifications
Christianstadt, 9
Landscron, 9
fortresses, 194
banks of the Scheldt, 221
Maestricht, 225
forts, 91, 138, 204
Algièrs, 202
Br., Spanish seek surrender, 37
Cruithanz, 9
Dutch, 32
Frederick Henry, 96
Frederik Henrik, 226
Kruischans, 96, 226
Leiskenshoek, 226
Liefkenshoek, 96
Lillo, 4, 9, 10, 96, 226
Muscle Shoals, No. Car., 37
M'Intosh, 19, 67, 232
Pitt, 144, 149, 196, 222, 232
Point Pleasant, 145
San Isadore, 112
Scheldt, demolished, 154
Stoitagre, 9
Foster
Capt, 52
J., 10, 239, 261
found
bolt of osnaburgs, 2
box, 165, 170, 173
horse, 123, 167
horses, 94, 96, 146, 156, 157, 217, 219, 223, 225, 230, 235
Negro man, 193
saddle, 211, 219, 220
Four Indians Pass, 153
Four Mile Run, 119, 235
fowl, 170, 199
Fowler
John, 52, 238
fowling pieces, 7, 49
Fox, 92
Mr., 92
Mr., and Empire, 71
fox-dog, 213
frails, 49
France, 3, 6, 31, 43, 48, 105, 129, 130, 141, 147, 164, 187, 201, 204, 223, 225, 235
10,000 troops to Hispaniola, 221
30,000 man camp vs. Belgrade, 65
30,000 men in Moravia, 65
32 more men, cavalry regt., 227
40,000 troops for Holland, 10
60,000 men to Low Countries, 31
7 ships, 1500 men sail for East Indies, 56
70 million livres West Indies trade, 129
70,000 men at Colin, 65
Algiers' French captives, 202
Am.-Fr. trade arbitrators, 149
armed neutrality policy, 130
artillery horses released, 195
assistance to Dutch, 32
augmenting army, 221
Br. goods arrêt unpopular, 220
British flag insult, 227
British-French war, 195
cannot desert Dutch, 51
Cape Nicola Mole King's port only, 66
Cardinal de Rohan jailing, 213
champion the Dutch, 4
confederation invitation, 173
Court of Versailles, 9, 10, 65
cultivation of science, 226
Dauphin, 66
De Vergennes's politics prevail, 31
Dutch forces to transit, 61
eleven sail off Finisterre, 214
Emperor's reception prepared, 148
equipping fleets, 221
explorer de Peyrouse, and King, 124
extension of commerce, 226
fitting out 8 war ships, 55
fitting out Brest warships, 47
Fr. Ambassador, St. James, 263
Fr.-Am. bonds of union, 149
French Naval Armies, 19
French-English prejudices, 204
Great Britain, French version, 101
institutions for distress, 226
intercession, support, 227
King bans Voltaire book, 159
King emancipated Scots, Irish, 32
King mediates peace talks, 178
King protecting States General, 32
King receives balloon clock, 110
King receives T. Jefferson, 130
King to mediate, 214
King, Queen make balloon flight, 144
King's letter re: La Fayette, 154
King's letter to the Emperor, 76
King's interference with Austria, 18
La Fayette, 204
Louis XV, 130
Louis XVI, 204
mediation rejected by Austria, 32
merchant ship convoying, 125
morals, religion endangered, 159
Most Christian Majesty, 4, 226
naval personnel policy, 14
navy formidability sought, 227
negotiations with Great Britain, 201
not taking part, 42
offspring of King James, 226
Parliament of Paris, 154
peacetime land forces, 61
positions blocks vs. Austria, Prussia, 65
Prince born: Duke of Normandy, 92
Queen disapproves foreign policy, 20
Queen helps insolvent gambler, 147
Queen receives T. Jefferson, 130
Queen, German Emperor are siblings, 65
revolution in Ministry, 20
seeks navy formidability, 227
ships to Cape Breton, 180
silk manufactories, 252
smuggling nullifies arrêt, 220
spies in Ireland, 184
subjects, and United Provinces armies, 194
the arbitress of Europe, 56
to assist the Dutch, 91
to supply 25,000 men, 4
troops to French Flanders, 82
Vergennes favors Holland, 20
Versailles, Br. Amb. decamps, 196
West India fortifications, 196

France, new free ports
Guadaloupe: Point au Petre, 247
Hispaniola: Cape Francois, 247
Hispaniola: Cayet St. Louis, 247
Hispaniola: Port au Prince, 247
Tobago: Scarborough, 247
Francis
Frederick Eugene, 19
Franckfort, 46
Frankfort, Pa., 118
Frankfurt, 46
Frankland
Ann, 242
William, Rev., 242
Frankland, new state of, 140, 205
and Federal Government, 180
and North Carolina, 180
Congress' reception satisfies, 180
election of Assemblymen, 180
General Assembly meets, 180
Governor Martin's manifesto, 180
Kentuckians debate separation, 180
Martin's manifesto derided, 180
new Assembly's actions, 180
progress report for, 180
resolved on separation, 180
Va. Executive's measures against, 180
Franklin
B., President, Supr. Exec. Council, 197
B., Supreme Exec. Council, 197
Benjamin, Dr., 31, 48, 139, 149, 160, 164, 169, 175, 180
Benjamin, Dr., portrait, 154
Chief of Philosophers, 259
Counsellor, Phila., 197
Susannah, 49, 50, 60
Franks, 75
Fraser
Mr., 263
Frazer
J., 93, 114
John, 97
Frederick Co., 7, 12, 17, 22, 50, 52, 59, 69, 75, 81, 82, 118, 136, 138, 156, 166, 167, 171, 177, 216, 224, 229, 235, 240, 250, 256, 261, 267
Frederick of Prussia
ill, excruciating gout, 247
Frederick Parish, 52
Frederick Town
Committee of correspondence members, 198
manufacturers, gents., letter from, 198
tradesmen, mfrs.' petition, 228
Frederick, Lord Carlisle, 228
Frederick-Town, 2, 44, 83, 224
Fredericksburg, 7, 17, 20, 22, 28-30, 40, 44, 45, 49, 50, 59-61, 70, 89-91, 94, 99, 100, 147, 172, 177, 183, 187, 205, 211, 217-219, 230, 236
Fredericksburg Jockey Club, 142, 143, 152
Free Masons, 15, 101
Brethren, Royal Arch, 175
Brethren, Sublime Lodge, 175
Brother Benjamin Franklin, 175
Brother George Washington, 175
Brother Inspector, 175
Brother King of Prussia, 175
Brother Orator, 175
Deputy, 175
German elector hostile towards, 237
Grand Lodge of Pennsylvania, 175
Grand Master, 175
Grand Master of America, 175
Invited Brethren, 175
Junior Sublime Warden, 175
Lodge consecration: toasts (listed), 175
Lodge Room, 175
Master of Ceremonies, 175
New Lodge, 175
Officers, Lodge No. 2, 175
Officers, Lodge No. 3, 175
Officers, Lodge No. 4, 175
Officers, Lodge No. 8, 175
Officers, Lodge No. 9, 175
Past Masters, 175
St. John's Day celebration, 249
Sublime Lodge, Phila., consecration, 175
Sublime Secretary, 175
Sublime Senior Sublime Warden, 175
Sword Bearer, 175
The Thrice Puissant, 175
Treasurer, 175
Tyler, 175
Free Masons (N.Y.)
Brethren, 259
Chaplain, 259
Deputy Grand Master, 259
Grand Jun. Warden, 259
Grand Lodge Pursuivant, 259
Grand Master, 259
Grand Secretary, 259
Grand Sen. Warden, 259
Grand Stewards, 260
Grand Treasurer, 259
Junior Warden, 259
Knights Templar, 260
Lodges 169, 210, 212, 259
Lodges 2, 4, 5, 259
Music, 259
Past Grand Master, 259
Past Master, 259
Rev. Mr. Beach, 260
Royal Arch Ind. Lodge, 259
Secretary, 259
St. John, celebration, 259
Stewards, 259
Treasurer, 259
Free Masons, Edinburgh
Brethren, 190
Grand Master Mason, Scotland, 190
Masters, 190
Officers, 190
freebooters, 227
freedom, 126
freeholders, 35, 168, 265
freemen, 168
freight, 52, 98, 99, 181, 193, 200, 211, 219, 225, 239, 240, 250
for hire, 75
sought, 64
French
George, 104, 109, 110
French brandy, 109, 181, 229
French calicoes, 218
French cordials, 15, 85
French gloves, 74
French Islands, 155
French linens, 170
French man of war
retakes Dutch ship, sinks pirate, 105
French servants, 59, 61, 70
French West India
especially against Am. trade, 221
to prohibit all foreign trade, 221
friars, 65, 125
fricassees, 201
Frigates, 186
(Fr.) of the line, 47
(unk) 2 Spanish, 168
(unk) 2, from Ostend, 139
(unk) Br., his Majesty's, 158
(unk) British, 220
(unk) King's, pursues pirate, 111
(unk), English, 220
12, Black Sea, Russian, 241
6, French, 214
Agneda, 180
Alexander, 34 guns, 8 carronades, 139
British, (war) 84, 42
Hebe, 36 guns, 110
Matilda, 180
Mercury, 155, 242
Merlin, 18 guns, 110
Minerva, 190, 202
of Holland, 3
of Portugal, 209
San Leocadiz, 110

Santa Brigida, 202
Santa Casilda, 202
Spanish, 36 guns, 178
St. Lucia, 246
Thetis, 111
Winchelsea, 110
fringe, 80, 165, 217
frontier posts (Am.)
Br. perfidious conduct, 232
Britain's encroachments, 232
Frontigniac wine, 15, 24, 52
frost, 76
frows, 11
frugality, 232
fruit, 89, 237
Portuguese, 185
fruit trees, 75, 224
frying pans, 15, 81, 85, 136, 171
Fullerton
Richard, 117
Fullmer/Fulmore
Joseph, 104, 109, 110, 234
Fulton
Robert, 234
funeral orations, 187
fur trade
North West, importance, 190
Furber [Purber?]
Capt., 178
furnaces, 210
furniture, 16, 49, 53, 55, 61, 70, 73, 198, 217, 219, 235, 245, 252
furniture checks, 58, 79, 165, 217, 218
furniture, copper plate, 197
furniture, household, wooden, ready made, 197
furs, 58, 135, 150, 168, 178, 194
Fusdan
Mr., horse driven saw mill, 42
fustian jackets, 59
fustian waistcoats, 131
fustians, 6, 12, 49, 58, 79, 81, 108, 132, 136, 151, 165, 170, 217, 218, 249

G

Gadderer
Capt., 178
Gainsborough
great fall of snow, 36
Galata, 75
Galiots
Algerine, 209
Gallagher
Mr., horse rider, 260
gallons, 6, 11, 15, 21, 28, 38, 44, 52, 58, 63, 78, 84, 88, 108, 122, 131, 136, 142, 160, 169, 181, 187, 198, 223, 228, 239, 254, 261
Galloway
David, 91, 100
David, Jr., 89
gallows, 130, 163
Galvez
Don, Admiral, 52
Don, Havana Governor, 27, 37, 110
gaming, 122
Gaolers, 54, 251, 256, 261
gaols, 15, 24, 44, 50, 54, 55, 64, 70, 83, 85, 123, 135, 161-163, 165, 172, 177, 178, 193, 200, 207, 212, 217, 251, 261
Kingston, 37
gardens, 33, 53-55, 64, 94, 99, 118, 161, 182, 193, 218, 224, 267
Gardiner
Joseph, 255, 261, 267
Sylvester, Dr., ex-Boston, 32
Gardner
C., 239
S., 48
Gardoqui
James, Spanish Minister to U.S., 56
Garlick
J., 38
garments ready-made, men's, women's, 185
garrisons, 18, 37, 61, 77, 96, 121, 129, 201, 232
Antwerp, 3
Belgrade, 65
Ceylon, 247
Ft. M'Intosh, 67
Havana, 27
Jamaica, 101
garterings, 11, 33, 49, 58, 79, 151, 165, 218
garters, 7, 74
Gaspee Bay, 5
Gaspez de Villaquesa
Don Gaspez, Fleet Surgeon Major, 62
Gates
Horatio, 84
Gatewood
William, 30
Gauntt
Thomas, 84
Gautice
J., 126
gauze ribbons, 28
gauzes, 6, 7, 12, 15, 28, 33, 49, 58, 80, 81, 98, 99, 103, 123, 125, 132, 136, 142, 146, 151, 155, 165, 170, 197, 218, 239
Gay
Charles, 234
Geal
Peter, 212
gears, 126, 132, 229
geers, 223
General Assembly, 2, 10, 13, 17, 20, 24, 31, 35, 37, 53, 57, 63, 83, 119, 132, 156, 157, 167, 188, 205, 224, 225, 235, 265, 361
Pennsylvania, 181, 210, 254
Rhode Island, adjourned, 228
Geneva, 229
Genoa, 249
Gensang, 12, 52, 168
gentian, 29
Gentleman's Magazine, 107
George-Town, Md., 2, 8, 12, 13, 15, 26, 30, 38, 40, 41, 44, 49, 52, 63, 64, 70, 71, 78, 79, 82-86, 93, 99, 104, 119, 122, 124, 126, 133, 152, 153, 161, 166, 167, 172, 176, 181, 199, 212, 218, 219, 224, 230, 235, 255, 262, 267
Addition to, 41, 49
George-Town Academy, 85
lottery, 12, 13, 23, 26, 30, 105
Georgia, 24, 182, 222
Assembly, and Tenasee's great bent, 205
attempted Spanish invasion, 162
bounty lands' location, 141
covets Spanish Florida, 243
under Russia, skirmishes, 46
Georgia Company, 205
Georgia-Indians
soil rights, 253
treaty terms, 253
white's trespass on Indians, 253
Georgians
lawless and licentious, 163
German cords, 12, 59, 109
German Flatts, 113
treaty talks at, 113
German flutes, 256
German linen, 80
German mercenaries (for G.B.)
Am. war deaths: 11,853, 51
German osnaburgs, 15
German Princes, 194
negotiating a league, 162
German steel, 1, 33, 81, 98, 146, 181
German ticklenburgs, 100
Germanic League
Polish joining unlikely, 243
Germany, 4, 111, 129, 157, 168, 195, 196, 221
barter with Bavaria, 147
declares war on States Gen., 9
declares war on States of Holland, 32

ecclesiastics, 9
Electors side with Austria, 42
Emperor funds collection, 37
Emperor of, 207, 227
Emperor's circular letter, 13
Germanic body in ferment, 9
Princes form league, 168
Protestant Electors, 9
Protestant interest, 168
Gervais
Col., 149
John L., Hon., 56
Mr., 19
Gibbes
William H., Esq., 149
gibbet, 37
Gibney
Hugh, 72, 104, 109, 110
Gibraltar, 55, 139, 162, 194, 221, 226
fortifications rebuilding, 111
Governor protects Fr. ship, 243
Gibralter, 66, 67
Gibson
J., 222
James, 234
John, 24, 85, 132
Gilbert
Mr., 92
Gildart
Francis, 216
Gill
John, 83
John, Capt., 159
Gillis
Capt., 96
Gilpin
Col., 234
George, 48, 84
George, Col., 235
Mr., 224, 225, 235
gilt buttons, 100, 151
gilt letter paper, 2, 12, 17
gilt looking-glasses, 49
gilt pins, 74
gilt watch chains, 219
gimblets, 74, 136, 151
gimlets, 80, 165, 171
gimped fringe, 80
gin, 1, 15, 85, 142, 151, 155, 250, 254
ginger, 15, 80
ginseng
a lucrative trade, 254
cultivation, curing, 254
ginseng to London (lbs.)
Baltimore 2000, 62
Maryland 650, 62
New York 350, 62
Philadelphia 300, 62
Potomack 1764, 62
United States, 5064, 62
girths, 74, 80, 136, 151, 171
girthweb, 171, 197
Gisborough, 199, 207, 212, 219, 230
Glasgow, 24, 43, 56, 78, 93, 97-100, 102, 105, 109, 115, 122, 228, 261
dollar value falls, 107
Glasgow-Square, 28
glass, 6, 7, 91, 95
glass punching
tools for, 236
glass ware, 1, 7, 11, 15, 49, 74, 81, 100, 137, 151, 165, 169, 171, 192, 219
Glasscock
Peter, 267
glasses, 81
Glauber salts, 2, 29
Glebes
Henrico Parish, 48
Glenn
John, 31
Gloucester, 20, 63, 114, 118, 122, 239
Gloucester cheese, 100
Gloucester Co., 123, 124, 128, 138, 142, 147, 171
Glover
Thomas, 234
Glover's Reef, 93
gloves, 6, 7, 16, 28, 58, 73, 74, 80, 81, 99, 123, 132, 136, 165, 170, 218, 239
leather, 197
silk, 197
glue, 81, 171, 185, 197
Goddard
Mr., 17
Godfrey
P., 78, 192
Godfrey's cordial, 29, 85, 133, 143, 147, 152, 162, 167, 172, 177, 183, 188, 193, 200, 207, 212, 255, 262
Godolphin Arabian, 39
Godolphin, Lord, 60
Godwin
Kinchen, 31
Gogherty
Patrick, 131, 133, 143
gold, 40, 66, 69, 90, 97, 110, 141, 203, 223, 260
gold broaches, 11
gold coins
dug up with diamond, 147
gold prices, 52
gold sleeve buttons, 16
gold watches, 49, 119, 122, 124, 197
gold, wrought, 185, 197
Goldsmiths, 40, 41, 49, 54
Goldthwait
Catherine, 32
Mr., 32
Thomas, Esq; ex-Penobscot, 32
[son], age 24, 32
goloshoes, 197
Golphinton
Commissioners, Indians meet, 253
Gonge
Sieur Lamy, builds balloon clock, 110
Goodwin
N., 239
Nash, 223
Nathaniel, 225, 235
O., 43, 83
Goolding
Patrick, 29, 34, 40
Goose Creek, 64, 65, 75, 85, 103, 192
Gordon
George, President, Prot. Assn., 207
Lord George, 10, 23, 26, 139, 263
Lord, and John Adams, 143
Lord, to protect Dutch, 10
Goree, 10
Gorham
Nathaniel, 117
Gormly
Samuel, 234
Gorsuch's Point, 53
gospel
to preach, 196
Gottenburg, 20, 83
gouges, 74, 80, 151, 171
gout, 247
Governors, 21, 38, 44, 57, 63, 88, 141, 144, 215, 228
Maryland, 210, 228
New Jersey, 210
Pennsylvania, 16
Vermont, 254
Gower
Earl, 32
gown
plaid, 82
Graaf, 105
Grafton
Duke of, 32
Graham
Catherine MacAulay, 93
John, 119, 121, 124, 234
M'Cauley, Mr. & Mrs., 126
Richard, 17, 40, 75
grain, 2, 103, 141, 166, 196, 266
England stockpiling, 31
fermented, 10
malted, 185
Grame

Capt., 24, 141
grammar, 98, 160
granaries, 29, 69
Grand Pensioner
Dutch diplomatic conduit, 14
Grand Seignior, 75
grass, 193, 224
Gravenhague, 10
Gravesend, 63, 141, 160, 192
Gray
Daniel, 137
Mr., 158
Grayson
William, 216
Great Britain, 71, 144, 153, 155, 160, 208, 245, 248, 251, 252, 257, 262
absurdly long cause ends, 148
Act [protecting] Iron, Steel Making, Workers, 236
African coast outrages, 253
Algerines stop English ship, 194
altered Irish propositions, 184
Am. Emb. denigrated, 163
Am. war diminished G.B. status, 56
Am.'s rancorous step-mother, 149
anti-Pitt ballad, 247
board to study G.B.-U.S. trade, 112
Br. Amb. decamps Versailles, 196
Br.-Irish commercial agreement, 184
British flag, Fr. insult, 227
British-French war, 195
cavalry, 101
Chancellor, 184
Chancellor of the Exchequer, 92, 238
commercial expedition, N.W. Am. coast, 194
commercial expedition, South Seas, 194
Commissions, Loyalist claims, to Nova Scotia, 163
credit, 101
desertion penalties, critique, 252
dissensions embolden France, 221
dry season's effects, 203
Dutch Ambassador, 143
Eden's Am. trade views, 92
English manufactures superior, 178
English trade monopolies, 158
Envoy to U.S. Temple, 194
equal Irish privileges, 184
execrable poor laws, 168
fleet fitting out, Spithead, 214
Foster, Chancellor of Exchequer, 195
Fox's Am. trade views, 92
Fr. prohibition spurs Br. trade, 178
French-English prejudices, 204
George III , 87
good Queen Bessy, 62
hardware, woolens, 194
his Britannic Majesty, 9
House of Commons, 153
House of Lords, 139, 168
House of Peers, 101
incapable vs. Irish potato boats, 221
Ireland, commercial arrangements, 56
Irish affairs, 263
Irish propositions, 214
Jamaica-Spanish provinces trade, 101
Jenkins' Am. trade views, 92
King assents to Newfoundland trade bill, 101
King as German elector, 9
king continues provisioning Loyalists, 164
King of, 43
King restocking Windsor, 220
King William, 148
King, Irish Resolutions, 189
King, J.Adams' audience, 128
King, Mr. Adams private talk, 179
King, Prince of Wales, Marriage, 247
King, toddler, chat, 243
levee, St. James's, 189
Lord Chancellor, 139
Lords of the Treasury, 105
manufacturing interests, 184
militia's one month muster, 42
Mint, Tower, 105
Mr. Pitt's budget, 47
national debt, illustrated, 254
naval officers seek service, 214
navy order of battle, 42
navy recruiting methods, 214
navy ships, deployment, 101
negotiations with France, 201
Negro trade income, 101
new guineas, half guineas, 105
Parliament, 143, 252
Parliament adjourned, 214
Parliament only to repeal, alter laws, 46
Parliaments Irish propositions, 168
Pitt 's Am. trade views, 92
Pitt budget omits lottery, 130
Pitt party defeats Bedford's, 32
Pitt prepares commercial regulations, 42
Pitt proposes bachelor tax, 130
Pitt's bill, Loyalist claims, 163
Pitt's Loyalist plan successful, 154
Pitt's Loyalist relief act, 153
Pitt's pre-Parliament list, 226
Pitt's sinking fund future, 184
Pitt's Loyalist bill, critique of, 158
Pitt's Newfoundland trade bill, 101
Pitt's policy on the poor, 47
Portsmouth naval review, 178
Prime Minister, 23
Prince of Wales jailed, 153
Prince to be Post Captain, 178
Privy Council, 231
Queen receives Mr. Adams, 179
refuses payment, Am. negroes, 160
revised penalties, deserters, 231
Royal Academy, 259
Royals' attendants mocked, 148
Scottish, Irish plans compared, 168
ships, to watch French ships, 158
sinking fund, 184
St. James levee, 194
St. James's, 148
surrender African sites, 227
to keep N.W. posts, 221
trade policy distresses U.S., 102
trade with America debates, 92
Treasury, 184
treaty of peace with Am., 221
U.S. non-compliance, peace treaty, 160
Great Britain & Ireland peacetime land forces: 58,000, 61
great coats, 143, 192, 255
Great Falls, 10, 94, 131
Great Miami, the, 222
Great-Hunting Creek, 1
Greece, 153
Greek testaments, 170
Green
Capt., 56, 78
F., 17
Frederick, 123
J., 24, 233
Nathaniel, 45
S., 17
Green Briar
relief party, Pt. Pleasant fort, 145
green tea, 81, 103, 109, 115, 120, 137, 171, 181, 206, 211, 217, 223, 234
Greene
Gen., nephew of, 135

Gen., toured Georgia, East Floridargia, 77
Nathaniel, 50, 60
William, elected Gov., R.I., 87
Greenhead, 235
Greenough's tincture, 29
Greenway Court, 216
Gregor
John, 234
Grenada, 63, 92, 93, 101, 154, 159, 173, 224
Grenada rum, 94, 95, 98, 100, 105, 156
Gresham
Mr., 158
Gretter
Elizabeth, 48, 55
John, 229, 231
Michael, 6, 9, 18, 54
Mrs., 6, 98
greyhounds, 54
grid irons, 15, 251
Griffing
M., 93, 118
Moses, Capt., 234
Griffith
David, 17, 21-23, 26, 52, 55, 64, 82, 86, 91, 95
David, Rev., 12, 234
Dr., Rev., 250, 257, 262
Griffiths
William, Dr., 19
Grimes
John, 115, 116, 124
grindstones, 49
grist mills, 176
Groat Market, 196
groceries, 100
grog, 163
Groningen
supports confederacy, 194
grooving planes, 11
Grosvenor Place, 220
Groz Niklos, 116
grubbers, 1
guaci, 29
Guadaloupe, 247, 249
Guadaloupe-Martinique
30 Am. ships seized, sold, 164
Guelderland
Province, most obstinate, 110
speeds defence activity, 51
Guelders, 201
Guelphi
Don Pedro, 14
Guinea, 10
Guineaman (ship type)
(unk) from Cork, 128
guineas
counterfeit French, 24
guitars, 256
gum camphor, 29
gun boats, 140
gun carriages, 189
gun locks, 74, 171
gun powder, 194, 248
Gunnell
John, 84
gunnery
new optical device for, 67
gunpowder, 1, 74, 80, 81, 100, 132, 136, 137, 189
gunpowder tea, 146
guns, 15, 135, 191, 245, 252
48-pounder, 3
Gustavus
Samuel, 19
Gutro
J., 135
Gyllenspetz
Capt., 49
J., 48, 78

H

haberdashery, 192, 230
Habit Makers, 25, 26, 35, 98, 101, 109, 110
habits, Turkish, 208
hackney coach tax
inspires anti-Pitt ballad, 247
Haddo
Lord, Grand Master Mason, 189
Hadley's quadrants, 33, 251
Haerlem checks, 218
Haerlem oil, 29
Hagely
George, 255, 262, 267
Hager's-Town, 2
Hague, 2-4, 13, 46, 51, 55, 61, 76, 82, 96, 128, 148, 194, 195, 213, 214, 221, 225, 241, 246
6000 march to Scheldt, 221
Austrian minister at, 13
conciliation success unlikely, 51
contraband in diplomatic mail, 221
Emperor's preparations alarming, 221
Emperor's intentions hostile, 221
Kalatchow letter replied to, 46
matters at disagreeable extremities, 221
news from Germany, 51
peace a certainty, 124
tumult ringleaders taken, 213
Haig
George, 37
Haintrammach
Maj., 222
hair brooms, 7
Hair Cutters, 34, 40, 45
Hair Dressers, 40, 45
hair manufactures, 197
hair pins, 74, 80, 218
hair powder, 6, 58, 74, 123, 185, 197, 218, 239
hair sieves, 74, 81, 151
hair sifters, 80, 165
hair, false, 196
hairbines, 170
Halden/Halder
Capt., 99
T., 78, 141
Haldiman
Gen., 91
Haldimand
Gen., to survey Newf. fortifications, 110
Hale
J., 130, 135
late Brigade Cmdr., 258
half chests, 90
halfthicks, 165
Halifax, 19, 67, 78, 87, 107, 129, 164, 242, 261
flagrant treaty violation, 134
Loyalist claims commissioners, 238
Virginia, 19
Yorkshire, Eng., 201
Halifax Company, 121
Halifax Journal, 150
Hall
Dick, 49
Jonathan, 235
Mr., 206
Richard B., 39, 45, 49
Hallam
and Henry, theatre mgrs., 145
Hallott
A., 72
halters, 81
hamberlines, 1
Hamburg, 34, 40, 45, 51, 52, 93, 134, 227
timber ships, 227
Hamil Mamed Pacha
Grand Vizier, Turkey, 163
Hamilton
Gawin, 31
Henry, 62
Robert, 211, 219, 225
hammers, 11, 74, 81, 136, 171
Hammersley
Mr., 191, 192
Hammond
A.S., Sir, 195
E., 63, 73
Hamon
Reuben, Jr., 140
William H., 234
Hamp
B.A., 230, 240

hampers, 7, 58, 63, 64, 90, 108, 131, 136, 181
Hampshire Co., 17, 74, 88
Hampstead, 121
Hampstead, Long island, 214
Hampton, 135
Hanau, 46
  Emperor's equipage arrives, 46
Hanau mercenaries
  died in Am. war: 981, 52
Hanby
  John, 217
Hancock
  and Adams, 144
  John, 117
  John, Pres., U.S. Senate, 228
handbills, 31
Handel (composer)
  Messiah, 121
handkerchiefs, 1, 6, 7, 12, 15, 21, 49, 58, 73, 74, 79-81, 88, 98, 99, 103, 108, 132, 136, 146, 147, 151, 170, 197, 218, 239
handles, 171
handsaw files, 136, 151, 218
handsaws, 80, 81, 136, 165, 171
hangings, paper, 197
Hannah
  Alexander, 234
  Elizabeth, 7
  Mrs., 234
Hanover
  Electorate of, 168
  House of, 159
Hanson
  John, 234
  S., 261, 267
  T., 261, 267
  Thomas H., 18, 23, 44, 50, 54, 60, 64, 70
harbour, 174
hard of hearing, 131
Hardage
  William, 45, 50, 54, 60, 64
Hardin
  John, 193, 200, 207
Hardisty
  Samuel, 255, 262, 267
hardware, 1, 6, 7, 12, 49, 58, 59, 82, 98, 100, 132, 146, 194, 211, 230
Hardy
  Samuel, Hon., 191
Haring
  John, Hon., 43
Harmar
  Col., 144
Harmer
  Col., 232
Harmony-Hall, 33
harnesses, 44, 127, 177, 206
Harper
  Capt., 7, 48-50, 58, 60, 88, 90, 91, 100, 108, 115, 120, 126, 131, 143, 146, 153, 164, 165, 177, 212, 251, 256, 262, 266
  Col., 198, 207
  Edward, 1, 9, 12, 119, 124, 128, 233, 235, 236, 245
  John, 84, 235, 236, 245
  John, Sir, 33
  Mr., 69, 133, 147, 160, 171, 181, 212
  S., 233
  Samuel, 211, 219, 225
harpsichords, 256
harpy, 14
Harrison
  Benjamin, 31, 198
  Burr, 104, 109, 115, 120
  Capt., 5
  Carter Bassett, 31
  Carter Henry, 31
  Cuthbert, 69, 85
  Joseph W., 84, 234
  Michael, 198
  Mr., 181
  Richard, 84
  Richard, Am.Cons., Cadiz, 222
  William, 228
Harrowgate
  mineral waters of, 154
Hart
  Jonathan, Capt., 179
Hartford, 42, 56, 62, 149
  General Assembly not called, 42
Hartford, Conn., 16
Hartlepool, 36
  gales grounds 16 ships, 36
Hartley
  Mr., 39
Hartshorne
  Master, 72
  William, 11, 14, 18, 25, 53, 73, 81, 82, 84, 86, 94, 95, 105, 115, 116, 124, 131, 132, 138, 143, 147, 152, 157, 165, 167, 170, 172, 177, 183, 198, 234-236, 245, 251, 257, 262
Harvie
  John, 182
Harwich, 154
Haskell
  Capt., 2, 6, 9, 12, 13, 17
  W., 5, 20
hat hooks, 74
Hatch
  Emir, Caravan of Mecca cdr., 111
hatchets, 1, 15, 197
hatchways, 252, 257
hats, 1, 6, 7, 11, 15, 21, 49, 58, 73, 80, 81, 88, 99, 103, 123, 127, 131, 132, 136, 146, 151, 161, 165, 170, 192, 206, 211, 217, 218, 223, 230, 234, 239, 250, 251
  beaver, 185, 197
  beaveret, 197
  castor, 185, 197
  wool, 185
Hatter's trimmings, 218
Hatters, 89
Haufman
  Carsten, Capt., 151
hautboys, 256
Havana, 27, 52, 56
  1000 troops to New Orleans, 27
  Don Galvez, Governor, 110
  Governor Don Galvez, 37
  open to Am. ships, 113
  reopened to Am. ships, produce, 92
Havana garrison
  manned by militia, 27
Havana Governor
  to attack Musquito Shore, 37
Havanna, 180
  3 millions for debt payments, 180
  arsenal burned to ground, 189
  dysentery kills, 162
Havre, 139
Havre-de-Grace, 149, 223, 225, 235, 239
Hawes
  Samuel, 30
Hawkins
  Col., toured Georgia, East Florida, 77
  George Fraser, 198, 207, 212
  Mr., 75
  Susanna T., 198, 207, 212
  Thomas, 84
Hawling
  Mr., 25
Hawling's Bottom, 25
hay, 2, 33, 149, 170, 203
Haycock
  William, 218, 219, 230
Hayden
  W., 44
Haye
  Capt., 116
Hayes
  Mr., 17
  Mr., Boston broker, 4
Hayes's, 245
Hays
  John, 31
Hazard, 184
Hazelhurst
  Isaac, 4, 97
Head of Bohemia, 17
Head of Elk, 17, 45
Headboroughs, 54

Heale
William, 69
health, 5
Heard
James, 69, 70
hearth brushes, 80
heaven, 208
Hebrew
letter written in, 196
Heideck
John Joseph, 196
Helfintche Zouchte, 201
Hellstedt
Charles, 44
Helmes
Jacob, 54
Hemp, 8, 24, 113, 126, 156, 202, 261, 267
hempen rolls, 100
Henderson
Alexander, 31, 36, 39, 41, 49, 84, 132
Hendricks
James, 73, 81, 82, 137, 138, 147
James, Col., 216
Henn
Justice, 138
Henrico Co., 126
Henrico Parish, 48
Henry
and Hallam, theatre mgrs., 145
Don, found Cape Verd, 190
John, Hon., 228
Patrick, 44, 57, 88, 228
William, 214
Henshaw
W., 193, 200
Hepburn
Mr., 138, 147
Nancy, 48
William, 53-55, 60, 64, 84, 94, 136, 138, 147, 156, 157, 162, 171
Herbert
William, 14, 80, 84, 118, 206, 212, 219, 223, 225, 231
Herchell
Henry, 19
Hereford
William, 199, 207, 212, 219
Hermelin
Baron, 19
herrings, 2, 25, 199, 207, 212
Hesse Cassel
peacetime land forces, 61
Prince Frederick appointed, 31
Hesse Darmstadt
Prince of, 201
Hessian rolls, 218
Hessians, 151
died in Am. war: 6500, 52
Hevein
theatrical gentleman, duel, 158
Hewes
Aaron, 250, 256, 262
Hewit
Counselor, 138
Hewitt
Martha, 216
Hewson
Capt., 169
Hibernian Magazine, 193, 225
hides, 89
Hierro
Don Calderon, Gov., 27
Higginson
Miss, 233
High Bridge, 196
High Mightinesses, 3
Hill
Clement, 177, 178, 188, 193, 200, 207, 212
J., 5
L., 72
Hill's balsam, 29
Hindman
William, 228
Hindoos, 213
Hindostan, 213
hinges, 15, 74, 136, 165, 171
hints
early rising adds life, 145
hips, bolstered, 196
Hispaniola, 10, 15, 19, 20, 24, 116, 247
foreign trade ban, 116
history books, 136
Hite
George, 84
Hixon
Timothy, 217, 219, 230
William, 217
Hoak
Peter, Dr., 234
Hobb's Hole, 165, 170, 173, 211
hobby horse, 201
Hock, 1
hoes, 132, 136, 171, 251
Hogan
John, 127
Hogarth, 183
Hogg
Peter, 156
hogs, 2, 73, 166, 167, 170, 198
hogsheads, 6, 8, 11, 15, 28-30, 33, 35, 52, 53, 58, 68, 79, 85, 88, 89, 94, 98, 99, 103, 108, 114, 115, 118, 122, 131, 136, 142, 151, 155, 156, 160, 164, 166, 169, 181, 188, 198, 206, 211, 217, 223, 224, 234, 238, 239, 246, 250, 254, 257, 262, 263, 266
barrels, 156
contents of, 246
Hoilckte
Lt. Col., 247
Holiday
James, 234
Holland, 15, 18, 23, 33, 43, 47, 130, 201
aggressions in, 208
coals purchased from England, 47
province of, demography, 14
States of, 2
United Protestant States of, 23
Vergennes favors, 20
Holland duck, 1, 146
Hollands, 7, 58, 74, 79, 81, 88, 136, 151, 165, 170, 217
Holliday
Capt., 43
Mr., 234
Hollins
John, 254
Hollinsbury
Richard, 234
hollow iron ware, 115
hollow planes, 11
hollow ware, 28
Holme's Run, 1
Holmes
James Cunningham, 155
Joseph, 8, 11, 12, 17, 50, 84, 143
Stephen, 234
Holton
Samuel, Congress' Pres., P.T., 154
homespun, 126, 179
Honduras, Bay of, 93, 116
honey, 85, 133, 143, 147, 152, 162, 167, 172, 177, 183, 188, 193, 200, 207, 212, 255, 262
honey-combs, 49
honeycomb cord, 218
honeycombed velverets, 58
Hooe
Col., 114, 156, 157, 162, 182, 250, 255
Gerard, 53, 60, 64, 65, 75
Henry D., 22
Mr., 239
Richard T., 26
Robert T., 12, 17, 22, 84, 118
Robert T., Col., 103
Hooe's Ferry, 53, 126, 128, 137
Hooe's warehouse, 182
Hooff
Lawrence, 109, 110, 120, 124
hooks, 197, 251
hooks and eyes, 171
Hooper's pills, 29
hoops, 196

carriage, 197
hickory, 179
Hoorne
2 cavalry companies, 2
Hop
Baron, 13
Hope
Brig. Gen., 248
Hopkins
John, 31
Stephen, Hon., 141
hops, 1, 13, 266
Horace, 16, 170
Mr., 22, 26
horn combs, 74, 80, 136, 165, 170, 218
Hornblower
Josiah, 210
horse bells, 165
horse harness, parts of, 197
Horse riders, 260
horse whips, 171
Horse-Lick, 44
Horsemen, 185
horses, 28, 66, 69, 70, 73, 76, 85, 94, 96, 101, 127, 142, 145, 159, 164, 166, 167, 170, 171, 184, 193, 198, 203, 213, 229, 230, 254, 256, 263
£200 each for Am. war, 51
Apollo, 39
Apollo's Dam, 60
Bajazet, 206
Bald Galloway, 39
Barb, 33
Bet Bouncer, 192
brands, 142
breeding, 39, 48, 70, 74, 81, 85, 86, 91, 95, 100, 104
brushes, 151
Careless, 33, 191
Chatham, 60
Cottingham, 39
Crab, 39
Cub, 74, 81
Cullen Arabian, 33
Cumberland, 192
Ebony, 60
Eclipse, 33, 39, 45, 49, 206
Fearnought, 60
for rent, 25, 26, 35, 40, 75
for sale, 2, 7, 29, 44, 45, 49, 53, 54, 94, 126, 132, 133, 177, 181, 188, 192, 199, 206, 212, 223, 266
found, 94, 146
Godolphin Arabian, 60
hobby, 201
Hotspur, 186, 192
Ironsides, 191
Jenny Dismal, 60
Magnolio, 39, 45, 49, 54
Morton's Traveller, 39
North-Country Diamond, 33
Obscurity, 33, 40, 45, 86, 91, 95, 100, 104
Old Child Mare, 33
Old Dismal, 60
Othello, 39, 60
Paul Jones, 192
Phoebe, 39
Polydore, 192
races, 68, 75, 142, 143, 147, 152, 153, 157, 167, 182, 183, 187, 188, 196, 201, 232
Ranger Arabian, 39
Regulus, 39, 60
Republican, 59, 65, 70
runaway, 178, 188
Selima, 39
Snake, 39
sorrel, 142, 143
Spry, 186, 191
stalls for, 267
stealing, 21, 52, 196
stolen, 17, 22, 30, 119, 121, 122, 127, 133, 137, 138, 142, 143, 147, 152, 153, 156, 157, 161, 162, 167, 172, 177, 192, 217, 219, 224, 230, 235, 261
strayed, 6, 12, 13, 18, 22, 23, 30, 34, 40, 45, 89, 91, 98, 100, 104, 109, 119, 121, 122, 127, 133, 137, 138, 142, 143, 147, 152, 157, 162, 172, 193, 200, 217, 219, 230
Targuin, 191
taxes on, 20, 21
Traveller, 206
True-Whig, 60
Union, 206
Whitefoot, 60
Young Selima, 60
horses, artillery, 195
horsewhips, 7, 80
Horsham, 226
"No Irish propositions!", 226
"No shop tax!", 226
hose, 6, 7, 12, 59, 98, 99, 123, 146, 151, 165, 170, 217, 218, 239, 250, 254
silk, 197
hosiery, 73, 192, 230
hospitals, 34, 35, 45
hostlers, 123, 210
hotels, 42, 76
Comte de Mercy arrives, 42
Dutch, 208
Piccadilly, 128
Hough
Mr., 146
hour glasses, 74
house jack, 197
House of Delegates, 234, 266
Maryland, 222
House of Delegates (Va.)
Act, Incorp. Episcopal Church, 23
Bill, provision for teachers of Christian religion, 30
John Beckley, Clerk, 31
vote record, Teachers of Christian religion bill, 30
household furniture, 2, 55, 61, 70, 73, 217, 219, 235, 256
household goods, 185
housekeepers, 142, 143, 152, 157, 265
houselines, 1
houses, 69, 98, 99, 108, 109, 116, 124, 127, 132, 138, 198, 199, 205, 229, 235, 255
brick, 57
for rent, 8, 25, 44, 49, 50, 54, 55, 60, 64, 79, 82, 86, 123, 136, 161, 219, 229, 230, 235, 236, 245, 251, 257, 262
for sale, 22, 94, 199, 207, 212, 219, 231
Howard
Henry, 89
Howe
Gen., 24, 203
Robert, Maj. Gen., 149
Howell
Samuel, 97
Hubbard
James, 31
Hubble
William, 16
Hudnall
Ezekiel, 60, 64, 70
Hudson's Bay
ships, 4
Huertas
Francis, 62
Huff
John, 29, 30, 35, 45, 49, 50
Huger
Daniel, 37
Hughes
Frances, mariner, 24
Francis, Capt., 19
G., printer, 190
H., 48, 155, 233
Henry, Capt., 188, 193, 200
Huie
A., 102
Alexander, 115
Humane Society
fêtes its rescuees, 150
Humphreys
J., 126
William, 146, 147, 157

Humphries
J., 24, 38, 63, 78, 88, 114, 141, 155, 169, 187, 222
Ralph, 30
Humpton
Richard, 117
Hungary, 51
Austria Emp.'s edict for, 233
servitude abolished, 233
subjects' new rights (listed), 233
tobacco culture, 116
Hunter
Elizabeth, 234
George, 216
John, 234, 235
Moses, 30, 84
Nathaniel C., 58, 61, 70
William, Jr., 2, 9, 14, 17, 18, 24, 48, 50, 58, 60, 73, 79, 80, 82, 85, 91, 95, 96, 108, 132, 223, 230, 234, 236, 239, 240, 250, 257, 262, 266, 267
hunters, 49
hunting, 232, 266
Hunting Creek, 119
husbandry, 246
Hussan Bey, 111
hussars, 20
Hussey
Mr., Recorder, 19
Hutchings
Mr., 192
Hutchins
Capt., 196, 232
J., 88
Thos., Geographer, Surveyor Gen., 149
Hyde
Mr., 211
Hyder
pillage, 231
hydrometers, 136
hydrophobia
soap suds prevent, 243
hyson tea, 49, 64, 73, 74, 90, 98, 103, 108, 109, 115, 120, 131, 146, 156, 165, 171, 181, 206, 211, 217, 223, 234, 239

I

immigrants
200 from Amsterdam, 159
300 from Amsterdam, 160
Imperial Internuncio, 162
Fr. Amb. to work with, 162
Imperial Troops, 43
importation, 35, 57, 67, 245
Importers, 257, 262, 263
imports, 88
states ask non-import association vs. G.B., 72
imposts, 4, 88, 150, 254
India, 23, 101, 159, 194, 213, 214, 231, 242
assassinations, overthrows, 129
Irish ships to, 196
news dispatch to, 37
India British Forces
Meadows, Maj. Gen., 24
India chintzes, 49
India Company
desertion penalties, 252
Directors of, 231
fire loss, 2 ships, tea whse., 126
India Goods, 8, 99
India handkerchiefs, 81
India nankeens, 81, 100
Indiaman, 3
Indiaman (ship), 66
Indian affairs
Commissioners of, 113
Indian confederacy mover
Joseph the Mohawk King, 247
Indian Corn, 2, 15, 22, 44, 49, 69, 104, 112, 156, 182, 199, 224
mills, 165
Indian country, 232
Indian persian gown, 86
Indian River, 164
Indians, 121, 150, 161, 232
almost uninterrupted quiet, 204
and white people: a view, 261
Buenos Ayres, 189
Cherokee, 140, 196, 261
Cherokees, 205
Chicasa, 205
Chicasas, 205
Chief Cornplanter, 144
chief protection, 232
commissioners appointed, 205
confederated against U.S., 247
Creek, 140, 205, 247
Del. warrior, murder trial, 232
Delaware warrior, detained, 232
Delawares, 196
hunting grounds, 145
Indian Affairs Commissioners, 149
Lower Creeks, 253
Mingos, 196
Mississippi's banks, tribes, 247
Mohawk, 247
Mosghes [or, Mofghes-Eds.], 247
Oneyday, 113
Racoon Bottom ambush, 145
rumours of, 196
Shawanese, 196
Shawanese, Six Nations united, act, 145
Six Nations' dissatifaction, 144
southern tribes, 205
treaty at the Great Miami, 222
Treaty in Georgia, 253
tribes back of Florida, 247
tribes back of Georgia, 247
tribes on the Ohio, 247
Tuscarora, 113
U.S. Commissioners to, 140
Upper Creeks, 253
indigo, 81, 98, 104, 171, 201, 239, 243
Indostan
Mahratas, 66
Nizam, 66
Tippoo, 66
industry, 232, 233, 258
infants, 208
infidelity
of person of high rank, 163
influenza, 134
Ingersol
Jonathan, Capt., 154, 173, 174
Ingraham
J., 5, 43, 63, 73, 97, 107
Mr., 137
ink cake, 256
ink chests, 256
ink holders, 34, 40, 45
ink pots, 80, 256
ink stands, 2, 13, 17, 74
inkpowder, 2, 7, 13, 17, 59, 74, 81, 151, 170, 218, 256
Innis
Capt., 155
inns, 169, 172, 177, 183
inns of court, 153
inquisitions
Portuguese, 208
Spanish, 208
insects, 33, 78
Inspectors, 21, 38
Inspruck, 139
instruments, 58, 256
surveying, 185
insurance, 261
on N.Y. remittances, saved, 155
insurance (maritime)
Barbary corsairs affect rates (listed), 56
Barbary pirates cause rate change, 56
insurance rates
up 8-10% in Levant ports, 46
insurance, marine
20% on Dutch ships, 10
insurrection
in Utrecht, 195
intelligence, 200
intestines, 237
intoxication, 72, 125, 141
inundations
damage done by, 225

invoice books, 256
Inward Entries, 5, 10, 15, 20, 24, 27, 33, 38, 43, 48, 52, 58, 63, 67, 72, 78, 83, 88, 93, 97, 102, 107, 114, 118, 122, 126, 130, 135, 141, 150, 155, 160, 164, 169, 176, 181, 187, 192, 198, 205, 210, 216, 222, 228, 233, 239, 249, 254, 261
ipecacuanha, 29
Ipswich, Mass., 19
Ireland, 5, 10, 14, 27, 32, 71, 85, 96, 101, 129, 145, 158, 195, 222, 227, 238, 260
150 troops to St. Vincent's, 96
2 regiments to foreign service, 96
200 troops to Barbadoes, 96
250 troops to St. Kitt's, 96
300 troops to Antigua, 96
3000 troops to Leeward Is., 96
altered Irish propositions, 184
an imperial diadem, 173
Attorney Gen. says congress illegal, 55
Br. officers wound Dubliners, 244
commercial propositions, reaction to, 168
Commercial Settlement, 189
counterfeit half guineas, dollars, 66
Court of King's Bench, 18
credit revolution's effects, 14
emancipation's trade effects, 158
equal privileges as G.B., 184
favorable news from, 42
French spies, emissaries, 184
Gr. Britain, commercial arrangements, 56
guineas to America, returned, 148
his Majesty, Pitt, popular, 159
House of Commons, 56
improvements; arts, manufactures, 148
independence, perils of, 203
Legislature's overturn design, 148
Lord Gordon's letter on, 263
new system for, 76
new taxes astonish, alarm, 67
omnipotent Parliament sought, 195
Parliament, 139, 173, 184, 189
Parliament meets on trade, 14
Parliament's new taxes, 86
pension list like Noah's ark, 101
Prime Serjeant, 19
Privy Council, 148
protecting duties, 19
Protestant landholders uneasy, 159
refusing commercial treaty, 196
return to captivity, 173
Right Hon. Attorney General, 19
rights of, listed, 173
ships to India, 196
should assist paying Eng. debts, 82
Solicitor General, 19
spirit of volunteering subsists, 148
St. Patrick, patron saint, 258
trade bill, 87
West Indies smuggling trade, 158
Irish beef, 229
Irish Brigade, 27
volunteer for Holland, 23
Irish linens, 6, 7, 11, 12, 15, 28, 33, 53, 55, 58, 59, 61, 74, 79-81, 98, 100, 103, 131, 132, 136, 142, 146, 151, 155, 165, 170, 206, 211, 218, 219, 229
Irish mess pork, 229
Irish servants, 33, 35, 45, 69, 71, 73, 82, 89, 91, 105, 123, 124, 127, 128, 131, 133, 137, 143, 146, 217, 219, 225, 230, 231, 240
Irish sheetings, 15, 100, 146, 151, 170
Irishmen, 122, 251, 256, 261
Irkutsh, 76
iron, 86, 135
cast, 185
from Sweden, America, 101
smelting furnace improvement, 101
trade become lucrative, 101
iron buckles, 230
iron candlesticks, 218
iron castings, 34, 49
iron dogs, 52
iron forge
new, opened, shown, 51
iron hollow ware, 28
iron hoops, 266
iron locks, 69
iron pots, 6, 81, 82, 132, 136, 151, 251
iron tea kettles, 74
iron ware, 115
iron works, 137, 224
ironing, 183, 230
ironmongery, 12, 73, 81, 100, 192, 230
irons, 218
Irvine
James, 190, 261, 267
Irwin
James, 234
island (Br. West Indies)
seized Am. ship, cargo, 102
island (Br.)
fired on Am. ship, 102
islands, 87
Antigua, 96
Azores, 197
Azores., 190
Bahama, 62
Bald Tusket, 107
Baleiro, 36
Barbadoes, 96
British West India, 201
Cape Breton, 87
Cape de Verd, 43
Ceylon, 247
Cumberland, 77
Fayal, 197
French West India, 221
Grenada, 154
Hierro, 27
Hispaniola, 19
Isle of Bourbon, 56
Java, 87
Leeward, 96
Madeira, 51
Madera, 190
Martinique, 96
Mauritius, 56
Porto Santo, 190
Prince's, 190
Providence, 144
Sandwich, 124
St. Christopher's, 113
St. Thomas, 190
Torry, 96
Turk's, 101
Turk's, 185
West India (Br.), 87
West India (Fr.), 196
West Indies, 164
Western, 190, 191, 222
Windward, 159, 164
Isle of May, 155
Israel
descendants of, 196
tribes of, 208
Italian flowers, 99
Italian Morocco slippers, 99
Italian religion, 208
ivory combs, 74, 80, 136, 165, 170, 218

J

jack planes, 11, 80
jackal, 213
jacket buttons, 219
jackets, 25, 73, 89, 95, 103, 127, 142, 143, 146, 161, 172, 176, 177, 217, 255

jacks, 151
house, 197
Jackson
D., 103
Harry, 59, 64, 65
S., 210, 228
W., 135
William, 117
Jalap, 2, 29
Jamaica, 47, 52, 61, 63, 66, 87, 101, 129, 145, 148, 158, 159, 163, 164, 192, 210, 221, 233, 245, 249, 250, 261
4,000,000 acres, 260
absorbed in vice, 196
Alured Clarke, Gov., 214
declining commerce, 158
general embargo, all vessels, 214
Governor of, 37
horse racing, 196
Lord Dunmore, Gov., 96
Lt. Gov., 61
Lt. Gov. placating God, 243
many favor Am. trade, 204
many plantations damaged, 191
militia called up, 37
most dreadful hurricane, 191
non-export act's effect, 238
poetic description of, 260
regiment strength to 500, 61
restrictions on rums, sugars, 158
seeks Am. supplies, 203
sends troops to Musquito Shore, 37
sugar cane crop, 66
supplies halted, 238
troop augmentation, 96
Jamaica (Annoto Bay) loss
2 ships, 191
Jamaica (Greenwich) on shore
1 packet, 1 ship, 191
Jamaica (Rocky Keys) dashed on
2 brigs, 4 sloops, 191
ship, 2 schooners, 191
Jamaica (West End) on shore
ship, schooner, 3 brigs, 191
Jamaica (West End) total wrecks
ship, schooner, 3 brigs, 191
Jamaica losses
bodies, whole and part, buried, 191
several (unk) lost, on shore, dismasted, 191
Jamaica mahogany, 211
Jamaica rum, 2, 17, 18, 34, 166, 167, 250, 256, 262
Jamaica spirits, 6, 11, 15, 21, 24, 26, 28, 35, 38, 44, 45, 49, 52, 54, 58, 60, 63, 78, 81, 84, 88, 108, 109, 122, 131, 136-138, 142, 147, 160, 169, 171, 181, 187, 198, 211, 219, 223, 225, 228, 229, 239, 250, 254, 261, 266
James
Capt., 135
Hugh, Dr., 19
Reuben, 130
James's powders, 29
Jameson
Col., 15
Jamieson
Andrew, 234-236, 245
Janissary Aga, 111
Janney
Joseph, 84, 166, 167, 177, 217, 219, 230, 235
Japan, 194
japanned hair pins, 74
japanned snuffers, 80
japanned tea trays, 74
japanned waiters, 132
jars, 89, 115
Jay
Mr., Minister of Foreign Affairs, 116
Mr., portrait of, 154
jeanets, 49, 58, 73, 74, 81, 98, 100, 170, 218
jeans, 12, 49, 58, 73, 79, 81, 98, 100, 109, 136, 151, 165, 170, 218, 234, 250, 254
Jefferson
Col., in Paris residence, 130
Col., Min. Plenipo. to France, 130
Gov., 21
Thomas, 50, 239
Thomas, Algerine matter, 228
Thomas, Hon., 48
Jefferson Co., 59, 61, 70, 85, 91, 95, 104
Jeffries
Mr., balloonist, 125
Jenkin
Caleb, high sheriff, 101
Jenkins
Capt., 38
G., 130
Mr., 92
Jenkinson
Mr., politics of, 220
Jenningham
Henry, 234
Jenny
Capt., 93
Jericho, 208
Jerusalem
siege of, 213
Jesuit's drops, 29
Jesuits' bark, 89
Jett
Catharine, 199, 207, 212, 219, 225
Jewelers, 40, 41
jewelry, 40, 41, 49, 142, 151, 155, 197, 230, 256
jewels, 231
Jewish rabbi, 196
Jews, 121, 153, 196, 207
Dutch, 207
German, 207
King of the, 208
Portuguese, 207
Spanish, 207
Jiles
P., 234
jobbers, 122
Jockey Club purse, 186
jockey clubs, 60
John
Thomas, 78, 198
John II of Portugal, 190
Johns
Capt., 169
Richard, Capt., 79
Johnson
Benjamin, alias William, 163
Dr., 91, 120
Francis, 54, 83, 117
Francis, Col., 19
Johnston
Baker, 84
Capt., 228
D., 63, 107, 155, 192
Dennis, 251, 256
Dennis M., 103, 109, 115, 120
George, 94
James, 84
Thomas, 84, 261
William, 234
William, Maj., 103
Zachariah, 30
Joiners, 185
joiners' tools, 1, 11, 256
joiners' work, 185
Jolly
John, 234
Jones
Capt. (of Alexandria), 239
Charles, 234
David, Dr., 160
Edward, 223, 225, 235
Joseph (of Dinwiddie), 31
Joseph (of King George), 31
Paul, 400,000 livres prize money, 194
Paul, Kamchatka expedition, 194
Jordan
Mr., 46
Joseph, Mohawk King, 247
journals, 84, 86, 95, 100, 109, 115, 120, 133, 143, 147, 152, 162,

167, 172, 177, 183, 188, 193, 200, 207, 212, 255, 256, 262
Journeymen, 114
Journeymen Printers, 44, 55, 60, 65, 267
Joyce
Mr., Jr., 72
Judah, 208
Judea, 208
Judge of the Admiralty, 24
Judges, 187
jugs, 15, 74, 132, 136, 251
juries, 258
jury masts, 78
Justices, 54, 187
Justices of the Peace, 255
Justin, 170

K

Kaunitz
Count, letter to Austrian envoys, 201
infantry regiment of, 20
Prince of, 124
Prince, to Ratisbon, 231
Kean
Capt., 191
John, 156, 157, 167
John, delegate to Congress, 37
Keaquick
John, Capt., 112
Kearnes
John, 31
Keating
Mr., mutineer, thief, 163
Keaton
Maurice, murderer, executed, 37
Keefe
William, 127
Keeke
Claas, Capt., 135
keel, 264
kegs, 2, 250, 254
Keilly
John, 123
Keith
James, 14, 84, 234
Mr., 160
Kelly
James, 234
William, 172, 183
Kelly (witness to mutiny, theft), 163
Kelso
Capt., 97
Kendal cotton coat, 122
Kendal cottons, 170
Kennedy
David, 73, 82
Kennett's Antiquities, 170
kentings, 81, 136, 151, 218
Kentucky, 67, 113, 140, 144, 199, 207, 212
Commonwealth of, 140
people wish separation, 140
separation debated, 180
separation from Virginia, 113
settlement of, 84
Washington Co. measures, 180
kerseys, 6, 151, 165, 250, 254
duffils, 165
keys, 136, 165, 219
Keys
Mr., 73
Keys's Ferry, 25
kickshaws, 201
Kidd
Mr., proprietor, 67
kidskin gloves, 58
Kilkenny, 3
Kilkenny Co., 138
kilns, 151, 235
King
Elizabeth, 261
J., 27
Miles, 31
Rufus, 117
King and Queen Co., 239
King Charles the Second, 252
King George Co., 126, 128, 137
King George III, 107
King James
in France, offspring, 226
King of Prussia, 43, 76, 222
King of Sweden, 44
King Tamminy, 67
king's cords, 58, 74, 132
King's plates, 60
Kingsbury
Jacob, Ens., 179
Kingston, 19, 52, 61, 66, 87, 105, 116, 129, 148, 154, 163, 221, 243, 245
Custom House, 191
day of fasting, prayer, 243
day of humiliation, 243
gaol, 37
great hurricane damage, 191
Jamaica, 154
Kingston harbour losses
sunk: ship, brig, sloop, 191
Kingston loss on shore
2 schooners, 1 sloop, 191
3 ships, 4 brigs, 191
Kirby
James, Dr., 234
kirby fish hooks, 151
Kirk
James, 14, 251
Kirkleatham
great fall of snow, 36
Kirkpatrick
Thomas, 24, 26, 30, 85, 91, 95, 100, 132, 133, 143, 152, 157, 161, 234
kitchen furniture, 2, 73, 217, 219
kitchens, 2, 28, 75, 104, 118, 126, 132, 166, 176, 193, 199, 205, 224, 229, 250, 255
kittereen, 184
Kittery, 106
Kleinhoff
John, 137, 138, 147, 234
knap, 255
knee buckles, 11, 16, 136, 165, 171, 219
knee garters, 7
Knight
J., 52, 72
knitting pins, 74, 151
knives, 7, 11, 15, 57, 59, 74, 95, 151
knives and forks, 80, 81, 108, 151, 165, 171, 218
Knox
George, 234
Henry, Hon., 43
William, 17
Koenigstein
42,000 man camp, 76
Kozenzook, 19
Kruischans
Frederick Henry, 96
Kuskuscoes, 67

L

L'Orient, 33, 37, 56, 72, 77, 83, 93, 126, 155, 188, 190, 194, 211, 219, 220, 225, 228, 233, 240, 244
L'Orieth
Zachariah, 244
La Fayette, 204
Laborers, 160
laces, 7, 12, 15, 16, 19, 40, 81, 99, 123, 136, 165, 170, 219
chaise, 197
coach, 197
livery, 197
Lacey
Israel, 89, 91, 98
James, 120, 124, 127, 128
Laguira, 52
Laiezou
L., 97
Lake
T.J., 97, 107, 135
Lamb
Mr., Capt. U.S.A., 248
lamb gloves, 146

Lambert
  Capt., 98
  W., 160
Lamely
  William, 155
lampblack, 7, 9, 18, 21, 75, 86, 91, 185
lamps, 15
land
  condemnation of, 2, 13
  deeds, 1, 18, 23, 30, 40, 41, 49, 90, 115
  for rent, 166, 167
  for sale, 1, 2, 7, 9, 11-13, 17, 22-26, 30, 34, 40, 44, 45, 50, 53-55, 59-61, 64, 70, 73, 75, 81, 85, 86, 89-91, 94-96, 100, 103, 104, 109, 110, 115, 120, 123, 124, 126-128, 132, 137, 138, 142, 143, 147, 151-153, 156, 157, 162, 166, 170-172, 176, 177, 183, 188, 193, 199, 200, 205, 207, 217, 219, 224, 225, 229-231, 235, 236, 240, 245, 250, 251, 256, 257, 261, 262, 266, 267
  patents, 156, 167
  taxes on, 20
  warrants, 94, 218
landaus
  duties on, 184
landholders, 215
Landing waiters, 257, 262
landings, 29
  Elk-Ridge, 75
landlord, 134
Landscapes in Verse, 230
Landscron
  fortifications, 9
Land's End (Eng.), 77
Lane
  Hardage, 126, 133, 138
  John, 52
  Richard, 234
Langara
  Rodney's defeat of, 62
Langdon
  John, President, Senate, 134
languages
  English, 98, 196
  French, 59
  German, 59
  Greek, 98
  Latin, 72, 80, 91, 98
  Oriental, 196
Langworthy
  Mr., 17
Lankford
  Benjamin, 31
larceny, 83
Larder
  Daturic, 169
lasting shoes, 7, 28, 49
lastings, 12, 48, 132, 146, 170
lasts, 151, 171
Latham
  Robert, 234
lathe strings, 236
lathes
  turning, burnish, polishing, 236
lathing hammers, 80
Latin odes, 16
Latterman
  infantry regiment of, 20
law test
  Pennsylvania, 180
lawn aprons, 74, 99, 218
lawns, 1, 6, 7, 48, 74, 80, 98, 99, 108, 132, 136, 146, 165, 170, 197, 218
Lawrason
  James, 84
  Mr., 25, 26
Lawrence
  John, 43
  Mr., portrait of, 154
laws, 146
Le Roi
  Mr., engineer, 3
lead, 1, 146, 151, 171
lead pencils, 2, 170, 256
lead utensils, vessels, 185
leading lines, 171
leading strings, 208
Leakins's Lot, 224
leases, 225
Leath
  J., 160
leather, 171
leather bags, 74
leather breeches, 151
leather collars, 81
leather gloves, 136, 170
leather ink holders, 34, 40, 45
leather inkpots, 80
leather shoes, 6, 28, 74, 80, 99, 132, 136, 170, 239
  men's, 185
  women's, 185
leather, soal, 197
leather, wash, 197
Lebanon, Conn., 155
LeBrun
  Mon., 88
ledgers, 84, 86, 95, 100, 109, 115, 120, 133, 143, 147, 152, 162, 167, 172, 177, 183, 188, 193, 200, 207, 212, 255, 256, 262
Lee
  Arthur, Esq. Indian Comm'r, 20
  B., 5, 83
  Charles, 54, 83, 84, 123, 239
  Charles, Maj.-Gen., 127
  George, 234
  Henry, 40
  Henry, Jr., 216
  Richard, 31, 123, 124, 128, 138, 142, 147
  Richard B., 63
  Richard Bland, 31
  Richard Henry, 154, 216
  Thomas S., 78, 84
  Thomas Sim, 84
Leed's Town, 60, 187, 193, 200, 207
Leesburg, 29, 44, 50, 54, 59-61, 65, 70, 75, 85, 89, 91, 94-96, 100, 103, 104, 115, 126, 131, 141, 156, 157, 162, 199, 207, 212, 218, 219, 239, 240, 245, 251
Leeward Islands, 96
leggings, 127
Leghorn, 18, 51, 91, 111, 202, 231
Leghorn hats, 81
Leifkin
  D., 249
Leigh
  Henry, 234
Leiper
  George R., 234
Leiper's snuff, 136, 171
Leitrim, 96
LeJoyille
  Capt., 176, 186, 192
Lembourg
  Duchy of, 227
lemon squeezers, 171
lemons, 49, 89, 91, 96, 185
Leogan, 28
Lestevenon
  W. A., 13
letter books, 84, 133, 143, 147, 152, 162, 167, 172, 177, 183, 188, 193, 200, 207, 212, 255, 256, 262
Letter Paper, 2, 12, 17, 80
letters, 16, 109, 115, 182, 234, 236
letters to the Editor, 50
Levant
  Dutch trade in, 110
  famine relief methods, 196
  maritime insurance up 8-10%, 46
  plague remedies, 196
levee at St. James, 66
Levi
  Jew Elikao, 247
levies, 265
Lewis
  Andrew, 156
  Col., 150
  George, 21
  John, 17
  Mo(r)decai, 4, 97
  Samuel, Col., 145
  T., 28, 72

Thomas, 84
Thomas, Col., 145
Leyden
Baron of, 125
libraries, 256, 257, 267
licenses
ordinary, 20, 21
Liefkenshoek, 96
light house, 52
lightning, 118, 140, 141
metallic conductors, 140
Ligne
infantry regiment of, 20
Prince of, 61
Liguanea, 244
Lillo, 9, 10, 96, 129
lime, 28
limes, 211
limestone lands, 2
limestone quarry, 167
limestone water, 256
Lincoln
Maj. Gen., Hon., 114
Lincoln Co., 218, 219, 230
Lincoln's Inn, 26, 96
Lind
Arthur, 234
Linden
Baron, Dutch Amb., 227
Lindo
Elias, Esquire, 207
Lindsay
Opie, 218, 219, 230
Lindsey
Comm. asks Br. ship release, 111
John, Comm. Sir, 111
lindsey petticoats, 21
linen checks, 218
linens, 6, 7, 11, 12, 15, 28, 33, 49, 58, 69, 74, 80, 81, 98, 103, 108, 109, 135, 136, 160, 164, 165, 169, 172, 181, 192, 199, 206, 211, 217, 218, 223, 230, 234, 239, 250, 254
Flanders, 19
flax, 185
Lingan
James M., 84
linseed oil, 113
linsey jackets, 21, 95
linsey petticoats, 21, 95
linseys, 11, 132, 151, 165, 170, 218, 234, 239
Lintz, 46
liquorice, 29
liquors, 44, 59, 73, 75, 85, 156, 163, 170, 217, 260
Lisbon, 5, 10, 24, 32, 33, 48, 49, 51, 66, 68, 72, 73, 76, 78, 103, 110, 126, 141, 195, 206, 209, 212, 219, 225, 239, 240, 243, 246
American ships'demands, 18
English Consul at, 18
Queen grants Am. ships privileges, 67
Lisbon salt, 28, 30, 35, 68, 70, 181, 229
Lisbon wine, 49, 73, 81, 82, 94, 100, 103, 104, 118, 131, 156
Litchfield, 116
Litchfield Co., Conn., 43
literature, 80, 98, 160, 161, 256
Lithgow
Alexander, 40
Little
Capt., 125
Charles, 84
Little Falls, 53
Little Park, Windsor, 220
liturgy, 240
liver oil, 34
Liverpool, 20, 29, 33, 37, 40, 52, 56, 58, 63, 64, 66, 83, 85, 88, 91, 99, 100, 109, 112, 141, 155, 191, 192, 206, 210, 217, 220, 251, 256, 261, 262, 266
Liverpool ale, 64
Liverpool bottled ale, 11
Liverpool bottled beer, 6
Liverpool china, 6
Liverpool salt, 156, 229, 251
Liverpool ware, 165
livery lace, 197
livery stables, 161, 162, 172, 177, 183
livestock, 202, 203, 242
Livingston
Walter, 19
William, 118, 210
William, Gov., N.J., 113
Livingston's Manor, 116
Llewellin's warehouse, 69
Lloyd's Marine List, 97
loaf sugar, 6, 8, 11, 52, 64, 74, 81, 82, 103, 123, 136, 137, 142, 156, 171, 197
lock chains, 223
locks, 11, 15, 69, 74, 80, 136, 151, 165, 171, 182, 233, 252
Lockyer's pills, 29
Lodge
Joseph, 142
Lodge No. 39, 98, 101, 107, 160, 245, 250, 257, 262
Lodge, The, 217, 219, 230
Lodwick
Capt., 178
Loftenburgh
Capt, 32
lofts, 136, 250, 255
Lofwenburg
Peter, ship master, 51
log cabins, 235
log houses, 2
log tobacco house, 224
log-lines, 185
Logan
W., 149
Logil
Charles, Esq., 222
loglines, 1
logwood, 165
Br. cutters transgressed, 110
Lomax
John, 12, 13, 18, 23-26, 53, 109, 115, 120, 122, 127, 128, 156, 157, 162, 172
Mr., 37, 67, 78
London, 2, 3, 5, 6, 8-13, 15, 17, 18, 20, 23, 26-28, 30-36, 38-40, 42, 43, 45, 46, 48, 49, 51, 55, 56, 58, 61, 63, 66, 67, 72, 76-80, 82, 86, 88, 90, 91, 93, 96, 99, 101, 103-105, 109, 110, 112, 114-116, 121, 124, 126, 128, 130, 133, 138, 141, 144, 149, 150, 153-155, 158-162, 166, 168, 169, 173, 176, 178, 179, 181, 184, 188, 189, 192-194, 196, 200, 201, 203, 207, 211, 219-222, 225, 226, 228-231, 236, 237, 240, 243, 245-252, 254, 256-258, 261-263, 267
nobility and gentry, 145
Russian Ambassador, 247
St. Thomas's Hospital, 19
tobacco price (lb.) list, 63
Tower, 26
London coats, 127
London pins, 151
London playing cards, 218
London porter, 58, 90, 108, 131, 136, 165, 229
London volcabularies, 170
London, Court of
refuses relinquishing N.W. posts, 72
Londonderry, 43, 164
Long
Edward, 59
long boat, 159
Long Island, 214, 259
long-ells, 224
Longden
John, 151, 153, 157
Lonningfoot
parish of Lamplugh, 51
looking glasses, 1, 7, 11, 48, 49, 55, 74, 80
Loran
Capt., 178
Lord Carlisle, 39, 228

Lord George Gordon
letter on Irish affairs, 263
Lord Godolphin, 60
Lord Milford, 33
Lord North, 223
Lord Tracy, 33
Lordan
John, 145
lost
auditor's certificate, 79, 86
cow, 188
gold watch, 119, 124
saddle bags, 69, 70, 94, 100
lots
Carrollsburgh, 40, 41
for rent, 8, 21, 24, 26, 40, 41, 49, 52, 58, 68-70, 73, 81, 98, 100, 105, 108, 109, 126, 146, 169, 182, 187, 188, 192, 193, 199, 200, 211, 229, 234-236, 250, 251, 257, 261, 262, 266
for rent, George-Town, 122
for sale, 2, 23, 25, 26, 28-30, 35, 40, 45, 48, 49, 54, 55, 60, 61, 64, 68, 73-75, 79, 81, 82, 85, 86, 91, 95, 96, 98, 100, 103, 109, 114-116, 119-121, 124, 127, 131-133, 136, 138, 142, 143, 147, 151, 152, 155, 157, 161, 167, 171, 172, 176, 177, 183, 188, 192, 198, 199, 206, 207, 212, 219, 229, 230, 245, 257, 262, 266, 267
for sale, Dumfries, 29, 35, 45, 54, 60, 64, 70
for sale, Fredericksburg, 205, 230, 236
for sale, George-Town, 40, 41, 124, 133
for sale, Georgetown, 41
for sale, Leesburg, 59, 94, 96, 103
for sale, Norfolk, 28, 33, 35
for sale, Upper-Marlborough, 70
for sale, Winchester, 8
water, 126
lotteries, 12, 13, 23, 26, 30, 153
British, 130
Georgetown Academy, 85, 86, 105
loyalist relief, 154
Loudohn
Field Marshall, at Colin, 65
Loudon
Mr., 77
Loudon Co., 8, 17, 18, 23, 24, 26, 30, 34, 39, 54, 59, 63-65, 70, 75, 85, 86, 89, 91, 95, 103, 109, 115, 119, 120, 123, 124, 126, 128, 133, 137, 146, 171, 173, 176, 177, 183, 188, 193, 217, 218, 240, 267
Loughead
Capt., 233
Lougherey
Philip, 73, 82
Louis XVI., 204
Louisiana, 27
Louisiana frontiers
Americans settlers, 27
Love
Miles, 53
Samuel, 187
Samuel, Jr., 8, 142, 143, 152, 161
Low Countries, 3, 13
60,000 French coming, 31
Austrian forces in, 61
Imperial troops destined for, 20
Low Countries (Austrian)
flooded by Dutch waters, 32
Lowe
John, ordained, 214
Lowe's Masonic Sermons, 193, 200
Lower Creeks (tribes), 253
Lower Falls, 99, 177
Lower-Marlborough, Md., 7
Lowndes
Benjamin, 48, 55, 60
Christopher, 48, 55, 60
Francis, 48, 55, 60
Lownes
James, 234
Mr., 108
Lowry
Mr., 104, 109, 115, 120, 124, 128, 133, 138, 147, 152, 157, 161, 167
W., 12
William, 12, 13, 18, 58, 65, 84, 234, 240, 251
Lowth
Mr., 161
Loyalist
Pitt's bill for, critiqued, 158
widows, orphans, 158
loyalists, 62, 144, 153, 154
(Nova Scotia) in distress, 51
claims described, 247
claims, examination of, 163
claims: property, services, 238
East Florida, ask Spanish help, 87
king continues provisions to, 164
refugees, accursed, 121
Loyd
Col., 206
Lubeck
Prince Bishop of, dies, 168
Ludlum
Anthony, Capt., 112
Luis
Spain's Infant Don, 189
lumber, 71, 175, 190, 209, 249
Albany boards, 34
lump sugar, 15
Lunardi
Mr., balloonist, 14
lustrings, 15, 52, 58, 74, 79, 99, 132, 165, 170
Lutheran church
considerable loss to, 168
Luzerne
Marquis, Windward Is. governor, 159
Lycurgus
celibacy laws, 139
Lyle
Capt., 13
Col., 1
Hugh, 234
R., 234
Robert, 8, 49, 50, 60, 68, 70, 109, 115, 120, 216
Lyles
Henry, 64, 65, 74, 75, 84, 86, 104, 132, 133, 143, 170, 172, 177, 183, 192, 199, 207
Mr., 142, 245
William, 14, 79, 84, 86, 95, 99, 100, 109, 110, 115, 124, 132, 138, 143, 147, 152, 167, 172, 177, 183
William, Col., 137, 143
Lymington, 77
Lynn
Adam, 49, 55, 60, 108, 115, 120
John, 84
Lyon
Capt., 105
Dr., 33

M

M'Bride
Capt., 105
M'Cabe
Henry, 156, 157, 162, 171
Mrs., 156
M'Cahen
Hugh, 234
M'Candless
George, 206, 212
M'Cann
Capt., 191
M'Carty
Thaddeus, 59, 64, 65
M'Causland
Conolloy, Master (ship's), 164
M'Clain
T., 63, 68
M'Clay
John, 234
M'Clenachan
J., 228

John, 235, 240
M'Comb
Capt., 209
M'Connell
Matthew, 117
M'Coole
John, 136, 138
M'Crea
John, 187
Master, 72
Robert, 24, 85, 90, 132
M'Cready
James, 234
M'Cubbin
Zachariah, 53
M'Daniel
William, 7, 16
M'Daniel's Tavern, 7
M'Donald
Charles, 8
M'Dugal
Alexander, 234
M'Gachen
Mr., 85
M'Guire
Edward, 50, 68
McHenry
James, Dr., 19
M'Iver
Charles, 45
Mr., 30, 34, 40
M'Kean
Thomas, 117
M'Kellan
Capt., 245
M'Kenna
James, 239, 240, 251
M'Kenny
J., 135
M'Kewan
Michael, 8, 12, 17, 22
William, 84
M'Kinney
John, 234
M'Knight
Charles, Dr., 17
Mr., 25, 90
William, 79, 82, 86
M'Lean
Ewan, 210, 219, 225
Samuel, 2, 13, 18, 22
M'Lellan
Capt., 102
M'Mechen
David, 189
Mr., 188
M'Murray
Mr., 60, 61, 65, 75, 82, 91, 110, 120, 124
M'Nair
Ebenezer, 239
M'Pherson
D., 108, 115, 142, 143, 152, 182, 188, 193, 200, 224, 225, 235
Daniel, 1, 9, 13, 25, 26, 34, 81, 82, 84, 86, 89, 91, 96, 104, 109, 115
I., 108, 115, 142, 143, 152, 182, 188, 193, 200, 224, 225, 235
Isaac, 1, 9, 13, 25, 26, 34, 81, 82, 86, 89, 91, 96, 104, 109, 115
Samuel H., 22, 23, 30
M'Whir
Rev., 107
William, 80, 86, 91
William, Rev., 245
Macao, 87
Portuguese Governor of, 87
Swedes at, 87
macaroni (dandy)
confrontation with, 121
Macartney
Lord, Madras Gov., 189
Lord, oppressive management, 231
mace, 80, 81, 171
Machapungo, 176
machines
fresh water, 264
Machodick Neck, 235
Machodick warehouses, 170, 172, 183
MacIver
Colin, 88, 91, 100
Mackay
James, 222
mackerel, 1, 11, 13, 15, 28, 49, 103, 171
Mackrell
Mr., 246
Macky
Robert, 84
Macpherson
William, 117
Madden
Michael, 131, 133, 143, 188, 193, 200, 235
madder, 81
Maddison
James, 31
Madeira, 112
Madera, 48, 49, 91, 96, 103, 128, 181, 222
Madera
Isaac, 89
Madera wine, 2, 9, 17, 18, 63, 108, 137, 139, 142, 143, 152, 181, 182, 224, 228, 230, 240, 245, 251, 256
Madison
James, 20, 88
Madras, 66
Lord Macartney, Gov., 189
Madrid, 5, 13, 14, 36, 138, 189, 195, 221, 243, 246
Society of Natural History, 62
Maestricht, 3, 77, 96
indemnity for, 214
Prince Frederick appointed Governor, 31
treason against suspected, 76
Magaw, Samuel
Sec'y, Philosophical Soc., 20
magazine (publication), 201
magazines, 65, 194, 201
Magee
Mr., proprietor, Dublin Evening post, 67
magistrates, 27, 174, 202, 248
magnesia, 2, 29
Magruder
Basil, 70
Ninian Beall, 199
Thomas, 40, 64, 70, 71, 82
William B., 70
Magruder's Vale, 70
Maguire
Margaret, 85
Patrick, 85, 90
mahogany, 211
mahogany chairs, 217, 229
mahogany tables, 217
Mahomet, 122
Mahon, 168, 202
Capt., General of, 202
Mahony
Jeremiah, 234
maids, 196
mail, 182, 191
routes established, 169
savings, 180
mail service, 20
Maillebois
Count de, 128
M., 43
Making
Capt., 155
Makins
S., 176
Malaga, 112, 209
Algerine corsairs block, 158
Malston, Eng., 242
Malta
annual drubbing at Algiers, 91
man of war, Portuguese
convoying vessels, 209
Managers, 85
Manchester, 61, 102
against the Irish measures, 139
clock makers' petition, 139
concessions to Ireland excessive, 61
Duke of, family line, 258

tanners' petition, 139
Manchester cottons, 218
Manchester goods, 59, 206, 217, 219, 230, 251
Manchester gown patterns, 165
Manchester tapes, 79
Manchester, Duke of
St. Patrick: related, 258
mane combs, 219
mangoes, 231
manifests, 246, 251, 257
Manley
John, 181
Sarah, 181
Manly
George, 222
Mann
T., 33, 38, 48, 52, 103
Z., 63, 72, 78, 88, 118, 122, 135, 150, 160, 176, 181, 210, 216, 233
Zachariah, 64, 65, 75
manna, 29
manners, 5
mansion houses, 73
mantua silks, 81
manufactories, 14, 108, 131
china and earthenware, 159
Manufacturers, 102
Baltimore, 198
Boston, 198
Frederick Town, 198
manufactures, 57, 78, 130, 141, 181
American, encouragement, 155
American, extending, 208
English and Irish, 61
French, English, 204
increase population, 208
of America, 209
manumission, 113
maps
Kentucky, 84
M'Murray's, new of U.S., 47
U.S., 60, 61, 65, 75, 82, 91, 110, 120, 124
marble, 85, 107
marble chimney pieces, 80, 165
marble, polished, 185
Marblehead, 174
Marbois
Fr. Charge des Affaires, 154
March
Boston, 137, 138, 147
marine, 215
French, threatened, 164
Mariners, 175
Mariners' compasses, 33, 74
market house, 73, 99, 126, 192, 199, 361
markets, 109, 115, 170, 261
Oxford, 220
Markham
Bernard, 31
marking irons, 151, 171
Marlborough, 158, 223
marline spikes, 197, 251
marlines, 1
Marmora, 128
marriage, 116, 196, 200, 247
laws of Solon, 139
marriages
Arell, David, 72
Blewit, Mr., 173
Buel, Rev., 259
Caverly, Phoebe, 72
Chesley, Rebecca, 245
Chew, Betsy, 52
Don Juan, infanta of Spain, 110
Dudley, Frances, 93
Duke of York, 231
Dundas, John, 48
Gardiner, Sylvester, Dr., 32
Gildart, Francis, 216
Goldthwait, Catherine, 32
Goldthwait, Mr., 32
Harper, Edward, 233
Hepburn, Nancy, 48
Hewitt, Martha, 216
Higginson, Miss, 233
Hollins, John, 254
King, Elizabeth, 261
Lyle, Robert, 216
Martin, Ann, 216
Mason, John, 135
Mercer, John F., 20
Miller, Miss, 259
Moxley, Betsy, 48
Parsons, Polly, 135
Pope, Mr., 254
Princess Frederica of Prussia, 231
Primate, Mrs., 32
Ramsay, Dennis, Col., 216
Roberdeau, Nancy, 169
Robertson, John, 48
Ryan, Michael, 93
Sim, Robert, 261
Smith, Miss, 254
Spriggs, Sophia, 20
Swift, Jonathan, 169
Taylor, Jenny, 216
Townsend, Henry, 245
Weightman, Richard, 52
Younge, Miss, 254
Marrice
Maj., and his lady, 160
Marseilles cotton, 81
Marseilles quilting, 12, 58, 74, 79, 100, 132, 151, 165, 170
marsh
draining of, 2, 13, 17, 361
Marshall
John, 31
marshes, 170
Marsteller
Philip, 234
Martha's Vineyard, 264
Martin
Ann, 216
Col., 136
Gov., of Frankland, 180
J., 239
Mr., Indian Commissioner, 205
Mr., member, Georgia co., 205
S., 73, 103, 107, 155
Thomas, 52
Martinico, 33, 43, 237, 254
Martinique, 247
French troops on, 96
Superior Council Arrêt, 101
Martinique-Guadaloupe
30 Am. ships seized, sold, 164
Martins
S., 141
Martinsburg, 8, 98, 101, 109, 120, 161
Marvin
Capt., 88
Maryland, 10, 16, 19, 25, 27, 43, 53, 64, 78, 83, 84, 122, 125, 130, 131, 152, 161, 169, 170, 210, 222, 228, 240
credit kept up, 125
Gen. Ass'y, Comm. on Manufactures, 228
General Assembly, 228
ginseng export figure, 62
Legislature, 189
paper currency petition, 228
State Theatre to open, 145
tobacco price, London, 63
Marylanders
discontent with new govt., 4
Mason
George, 6, 12, 13, 22, 23, 30, 34, 40, 45
John, 40, 41, 49, 135
Thomson, 79, 86, 161, 162, 172
Masonic odes, 16
Masonry
emblems on ship's stern, 19
Masons (also see "Freemasons"), 160, 187, 193, 200, 245
Massachusetts, 19, 130, 134, 150, 228
3 breakaway counties, 121
Br. ship duties repeal, 226
cedes western land to U.S., 87
Daturic Larder, Dutch Consul, 169
discountenancing prophanity, irreligion, 113
duties on vellum, parchment, paper, 77
Gov., Stanhope feud, 164

Gov. Bowdoin, 228
impost law, 155
navig. act, Eng. reaction, 248
navigation act changes, 244
Nova Scotians steal from, 121
representatives, Congress: list of, 117
ruinous trade, navigation policies, 71
spermaceti oil bounty, 244
Stamp Act, considered, 83
treat Br. factors as G.B. ours, 87
yellow, brown oil, bounty, 244
Massachusetts Bay, 19, 145
Massachusetts Centinel, 222
Massachusetts Stamp Act
documents affected (list), 77
massacre
of Hierro castaways, 27
Massaredo
Don Joseph, 202
Massorado
Rear Admiral Don J., 178
Masters, 28, 40, 44, 49, 50, 60, 64, 65, 70, 73, 75, 95, 97, 98, 103, 115, 120, 131, 143, 165-167, 170-173, 183, 186, 206, 211, 219, 223, 225, 230, 239, 240, 246, 249-251, 256, 257, 262, 266, 267
masts, 159, 176, 189
Mate of a ship, 25
Mates, 159, 245
mathematical instruments, 136
mathematics, 98, 160
Mathew
Lt. Gen., 24
Mathews
Gen., & officers, execution, 214
John, 174
matrimony, 196
Matthew
John, mutineer, 159
Matthews
General, 18
John, Esq., 149
Mr., mutineer & thief, 174
Thomas, 31
Mattox Bridge, 199, 207, 212, 219, 225
mattresses, 123, 127, 132, 133
maxims, 254
Maxwell
Gov., 144
Gov., Bahama Islands, 62
May
William, 261
Mayo
Joseph, 126
William, 30, 31
Mayors, 14, 54
meadows, 1, 7, 22, 25, 29, 75, 89, 90, 99, 103, 119, 151, 166, 170, 171, 217, 218, 224, 229, 235, 250, 266
Maj. Gen., 24
measure, carpenters', 185
meat houses, 2, 151, 166, 193, 205
Mecca, Caravan of, 111
Mechanics, 32, 208
encouragement of, 155
Mecklenburg Co., 52
Medicines, 2, 8, 12, 13, 18, 22, 23, 26, 29, 30, 34, 35, 40, 58, 61, 65, 100, 126, 128, 136-138, 147, 165, 251
Mediterranean, 68, 80, 85, 115, 139, 206, 211, 227, 234, 239, 249, 250
Moors masters of, 91
Medway, 4
Medway squadron
Commodore Bowyer, cmdg., 195
Meeks
Edward, 32
meeting houses, 34
Groat Market, 196
High Bridge, 196
meetings, 11, 34, 45, 53, 55, 60, 63, 67, 70, 73, 75, 78, 83, 84, 96, 98, 101, 131, 160, 233, 239, 250, 257, 261, 262
Mellile
1774 siege of, 246
memorandum books, 256
Memorial and Remonstrance [Essay]
James Madison, author, 207
men of war
Dutch, 3
Spanish (2), 74 guns, 178
men's leather shoes, 185
Mendicant Friars
Austrian Netherlands, 65
Menonists, 31, 45
Mentz
Elector in desperate state, 134
Electorate Court of, 168
Mercer
John F., 40, 45, 49, 50
John F., Hon., 20
Robert, Capt., 105
merchant mills, 7, 34, 176, 229
merchant's notes, 75
Merchants, 17, 19, 35, 43, 46, 48, 57, 63, 64, 67, 70, 72, 75, 86, 87, 98, 101, 107, 110, 112, 134, 145, 150, 151, 158, 169, 190, 195, 201, 205, 210, 215, 216, 220, 223, 225, 228, 229, 233, 238, 247, 250, 253-255, 257, 261, 262
in Cork relieve shipping, 114
ruined by British, 113
Merryman
John, 53, 55, 64, 70, 75
Meshach, 144
mess beef, 58, 90, 229
mess pork, 58, 229
message cards, 256
messinets, 7
metal buttons, 49, 59, 127, 136
Methodists, 45, 249
Mexico, 93, 158
Miami, 232
Miami River, 149, 196
Michaelis
Christ. Fred., M.D., 20
microscopes, 6, 136
Middleburgh
Preliminary Articles, resolutions on, 241
Middlesex court day, 146
Middletown, 232
Middletown, Conn., 149
middlings, 235
Migazzi
infantry regiment of, 20
Milan, 10
Milford
Lord, 33
military, 16, 123, 222
Army, 215
Fairfax militia, 79
Invasion in 1781, 17
land warrants, 218
militia, 57
Pennsylvania line, 45
military certificates, 8, 21, 94, 100, 156
military claims, 193
militia
South Carolina, 92
uniforms, described, 258
militia certificates, 100
militiamen
massacre castaways, 27
Mill Creek, 193, 200
mill houses, 2, 176
mill saw files, 218
mill saws, 171, 197
mill seats, 2, 7, 53, 90, 99
millenary, 7, 230
Miller
Christian, Master (ship), 107
J.W., 44
John W., 234
Miss, 259
Peter, 255
W., 73
Millet
Pierre, to gallies for slave theft, 101
Milliners, 143

mills, 1, 2, 7, 29, 30, 33, 34, 40, 59, 64, 65, 75, 90, 99, 103, 104, 152, 170, 172, 176, 183, 229
barley shelling, 154
Bruce's, 94
grist, 116
horse snuff, 81, 86
paper, 102, 147
saw, 94, 96
Mills
James, 146, 147, 157
John, 118, 124, 127
Milton, 170
Minden, 194
Miner
Joseph, 169
mines, 119
Mingoes, 150
mining, 94
Minister of War, 43
Minister Plenipotentiary
Britain's to Brussels, 4
Minister Republic of Holland
High Mightinesses, 169
Lords the States General, 169
Minister to France, 48
Ministers, 31, 41, 52, 60, 85, 88, 90, 135, 145, 157, 164, 166, 222, 240, 255
Minorca, 102
mint, royal, 194
miser
a miser's creed, 140
mishaps, 121
Mitchel
Joseph, 120, 133
Joseph, Col., 161
Mitchell
Charles, 25
Randle, 80, 86, 91, 137, 138, 147, 192, 199, 206, 212, 219, 225, 230
Samuel, 26
Mitchemore
Capt., 141
mitts, 7, 58, 80, 99, 136, 170, 218
leather, 197
silk, 197
Moatt
Capt., 10
J., 10
Mochain
Sieur, Royal Academy of Sciences, 101
Mochain, Sieur
discovered a new comet, 102
modes, 12, 33, 58, 73, 74, 79, 81, 98, 99, 132, 136, 218
Mogador, 93, 246
Moggadore, 181
mohair, 132, 151, 170
Mohoba Bank, 164
molasses, 1, 6, 8, 11, 15, 21, 28, 30, 34, 35, 38, 41, 44, 49, 52, 58, 63, 64, 78, 84, 88, 108, 115, 122, 131, 136, 142, 156, 160, 165, 167, 169, 171, 175, 181, 187, 192, 198, 223, 224, 228, 239, 254, 261
molasses sugar, 166
mole
Algiers, 500 toises long, 66
monasteries, 65
Moncure
John, Rev., 166
money, 97
'annas, 213
copper, 140
copper, a, 233
counterfeit dollars in Ireland, 66
counterfeit French guineas, 24
counterfeit half guineas, Ireland, 66
dollar rate falls, Glasgow, 107
ducats, 133, 220
Dutch florins, 96
farthings, 140, 184
florins, 47, 116, 178, 225, 227
gold, 102
guineas, 56, 140, 148, 203, 254
half-crowns, 213
hard dollars, 173
livres, 194
Mexican large, 52
paper currency, 228
paper money, 227
paper money, evils of, 121
paper, approving view, 102
pence, 140
Pennsylvnia paper, 102
pezos, 247
pieces of eight, 52, 175, 189
pillar large and small, 52
pounds, 140
pounds sterling, 173
rupees, 66, 213
shillings, 140, 254
silver, 102
Spanish dollars, 168
money scales, 7
Monongalia Co., 54, 59, 61, 70, 85, 91, 95, 104
monopolies, 121
Monroe
James, 216
John, 161, 162, 172, 256, 262
Sarah, 255, 256, 262
William, 90, 91, 100, 104, 115
Montague
family line, 258
Montego Bay, 164
Montenegro Bay, Jamaica, 19
Montgolfier, the
[generic name, hot air ballon], 183
Montgomery
James, 31
John, 83, 122
Montgomery Co., Md., 104, 127, 138, 151, 153, 161, 167, 172, 177, 183, 188, 224, 225, 235, 240, 245, 251, 255, 257, 262, 267
Montreal, 261
English fortifying, 62
monuments, 107
Moor
Jacob, 137, 138, 147
Moore
a pirate, 135
Capt., 43
Jacob, 223, 225, 235
Mr., 114
P., 181
Reuben, 104
Stephen, Clonmell rep., 168
T.L., 117
William, Clonmell rep., 168
Moore's navigation, 33
Moore-Hill, 35, 39, 41, 49
moorings, 252
Moorish cruiser
captured 6 Am. ships, 66
Moorish King
Alley Courie, 10
Moors, 5, 186, 210, 237
capture French Governor's snow, 10
seize Venetian polacre, 91
morality, 5
morals, 31, 159
Moran
J.C., 254
Morarty
Maurice, 234
Moravia, 76
moreens, 12, 81, 132, 170, 218, 249
Morgan
Capt., 191
Mogran, 85
Morgan's Run, 59
Morgan's-Town, 54
Morie
P., 103
Morlaix, 176
Moro
Sieur, 2d in cmd., Susa, 46
Moro castle, 27
Moroccan export corn ships
Genoese, 247
Portuguese, 247
Spaniards, 247
Tuscans, 247

Morocco, 6, 43, 83, 111, 128, 180, 181
  basis for anti-U.S. acts, 112
  Chiappo, Venetian Consul, 247
  Emperor of, 246
  Mr. Barclay sent as Am. agent, 248
  new regulation, corn, 247
  sent E. Levi, Mogador, 247
  Spain's gift: 12 freed slaves, 246
Morocco shoes, 7, 49, 136, 170, 218
Morocco slippers, 218
Morocco-leather pocket-books, 33
Morris
  Thomas, 149
mortars, 171, 189, 194
mortars and pestles, 165
Morton
  John, 154
mould candles, 1, 63, 146, 181, 239
moulding planes, 80
Moulton
  Gen., 258
Moultrie
  William, Hon., 36
Mounsher
  W., 94, 100
Mount Vernon, 39, 93, 142, 206, 218, 222, 230, 236
Mount-Airy, Md., 90, 95, 101
Mount-Royal Forge, 53
mourning crapes, 170
mowing, 17, 45
Moxley
  Betsy, 48
  John, 17, 18, 23, 30
Moyes
  Dr., lecturer extraordinaire, 82
  Dr., water spouts, 264
Muenster treaty, 242
muffs, 197
Muhlenberg
  Henry, Rev., 20
Muir
  Capt., 239, 240, 251
  John, 40, 41, 45, 132, 230, 239, 240, 250, 257, 262, 267
Mulattoes, 64, 65, 90, 95, 100, 101, 103, 104, 109, 110, 116, 122, 127, 156, 161, 165, 172, 177, 183
Mull
  George, 156
mullet twine, 251
Mullingar, 260
Murad Bey, 75
murders, 18, 37, 43, 88, 130, 135, 145, 163, 209, 222, 223
Murphy
  William, 17, 256, 257, 267
Murray
  Capt., 19
  H., 138
  John, 8, 24, 26, 34, 35, 52, 55, 64, 156, 157, 162
  Patrick, 54, 55, 64, 94, 136, 161, 162, 172, 177, 183
Murry
  infantry regiment of, 20
Murtland
  John, 223, 230, 234
Muschett
  James, 86, 95
Muscle Shoals
  Spanish incursion at, 37
  western part So.Car., not No. Car., 47
Muscovado sugar, 6, 11, 15, 21, 28, 38, 44, 52, 58, 63, 64, 78, 79, 81, 84, 88, 94, 100, 101, 108, 115, 118, 120, 122, 131, 136, 142, 151, 155, 156, 160, 164, 169, 181, 182, 187, 198, 223, 228, 239, 254, 261
Muse
  Battaile, 25, 26, 34, 35, 69, 70, 94, 100
music, 93, 187, 256
music houses, 247
musical instruments, 185
muskets, 1, 158
Muskingum, 232
muslin aprons, 15, 99
muslin cords, 73
muslin stripes, 12
muslinets, 109
muslins, 6, 48, 49, 52, 58, 74, 80, 98, 99, 103, 125, 132, 142, 151, 155, 165, 170, 197, 249
Musquisack, 150
Musquito, 61
Musquito Indians
  Carthagena joins assault, 61
Musquito Shore, 110, 116
  Br.-Span. maritime courtesy, 129
  British logwood cutters, 110
  English-Spanish treaty, 106
  Jamaica reinforcing, 47
  loyalist refugee settlement, 121
mustard, 6, 81, 171, 185, 197, 219, 229, 239
mutton, 198
Myre
  Conrad, 17, 18, 23, 30

N

nabob
  English steals diamonds, 71
Nabob of Arcot, 231
nags, 7
nail rods, 171, 185
nails, 7, 8, 12, 15, 33, 49, 52, 74, 80-82, 98, 135-137, 142, 146, 151, 165, 171, 197, 239, 251
  ready made, 185
Nangomy, 103
nankeens, 12, 73, 81, 100, 141, 142, 146, 151, 155
Nansemond, 135
Nantasket Road, 149
Nantucket, 130
  England contracting benfits, list, 203
  envoy sails for England, 203
  requesting independence, 202
Nantz, 149, 227
  Consuls of, 190
napkins, 1, 6
Naples, 125, 194
  may suffer by Algerines, 202
  to join Algiers attack, 125
Naples & Sicily peacetime landforces: 30,000, 61
narrow hoes, 74
Narrows, the, 77
Nashville, 204
Nassau, 112, 144
  Prince of, 242
Nassau, New Providence, 62
national debt, 35
national prosperity, 215
Natural History, Society of, 62
natural wonders
  £700,000 sterling fire, 126
  amphibious animal, Chile, 13
  catastrophic lightning, 116
  Connecticut earthquake, 259
  earthquake lakes cause epidemic, 125
  epidemical dysentery kills 1000, 162
  Eur. drought severest in memory, 130
  extreme high tide, severe storm, 175
  fire loss, £300,000, 133
  gale, mid-Atlantic coast, 185
  great dearth in the Duab, 213
  Jamaica hurricane, 191
  lightnin destroys grist mill, 116
  lightning damages chimney, gable-end, 121
  lightning dismasts, wrecks ship, 258
  lightning enters school, kills, 140
  method: fresh, from salt water, 264
  monstrous child, description of, 62
  pestilential fog kills corn, 139
  plaster fumes fell family, 253

recent births, 4 generation, same family, 179
sea survival, cork apparatus, 238
soap suds bar hydrophobia, 243
sun, circled with suns, 116
violent earth tremors, 140
West Indies severe hurricane, 178
wind: 200 ships missing, 134
woman 4-years pregnant, 246
nature (also see "Natural Wonders"), 208
Navarre
French troops increasing, 189
Navarro
Joachin, 62
navigation, 7, 10, 29, 30, 40, 53, 55, 57, 60, 63, 70, 75, 78, 83, 94, 104, 131, 141, 170, 176, 182, 186, 188, 193, 200, 204, 210, 264
50 Am., West Indies sail safe, 162
Am. vessels, G.B. ports, 92
Bahamas refuses Am. ship, 148
Bahamas' Am. ship seizures, expulsions, 148
Barbary corsairs stop trade, 125
Barbary incursions incommode, 47
Cape Nicola Mole closed to Ams., 66
China seas, 87
discouraged, 71
East Indies bars Am. ships, 158
easterly winds stop America-bound, 114
eastern, 205
England's repeal of the act, 14
floating light near Cromer, 36
free ports to Americans, 37
Havana open to Am. ships, 113
Havana reopened to Am. trade, 92
laws for better regulation, 155
Mississippi, Spanish truculence, 56
new optical device for, 67
of the Mississippi, 27
of the Scheldt, 154
Pope opens to Am. ships, 113
restrictive act proposed, 125
ruinous policies, 71
ship loss, contrary winds, 134
Spanish bar New Orleans, 20
St. Kitt's seizes Am. ships, 144
to China, novel, 253
uncharted rocks, Torry Island, 96
Navigation Act, 150
Neal
Mrs., 122
Nebuchadnezzar
King, 144
necessary, 77
Neckar
Mr., 141
needle-worked aprons, 7
needles, 6, 7, 74, 80, 81, 165, 170, 172, 219, 251
needlework, 182
Negapatnam
negotiation for, 77
Negro cottons, 136, 151, 165, 217, 239, 250, 254, 255
Negroes, 12, 18, 23, 28, 30, 35, 44, 52-54, 57, 64, 65, 75, 86, 88, 91, 94, 95, 109, 110, 114, 120, 122-124, 127, 131, 133, 134, 138, 142, 143, 146, 161, 163, 165, 183, 192, 193, 198-200, 205-207, 211, 212, 219, 239, 244, 262
bill to bar importation, 244
for hire, 1, 198, 212, 219, 261
for rent, 230
for sale, 1, 6, 9, 12, 13, 18, 26, 30, 34, 39-41, 45, 53, 55, 61, 64, 70, 75, 94, 126, 128, 137, 142, 151, 155-157, 162, 166, 167, 170, 172, 181, 192, 198, 199, 211, 217-219, 223, 225, 250, 254, 266
from Africa, 184
from the West Indies, 184
quarters, 151, 170, 224
runaways, 17, 22, 25, 26, 50, 60, 85, 95, 133, 162, 165, 172, 176, 193, 261, 267
taken away, 21, 23, 30, 34
wench, 21, 23, 30, 34, 86, 95, 101, 123, 126, 131, 133, 138, 142, 151, 155-157, 162, 167, 183, 192, 200
Nekar
Mr., 129
Nelson
Hugh, 166, 167, 177
John, 267
Nathaniel, 31
Nelly, 267
Nepean
Mr., commissioner, 32
Nesbit
John, 4
Nesbitt
John M., 97
Netherlands, 42, 135
nets, 6
Neubro, 219, 225
Neubro furnace, 210
Neuilly bridge, 189
Neville
Lord, 220
New
Capt., 8, 141
T., 33
Thomas, 211
Thomas, Capt., 219, 225
New Andalusia, 140
New Brunswick
new settlers' progress, 178
supplying West India Is., 178
New England, 73, 102, 135, 233, 249, 254
trade, West Indies, 178
New England rum, 1, 8, 9, 13, 28, 49, 108, 115, 131, 137, 165-167, 171, 197, 239
New Exchange Enlarged, 224
New Hampshire, 5, 182, 222
Act, personal property for debts, 222
Brigade, Artillery, 258
Brigade, Light Horse, 258
brigades, militia, 258
Daturic Larder, Dutch Consul, 169
General Court, 222, 253
Great & Gen. Court session ends, 227
militia units, uniforms, 258
new punishment, petty crimes, 253
paper money disfavored, 227
regiment in Am. homespun, 179
New Haven, 56, 141, 179
New Jersey, 20, 210, 240
Congress to regulate trade, 238
foreign merchandise, duty on, 254
General Assembly, 238
raise 110 men,serve 3 years, 238
New London, 24, 66, 259
residence of Bishop, 130
New Orleans
1000 Havana troops coming, 27
Spaniards bar way to, 20
New Providence, 105, 148, 205
Collector, 175
Gov., 175
Judge of the Admiralty, 175
mistreatment, Am. ship, 175
New York, 4, 5, 10, 14, 15, 17, 19, 20, 24, 28, 32, 37, 38, 43, 47, 51, 52, 56, 62, 63, 73, 77, 78, 87, 88, 92, 93, 101, 107, 113, 114, 116, 121, 126, 130, 134, 149, 151, 153-155, 159, 168, 169, 173, 175, 179, 181, 182, 184, 185, 191, 192, 194, 196, 203, 208, 210, 214, 215, 221, 228, 230-232, 238, 240, 245, 248, 249, 251, 253, 256, 259, 261

Chamber of Commerce, 148
City Hall, 117
duties selling Negroes, 113
few English ships, 195
ginseng export figure, 62
Governor Clinton, 112
grants hemp bounty, 113
legislature dumps 5% bill, 51
Legislature orders frontier quota, 37
Mayor and corporation, 117
packets' free transport, Br. indigents, 37
trade very slack, 195
New York city
from, conveyance of mail, 169
New York duties
foreign cordage per cwt. 1/, 113
foreign hemp, cwt. 2/, 113
foreign linseed oil, gal. 4d, 113
pair of boots, 2/, 113
pair of shoes, 6d, 113
white rope or yarns, cwt., 4/, 113
New York troops, 232
Newbury, 140
Newburyport, 92, 174, 253
plaster fumes fell family, 253
Newcastle, 36, 196
100 ships lost in storm, 42
Duke of, and beggar, 243
Newenham
Edward, Sir, 9
Newfoundland, 43, 71, 154
Adm. Campbell, Gov., 110
Banks of, 134
Br. frigates fire on Am. fishermen, 107
Newfoundland banks, 66
Newgate, 62, 67, 75, 103, 161, 218
Newington Green, 180
Newman
Capt., 191
Newport, 43, 47, 104, 233
Newport, Md., 95, 100
Newspaper, Thoughts on a [Editorial], 200
Newspaper--2/3d
Massachusetts' new tax on, 77
newspapers, 38, 126, 182, 222, 242, 245, 249, 254, 261
Augusta, by G. Hughes, 190
Bahama Gazette, 27, 87, 113
Boston, 242
Calcutta Gazette, 252
Continental Journal, Boston, 83
Dublin, 55
Dublin Evening Post, 67
Dublin Morning Post, 67
Edinburgh Courant, 231
English, 184
essay on, 200
Exchange Advertiser (Boston), 125
French, 55
Gazette, 168
Gazette (Utrecht), 201
Halifax, 238
hint treason against Maestricht, 76
Irish, 148
Jamaica, 196
John Gill's, Boston, 159
London, 52, 155, 160, 259
London Morning Chronicle, 205
London Morning Post, 200
London Universal Register, 140
Maryland, 188
Maryland Journal, 115, 121
Massacusetts Spy, 149
New Haven Gazette, 43
New York, 92
New York Gazette, 93
Newbury, 140
Parisian, 252
Pennsylvania Packet & Daily Advertiser, 68
St. Christopher's Gazette, 113
subscriptions, 5
suppressed by Stamp Act, 118
VJ&AA, 5
Volunteer Journal (Cork), 118, 138
Niagara, 91, 144, 145
Nicholas
John, 30
Samuel, 117
Samuel, Maj., 17
Wilson Cary, 30
Nichols
William, 137, 138, 216, 219, 225
Wliliam, 211
Nicholson
Capt., 63
Nightingale
Mr., 4
Nimuegen, 201
nippers, 171
nitre, 29
Niven
Daniel, 32
Nixon
Capt., 5, 52
George, 141
J., 28, 93
James, 34
James, Capt., 40, 45
John, 4, 97
Noah
Elias, 98, 101
Noah's ark
like Irish pension list, 101
Noble
George, 256
Thomas, 261, 267
Noland
Mary, 167, 177
Philip, Jr., 166, 167, 177
Thomas, 167, 177
Noland's Ferry, 166, 167, 177
nonjurors
bill to relieve, 189
nonsopretties, 7, 15, 74, 218
Norborne Parish, 85, 90, 95
Norfolk, 28, 30, 60, 64, 70, 93, 144, 159, 175, 215
buildings water filled, 175
lost: lumber, merchandise, 175
lost: salt, sugar, corn, 175
ships drove from moorings, 175
tide, storm damage, described, 175
warehouses carried away, 175
Normandy, 19, 32
Norris
Malachi, 47
North
Lord, 71, 144
Lord, and America, 71
Lord, new connexions, 184
North Carolina, 47, 68, 72, 118, 141, 205, 218, 228, 233
Caswell, Governor of, 180
new Spanish post, 37
Plank Bridge, 47
Spanish incursion, 43
Tenasee great bent purchase, 205
North Carolinia
spirited remonstrances , 4
North Edisto, 112
North Riding, York Co., 242
North River, 153
Northumberland Co., 95
Norton
Daniel, Dr., 161
George F., 99, 104, 109
Mr., 54, 55, 60
Norwood
Capt., 206
Nosewell
Justice, 187
Notley Hall, 206, 212
Nourse
James, 172, 173, 183, 224, 225, 235
Joseph, 224
William, 172, 173, 183, 224
Nova Scotia, 5, 20, 43, 71, 87, 101, 117, 148, 164, 190, 242
Am. loyalists return to N.Y., 107
Jamaica seeks volunteers, 61
only Brit. trade, ships, 87
steals from Massachusetts, 121
novels, 126, 185
novices, 65

nunnery, 125
nuns, 74, 125
nuns' thread, 49, 151, 165
Nuremburg, 46
Nurses, 99
nutmegs, 80, 81, 171
nuts, 197

O

O'Brian
  Capt., 239
O'Donnel
  Capt., 210
O'Donnell
  Capt., 141
O'Kelly
  Col., 33
O'Neill
  Bernard, 40, 41, 50, 84
O'Reilly
  Comte, 140
O'Rourke
  Count, 26, 96
O-planes, 11
oars, 89, 189
oatmeal, 251
Obryan
  Richard, 222
Ocagna
  Don Vincent, Surgeon in Ordinary, 62
Occoquan, 99
Occoquan furnace, 210
occupations, 255
ochre, 74
Ocracock Bar, 186
Odes, 16, 22, 26
Officers, 43, 170
officers' certificates, 22
OG-planes, 11
Ogle
  Benjamin, 45, 50, 54, 60, 64
Oglethorpe
  Gen., founded Georgia, 162
  James, Gen., Cranham Hall, Essex, 162
Ohio, 47, 232
Ohio River, 145
  savages continue mischief, 113
oil, 1, 13, 67, 71, 108, 123, 162
  spermaceti, Am. exports to Fr., 149
oil, lindseed, 197
oil, scalding
  execution by, 214
Old Bailey
  address to convicts, 258
  Mr. Recorder, 258
Old Calabar, 128
Omond
  Robert, 234
Oost, 225
opium, 29, 246
oporto wine, 73, 81, 82, 94, 100, 103, 104
Oran, 189
  Bey's 8000 men, 14
  Moors' vandalism, theft, 14
Orange
  Prince of, 242
Orange and Nassau
  House of, 242
Orange Co., 94, 96, 104
orange peel, 29
oranges, 4, 49
orchards, 1, 2, 22, 89, 99, 151, 166, 176, 224
Orde
  Mr., 5
  Mr., propositions of, 86
  Thomas, Hon., 56
ordnance wharf, 163
organs, 59, 64, 65, 75
Oriental Company, The, 195
Original Writ
  Clerk of Common Pleas, 77
  Justice of the Peace, 77
Orphean Society, 187
Orrick
  Nicholas, 115, 116, 124
Orta, 197
  Cabral, J.F.F., Mayor, 198
Osburne
  John, 70
  Michael, 234
Osgoode
  Mr., Treasury Bd. Commissioner, 19
Osman
  M.B., Moroccan Amb., 246
  Mahomet Ben, 246
osnaburg shirts, 25, 122, 123
osnaburg thread, 11, 28, 33, 151
osnaburg trousers, 89, 123
osnaburgs, 1, 2, 6, 7, 9, 11, 15, 28, 49, 59, 74, 79-81, 100, 136, 142, 151, 153, 155, 161, 165, 170, 234, 239
Ostend, 4, 10, 105, 139
Ostokoi, 203
ostrich, 66
ostrich feathers, 6, 16, 99
Oswald
  Eleazer, Col., 17
  Mr., 187
  portrait of, West's, 154
Oswaldkirk, Eng., 242
out houses, 2, 75, 89, 99, 109, 123, 176, 199, 224
Outram
  Capt., 141
ovens, 82
Over Maeze, 225
overalls, 89, 192
Overseer's house, 1
Overseers, 94
Overseers of the Poor, 265, 266
Overton
  Capt., 92
Overyssel, 201
Ovid, 170
Owing
  Samuel, 33
oxen, 191
Oxen Hill, 161, 162, 172
Oxford
  sink of vice, profligacy, 5
Oxford market, 220
Oxley
  Mr., 39
oyster knives, 171, 218
oysters, 170

P

Pacha
  Porte's Governor of Egypt, 111
pacification
  Republic's steps towards, 227
pack saddle, 6
Packard
  S., 38, 78, 97, 150
Packets, 14, 65, 70, 75
  (unk) Fr., 117
  (unk) French, 37
  (unk) from Helvoetsluys, 154
  (unk) Nova Scotia, 204
  (unk) Spanish, 180
  at Calais, 42
  Carteret, 191
  Courier de la L'Orient, 155
  Courier de New York, 37, 56
  from Dublin via N.Y.packet, 14
  Greyhound, 107, 195
  his Britannic Majesty's, 37
  La Courier de l'Amerique, 4
  La Martinique, 126
  Le Courier de la Martinique, 93
  Le Courier d'Europe, 77
  Philadelphia, 249
  Port l'Orient-New York, 238
  Roebuck (Br.), 248
  Speedy, 20
  Swallow, 191
  the British, 4, 203
  the December Brit., 19
padesoys, 170
padlocks, 15, 218
  French, 19
pads, 6

Page
John, 171, 173, 183
Mann, 31
Mann, Hon., 20
Paine
Thomas, remunerated, 159
paint brushes, 80, 170
painter's colours, 197
painting, 108
paints, 1, 15, 100, 169, 196
Pajarate wine, 229
palace, 231
Palatine
villages flooded, 105
Palfrey
Col., 184
captured, 43, 47
Palinurus, 144
Pallas, 210
palsy, 226
Pancas
Miss, 160
Paolian rib, 58
Papal dispensation, 76
paper, 77, 132, 143, 152, 161, 167, 170, 177, 187, 188, 193, 200, 207, 212
paper hangings, 2, 7, 12, 17, 19, 22, 23, 30, 35, 45, 49, 54, 79, 197
paper mills, 102, 147
paper money
New Hampshire, disfavored, 227
paper, printing, 185
paper, sheathing, 185
paper, wrapping, 185
paper, writing, 185
Paradise, 123, 124, 128, 138, 142, 147
Paradise Lost, 170
parchment, 77, 139, 185
Paris, Fra., 3, 9, 13, 14, 18, 31, 46, 51, 55, 61, 76, 82, 101, 111, 112, 129, 134, 139, 144, 147, 159, 162, 173, 189, 194, 195, 201, 213, 214, 225, 227
3 capital houses bankrupt, 195
Academy of Sciences, 159
Am. remittances tardy, 196
assembly of the clergy, 213
baths for the poor, 226
change [Exchange] gloomy, 196
Duke of Dorset, Brit. Envoy, 56
Emperor, incognito, arrives, 42
Franklin's visit to, 139
negotiations stopped, 221
rage for ballooning, 51
parishes, 11, 65, 237, 265
Chester, 240
Fairfax, 11
Frederick, 52
Henrico, 48
Norborne, 85, 90, 95
Shelburne, 24, 26, 34
Parker
Mr., merchant, a suicide, 112
S., 20
Parliament, 3, 134
parlours, 126, 199
Parr
John, Capt., 87
Parramore
Thomas, 31
parrier (dog), 213
Parrott
A., 10
parsimony
Duke of Bedford's, 158
parsonage, 130
Parsons
James, Capt., 5
John, 187
Nancy, & Duke of Bedford, 158
Polly, 135
passages, 5, 29, 44, 60, 78, 97, 126, 127, 155, 166, 171, 176, 188, 192, 211, 224, 240, 245, 250, 266
passengers, 52, 114, 135, 176, 188, 211, 240
on ship, 28
sought, 34, 39
Passy, 139
paste work [jewelry], 197
pasteboards, 81, 185, 218
pasturage, 39, 59
pastures, 53
patent beaver, 49
patents, 156
Patrick
Capt., 169
J., 83
pattararoes, 243
Patten
Thomas, Capt., 191
patterns, 79, 165, 217, 251
Patterson
Capt., 191
William, Hon., 56
Patterson's Creek, 17
Patton
James, 21
Mr., 15
Patuxent, 20
Patuxent Iron Works, 127, 128, 137
Pauget
Peter, 19
paupers, 168
Paviett
B., 239
Payne
Mr., 94
Thomas, 20
W., 12, 17, 22, 26
Payne, Thomas
Author, Common Sense, 20
peace, 150, 215, 239
peach orchards, 1, 2, 151
Peale
Mr., 108
Pearce
Mr., 192
peas, dried, 185
pecoson land, 217, 219, 230
Peillon
Mon., 17
pelongs, 58, 81, 170
peltries, 190
pen knives, 7, 81, 151, 165, 171, 218, 256
pencils, 2, 13, 17, 74, 165, 170, 219, 256
Pendleton
Edmund, 50
J., Jr., 79
James, 31
Philip, 84
Penlerick
Capt., 191
Penn, 97
William, Sir, 149
Pennefather
Richard, Cashel Burgess, 168
William, Cashel Burgess, 168
Pennsylvania, 16, 57, 63, 85, 154, 181, 193, 210, 240, 254
2 companies, frontier troops, 232
70 men march to Fort Pitt, 222
Attorney General Bradford, 19
bank incorporation act repeal, 51
General Assembly
appoints State reps., 214
Clerk, S. Bryan, 97
honor, gratitude, common sense, 149
import duties, schedule of, 184
Legislature against dueling, 232
State surveyor, Cunningham, 196
Supreme Courts Prothonotary, 19
test law harmful, 180
trade control to Congress, 97
Pennsylvania, Univ. of
Teacher of Mathematics, 20
Penobscot
captors seek head money, 92
Penobscot affair
Chancellor of the Exchequer views, 92
Collier's views, 92
pens, 12, 59
Peoples
D., 10, 222, 228
pepper, 1, 80, 81, 136, 137, 146, 156, 165, 171, 250

pepper mills, 80
Pepperell
William, portrait of, 259
Pera (near Constantinople), 75, 241
perch hooks, 251
perfumes, 123, 196
Perkins
Capt., 141
T., 44, 63
Thomas, Capt., 52, 55
Perkinson
E., 126
Perrin
Joseph Marie, 58, 61, 65, 75
Perry
James, 103, 109, 110, 116
persian gauze, 28
persian quilts, 218
persians, 73, 79, 81, 99, 165, 218
perspective glasses, 6
Peru, 93, 158
perukes, 133
Peruvian bark, 2, 29, 58
pestilence, 195, 213
Peter
Robert, 84, 85, 122, 124, 133
Petersburg(h), 17, 46, 61, 76, 111, 116, 133, 162, 178, 243
Petit
Charles, 4, 20, 97
petitions, 132, 133, 143, 156, 157, 210, 225, 233, 361
General Assembly, 2, 13, 17
Petre
William, 217, 219, 225
petticoats, 6, 81, 95, 98, 131, 172, 229
Pettis
James, Capt., 185
Pettit
Charles, 63, 214
pewter, 100, 136, 171
pewter basons, 15
pewter dishes, 100, 151
pewter quarts, 218
pewter spoons, 59, 136, 151
pewter utensils, vessels, 185
pewter, wrought, 197
Peyton
Ann, 126
Francis, 31
J., 53, 60, 65
John, 63
phætons, 29, 211
Phedrus
Lion and the Lamb fable, 221
Philadelphia, Pa., 7, 10, 14, 15, 17, 19, 24, 25, 32, 33, 37, 43, 44, 47, 51, 56-58, 62, 63, 66, 68, 72, 75, 77, 82, 83, 87, 88, 92, 93, 96, 97, 99, 102, 103, 105-108, 113, 114, 117, 118, 125, 130, 132, 134, 135, 139, 144, 147, 149, 150, 155, 159, 160, 164, 169, 173, 175, 176, 180, 184, 187, 190-192, 194, 198, 203, 204, 209, 214, 216, 221, 222, 228, 229, 233, 235, 238-240, 244, 245, 248, 250, 254, 255, 261, 262, 265, 267
3-year old boy burns, 264
arrival of Dr. Franklin, 149
committee, merchants', traders' memo, 97
Executive Council, 169
ginseng export figure, 62
Merchants meet, 4
new paper money vital, 102
ships, 4
Spanish Amb. en route N.Y., 173
Supreme Executive Council, 197
Union Fire Company, 180
wardens office warning, 228
Philadelphia Bank
subscriptions, funding, 154
Philadelphus [pen name], 121
Philipsburgh, 53
Phillips
Joseph, Capt., 66
Philosophical Society
members, list of, 19
philosophical studies, 264
Phoenix, from ashes, 248
physic, 22, 26, 30
physic and surgery, 8, 239, 245, 251
physicians, 8, 19, 26, 34, 35, 40, 45, 114, 116, 124, 136, 138, 147, 239, 245, 247, 251, 255
piano fortes, 256
pianos, 59, 64, 65, 75
Piccadilly, 128
pickaxes, 16
pickled codfish, 34
pier glass, 16
pier-heads, 212
Pierce
B., 118
John, 215
piers, 251
Pilkington
Thomas, 234
pillage, 231
pillagers, 227
pillow fustians, 170, 217
pillow ticks, 151
Pilmore
Rev., 249
Pilot
John, 19
Pilot boats, 174
to conduct Russians, 195
Pilots, 135
pimento, 108, 131, 151, 165, 171, 211, 250
pincers, 171
pinchbeck watches, 49
pinchers, 136
pinching irons, 218
Pinckney
Charles, 37
pinking irons, 171
pins, 6, 7, 11, 12, 33, 80, 81, 136, 151, 165, 170, 218
pint silver cans, 16
Piper
Mr., 8
pipes, 1, 2, 6, 8, 11, 49, 63, 108, 142, 165, 181, 229, 266
piracy, 24
of schooner *Free-Mason*, 19
pirate schooner
hull, crew described, 205
pirates, 174, 239
Agreement, text of, 174
Algiers, 159
cast away six persons, 155
chase Nassau-bound sloop, 205
of Algiers, 65
pursued, caught, jailed, 135
Spain vamping up, 196
Piratical corsairs
seize slaver, 128
piratical crew
in public gaol, 174
Piscataway, Md., 130
pistols, 121, 158, 174, 223
duelling, wheat loads, 158
horseman's, 248
pit saw files, 165
pit saws, 165, 171
pitch, 104, 109, 115, 133, 142, 194, 224, 230
Pitt, 92
Capt., 125
Irish propositions by, 159
Mr., 71, 130
Mr., 1st Lord of the Treasury, 23
Mr., abused at Horsham, 226
Mr., coach windows broken, 226
Mr., trade bill, 101
W., Prime Minister, 24
William, mocked, 66
Pittsburg
an hundred buildings, 232
cheap provisions, 232
pleasantly situated, 232
plague, 27, 173, 196
broke out in Tripoli, 101
in Turkish fleet, 46
plaids, 165, 170
plain irons, 74
plains, 49, 165, 239
plaintiffs, 222
plane irons, 80, 171

planes, 11, 80, 219
Plank Bridge, No. Car., 47
planks, 59, 94, 108
  oak, for gun carriages, 189
  ship, 89
  yellow poplar, 187
plans, 85
plantation utensils, 70, 166, 170
plantation work, 1
plantations, 17, 23, 45, 90, 119, 142, 161, 198, 204, 228, 235
  British, rums, sugars, 158
  for rent, 119, 152, 153, 161, 199, 207, 219, 230
  for fale, 2, 8, 12, 13, 17, 22, 25, 26, 34, 75, 89, 91, 100, 105, 115, 121, 124, 161, 162, 166, 172, 217-219, 230
  marks, 263
  Portuguese, 251
  Spanish, 251
Planters, 4, 63
planting, 176, 199, 224
plants, 33
Plasterers' trowels, 171
plastering, new
  noxious fumes, 253
plated buckles, 6, 11, 28, 33, 59, 81
plated spoons, 28
plated ware, 197
plates, 15, 81, 151, 172
playing cards, 81, 184, 197, 218, 239, 256
plays (theatricals), 185
Pleasants
  Samuel, 75, 229
Plenipo
  the American, J. Adams, 140, 144
plough-lines, 81
Ploughman, 17
ploughs, 17
plumb pudding, 200
Plunket
  Mr., 251
plushes, 73, 218
pocket books, 7, 33, 69, 80, 256
pocket knives, 81
Poets, 201
poetry, 16, 81, 200
  "A Rural Ode", 70
  "Advice to a Young Lady, on Seeing Her Dance", 219
  "An Apostrophe to Dame Fortune", 188
  "An Epitaph on a COUNTRY COBBLER", 49
  "An Evening Soliloquy", 81
  "Death of Miss Ramsay", 216
  "Epigrams", 34
  "Epitaph on a Blacksmith", 206
  "Epitaph on Dr. Johnson", 120
  "Epitaph on Hogarth, in Chiswick Church-Yard", 183
  "Friendship: An Ode", 45
  "From the European Magazine", 104
  "From the Hibernian Magazine; The Extent of Life's Variety", 40
  "I Will Be Happy", 54
  "Jue d'Esprit on the Word Idea", 157
  "Life", 22
  "Lines Addressed to Ambition", 251
  "Night", 167
  "Ode to Virtue", 132
  "On a Good Conscience", 256
  "On Angling", 124
  "On Bribery", 7
  "On Seeing a Rose in October", 212
  "On taking the Bark, by a Lady", 199
  "On Truth", 12
  "Poetical Rondeau, Said to be Written by Mr. Gray", 152
  "Simplicity", 100
  "Soliloquy on a Spring Morning", 86
  "The Ant and the Caterpillar: A Fable", 64
  "The Bee, Written by Mr. Nicholls", 60
  "The Boy's Choice of a School-Master", 172
  "The Cot", 177
  "The Farmer and the Robin-Red-Breast", 267
  "The Incurable, To Doctor...", 235
  "The Maiden's Wish", 240
  "The Muses Ode", 230
  "The Setting Sun", 95
  "The Stage of Life", 75
  "The Summum Bonum, Or, Infallible Receipt for Happiness", 137
  "The Sure Way to Gain Esteem", 147
  "The Thunderstorm", 127
  "Thoughts on the Seasons", 161
  "To a Friend Who Pressed the Author to Marry...", 193
  "To Death", 115
  "To Stella", 91
  "Universal Discontent", 30
  "Verses Addressed to a Gentleman...", 262
  "Verses Presented by a Gentleman...", 225
  "Verses Written Extempore in Praise of a Goosequill", 25
  "Verses Written in a Lady's Prayer-Book", 109
  Verses Written on a Blank Leaf of Pope's Moral Essays, 143
Point au Petre, 247
Point Pleasant
  Indians kill five officers, 145
Point West, 250
poison
  execution by, 214
Polacres
  Venetian, Moors take, 91
Poland
  corn crops promising, 173
  Germanic League membership, 243
  Vienna, Petersburgh's influence, 243
police
  Rotterdam, policy, results, 168
Policy of Insurance--1/
  Massachusetts' new tax on, 77
polishing brushes, 236
  covered with gold, silver, 236
politicians, 153
politics, 220
Polk
  Charles, 234
  Charles Peale, 108, 115, 120
Polson
  John, 156
pomatum, 74, 218
Pondicherry, 160
Pool, Eng., 32
poor, 5, 12, 102, 107, 223, 254, 265
  Act to benefit, 265
  Br. laws execrable, 168
  theatre for relief, 37
poor rates, 265
Pope
  Benjamin, 31
  Conclave of the Holy See, 214
  instructions to Nuncio, 214
  Joseph, 132, 133, 138
  Mr., 143, 254
  open ports to Am. ships, 113
  Pius the 6th, 214
population
  produces manufactures, 208
pork, 52, 58, 90, 185, 197, 224, 229
porringers, 100
Port Farina, 194
Port Louis, Brittany, 19
Port l'Orient, 4
Port Royal, 37, 60, 116, 163, 211
Port Tobacco, 122, 127, 135, 245
Port wine, 11, 22, 23, 28, 30, 49, 73, 81, 104, 131, 137, 266
  red, 229
Port-au-Prince, 141
Porte, 134
  asked to control Dutch ship, 76

Porte-Russia
perfect harmony, 247
Portendie, 10
porter, 7, 22, 58, 63, 100, 108, 123, 127, 131-133, 155, 160, 164, 165, 171, 185, 197, 229
Charles, 31
Mr., 137
porterage, 255
Porters, 184, 255
portmanteau locks, 80
portmanteaus, 74, 182
portrait painting, 108
portraits, 115, 120
ports, 5, 27, 37, 48, 58, 63, 68, 70, 83, 103, 114, 126, 141, 145, 155, 160, 176, 181, 188, 192, 205, 206, 211, 229, 233, 245, 246, 250, 252, 257, 263
Portsmouth, 47, 111, 116, 148, 194
Vendue Master dies, 239
Portsmouth, N.H., 92, 106, 134, 140, 182, 227
from, conveyance of mail, 169
military spirit spreading, 179
Portugal, 186, 245, 246
12 sail squadron, protecting, 226
6 frigates cruise against Algerines, 226
African discoveries, 190
annual drubbing at Algiers, 91
Don Louis, son, Queen Isabella, 76
John II, 190
line of battle ship, cruising, 226
may suffer by Algerines, 202
Mediterranean squadron, 195
peacetime land forces, 61
Prince Henry's voyage, 190
Queen Isabella, 76
Queen to protect trade, 195
royal marriage, 110
trade policy for Ireland, 139
warships to Sacre Bay, 195
Portugal-Spain
royal marriage, effects of, 138
Portugual
measures against Algerines, 254
Queen rewards frigate crew, 243
ships take Algerine corsair, 243
Portuguese, 186
Portuguese vessels
Algerine cruisers, 191
post
Charleston-Augusta, 190
Post-Master General, 182
British, 129
post-office, 34, 182, 234, 236
Post-Rider, 29, 30, 35, 45, 49, 50
post-riders, 180
postage, 180
postulants, 65
potatoes, 1, 13, 66
Potomack
ginseng export figure, 62
opening of, 188
Potomack Co., 10, 84, 94, 96, 101, 131, 133, 143, 152, 198, 207, 212, 219
Potsdam, 168, 248
Potts
John, 101
John, Jr., 84, 94, 96, 101, 198, 207, 212, 219
John, of Potts Grove, 261
Ruth, relict of John, 261
Potts Grove, 261
Pounce, 2, 13, 17
poverty, 209
as a virtue, 260
powder, 15, 151, 171, 230, 239
hair, 185, 197
powdering puffs, 218
Powell
James E., Gov., 144
Leven, 84, 85, 91, 95, 123, 124, 133
Leven, Col., 103
Richard, 107
power of attorney, 25, 156
Powhatan, 126
Powles valley
Indians kill 6, abduct one, 121
Poyer
Philip, 156, 157, 167, 234
Practitioners, 29
Praslin
Duke of, 130
Prat
Mr., negotiator in Ireland, 32
Pratt
John, Lt., 179
Mr., 230
Mr. Michael, 179
Shubael (Dr.), 141, 234
prayer books, 2, 13, 17, 163, 170
Prebendaries, 139
Preiss, 46
Prejudice, thoughts on [editorial], 204
Prelate, Upper Austrian
denied pilgrimage permission, 158
Prentiss
Henry, 250
Presbyterian Meeting House, 107, 235, 245
Presbyterians, 45
offer Bishop meeting house, 130
Presbyters, 214
Presidents, 78, 84, 88, 94, 96, 101, 182, 188, 193, 198, 200, 210, 255
press
paper, kills worker, 102
Press, Liberty of the
Stamp Act impinges on, 83
presses, 19
beds and punches for, 236
cutting out, 236
for giving impressions to metal, 236
for horn buttons, 236
piercing, 236
piercing, beds and punches for, 236
Presto
William, 238
Prettie
Henry, Tipperary rep., 168
Preyst
infantry regiment of, 20
Price
Benjamin, 33
Dr., "Observations...Am. Revolution", 180
Dr., essay on Am. Revolution, 154
Dr., political confessor, 140
Dr., Political Magazine comment on, 154
Mrs., 137
Oliver, 21, 99, 119, 121, 124, 234, 250
Richard, Dr., 180
Richard, Rev., 20
prices of goods, 6, 11, 15, 21, 28, 38, 44, 52, 58, 63, 78, 84, 88, 108, 122, 131, 136, 142, 160, 169, 181, 187, 198, 223, 228, 239, 254, 261
Priddie
Mr., schooner *Hazard*, owner, 178
Priestly
Dr., doctrine of resurrection, 82
Joseph, Rev., 20
Priestman
Capt., 43, 192
Priests
Italian, poisoning by, 208
priests, celibacy of, 134
Primate
Mrs., 32
primers, 185, 197
Prince
B., 107, 114
Capt., 108, 110, 120
Prince de Ligne
Gov. of Antwerp, 195
Prince George Co., 239
Prince George's Co., Md., 39, 70, 90, 119, 121, 133, 138, 146, 147, 157, 176, 198, 199, 207, 212, 217, 219, 230

Prince of Conde
seeks army command, 31
Prince of Kaunitz
delay pending Russia response, 42
Prince of Ligne
Cmdr., Austrian forces, Low Countries, 61
to attack Scheldt forts, 221
Prince of Nassau Weilbourg
replaced by Prince Frederick, 31
Prince of Orange, 2
to attack Low Countries, 55
Prince of Orange, Stadtholder, 247
Prince of Wales
Carleton House completion, 247
Prince William Co., 1, 7, 9, 16, 18, 22, 40, 59, 123, 128, 132, 133, 138, 166, 167, 177, 267
Princes, 144
princes stuff, 132
Princeton, N.J., 20
Prince's Island, 190
Principals, 240
printed calicoes, 58, 230, 239, 255
printed cottons, 58, 80, 165, 170, 230
printed handkerchiefs, 49, 58, 165
printed linens, 6, 11, 33, 58, 80, 98, 103, 109, 165, 170, 218, 239
printed Marseilles quilting, 58
printed quiltings, 217
printed sermons, 240, 251, 257, 262, 267
printed velverets, 49, 217, 255
printed velvets, 136
Printers, 15, 17, 25, 26, 40, 44, 45, 50, 55, 60, 64, 65, 67, 68, 84, 118, 123, 126, 131-133, 159, 182, 187, 193, 198, 200, 207, 212, 217, 219, 255, 262
Printing, 5, 8, 9, 13, 16, 18, 23, 26, 30, 35, 41, 45, 50, 55, 60, 65, 70, 75, 82, 86, 91, 95, 100, 105, 110, 115, 120, 124, 127, 133, 138, 143, 147, 153, 157, 162, 167, 172, 177, 183, 188, 193, 200, 207, 212, 219, 225, 230, 235, 240, 245, 251, 257, 262, 267
printing paper, 185
printing-office, 2, 7-9, 11, 12, 16, 17, 21-23, 29, 30, 45, 49, 54, 55, 60, 68, 75, 81, 82, 86, 91, 95, 98, 100, 109, 110, 115, 120, 122, 124, 133, 143, 147, 152, 161, 162, 167, 171, 172, 177, 183, 188, 192, 193, 199, 200, 207, 212, 219, 230, 234, 235, 240, 241, 245, 251, 255, 257, 262, 267
prisoners, 54, 93
break jail, 135
prisons, 54
building of, 40, 41
Privateers, 107
in Ostend's harbour, 4
privy seal
brought by Mr. Nepean, 32
prize ship
Lord Howe, 248
proclamations, 88
Proctor
Thomas, 17
produce, 1, 2, 8, 57, 67, 70, 73, 90, 94, 104, 146, 165, 176, 181, 192, 230, 240
Professors, 20, 196, 255
Promissory Notes of Hand, 6£ or greater--3d
Massachusetts' new tax on, 77
Proprietors, 83, 94, 257, 262, 263
prosperous, 134
woman, victimized, rescued, 134
Protestant Association, 23, 208
President: George Gordon, 207
Protestant Episcopal Church, 52, 60, 65, 85, 88, 240
Protestants
Dutch, Lord Gordon protects, 10
interest in Germany, 168
Prothonotaries, 19
Prouting
Capt., 226
Providence, 38, 48, 130, 144, 150, 210, 228, 239
General Assembly of, 144
Maxwell, Gov., 144
Powell, James Edward, Lt. Gov., 144
Providence, R.I., 141, 185, 190, 249
Provost, 17
proxy, 84
prunellas, 249
Prussia, 43, 76, 111, 222
40,000 troops for Holland, 10
afraid of France, 42
armies, 76
Bavarian barter, remonstrance, 147
Frederick, 242, 247
his Prussian Majesty, 194
jealous, Austria expansion, 227
King begins encampments, 82
King dangerously ill, 91
King heads German league, 168
King of, 4, 173, 175, 214
joining Dutch, 3
orders provisions for army, 76
views on Stadtholder, 242
league hostile to Emperor, 201
may war with Austria, 130
no Austrian troops, 3
Old Frederick's mind, 26
Prince Henry of, 13
Prussian Majesty, 3
Prussia's Minister at Vienna, 76
review of the troops, 248
signs preliminary peace accord, 112
the Emperor, the Dutch, 91
troops on the move, 42
Wesel troops on alert, 241
Prussia peacetime
land forces: 224,434, 61
Prussian flag
Dutch sailing under, 4
psalm books, 197
psalters, 2, 13, 17, 170, 185, 218
public auction, 64, 126, 166
public buildings, 2, 13, 126
public good, 209
public houses, 109, 115
for rent, 120, 122, 127, 128
public peace, 258
Public Vendue, 1, 2, 13, 17, 25, 28, 33, 48, 53-55, 58, 69, 73, 79, 85, 98, 108, 114, 118, 119, 122, 127, 131, 132, 136, 137, 142, 146, 155, 160, 164, 169, 176, 181, 187, 192, 199, 206, 211, 217, 223, 229, 234, 250, 254, 261, 266
pudding, plumb, 200
puffs, 218
pullies, 171
Pumage, Normandy, 19
pump geer, 197
pump tacks, 171
pumps, borings of, 197
puncheons, 49, 63, 108, 155, 160, 164
punishment
petty crimes, 253
whipping and death, deserters, 231
Purber [Furber?]
Capt., 178
Purcell
Reuben, 239
purses, 74, 91

Q

quadrants, 33, 159, 258
Quakers, 31, 45, 180
Quantico, 98, 115, 234
quarantine
of 40 days, 3 vessels, 202
quarries, 167
quarter casks, 11, 49, 89, 108, 118, 131, 142, 156, 229, 250
quarter chests, 33, 68, 98, 103, 108, 156

quarter hour glasses, 74
Quarter-Master, 38
Quebec, 71, 154, 248, 261
  Americans-Quebecois illicit trade, 62
  Castle of St. Louis, 248
  N.E. storm ruins buildings, ships, 4
  West Indies (br.), 71
Queen Elizabeth, 252
queen's china, 1, 103
queen's cords, 49, 58, 165, 218
queen's ware, 7, 11, 15, 24, 28, 49, 74, 81, 132, 136, 137, 151, 160, 164, 165, 169, 171, 192, 239, 251, 266
quills, 7, 12, 59, 80, 165, 218, 239, 256
quiltings, 74, 100, 217
quilts, 99, 170, 218
quintals, 116
Quirk
  Capt., 114
  R., 28, 73
  Richard, Capt., 234

R

rabbi, Jewish, 196
rabbit planes, 11
races, 68, 75
Racoon Bottom
  Indians kill five at, 145
Radcliff Highway, 23
Ragusa
  gets Russian Consul, 133
  Turkish yoke, 133
Rahab, 208
Raimond
  Jean, monstrous baby, 62
raising planes, 11
raisins, 89, 115, 185, 197
Ralls
  George, 75, 86
Ramsay
  Ann, 48
  Capt., 155
  David, Senate Chairman, 228
  Dennis, 59, 84, 114, 116, 218
  Dennis, Col., 182, 216
  James, 94, 100, 101
  Nathaniel, 228
  Sally Douglass, 216
  William, 8, 15, 48, 103, 109, 110, 120, 124
Ramsey
  David, delegate to Cong., 37
  Dr., 17
Randall
  Sec'y, Am. Embassy, Paris, 249
  Thomas, of New York, 249
Randolph
  Edmund, 182
  H., 79
ranging, 266
Rankins
  Benjamin, 22, 23, 30, 34, 95, 101
rape
  perpetrator caught, jailed, 118
Rappahannock, 44, 72, 141
Rappahannock-Mountain, 99
rasors, 7, 74, 81, 151, 165, 171, 218
Rasp House (Rotterdam), 168
rasps, 171
rat traps, 74, 171
ratteens, 12
rattinets, 81, 100, 132, 170, 218
rattle, child's, 208
ravens duck, 1, 15, 170
Rawlings
  Isaac, 212, 219, 225
Rawlins
  John, 151, 157
Read
  J., 28
  J. delegate to Congress, 37
  Jacob, 37
  Thomas, 234
reading, 90, 160
  N.Y. troops transit to frontier, 154
real estate
  deeds, tax on, 77
reap hooks, 11
reaping, 45
reaping hooks, 184
rebuses, 16
receipt books, 256
Recorders, 14
Rectors, 140, 158, 240
redwood, 81
Reed
  Gen., 258
  Joseph, 63
  O., 103, 107
Reeder
  Mr., 107, 131
  Thomas, 94, 96, 229, 230, 236, 245, 251
refugees
  Am. loyalists, lottery for, 130
Regency of Tuscany
  adds 15 gallies vs. Algiers, 238
regiments
  2 English to N.W. frontier, 121
  20th foot, 3
  29th, to relieve 8th, 91
  31st, to relieve 8th, 91
  8th, holds N.W. forts, 91
  8th, relieved by 2 regts., 121
  Bender, to Holland frontiers, 221
  British, 144, 231
  cavalry, Fr. adds 32 men each, 227
  cavalry, Vanderhoop's, 201
  Colonel of Berwick's, 226
  Deutschmeister, 46
  first American, 222
  Hesse Darmstadt's infantry, 201
  Hessian, 128
  Irish, 231
  Preiss, 46
  Tillier, 46
regiments (Dutch)
  2-Batavia, 247
  2-Cape of Good Hope, 247
  to Trincomale, 247
Reily
  Stevens, 18
Reischach
  Baron, 13
religion, 41, 159, 180, 245
  Italian, 208
religious freedom, 50
Remnant
  John, 234
Rennes, 189
Republic of Holland, 3, 4, 91, 227, 241
  3 Mease bailiwicks to Austria, 55
  500 immigrants to Phila., 159
  64 ships crewed by 11,520, 202
  80,000 French, Prussian troops reinforce, 10
  accord with Austria, 125
  activating all war ships, 46
  Ambassador at Vienna recalled, 10
  Ambassador to St. James, 143
  and the Emperor, 91
  Armed Neutrality policy, 105
  army, 3
  Austria accommodation certain, 129
  Austria captures 250 Rhinegrave of Salm men, 55
  Austria declares war on, 4
  Austria, amicable adjustment, 130
  Austrian affairs settled, 154
  Austro-Dutch dispute amicable, 162
  breaks Lillo dike, drowning several, 10
  cabals, 196
  Civil Government tottering, 196
  complaint against Stadtholder, 195
  concessions for flag affront, 154
  confederation invitation, 173
  Court mourns Queen of Sardinia, 241
  declaration of war by, 13
  demands of Joseph II, 110

demands of Venice 600,000 florins, 47
Dutch army desertions, 196
Dutch loan interest, 42
Dutch reinforcing E.Indies, 246
Dutch to give Austria Maestricht, 55
editorial on, 92
Emperor disposed to agree, 61
Emperor far from accommodation, 61
Emperor's demands of, 96
Emperor's list of demands, 96
Emperor's unreasonable terms, 196
endorses Dutch colony in N.Y., 153
French King to mediate, 214
get Palatine flood complaint, 105
Groningen deputies decamp, 243
High Mightinesses, 2, 3, 76, 128, 214, 225
House of Orange, 195
Imperial, Dutch troops clash, 10
internal spats hinder peace accord, 110
leurs Hautes Puissances, 208
Low Countries, 3, 13
new dragoon regiment, 128
peace with Emperor rumor, 96
Prince of Orange, 2, 4
  critical of defence, 105
  Nassau, 242
Prince Stadtholder, 3, 46, 148
reponse to Austrian demands, 125
Scheldt resolution, 138
Serene Highness Utrecht letter, 201
Serene Highness' defence plan, 128
Stadtholder, 3, 242
  appoints Maestricht's Gov., 31
  letter criticized, 195
  unbalanced, 196
Stadtholder's affairs worsen, 195
Stadtholder's tenure basis, 91
States General, 2, 9, 13, 14
  to Austrian demands: no, 82
  mediators, 194
Swiss recruits captured by Austria, 55
ten millions florins to Austria, 154
two ambassadors to Vienna, 148
United Provinces, 47
Utrecht deputies decamp, 243
Venetians arm against, 93
Venice targets Levant trade, 110
Venice targets Levantine trade, 110
vitals sapped from within, 91
war with Austria seems sure, 76
weak, defenceless, 105
wish successful peace negotiations, 113
Zealand deputies decamp, 243
Republic of the United Provinces
  Ministers Plenipotentiary of, 13
Republic of Venice
  treaty with Russia, 194
  Turkey 's threat, 194
residences, 53, 90, 218, 255
resolutions, 150
resurrection
  Priestly's doctrine, 82
Resurvey on Dogwood-Plains, 44
Resurvey on Horse-Lick, 44
Resurvey on Sugar-Bottom, 44
Resurvey on Walnut-Level, 44
returns, 29, 43, 48, 96, 107, 186, 211, 249, 257
  broke gaol, 162, 172, 177, 178
  from England, 240
  of books, 103, 109, 110, 120, 124, 128
  of letters, 86, 91
  of lost gold watch, 119, 122, 124
  of peace, 16
  of runaways, 26, 50, 54, 60, 64, 65, 71, 75, 82, 91, 95, 100, 101, 104, 109, 110, 115, 120, 124, 127, 128, 133, 137, 143, 146, 147, 151, 153, 157, 161, 167, 172, 177, 183, 188, 193, 200, 207, 219, 225, 230, 231, 240, 267
  of stolen horses, 167, 225, 235
  of stolen silver can, 55, 60
  of stolen yawls, 91, 96
  of strayed cow, 188
  of strayed horses, 91, 98, 104, 109, 121, 127, 133, 138, 142, 147, 153, 157, 162, 172, 178, 188, 193, 200
  of unsold tickets, 85
  Overseers of the Poor, 265
  to England, 12, 361
Reussel, 226
revenue law, 20, 24
Revenue Officers
  his Majesty's, 87
revolt
  Indians against Spanish Govt., 129
Revolution, American
  Price's views on, 180
Revolutionary War, 32, 50, 56, 62, 71, 135, 139, 154, 159, 180, 205, 215, 260
rewards, 6, 9, 12, 13, 16-18, 21-23, 25, 26, 30, 34, 35, 40, 41, 44, 45, 49, 50, 54, 55, 59-61, 64, 65, 70, 71, 73, 75, 81, 82, 85, 86, 88, 89, 91, 95, 96, 100, 101, 103, 104, 109, 110, 116, 120-124, 127, 128, 131, 133, 137, 138, 142, 143, 146, 147, 151-153, 156, 157, 161, 162, 165, 167, 172, 177, 178, 183, 188, 193, 200, 207, 211, 217, 219, 224, 225, 229-231, 235, 240, 261, 267
Reynst
  Admiral, 9
  Vice-Admiral, 2
Rhine
  circle of the Upper, 168
Rhode Island, 1, 4, 24, 33, 45, 52, 88, 97, 103, 107, 126, 135, 141, 155, 222, 228, 249, 254
  £19,390 1 6 9 for U.S. debt, 228
  £20,000 tax for U.S. debt, 228
  General Assembly adjourned, 228
  passed the 5% act, 47
Rhode Island cheese, 13, 33
rhubarb, 2, 29
rib delures, 58
ribbons, 7, 11, 12, 15, 28, 33, 49, 58, 73, 74, 80, 81, 98, 99, 123, 125, 136, 151, 197, 239
rice, 10, 67, 135, 142
  duty on, 71
Rice,
  B., 33
Richards
  George, 5, 8, 10, 13, 18, 21, 23, 26, 30, 35, 40, 45, 50, 55, 60, 65, 70, 75, 82, 86, 91, 95, 100, 105, 110, 115, 120, 123, 124, 127, 133, 138, 143, 147, 153, 157, 162, 167, 172, 177, 183, 187, 188, 193, 200, 205, 207, 212, 219, 225, 230, 235, 240, 245, 251, 257, 262, 267
  Mr., 171
Richardson
  Thomas, Capt., 122
Richey
  William, 10
Richie
  Capt., 77
Richland, 102
Richmond, 11, 17, 23, 30, 40, 43, 44, 47, 52, 78, 79, 83, 88, 93, 121, 130, 135, 175, 182, 198, 215, 222, 266, 267
  ball, at the capitol, 249
  balloon ascension, 228
  capitol square, 228

Commissioners, public buildings, 145
Common Hall, 145
Ebenezer, 245, 251
Ebenezer, Dr., 239
Free Masons' celebration, 249
G., 78, 130
General Court sentencing, 238
Masons lay capitol cornerstone, 145
Privy Council, 145
Shockoe Hill, 228
Riddick
Willis, 31
Ridgely
Henry, Jr., 84
Richard, 228
riding carriages, parts of, 197
riding chairs, 197
riding chaises, 104
riding hats, 49
Rig
B., 181
Rigg
Richard, 136, 138
rigging, 69
yarn, 185
rights, 36
Riley
Patrick, 127
Ring, The, 228
Rio de la Hache, 129
Rippon-Lodge, 16
rivers, 146, 167
Bender, 82
Black, 47, 52
Camouchie, 253
Charles, 118, 248
Cheat, 59
Conecocheague, 239
Cumberland, 121
Danube, 201, 226
Eastern Branch, 155, 160, 199, 230
Gasper's, 94
Humber, 195
Indian, 164
James, 8, 24, 33, 97, 141, 169, 182, 188, 193, 200, 205, 261
Kentucky, 177
Little, 99, 103, 137, 176
Maese [sic], 61
Mease, 55
Medway, 4
Miami, 149, 196, 232
Mississippi, 20, 47, 56, 205, 247
Monongalia, 54, 59
Mountaise, 76
North, 104, 153
North Branch, 10, 94
North Edisto, 112
Ohio, 11, 113, 145, 156, 157, 167, 193, 200, 207, 232, 247
Patapsco, 53
Patuxent, 43
Potomack, v, 2, 5, 7, 10, 25, 29, 30, 40, 44, 50, 53-55, 60, 63, 64, 70, 73, 75, 78, 83, 88, 94, 98, 99, 103, 104, 114, 119, 123, 126-128, 137, 152, 166, 170, 177, 188, 199, 217, 230, 235, 264
Rappadan, 94
Rappahannock, 7, 135, 187
Santee, 233
Scheldt, 2-4, 9, 13, 14, 42, 51, 55, 76, 96, 138, 154, 221, 226, 238, 242
Seine, 139, 189
Seneca, 224
Shenandoah, 21, 23, 30, 34, 118
St. John's, 87
St. Mary, 253
St. Mary's, 77, 87
Susquehanna, 149
Tenasee, 205
Weluwe, 201
roads, 94
from Col. Powell's, 103
from the back country, 229
from Winchester, 7, 104
public, 25, 176
to Colchester, 83, 103
to Frederick-Town, 224
to Leesburg, 89
to Snicker's Gap, 85
to South Carolina, 218
to Staunton, 75, 229
to Winchester, 218
Roane
Spencer, 30
roast beef, 200
roasting jacks, 98
Rob
J., 192
James, 171, 172, 183
robberies, 83, 160, 165
Roberdeau
Daniel, 84, 211, 219, 225, 251, 266
Gen., 169
Mr., 119
Nancy, 169
Roberts
Capt., 192
E., 240
Robertson
Benjamin, 239
Capt., 25, 114, 205
J., 44, 58, 118, 126
John, Capt., 48
Joseph, 115, 116, 124
Justice, Hon., 138
W., 58
Robileund
charnel house, described, 213
half the inhabitants dead, 213
Robinson, 23
Edward, 23
Moses, 254
Mr., 230
T., 126
Rochefort, 124
Rock of Lisbon, 191
Algerine cruisers, 191
Rockingham Co., 137, 138, 147, 234
Rodney's cord, 218
Rogers
John, 175
William, Rev., 117
rollers
of metal, 236
Rollins
D., 135
rolls, 1, 15, 151, 170, 218
romal handkerchiefs, 58, 81
romals, 251
Roman Catholics, 84, 86, 95
penal laws against, repeal, 159
Roman fleet, 184
romances, 126, 185
Romans
King of the, 23, 207
Rome, 153
ladies of, 260
peacetime land forces, 61
pilgrimage to denied, 158
republic of, 260
Ronald
William, 31
rooms
for rent, 109, 212, 219
rope, 6, 189
white, 185
ropemaking, 6, 9, 12, 13, 18, 23
Roper
Nicholas, 34, 171
Thomas, 44, 50, 54, 60, 65, 70
ropewalks, 6, 261
Rorke
Bryan, 138
Mr., jailed, fined, 67
Rosegill, 34
Rosewell, 171
Rosier's Creek, 170
Rosiere
Capt., 191
Ross
David, 182
John, 4, 97
Rosseau, 179
Rotch
William, Nantucket envoy, 203

Rotterdam, 9, 128, 178
garrison, 2
vagrants jailed, banished, 168
Rouen, 139
Parliament of protests King's Am. trade policy, 129
Round House, 53
Round O [place name], 231
round planes, 11
Roundhill Church, 170, 172, 183
Rousillon
French troops increasing, 189
rover, Algerine, 228
Row
A., 20, 24
Rowand
John, 235, 240
Thomas, 235, 240
Royal Academy exhibit
Brown, 259
Copley, 259
landscapes, 259
Loutherbourg, 259
portraits, 259
Stewart, 259
West, 259
Royal Navy
Acting Lieutenants, 23
Lieutenants denied Austria service, 31
Mates, 23
Midshipmen, 23
seamen, 23, 24
volunteers, 23
Royal Refugee woods, 204
royal ribs, 7, 49, 170
Royston
John, 234
Rozer
Henry, 40, 41, 49, 206, 212
Rudiman's Rudiments, 170
Ruffin
Edmund, 31
rugs, 136, 151, 165, 218, 239
rules, 74, 171
rum, 1, 2, 6, 8, 9, 11, 13, 15, 17, 18, 21, 24, 26, 28, 33-35, 38, 44, 45, 48, 49, 52, 54, 55, 58, 60, 63, 64, 69, 71, 78, 79, 81-84, 86, 88, 91, 94, 95, 98, 100, 101, 103, 105, 108-110, 115, 118, 120, 122, 124, 127, 128, 131, 136-138, 141, 142, 147, 151, 152, 155-157, 159, 160, 162-164, 166, 167, 169, 171, 172, 175, 177, 181-183, 185, 187, 188, 192, 193, 197-201, 206, 211, 217, 223, 224, 228, 234, 239, 250, 254, 256, 261, 262
foreign, 197
Rumney
Mr., 230
William, Dr., 24, 26, 35
rumps, cork, 196
rums, 158
Rumsey
James, 84, 115, 116, 124, 198
runaways, 6, 8, 12, 16-18, 22, 23, 25, 26, 30, 33-35, 41, 44, 45, 49, 50, 53, 54, 59-61, 64, 65, 69-71, 75, 82, 85, 86, 89-91, 95, 100, 101, 103-105, 109, 110, 115, 116, 120, 122-124, 127, 128, 131, 133, 138, 142, 143, 146, 147, 151-153, 157, 161, 162, 165, 167, 172, 176-178, 183, 188, 193, 200, 207, 217, 219, 220, 225, 230, 231, 261, 264, 267
Russel
C.C., 15
Russel's Sermons, 2, 13, 17
Russell
Benjamin, 234
Charles, Capt., 48
russels, 12, 59, 100, 151
Russia, 31, 42, 46, 86
13-ship Black Sea sqn., 241
9 warships to Elsineur, 195
alliance with Austria, 4
Black Sea fleet stronger, 241
China quits commerce with, 76
Consul at Ragusa, 133
corn crops promising, 173
Crimea weary of, 196
Czarina, 247
designs on Poland, 93
Empress of, 4, 9
Empress sees hostile designs, 92
Empress' letter to King of Prussia, 46
Empress' support of Austria, 133
Great Duke's children, 93
on German-Bavarian barter, 147
peacetime land forces, 61
real intent unclear, 51
revenge upon, 13
Tartar cavalry to Austria, 178
treaty with Venice, 194
Turks' movements disturbing, 111
Russia drillings, 15, 80
Russia duck, 1
Russia sheetings, 11, 15, 80, 100, 136, 146, 170
Russia-Turkey
perfect harmony, 247
Russian Black Sea force
15 frigates, 36-50 guns, 241
2 ships, line, 74 guns: Cherson docks, 241
3 ships of the line, 74 guns, 241
4 or 5 five cutters, 241
Ruther
Christian Henry, 192, 212, 219, 230
Rutherford
Thomas, 85
Rutland
his Grace of, 148
[Duke of], 14
Rutledge
John, Hon., 118
M.E., slave non-importation, 244
Ryan
James, 17
John, 234
Michael, Col., 93
rye, 190
Rye, Sussex, 246

S

sackings, 165
Sackville
Lord Viscount, 237
Lord (the Younger), 237
Lord, speech, Irish trade, 168
sacraments, 237
Sacre Bay, 195, 243
sacrophagus, 107
sad irons, 151
saddle bag locks, 80, 151
saddle bags, 69, 70, 94, 100
saddle cloths, 74, 80, 136, 151, 197
saddle horses, 75
saddle housings, 151
saddle straps, 80
Saddlers, 198
Saddlers' fringe, 165
Saddlers' hammers, 171
Saddlers' tools, 15, 218
Saddlers' ware, 15
saddlery, 81, 103, 132, 192, 230
saddles, 11, 74, 80, 81, 94, 126, 132, 151, 156, 171, 197, 198, 211, 219, 220
sagathees, 81, 170
sago, 29
sail canvas, 224, 251
sail duck, 1, 104, 142
sail needles, 170, 251
sail twine, 1
sailcloth, 33, 170, 181, 189
Sailmakers, 115
Sailors, 27, 216, 233
sails, 69, 156, 159, 185, 194
Salee, 128
Salem, 20, 83, 173, 179, 203, 228, 237
Saletine rover
takes Salem brig, 237

Salinas y Moniho
Don Francisco, 246
Salisbury, 142, 143, 152
Salisbury cloths, 12
Salm
Rhine-Graaf of, 76
Salmon's grammar, 136
Saloman
Nathan, 207
salt, 1, 2, 6, 11, 15, 21, 28, 33, 38, 44, 49, 52, 58, 63, 68, 70, 77, 78, 81, 82, 84, 88, 89, 94, 100, 104, 108, 122, 131, 136, 142, 156, 160, 169, 175, 181, 187, 198, 206, 211, 223, 224, 228, 229, 239, 251, 254, 261, 264
blown, 266
Turks island production, 101
salt beef, 198
salt licks, 150
salt marshes, 170
salt of Hartshorn, 29
salt of tartar, 29
salt of wormwood, 29
salt pork, 198
saltpetre, 16, 171
salvers, 74
Samblas Indians, 62
annexation of territory, 62
attacked by Spaniards, 61
humble Spain, 61
sand glasses, 1
Sanderson
Mr., 230
R., 126
Sandford
Robert, Capt., 79
Sanduski, 196
Sandy Hook, 4, 174, 228
Sanford
Jeremiah, 119
Richard, 152, 153, 157
Santa Fee
Indians in revolt, 129
Sanz
Don Antonio Claracony, 27
Sardinia peacetime
land forces: 40,000, 61
sarrandines, 7
sarsaparilla, 12
sarsenets, 58, 79, 99, 165, 170
sash planes, 11
Sastingen, 226
satin florentines, 49
satinets, 12, 58, 73, 165, 170, 217, 249
satins, 12, 58, 79, 99, 132, 141, 165, 170, 218
saucers, 81
Saunders
John, 59, 65, 70
Saunderson
R., 118
Savage
Capt., 176
Nathaniel Lyttleton, 25
Thomas M., 131, 133, 143, 234
Savanna(h), 77, 162, 182, 190, 205, 243, 253
conveyance of mail to, 169
Savary
Peter, 120, 121, 133
saw files, 165
saw mills, 34, 94, 96, 176, 177
horse powered, 42
sawing, 95
saws, 11, 33, 74, 171
Sawyer
Comm., 129, 242
T., 47
T., lost at sea, 47
Sawyers, 1, 33
Saxony
Elector of, 173
Elector of, asked for 12,000 troops, 76
peacetime land forces, 61
Sayers
Robert, 31
scaffolding, 233
scaffolds, 121
scale beam, 197
scales, 7, 33
scandal, 201
scantling, 28
Scarborough, 247
J., 118
scents, 196
Scheldt, 13, 226, 238, 242
Austrian navigation of, 154
Austro-Dutch ship incident, 37
must be open: Austria, 51
opening of, 3, 76
opening the, 19
sovereignty of, 14, 96
the opening of, 42
Schnitzell
George, 84
school house
building of, 160
schools, 7, 30, 34, 90, 91, 98, 101, 109, 153, 160, 210
books, 161
College in Bermuda, 5
College of Nassau Hall, 20
college, Western Shore, Md., 188
dancing, 6, 12, 13, 141
Georgetown Academy, 85
grammar, 93
Latin, 72, 80, 86, 91, 187
scandal, Sheridan's, 71
Schooners, 170, 173, 187
(unk) bottom upwards, 186
(unk) bound for Norfolk, 47
(unk) from Boston, 209
(unk) from Eustatia, 102
(unk) from New England, 186
Abigail, 249
Adams, 20, 24, 222
Adventure, 118, 126
Amity, 159, 174
Barbadoes, 67, 69, 70, 88, 130, 150, 222, 254
Betsey, 126
Bumper, 245
Cynthia, 228, 254
Eagle, 210, 233
Ellicott, 10
Fan-Fan, 92
Favorite, 191
Fly, 135
Free Mason, 24
formerly *Nancy*, 19
General Campbell, 191
General Jones, 68
Governor Parr, 160
Greyhound, 141
Harrington, 15
Hazard (Mr. Priddie's), 178
Henrietta, 239
Holland, 191
Hope, 24
Hopewell, 181
Industry, 10, 159, 239, 261
Jane (Messrs. Stack & M'Namara's), 178
Jesse, 93, 164, 192, 245
Judith, 222, 233
Keats, 107
Lottery, 33, 48, 52, 63-65, 72, 75, 78, 88, 103, 118, 122, 135, 150, 160, 176, 181, 210, 216, 233
Maria, 222
Mary, 63, 68, 107, 155, 192, 239
Matilda, 148
Molly, 79, 145, 251, 256
Nancy, 103, 126, 155
now *Free Mason*, 19
Nelly, 27
Nepa, 160, 181
Olive-Branch, 135
Peggy, 28, 73, 114
Pilgrim, 187
pirate, casts away six, 155
Polly, 24, 38, 78, 150
Roving Nancy, 60, 64, 70
Ruth, 52
Sally, 135, 141
St. George, 63, 65, 69, 70, 75, 150
Success, 20
Surprize, 97

Swallow, 254
Sweet, 174
Tryal, 216
Venture, 118
Virginia, 15, 18, 26, 38, 107
Schram
Capt., 77
Schweidnitz
Prussian army of 80,000, 76
sciences, 136, 256
Royal Academy of, 102
Scindia
Majee, 129
scissors, 7, 74, 81, 151, 165, 171, 218
Scituate, 203
sconces, 171
Scorer
John, 160
Scotch barley, 2, 251
Scotch regiment
Lord Lewis Drummond, cmdg., 26
Scotch threads, 58, 136, 170, 218
Scotland, 27, 117, 222, 252, 257
arming themselves refused, 159
Counties and Boroughs, 220
greatest discontents, 248
pre-Parliament resolutions, 220
selfish, cool, intrepid, ingenious, 32
Scott
Alexander, 160
Capt., 72
E., 22
Eliza, 22, 23, 30
George, 84
J., 166, 167, 177
James, Rev., 16, 18, 26, 166
John, Rev., 22, 23, 30
W., 93, 130, 150, 155
William, 84, 99, 104, 109, 177, 188, 234
scrapers, 197
screw making
pins and stocks for, 236
screw planes, 11
screw plates
iron or steel, 236
screws, 171
Sculptors, 107
Scutari
Bashaw of, 194
scythes, 1, 80, 82, 85, 100, 184, 197
sea otter, 194
sea weed, 33
Seabury
Samuel, Rev. Bishop, 117, 130, 149, 179, 214
Parsonage residence, 130
seale beams, 171
sealing wax, 2, 12, 17, 74, 151, 165, 170, 218, 256
seals, 165, 219
seamans' assistants, 33
Seamen, 87
seas
Adriatic, 113
Baltic, 3
Black, 111, 226, 241
Mediterranean, 227, 231, 243, 252
Seaton, Eng.
gale wrecks ships, 36
Sebastonopolis
Admiral's ship near complete, 241
secular poems, 16, 22, 26
Sedgwick
Theodore, 117
seeds, 209
Segodin, 116
seine, 251
man walked across, 189
seine twine, 1, 16
seines, 185
Selden
Miles, 23
Miles, Rev., 48
Selectae e Veteri, 170
Selim Effendi
the Chiaux Bachi, deposed, 76
seminaries, 31
Senate, 234, 266
Senators, 191, 198
Seneca, 94, 261
Seneca, Md., 8
senna, 29
Sequeville
Sieur, 130
sequin tea, 73, 103
serges, 165, 170, 218, 249
sermons, 187, 193, 200, 240, 251, 257, 262, 267
servants, 18, 23, 33, 35, 45, 59, 61, 69, 70, 73, 82, 89, 91, 105, 122-124, 127, 128, 133, 137, 143, 146, 147, 153, 172, 183, 193, 217, 219, 225, 230, 231, 237, 240, 251, 264
servants caps, 132
servers, 151
sewing, 172
sewing silk, 7, 33, 49, 81, 132, 136, 170, 218
sewing twine, 146
Seymour/Seymore
Capt., 69
J., 67, 88
shades, 15
Shadrach, 144
shags, 49, 192
Shakespeare
William, 234
shalloons, 7, 73, 79, 81, 100, 132, 136, 146, 165, 170, 218, 230, 239
Shallust, 170
shammy gloves, 218
Shaon
David, 119, 251, 256
shaving
heads, eyebrows, 264
shaving boxes, 80, 218
Shaw
Mrs., 210, 219, 225
Shawanese, 150
Shawanese Chiefs, 150
Shawanese town
council at, 144
shawls, 49, 197
Shawman
William, Col., 9
sheathing paper, 185
sheds, 29
sheep, 33, 73, 149, 170, 198
as monster's food, 14
sheep shears, 74, 171
Sheerness, 195
sheers, cutting
metal, 236
rolled metal, silver thereon, 236
rolled steel, 236
sheet copper, 1
sheet lead, 1
sheet tin, 1
sheet-iron, 185
sheetings, 59, 80, 81, 88, 98, 100, 123, 230
Sheets
Jacob, 192, 200, 207
Shelburne, 107, 148, 149, 164
Earl of, 32
Lord, 32
loyalists need provisions, 51
Shelburne Parish, 24, 26, 34
Shelley
John, Sir, 39
shells, 28, 147, 231
Shenandoah, 45, 50, 54, 60, 64, 94, 95
Shenandoah Co., 57, 104, 109, 115, 120, 132
Shepherd
Abraham, 84
Sheridan
Counselor, 19
Mr., dramatist, 145
Mr., on Ireland, 173
Sheriffs, 17, 21, 54, 66, 161, 162, 172, 177, 178, 233, 265
County, 31
Sherman
Col., 232

sherry, 228
Sherwin
  Samuel, 30
Shetland hose, 224
Shields
  gale grounds 60 ships, 36
shingles, 108, 179
ship
  (unk) Phila., with tobacco, lost, 4
  14 sail arrived, dismasted, 56
  156 ships lost, damaged by storm (Eng.), 36
  6 seized by Moores, 66
  93 of 100 women die, 164
  Am. brig lost near Wicklow, 52
  Am. brig sinks Br. revenue cutter, 238
  and cargo lost, only 3 saved, 77
  British, 150, 261
  British built, 206, 211
  carrying tobacco, 245
  convicts marooned, killed ashore, 43
  copper bottomed, 250
  crew mutinied, 128
  crew sick, 216
  crew, hull, cargo loss, 105
  crew, passengers enslaved, 163
  dismasted by lightning, 116
  Dutch prisoners die on, 168
  emigrants offloaded, sinks, 43
  entirely lost, all perished, 77
  French, 233
  gale sinks 30, grounds 50 ships, 36
  gale, Atlantic seaboard, damage by, 185
  grounds, breaks, 181 die, 164
  heavy hurricane losses, 191
  in distress, 19
  leaking, into Grenada, 154
  lightning dismasts, starts leak, 258
  lost bowsprit, sails, 10
  lost her bowsprit, 93
  lost mast, oars, forecastle, 249
  Master, Mate drowned; cargo, ship saved, 36
  masts, 90, 176
  merchantman, 181
  mishap at sea, 63
  mishaps, 78, 97, 175, 176
  mutiny, seizure, castaways, 159
  of the line, French, 214
  of war, St. Ildephonso, 202
  of war, St. John Nepomuceno, 202
  onto Bahamas reefs, 4
  overset, 112, 233
  overset by gale, lost, 92
  passage, 181, 192
  Philadelphia built, described, 19
  piratically run away, 107
  repairs, 257
  seized, 175
  seized in St. Lucia, 145
  Shillelah believed sunk, 47
  speaking, 10, 24, 93, 105, 125, 128, 159, 185, 186, 249, 258
  stove to pieces, 190
  sunk, 249
  taken over, 15
  totally lost, Glover's Reef, 93
  West Indies hurricane loss list, 178
  with tobacco, 263
  wreck, 186, 205
ship bread, 235
ship building, 71
Ship carpenters, 175
Ship carpenters' axes, 74
Ship of the line
  Russian, Black Sea, 241
ship speaking, 66
Shipchandlers, 251
Shippen
  Edward, Jr., 160
Ships, 121, 126, 223
  (Fr.) of the line, extraordinary, 47
  (unk), 27
  (unk) 3, of Woods, Blasden lost, 178
  (unk) Am., Boston-Cadiz, 210
  (unk) Am., large, from Boston, 205
  (unk) Am., St. Ubes-Boston, 210
  (unk) Austrian, up Scheldt, 13
  (unk) Br. from Constantinople, 194
  (unk) Br. men of war, 163
  (unk) from Bordeaux, 110
  (unk) Nantucket whalers, 130
  (unk) new, from Brest, 163
  (unk) of Liverpool, 66
  (unk) of war (Fr.), 139
  (unk) Portuguese, 60 guns, 195
  (unk) Russian, 2-decker, 76 guns, 195
  (unk), from Nova Scotia, 180
  2 Dutch, of 16 guns, 9
  Abby, 63
  Achilles, 195
  Active, 192
  Aldborough, 10
  Alexander, 107, 191
  Alexandria, 192, 206, 217
  Algarve, 30 guns, 195
  Amelia, 48, 90, 99, 104, 109
  Amity's Production, 191
  Ann, 88, 102, 115, 116, 124
  Apollo, 194
  Astrea, 27, 29, 30, 40, 78, 228
  Atlantic, 159, 173
  Bacchus, 226
  Batavia, 151, 153, 161
  Belisarius, 52
  Bethia, 125
  Blandford, 97
  Bravoura, 80 tons, 47
  Brisk, 18 guns, 129
  Britannia, 98, 109
  Bull Dog, 116
  Carolina, 164, 198
  Cato, 97
  Ceres, 28, 30, 35
  Cesar, 73, 81, 82, 86
  Chance, 33
  Charming Peggy, 192, 212, 219, 220, 230
  Cincinnatus, 67
  Citta de Vienna, 112
  Commerce, 105
  Courier de l'Amerique, 227
  Dauphin, 222, 239
  Diligence, 116
  Duke de la March, 243
  Duke of Buccleugh, 77
  Dutch, 176
  Eagle, 72
  Empress of China, 78, 87, 92, 168
  Faithful Steward, 164
  Fanny, 92, 112, 123
  Favourite, 159
  Flora, 116
  Fortune, 78, 99, 109, 141
  Friends, 230, 239, 240, 250, 257, 262, 267
  Friendship, 43, 93
  George, 105, 125
  Glasgow, 169
  Grace, 52
  Grand Turk, 154
  Grandbourg, 176, 186, 192
  Grange, 192
  Harmony, 67, 160
  Hazard, 8, 33, 141, 211, 219, 225
  Heer Adams, 33
  Helena, 24
  Hendrick, 125
  Henry, 83, 93, 191, 249
  Hope, 38, 44, 49, 50, 77, 83, 114, 229, 230, 235, 245
  Hussard, 220
  Iphegenia, 116
  Iris, 24, 141
  Irish Volunteer, 47, 198
  Irresistable, 74 guns, 195
  Jamaica, 191
  Janet, 93, 99, 105, 109, 110, 115, 120
  Janus, 116
  Jason, 36 guns, 4
  Jenny, 68
  Johanna Florentina, 206, 212

John Baptist, 249
Kitty and Polly, 214
Leda, 20, 78
Liberty, 28
Lily or *Lilly*, 25, 58
Lion, 78
London Packet, 160, 164
Lord Howe, 248
Lydia, 97
Lyon, 33
Marquis de la Fayette, 192
Martha, 73, 82
Mary, 72, 73, 81, 82, 86, 95, 166, 167, 172, 216, 223, 225, 235, 239
Mary and Ann, 191
Mary Ann, 43, 192
Matty and Betty, 105
Merchant, 228
Mercury, 62, 164
Messenger, 192
Minerva, 141, 169
Molly, 191
Nancy, 97, 185
Neptune, 97, 125
Ocean, of Glasgow, 43
Olive Branch, 191
Orange, of 50 guns, 4
Pallas, 141, 210
Paragon, 48, 52, 155, 188, 193, 200, 233
Peace and Plenty, 238
Pearce, 43
Peggy, 5, 164, 166, 167, 172, 183, 222
Philadelphia, 160
Plymouth, 52
Polly (Friends), 113
Postilion (Fr.), 4
Potomack, 63, 229, 230, 236, 240
Potomack Planter, 79, 82, 95, 169
Rambler, 209
Ranger, 72
Rappahannock, 28, 30, 40
Resolution, 178
Roebuck, 249
Salisbury, man of war, 110
San Josef, 24 guns, 195
Shillelah, 47
Speedwell, 108, 110, 120
Spooner, 178
square rigged vessels, 203
St. Ann, 164, 233
Stanley, 33, 58, 80, 82, 86, 104, 109, 110
Swan, his Majesty's, 116
Tartar, 27
Thetis, 155
Thomas, 178
Three Brothers, 96, 155
Three Cranes, 173
Three Friends, 24, 159
Triton, 28, 37, 49, 72, 135
Tweed, 141
Tyger, 5
Union, 43, 125, 181, 188, 193, 200, 211, 219, 225, 228
United States, 160
Van Berkel, 113
Virginia, 72
Virginia Hero, 63
Virginia Packet, 139
Vrow Geertruydenberg, 105
Washington, 37, 176
Watson, 44
Weazle, 16 guns, 129
William, 125
York, 141
Young Daniel, 67, 68, 70, 103
Zaal Bloom, 44 guns, 4
shipyards, 53
shirting, 151
shirts, 1, 11, 15, 25, 33, 58, 89, 120, 127, 131, 143, 146, 161, 177, 230, 255
Shoan
  David, 124
Shockoe Hill, 228
shoe brushes, 80
shoe buckles, 11, 165, 171, 192, 219
shoe knives, 171
shoe thread, 239
shoe vamps, 197
shoe-tacks, 81
Shoemakers' hammers, 80
Shoemakers' pincers, 171
Shoemakers' tools, 165, 218
shoes, 1, 6, 7, 11, 21, 28, 33, 34, 49, 58, 59, 70, 74, 80, 81, 89, 98, 99, 103, 108, 123, 127, 131, 132, 135, 136, 146, 147, 151, 161, 170, 177, 192, 197, 206, 211, 217, 218, 223, 230, 234, 239, 251
  high heeled, 196
  leather, 185
  stuff, 185
shop furniture, 12, 13, 18, 22, 23, 26, 30, 35, 40
shop tax
  Scotch shopkeepers resist, 221
shops, 69
Short
  John, 34, 35, 45, 361
  Mr., 93, 114
shot, 7, 15, 74, 80, 81, 100, 132, 136, 137, 146, 165, 171, 218, 230, 239
  musket, 189
shovel and tongs, iron, 197
shovels, 1, 11, 15, 80, 82, 85, 136, 151, 165, 171, 251
Shreve
  Benjamin, 14, 84
  Mr., 25, 26
Shugars
  Martin, 239
Siberia, 76
sickles, 80, 82, 100, 184
Siddons
  Mrs., 148
side-board slabs, 80, 165
sieves, 7, 58, 74, 80
sifters, 136
Siie
  Jean Baptist, J., Paris, 20
Silesia, 214
Silesias, 151
silk, 6, 49, 58, 74, 98, 103, 108, 125, 132, 136, 151, 151, 197, 239
  Fr. silk manufactories, 252
  machine, at Derby, described, 252
  Piedmontese Reel, 252
silk culture
  South Carolina experiment, 227
silk ferrets, 7
silk gauzes, 49
silk gloves, 170
silk handkerchiefs, 15
silk mitts, 7, 58
silk petticoats, 6
silk stockings, 58
silver, 40, 90, 97, 141, 254
silver buckles, 161
silver buttons, 136
silver cans, 16, 54, 55, 60
silver clasps, 33
silver oar, 163
silver prices, 52
silver thimbles, 171
silver watches, 11, 33, 177, 197
silver, quick
  Spanish contract to Austria, 162
silver, wrought, 197
silvered watch chains, 219
silverets, 7
Sim
  Joseph, 84
  Robert, 75, 81, 82, 261
Simmons
  T., 20, 44
Simms
  Charles, 57, 84, 118
Simons
  Maurice, Col., duelist, 231
Simpson
  Mr., Marshall of Court of Admiralty, 163
  Richard, 224

Sinclair
James, 234
John, 24
single planes, 11
singlo tea, 73
sinners, 88
sirkins, 229
size sticks, 171
skeleton wire, 170
skillets, 80
Skinner
Alexander, 199, 207, 212
Skinners, 155
skins, 12
skirts, 69
Slacom/Slacum
Capt., 73
G., 72, 93, 155
Gabriel, 73
slates, 74, 132, 151, 165, 170, 219, 256
Slaughter
a pirate, 135
slaughter houses, 220
slavery, 5, 126, 205, 222, 238, 252, 260
requires remedy, 148
States of Europe ripe for, 31
slaves, 34, 40, 45, 53, 85, 95, 121, 122, 127, 128, 142, 164, 189, 213, 246
3 Am. Captains, Algiers, 221
Africa coast, sold, 129
Christian, blown up by Algerines, 111
for sale, 16, 26, 33, 73, 81, 86, 161, 171, 173, 183, 199, 207, 212, 219, 225, 235, 240
N.Y. regulations, 113
Old Calabar, 128
slave ship casualties, 116
stealing of, 101
taxes on, 20, 21
sledge hammers, 171
sleeve buttons, 80, 81, 136, 171
sleeves, 69
Sleigh/Sliegh
W., 88, 107
slippers, 100, 197, 218
stuft, 185
slit-iron, 185
slitting mills
roles, slitters, beds, 236
Sloates
Jacob, 234
Sloopa
Edward, 63
Sloops, 141, 175, 205
(Br.) of war, 47
(Fr.) of war, 243
(unk) Capt. James Pettis, 185
(unk) Capt. Robertson's, 205
(unk) from Rhode Island, 159
(unk) from Washington, 186
(unk) of war, 111
(unk) of war (Br.), 139
(unk) St. Eustatiasloop, 43
(unk) supposed pirates', 205
(unk) Virginia built, 185
Active, 4
Anchorsmith, 24, 130
Ant, 254
Bathsheba, 43, 73, 97, 107
Betsy, 5, 63, 88, 114, 135, 192, 210, 228
Betty, 249
Charming Polly, 63, 83, 114, 160, 164, 192, 198
Commerce, 38
Delaware, 185
Diligence, 73
Dolphin, 10, 33, 58, 68, 93, 118, 150, 187, 198, 222, 228
Dove, 78, 97, 150
Edward, 73
Empress of China, 253
Experience, 44
Experiment, 181, 253
Favorite, 181
Fitz William, 239
for sale, 29, 164, 240
Friendship, 103, 107
General Washington, 97, 107, 135
Goodluck, 141
Hero, 78, 88, 114, 126, 141, 155, 169, 187, 222
Hetty and Matilda, 44
Industry, 160, 164, 171, 172, 183, 192
Judith, 73, 103, 107, 141, 155
Lark, 10, 141, 150
Little Tom, 228
Lottery, 38
Molly Beverly, 68, 93, 103, 135, 141, 205
Nancy, 38, 205
Night Ramble, 141
Nightingale, 118
Phebe, 145, 175, 181
Phoebe, 63, 83
Pimento, 88
Polly, 1, 10, 13, 63, 68, 72, 103, 114, 118, 126, 130, 135, 239
Ranger, 176, 216
Rising Sun, 258
Sally, 78, 114, 122, 191, 192
Sally Moore, 181
Speedwell, 93, 107, 114, 155
St. George, 63
Surprise, 103, 210, 249
Susanna(h), 20, 48, 52
Three Friends, 112
Three Sisters, 228, 235, 240
Unity, 175
Vulcan, 228
Washington, 176, 187, 222, 228
William, 155
sluices
in Flanders, 96
on the Maese, 96
small-pox, 131
in Litchfield Co., Conn., 43
Smallwood
William, Hon., 228
Smith
Alexander, 255, 262, 267
brother (Free Mason), 175
Capt., 123, 141, 254
Col., Sec'y to Amb. J. Adams, 128
Edward, 11, 84
George, 99
John, 126, 127, 179
John, Hon., 254
Margaret, 126
Melancton, 43
Miss, 254
Mr., 211
Patrick S., 84
Rev., 17
Samuel S., Rev., 20
Thomas, 31
W.B., 122, 150
William, 179, 230, 231, 240
William Baxter, Capt., 234
Smith's shops, 1, 104
Smith's-Shop-Field, 24
Smiths' anvils, 94
Smiths' hammers, 171
Smiths' tools, 11
smoaking tobacco, 239
smoothing irons, 6, 15
smoothing planes, 11, 80
smuggling, 201, 203
saved £9000 tobacco duty, 238
tobacco, India goods, 238
Smyrna
Dutch warship unsettles, 76
plague report in error, 173
snaffle, 218
snakeroot, 12, 88, 126
Snicker's Gap, 85, 119, 124, 137
Snickers
Capt., 191
Snickers's Ferry, 256
Snipes
William Clay, duelist, 231
William Clay, Round O, 231
Snowden
Thomas, 127, 128, 137
snowdenets, 58
Snows
Amelia, 103
Lady Johnston, 103
Resolution, 48-50, 60, 78

Sophia Magdalena, 32, 51
snuff, 171, 185, 219, 239
  new, from coffee, cream, 162
  Spanish, 162
snuff boxes, 74, 80, 151, 165, 171, 228
snuffers, 80, 165, 171, 218
soap, 1, 6, 11, 15, 28, 33, 49, 81, 94, 98, 103, 108, 137, 142, 151, 155, 160, 164, 165, 169, 171, 185, 218, 229
  Castile, 185
  hard, 197
soap-boiling business, 218
Society of Cincinnati, 255
Society of Friends, 57
Socius, 68
sofas, 98
soldier's certificates, 22, 54, 131, 170
soles, 98
Solicitors, 21, 38
Solomon
  on Diligent Men, 140
Somersall
  Anthony, Sr., Esq., 178
Somerset Co., Md., 67
songs, 16
Sons of St. Patrick, 37
Sool
  William, 234
sorcery
  laws against, 196
Souchong tea, 8, 49, 90, 108, 109, 115, 120, 131, 156, 165, 171, 239
souflee, 7, 12, 58, 74, 218
soul, 82
soundings, 164
South America, 140, 245
South bridge, 189
South Carolina, 19, 52, 93, 112, 113, 125, 218, 227, 228, 233, 240
  Act on sales under executions, 222
  ban on Negro importing, 244
  Carolinians denigrated, 125
  delegates, U.S. Congress, 37
  flora, fauna collected, 37
  General Assembly, 222
  Governor, Lt. Gov., 37
  no crops last year, 113
  organizing a militia, 92
  Privy Council members, 37
  silk cultivation, 252
  silk culture experiment, 227
Southall
  Turner, 30
Southard
  William, 126, 133, 138
spades, 1, 11, 16, 51, 80, 82, 165, 171, 197, 251
Spain, 5, 27, 129, 186, 191, 201, 202, 245
  16 sail to guard straits, 221
  Algerine policy displeases Lisbon, 195
  Algiers campaign, 36
  Algiers squadron command change, 66
  Algiers' preparation vs. Spain, 66
  Ambassador, at U.S. Congress, 116
  and Regency of Algiers, 46
  annual drubbing at Algiers, 92
  arms poorly regarded, 62
  Charles III, 87
  cross, Order of Charles III, 36
  debts to individual Ams., 173
  defeat of its Armada, 62
  duty to Royal flag, 184
  gift: 12 freed slaves, 246
  His Most Catholic Majesty, 37
  Infant Don Luis, 189
  King, 110, 208
    decorates officers, 36
    promotes officers, Algiers action, 36
    wants Algiers peace, 178
  King's brother dies, 195
  Mississippi navigation rights, 56
  Morocco rapprochement, 246
  plans attack on Algiers , 56
  postpones Algiers attack, 159
  reinforcing Minorca, 221
  royal marriage in, 76, 110
  Spanish Legation, New York, 116
  the infanta Charlotta Louisa, 76
  triple defeats at Algiers, 62
  uses Fr. peace mediator, 178
  vamping up pirates, 196
  war ship Captains' duty, 184
  warlike preparations, 221
  with Naples, war on Algiers, 125
Spain peacetime
  land forces: 98,000, 61
Spain-Algiers Peace, 189
  terms, schedule of, 189
Spain-Portugal
  royal marriage, effects of, 138
Spalding
  Dr., 244
Spaniards, 239
  attack Samblas Indians, 61
  set up No.Car. post, 37
Spanish Ambassador, 181
Spanish brandy, 8, 109
Spanish floating batteries
  Elliott's destruction of, 62
Spanish inquisition, 208
Spanish Main, 61, 129
Spanish wool, 196
spars, 185
Spartans, 121
Speakers, 187, 222
specie, 21, 170
specie certificates, 169
spectacles, 7, 74, 80, 81, 136, 165, 171, 218
spelling books, 7, 136, 170, 185, 197, 218, 256
spermaceti candles, 34, 52
spice mortars, 171
spies, 215
  Joshua's, 208
spikes, 136, 197, 251
spinets, 256
spirits, 6, 11, 15, 21, 28, 38, 44, 52, 53, 58, 63, 78, 84, 88, 108, 118, 122, 131, 133, 136, 137, 142, 156, 157, 160, 162, 169, 181, 187, 198, 219, 223, 225, 228, 239, 254, 261, 266
  distilled, foreign, 197
  volatile, 237
Spithead, 43, 110, 178
  fleet's cruise short, 178
Spooner
  N., 103, 155, 205
  Paul, 254
spoons, 28, 59
Spotswood
  Gen., 191, 192
Spotsylvania Co., 89, 91, 100
sprigged muslins, 99, 170
spriggs, 251
Spriggs
  Richard, 20
  Sophia, 20
spring goods, 58, 60, 64, 65, 73, 75, 98
springs, 1, 2, 115, 119, 151, 171, 176, 224, 235, 256
spruce, 1, 13
spurs, 7, 59, 80, 165, 171, 218
spy glasses, 1, 33, 136
squares, 54, 165
squeezers, 171
Squire
  Richard, 174
  Richard, mutineer, 159, 174
Squire's elixir, 29, 85, 133, 143, 147, 152, 162, 167, 172, 177, 183, 188, 193, 200, 207, 212, 255, 262
St John's, 77
St. Algesiras
  town rebuilding, 111
St. Ann Parish
  severest hurricane since 1772, 178

St. Augustine, 27, 77, 129
reception for Gen. Greene, details, 77
St. Barb
Capt., 28, 30, 35
St. Bart.'s
much damage in country, 179
ship damage, 179
Swedish Gov. house down, 179
St. Bartholomew, 179
seized by Swedish inhabitants, 66
St. Christopher's, 150
condemned ships, cargo, to be sold, 113
St. Clair
Arthur, 117, 214
St. Croix, 24, 107, 192, 228, 251, 256
St. Croix rum, 224
St. Domingo
M. De Marbois, Intendant, 159
St. Eustatia, 28, 43, 93, 126, 141, 155, 205, 211
St. Eustatius, 211, 219, 225, 233, 251, 256
St. George's, Bermuda, 101, 134, 144
St. George's, Grenada, 92, 101
St. James, 110
£50,000 race wagers, 14
St. James, Court in
King and Queen, 264
Lord Caermarthen, 264
Lord Cambden, 264
Lord Gordon snubbed, 264
Lord Sydney, 264
Pitt, Mr., at, 264
St. James's levee, 66
St. John the Baptist, 107
St. John the Evangelist, 245
Masonic celebration of, 259
St. John's
condemned ships, cargo to be sold, 179
land damage, trees, 179
ship damage
sloop went to pieces, 179
sloop, drove to sea, 179
Vice Admiralty Court condemns 2 ships, 179
St. John's Lodge, 187
St. John's, Antigua, 140
St. Juan, 246
St. Kitt's, 43, 96, 145, 159, 178, 205
forbids Am. ship water, 102
hurricane damage, 178
St. Ann Parish, 178
seizing Am. vessels, 144
St. Louis
order of, to Count O'Rourke, 96
St. Lucia, 145, 175, 181
increasing the garrison, 96
per Arrêt, seizes vessels, 92
seizes 3 Am. ships, 130
St. Martin's, 66
14 sail arrived, dismasted, 56
St. Mary's Co., Md., 69, 70, 161, 162, 172, 177, 178, 245
St. Michael's church
Charleston, 121
St. Patrick
Duke of Manchester, kin, 258
patron Saint, Ireland, 258
St. Paul
tomb of, 158
St. Paul's Church-Yard, 191
St. Peter
tomb of, 158
St. Peter Parish
severest hurricane since 1772, 178
St. Petersburgh, 46
St. Pierre, 247
St. Roque
posts being rebuilt, 111
St. Thomas, 190
custom house officers dismissed, 173
St. Ubes, 83, 222, 239, 249
stables, 2, 29, 94, 96, 104, 151, 161, 162, 172, 177, 183, 193, 199, 205, 210, 250, 255, 267
Stadtholder
Prince, 3
toured Holland's frontiers, 3
Stafford
Capt., 33
Stafford Co., 2, 7, 12, 13, 26, 30, 59, 90, 95, 96, 104, 109, 115, 120, 124, 127, 132, 138, 143, 147, 152, 157, 162, 165, 177
stage-office, 81, 217, 219
stages, 15, 21, 44, 115, 182, 255
Stagg
John, 32
stairs, 170
stalls, 224
Stamford
Earl of, chairs gala, 150
Stamp Act
lost America to England, 66
suppress newspapers, 118
stamps
dog head, 236
fraud by hatter, 116
hammers and anvils for, 236
hand, 236
iron rods for, 236
pulley, 236
screws for, 236
stamps, tax
hatter's fraud, 116
Stanhope
Capt., 155, 242
Capt., and Mass. Gov. feud, 164
Cmdr. (ship's), 149
Stantown, 104
starch, 6, 185, 197
Stastinger, 96
States
new, European division of, 184
States of Holland, 24, 46
Dutch Ambassador, 24
editorial on, 92
Statesmen, 191
stationary, 73, 100, 256, 257
Staunton, 75, 229
stays, 7, 28, 33, 74, 99, 132, 136, 165
stealing, 54
Steddikorn
Simon, 102
Steed
John, 172, 183
steel, 15, 33, 81, 86, 98, 137, 171
British, 185
steel spring rat traps, 74
steel wire, 1
steels, 171
steelyards, 80, 165, 197
Steiner
Jacob, 198
stem, 264
Stephens
Adam, 156
Capt., 239
Isaac, 222
Richard, master (ship's), 222
Stephensburg, 256
stern post, 264
Steuart
A., 118, 150
H., 86, 95
Stevenson
John, Dr., 43
Steward
A., 187, 198, 222, 228
Stewart
A., 68, 93
Charles, 12, 13, 18, 26, 30, 34, 40
David, 57, 84
David, Dr., 234
George, 174
John, 166, 167, 172
Mr., 251
Mr., artist, 153
O., 58
stick wire, 170
still houses, 176
stills, 176
copper worms for, 197
stirrup irons, 171, 218
stirrup leathers, 74, 80, 151

Streit
Christian, 157, 167
strings, 165
leading, 208
Strong
David, Capt., 179
Strother
French, 30
Stuart
Archibald, 30
James, 206, 212
William Gibbons, 126, 132, 138, 143, 152, 157, 161, 167, 172
Stubblefield
Joanna, 53, 55, 61
Thomas, 53
stuff breeches, 89
stuff petticoats, 6, 229
stuff shoes, 6, 58, 99, 151, 230
stuffs, 132, 192
Sublime Porte, 162
subscribers, 99, 115, 131, 133, 143, 152, 205
subscriptions, 22, 78, 83, 84, 94, 123, 187, 193, 200, 212
circulating library, 256, 257, 267
for printing, 16
Newspaper, 5
Sufa
again bombarded, 231
bombardment, itemized, 231
sugar, 1, 6, 8, 11, 15, 21, 24, 28, 29, 38, 44, 52, 58, 63, 64, 67, 69, 73, 78, 81, 84, 88, 89, 94, 98, 100, 101, 103, 108, 115, 118, 120, 122, 131, 134, 136, 137, 142, 146, 156, 158, 160, 167, 169, 171, 175, 178, 179, 181, 187, 192, 198, 199, 201, 206, 211, 217, 223, 224, 228, 229, 234, 239, 243, 250, 254, 261
refined, 185
sugar lands, 229
sugar nippers, 171
Sugar-Bottom, 44
Sugarland Run, 218
suits, 11
sulkeys, 197
sulkies, 94
Sullivan
Gen., death report wrong, 228
Giles, 181
Giles, Capt., 188, 193, 200, 211
John, Hon., 222
Sullivan Co., 205
sulphur, 15
sulphur of Antimony, 29
summer wear, 49
Summerhill, 66
Sumpter
Thomas, So.Car. Privy Council, 37
Sunda, Straits of, 87
supercargoes, 87
Superintendents, 188, 193, 198, 200
surcingles, 74, 80, 151, 218
Surgeon's instruments, 12, 13, 18, 23, 30, 35, 40
Surgeons, 20, 62, 237, 255
surgery, 8, 239, 245, 251
woman, 70, breast cancer removed, 203
woman, 73, leg amputation, 203
Surinam, 38, 63, 103, 126, 210, 239, 254
Surrene, 189
surtout coats, 59, 89
surtouts, 131
surveying
new optical device for, 67
Surveyor's compass, 136
Surveyors, 53, 175, 196, 232
at Fort Pitt, 232
running the east-west line, 232
Surveyor General, 232
surveys, 156, 157, 167, 170, 175, 193
Susa, 46
Venetian squadron bombards, 18
Susmilch
political arithmetician, 14
Sussex, 246
Sussex Co., N.J.
import on foreign goods, 254
Suter
James, 224, 225, 235, 240, 245, 251, 257
Sutton
John, 118, 120, 124, 128, 138, 152, 153, 176, 177, 188
Sutton, Mass., 37
Swain
Capt., 77
Swan
Thomas, 234
swanskins, 11, 73, 165, 170, 218, 255
Sweden, 19, 44, 86
artillery useless in capitol, 9
de Vergennes caused revolution, 129
iron, 101
King dear to people, 9
King of, 173
King of, privileges to Ams., 125
Minister of State de Creutz, 9
puts frontier on alert, 9
Sweden peacetime
land forces: 49,000, 61
Sweden, gifts to Dey
ammunition, warlike stores., 252
artillery, arms, 252
Sweden-Algiers
Swedish ship security, 252
Sweden-Turkey
treaty of commerce, 252
Swedish
timber ships, 227
Swedish bar iron, 266
Swedish iron, 171
Swedish nails, 52
sweet oil, 100
Sweet Springs, 145
Swift
Foster, 114, 116, 124
Jonathan, 7, 28, 30, 35, 50, 58, 60, 75, 90, 91, 100, 103, 108, 115, 120, 131, 133, 143, 146, 147, 153, 165, 167, 169, 177, 192, 199, 206, 211, 229, 240
Swin, 242
Swink
William, 6, 9, 18
Swiss cantons
auxiliaries from, 61
Swiss officers, men
captured by Austrians, 46
Swope
Michael, 234
sword, 231
Sydney
Lord, 263
Symmes
John Cleves, 210
Synope, 241

T

table ketches, 171
table knives, 7, 15, 81
Table of Dollars, 255
table planes, 11
table spoons, 11, 100, 136
table steels, 171
tablecloths, 6, 12, 15, 74, 80, 100, 146, 170, 218
tables, 16, 217
tables, E.O., 180
tables, polished marble, 185
tackle, 197, 245, 252
tacks, 171
taffetas, 7, 81, 249
Tail
Peter, 234
Tailors' shears, 165, 171
Tailors' thimbles, 171
Tailors' threads, 170
tallow, 185, 218
tallow candles, 8, 52
Tallow Chandlers, 218
Tallowchandlers, 168
tamboured muslins, 80

tammies, 12, 49, 59, 79, 81, 100, 136, 151, 170, 218, 230, 239
tan yard, 2, 89
Tangiers, 5, 83, 93, 111, 176, 186, 194, 247
Tanners, 139, 251
tanners' oil, 11
tap borers, 74, 80
taperbits, 74
tapes, 6, 7, 15, 28, 33, 49, 74, 79, 81, 88, 151, 165, 170, 218
tar, 1, 104, 109, 115, 133, 142, 224, 230
tares, 257
tarpaulin canvas, 251
tarring and feathering, 158
tartar, 2
tartar emetic, 29
Tartary tribes, 111
Tasker
  Col., 60
tassels, 217
tastes, 170
Tate
  Capt., 194
Tattersall
  Mr., 39
  Richard, 39
Tavernkeepers, 239
taverns, 54, 172, 210, 212, 217-219, 224, 267
  at Marblehead, 174
  Byrne's, 169
  Cape's, New York city, 117
  Castle Inn, Chesterfield, 173
  Cherry's, 172
  city (Phila.), 4
  City Tavern, 175
  Fountain, 98, 101
  Kettle Drum, Radcliff Highway, 23
  licenses, taxed, 20, 21
  Lomax's, 25, 67, 78, 109, 115, 120, 122, 127, 128, 156, 157
  London Tavern, 150
  Lyles's, 245
  M'Candless's, 206
  M'Daniel's, 7
  M'Guire's, 29
  Reeder's, 6, 107, 131
  Roper's, 29, 240
  Tebbs', 49, 50, 60
  Ward's, 25, 94
  Wise's, 25, 58
Tax Collectors, 21
taxes, 24, 38, 42, 203, 208, 222, 233, 265
  Bahamian, unconstitutional, oppressive, 113
  by Irish Parliament, 86
  cargo, 67
  collection in 1785, 20
  commutation, 3
  deficiencies, 3
  hackney coaches, Dublin, 247
  land, 31
  on bachelors, 130, 158
  on coals, 47
  on emigrants, 66
  on Ireland, proposed, 96
  on maid servants, 130
  on shipping, 52
  Scot shopkeeps resist shop tax, 221
  shop, 143
  upon widowers, 139
Tayloe
  John, Hon., 210
Taylor
  Archibald, 187
  Capt., 112
  George, 107
  Jenny, 216
  Jesse, 58, 60, 65, 68, 73, 82, 103, 104, 109, 110, 115, 206, 212, 219, 225, 234, 240, 251
  Jesse, Capt., 49, 216
  John, 219, 225
  John (of Southampton), 31
  Master, 72
  Mr., 254
  William, 103, 109, 115, 182, 188, 193, 200, 218, 225, 230, 235, 240
Taylors, 25, 26, 35, 59, 98, 101, 109, 110, 114, 151, 210, 219, 235
Taylors' thread, 151
Tazewell
  Henry, 31
tea kettles, 52, 74, 80, 132, 136, 151, 171, 218
tea pots, 52
tea trays, 151
tea, Hyson, 185
Teachers, 31, 41, 80, 141
  dancing, 93
teas, 1, 8, 15, 28, 33, 49, 58, 64, 68, 73, 74, 81, 83, 90, 98, 103, 108, 109, 115, 120, 26, 131, 132, 137, 141, 142, 146, 151, 155, 165, 171, 181, 192, 206, 211, 217, 223, 234, 239, 250, 251, 254
  Bill on, 3
  European, 185
  West Indies, 185
teaspoons, 11, 74, 100, 136
Tebbs
  Deskin, 132, 133, 138
  Foushee, 73, 74, 81, 86
  William, 49, 50, 60
  Willoughby, 74, 81, 86
teeth, artificial, 196
Telfair
  Mr., Georgian, 253
temperance, 125
temperature of air, 5
Temple
  Hon. Mr., Br. Consul, 228
  J., Br. Consul General in U.S., 244
  Mr. John, Br. Consul to Am., 66
  Mr., Envoy, 194
  Mrs., dau. Mass. Gov., 228
  the Earl, 32
temple spectacles, 74, 171, 218
Temple, the (law), 116
tenants, 224
Tenasee's great bent
  private company to buy, 205
tenders (small boats), 214
tenements, 109, 119, 132, 229
  for rent, 99
  for sale, 104
Teneriffe, 27
  Governor of, 43
Teneriffe wine, 81, 137, 156, 230, 236, 266
Teschen
  Treaty of, 76
testaments, 136, 151, 170, 185, 218, 256
Texel, 47
Thaddeus
  Brig. Gen., Kozenzook, 19
Thames, 135
Thaxter
  Thomas, Dr., 203
theatre
  American Company of Comedians, 145
  Drury lane, 148
  duel, itinerant actors, 158
  relief of the poor, 37
  Roman Father, tragedy, 56
  school for scandal, 71
  state theatre in Maryland, 145
thicksets, 136, 217
thieves, 135
thimbles, 74, 80, 165, 171, 197, 219, 251
Thomas
  Alexander, 156, 157, 172
  Dr., 44
  John, 211, 219, 220
  Mr., 234
  Philip, 84, 198
Thompson
  Capt., 191
  Charles, 215
  Garland, 59, 61, 70
  J., 176, 187
  R., 141
  Richard, 40, 41, 49, 64, 70
  W., 193, 200, 207

Thomson
Charles, 38, 63
Charles, Sec'y of Congress, 32
Charles, Sec'y, U.S. Congress, 154
George, 187
Thorne
Michael, 234
Thornton
Anthony, Col., 69
Francis, Col., 74
John, 8, 31
S., 228, 254
William, 31
Thoughts on a Newspaper [Editorial], 200
Thrashill
James, 165
threads, 6, 7, 12, 15, 74, 80, 81, 98, 103, 108, 132, 135, 136, 151, 165, 218
three-story brick houses, 127, 128, 137, 212, 235
for rent, 266
three-story brick stores, 236
for rent, 245
Throckmorton
Capt., 99, 104, 109
John F., 90, 109, 115
John Fisher, 103
John, Capt., 48
Robert, Jr., 161
thumb latches, 74, 171
Tibullus, 16
ticklenburgs, 80, 100, 146, 151
ticks, 98
tierces, 8, 11, 15, 229
tiffanies, 74
tiffany, 170
tile, china, 197
tile, marble, 197
Tillier, 46
timber, 1, 2, 5, 59, 74, 75, 90, 151, 224, 227, 229
ship, 202
timber ships
Hamburg, 227
timothy, 1, 2, 119, 151, 217, 224, 250
tin, 74
tin plates, 146
tin utensils, vessels, 185
tin ware, 15, 100, 132, 171, 197
Tipperary
freeholders, freemen, 168
tippits, 197
Tippo Saib
concubine execution method, 252
kills 32 British officers, 18
poisoning attempted, 252
Tippoo
struck rupees on his own name, 66
tithables, 265
tobacco, 2, 6-8, 11, 12, 15, 21, 22, 24, 28, 38, 43, 44, 49, 52, 58, 63, 67-70, 75, 78-80, 82, 84, 86, 88-90, 95, 98, 99, 103, 104, 108, 109, 114, 115, 118, 122, 131, 135, 136, 142, 146, 156, 160, 166, 167, 169, 170, 172, 181, 187, 188, 198, 205, 206, 211, 223, 224, 228, 229, 234, 235, 239, 252, 254, 256, 257, 261, 262
Carolina, 63
certificates, 263
duplicate notes for, 38
duties on, 245
duty on, 71
for hire, 38, 52, 100, 181, 188, 193, 200, 211, 219, 225, 230, 250, 257, 267
grown in Hungary, 116
inspection, 37
manufactured, 185, 197
Maryland long leaf , 63
Maryland middle brown, 63
Maryland yellow, 63
price (lb.), London list, 63
separate, 262
shipping, 263
taxes on, 38
Virginia, James River, 63
Virginia, York River, 63
warrants, 262
Tobacco Act, 251, 257, 262
tobacco boxes, 151, 165, 171
tobacco duty
pernicious effects, 238
tobacco houses, 170, 224
tobacco notes, 69
tobacco to London (lbs.)
Georgia 885, 62
Maryland 43,000, 62
New York 2,418, 62
Philadelphia 4204, 62
U.S., 724,796, 62
Virginia 674,089, 62
tobacco warehouses, 205
Tobacconist's utensils, 266
Tobin
Thomas, 198, 207, 212, 234
Tocherepow, 116
tolls, 11
tombs, 173
St. Peter and St. Paul, 158
Tomkins
John, 54
tongs, 85, 151, 171
Tonyn
Gov., 27
Tool Act, 241
tool or utensil (any)
used in iron, steel mfg., 236
tools, 1, 11, 16, 218
tools, utensils-iron, steel mfg.
models or plans, of, 236
tooth brushes, 218
topography, 84
Toppan
C., Speaker, Hse. of Representatives, 134
Torge
R., 155
tories
threatened with starving, 191
Torrington
Earl of, at Brussels, 61
Earl of, Br. Amb. at Brussels, 124
Lord Viscount, 4
tortoishell, 74
tortoishell combs, 218
tortoishell watches, 49
Tortola, 181
Toulon, 125, 190
toupee irons, 218
tow linens, 151, 161
toweling, 218
Towell
Mark, 28, 40
Towers
Capt., 160
Towles
Thomas, 31
town meeting, 67
Town-Run, 22, 23, 30
Townsend
Henry, 84, 152, 153, 161, 245
John, 122, 160
townships, 93
toy shop, 201
toys, 74, 194
children's, 197
trace ropes, 136
traces, 81, 171
Tracy
Lord, 33
trade, 57, 101, 176, 188, 191, 215, 239
Algerines halt U.S.-Medit., 227
Am. Amb. ignorant in, 163
Am. carrying, protective act, 125
Am. remittances tardy, 196
Am.-Fr. arbitrators, 149
Am.-Swedish reciprocity, 125
American corn imports, 163
armed Barbary vessels block, 201
Br.-Fr. negotiations, 201
central authority to Congress, 72
Charleston Chamber's policy committee, 148
Chicasas soliciting, 205

China quits Russian commerce, 76
Dutch colony for, 153
English monopolies, 158
European luxury, 62
Europe's East India, threatened, 168
Fr. prohibition spurs Br. trade, 178
Fr. West India prohibits foreign, 221
French, increasing, 243
French, threatened, 164
fustian, 61
G.B. against Am.-West Indies , 87
G.B.-Am., deterrents, 158
G.B.-U.S., 87
ginseng, lucrative, 254
into Indian country, 19
Irish smuggling, 158
Irish trade bill, 87
Jamaica's declining state, 158
La Fayette improves Fr.-Am., 149
many Jamaicans favor Am. trade, 204
Mass. duties repealed, 226
Mr. Pitt's Newfoundland bill, 101
Nassau wants few Am. goods, 27
Negro trade, 101
New Brunswick-West Indies, 178
New England-West Indies, 178
New York's very slack, 195
policy (Br.) distresses U.S., 102
Portugal-Ireland, 139
R.I., Nantucket oil to England, 162
resolutions re: Ireland, 168
restoration of, 78
ruinous policies, 71
ruinous, alarming state, 198
U.S. Congress to regulate, 113, 134
U.S. stops U.S.-G.B. trade, 72
West Indies, American, 168
Traders, 58
tradesmen, 24, 32, 67, 89
Baltimore, 198
Boston, 198
train oil, 15, 52, 89, 142
Transports
Mercury, 36 guns, 149
Transylvania
inactive confusion, 92
Trapani, 47
Travellers, 169, 210
Travers
Charles, 19, 24
H., 187
treason
charge of high treason, 101
misprision of Loyalists attempting return, 107
Treasurers, 11, 94, 131, 142, 182, 188, 210, 212
Treasury, 182, 215
Board of J.L. Gervais declines being Commissioner , 56
treaties, 35, 186, 215
of Muncaster, 46
1756, 3
1783; G.B. says U.S. noncompliant, 72
Aix la Chapelle, 1731, 14
alliance: Venice, Russia, Vienna, 111
American, West's portrait, 154
amity, Frankland-Cherokees, 140
at great Miami, proposed, 149
Austro-Dutch conditions, listed, 154
Barrier, 9
Br.-Am. peace, 221
commerce, 141
commerce, Sweden-Turkey, 252
commercial, Ireland refuses, 196
commercial, U.S.-G.B., 72
contravening of, 13
Definitive, of Peace, G.B.-Am., 160
flagrant violation by Halifax, 134
G.B.- Germanic Powers, 227
Indian, Fort M'Intosh, 19
Indians' non-compliance, 145
Muenster/Munster, 13, 14, 226, 242
N.W. Indians' upset over, 144
of Teschen, 76
Russia-Venice, 194
talks with Indians, 62
Trenton
decree, 1782; Susquehanna land, 150
Trenton, N.J., 17
Tresenthen
William, Capt., 159, 173
Treves
Elector of, 173
trevits, 15
Trieste
Levant ships quarantined, 173
Trigg
John, 30
trimmings, 74, 100, 136, 151, 218
Trinity Church
Holy Orders administered, 179
Trinity College, Dublin
Prof. of Chymistry Percival, 20
trinkets, 194
Triplett
Daniel, 142, 182, 188
Simon, 85, 91, 95
Tripoli
4 refugee ships depart, 196
only prof. of medicine departs, 196
pestilence redoubles, 195
plague and famine, 196
plague broke out, 101
Tripoli, Regency of, 47
Tristan
Nuna, doubled Cape Verd, 190
troop movements, 2
Troops
Capt., 97
trousers, 127, 146, 161
trowels, 171
trumpery, 125
trunk locks, 74
trunks, 83
Trustees, 187, 239
Truxillo, 116, 129
Truxton
Capt., 160, 164, 210
Tucker
Capt., 97, 249
Tuition, 7
tully garterings, 218
tumblers, 81
Tunis
Bey of, 9
expects Venetian fleet, 194
indemnification for flag insult, 9
pestilence abates, 195
receives gifts (listed), 194
Turberville
John, 123, 127, 128
Turk's Island, 150, 176, 210
Turkey
2d rank Minister to Madrid, 46
3000 on Danube works, 226
6000 Janissaries at Belgrade, 93
Acaugi Bachi to Algiers, about Spain, 46
Achmet IV, Sultan, 208
anarchy, tyranny, 196
and Imperial Courts, 197
Bashaw of Belgrade, 203
Bashaw of Scutari, 194
Burgudore-Black Sea canal, 226
Captain Pacha's fleet has plague, 46
cruelty and dissipation, 196
despotic Empire endangered, 197
Divan, 46, 162, 194
frontier movements, 162
frontiers with Austria, 201
government change, policy change, 162
Grand Seignior, 46, 75, 208

Grand Vizier
executed, 163
misfortune, 203
Great Master of the Universe, 163
march troops towards Bender, 82
might side with Tunisians, 194
peacetime landforces, 61
Porte, 65, 197
Porte uneasy over Russia, 241
prepares for war, by sea, land, 93
Russia's depredations, 208
Seraglio gate
barbarites, 203
Vizier's head, 163
Soleiman Effendi now Tefterdar, 203
Spain asks Porte's aid with Algerines, 47
Sublime Porte, 162
calendar, 46
revolution, 203
Sultan, 203
Tefderdar, 203
Tefderdar Faizi Ismael deposed, 203
Turks take Am. ships near Cadiz, 106
Turkey-Sweden
treaty of commerce, 252
Turks
threat to Am. shipping, 56
Turky oil-stones, 171
Turk's Island, 185
Turlington's balsam, 29
Turner
Gregory Page, Sir, 143
M., 210
turpentine, 1, 89, 104, 109, 115, 133, 142, 224
Tuscany
Regency of, 238
Tuscany peacetime
land forces: 3,000, 61
Tuvache
Capt., 117
Twentyman
Thomas, 37
twine, 1, 6, 16, 146, 185, 251
Twining
Nathaniel, 15, 21, 217, 219
twist, 7, 12, 49, 79, 132, 151, 165, 170, 218, 239
two-story brick houses, 28, 81, 86, 132, 224, 250
for rent, 255
Queen Street, 2
two-story stone houses, 85
Tyndal
Capt., 166
J., 164, 222
types, 119
Tyrie
Capt., 93

U

U.S. board of treasury
duties, personnel, 260
U.S. Congress, 4, 43, 144, 173, 194, 196, 205, 232
(9) representatives in town (N.Y.), 10
and Frankland, 180
appoints H. Knox minister of War, 43
appoints treasury commissioners, 19
board of treasury, 260
Br. Cons.Gen.'s credentials, 244
Commissioners, Indians meet, 253
condemns Ohio land seizing, 154
contemplates luxury tax, 153
disposal of western territory, 93
domestic debt payment, 208
Dutch colony petition, 153
Grand Committee, Supplies, 186
Indepence Day dinner, 117
Indepence Day dinner's toasts, 117
J. Hancock, Senate Pres., 228
Kentucky deputation to, 140
mail routes, 169
military claims chargeable to U.S., 87
possibly pay off Turks, 107
President of, 145
reponds to Boston (trade) petition, 102
Roger Ogden to be Dep. Sec'y, 113
Secretary, 116
Chas. Thomson, 32
Senate Chmn, D. Ramsay, 228
six States present, 5
Spain, Mississippi navigation, 56
standard of weights and measures, 169
to buy off Barbary pirates, 56
to regulate trade, 134
vesting with commerce authority, 97
votes Thomas Paine award, 159
welcomed by NY Artificers, Tradesmen, MechanicsCongress, 32
U.S. Post Master Gen.
to contract mail carriers, 169
U.S. public debt
Total: $3,000,000, 186
U.S. requisitions, quotas
Connecticut, $264,182, 186
Delaware, $44,886, 186
Georgia, $32,060, 186
Maryland, $283,034, 186
Massachusetts, $448,454, 186
New Hampshire, $105,416, 186
New Jersey, $166,716, 186
New York, $256,486, 186
No. Carolina, $218,012, 186
Pennsylvania, $410,378, 186
R.I., Providence Plantations, $64,636, 186
So. Carolina, $192,366, 186
Virginia, $512,974, 186
Uhler
Valentine, 229, 231
umbrellas, 123, 197
Undertakers, 99
Underwriters, 181
uniform companies (Charleston, S.C.), 258
uniforms, militia, described, 258
United Low Countries peacetime land forces: 37,000, 61
United Netherlands
joins France, Prussia, 4
Minister Plenipotentiary of, 169
United Provinces
high population's bases, 14
United States, 128, 149, 254
Algerines declare war on, 190
Am.-Fr. trade arbitrators, 149
Amb. signs Austro-Dutch accord, 112
Americans-Quebecois illicit trade, 62
Barbarians' insults, abuses, 93
board of treasury, 93
Board of Treasury, weights & measures, 169
Br. doomsday prophesy, 184
centralized trade authority to Congress, 72
debt, payment schedule , 186
department of foreign affairs, 244
desires N.E. oil to G.B., 162
domestic debt, 208
English oppose Am. claims in N.W., 62
Florida may rupture, 163
Fr.-Am. bonds of union, 149
frontier artillery uniform design, 92
frontier infantry uniform design, 92
G.B. to keep N.W. posts, 72

Geographer to, 149
ginseng export figure, 62
House of Commons debates trade, 92
Independence Day celebrations, 117
iron, 101
Map, M'Murray's, new, 47
military uniforms, distress about, 92
Min. Plenipo. to Britain J. Adams, 128
Minister of War, 92
no federal town soon, 56
no improved system, 154
Paymaster General, 87
peace treaty non-compliance, 160
President entertains Spanish Amb., 117
public indebtedness, 186
rewards Thomas Paine, 159
Secretary for Foreign Affairs, 169
should bar Br. goods, 173
states, requisition on, 186
Surveyor General, 149
threatened by luxury, sloth, 125
trade with Spanish dominions, 93
universities, 153, 255
Upper Creeks (tribes), 253
Upper Marlborough, 60, 70, 176, 178, 188, 193, 261
Urbanna, 146, 147, 157
Ushant, 139
Ustufchna, 116
utensils and vessels
lead, 185
pewter, 185
tin, 185
utopianism, 180
Utrecht, 61, 125, 201
burghers persist in policy, 195
citizens request troops, 201
Colleges of State arming, 18
confidence in magistrates lost, 202
dangerous insurrection, 195
Deputies of the States, 201
Deputies request troops, 195
Dom tower, 201
regents to restore harmony, 202
supports confederacy, 194
troop rumors, 201

V

vagrants, 266
Valentine
Thomas, 161, 162, 172, 177, 178
valerian, 29
Valkhamecht
Mr., Dutch Consul, N.Y., 153
Vallance
Capt., 159
Valle
Don Gonzallo, took Azores, 190
Van Berkel
M., 135
Van de Perre
P.E., 13
Van Gelder
P.M., 107
Van Kreutznacht
Aulic Counsellor, 157
Emperor's punishments of, 157
Van Leyde
P., 13
Van Leyden
Dutch Minister, Vienna, 214
Van Lynden
Baron, 23
Van Monster
General Baron, Governor, 105
Vander Hoop
Major General, 201
Vanmiter
Isaac, 30
Vannost
brother (Free Mason), 175
vassal, 233
Vaz
Tristane, finds Porto Santo, 190
Veale
E., 68
Vecchia, 113
vegetables, 200, 202
Veldt Marshal
Fr. subjects exempt from, 194
Vellore
Killadar of, 231
vellum, licenced, 77
velverets, 7, 49, 58, 79, 81, 165, 217
velvets, 7, 49, 74, 81, 132, 136, 151, 170, 197, 218
Vendue-Master, 1, 11, 24, 28, 30, 33, 35, 48, 54, 55, 58, 69, 70, 73, 79, 98, 103, 108, 114, 118, 119, 122, 127, 131, 137, 142, 146, 151, 155, 161, 165, 169, 176, 181, 187, 192, 199, 206, 211, 217, 223, 234, 239, 250, 255, 266
vendue-office, 24, 28, 48, 55
Vendue-Store, 1, 6, 11, 33, 58, 60, 64, 69, 73, 79, 98, 100, 103, 108, 109, 114, 118, 119, 122, 127, 131, 142, 151, 155, 160, 164, 169, 176, 181, 187, 192, 199, 206, 211, 217, 223, 234, 250, 254, 255, 266
Venetian Consul, 9
Venetian fleet
Chevalier Emo, Cmdg., 194
Venice, 9, 46, 47, 110, 133, 231
30 Sclavonian xebecs, 110
alliance with Russia, Vienna, 111
annual drubbing at Algiers, 91
arms against Holland, 93
augments maritime armament, 133
Doge seized, officials jailed, 202
needs 2 million ducat loan, 133
peacetime land forces, 61
spiritual council instigates coup, 202
squadron, Chevalier Emo cmdg., 47
venison, 233
Vera Cruz, 180
verdigrease, 1
Vergennes
Count, Fr. Prime Minister, 66
Mons., 76
Vermont, 254
legislature grants coining rights, 140
legislature, 17 days, 21 acts, 121
Versailles, 110, 201
Court of, 227
seeks armament readiness, 51
vessels, 49, 69, 73, 83, 86, 88, 91, 95, 99, 109, 121, 136, 141, 145, 150, 155, 181, 186, 206, 211, 212, 215, 219, 225, 239, 245, 252, 263, 266
American Bottoms, 67
British, 64
coasting, 57
for sale, 64
registers, tax on, 77
unloading, 24
vestries, 31, 52, 85, 266
abolishment of, 17, 22, 26
dissolved, 11
vestrymen, 12
Vettenhal's and Christie's Latin Grammars, 170
vices, 11, 31, 94, 171
victualers, Dutch, 247
Vidler
Edward, 146, 151, 157
Vieller
Edward, 16, 18, 23

Vienna, 4, 43, 51, 61, 93, 96, 101, 116, 124, 125, 133, 139, 157, 162, 178, 201, 208, 214, 242, 243, 246
- artillery, martial stores arrive, 201
- association, dress regulation, 157
- Dutch Ministers affronted, 214

Vierset
- infantry regiment of, 20

villains, 120
vineyards, 174
violincellos, 256
violins, 1, 95, 256
Virgil, 14, 16, 170
Virginia, 20, 25, 36, 43, 45, 53, 63, 66, 78, 89, 97, 105, 135, 141, 148, 155, 159, 169, 192, 205, 230, 238, 240, 245, 251, 256
- credit kept up, 125
- elects Gen. Assembly Speaker, 198
- General Assembly, 207
- Government, and Kentucky, 180
- great personage from, 189
- Kentucky seeks separation, 113
- reward for escaped prisoners, 135
- ships, 4
- Tenasee great bent purchase, 205
- tobacco price, London, 63

Virginia cloth jackets, 172
Virginia cotton breeches, 123
Virginia currency, 198, 211, 216
Virginia General Court sentencing, 238
- Burcher, Katey, stealing, 239
- Fowler, John, robbery, 238
- Presto, William, robbery, 238
- Purcell, Reuben, stealing, 239
- Wood, Nicholas, stealing, 239
- Wyatt, John, stealing, 239

Virginia Journal and Alexandria Advertiser, 5
- first year completed, 5

virgins, 196
virtues: industry, frugality
- vital: indepence, liberty, 232

vitriol, 1
Voce
- Col., 45

Voltaire
- King bans 31st book, 159

Voltaire's Miscellanies, 119
volunteers, 174
von Sprengporten
- plan for dragoon regt., 128

Vrendoven, 96
- Outer Maese, 96

W

Wade
- W., 103, 135, 141, 205

wafers, 2, 12, 17, 59, 74, 81, 165, 170, 239, 256
Waggoner
- Andrew, 156

Waggoners, 22
waggons, 94, 126, 127, 133, 138, 181, 199, 217, 223-225, 229, 235, 263
waistcoat patterns, 74, 217
waistcoats, 17, 69, 122, 123, 127, 131, 146, 192, 221, 230
waiters, 171
Walemen, 145
Wales
- Andrew, 7, 123, 156, 157, 167, 206, 212, 219, 225, 251, 256, 262, 266, 267
- Leven, 234
- Mr., 88, 91, 100, 123

Walke
- Thomas, 31

walking canes, 185
Wall
- George, Col., 20
- William, 216

Wallace
- Capt., 198

Waln
- Nicholas, 160

Walnut-Level, 44
Walworth
- deadly swindle fails, 248
- namesake's ominous portent, 173
- within two miles of London, 173

wampum, 150
wanted
- Apprentices, 8, 54, 55, 98, 101, 109, 110, 235
- Barkeeper, 192, 199, 207
- books lent, 128
- charge of mill, 29, 30
- charter, 206
- charters, 219, 234, 240, 251, 256
- Clerk, 131, 165, 240, 251
- dray driver, 199, 206
- employment, 182, 188, 193, 217, 219, 230, 239
- hemp, 261, 267
- Journeyman Printer, 255, 262, 267
- milch cow, 116
- Minister, 60, 65, 85, 90, 95
- Negro wench, 183, 192, 200
- Negro women, 126, 165
- Negroes, 198, 207, 212, 219, 261
- owners of goods, 90
- return of books, 119
- wet nurse, 99

Wanton
- George, Capt., 148

wants, human
- acerbic list of, 149

war, 36, 191, 250
- British-French, 195

war in Europe
- contrary news accounts, 62

war with Holland, 33
Ward
- Mr., 94
- William, 24, 25, 123, 124

Warden
- William, 120, 124, 127, 128

wardens office, Phila.
- the Brown, navig. aid, 228

wares (see heading)
warehouse officers, 262
warehouses, 38, 69, 79, 90, 102, 132, 133, 156, 157, 162, 170, 172, 182, 183, 205, 211, 225, 257, 262, 263, 266
- for rent, 223, 231, 250
- for sale, 146, 147, 157
- public, 250

warming pans, 151, 165, 218
Warner
- Capt., 185

warnings
- bond to John Dundas, 211
- bonds from John Dundas, 219, 225
- bonds of John Murtland, 223, 230, 234
- bonds of Samuel Hardisty, 262, 267
- bonds to Alexander Smith, 255, 262, 267
- bonds to George Hagely, 255
- bonds to Henry Yost, 199, 207, 212
- bonds to Peter Glasscock, 267
- credit to Nelly Nelson, 267

warrants, 21, 25, 26, 28, 69, 94, 218
- for sale, 40, 41, 50, 60

Warsaw, 243
Warwick Co., 135
Warwickshire, Eng., 151
wash leather, 197
- gloves, 28

washballs, 218
washing, 126, 183, 230
Washington, 68, 104, 140
- Bailey, Col., 2, 7, 90
- Gen., 108, 198
- General, 16
- General, aide de camp Smith, 128

George, 17, 69, 78, 84, 93, 94, 142, 143, 152, 157, 206, 218, 230, 236
George, hires Walworth house, 173
John Augustine, 119, 124
Lund, 39, 45, 49, 54, 84
Master, Art of War, 259
Washington Co., 44, 50, 54, 60, 64, 70
Washington Co., Md., 2
Washington Co., Pa., 193
Washington College, 240
Washington cords, 58
Washington, General
Aid-de-Camp to, 144
Washington, N.C., 233
Washington's Mill, 170, 172, 183
Wassenar
Comte, Dutch Deputy, 208
waste books, 256
watch chains, 80, 165, 171, 219, 239
watch crystals, 239
watch house, 153
watch keys, 80, 171, 239
watch seals, 80, 219, 239
watch springs, 239
watch strings, 80
watches, 11, 40, 49, 54, 119, 122, 124, 177
gold, 197
silver, 197
Watchmen, 153
water, 145, 151, 155, 176, 224, 229, 250, 266
stagnation of, 10
water pitchers, 1
water spouts, 264
Dr. Moyes' lectures, 264
water wheels, 253
Watermen, 146
Waters
John, 251, 256, 261
William, Capt., 24
Watkins
Capt., 206, 217, 251
J., 210
John, 206
William, 31
Watson
Capt., 97
Ebenezer, 234
James, 187
Josiah, 44, 45, 54, 211, 223, 234
Mr., 69, 94, 101, 181, 212, 219, 225
Robert, ship's mate, 159
wax, 185
weather (also see "Natural Wonders"), 176
earthquakes, 245
heavy gusts, 118
hurricanes, 249
stages in, 182
violent wind, 175, 176
wind at sea, 5
weaving, 91
Webb
J., 160
John, 54
Webster's Grammatical Institute, 161, 167, 172
Wedzell
Frederick, 255
Weede
Maj., 17
Weedon
G., 170, 172, 183
Nathaniel, 176, 177, 188, 193
Weekly Magazine, 143
Weightman
Richard, 52, 98, 101, 109, 110
weights, 257
weights and measures
fixing the standard of, 169
Welch
Capt., 185
J., 228
Welch gentleman, 144
welfare, 233
wells, 118
Richard, 4, 97
Welwyn, 122
wenches, 1, 21, 23, 30, 34, 86, 95, 101, 123, 126, 127, 131, 133, 138, 142, 151, 155-157, 162, 167, 183, 192, 200
Werington
John, 8
West
Doctor, 264
George, 130
John, 156
Mr., artist, 153
Mrs., 130
N., 27, 78
Nancy, 181
Nathaniel, Capt., 29, 40
Roger, 84, 181, 217, 219, 230
T., 78
West Friesland, 46, 241, 242
West India Company (Denmark), 173
West Indies (Br.), 204
West Indies (Fr.)
produce to Br. dominions, 201
West Point, 232
West Point-Fort Pitt
70 men, 36-day march, 232
West-India Goods, 24, 26, 29, 35, 58, 90, 91, 100
West-India rum, 1, 9, 13, 24, 26, 28, 34, 35, 44, 45, 54, 60, 64, 89, 103, 108, 115, 120, 127, 136, 137, 142, 151, 155, 160, 164, 169, 171, 182, 188, 193, 200, 239
West-India trade, 57, 164
West-Indies, 4, 15, 43, 97, 107, 108, 110, 120, 128, 135, 141, 150, 155, 162, 164, 168, 201, 202, 216, 239, 240, 249, 261
commodities, Fr. undersell, 243
free ports to Americans, 37
hurricane relief, 190
Irish smuggling trade, 158
new fortifications, 196
produce, 223
produce to British, 201
ships from, 4
trade liberties, 129
Western Country, 94
connexion with, 189
new settlers unopposed, 209
politics abridged, 180
savage wilderness to civilized field, 210
savages peaceful, but deceitful, 209
Western islands
Algerine cruisers, 191
Western Isles, 222
Western Shore, Md., 188
western waters, 25, 26, 40, 41, 50, 57, 59, 60, 104
Westmeath, 260
rash promise, in liquor, 260
Westminster, 5
election, 195
Westminster Abby, 107
Westminster Hall, 228
Westminster, High Bailiff
Thomas Corbet, Esq., 61
Westminster, votes for
Fox, C.J., Hon, 61
Lord Hood, 61
Wray, Cecil, Sir, 61
Westmoreland Co., 82, 86, 119, 123, 127, 128, 161, 162, 165, 172, 177, 183, 199, 207, 212, 219, 225, 235
Westphalia, 9
Westwood, 16
wet goods, 24, 48, 55, 68-70, 98, 103, 108, 114, 118, 122, 127, 131, 137, 142, 151, 155, 160, 164, 169, 181, 206, 211, 217, 218, 223, 234, 250, 254, 266
whale fishery, 71, 203
whale oil, 67
whalebone, 81
Whalemen, 145
whales
8 killed nearby, 101
whaling geer, 197

whaling voyage, 264
wharf, 54, 64, 79, 94, 98, 223, 225, 231, 250
building, 119, 124
Conway's, 29, 34
Copelano's, Halifax, 107
County, 60, 68
ferry, 136
Fleming's, 182
Gilpin's, 224, 225, 235
Harper & Keith's, 160
Harper & Watson's, 69, 181, 212
Harper's, 7, 48-50, 58, 60, 88, 90, 91, 100, 108, 115, 120, 131, 133, 137, 143, 146, 147, 153, 164, 165, 171, 177, 198, 207, 212, 251, 256, 262, 266
building of, 126
Hooe & Harrison's, 187, 193
Hooe's, 156, 239, 250
Lyle's, 1, 13
Princess street, 55
Roberdeau's, 119
Wharf builders, 251, 256
Wharton
Charles H., 240
Thomas, 234
wheat, 2, 6, 7, 11, 15, 18, 21, 22, 28, 38, 43, 44, 49, 52, 58, 63, 70, 78, 84, 88, 103, 108, 116, 122, 131, 136, 142, 156, 160, 167, 169, 170, 181, 182, 187, 192, 198, 199, 203, 206, 213, 223, 228, 239, 254, 261
wheel work, 95
wheels, water, 253
wherry, 163
whip saws, 136
whipping, 231
whipping post, 83
whips, 197
carriage, 185
horsemen's, 185
whist (game), 130
White
Alexander, 75, 81, 82, 84, 229, 235, 240
Capt., 191
Francis, 255, 262, 267
Nicholas, 198
White Horse, 108
white lead, 1, 165
White-Oak Spring, 224, 225, 235
Whitechapel needles, 80, 219, 251
Whitehaven, 27, 28, 51, 72, 73, 81, 82, 86, 103, 107, 114, 135, 164, 166, 222, 229, 230, 235, 245
Whitesmiths, 146
Whiting
Henry, 69
Whitlock
theatrical gentleman, duel, 158
Wholesale, 8
Wicklow, 52
Wicklow, Ire., 222
widowers, 200
tax upon, 139
widows, 196, 200
and orphans, Loyalists', 158
Wigan checks, 88
Wilcox/Wilcocks
Jacob, Lt., 179
John, 4, 97
wild fowl, 170, 199
wildbores, 59
wilderness, 254
Wilkinson
Elizabeth, 265
John, 265
Nathaniel, 30
Willet
Capt., 160
Williams
Elisha, 256, 261, 267
H., 15
Mr., 223
Rev., 259
Williamsburg, 8
Willis
Francis, Jr., 69
Richard, 25, 26, 34
W., 10
Willoughby Bay, 179
Wills
John Scasbrook, 31
Wilmington, 141
Wilson
Goodrich, Vendue Master, 239
James, 63, 214, 216, 225, 235
Master, 72
Thomas, 187
William, 29, 30, 35, 45, 49, 50, 54, 60, 63-65, 68, 70, 75, 98-100, 105, 109, 110, 115, 181, 188, 198, 200, 207, 212
wilton cloths, 81
Wimmer
John, 192, 200, 207
Winchester, 7, 8, 11, 12, 17, 29, 30, 34, 35, 45, 49, 50, 52, 54, 55, 60, 65, 74, 75, 83, 100, 104, 143, 156, 157, 161, 167, 171, 173, 183, 193, 200, 207, 212, 217-219, 225, 229, 235, 240, 256
Winchester races, 68, 75, 152, 153, 157, 167
window glass, 7, 15, 81, 85, 137, 151, 171, 230
window pullies, 171
window screws, 171
Windsor Castle, 110, 220, 243
Royals, boy, breeches, 243
Windsor chairs, 176, 187, 193, 200, 217
Windward Islands, 160
new Governor appointed, 159
windward rum, 6, 11, 15, 21, 28, 38, 44, 52, 58, 63, 78, 84, 88, 108, 122, 131, 136, 142, 156, 160, 169, 181, 187, 198, 223, 228, 239, 254, 261
wine, 2, 49, 109, 118, 122, 135, 160, 164, 169, 171, 181, 192, 240, 245, 251, 256, 266
Madera, 139, 197
non-Madera, 197
Portuguese, 185
wires, 74
Wise
John, 98, 109, 115, 120, 122, 127, 128
Mr., 25, 58, 205
Peter, 14, 99
Wise, or Wiseman, 174
witchcraft
laws against, 196
Witham
B., 222
Woffenar
Baron, Ambassador to Vienna, 124
Baron, next Dutch Amb. to Vienna, 124
Comte de, Amb. to Austria, 125
Wolf-Run, 22, 99
Wolfe
Gen., 154
wolves, 57
women
flogged, 231
wiles, law against, 196
womens' leather shoes, 185
wood, 145, 152
Wood
John, 104, 109, 110
L., Jr., 21
Nicholas, 239
wood cutting, 18
wood screws, 171
wood-axes, 85
woodlands, 1, 166
Woodrow
P., 83
woods, 22, 205, 217
Woods
J., 33
John, Capt., 58
Mrs., ship owner (3), 178
Woodstock gloves, 74
Woodville, 75, 81, 82, 250, 257, 262
woodyard, 90
Wool
Jeremiah, 32

wool cards, 74, 185
wool, Spanish, 196
woollens, 192, 194, 217, 224, 225, 230, 235, 251, 255
Spansh, 139
Yorkshire, 139
Worcester, 84, 87
working clothes, 59
Wormeley
James, 34, 171
Ralph, 35, 45
Ralph, Jr., 171, 172, 183
worms for stills, copper, 197
wormwood salt, 29
worsted furniture checks, 79
worsted stockings, 81
Worthington
Charles, 2, 84
Worthington's Run, 224
wrapping paper, 81, 185
Wray
George, 31
wreath of flowers, 54
Wright
Mr., 70
Robert, 64, 65, 75
William, 147, 153, 234
writ of execution
taxes on, 77
writing, 90
writing paper, 2, 7, 12, 17, 59, 74, 80, 81, 143, 151, 165, 185, 218, 239, 256
wrought buckles, 81
Wulfert
agent, lacks 2 tons gold, 110
Würtemburg peacetime
land forces: 6,000, 61
Wyatt
John, 239
Wybrants
Capt., 68, 70
S., 68, 103
Wyllis
Samuel, Col., 16
Wyllys
John P., Maj., 179
Wynkoop
Cornelius, 84
Wythe
George, 50

X

Xebecs, 106, 190
30 Sclavonian, Venice, 110

Y

yarn stockings, 1
yarns, 165
foreign, 197
Yates
Robert, 127, 128, 137
yawls, 89, 91, 96
yeast, 266
Yeocomoco, 80
York
Duke of, 231
York Co., 8, 166, 167, 177, 222
York Co., Eng., 242
Yorkshire, 201
woolen manufactory's orders, 139
Yorkshire coverlets, 151
Yost
Henry, 199, 207, 212, 255, 262, 267
John, 255
Young
C., 48, 52
Capt., 37, 58
Dr., 122
G., 58
George, 64
Mr., 211
Notley, 40, 41, 49
Young Man's Companion, 170
Younge
Miss, 254
Younghusband
Robert, Master, Mate, 112

Z

Zane
Col., 224
Isaac, 31
Mr., 30
Zealand, 3
zedoary, 29
Zeeland
augmenting miners corp, 241
raising another Artillery co., 241
Zeeland, States of
disapprove [peace] preliminaries, 227
peace terms objections (list), 227
Zevenhuysen, 220
Zolicoffer
Mr., banker, 9
Zoroaster, doctrines of, 264

No Surname

[]
Ann, 86, 91
Bet, 86, 91
Cab, 2
Caleb, 120, 133
Capt., 5, 43
Capt. of Ship Alexandria, 192
Capt., from London, 5
Capt., of Ship Washington, 176
Cub, 85
Davy, 53, 60, 64, 65, 75
Dick, 34, 85, 91, 95
Dick, black boy, 159
Edward, 34
Emanuel, 95
Evelina, 228
George, 161, 162, 172
Harry, 59
Jacob, 25, 26, 44, 50, 54, 60
James, 95
Joe, 127, 138, 151, 153, 161, 167, 172, 177, 183, 188
Kate, 95, 101
Lad, 122
Laz, 34, 40, 45
Maria, 131, 133, 138
Michael, 176, 193, 200, 207, 212
Molly, 172, 177, 183
mutineer, thief, 174
Nat, 122, 127, 128
Ned, 122, 143
[Negro], 147
Nelly, 123, 127, 128
Nick, 90, 95, 101
Peter, 8, 12, 17, 22
Sancho, 103, 109, 110, 116
Sarah, 261, 267
Stuart, mulatto, 159
Tawny woman, 152
three black boys, 159
Tom, 54
Will, 17, 18, 26, 30, 34, 35, 41, 49, 54, 122, 127, 128
Will, black boy, 159
Winny, 109, 110, 120, 124
Zack, 122, 127, 128

Heritage Books by James D. Munson:

Alexandria, Virginia: Alexandria Hustings Court Deeds, 1783–1797

Alexandria, Virginia: Alexandria Hustings Court Deeds, Volume 2, 1797–1801

Heritage Books by Wesley E. Pippenger and James D. Munson:

The Virginia Gazette and Alexandria Advertiser: *Volume 1, September 3, 1789 to November 11, 1790*

The Virginia Journal and Alexandria Advertiser: *Volume I (February 5, 1784 to January 27, 1785)*

The Virginia Journal and Alexandria Advertiser: *Volume II (February 3, 1785 to January 26, 1786)*

The Virginia Journal and Alexandria Advertiser: *Volume III, (March 2, 1786 to January 25, 1787)*

The Virginia Journal and Alexandria Advertiser: *Volume IV, (February 8, 1787 to May 21, 1789)*

Heritage Books by Wesley E. Pippenger:

Alexander Family: Migrations from Maryland

Alexandria (Arlington) County, Virginia Death Records, 1853–1896

Alexandria City and Arlington County, Virginia Records Index: Vol. 1

Alexandria City and Arlington County, Virginia Records Index: Vol. 2

Alexandria County, Virginia Marriage Records, 1853–1895

Alexandria Virginia Marriage Index, January 10, 1893 to August 31, 1905

Alexandria, Virginia Marriages, 1870–1892

Alexandria, Virginia Town Lots, 1749–1801 Together with the Proceedings of the Board of Trustees, 1749–1780

Alexandria, Virginia Wills, Administrations and Guardianships, 1786–1800

Alexandria, Virginia 1808 Census (Wards 1, 2, 3, and 4)

Alexandria, Virginia Death Records, 1863–1896

Alexandria, Virginia Hustings Court Orders, Volume 1, 1780–1787

Connections and Separations: Divorce, Name Change and Other Genealogical Tidbits from the Acts of the Virginia General Assembly

Daily National Intelligencer *Index to Deaths, 1855–1870*

Daily National Intelligencer, *Washington, District of Columbia Marriages and Deaths Notices (January 1, 1851 to December 30, 1854)*

Dead People on the Move: Reconstruction of the Georgetown Presbyterian Burying Ground, Holmead's (Western) Burying Ground, and Other Removals in the District of Columbia

Death Notices from Richmond, Virginia Newspapers, 1841–1853

District of Columbia Ancestors, A Guide to Records of the District of Columbia

District of Columbia Death Records: August 1, 1874–July 31, 1879

District of Columbia Foreign Deaths, 1888–1923

District of Columbia Guardianship Index, 1802–1928

District of Columbia Interments (Index to Deaths) January 1, 1855 to July 31, 1874

District of Columbia Marriage Licenses, Register 1: 1811–1858

District of Columbia Marriage Licenses, Register 2: 1858–1870

District of Columbia Marriage Records Index
June 28, 1877 to October 19, 1885: Marriage Record Books 11 to 20
Wesley E. Pippenger and Dorothy S. Provine

District of Columbia Marriage Records Index
October 20, 1885 to January 20, 1892: Marriage Record Books 21 to 30

District of Columbia Marriage Records Index
January 20, 1892 to August 30, 1896: Marriage Record Books 31 to 40

District of Columbia Marriage Records Index
August 31, 1896 to December 17, 1900: Marriage Record Books 41 to 65

District of Columbia Probate Records, 1801–1852

District of Columbia: Original Land Owners, 1791–1800

Early Church Records of Alexandria City and Fairfax County, Virginia

Essex County, Virginia Guardianship and Orphans Records, 1707–1888: A Descriptive Index

Essex County, Virginia Marriage Bonds, 1804–1850, Annotated

Essex County, Virginia Newspaper Notices, 1738–1938

Essex County, Virginia Newspaper Notices, Vol. 2, 1735–1952

Essex County, Virginia Will Abstracts, 1751-1842 and Estate Records Index, 1751–1799

Georgetown, District of Columbia 1850 Federal Population Census (Schedule I)
and 1853 Directory of Residents of Georgetown

Georgetown, District of Columbia Marriage and Death Notices, 1801–1838

Husbands and Wives Associated with Early Alexandria, Virginia
(and the Surrounding Area), 3rd Edition, Revised

Index to District of Columbia Estates, 1801–1929

Index to District of Columbia Land Records, 1792–1817

Index to Virginia Estates, 1800–1865
Volumes 4, 5 and 6

John Alexander, a Northern Neck Proprietor, His Family, Friends and Kin

Legislative Petitions of Alexandria, 1778–1861

Pippenger and Pittenger Families

Proceedings of the Orphan's Court, Washington County, District of Columbia, 1801–1808

Richmond County, Virginia Marriage Records, 1854–1890, Annotated

The Georgetown Courier *Marriage and Death Notices:*
Georgetown, District of Columbia, November 18, 1865 to May 6, 1876

The Georgetown Directory for the Year 1830: to which is appended, a Short Description of the Churches, Public Institutions, and the Original Charter of Georgetown, and Extracts of the Laws Pertaining to the Chesapeake and Ohio Canal Company

The Washington and Georgetown Directory of 1853

Tombstone Inscriptions of Alexandria, Volumes 1–4

Virginia's Lost Wills: An Index

Westmoreland County, Virginia Marriage Records, 1850–1880, Annotated

www.ingramcontent.com/pod-product-compliance
Lightning Source LLC
Chambersburg PA
CBHW081345230426
43667CB00017B/2732

* 9 7 8 1 8 8 8 2 6 5 9 1 0 *